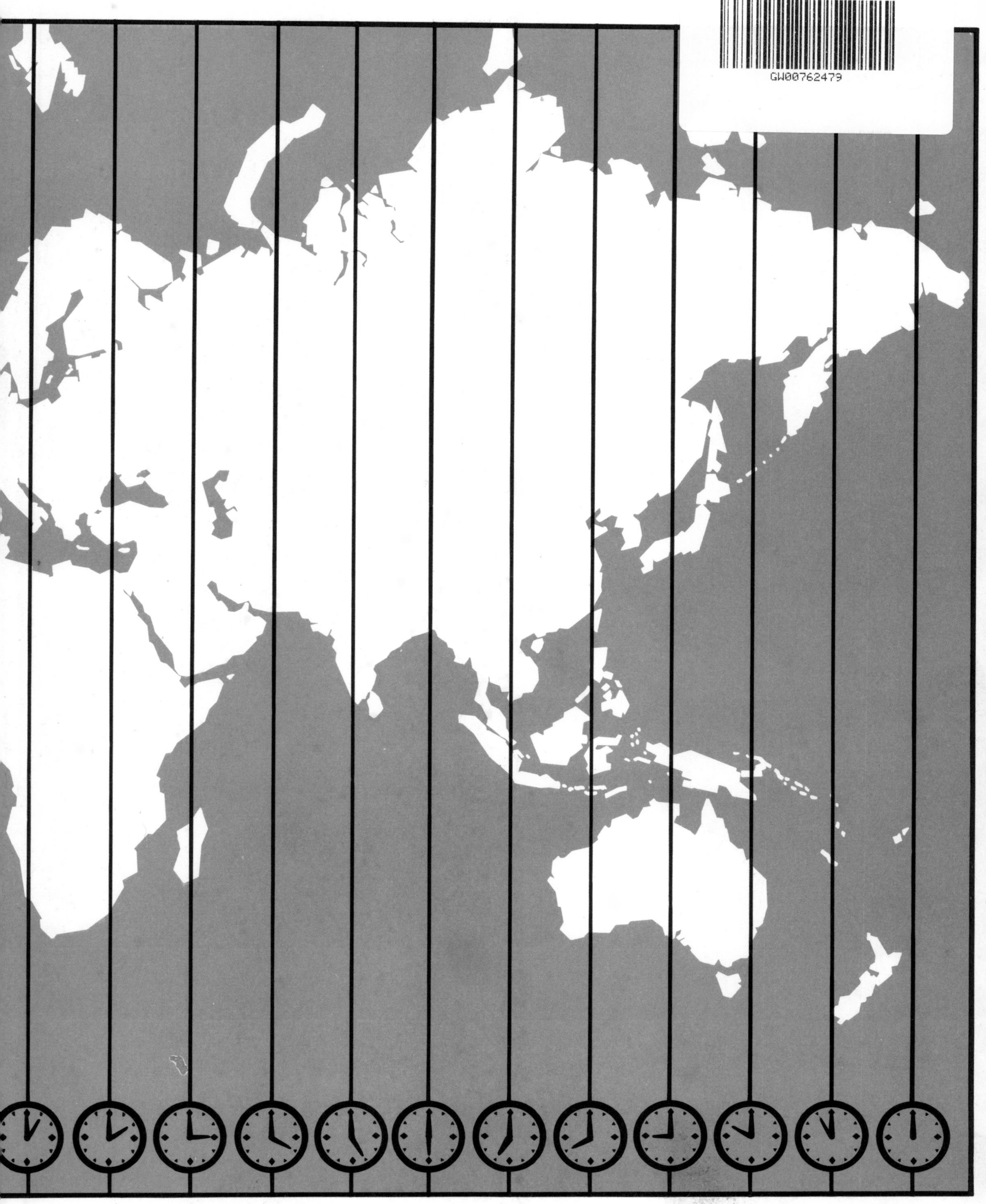

THE HAMLYN PICTORIAL ATLAS FOR CHILDREN

THE HAMLYN PICTORIAL ATLAS FOR CHILDREN

HAMLYN

Key to regional maps

K E N Y A	Featured country
U G A N D A	Other countries
CASABLANCA	Principal city
Wolverhampton	Other cities or large towns
Belmopan	Other towns
Brazzaville	Capital cities underlined
	International boundary
	River and lake
	Seasonal river and lake
Mt. Toubkal 4165m.	Mountains with peak

Abbreviations

Franc CFA Franc de la Communauté financière africaine
Franc CFP Franc de la Communauté financière pacifique

Edited and written by Philip Steele B.A., and Keith Lye B.A., F.R.G.S.

This edition first published 1989 by
The Hamlyn Publishing Group Limited
Michelin House, 81 Fulham Road, London, SW3 6RB, England

ISBN 0 600 56340 5

Printed in Czechoslovakia
The basis of this was *The Pictorial Atlas for Children*
published by Deans International Publishing.
52063/2

Contents

Africa

The African continent has long been a source of fascination to the rest of the world. Fossils have shown that the human race may have evolved in Africa. The Nile valley was the centre of one of the world's first great civilizations, and in the classical era the coasts of North Africa were influenced by the marvellous cultures of Greece, Rome and Carthage. Arabs and, much later, Europeans traded around the coasts of the continent. But to Europe, the interior of Africa was a mystery, cut off by burning deserts and impenetrable forests, by swamps and mountains, by hostile warriors and by wild animals. Similarly, the great kingdoms and ancient cultures that flourished in the African interior had little access to the outside world. For centuries, European maps of Africa showed the interior as blank, except for such enigmatic captions as *'hic sunt leones'*, 'here there are lions'. The tales that emerged from trading parties and lone explorers was of a land populated by monstrous animals and of all kinds of fantastic marvels.

Today the wildernesses of the world have been largely tamed, and the map of Africa is no longer blank. But early European explorers in search of the source of the River Nile put their lives at risk when setting out into the unknown. Today air travel and communications have opened up the most inaccessible places. Africa may not be the uncharted wilderness that it once was, but it is nevertheless a continent of spectacular beauty, and just as fascinating as it always has been.

The northern coastline of Africa consists mostly of a fertile strip enjoying a Mediterranean climate. In the north-west lie the folded Atlas ranges. Sprawling across the whole of the interior of North Africa lies the world's largest desert, the Sahara. This vast tract of sand and stone is about 8,400,000 km² (3,243,000 mi²) in area, nearly as large as the United States. The Sahara has not always been the arid wasteland that it is today. Rock paintings of 6,000 years ago feature hunting scenes and savannah animals, while those of later periods feature herdsmen. In ancient times, the region alternated between periods of drought and periods of fertility.

In north-eastern Africa, the valley of the world's longest river, the Nile, cuts across the Sahara. The Nile contains water from the volcanic mountain ranges and huge lake systems of eastern Africa, and from the high mountains of Ethiopia. Running the length of eastern Africa, north to south, lies the great chain of rift valleys, caused by the slipping of huge sections of the Earth's surface between massive faults. In places, the valley floor has been filled by water, creating a series of lakes.

South of the desert region of North Africa lies the rolling grassland of Africa, the domain of lion, antelope, elephant, zebra, giraffe and rhinoceros. This is savannah, dotted by trees, such as the thorny acacia and the baobab. In the equatorial zone, the savannah merges into dense rain forest. This hot, humid part of the continent is dominated by the great River Zaire (Congo). To the south, the pattern of climate and the zones of vegetation repeat that of the north, although other factors, such as wind patterns, ocean currents and altitude also have their effect. In the tropical belts are highlands reaching more than 4,000 metres (13,120 feet).

Most of southern Africa consists of high plateaux. The southern perimeter of the plateaux is tilted upwards forming

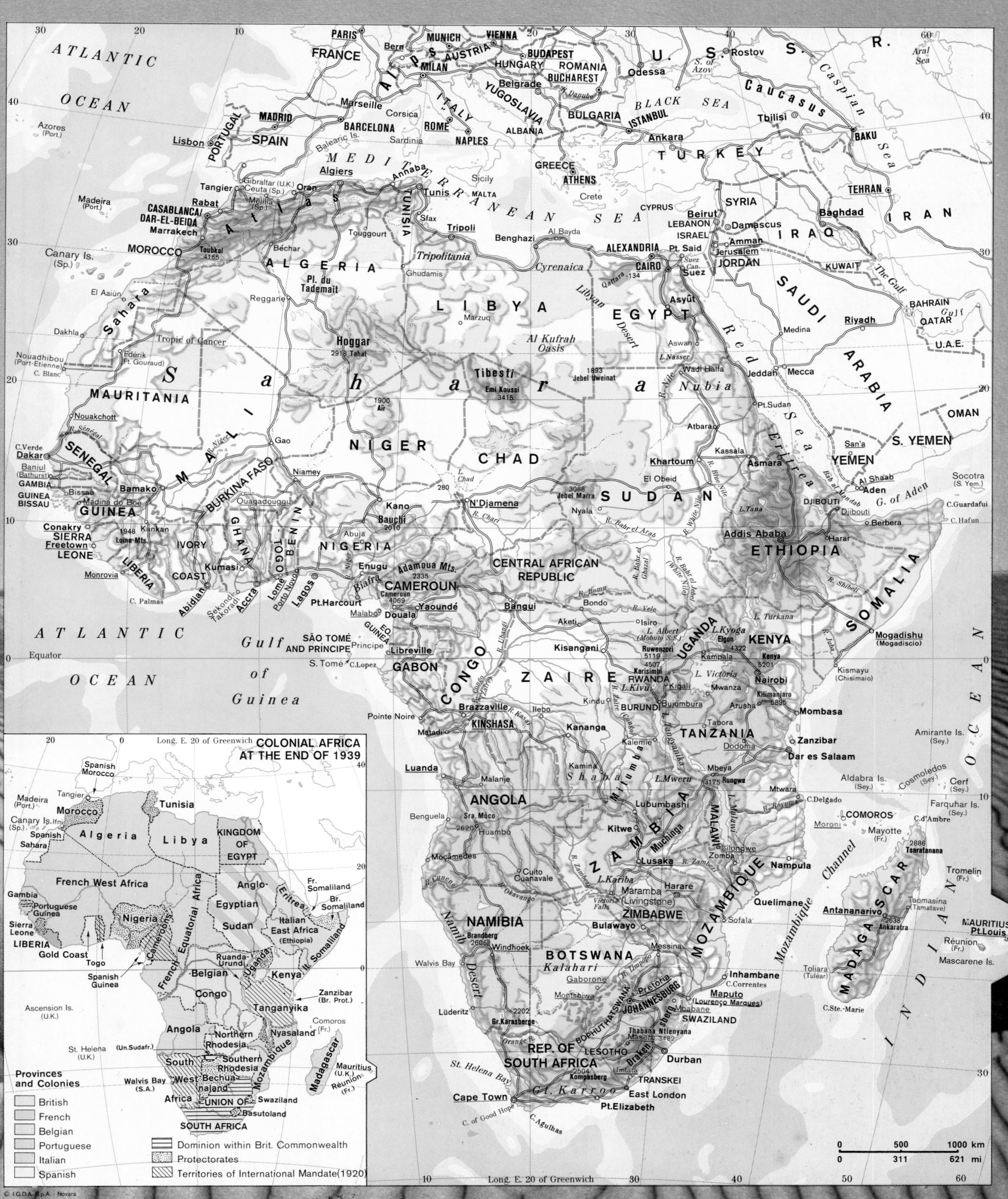
ATLANTIC OCEAN
PARIS
FRANCE
Bern
MUNICH
VIENNA
AUSTRIA
Alps
MILAN
BUDAPEST
HUNGARY
ROMANIA
BUCHAREST
U. S. S. R.
Rostov
Odessa
S. of Azov
Aral Sea
Caspian Sea
Caucasus
Belgrade
YUGOSLAVIA
R. Danube
BLACK SEA
Marseille
Corsica
ITALY
ROME
NAPLES
ALBANIA
BULGARIA
ISTANBUL
Tbilisi
BAKU
Azores (Port.)
PORTUGAL
MADRID
SPAIN
Lisbon
BARCELONA
Balearic Is.
Sardinia
Ankara
TURKEY
MEDITERRANEAN SEA
Algiers
Sicily
MALTA
GREECE
ATHENS
Crete
Madeira (Port.)
Gibraltar (U.K.)
Ceuta (Sp.)
Tangier
Oran
Annaba
Tunis
Melilla (Sp.)
Rabat
CASABLANCA/DAR-EL-BEIDA
Marrakech
Atlas
TUNISIA
Sfax
CYPRUS
SYRIA
Beirut
LEBANON
Damascus
ISRAEL
IRAQ
Baghdad
TEHRAN
IRAN
MOROCCO
Toubkal 4165
Canary Is. (Sp.)
Béchar
Touggourt
Tripoli
Benghazi
Al Bayda
ALEXANDRIA
Pt. Said
Amman
Jerusalem
JORDAN
KUWAIT
The Gulf
ALGERIA
Tripolitania
Cyrenaica
CAIRO
Suez
Suez Can.
Qattara -134
Ghudamis
Pl. du Tademaït
El Aaiún
Sahara
Reggane
LIBYA
Marzuq
Libyan Desert
EGYPT
Asyût
SAUDI ARABIA
Medina
Riyadh
BAHRAIN
QATAR
U.A.E.
Gulf
Dakhla
Tropic of Cancer
Hoggar
2918 Tahat
Al Kufrah Oasis
Aswan
L. Nasser
Wadi Halfa
Red Sea
Jeddah
Mecca
Nouadhibou (Port-Etienne)
C. Blanc
Fdérik (Ft. Gouraud)
Sahara
Tibesti
Emi Koussi 3415
1893 Jebel Uweinat
Nubia
R. Nile
MAURITANIA
1900 Aïr
Pt.Sudan
OMAN
Nouakchott
R. Sénégal
MALI
R. Niger
Gao
NIGER
Atbara
Eritrea
San'a
S. YEMEN
C.Verde
Dakar
SENEGAL
CHAD
Khartoum
Kassala
Asmara
YEMEN
Banjul (Bathurst)
GAMBIA
Bissau
GUINEA BISSAU
Bamako
BURKINA FASO
Niamey
L. Chad
280
El Obeid
R. Blue Nile
SUDAN
Bab al Mandab
Al Shaab
Aden
Socotra (S. Yem.)
G. of Aden
GUINEA
Madina do Boe
Ouagadougou
Kano
N'Djamena
3088 Jebel Marra
Nyala
R. White Nile
L.Tana
DJIBOUTI
Djibouti
C.Guardafui
Berbera
C. Hafun
Conakry
SIERRA LEONE
Freetown
1948 Loma Mts.
Kankan
GHANA
TOGO
BENIN
Bauchi 2010
Abuja
R. Chari
R. Bahr el Arab
Addis Ababa
Harar
IVORY COAST
NIGERIA
LIBERIA
Monrovia
Kumasi
Enugu
Adamoua Mts. 2335
CENTRAL AFRICAN REPUBLIC
R. Bahr el Ghazal
R. Bahr el Jebel (White Nile)
ETHIOPIA
R. Shibeli
SOMALIA
C. Palmas
Abidjan
Sekondi-Takoradi
Accra
Lomé
Porto Novo
Lagos
Biafra
CAMEROUN
Cameroun 4069
Pt.Harcourt
Malabo
Douala
Yaoundé
Bangui
R. Bomu
Bondo
R. Uele
L. Turkana
ATLANTIC OCEAN
SÃO TOMÉ AND PRINCIPE
Principe
EQ. GUINEA
Libreville
Gulf of Guinea
Aketi
Isiro
L. Albert (Mobutu S.S.)
UGANDA
L. Kyoga
Elgon
KENYA
4322
Mogadishu (Mogadiscio)
R. Juba
Equator
S. Tomé
C.Lopez
GABON
CONGO
R. Ubangi
Kisangani
Ruwenzori 5119
Kampala
Kenya 5201
4507 Karisimbi
RWANDA
L.Kivu
Kigali
L. Victoria
Nairobi
Kismayu (Chisimaio)
ZAIRE
R. Congo (Zaire)
Kindu
Bujumbura
BURUNDI
Mwanza
Kilimanjaro 5895
Arusha
Mombasa
Pointe Noire
Brazzaville
R. Kasai
Ilebo
Matadi
KINSHASA
Kananga
Tabora
TANZANIA
Zanzibar
Kalemie
L. Tanganyika
Dodoma
Dar es Salaam
Amirante Is. (Sey.)
INDIAN OCEAN
Luanda
Kamina
Shaba
Mitumba
L. Mweru
Mbeya
3175 Rungwe
Aldabra Is. (Sey.)
Cosmoledos (Sey.)
Cerf (Sey.)
Malanje
ANGOLA
Lubumbashi
L. Malawi
Mtwara
R. Rovuma
C.Delgado
Farquhar Is. (Sey.)
Benguela
Sra. Môco
2620
Huambo
Kitwe
ZAMBIA
Muchinga
MALAWI
Moroni
COMOROS
C.d'Ambre
Mayotte (Fr.)
2886 Tsaratanana
Moçâmedes
R. Cunene
Cuito Cuanavale
R. Okavango
R. Zambezi
Lusaka
Lilongwe
Zomba
Nampula
Mozambique Channel
L.Kariba
Maramba (Livingstone)
Victoria Falls
Harare
ZIMBABWE
MOZAMBIQUE
Quelimane
Tromelin (Fr.)
Antananarivo
Taomasina (Tamatave)
MADAGASCAR
2638 Ankaratra
NAMIBIA
Namib Desert
Brandberg 2606
Windhoek
Bulawayo
Sofala
MAURITIUS
Pt.Louis
Réunion (Fr.)
Mascarene Is.
Walvis Bay
BOTSWANA
Kalahari
Messina
R. Limpopo
Gaborone
Pretoria
Inhambane
C.Correntes
Toliara (Tuléar)
Molopo
Mopashiwa
BOPHUTHATSWANA
JOHANNESBURG
Maputo (Lourenço Marques)
Mbabane
SWAZILAND
C.Ste.-Marie
Lüderitz
2202
Gr.Karasberge
Orange R.
Thabana Ntlenyana 3482
Maseru
LESOTHO
REP. OF SOUTH AFRICA
Drakensberg
Durban
Umtata
St. Helena Bay
2504 Kompasberg
TRANSKEI
Cape Town
Gt. Karroo
East London
Pt.Elizabeth
C. of Good Hope
C. Agulhas
0 500 1000 km
0 311 621 mi
Long. E. 20 of Greenwich
COLONIAL AFRICA AT THE END OF 1939
Spanish Morocco
Tangier
Madeira (Port.)
Morocco
Tunisia
Canary Is. (Sp.)
Ifni
Spanish Sahara
Algeria
Libya
KINGDOM OF EGYPT
French West Africa
Anglo-Egyptian Sudan
Eritrea
Fr. Somaliland
Br. Somaliland
Italian East Africa (Ethiopia)
It. Somaliland
Gambia
Portuguese Guinea
Sierra Leone
LIBERIA
Gold Coast
Togo
Nigeria
Cameroons
French Equatorial Africa
Spanish Guinea
Ruanda-Urundi
Uganda
Kenya
Belgian Congo
Zanzibar (Br. Prot.)
Ascension Is. (U.K.)
Tanganyika
Comoros (Fr.)
Angola
Northern Rhodesia
Nyasaland
Mozambique
Madagascar
St. Helena (U.K.)
(Un.Sudafr.)
South West Africa
Southern Rhodesia
Bechuanaland
Mauritius (U.K.)
Réunion (Fr.)
Walvis Bay (S.A.)
UNION OF SOUTH AFRICA
Swaziland
Basutoland
Provinces and Colonies
British
French
Belgian
Portuguese
Italian
Spanish
Dominion within Brit. Commonwealth
Protectorates
Territories of International Mandate(1920)

The biggest lakes

Lake Victoria: 68,100 km²; 26,295 mi² (between Kenya, Tanzania and Uganda); **Lake Tanganyika:** 32,893 km²; 12,701 mi² (between Zambia, Burundi and Tanzania); **Lake Malawi (Nyasa):** 30,800 km²; 11,893 mi² (between Mozambique, Malawi and Tanzania); **Lake Chad:** 16,300 km²; 6,294 mi² (between Chad, Cameroun, Nigeria and Niger); **Lake Turkana:** 8,600 km²; 3,320 mi² (between Kenya and Ethiopia); **Lake Mobutu Sésé Séko:** 5,400 km²; 2,085 mi² (between Uganda and Zaire).

rugged mountains, such as those of the Drakensberg range. But the Cape ranges in the south-west are fold mountains. Central-southern Africa is occupied by a semi-desert region, the Kalahari, while the Namib desert in Namibia is one of the world's bleakest.

The flora and fauna of Africa includes some of the world's most remarkable

African art

The first great examples of African art are the beautiful murals painted in the tombs of ancient Egypt. They depict everyday scenes as well as mythological ones. In Nigeria, clay sculptures dating back nearly 3,000 years have been found at Nok. The Arab invasion of North Africa resulted in a flourishing culture, expressed artistically in the intricate decorative work of Islam. The black peoples of western and southern Africa often expressed themselves in wood, producing remarkable masks, sculptures and figurines in abstract or stylized forms. In their work, the artists sought to establish a communication with divinity, and to honour the religious traditions of the community in which they lived. Metalwork included the famous Benin bronzes of Nigeria and the decorative gold weights of the Ashanti in Ghana.

Above: A cotton depot in southern Burkina Faso (Upper Volta). More than 80 per cent of the work force in Burkina Faso is employed on the land, and cotton is an important cash crop.

Right: These dancers from Mali continue one of the oldest religious traditions on the continent – that of the Dogon people. Their masks represent the spirits of animals, buildings and of their ancestors.

The highest mountains

Kilimanjaro: 5,895 m; 19,341 ft (in Tanzania); **Kenya:** 5,201 m; 17,064 ft (in Kenya); **Ruwenzori:** 5,119 m; 16,795 ft (between Zaire and Uganda); **Ras Dashan:** 4,620 m; 15,157 ft (in Ethiopia); **Meru:** 4,566 m; 14,980 ft (in Tanzania); **Elgon:** 4,322 m; 14,180 ft (between Kenya and Uganda); **Toubkal:** 4,165 m; 13,665 ft (in Morocco); **Cameroun:** 4,069 m; 13,350 ft (in Cameroun); **Thabana Ntlenyana:** 3,482 m; 11,424 ft (in Lesotho).

The longest rivers

Nile: 6,671 km; 4,145 mi; flows into the Mediterranean (Egypt); **Zaire (Congo):** 4,200 km; 2,610 mi; flows into the Atlantic Ocean (Zaire); **Niger:** 4,160 km; 2,585 mi; flows into the Atlantic Ocean (Nigeria); **Zambezi:** 2,660 km; 1,653 mi; flows into the Indian Ocean (Mozambique); **Orange:** 1,860 km; 1,156 mi; flows into the Atlantic Ocean (Republic of South Africa); **Volta:** 1,800 km; 1,118 mi; flows into the Atlantic Ocean (Ghana); **Limpopo:** 1,600 km; 994 mi; flows into the Indian Ocean (Mozambique).

The main islands

In the Indian Ocean: **Madagascar:** 587,000 km²; 226,654 mi² (off Mozambique); **Socotra:** 3,579 km²; 1,382 mi² (off Somaliland); **Réunion:** 2,510 km²; 969 mi² (east of Madagascar); **Mauritius:** 1,865 km²; 720 mi² (east of Madagascar); **Zanzibar:** 1,658 km²; 640 mi² (off Tanzania); **Gran Comoro:** 1,148 km²; 443 mi² (off Mozambique).
In the Atlantic Ocean: **Bioko:** 2,017 km²; 779 mi² (off Cameroun); **Tenerife:** 1,929 km²; 745 mi² (off Morocco).

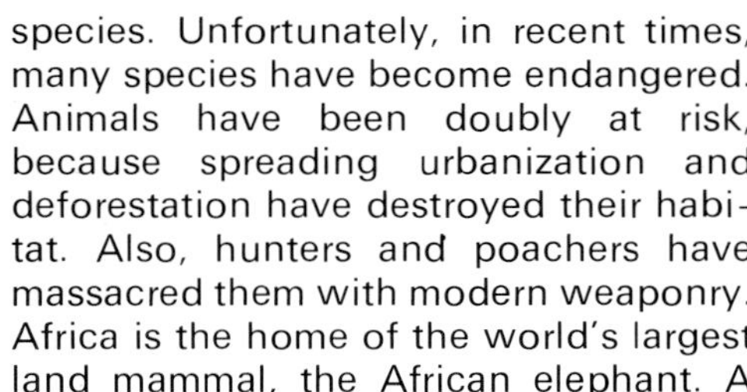

species. Unfortunately, in recent times, many species have become endangered. Animals have been doubly at risk, because spreading urbanization and deforestation have destroyed their habitat. Also, hunters and poachers have massacred them with modern weaponry. Africa is the home of the world's largest land mammal, the African elephant. A

male averages over 5·5 tonnes (5·4 tons) in weight. Africa also has the world's largest bird, the flightless ostrich, which has been known to reach a height of 2·74 metres (9 feet). To protect such animals from possible extinction, many African countries have set aside huge areas as national parks or reserves. There is the Serengeti and many others in Tanzania, Tsavo and Amboseli in Kenya, Luangwa Valley in Zambia, Virunga in Zaire and the Kruger National Park in South Africa. The largest reserve in Africa is the Etosha in Namibia, which now covers an area of 99,525 square kilometres (38,429 sq miles).

Compare the main map of Africa on p. 7 with the inset map on the same page, which shows the political boundaries of the continent before the Second World War. No other continent has experienced such rapid change in recent years. Africa is at the same time an ancient and a new continent.

The first great African civilization was that of ancient Egypt, which flourished along the banks of the River Nile as early as 3000 BC. Its monuments and paintings reveal a supreme cultural achievement. The northern coast of Africa later became part of a Mediterranean-based culture under Carthage and Rome.

But what was happening in the mysterious interior? A civilization was flourishing in the Nok region of northern Nigeria in about 900 BC. In central and southern Africa, Hottentots and Bushmen were gradually conquered or overrun by Bantu-speaking peoples, who advanced southwards from the region that is now Cameroun in successive waves between the first century BC and the 18th century AD. The most famous memorial to their historical achievements is the ruin of Great Zimbabwe, which was the centre of a civilization in the Middle Ages.

With the Arab invasion of the northern coast in the seventh century AD, Islam spread south along the Saharan caravan routes. In the Middle Ages, a number of powerful West African kingdoms flourished to the south of the Sahara, including Ghana, Kanem-Bornu, Mali and Songhai. The names Ghana and Mali have been used for two modern nations. Further medieval kingdoms and empires flourished in Zaire and in central southern Africa, notably that of the Kongo. The 19th-century explorer John Hanning Speke found long-established kingdoms in the Uganda region, such as Bunyoro and Buganda.

When, in 1498, the Portuguese

explorer Vasco da Gama rounded the Cape and sailed up the east African coast, it was the beginning of a new era for Africa. From then until the 20th century, European countries exploited the continent, its people and its resources. Gold was the original lure, and then the lucrative and wretched slave trade, carried out by Europeans and Arabs alike. Land was another powerful incentive for the European invaders. The Dutch founded Cape Town in 1652 and soon their farmers were penetrating the interior.

In the 18th and 19th centuries, Britain and other European countries were in the forefront of scientific and technological advances, known as the Industrial Revolution. The new factories required cheap raw materials from overseas, a cheap labour force and a ready overseas market for goods. To achieve these things, the countries of Europe began a scramble for colonies all over the world. The chief colonial powers in Africa were Britain, France, Portugal, Germany, Belgium, Spain and Italy. Many African peoples put up a fierce resistance to colonial rule. The Zulus of southern Africa and the Ashanti of western Africa took on the whole might of the British army, as did the Sudanese troops of El Khalifa at the Battle of Omdurman in 1898. But in 1884 the European powers met in Berlin and divided up Africa between them. They paid scant regard for the cultural traditions of the continent. Many of today's political borders date from the colonial period, and cut right across ethnic groupings, a frequent cause of unrest and instability.

In the 20th century, the European powers were weakened by two World Wars, and gradually the peoples of Africa began to reassert their aspirations and desire for independence. In places, the colonial authorities relinquished power peacefully. In others, it took long guerrilla wars or political struggle to achieve independence. Today the European powers have withdrawn, although a white minority government still controls

Above and left: Two examples of the unique African fauna – giraffes and flamingoes. There are more than 200 national parks to protect the animals and their natural environment. But they are only of limited use. They provide a degree of protection against hunters and poachers, but they cannot prevent the wholesale alteration of the environment elsewhere.

Above centre: The dense vegetation of the equatorial rain forest. Much of the Zaire region of central Africa is covered by forest.

Right: The cheetah is the fastest animal on four feet. Top right: The king of the beasts, the magnificent lion. Centre right: The white rhinoceros. Bottom right: The mighty jaws of the hippopotamus.

the Republic of South Africa. Although the colonial powers have withdrawn, Africa remains a battleground between East and West. And, despite independence, most of Africa remains poor, while most of Europe is rich. But many African countries have resisted 'neo-colonialism', whereby European interests sought to retain effective control after independence, and set about a policy of Africanization. Instrumental in establishing solidarity between the countries of Africa has been the pan-African movement, which culminated in the formation of the Organization of African Unity (OAU).

Africa is a huge continent, and inevitably there has been a series of differences and major conflicts between the various countries in the post-colonial era. Political systems of all kinds have been adopted, with varying degrees of success. Some countries have been fortunate enough to possess rich natural resources, such as oil, and so they have been able to finance a programme of social and industrial improvements. Other countries have been beset by dreadful poverty, or suffered from drought, famine and civil war. As cities have grown and industry has been developed, ancient ways of life have drastically changed. The industrial powers supply financial and practical aid to the countries of Africa, but it is often insufficient and the practical aid is not always appropriate to local needs.

But despite these huge problems, real progress has been made in a number of areas, such as medicine and health care. The World Health Organization (WHO) now claims that smallpox is totally eradicated, and programmes against other diseases have made an impact. But malaria, cholera, bilharzia, sleeping sickness and other diseases still kill or sap the vitality of many African people. While swamps can be sprayed with pesticide to kill mosquitoes, an equally important way of tackling health problems is to introduce local programmes of health education, as many African countries have now done. Unfortunately, health problems, such as malnutrition and starvation, require rather more radical solutions.

Another field of great advance has been education. During the colonial period, most countries provided only the most rudimentary education for African children. Initially, most schools were run by missionaries. When more advanced colleges were founded, they were open only to a few students, and largely geared to European examination systems. Today there is widespread free primary and secondary education in

The principal countries

This table shows the principal countries on the African continent, but leaves out a number of the smaller nations: Cape Verde, Comoros, Djibouti, Gambia, Guinea-Bissau, Equatorial Guinea, Mauritius, São Tomé and Principe, Se .helles, and Swaziland. Territories wnich are not independent include the Spanish enclaves of Ceuta and Melilla, the British Saint Helena, and the French Réunion. The Republic of South Africa considers the following Homelands to be independent republics: Bophuthatswana, Transkei, Ciskei and Venda.

The total area of the African continent is 30,330,000 km² (11,711,000 mi²).

Africa, and many fine universities. Finances are obviously a problem – text books are expensive all over the world, as are laboratory equipment and teaching aids. Legacies of the colonial era often remain in the educational structure or in the language of instruction (often French or English). Increasingly, however, the curricula are based upon local requirements. The whole future of Africa rests upon its educational system.

An educated Africa has led to the appearance of a fine body of modern literature. Traditional African tales are a fascinating mixture of myths, legends, epics and fables, passed down by word of mouth from one generation to the next. Written texts appeared in Ethiopia in ancient times and, in areas of Islamic influence, Arabic script was adapted to local use, as by the Swahili on the coast of East Africa. Modern works of literature are written in many languages, from English and French, to Swahili and Hausa. Many authors choose to write of the struggle for independence and of contemporary society. These concerns are reflected in many of the novels by the Kenyan writer Ngugi wa Thiongo, such as *Petals of Blood.* Other writers who have received international recognition include the Guinean, Camera Laye, and the Nigerian, Chinua Achebe.

In other fields of artistic expression, Africa has long had an influence on the rest of the world. The fascinating rhythms of African drumming, folk dance and music have survived into the age of the recording studio, and also passed into the popular music culture of the Americas, in jazz, blues, calypso and reggae. The outside world has also influenced African music, and today many

Flag	State	Capital	Area	Population	Economic Resources
	Algeria	Algiers	2,381,741 km² (919,646 mi²)	21,460,000	Oil, natural gas; fishing; vines; olive trees; citrus fruits; cereals; sugar-beet.
	Angola	Luanda	1,246,700 km² (481,380 mi²)	8,756,000	Diamonds; oil; iron; coffee; cotton; tobacco; palm-oil; sugar-cane.
	Benin	Porto Novo	112,622 km² (43,486 mi²)	4,043,000	Coffee; ground-nuts; copra; bananas; cotton; palm-oil; maize; millet; manioc; fishing.
	Botswana	Gaborone	600,372 km² (231,818 mi²)	1,070,000	Manganese; diamonds; nickel; asbestos; cereals, citrus fruits; stock-breeding.
	Burkina Faso	Ouagadougou	274,200 km² (105,875 mi²)	6,700,000	Gold; manganese; groundnuts; cotton; millet; maize; sesame; tobacco; stock-breeding.
	Burundi	Bujumbura	27,834 km² (10,747 mi²)	4,920,000	Coffee; cotton; tobacco; sorghum; maize; manioc; stock-breeding; fishing.
	Cameroun	Yaoundé	475,442 km² (183,579 mi²)	10,191,000	Cocoa; coffee; groundnuts; rubber; palm-oil; fishing; stock-breeding; timber.
	Central African Republic	Bangui	622,984 km² (240,549 mi²)	2,520,000	Diamonds; coffee; groundnuts; cotton; rubber; palm-oil; timber.
	Chad	N'Djamena	1,284,000 km² (495,782 mi²)	5,120,000	Salt; tin; cotton; cereals; rice; manioc; natural resins; stock-breeding.
	People's Republic of the Congo	Brazzaville	342,000 km² (132,054 mi²)	1,740,000	Oil; potash; zinc; lead; gold; copper; groundnuts; coffee; cocoa; cereals; timber.
	Egypt	Cairo	1,001,449 km² (386,683 mi²)	48,000,000	Cotton; sugar-cane; cereals; citrus fruits; dates; bananas; vegetables; textiles.
	Ethiopia	Addis Ababa	1,221,900 km² (471,804 mi²)	40,000,000	Platinum; gold; coffee; tobacco; cotton; fishing; salt; food processing; textiles.
	Gabon	Libreville	267,667 km² (103,352 mi²)	1,370,000	Manganese; iron; uranium; oil; timber.
	Ghana	Accra	238,537 km² (92,105 mi²)	12,210,000	Manganese; gold; diamonds; cocoa; coffee; rubber; palm-oil; coconut-oil; fishing.
	Guinea	Conakry	245,857 km² (94,931 mi²)	5,410,000	Diamonds; bauxite; bananas; pineapples; tobacco; coffee; groundnuts; palm-oil; cereals.
	Ivory Coast	Abidjan	322,463 km² (124,510 mi²)	8,890,000	Manganese; coffee; cocoa; bananas; pineapples; palm-oil; coconut-oil; cereals.
	Kenya	Nairobi	582,646 km² (224,973 mi²)	19,500,000	Sweet potatoes; manioc; bananas; stock-breeding; food processing; tourism.
	Lesotho	Maseru	30,355 km² (11,721 mi²)	1,470,000	Diamonds; maize; wheat; sorghum; tourism; stock-breeding; wool; skins; leather.
	Liberia	Monrovia	111,369 km² (43,002 mi²)	1,992,000	Diamonds; iron ore; mining; manioc; rice; bananas; palm-oil.
	Libya	Tripoli	1,759,540 km² (679,399 mi²)	3,500,000	Oil, natural gas; cereals; tomatoes; olives; dates; sheep and goats.
	Madagascar	Antananarivo	587,041 km² (226,670 mi²)	9,740,000	Graphite; rice; coffee; sugar-cane; cotton; sisal; tobacco; stock-breeding.

Flag	State	Capital	Area	Population	Economic Resources
	Malawi	Lilongwe	118,484 km² (45,749 mi²)	6,600,000	Tea; tobacco; sugar-cane; cotton; maize; groundnuts; tobacco.
	Mali	Bamako	1,240,000 km² (478,793 mi²)	7,720,000	Cotton; sugar-cane; millet; rice; groundnuts; fishing; stock-breeding.
	Mauritania	Nouakchott	1,030,700 km² (397,977 mi²)	1,830,000	Iron; copper; cereals; gum arabic; stock-breeding; fishing.
	Morocco	Rabat	446,550 km² (172,423 mi²)	21,465,000	Phosphates; cereals; citrus fruits; vegetables; stock-breeding; sugar; tourism.
	Mozambique	Maputo	801,590 km² (309,513 mi²)	13,140,000	Cereals; manioc; coconuts; bananas; groundnuts; citrus fruits; coal.
NOT DECIDED	**Namibia (South-west Africa)**	Windhoek	824,292 km² (318,278 mi²)	1,066,000	Diamonds; copper; tin; lead; manganese; fishing; stock-breeding and associated industries.
	Niger	Niamey	1,267,000 km² (489,218 mi²)	6,270,000	Uranium; millet; sorghum; cotton; stock-breeding; timber; skins.
	Nigeria	Lagos (Abuja capital designate)	923,768 km² (356,688 mi²)	88,847,000	Oil, natural gas; coal; cocoa; palm-oil; groundnuts; cotton; tobacco.
	Rwanda	Kigali	26,338 km² (10,170 mi²)	5,650,000	Tin; natural gas; tungsten; coffee; tobacco; groundnuts; maize; manioc; skins; leather.
	Senegal	Dakar	196,192 km² (75,754 mi²)	6,300,000	Phosphates; groundnuts; sorghum; millet; rice; fishing; food industry.
	Sierra Leone	Freetown	71,740 km² (27,700 mi²)	3,643,000	Diamonds; iron-ore; manioc; cereals; coffee; cocoa; palm-oil.
	Somali Republic (Somalia)	Mogadiscio	637,657 km² (246,214 mi²)	6,248,000	Bananas; cotton; groundnuts; fishing; cattle; sheep; camels; timber.
	Republic of South Africa	Cape Town Pretoria	1,221,037 km² (471,471 mi²)	30,844,000	Gold; diamonds; other minerals; cereals; potatoes; fruit; manufactures.
	Sudan	Khartoum	2,505,813 km² (967,553 mi²)	21,440,000	Cotton; sorghum; groundnuts; sesame; tomatoes; cattle; sheep; goats.
	Tanzania	Dodoma	945,087 km² (364,920 mi²)	20,000,000	Diamonds; lead; coal; coffee; pineapples; bananas; sisal; stock-breeding.
	Togo	Lomé	56,785 km² (21,926 mi²)	2,890,000	Iron; chromite; bauxite; coffee; cocoa; palm-oil; cotton; groundnuts; citrus fruits.
	Tunisia	Tunis	163,610 km² (63,174 mi²)	6,966,000	Olives; vines; citrus fruits; dates; sugar; phosphates; oil; iron; lead; zinc; salt.
	Uganda	Kampala	236,036 km² (91,139 mi²)	13,990,000	Copper; cotton; millet; manioc; maize; coffee; tea; tobacco; groundnuts; cattle.
	Zaire	Kinshasa	2,345,409 km² (905,617 mi²)	31,940,000	Diamonds; copper; gold; lead; cereals; groundnuts; coffee; tomatoes; citrus fruits; tea.
	Zambia	Lusaka	752,614 km² (290,602 mi²)	7,539,000	Copper; manganese; lead; zinc; tin; tobacco; timber.
	Zimbabwe	Harare	390,580 km² (150,812 mi²)	7,878,000	Gold; steel; asbestos; tobacco; cotton; meat.

African bands use electric guitars and western instruments. The popular music of western Africa, which has evolved from the highlife music of the 1950s, now has a world-wide audience.

African art, with its beautifully carved wooden masks in both realistic and abstract styles, has also had a significant impact on the western art world through such artists as Amedeo Modigliani and Pablo Picasso. African architecture is as varied as the landscape in which it is built. There are the round, thatched mud huts of many parts of the African countryside, the skyscrapers of Lagos and Nairobi, the picturesque, narrow streets and mosques of the island of Lamu in Kenya, the tents of Saharan nomads, and the flat-roofed mud houses of Egypt.

The religions of Africa are many. Christianity has one of its oldest centres in Ethiopia, where, together with Egypt, the Orthodox (Coptic) tradition still continues. Christianity is also widespread elsewhere in the continent, as the result of the missionary expeditions which accompanied the colonial expansion of the European powers. Most of the principal Christian sects are represented. Islam is established throughout the north of the continent and along the eastern coast. The traditional religions of Africa are also still widely practised. These vary greatly, but often include monotheism and creation stories, a pantheistic reverence for the divine spirit in aspects of nature, respect for one's ancestors, and magic.

Historically, the physical geography of Africa separated its peoples from each other. The lack of easy communications in many areas hindered the development of centralized nations, so a vast range of dialects and languages developed. The southern part of the continent is dominated by languages of the Bantu group, with the exception of areas where the Bushman and Hottentot cultures survive. Swahili is spoken as a lingua franca over much of East Africa, while Lingala is an important language of the Zaire region. European languages of southern Africa include English and Portuguese. Afrikaans, a South African language, evolved from the Dutch spoken by early settlers. In West Africa there are several families of languages: Fula, Mande, Wolof, Kwa, Gur and Akan. Among the most important West African tongues are Yoruba and Hausa, spoken in the Nigeria region. Colonial languages of West Africa include English and French. The north of the continent is dominated by the Arabic language, which is spoken from Morocco to Egypt, and also in many other parts of Africa.

Algeria

El Djemhouria El Djazaïria Eddemokratia Echaabia

Algeria is a large country in North Africa. Its coastline on the Mediterranean Sea extends about 1,000 kilometres (620 miles). Algeria stretches deep into Africa and its southern borders are shared with Niger and Mâli. To the west lie Morocco and Mauritania, while Tunisia and Libya are to the east.

Along the coast is a fertile zone, a green area of vineyards and olive groves sheltered from the desert winds by the mountains to the south. This northern region is known as Tell Atlas, a gentle landscape enjoying a Mediterranean climate. As one travels south, one enters a region of high plateaux, and the green landscape gradually gives way to barren rock. This harsher country rises to the mountain range of the Saharan Atlas, whose peaks, at around 2,000 metres (6,562 ft) are often covered with snow.

Beyond the mountains is the world of the desert, mysterious and inhospitable, where there is hardly ever any rainfall and temperatures average 13°C to 37°C (55°–99°F). This vast, rolling wasteland of sand and rock is broken in the south by the mountainous region of Hoggar.

However desolate an area the Sahara may seem, it has in fact turned out to be a vast store of natural resources, and the key to wealth for modern Algeria. Large deposits of oil and natural gas are currently exploited. Crude oil is piped directly to coastal ports, and natural gas is liquefied and then exported. Chemical and manufacturing industries are being rapidly developed.

The people of Algeria are Muslims, of Arab and Berber (Kabyle and Tuareg) stock. Most people speak Arabic. Most of the million French residents who lived in Algeria prior to independence have returned to their native country, and many Algerians now work in France. Industrialization in Algeria has meant that many peasants have moved away from the land to the cities. However, in rural areas, the traditional pattern of life continues unchanged. In the agricultural land of the north, people are farmers, living the settled life of villagers. In the drier regions, people spend much of the year wandering with their herds before returning to their land. In the desert live true nomads, wandering endlessly with their herds and camels.

The North African coast has always attracted trade and settlement. For centuries, the Berbers traded north to south, their long caravans of up to 6,000 camels bringing gold from the interior or taking salt from the coast.

Social reform and economic power have radically changed the country but the country holds to traditional Islamic values. Family life still dominates society.

Oil wealth has made possible – and necessary – the development of communications within this land of difficult terrain. Railways link the towns of the north, and the roads extend south into the desert. Oran and Annaba are the chief ports.

Below: The harbour at Algiers.

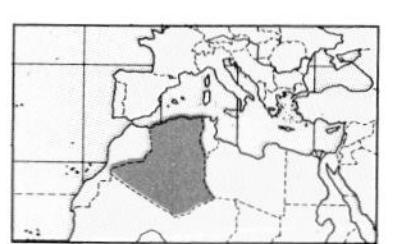

Area: 2,381,741 km² (919,646 mi²)
Population: 21,460,000
Capital: Algiers (Alger, El Djezair) (pop. 2,160,000)
Currency: dinar

Angola

República Popular de

Lying on the Atlantic Coast in south-central Africa, Angola is bounded by Namibia, Zambia and Zaire. It also includes the enclave of Cabinda, between Congo and Zaire. Most people, including the Ovimbundu, Kongo, Mbundu, Lunda and Chokwe, speak Bantu languages. The official language is Portuguese.

A major colony of Portugal for 400 years, the recent history of the region has been one of strife. A 14-year war against the colonial forces culminated in independence in 1975. But independence was marred by bitter civil war between the various factions seeking control of the country, namely the socialist MPLA, the FNLA and UNITA. The first organization was at length successful in fighting off the challenge of the other two.

Behind the coastal strip are plateaux and highlands, which drop down to the river basins of the Zaire and the Zambezi. To the south lies desert.

The climate is suitable for the cultivation of coffee, sugar-cane, cotton, and groundnuts. The northern forests supply timber such as mahogany, and palm-oil. Mineral wealth is considerable, diamonds, oil and iron-ore being present in quantity. Other minerals include copper and manganese. Chief imports are textiles, foodstuffs and steel.

Area: 1,246,700 km² (481,380 mi²)
Population: 8,756,000
Capital: Luanda (pop. 700,000)
Other towns: Huambo, Lobito, Benguela
Currency: kwanza

Benin

République Populaire du

The People's Republic of Benin is a small country on the coast of West Africa, bordering upon Nigeria, Niger, Burkina Faso and Togo. It was known as Dahomey until 1975, and was under French rule from 1892 until 1960, when it became fully independent. French is the official language, but many African languages, such as Fon, Adja, Bariba and Yoruba, are also spoken. Benin is densely populated, and is the home of many ethnic and language groups.

As in Nigeria, the climate in the south of the country is humid and tropical, with lush forests stretching back from the sandy coast. The clay soil of central Benin gives way in the north to a sandy, dry plateau.

Most people in Benin make their living by farming. They grow sweet potatoes and yams, cassava and millet. Palm-oil is widely produced for cooking, and it is also the country's chief export, being used in the manufacture of soap, wax and other products. Groundnuts, coffee and cotton are exported. There is little heavy industry or mining. The oil resources are now being developed.

Area:
112,622 km²
(43,486 mi²)
Population:
4,043,000
Capital:
Porto Novo (pop. 208,000)
Other towns:
Cotonou
Currency:
franc CFA

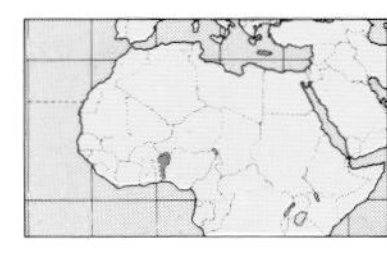

Botswana

Republic of

Right in the centre of southern Africa lies the Republic of Botswana. For the most part it is an arid country. In the south is the inhospitable Kalahari. This semi-desert is the home of the nomadic Bushmen or San people, who live by hunting. In the north-west of the country lie the vast swamps of the Okavango Basin, remarkable for their wildlife. Some forest grows in the northern region. Cattle provide much of the country's wealth, but a mining industry has recently been developed, based on coal, copper, nickel and diamonds.

The country takes its name from the Tswana peoples, who form the largest part of the population. It was formerly known as Bechuanaland, and as such was declared a British protectorate in 1885. It became independent from Britain in 1966, but remains a member of the Commonwealth. English is the official language of government, but most people speak Setswana.

A rail link between Mafeking and Bulawayo via Gaborone was built in the colonial period, and today a new road runs from Nata to Kazungula in Zambia.

Burkina Faso – *see Upper Volta, page 48*

In Botswana the people rely on their own crops to sustain them. Here a small boy shows his spinach crop.

Area:
600,372 km²
(231,818 mi²)
Population:
1,070,000
Capital:
Gaborone (pop.
Other towns:
Francistown,
Lobatse
Currency:
pula

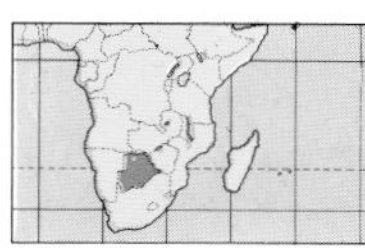

Burundi

Burundi is a tiny country on the eastern shore of Lake Tanganyika, bordered by Rwanda, Tanzania and Zaire. It was founded as a kingdom in the seventeenth century. Occupied by Germans in 1885, it passed to Belgium after the First World War, together with Rwanda (as Ruanda-Urundi). After the Second World War, it became a United Nations Trust Territory. It became an independent kingdom in 1962, but four years later it became a republic, after a military coup.

The chief language is Kirundi. Most of the people are Hutu, but power lies with the Tutsi minority. Coffee and cotton are the chief export crops.

Area:
27,834 km²
(10,747 mi²)
Population:
4,920,000
Capital:
Bujumbura (pop. 157,000)
Currency:
franc

Cameroun

République Unie du

The highest mountain in West Africa is Mount Cameroun. At 4,069 m (13,350 ft), it rises near the coast of the United Republic of Cameroun, on the Bight of Biafra. There are more mountains in the mid-north of the country, plains in the south, and a central plateau. The far north of the country borders upon Lake Chad. Cocoa and coffee are grown widely. Agriculture, forestry, fishing, mining and light industry are all important.

After three centuries of terrorization and plunder by European slave traders, this region became a German territory in 1884. After the First World War, it was ruled by Britain and France until independence in 1960–61. Both English and French are widely spoken today. The many ethnic and language groups include the Bamiléké, Fulbe and Bassa peoples.

Area:
475,442 km²
(183,579 mi²)
Population:
10,191,000
Capital:
Yaoundé (pop. 337,000)
Other towns:
Douala
Currency:
franc CFA

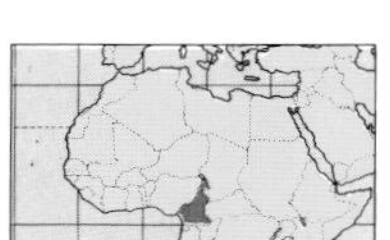

Cape Verde

República de Cabo Verde

This republic consists of a number of islands in the Atlantic Ocean, off the coast of West Africa. A former colony of Portugal, Cape Verde gained independence in 1975. The Portuguese-African population lives from farming and fishery.

Area:
4,033 km²
(1,557 mi²)
Population:
324,000
Capital:
Praia (pop. 37,500)
Currency:
escudo

Central African Republic

One of Africa's poorest countries, the Central African Republic lies at the heart of the continent. The north is dry and very hot; the south is humid. Coffee, cotton, millet and tobacco are all grown, but mineral deposits, notably uranium and diamonds, are of great importance. Before independence, the country was a French colony known as Ubangi-Shari. Ties with France are still close, and French is an official language. Arabic is widely spoken in the north, and Sango in the west.

For three years from 1976, the country was known as the Central African Empire. But when the self-proclaimed emperor Jean Bédel Bokassa was deposed in 1979, the country became a republic once more, under its original president, David Dacko. In September 1981 Dacko was ousted by the commander of the army, General André Kolingba.

Area:
622,984 km²
(240,549 mi²)
Population:
2,520,000
Capital:
Bangui (pop. 390,000)
Other towns:
Bangassou, Bambari
Currency:
franc CFA

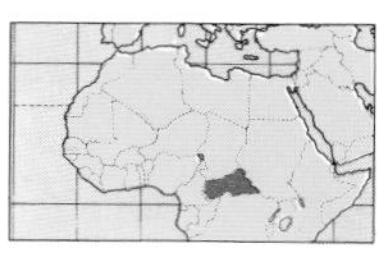

Below left: The cattle farmers of Cameroun travel long distances to get their cattle to market. Below right: A rubber tapper working in Central African Republic.

Chad

République du Tchad

The Chad Republic is a large country in the centre of northern Africa. It stretches from the harsh wastes of the Sahara in the north to the rolling grasslands of the south. The marshy south-west of the country borders the shallow waters of Lake Chad, which provides fish and the mineral natron.

The country includes the homelands of many peoples: Arabs, Fulani (or Fulbe), Hausa, Kanuri and Sara-Bòngo-Bagirmi. As in many countries in this region, Islam is practised alongside traditional African religions, and Christianity.

Full independence from France in 1960 did not bring peace to Chad, which has had a troubled history arising from its ethnic and religious diversity. A bitter civil war involved French troops on the government side for a time. President Ngarta Tombalbaye was killed in April 1975, and the general who followed him, Félix Malloum, was in turn ousted by Goukouni Oueddei. But in 1982, forces led by Hissène Habré seized N'Djamena and Habré became president. However the country was not united, and suffered also during fighting against Libya, Chad's powerful neighbour. The country has remained poor.

Area:
1,284,000 km²
(495,782 mi²)
Population:
5,120,000
Capital:
N'Djamena (Fort-Lamy) (pop. 303,000)
Other towns:
Moundou, Sarh (Fort-Archambault), Abéché
Currency:
franc CFA

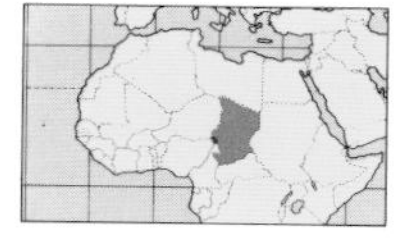

Comoros

Formerly a French protectorate, these three islands in the Indian Ocean between Madagascar and the African mainland, became independent in 1975. The capital, on Gran Comoro, is Moroni. Vanilla, cloves and sisal are among the chief products.

Right: Irrigation is important in the agriculture of Chad. Millet, cotton and groundnuts are grown.

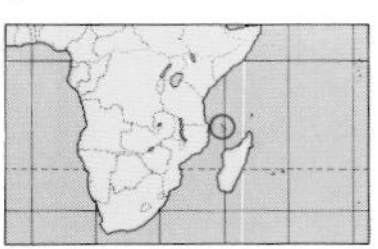

Congo

République Populaire du

Lying on the west bank of the River Zaire, and its tributary, the River Oubangui, the People's Republic of Congo lies on the equator. It is a hot, steamy land, much of which is swamp or forest, although there is also some grassland. The coastline stretches for a short distance along the Atlantic. Timber, mining, agriculture and fishery are all important industries.

The peoples of the Congo, including the Kongo, Téké, Sanga (Gabonais) and Bobangi, all speak Bantu languages, but French is the official language. The Congo was under French rule from 1880 until 1960. After independence, the new republic was called Congo-Brazzaville to distinguish it from Congo-Kinshasa (now Zaire).

The capital, Brazzaville, across the river from Kinshasa in Zaire, is linked to Pointe-Noire on the coast by road and rail.

Area:
342,000 km²
(132,054 mi²)
Population:
1,740,000
Capital:
Brazzaville (pop. 422,000)
Other towns:
Pointe-Noire
Currency:
franc CFA

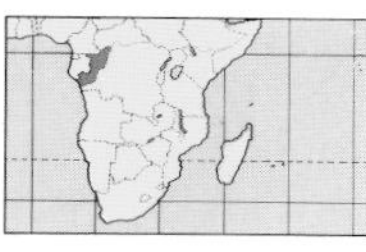

Djibouti

Jumhouriyya

The Republic of Djibouti is a small country on the north-eastern African coast. The climate is hot and dry and most of the land is desert. The people are Muslims, and made up chiefly of two main ethnic groups: the Issa people (a Somali clan), and the Afars, or Danakil, who are nomadic herders of goats, sheep and cattle. The town of Djibouti is an important port on the Gulf of Aden, with an airport and rail links to Ethiopia. Its position below the entrance to the Red Sea places it on the shipping routes to the Suez Canal. From 1881 onwards, the country was known first as French Somaliland and, later, as the French Territory of the Afars and the Issas. Since independence in 1977, the French have retained military bases in the new republic.

Area:
23,000 km²
(8,880 mi²)
Population:
340,000
Capital:
Djibouti (pop. 150,000)
Currency:
franc

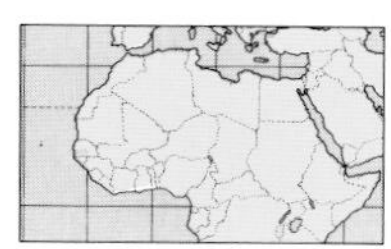

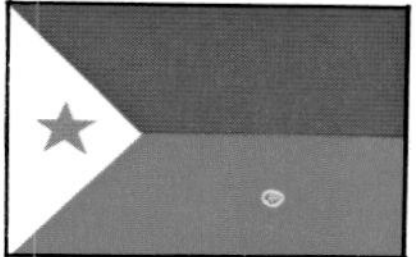

Above: Elephantine Island lies in the Nile at Aswân. In ancient times, the flood level of the great river was measured here.

Egypt Arab Republic of

Some 450 years before the birth of Christ, the Greek historian Herodotus wrote that the land of Egypt was the 'gift' of the River Nile. The same might just as well be said today. One look at the map will show that the Arab Republic of Egypt, as this Mediterranean country is officially called, is bounded on all sides by arid wasteland. The Libyan desert lies to the west, the Nubian desert to the south, and the Red Sea and the Arabian desert to the east. Egypt would also be desert were it not for the River Nile, because the rainfall is scarce, the sky is nearly always clear, and temperatures are always high, even in winter.

But through the middle of this immense stretch of desert runs the Nile, the longest river in the world. From its sources in central Africa, the Nile flows 6,671 kilometres (4,145 miles), through the swamps of southern Sudan and the burning temperatures of the Nubian Desert, before winding northwards through Egypt to the Mediterranean. North of Cairo, the river forms a huge fertile delta region.

Every summer throughout the ages, the rains of equatorial Africa have swollen the river to a mighty flood. When the waters receded, they left behind a rich

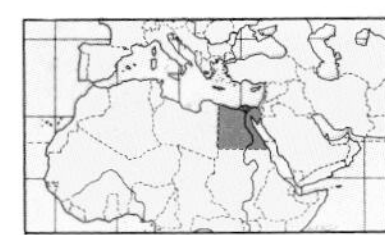

Area:
1,001,449 km²
(386,683 mi²)
Population:
48,000,000
Capital:
Cairo (pop. 8,540,000)
Other towns:
Alexandria, El-Giza, Subra-El Khema, El-Mahalla el Kubra, Tanta, Port Said, El Mansûra, Asyût, Zagazig, Suez, Damanhur
Currency:
pound

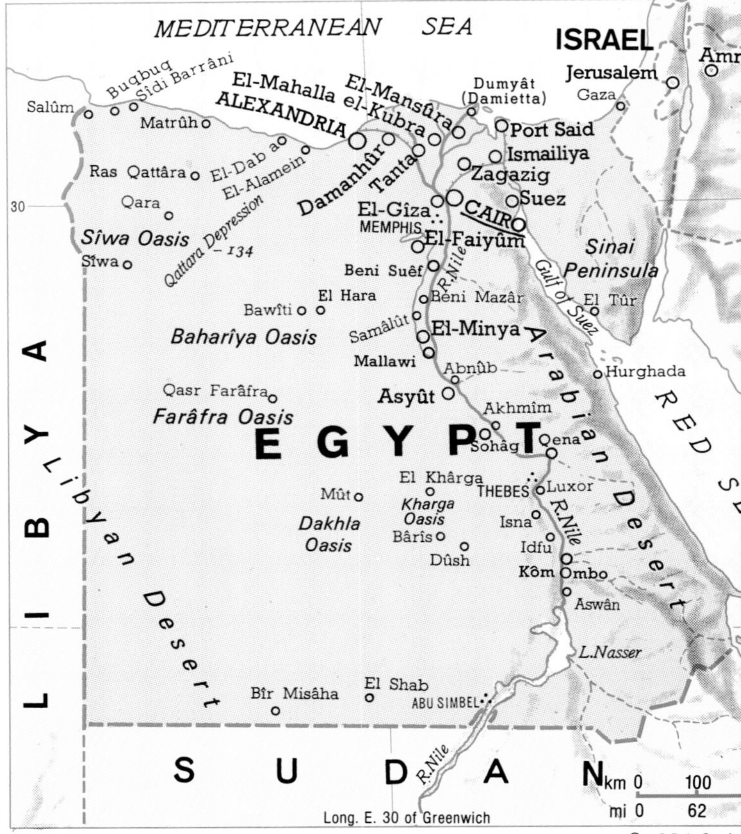

alluvial silt, which provided a rich soil, ideal for farming. Although the Nile valley occupies only one-thirtieth of Egypt's total territory, this fertile strip is the home of nearly all Egyptians. Farms, villages and then towns and temples arose on the banks of the Nile, giving birth to one of the greatest civilizations the world has known.

Today the waters of the Nile are still being harnessed, and the flood is regulated by a system of barrages. Irrigation is now highly efficient. Some 3,000,000 hectares (7,413,000 acres) already receive water in this way, and this figure is expected to increase.

The greatest feat of engineering in modern Egypt has been the construction of the Aswân High Dam. Built with Soviet assistance in the 1960s, this 122-metre (400-ft) high dam lies to the south of the 1902 dam and it has created a huge artificial inland sea, Lake Nasser, which is 500 kilometres (311 miles) long and contains 157,000 million cubic metres (about 600,000 million cubic feet) of water. During the construction of the dam in 1968, huge statues at the ancient temple of Abu Simbel had to be raised above the rising waters of Lake Nasser. Funded by UNESCO, this feat of engineering was almost as remarkable as the building of the dam itself. The dam's capacity for generation of power, and the industrial possibilities arising from that capacity, are formidable.

Industrialization is rapidly changing the face of Egypt, Africa's second most industrialized nation. But even so, more than half of the population still works on the land. Peasants still farm the land as they have done for centuries, although today they are often organized in co-operative units. Cotton, sugar-cane, dates, fruit and vegetables are the chief crops.

The people of modern Egypt are mostly of Arab origin, speaking Arabic and following the Islamic faith. There is a sizeable minority of Coptic Christians. There are some nomadic Bedouin, and, settled on the Mediterranean coast, there is a small minority of Greek origin. The history of Egypt is a remarkable one, which has had an incalculable influence on subsequent world history.

Because of the River Nile and the fertile soils in its valley, Hamitic peoples began to farm the region some 6,000 years ago. The empires of ancient Egypt were ruled by a pharaoh, or divine king, and 31 dynasties were recorded between 3100 and 332 BC. The first 10 dynasties were based on the city of Memphis, on the west bank of the Nile. The founder of Memphis was Menes, who united the

Above: El Giza on the outskirts of modern Cairo. Behind the mysterious statue of the Sphinx (top), rise the pyramids (below), tombs built for pharaohs of the third millennium BC.

country and constructed a dam on the river. Already art and culture were highly developed.

Perhaps the world's most famous ancient monuments are the pyramids. The earliest was built at Saqqara in about 2680 BC, by Imhotep, adviser to King Zoser of the third dynasty. The finest are to be seen at El Giza, on the outskirts of modern Cairo. These are the royal tombs of Cheops (Khufu), Chephren (Khafre) and Menkaure. The highest is that of Cheops. Originally 144 metres (472 ft) high, it took 20 years to build. Large groups of workers were used, carrying blocks of stone on heavy sledges, which were hauled along on rollers. Close to the pyramids rises the Sphinx, a colossal monster sculpted out of stone, having the head of a human and the body of a lion.

These monuments not only reveal the artistic and mathematical skill of the Egyptians, but also their religious feelings. They worshipped the Sun, the Moon, the Sky and the Nile, as well as a host of animals, which, they believed, embodied deities. Perhaps the best known example of the latter is the sacred bull Apis (Hapi) of Memphis, which was worshipped as an incarnation of the god Ptah. Egyptians believed strongly in the afterlife, and in the survival of the spirits of all living creatures after death.

It is largely because of this faith that today we have such an extensive knowledge of what life in ancient Egypt must actually have been like. In order that the dead should have a safe passage to the next world, all their possessions, including furniture, weapons and jewellery, were placed with them in the tomb, and food was left for them to eat on the way. As these tombs have become uncovered in the last two centuries, they have revealed a fascinating portrait of a lost world.

The bodies of important persons were embalmed, or 'mummified', to protect them against deterioration. Internal organs were removed, and the corpse was filled with aromatic disinfectants, then wrapped with bandages soaked in scented oils, and finally laid to rest in a painted sarcophagus. Prepared in this careful way, many mummies have remained intact until today.

The religious rituals, dedicated to the gods and to the deceased, were the tasks of the priests. They belonged to the most powerful caste in the country, because it was from these priests that the pharaohs chose their principal advisers. The warriors were another important caste, who formed the cadre of the army and held high offices at court. But the great majority of the common people enjoyed no such privileges. They worked in the fields and lived in crude huts made of mud. Despite their wretched living conditions, they had to give up part of their harvest to the pharaohs. For those unwilling to do so, there were harsh punishments. These social conditions remained unchanged throughout the history of ancient Egypt.

The Kingdom of Memphis was succeeded by the Middle Kingdom, which survived some 400 years. Its capital was at Thebes, near the modern town of Luxor. The Middle Kingdom, however, fell to Hyksos, invaders of Asian origin who ruled the country from about 1674 BC until 1567 BC. They were expelled. Under such pharaohs as Thutmose III of the 18th dynasty, civilization reached a peak. And under Rameses II of the 19th dynasty, spectacular temples, such as that at Karnak, were constructed. Rameses III extended the Egyptian empire and might possibly have been the pharaoh at the time of the Biblical exodus.

Eventually the great empire crumbled. Egypt was split into a number of small states which were repeatedly invaded by the Ethiopians and other neighbouring countries. However, in the seventh century BC, a great ruler, Psammetichus, re-established unity. Under Nekao, Phoenician seamen were sent upon an expedition to circumnavigate Africa.

In 525 BC, the country was invaded by Cambyses (Kambujiya), King of Persia. The Persian domination ended with the conquest by Alexander the Great. This great Macedonian ruler, whose empire stretched to India, gave his name to the city of Alexandria, which he founded on the Nile delta in 331 BC. Here the Greek-Macedonian dynasty of the Ptolemies became established upon the death of Alexander. The city became a great

Left: A relief from the back of the throne of Tutankhamun, inlaid with precious stones. This boy-ruler died about 1340 BC and was buried at Thebes.

centre of culture and learning. After centuries of splendour, this dynasty was defeated by Rome and, in 30 BC, Egypt became a province of the Roman empire. Eventually Egypt became Christian – the first monastic orders were founded in the vicinity of Thebes.

In AD 638, the Arabs invaded Egypt, thereby introducing a cultural identity which has survived until today. The country became predominantly Muslim, and Caliphates of great splendour were established. One leader in particular became famous throughout Europe for his chivalrous behaviour during the Crusades. This was Saladin (Salah-ed-din Yussuf ibn Ayub), a man of Kurdish origin who lived from 1137 to 1193. His citadel still stands in modern Cairo. In the 13th century, the Mamelukes, originally Circassian slaves who had been trained into a military elite, seized power. They ruled until the Turkish conquest of 1517, and even managed to retain power and influence under the new Turkish rulers.

The story of modern Egypt probably begins with Napoleon Bonaparte. In a bid to crush British supremacy in the east, he invaded Egypt in 1798–9. In the long term, the expedition was a military and political failure, but from a scientific view it was invaluable. With an inspiration rare among soldiers, Bonaparte allowed a group of learned men and artists to follow the expedition. They made sketches and detailed drawings of the ancient monuments. Europeans suddenly became aware of the wealth of culture awaiting discovery in the African continent, and the study of Egyptology was born. There was one major problem. Nobody could understand the inscriptions on the ancient monuments. Three alphabets were used by the ancient Egyptians: the hieroglyphic alphabet, composed of over 3,000 ideograms and phonetic symbols; the hieratic or sacerdotal alphabet, an abridged form of hieroglyphics used by the priests; and the vulgar or popular alphabet, which developed as a simpler version of the other alphabets, and was used in private communications. All were equally incomprehensible.

The code was broken by a lucky accident. A French officer from the corps of engineers, M. Boussard, found a black basalt slab near Rosetta, on the Nile delta. It bore three inscriptions – one in hieroglyphics, one in demotic, and one in Greek. Some 23 years later, the French scientist Jean François Champollion succeeded in deciphering the puzzle, and the world of ancient Egypt was revealed.

Below right: The modern face of Cairo, the capital, with its hotels, office blocks and flats. Tree-lined roads border the River Nile. Cairo is the largest city on the African continent.
Below left: A view of traditional Cairo. From the minarets of these mosques, the faithful are summoned to prayer five times a day.

Whilst Europe was becoming engrossed in the culture of ancient Egypt, Egypt was becoming aware of the technological advances made by modern Europe. In 1805 the Turkish governor, Mohammed Ali, introduced a programme of modernization, and, in 1841, Egypt broke away from the Ottoman Empire. In 1859, the Khedive Ismail approved the project to cut a canal through the Isthmus of Suez, in order to connect the Mediterranean and the Red Sea. This project, originally contemplated by the pharaohs, was carried out by the French engineer Ferdinand de Lesseps, and opened in 1869. A revolt by Arabi Pasha in 1882 led to military occupation by the British, who saw the strategic importance of the country. In 1914, Egypt became a British Protectorate. Independence as a monarchy came in 1921, under Fuad I. But the country remained very much within the British sphere of influence. Under King Faruk, British troops remained in the Suez Canal Zone. In the Second World War, Egypt became one of the principal theatres of war, and Egyptian and British forces defeated the Italians and Germans.

Faruk's corrupt government was finally overthrown by the army in 1952, and a presidential republic came into being in 1953. Gamal Abdel Nasser assumed power in 1954 and was formally elected president in 1956. Britain had previously agreed to withdraw all troops in Egypt, but when Nasser nationalized the Suez Canal in 1956, Britain, France and Israel intervened militarily. This ill-judged exercise came to an end when international and domestic opinion forced the Europeans to withdraw.

Nasser was the leader of the Arab world, and Egypt embarked upon a programme of union with other Arab states. However, brief periods of union with Syria and with the Yemen were frustrated in 1961. The ensuing 20 years were a period of great tension in the Middle East, as a result of the creation of the state of Israel in post-war Palestine. Israel and Egypt fought bitter wars in 1967 and again in 1973. Nasser died in 1970. His successor, Anwar as-Sadat, proved to be another politician of international stature. Sadat launched a peace bid in 1977, during the course of which he made a historic visit to Israel. Many Arabs viewed Sadat's initiative as appeasement, and he was assassinated at the height of his power in 1981. He was succeeded by President Muhammad Hosni Mubarak.

The future of Egypt depends on a number of factors, political and economic. For stability, the huge masses of poor peasants must derive benefit from the rapid progress Egypt has made in industrialization. Some kind of lasting accord must be achieved with Israel and other countries of the Middle East. However, the Islamic fundamentalism reintroduced by the Ayatollah Khomeini in the Iranian revolution of 1979 has implications which no Arabic leader can afford to ignore.

Certainly Egypt is now a major power in the world. As a growing number of international tourists discover, the country is rapidly becoming modernized. In a city such as Aswân, modern streets lie side-by-side with the traditional world of the bazaar. In Egypt, one is constantly aware of this juxtaposition of ancient and modern. Skyscrapers and hotel blocks share the Cairo skyline with the minarets of antique mosques, and jet aircraft fly over a Nile still plied by feluccas, the beautiful lateen-rigged sailing boats of old Egypt. The dusty streets are thronged with teeming crowds as they always have been, and the markets and cafés are bustling with life.

Cairo is the capital of Egypt, and it is also the largest city in Africa. Its universities are famous throughout the Arab world, and it is a centre of business and administration. Rail and roads link Cairo with the cities of the coast and delta. Chief among these are Alexandria, a huge port on the Mediterranean and a seaside resort popular with Egyptians, and Port Said, at the head of the Suez Canal. The road and rail links continue south along the Nile valley to Beni Suef, El Minya, Asyût, Sohâg, Qena and Aswân. A steamer links Aswân with the Sudanese rail network at Wadi Halfa, at the southern end of Lake Nasser. The rest of the country is mostly desert, as it always has been – a rough drive or camel-ride from one oasis to the next.

Left top: Black tea and coffee are drunk in the busy cafés of Cairo's old quarter.
Below: Along the River Nile, village life continues as it has for centuries.

Equatorial Guinea

República de Guinea ecuatorial

The Republic of Equatorial Guinea includes the Rio Muni region on the mainland of West Africa, between Gabon and Cameroun. It also includes islands in the Bight of Biafra, the most important of which is Bioko (previously known as Fernando Póo and later, Macias Nguema Biyoga). Some islanders are Bubi, descendants of the original inhabitants, while most mainlanders are Fangs. It is a former Spanish colony, and Spanish is the official language. Forests provide hardwood, such as ebony and mahogany. Cocoa, coffee, sugar-cane and tobacco are all cultivated.

Area:
28,051 km² (10,831 mi²)
Population:
398,000
Capital:
Malabo (Santa Isabel) (pop. 25,000)
Other towns:
Bata, Mbini
Currency:
ekuele

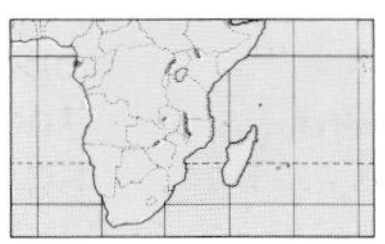

Ethiopia

Ethiopia is a country long famous in myth and legend. To the ancient Greeks the Ethiopians were a strange, magical race said to live on the edge of the known world. The emperors of Ethiopia claimed to be descendants of King Solomon and the Queen of Sheba. Early European explorers, such as the Scot, James Bruce (1730–94), who came to the country in search of the source of the Blue Nile, found an extraordinary land with an ancient Christian civilization.

Despite a military incursion by Britain and an invasion bid by Italy in the nineteenth century, Ethiopia, with the exception of Eritrea along the Red Sea, was the only region of Africa to avoid colonization by the European powers. Italy under Mussolini invaded Ethiopia in 1935, but was expelled in 1941. In 1974 the last emperor of Ethiopia, Haile Selassie, was deposed by the army. The army leaders proclaimed a republic and introduced radical reforms. However, the Eritreans, who had been fighting for independence since 1962, continued the war against the new rulers. Refugees from Eritrea poured into neighbouring Sudan. Further fighting broke out in the Ogaden region in the south in 1977, where Somalia supported the secessionist claims of Ethiopian Somalis.

Despite these troubles, Ethiopia still represents to many peoples of African descent the mystical homeland of the African peoples. The Rastafarians of Jamaica still revere Haile Selassie (formerly called Prince Ras Tafari) as a divine figure. In fact, the peoples of Ethiopia include a wide range of ethnic and language groups, including Cushitic peoples, such as the Gallas and Somalis, and Semitic peoples, such as the Tigreans and Amharas. Amharic is the official language.

Ethiopia is a largely cool, moist mountainous land of high plateaux, divided by the Rift Valley. The largest of the country's many lakes is Tana, which is the source of the Blue Nile. The plateaux are surrounded by hot, arid lowland regions, such as the coastal plain of the Red Sea. Ethiopia is a country of farmers. Coffee and cotton are major crops, and millet, maize and sugar-cane are also cultivated.

Drought and crop failure are common. The famine of 1984–5 shocked the conscience of the world.

Area:
1,221,900 km² (471,804 mi²)
Population:
40,000,000
Capital:
Addis Ababa (pop. 1,277,000)
Other towns:
Asmara, Diredawa
Currency:
birr.

Ethiopia has a strong Christian religious tradition. This is an Orthodox church in Bahar Dar.

Gabon

République Gabonaise

The Gabonese Republic lies on the Atlantic coast of Africa, between Cameroun and the Congo. The equator runs across the centre of the country, which, behind the marshy coastline consists of hills and valleys. The country has a wet, tropical climate, the rain forests producing valuable hardwoods. But the main wealth of Gabon lies underground: iron-ore, uranium and oil. Gabon is a member of OPEC, the Organization of Petroleum Exporting Countries, and its new-found wealth from oil has made it one of the fastest developing countries on the African continent.

Most of the population belongs to the Fang people, but the Echira and Adouma are also sizeable ethnic groups. The French began to infiltrate the Gabon region in the nineteenth century, and ruled it as a colony from after the First World War until 1958. Full independence came in 1960. The French remained politically and economically involved in the fortunes of Gabon, and French is the official language. Omar Bongo has served as president of the republic since 1967.

Area:
267,667 km²
(103,352 mi²)
Population:
1,370,000
Capital:
Libreville (pop. 350,000)
Other towns:
Port Gentil, Lambaréné
Currency:
franc CFA

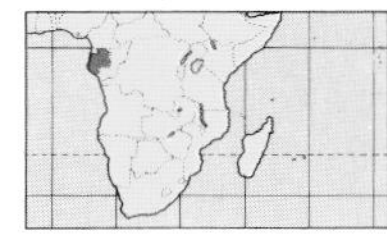

Central Western Africa.

Gambia

Republic of

The smallest country in Africa, the Republic of Gambia is a tract of land adjoining the banks of the Gambia River. It stretches for 480 kilometres (298 miles) into the interior and is surrounded by the Republic of Senegal. As with so many African countries, its boundaries reflect the history of European imperialism rather than local considerations.

The Portuguese were the first Europeans to discover the area, in the fifteenth century. In the sixteenth century, England recognized the trading possibilities of the river. After two centuries of competition from France and Portugal, the region was awarded to the British by the Treaty of Versailles in 1783. It eventually became a British colony, later achieving full internal self-government in 1963, and becoming an independent member of the Commonwealth in 1965. In 1970 the Gambia became a republic within the Commonwealth. In 1981 the Confederation of Senegambia was formed, with the aim of integrating the economies and armed forces of Senegal and the Gambia. Despite this close political alliance, both countries are still independent nations.

The largest ethnic group in Gambia is the Mandingo, followed by Fulbe (Fulani), Wolof, Djola and others, but English is the official language. Many are farmers, working fields of groundnuts and cotton for export. Maize, rice and millet are grown for food. The tropical climate is pleasant, and the capital Banjul (formerly Bathurst) has become a popular tourist centre.

Area:
11,295 km²
(4,361 mi²)
Population:
695,886
Capital:
Banjul (pop. 50,000)
Currency:
dalasi

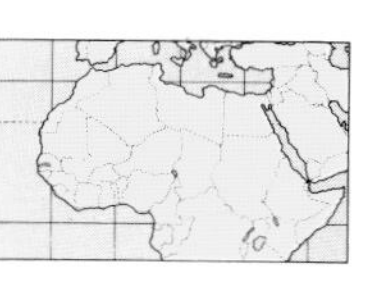

Ghana

Ghana was a powerful empire that flourished in West Africa during the early medieval period. Its name was adopted by the British colony of the Gold Coast, when it became independent in 1957. Gold played an important part in the region's history, because it was gold that first attracted Europeans to the area. From the fifteenth century onwards, the Portuguese, English, French, and Dutch fought each other in order to capture the rich rewards of trade along this coast. Soon they were dealing not only in gold, but also in human lives.

Slaves were taken by Europeans all along the coast, and shipped off to the new colonies in the Americas. The ships were so closely packed with bodies that many slaves died on the voyages. Firearms, alcohol and European manufactured produce were inducement for some local peoples to wage war upon the others, and so provide slaves for the European traders. This trade in misery continued until the last century.

From about 1670, the Ashanti kingdom of central Ghana became powerful, trading with the British on the coast and Arab caravans in the north. Its capital was at Kumasi, and it maintained its power for some two hundred years. Its chief resource was gold, and the high artistic quality of its brasswork, textiles, wood carving and pottery remain an inspiration

Above: Hardwood for export lines the quayside at Takoradi, one of the busiest ports on the Gulf of Guinea.

Below: This shows part of the funeral ceremony for a king of the Akan people. Red is the colour of mourning.

to modern craftsmen. The Ashanti fought a number of fierce battles against the British before colonization. Britain finally took control of the whole region in 1901. Independence was achieved in 1957. Ghana, as it was renamed, was the first of Britain's African colonies to achieve independence. The first prime minister was a remarkable man, Dr. Kwame Nkrumah (1909–72). As early as 1949 he founded the Convention People's Party and campaigned for self-determination. The British jailed him for his political activities, but he became a key figure in the new Africa. In 1960 Ghana became a republic. In 1966 Nkrumah's government was overthrown and accused of corruption, and there began a series of alternating military and civilian **governments. In 1979 the Supreme Military Council was overthrown by Flight-Lt. Jerry Rawlings. Rawlings allowed elections, which were won by Dr Hilla Limann. He later reassumed power, however, claiming that corruption had again got out of hand.**

Gold mining is still an important industry in Ghana. The Dunkwa region is rich in resources, and manganese, bauxite and industrial diamonds are produced. Today Ghana depends heavily on its cocoa crop for its wealth. Palm-oil, groundnuts, fruits, maize, rice and other crops are grown by the country's many farmers. The country is self-sufficient in maize and rice. Forests provide hardwoods for export. The sea and inland lakes provide fish, an important source of food. Light industry plays an ever more important part in the economy.

Ghana occupies a low-lying part of the Gulf of Guinea coastline, and stretches inland for some 700 kilometres. Behind the sandy coast lies a belt of forest and rivers. The dry north of the country is largely savannah. Dominating the map of Ghana is Lake Volta, an artificial lake caused by the damming of the Volta River at Akosombo. This is a vast hydro-electric scheme: the power generated provides electricity for industrial and domestic use within Ghana, and is also used in the neighbouring countries of Togo and Benin. Important sea ports are at Takoradi and at Tema, near Accra, the capital. Accra is the site of an international airport.

English is the official language of Ghana. Many people, including the Twi, Fante and Ashanti groups, speak languages belonging to the Akan family. Many other languages and dialects are also spoken.

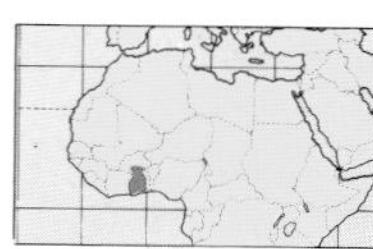

Area:
238,537 km²
(92,105 mi²)
Population:
12,210,000
Capital:
Accra (pop. 851,614)
Other towns:
Kumasi, Sekondi-Takoradi, Tamale, Cape Coast, Sunyani, Ho
Currency:
cedi

Women returning from market along Ghana's beautiful shoreline.

Guinea

République Populaire et Révolutionnaire de Guinée

The Popular and Revolutionary Republic of Guinea lies on the bulge of western Africa. The Atlantic coastline is made up of islands and swamps. Behind these lowlands are plateaux, high plains and mountains in the south-east. The sources of the Niger, Gambia and Senegal rivers are in the Fouta Djallon plateau. Mount Nimba, near the border with Liberia and the Ivory Coast, is 1,752 metres (5,748 ft) high.

The land contains various mineral resources. Bauxite, the rock from which aluminium is obtained, is the most important. Iron ore, diamonds and uranium are also mined. With Guinea's tropical climate, agriculture is also a vital industry. Coffee, bananas and pineapples are all grown for export.

The peoples of Guinea include the Fulbe (Fulani), Malinke (Mandingo) and Soussou. The country was a French colony from 1891 until 1958, when it became independent under the leadership of Sékou Touré. France withdrew aid when Guinea decided to sever its links with France, so Guinea instead went for aid to the Communist bloc. It became a neutral country, following a 'non-aligned' policy – that is, it favoured neither east nor west. A military coup followed the death of Sékou Touré in 1984. The President of Guinea is now Col. Lansana Conté.

The capital of Guinea, Conakry, is on the coastal island of Tombo. It is an industrial centre, and is linked to the town of Kankan by rail. Conakry has an international airport.

Area:
245,857 km² (94,931 mi²)
Population:
5,410,000
Capital:
Conakry (pop. 763,000)
Other towns:
Kankan, Kindia
Currency:
syli

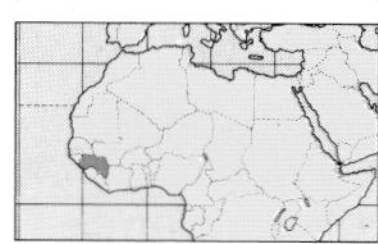

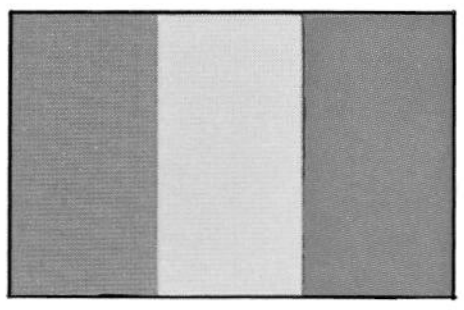

Left: Children play in the surf of Guinea's tropical Atlantic coast.

Below: Countries of the West African coast.

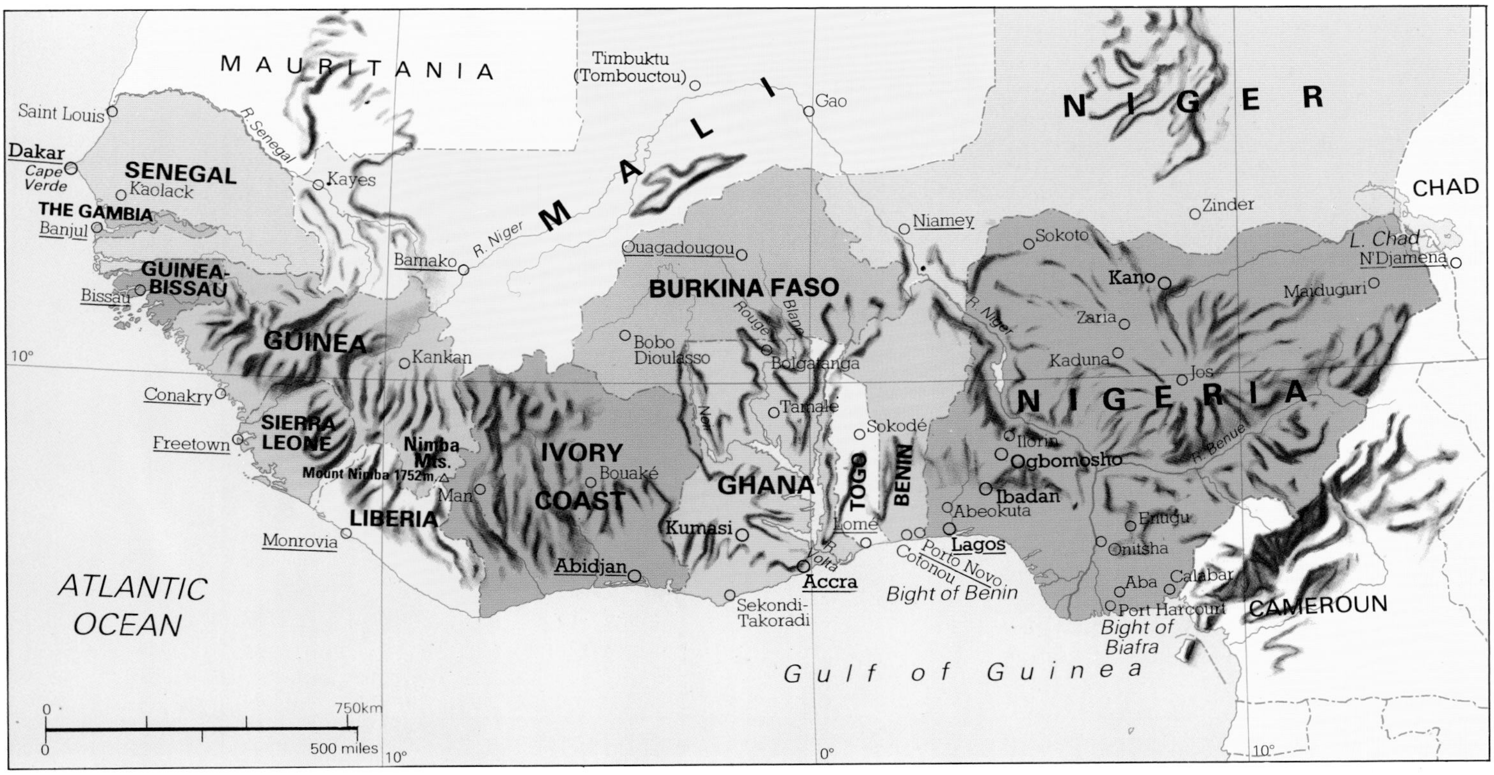

MAURITANIA
MALI
NIGER
CHAD
SENEGAL
THE GAMBIA
GUINEA-BISSAU
GUINEA
SIERRA LEONE
LIBERIA
IVORY COAST
BURKINA FASO
GHANA
TOGO
BENIN
NIGERIA
CAMEROUN
Saint Louis
Dakar
Cape Verde
Kaolack
Banjul
Bissau
Conakry
Freetown
Monrovia
Kayes
Bamako
Kankan
Nimba Mts.
Mount Nimba 1752m
Man
Bouaké
Abidjan
Timbuktu (Tombouctou)
Gao
Niamey
Ouagadougou
Bobo Dioulasso
Bolgatanga
Tamale
Kumasi
Sekondi-Takoradi
Accra
Lomé
Sokodé
Cotonou
Porto Novo
Lagos
Abeokuta
Ibadan
Ogbomosho
Ilorin
Kaduna
Zaria
Kano
Sokoto
Zinder
Jos
Maiduguri
L. Chad
N'Djamena
Enugu
Onitsha
Aba
Calabar
Port Harcourt
R. Senegal
R. Niger
R. Benue
R. Volta
Bight of Benin
Bight of Biafra
Gulf of Guinea
ATLANTIC OCEAN
10°
0°
0
750km
500 miles

Guinea-Bissau

Lying between the Republic of Guinea and Senegal on the West African coast is the small Republic of Guinea-Bissau, so called to distinguish it from its neighbour. Behind the Bijagos archipelago lies a deeply indented coastline. Rivers lead through a belt of forest to a swampy interior.

The Portuguese came to this coast as early as the fifteenth century, and established a colony in 1814. The peoples of Guinea-Bissau include Balante, Mandingo (Malinke), Fulbe (Fulani) and Mandjako, but Portuguese is the official language. Guinea-Bissau did not gain independence until 1974, after a 12-year war. Their leader, Amilcar Cabral, was killed in 1973 and so the first president of the new republic was Luiz Cabral. Cabral was overthrown in 1980 by General João Bernardo Vieira.

The economy of Guinea-Bissau depends upon farming. Rice is a major crop, as is maize. Coconuts, groundnuts, cassava and palm-oil are produced, and cattle are reared. Bauxite has been found in the south, as in the neighbouring Republic of Guinea. Produce is exported through Bissau, a busy port in the north of the country.

Area:
36,125 km²
(13,949 mi²)
Population:
844,000
Capital:
Bissau (pop. 109,500)
Currency:
peso

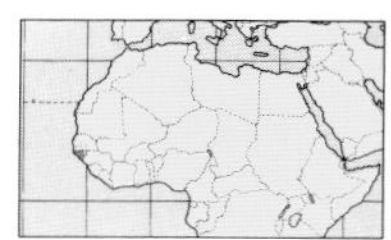

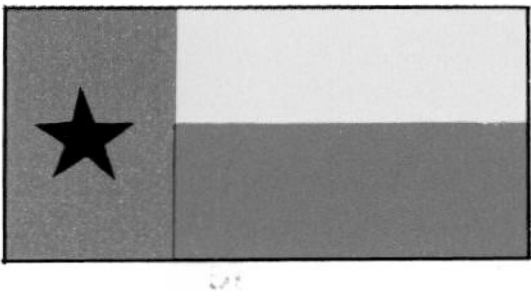

Ivory Coast République de la Côte d'Ivoire

Ivory Coast is a hot, humid country. It shares frontiers with five other nations: Ghana, Burkina Faso, Mali, Guinea and Liberia. Savannah covers the north. As one travels south, one passes through farmland before reaching the rain forests of the coast. These forests provide large amounts of timber for export, and also rubber. Other produce sold abroad includes cocoa, coffee, cotton, pineapple and palm-oil.

Although most people make their living from farming, either for export or simply to meet their own needs, many live in the large industrial city of Abidjan. This busy centre, the country's capital, is home for more than a million people. Abidjan is a port, being linked to the coast by a canal. It has an oil refinery and an international airport.

About 60 languages and dialects are spoken, including the Akan language group. Many people follow the traditional religions of their ancestors. Others are Muslims or Christians.

The rivers which lead into the interior from the Atlantic coast attracted European traders, and the French colonized the region at the end of the 19th century. After the Second World War, many African countries began a struggle to become independent from European occupation. In Ivory Coast this struggle was led by Félix Houphouët-Boigny, who became president when his country became fully independent in 1960. Unlike its neighbour, the Republic of Guinea, Ivory Coast remained closely involved with France. In 1959, Houphouët-Boigny helped form the Conseil de l'Entente. This association of former French colonies included Ivory Coast, Benin, Niger, Burkina Faso (Upper Volta), and, later, Togo. French remains the country's official language.

The only political party in the country is the *Parti Démocratique de la Côte d'Ivoire.* Election of delegates to the National Assembly, which has 147 members, takes place every five years. The country has had a stable government since independence, and this has helped to make the country relatively wealthy. But the Ivory Coast does face problems common to many African countries. For example, many industrial and commercial companies are under foreign control. Also, the development of industry has caused great changes in the traditional way of life, especially by turning country people into city-dwellers.

Area:
322,463 km²
(124,510 mi²)
Population:
8,890,000
Capital:
Abidjan (pop. 1,850,000)
Capital designate:
Yamassoukro
Other towns:
Bouaké, Daloa
Currency:
franc CFA

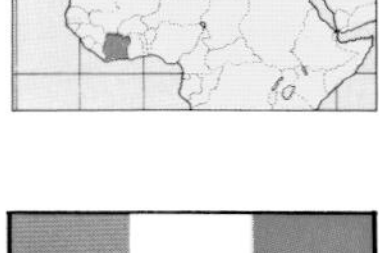

Abidjan, chief port and capital of Ivory Coast.

Kenya

Jamhuri ya

The Republic of Kenya lies on the eastern coast of Africa, bordering the Indian Ocean. It is a beautiful, open country which is teeming with wildlife. Zebra and wildebeeste still graze the huge tracts of such national parks as Tsavo and Amboseli. Elephant, lion, rhinoceros and buffalo are among the magnificent creatures that not long ago were free to roam across the land. But they have been ruthlessly hunted, and today Africa's wildlife is in danger. Forests have been cut down; huge cities are springing up; and poachers shoot elephants in order to sell the ivory for trinkets. Today national parks have been set aside in many African countries. The reserves of Kenya, and its neighbour Tanzania are among the last havens for African wildlife.

The coast of Kenya is made up of a fertile strip, fringed by white beaches. The Arabs colonized this coast about 1,200 years ago. The coast includes the island of Lamu in the north (an ancient centre of Islamic culture), the tourist resort of Malindi, and the city of Mombasa in the south. Mombasa, a centre of trade, is the major port of East Africa. It is a cosmopolitan city, with many inhabitants of Indian and Arab ancestry.

North-eastern Kenya is largely desert and arid bush country. In the north-west is a huge area of inland water – Lake Turkana (formerly Lake Rudolf), which is around 8,600 km ^{2} (3,320 mi^2) in area. The south-west lies on the equator. But it is mostly high land, and so the climate is more temperate than elsewhere. To the south-west of Mount Kenya, which is 5,201 metres (17,064 ft) high, lies the capital, Nairobi. It is a large city of about a million people and a centre for business, government, administration, and education.

A variety of ethnic and language groups make up the Kenyan nation. The Kikuyu form the largest group. The Luo, Luhya and Kamba are also numerous. In the north-east are the Turkana people, and in the south, straddling the border with Tanzania, are the famous Masai, who are known as warriors and cattle herders.

In many African countries, language is a major problem, because it divides the people. Kenya is an example. The peoples of the region speak many languages and dialects, including Kikuyu and Masai. English, the language of the colonial settlers, is also widely used as the language of trade and education. But today the official language is Swahili. Swahili is the language of the East African coast. It is spoken over a wide area, and has become one of the most useful languages in Africa. Swahili is a Bantu language, including many words from Arabic, and some other words from Urdu, Gujarati, Persian, English and Portuguese. Swahili is the language favoured by many of Africa's greatest writers.

The British first came to East Africa as traders and explorers, like the Arabs and the Portuguese before them. But soon settlers arrived, attracted by Kenya's rich farmland. In the early years of the 20th century, the British settlers built a railway and moved into the interior. African resistance to British rule came to a head in the 1950s with the Mau Mau rebellion, a violent confrontation between Kenyan guerrillas and British forces which lasted some eight years. Independence was finally won in 1963, and the first prime minister was Jomo Kenyatta. Kenyatta was a veteran of the struggle for independence, who had been jailed by the British. In 1964 Kenya was declared a republic. As president, Kenyatta became influential as the 'grand old man' of African politics. Upon his death in 1978, he was succeeded by the vice-president Daniel Arap Moi.

An attempt in 1967 to form an East African Economic Union with Kenya's neighbours, Uganda and Tanzania, failed, because of disagreements about policies. For example, Tanzania

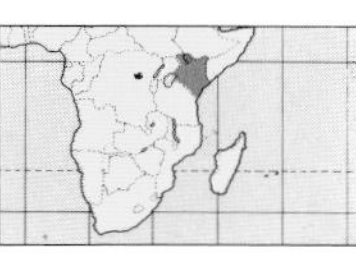

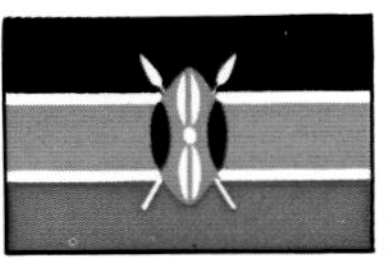

Area:
582,646 km^2
(224,973 mi^2)
Population:
19,500,000
Capital:
Nairobi (pop. 1,200.000)
Other towns:
Mombasa, Kisumu, Nakuru, Meru, Eldoret, Thika
Currency:
shilling

Above left: The skyline of modern Nairobi.

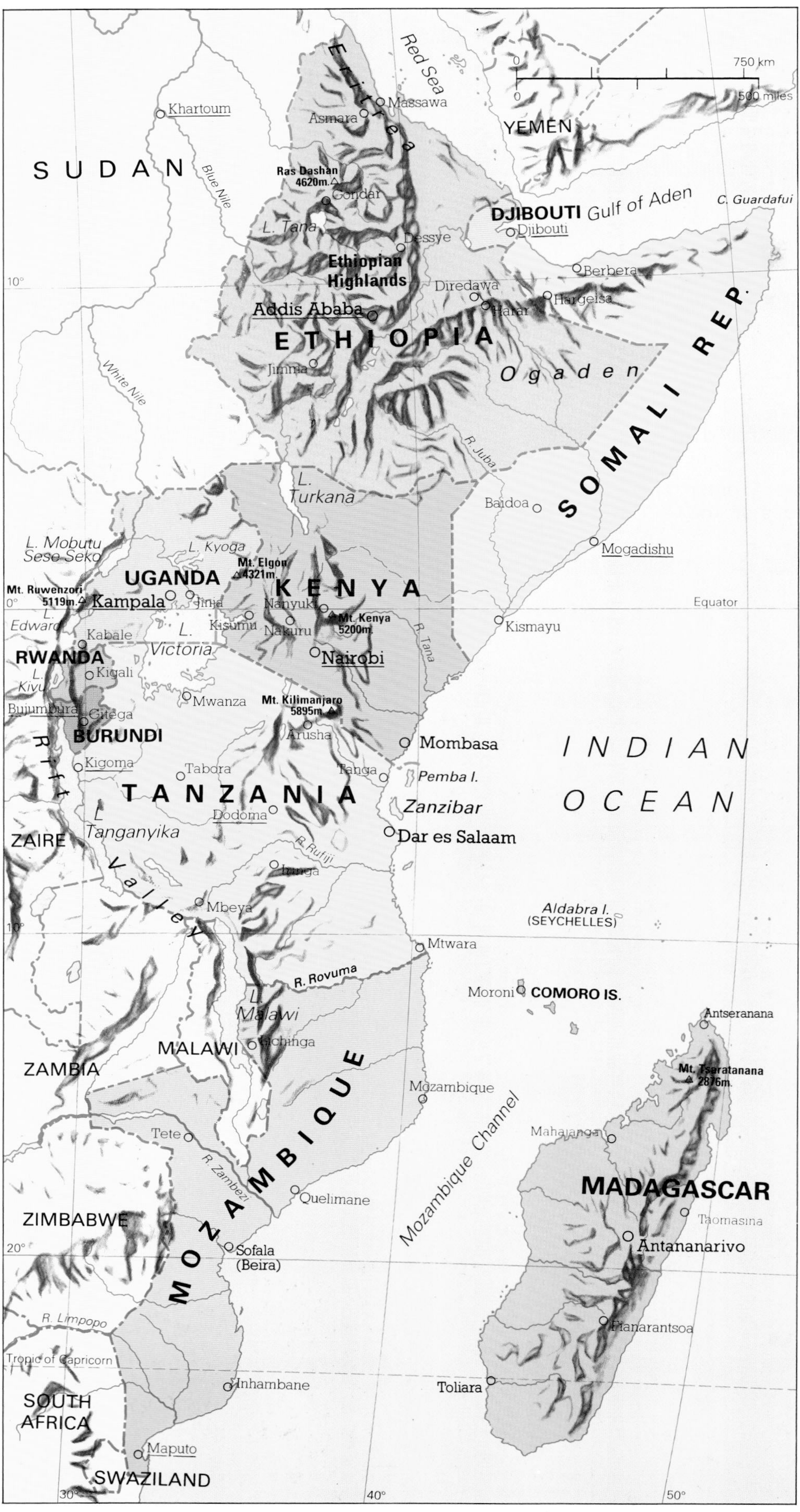

Countries of the Swahili coast and the Horn of Africa.

attempted to follow a programme of socialist reforms, whilst Kenya developed along capitalist lines. The Kenya African National Union (KANU), the party led by Kenyatta, suppressed opposition. In 1982, Moi put down an attempted coup by some members of the armed forces.

Kenya is a powerful economic force in East Africa. It lacks the massive income from oil enjoyed by such countries as Nigeria. Kenya's oil is imported through the port of Mombasa, which has a refinery. But it does have a few mineral resources, including fluorspar, galena (lead ore), salt, limestone and a little gold. Electricity is provided by hydro-electric schemes. Light industry flourishes in the cities and a variety of consumer goods are produced. Tourism is becoming more and more important.

Agriculture remains the most important activity in Kenya. The wide range of produce reflects the varying climate of the regions. Kenya produces bananas and pineapples, barley and wheat, coconuts, sisal (a fibrous plant used for making ropes and twine), cotton, maize and tea. Coffee is the leading export crop. Cattle farming provides meat, hides and dairy produce. Many city-dwellers keep small-holdings or plots of land in the country to supplement their income.

Kenya has a good communications network. Many roads are surfaced and in good repair. Train, coach or air services link the larger towns, and Nairobi has an international airport.

Lesotho
Kingdom of

The Kingdom of Lesotho is a small country in south-eastern Africa, bordered on all sides by the Republic of South Africa. The Drakensberg range is in the east, and the Maloti Mountains are to the north. Most of Lesotho is highland, crossed by the Orange and Caledon river systems.

The economy of Lesotho is based on agriculture. The capital, Maseru, is the only major city. Grain and vegetable crops are grown and cattle, sheep, goats, pigs and poultry are raised. But as in many African countries, the soil is poor and many farmers can provide food for their families, but little more. Lesotho's geographical position means that its affairs are closely connected with those of the Republic of South Africa. Many workers from Lesotho work across the border in South African towns and mines. Tourism is increasingly important, and oil and mineral resources are being developed.

Most people in Lesotho are Basotho, and both Sesotho and English are spoken. The Basotho nation had its origins in the early nineteenth century. It became the British protectorate of Basutoland in 1884, but regained independence as a monarchy within the Commonwealth in 1966.

The soil of Lesotho is very poor, and the farmers must cope also with difficult mountainous terrain.

Area:
30,355 km²
(11,721 mi²)
Population:
1,470,000
Capital:
Maseru (pop. 45,000)
Currency:
loti

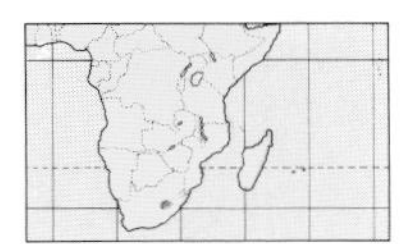

Liberia
Republic of

The Republic of Liberia lies on the Atlantic coast of West Africa, on the corner of the bulge. Slave traders raided the coast in the eighteenth century. When many slaves were freed in the United States, a small group returned to Africa to form a colony near the present site of Monrovia in 1822. Liberia became an independent republic in 1847. Local people resisted the American blacks, who formed an influential elite. Despite exploitation by foreign business interests, the country remained intact, under the modernizing influence of William Tubman, who served as president from 1944 to 1971. He was succeeded by William Tolbert, who was displaced when a military coup, led by Samuel K. Doe, occurred in 1980.

The climate of Liberia is equatorial. The north of the country is hilly savannah. The coastal strip is low-lying and the centre consists of grassland and forest. A series of rivers cross the country. Rubber is a major product, although iron-ore is the chief export. Cocoa and coffee are grown, and timber is another important product. Exports pass through the port of Monrovia, the country's capital. Many Liberians speak English, the official language, but a number of African languages are also spoken. The chief ethnic groups are the Kpelle and Bassa.

West Point, in Monrovia, capital of Liberia.

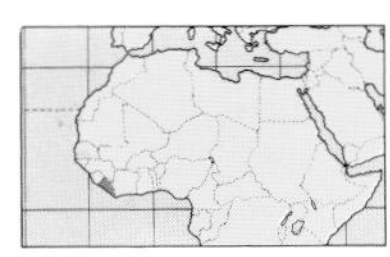

Area:
111,369 km²
(43,002 mi²)
Population:
1,992,000
Capital:
Monrovia (pop. 425,000)
Other towns:
Buchanan
Currency:
dollar

Libya

Socialist People's Libyan Arab Jamahiriyah

The Socialist People's Libyan Arab Jamahiriyah occupies the central section of the North African coastline. It borders the Mediterranean Sea and extends southwards into the heart of the Sahara. The country is six times the size of Italy, for example, although less than 3,000,000 people live there, because most of the country is uninhabitable desert.

Libya is divided into three historic regions. In the west is Tripolitania, which takes its name from Tripoli, the capital and the largest city in the country. The hinterland consists of an oasis-filled plain which gradually rises to a height of 1,000 metres (3,281 ft) before levelling out into arid semi-desert. The coast runs westward along the Gulf of Sirte to the eastern region of Cyrenaica, next to the Egyptian border. The coast between Benghazi and Tubruq (Tobruk) is rocky, and inland there is a limestone plateau called the Jebel Akhdar. This area contains many normally dry watercourses. The only agriculture possible in this harsh country is in the coastal regions of Tripolitania and Cyrenaica.

To the south-east, extending into Egypt, lies the Libyan Desert, a desolate region of gravel, sand and burning-hot temperatures. Only the oases of Al Kufrah relieve the monotony of the south-eastern landscape. The third province is Fezzan. It is largely occupied by the Sahara, with minimal rainfall and a raging desert wind, called the *ghibli*.

The frontiers of countries can reveal much about their history as well as their geography. The straight lines of Libya's eastern and southern borders suggest that they pass through a featureless landscape and that they are the result of the deliberations of modern politicians. Indeed, the modern state of Libya is the result of political treaties made in this century, but the history of the region can be traced back to ancient times.

Rock paintings have been found in Fezzan dating from before 3000 BC. The Phoenicians colonized the coast of Tripolitania, and the Greeks settled on the east coast. The name Libya comes, in fact, from the Greek word used to describe all the territory west of Egypt. Most splendid of the cities founded by the ancient Greeks was Cyrene. Archaeological digs have uncovered the fascinating civilization of this period. Magnificent examples of Greek architecture include the sanctuary of Apollo, the great temple of Zeus and the most ancient theatre in the African continent.

Between 100 BC and AD 100, the Romans colonized Tripolitania and Cyrenaica. Eventually they captured Fezzan (Phasania) as well. Byzantine rule followed, and then, in the seventh century, the Arabs invaded. Resistance by the native Berber population was overcome between AD 669 and 675.

In 1143, the Normans succeeded in capturing Tripoli but were soon expelled. Spain took Tripoli in 1510, but after years of fierce resistance, Emperor Charles V entrusted his possession to the Knights Hospitallers, whose base was then at Malta rather than Rhodes. In 1551, they were beaten by the Turks, and Tripoli became a centre for the dreaded corsairs, privateers who preyed upon the shipping of the Christian countries.

Turkish rule lasted until 1911, when the Italians invaded. Resistance was sustained, but eventually the country was subdued and Libya gained her current borders. In 1943, Libya was taken by the British in the desert campaign of the Second World War. In 1951, under the auspices of the United Nations Organization, Libya became an independent kingdom ruled by Idris I.

At the end of the 1950s, a discovery was made which was to transform the country – huge reserves of oil. Libya soon developed into a major economic power, and an important voice in the Arab world. The corrupt monarchy was overthrown in 1969 by an army officer, Muamar al Gadaffi (Qadhafi), a militant Islamic revolutionary who undertook radical reform of the country. Gadaffi's support for revolutionary causes led to accusations of terrorism. In 1986 this led to the USA bombing Libya. Libya is Africa's second largest oil producer. Petro-chemical industries are expanding, and industrial capacity in other fields is also being improved. There is limited agricultural production (dates, olives, fruit and grain), but most of the country is barren. Only 1·4 per cent of the land is farmed and food is the major import.

Communications within Libya are good. Roads link the towns along the coast and the chief towns of the interior, Ghudamis (Ghadames) and Sabhah (Sebha) are linked with the coast. Airfields provide internal and external services. The chief ports are the capital, Tripoli, and Benghazi.

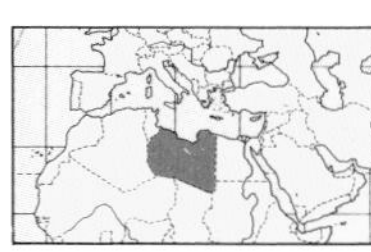

Area:
1,759,540 km² (679,399 mi²)
Population:
3,500,000
Capital:
Tripoli (pop. 980,000)
Other towns:
Benghazi, Misratah, Zawia (Zavia)
Currency:
dinar

The ruined forum at Leptis Magna, near the modern town of Al Khums (Homs).

Madagascar

Democratic Republic of

Area:
587,041 km²
(226,670 mi²)
Population:
9,740,000
Capital:
Antananarivo (pop. 400,000)

Other towns:
Taomasina, Mahajanga, Fianarantsoa, Antsiranana
Currency:
franc malgache (FMG)

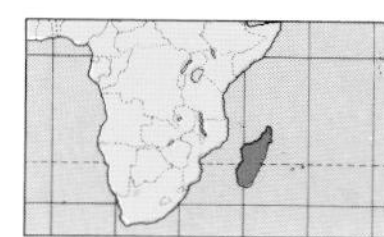

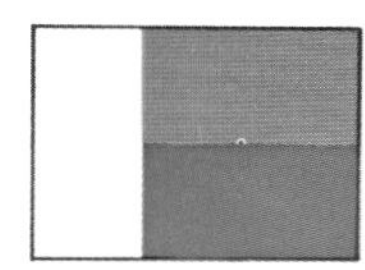

The islands off the eastern coast of Africa are beautiful, exotic places. They are on the ancient trading routes of the Indian Ocean, and their cultures have over many centuries linked the peoples of Africa and Asia. The largest of these islands is Madagascar, which makes up most of the Democratic Republic of Madagascar. The people of Madagascar are a mixture of Arabs, Indonesians and African peoples. The largest ethnic group is the Merina. French, Chinese and Indian immigrants have also settled on Madagascar.

The Merina people dominate the island's history. In the late eighteenth century, their king, Andrianampoinimerina, conquered his rivals and founded a united kingdom. Remains of the island's stormy past may still be seen in the strong defences surrounding hill villages. With the European colonization of the African continent in the late nineteenth century, the French declared the country a protectorate, but it became independent in 1960.

The first president was Philibert Tsiranana, whose party retained power for 12 years. In 1972, a military government under General Ramanantsoa took power, but he handed over to Colonel Ratsimandrava in 1975. After Ratsimandrava was assassinated, Didier Ratsiraka emerged as leader.

The island of Madagascar is 385 kilometres (239 miles) from the African mainland, and has a tropical climate. Rain forest covers the eastern coastal strip. The western part of the island is low-lying, separated from the east by a high plateau. The peak of Ankaratra rises to a height of 2,638 metres (8,655 ft) to the south of the capital, Antananarivo (Tananarive). The Tsaratanana Massif in the north of the island reaches 2,876 metres (9,436 ft). The south-west is semi-desert.

Wildlife thrives in the forested regions. Here live the true lemurs, such as the aye-aye and indri. These strange creatures are primitive primates, which live in trees. There is a national park in the far north, in the Mont d'Ambré region.

Agriculture is the mainstay of life in Madagascar. Rice is grown very widely, and is the staple food. Cassava, maize, coffee, sugar-cane and sweet potatoes are also cultivated. Exports include coffee and such luxuries as cloves and vanilla. Cattle are farmed in the west. Industry is small-scale, although oil-refining is important.

The houses of the Merina people (above) contrast strongly in their architectural style with the typical village huts of northern Madgascar (below).

Malawi

The Republic of Malawi is a long, thin-shaped country lying in eastern Africa, on the shores of Lake Malawi. This large stretch of water, which is still called Lake Nyasa in neighbouring Tanzania, was first made known to Europeans when it was discovered by David Livingstone, the Scottish missionary and explorer, in 1859. It lies in the Rift Valley, that huge depression that scars the eastern part of the African continent. Malawi shares borders with Zambia, Tanzania and Mozambique. Having no coastline, most imports and exports travel in and out by rail through ports in Mozambique. Much of Malawi consists of a plateau, with mountainous regions in the north and in the south, where Mount Mulanje, Malawi's highest peak rises to 3,000 metres (9,843 ft) to the east of Blantyre.

Coffee and tea are grown on the hillsides, but the most important crop is tobacco. Sugar-cane, groundnuts and cotton are also cultivated, and maize, cassava, millet, rice and fish provide food in the home. Malawi is primarily an agricultural country. Many people seek work in the industrial centres of Zambia, Zimbabwe and the Republic of South Africa.

Many peoples live in Malawi. There is the Nyenja-Chewa ethnic group, whose Bantu language is the one most widely spoken in the country, and the Yao, Tombe and Tumbuka peoples. Malawi is densely populated.

Malawi was the site of the Maravi empire in the sixteenth century. Later, its history was one of constant strife, as various peoples tried to gain control of the region. As in many parts of eastern Africa, Arab slave traders profited from and contributed to the unrest by their ruthless dealing in human misery. Malawi, or Nyasaland, as it was formerly called, became the British Central African Protectorate in 1892, and in 1953 it was taken into the Central African Federation with Northern and Southern Rhodesia (now Zambia and Zimbabwe). A struggle for independence was led by Dr Hastings Kamuzu Banda, who was gaoled for his activities in 1959. But his dream of an independent country came true in 1964. In 1966, Malawi became a republic within the Commonwealth. Dr Banda was the first president, and he became president for life in 1970. Malawi is a one-party state. Members of the Malawi Congress Party, the only party, are elected to serve five-year terms in the National Assembly.

The capital of Malawi is now the city of Lilongwe, but the largest city, Blantyre-Limbe, remains the chief industrial and commercial centre, with a population of about 222,000. Both Lilongwe and Blantyre are on the rail system, which is linked up to the railways of Mozambique by a bridge over the Zambezi River. **The port of Sofala (Beira) in Mozambique handles much of Malawi's trade. The Liwonde-Nayuchi railway line links up with the port of Nacala.**

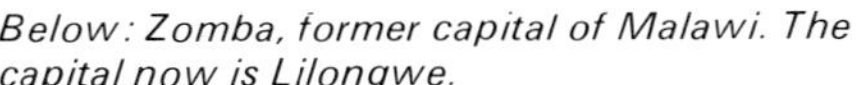

Below: Zomba, former capital of Malawi. The capital now is Lilongwe.

Above: A view of Malawi, from Mount Mulanje, the highest point in the country.

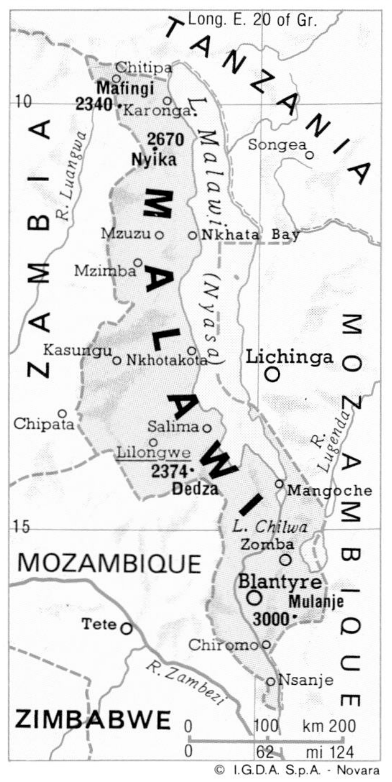

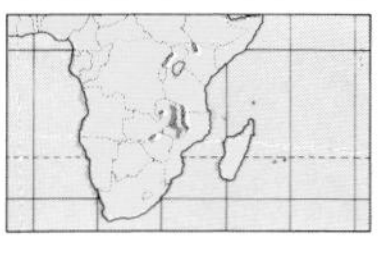

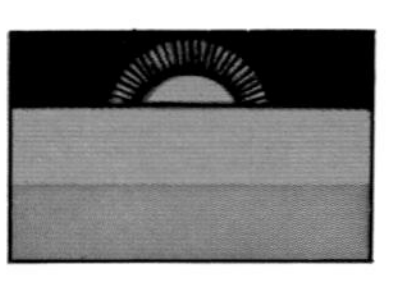

Area: 118,484 km² (45,749 mi²)
Population: 6,600,000
Capital: Lilongwe (pop. 103,000)
Other towns: Blantyre-Limbe, Zomba, Mzuzu
Currency: kwacha

Mali

République du

To many people in Europe, the name Timbuktu sums up the whole mystery of ancient Africa, the great continent whose interior remained unknown for so long. Timbuktu is, in fact, in central Mali, and is the last town seen by travellers before they enter the empty wasteland of the Sahara to the north. For centuries Timbuktu was of great importance to the trade caravans which crossed the Sahara.

The ancient empire of Mali was founded by Sundiata in the early 12th century. From 1883 until independence in 1958, the region was under French rule, and known as the French Sudan.

The Republic of Mali is a predominantly Islamic country. Most people are black Africans, including the Bambara, Mandingo (Malinke), Dyula, Songhai and Dogon peoples. Nomadic Tuaregs and Arabs live in the northern regions. The official language is French.

Running across Mali is the River Niger. The bend in the Niger creates a fertile region in the centre, to the south of Timbuktu. The south of the country is savannah, and the River Senegal crosses the western border. Chief exports are cotton, groundnuts, live animals, grain and fish.

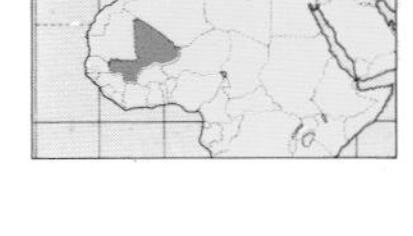

Area:
1,240,000 km² (478,793 mi²)
Population:
7,720,000
Capital:
Bamako (pop. 404,000)

Other towns:
Ségou, Mopti, Sikasso, Kayes
Currency:
franc

Below: A cheerful pineapple seller in Bamako, Mali.

Mauritania

République Islamique de Mauritanie

The Islamic Republic of Mauritania is a large country on the Atlantic coast of North Africa. Much of the country is uninhabitable desert – the sandy, stony wastes of the Sahara. This is the home of Berber and Arab nomads, who wander with their camels and herds of sheep and goats from oasis to oasis. There is sufficient rainfall in the south for some agriculture. Groundnuts, dates, rice and millet are all cultivated. The southern peoples, including the Wolof, Peul (Fulani) and Sarakole groups, are mainly black Africans.

Independence from France was achieved in 1960. In 1976, Spain withdrew from Spanish (now Western) Sahara to the north. By agreement, Mauritania and Morocco shared out this territory between them, but the Polisario guerrilla movement in Western Sahara forced Mauritania to relinquish its claim to the region in 1979.

Agriculture and fishing provide some of Mauritania's assets, but the greatest potential lies in the mineral resources available – copper and iron ore, which is by far the leading export.

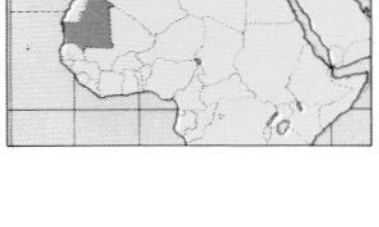

Area:
1,030,700 km² (397,977 mi²)
Population:
1,830,000
Capital:
Nouakchott (pop. 135,000)

Other towns:
Nouadhibou, Kaédi
Currency:
ouguiya

Above: Islamic art shows its influence with this decorative finger-wall-painting, a feature of a house in Oualata, Mauritania.

Mauritius

This group of islands in the Indian Ocean lies to the east of Madagascar. Once a French and then a British colony, Mauritius became independent within the Commonwealth in 1968. Its economy relies on sugar and tourism.

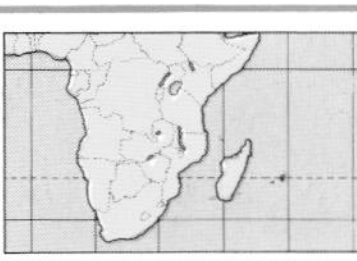

Area:
2,045 km² (790 mi²)
Population:
973,000
Capital:
Port Louis (pop. 150,000)

Currency:
rupee

Morocco

al-Mamlaka al-Maghrebia

Most countries in North Africa have been completely dominated by Arab culture. In Morocco, however, the culture of the Berbers, the original inhabitants, has survived relatively intact. The Berbers are a proud people and they have not readily submitted to the authority of invaders. Although the majority of the Moroccan population is now Arab, and Arabic is the official language, the Berber language is still widely spoken in the mountains of the interior.

At the end of the seventh century, the Arab penetration began. For the first time in their history, the Berbers adopted an alien religion and culture. Even so, in 739, under the leadership of Maysara, the tribes broke away from the Arab caliphate whilst retaining the Islamic religion. The great period of Berber power began in 786, with the rule of Idris-ibn-Abdullah, who succeeded in unifying the feuding and quarrelling tribes. The Almoravid and Almohad dynasties of the early Middle Ages controlled most of the Maghreb region of North Africa and much of Spain as well. In the late Middle Ages, European Christians reversed the balance of power and succeeded in occupying much of the Moroccan coast. But this territory was lost to the Sa'di dynasty in the 16th century. Morocco's present king Hassan II, belongs to the 'Alawi dynasty, which dates from the 17th century.

But this autonomy was interrupted during the colonial period. After France took Algiers in 1830, it sought to extend its rule into Morocco. But in the 19th century, the scramble for overseas colonies by the European powers was like a slow game of chess. Only when France had agreed to accept Britain's interest in Egypt, Italy's interest in Libya, and Spain's interest in gaining a foothold in northern Morocco, was the road clear. The greater part of Morocco became a French protectorate in 1912, although Tangiers was under international administration.

An independence movement developed before the Second World War. After a long and bitter struggle, independence came to the whole country in 1956. The restored monarchy faced many problems at home and abroad, not least the fighting of a desert war. This was sparked off by the claims of Morocco and Mauritania to the mineral-rich area of Western Sahara when it was vacated by Spain in 1976. These claims were resisted by Saharan guerrillas and Mauritania withdrew in 1979. This left Morocco in charge of all of Western Sahara, but the war continued, with Algeria supporting the guerrillas.

In independent Morocco the monarchy has directly intervened in the political process. The 1972 constitution, voted in by a referendum, gives ultimate power to the king. Representatives of trade unions, commercial and other interests participate in government.

Morocco's economy has undergone many difficulties on the road from colonialism to self-reliance. The 1970s saw considerable progress, largely due to mineral production. Morocco is now third in the world league of phosphate producers. Iron ore, lead, zinc and manganese all earn money, and there are also reserves of oil, tin, copper and other minerals.

More than half of the people work on the land. Agricultural produce includes vines, cereals, olives, dates, figs and citrus fruits. Sheep and goats are raised on a large scale. Forestry and fishing are of increasing importance, as are textile production, food processing and the chemical industry. The manufacture of fertilizers is particularly important. Probably the thing most people associate with this region is the fine goatskin leather known as morocco. Others may think of daggers inlaid with silver and enamel, carpets from Rabat, or precious, glazed ceramics. The traditional crafts certainly make their contribution to the economy, and go hand in hand with the development of international tourism.

Morocco has two coastlines. The Atlantic coastline is low-lying and sandy, while much of the Mediterranean coast is indented, with high cliffs. Much of the country is mountainous. The northern coastal range, the Rif, lies between the Strait of Gibraltar and the River Moulouya. Reaching a height of 2,456 metres (8,058 ft) at Mount Tidirhine, this range is structurally similar to that of the mountains in southern Spain.

Parallel with the Atlantic coast are three important mountain ranges: the Middle (Moyen) Atlas, the High (Haut) Atlas and the Anti-Atlas. The High Atlas contains one of Morocco's natural wonders, Mount Toubkal. At 4,165 metres (13,665 ft), it is the highest peak in North Africa. Between these mountains and the Atlantic Ocean lie a series of fertile plains, which are densely populated. The largest of these is in the north-east, bisected by the River Sebou. Behind the High Atlas lies yet another mountainous region, Jebel Sarhro.

The south of Morocco is desert, which covers a massive area if the disputed territory of Western Sahara, which Morocco has annexed, is taken into account. Here, there are many sand dunes, and the temperatures soar above 50°C (122°F). There is little rainfall.

The capital of Morocco is the ancient city of Rabat, but the really large centres of population are Casablanca, Kenitra and Fès (Fez). Casablanca is a port on the Atlantic and is really the commercial and industrial centre of the country, with 2,357, 200 inhabitants. The major cities are linked by road and rail, and by air to the outside world. Morocco's chief trading partners are the members of the European Economic Community and the United States.

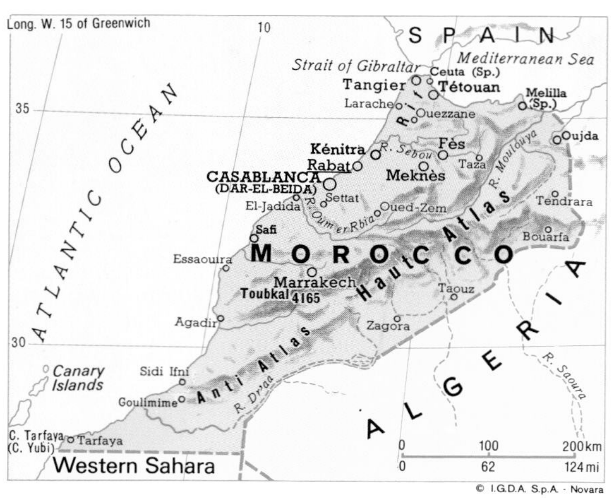

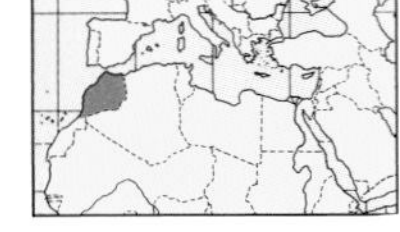

Area: 446,550 km² (172,423 mi²)
Population: 21,465,000
Capital: Rabat (pop. 865,000)

Other towns: Casablanca, Marrakech, Fès (Fez), Meknès, Tangiers (Tanger), Oujda
Currency: dirham

Mozambique

República Popular de Moçambique

The People's Republic of Mozambique occupies a long section of the East African coastline running from Tanzania in the north, to the Republic of South Africa in the south. It is separated from the island of Madagascar by the Mozambique Channel. The mighty Zambezi River cuts across the centre of the country, providing hydro-electric power at the Cabora Bassa dam, and forming a delta where it reaches the sea. The broad coastal lowlands give way to higher ground in the west.

Agriculture is now being organized on a collective basis. The main crops are copra (coconut kernels which are processed for oil), sugar, tea, cashew nuts, cotton and sisal (a fibrous plant used in making rope and twine).

Mozambique is ruled by a Marxist government under President Samora Machel, whose FRELIMO movement fought a 10-year war to free the country from Portuguese rule. Independence in 1975 put an end to 470 years of Portuguese involvement in the region.

Swahili is widely spoken, but Portuguese remains the official language. The people belong to a variety of ethnic groupings, including the Yao, Makonde, Nyanja and Makua-Lomwe. The country takes its name from the island port of Moçambique (Msumbiji) in the north.

Area:
801,590 km²
(309,513 mi²)
Population:
13,140,000
Capital:
Maputo (pop. 850,000)
Other towns:
Beira, Inhambane, Quelimane
Currency:
metical

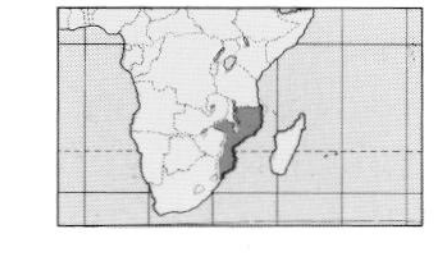

Namibia

Running along the Atlantic coast of southern Africa is a huge strip of empty wasteland – the Namib Desert. This desert and the land behind it form the country of Namibia, previously known as South-West Africa. This is the home of the Ovambo people, and a number of other ethnic groups, including Damara, Kavango, Herero, Nama, Bushmen and Europeans.

The climate is not really conducive to agriculture on a large scale, although livestock is raised commercially. Fishing and mineral production, however, are significant. Diamonds, copper, zinc and lead are mined in the region.

Namibia has been the focus of international discord for some years. A German protectorate before the First World War, Namibia has been administered by the Republic of South Africa since 1920. The United Nations Organization disputed their claim and, in 1971, the International Court of Justice ruled that South African control was illegal – a decision rejected by the South Africans, who nevertheless conceded the principle of independence.

Area:
824,292 km²
(318,278 mi²)
Population:
1,066,000
Capital:
Windhoek (pop. 65,000)
Currency:
rand

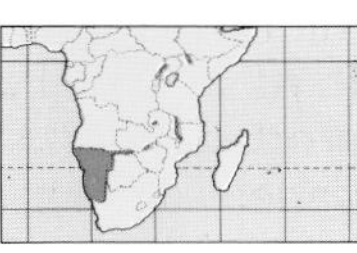

Niger

République du

A large section of the southern Sahara is taken up by the Republic of Niger. This country stretches between Algeria and Libya in the north, and Nigeria, Benin and Burkina Faso in the south. The north is desert, broken by the Aïr mountains. The desert is the home of Berbers called Tuaregs. These people are nomads who have learned to eke out an existence in some of the world's harshest terrain. The south-west is more fertile. Here the River Niger flows across the Mali border, and forms part of the frontier with Benin. The rest of the south is savannah.

Most of the population is Muslim. Ethnic groups of Niger include Hausa, Peul (Fulani), Kanuri and Djerma-Songhai. French is widely spoken, because Niger is a former French colony, and links with France remain strong. Before colonization this region was dominated by a number of small Islamic states. A supreme military council under the president, Colonel Seyni Kountché has ruled Niger since 1974. Most people are farmers and groundnuts are the chief cash crop. Cattle, sheep and goats are raised.

Area:
1,267,000 km²
(489,218 mi²)
Population:
6,270,000
Capital:
Niamey (pop. 225,000)
Other towns:
Zinder, Maradi
Currency:
franc CFA

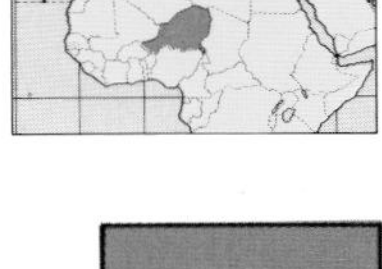

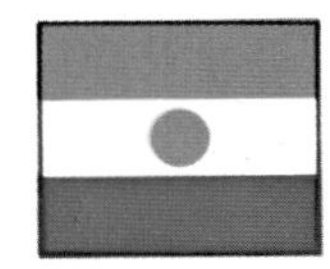

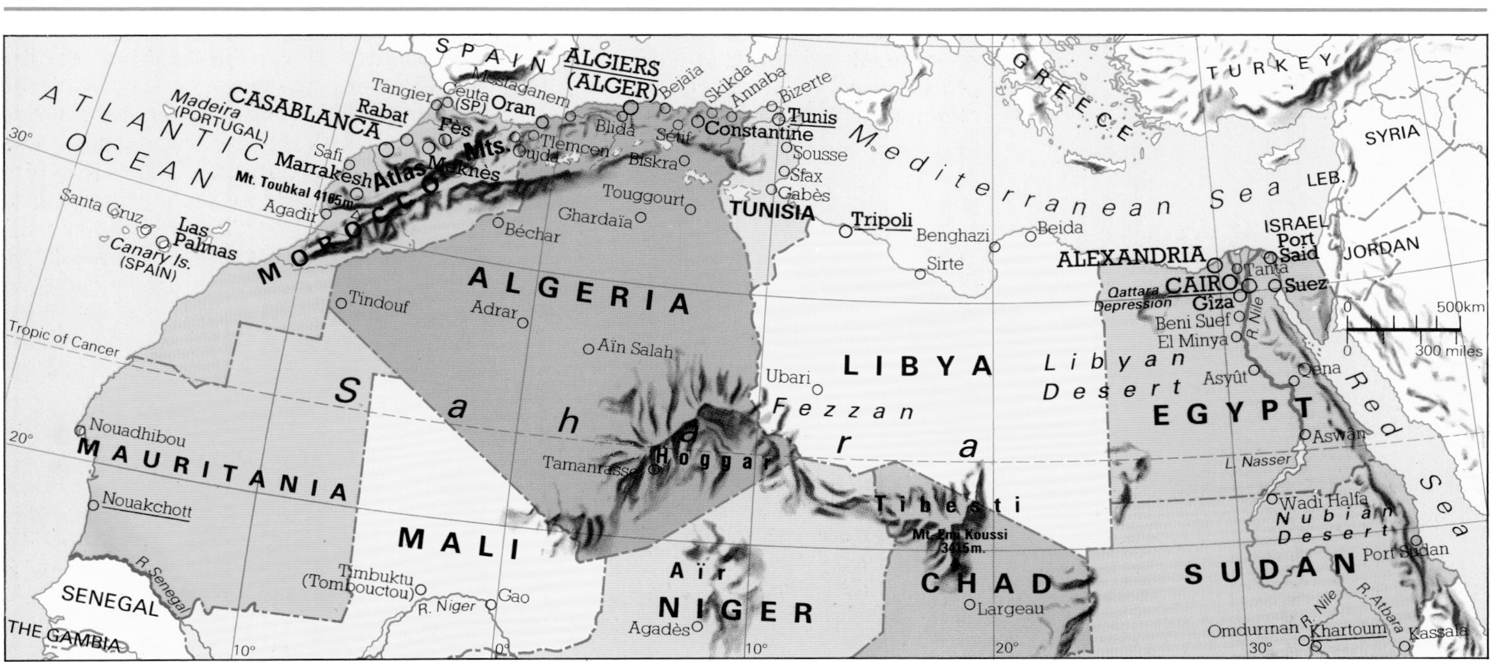

Nigeria

Federal Republic of

Above left: A terracotta head of a queen from Ife.
Above right: A Benin bronze head of a queen mother.

At the end of its 4,160 km (2,585 mi) journey to the Gulf of Guinea, the River Niger splits into a fine network of waterways. Behind this watery, humid coastline lies a large, fascinating and powerful country, the Federal Republic of Nigeria. As one travels inland from the swamps and forests of the south, the country becomes progressively drier, until one reaches the rolling, dusty plains of the north. The climate is hot, with a rainy season from July to October. A dry wind known as the 'harmattan' blows south from the Sahara during the dry season, but brings little relief because it carries with it dust and sand.

Nigeria is a land of contrasts: in climate, in peoples and culture, and in economics. There are about 250 ethnic groups in the country. Major groups include the Yoruba in the south-west, the Igbo in the south-east, and the Hausa, Fulani and Kanuri of the north. With such a bewildering variety of languages, the government decided to retain the old colonial language of English as the official tongue and as the medium of instruction in the schools. Most northerners are Muslims, while many southerners are Christians. The traditional religions of the south are also practised.

The diversity of the country has led to considerable difficulties in the years since independence. North and south have struggled for dominance, and in 1967 the south-east tried to break away from the federation. This move resulted in the Biafra War, in which about a million people are thought to have died before the federal government reasserted control over the region.

At the time when the ancient Greeks were founding the culture of Europe, an ancient civilization also flourished in the Nok region of northern Nigeria. The coast of the Gulf of Guinea was always an important cultural centre, and it was also a vital trading area because of its network of rivers. But, unhappily, Europeans obtained slaves from this part of West Africa and shipped them to the new colonies in the Americas. This brutal traffic brought untold misery to the area, encouraging warfare amongst the peoples of the region.

The British began to move into the area in the nineteenth century, at about the same time as the Islamic Caliphate of Sokoto was established in the north of the country. The coastal area was declared a British protectorate in 1893, and the colony of Southern Nigeria was formed in 1900. Six years later the north became a protectorate, and in 1914 the two halves of the country were united into a single colony.

Independence was achieved in 1960. In 1963 Nigeria became a republic within the Commonwealth, under Sir Abubakar Tafawa Balewa. A succession of military governments ensued. From 1979–83 there was a period of democracy under Shehu Shagari, but in early 1984 a Supreme Military Council again took power. The economy of Nigeria has been developed along free enterprise lines. Traditionally, Nigeria relies on farming, fishing and forestry. Cocoa, palm-oil, cotton and rubber are all important crops. Oil is the key to wealth in the modern world, and

© I.G.D.A. S.p.A. - Novara

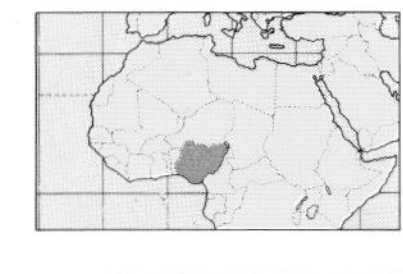

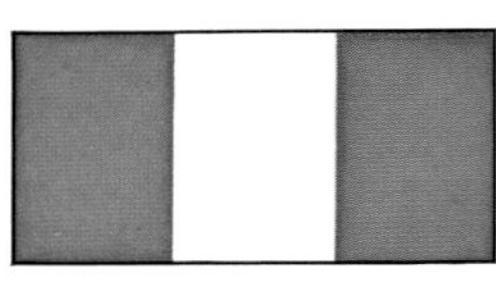

Area:
923,768 km² (356,688 mi²)
Population:
88,847,000
Capital:
Lagos (pop. 3,000,000)
Other towns:
Ibadan, Ogbomosho, Kano, Oshogbo, Ilorin, Abeokuta, Port Harcourt, Zaria, Ilesha, Onitsha, Iwo
Currency:
naira

Nigeria's oil wells financed modernization and industrialization within the country, but falling prices were to create many economic problems. There is an extensive road, rail and air route network, but the building of a new capital at Abuja, in the centre of the country, to replace the congested streets of Lagos, had to be abandoned.

The cost of living is extremely high, and alongside the wealth is poverty and hardship. Massive social problems exist. Nigeria is densely populated, particularly in the south, which is the centre of oil production, industry and commerce. The growth in the population is high, at 3·2 per cent per year (1975–79). At this rate, the country's population will double in only 22 years.

The fact that Nigeria has such economic potential has made it one of the most influential countries in Africa, and given it a powerful voice in international affairs.

The culture of Nigeria is rooted in a rich and varied tradition. The sculptures of Nok, Ife and the bronzes and other carvings of the ancient Kingdom of Benin remain unsurpassed. West African masks and pottery have had a great influence on European artists and craftsmen of the twentieth century. Nigerian authors, such as Chinua Achebe, have been among the leading writers of the post-colonial period in Africa. Despite the rapid industrialization of their country, most Nigerians still live in the countryside, and the traditional culture and way of life is still very much in evidence, whether in style of dress – the traditional textiles of Nigeria are magnificent – religious customs, or in colourful festivals.

Education is a major concern of the 19 state governors and Houses of Assembly. There are 13 universities in Nigeria, as well as polytechnics and an extensive programme of primary and secondary education. As with many African countries, education is probably the key to the future.

However, education like all other social services is expensive, and problems in financing many worthwhile projects arose in the early 1980s, as oil prices began to fall as part of the World depression.

Right top: Horsemen salute the Emir at Katsina, north Nigeria.
Right below: Oil drilling, the source of much of Nigeria's wealth.

Rwanda

Republic of

Africa is a continent of wide, open spaces. But the Republic of Rwanda is comparatively crowded, with 4,500,000 people living in an area the size of Albania. The Hutu form 90 per cent of the population. Most of the rest are Tutsi, although there are a few Twa (pygmies).

The western part of Rwanda is mountainous. The volcanic ranges along the Rwanda-Zaire border provide one of the few remaining havens for the gorilla, that giant ape which hides a gentle nature under a ferocious looking exterior. Lake Kivu runs north to south. It is one of the chain of lakes which fills the great Rift Valley. To the east are plateaux.

The climate is equatorial, and food crops include bananas, sweet potatoes and sorghum (a cereal crop). Tea, coffee and cotton are exported. There is some mining, but little industry. Most people live off what little food they are able to grow.

Rwanda and Burundi (formerly Ruanda-Urundi) have been the home of the Hutu people for many centuries. They were conquered by the Tutsi about 400 years ago, and the newcomers became their feudal overlords. After colonization by Germany, Ruanda-Urundi was ceded to Belgium in the First World War. The Belgians continued to administer the country by international agreement until 1962. Three years previously the Hutu in Rwanda had risen up against Tutsi domination. The Tutsi king fled in 1960 and, under the new republic, power was restored to the Hutu.

Area:
26,338 km² (10,170 mi²)
Population:
5,650,000
Capital:
Kigali (pop. 157,000)
Currency:
franc

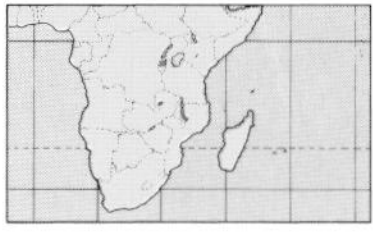

São Tomé e Principe

These islands are in the Gulf of Guinea. Independence as a republic in 1975 ended more than 450 years of rule by Portugal. Copra from coconut palms and palm-oil are the major exports.

Area:
964 km² (372 mi²)
Population:
110,000
Capital:
São Tomé (pop. 25,000)
Currency:
dobra

Senegal

République du Sénégal

The River Senegal, which reaches the Atlantic Ocean at the port of Saint-Louis, forms the northern border of Africa's westernmost country. The Republic of Senegal extends southwards from Saint-Louis to Ziguinchor. The country does not include the valley of the Gambia River. This region remains a separate sovereign state. However, in 1981, Senegal and Gambia embarked upon a close economic and political alliance, the union being known as the Confederation of the Senegambia.

Senegal is named after the Zenaga people who lived there in ancient times. In the Middle Ages, the region was dominated by the Fulani and Wolof peoples, and by Portuguese traders. Other European powers also became involved in the region, including the Dutch in the 17th century, the British in the 18th, and the French, who ruled the territory from 1817 until 1958, when Senegal voted to become an independent republic within the French Community. Under the 1978 constitution, Senegal is a multi-party democracy.

Groundnuts are Senegal's major export. Mining produces valuable phosphates, and the country also has a sizeable industrial output, centred on the capital Dakar. Oil is refined at Cayar.

Senegal is primarily an Islamic country. French, the official language, is still widely spoken. The African languages of the region fall into the West Atlantic, Mande and Fulfulde groups.

Area:
196,192 km² (75,754 mi²)
Population:
6,300,000
Capital:
Dakar (pop. 979,000)
Other towns:
Thiès, Kaolack, Saint-Louis, Ziguinchor
Currency:
franc CFA

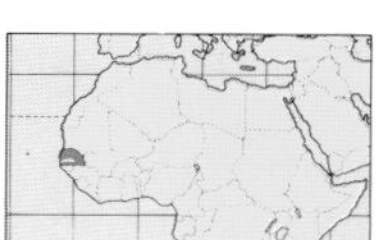

Below: Saint-Louis, Senegal.

Seychelles

Farming and tourism are the mainstay of life in the Seychelles, a group of islands in the Indian Ocean. Cinnamon, copra and guano are exported. A republic since 1976, the Seychelles is a member of the Commonwealth.

Area:
280 km² (108 mi²)
Population:
70,000
Capital:
Victoria (pop. 23,000)
Currency: rupee

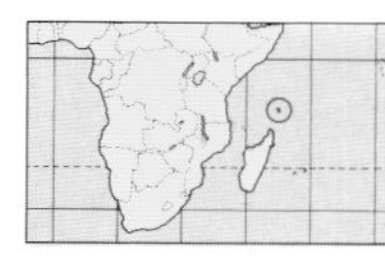

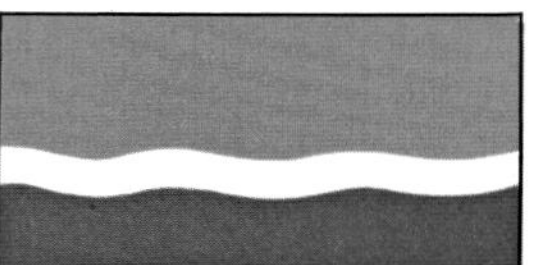

Sierra Leone

Republic of

The capital of the Republic of Sierra Leone is called Freetown. Like Liberia, Sierra Leone was founded to provide a home for freed slaves who were able to return to Africa from the colonies of the New World. In 1787, the Freetown region was purchased from King Naimbanna as a colony for the Creoles, as the freed slaves were known. Sierra Leone became a British colony in 1808, and the Creoles became an educated elite. The original African peoples of the country, mostly Temne and Mende, regained influence with independence in 1961. Two political parties contested each other for government, the Sierra Leone People's Party (SLPP) and the All People's Congress Party (APC). In 1978 Sierra Leone adopted the constitution of a one-party republic, with the APC in control. The country is a member of the Commonwealth.

Sierra Leone lies between Guinea and Liberia on the Atlantic coast of Africa. Freetown is situated on a large, natural, deep-water harbour. A low, hot and wet coastal strip gives way in the interior to drier highlands and plateaux. The climate varies with the altitude. Cocoa, palm-oil, coffee and ginger are exported, and maize and cassava are also widely grown. Rice is the staple food. Mineral resources include diamonds, bauxite, rutile (titanium dioxide), and iron-ore.

The official language of Sierra Leone is English. There is a university with two colleges – Fourah Bay, founded in 1827, and Njala, founded in 1964. There is a widespread programme of primary and secondary education.

Area:
73,326 km²
(27,925 mi²)
Population:
3,643,000
Capital:
Freetown (pop. 316,000)
Other towns:
Koidu, Bo, Kenema, Makeni
Currency:
leone

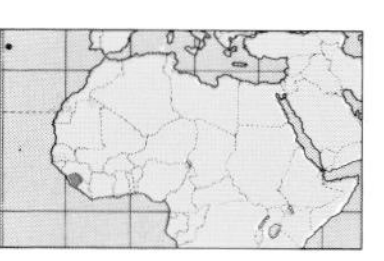

Elaborate masks are used in religious rituals by dancers of Sierra Leone. Masks such as these influenced European artists at the turn of the century.

Somalia

Al-Jumhouriya As-Somaliya Al-Domocradia

The Somali Democratic Republic is Africa's easternmost country. It lies on the Horn of Africa, that large area of land projecting into the Indian Ocean in north-eastern Africa. It shares borders with Kenya, Ethiopia, and Djibouti. It is a hot land, subject to periodic droughts. These can be major human disasters, because many people are nomadic herders, whose livestock graze the uplands and southern plains. The Juba and Shibeli Rivers provide a real lifeline in the south. Much of Somalia is arid land. To the north lies a high plateau. Crops grown include bananas, sugar-cane, fruit and maize. The Somalis are Muslims, as is the Arabic minority. In Africa, frontiers often divide peoples. For example, almost as many Somalis live in the surrounding countries as in Somalia itself. The Somali nation was founded in the 16th century, but during the colonial era it was divided between Britain, Italy, France and Ethiopia. British and Italian Somaliland were reunited upon independence in 1960. Somalia had a parliamentary democracy until 1969, when a coup heralded rule by a supreme revolutionary council. In 1977 power was passed to the praesidium of the Somali Revolutionary Party, who, under a new constitution, called a National Assembly in 1980.

Somalia has had uneasy relations with her neighbours in recent years. An invasion of Ethiopia was launched in 1977, in support of Somali guerrillas who wanted to secede from that country, but was repelled by Ethiopia.

Area:
637,757 km²
(246,214 mi²)
Population:
6,248,000
Capital:
Mogadishu (Mogadiscio) (pop. 600,000)
Other towns:
Hargeisa, Kismayu (Chisimaio), Merca, Berbera
Currency:
shilling

Much of Somalia is arid, but crops such as bananas are grown, also maize and sugar-cane.

South Africa
Republic of

The vast continent of Africa reaches its southernmost point at Cape Agulhas, below the Cape of Good Hope. Behind this lies the Republic of South Africa, a large country stretching from the Atlantic to the Indian Ocean. It is bounded to the north-west by Namibia (which as South West Africa has been administered by the Republic since 1915). To the north lie Botswana and Zimbabwe, and to the north-east are Mozambique and Swaziland. South Africa entirely surrounds Lesotho, an independent kingdom.

Much of South Africa is taken up by the grasslands of the highveld. There are tracts of mountainous country, from the famous flat top of Table Mountain, which rises to 1,082 metres (3,550 ft) above the city of Cape Town, to the Drakensberg range in the east, which rises to 3,350 m (10,991 ft). A series of parallel ranges, including the Groot Swartberge, stretch inland from the southern coast. The chief river of the Republic is the Orange. Rising in the Drakensberg Mountains, it flows westward for 1,860 kilometres (1,156 miles) across the centre of the country, reaching the Atlantic at Alexander Bay on the Namibian border. Its biggest tributary is the Vaal, which runs from south-eastern Transvaal for 1,120 kilometres (696 miles), joining the Orange River near Douglas. Desert areas include the Kalahari, which extends over the border from Botswana, and the Great Karroo of the south-west.

The high plateau character of much of the country means that the climate is fairly temperate, and in places pleasantly warm. Rainfall is high along the south-eastern coast. The presence of good agricultural land enables a wide range of crops to thrive in various parts of the country, including citrus fruits, bananas, apples, sugar-cane, groundnuts, maize and other grain crops. Vineyards provide wines and sherries for export. Cattle are raised in many areas.

The Republic of South Africa is the most industrialized land in the continent, with considerable iron and steel production. The economy is substantially financed by the extraction of precious minerals, which bring in large foreign earnings. Coal is mined in the Witwatersrand region of southern Transvaal, as is gold – the presence of which drew large numbers of prospectors from Europe in the last century. Today, miners, sometimes as much as four kilometres (2·5 miles) below the surface, produce more gold than in any other part of the world. Kimberley, in northern Cape Province, is the centre of the diamond industry, and diamonds form another extremely valuable resource. Silver, chrome, tin, uranium, asbestos, platinum, copper, iron-ore and manganese are also mined.

The peoples of South Africa come from a wide variety of ethnic backgrounds. Among those of African origin, the most numerous are the Xhosa, Sotho and Zulu. The Europeans are predominantly of Dutch descent (Afrikaners) or of British descent. There are large minorities of Asians, and many people of mixed descent, called Coloureds. Bantu languages are the most common. There are also Asian languages, such as Hindi and Urdu, but the official languages are English and Afrikaans. The latter is spoken by two-thirds of the white population.

The first people to inhabit this region were probably Bushmen and Hottentots. Between the 12th and 19th centuries, such Bantu peoples as the Sotho and the Nguni moved south into the area. During the 17th century, religious and political upheavals in Europe caused many people to start a new life in other parts of the

Above: A square in the middle of Cape Town, South Africa's legislative capital. Pretoria is the seat of government. It was to Cape Town that the first European settlers came.
Below: Roads and railways line the wharves at Durban in Natal.

world. Many went to North America, but a number of Dutch settlers, as well as some Germans and French Huguenots, moved to South Africa. The Dutch East India Company arrived on the Cape in 1652, and in the following decades farmers began to settle the interior. The British began occupation of the Cape between 1795 and 1806.

The 19th century was one of turmoil. In 1818 a powerful kingdom was formed in the east when Shaka became ruler of the Zulu nation. A brilliant soldier, Shaka conquered the other peoples of the region, causing large numbers of them to flee to other parts of southern Africa. Differences soon broke out among the white settlers between the British administrators and the Dutch farmers. The latter set out in covered wagons drawn by oxen to set up new colonies elsewhere: the Orange Free State, the South African Republic (Transvaal) and Natal. The latter was annexed by the British. Among the pioneers, this migration became known as the Great Trek. The British eventually conquered the Zulus in the war of 1879. There were also two wars in 1880-81 and 1899-1902 between the British and the Dutch settlers, or Boers as they were known, from the Dutch word for 'farmer'. Following the second of these bitter conflicts, an independent Union of South Africa was formed in 1910.

In 1936 the South African government passed laws restricting the electoral and territorial rights of the African population. The National Party, which took office in 1948, took this a stage further with their policy of *apartheid* or 'separate development'. Racial segregation was practised in all aspects of everyday life. In 1960 the white population voted in favour of making South Africa an independent republic. South Africa became a republic in 1961 and ceased to be a member of the British Commonwealth.

Under a continuing policy of *apartheid,* 'Bantustans' or homelands, for the African population have been established. Of these, Transkei, Bophuthatswana, Venda and Ciskei have internal governments with limited powers, and are termed republics. They are not, however, economically self-sufficient, because large numbers of workers are employed outside the Bantustans in industry. These designated areas form about 14 per cent of the land areas of the Republic, although the African peoples form about 70 per cent of the population. **The House of Assembly is made up of 178 members, headed by a Prime Minister with wide-ranging powers. Members are voted to office by Whites only. Recent reform allowed a degree of representation to people of mixed race through a Coloured House of Representatives, which has 85 members, and to Asians, through an Asian House of Representatives, which has 45 members. Black South Africans are denied the vote and have no representation in parliament. The 1970s and 1980s have seen increasing civil unrest in the Black townships, and further isolation of South Africa by the international community.**

Today the Republic of South Africa has two capitals. The legislature is based upon Cape Town, and government administration is based at Pretoria. The former city is built upon the peninsula between Table Bay and False Bay, in a spectacularly beautiful position. It is a port and industrial centre, as well as being a centre of university life. Pretoria lies in the north-east, and is the former capital of the Transvaal Republic.

The largest town in South Africa is Johannesburg, in the Witwatersrand. Once a boom town of the 19th century gold rush, it is now an industrial and business centre. In the south-east, on the Indian Ocean, is the largest port, Durban, in the province of Natal. The Republic has a good system of communications. An extensive network of railways covers the country, with about 30 per cent electrification. There are good roads and both internal and international air services.

As an urban nation – about half of its people are city dwellers – South Africa has made provisions for the protection of its wildlife. The origins of the Kruger National Park go back to 1884, when 'Oom' Paul Kruger, president of the South African Republic (Transvaal), envisaged a nature reserve in this part of the country. It was officially inaugurated in 1926. Its wildlife includes giraffe, lion, leopard and antelope. Another important conservation area is in the arid, sandy north-west of the Republic. This is the Kalahari Gemsbok National Park, which takes its name from one of its many inhabitants, the gemsbok, a large long-horned antelope with a tufted tail.

The flora of South Africa is as remarkable as its fauna. The most famous of its blooms is the protea, which is a national emblem.

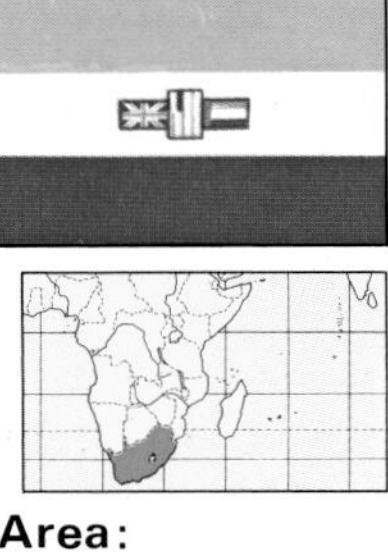

Area: 1,221,037 km² (471,471 mi²)
Population: 30,844,000
Capitals: Cape Town (pop. 1,108,000) Pretoria (pop. 563,384)
Other towns: Johannesburg, Durban
Currency: rand

Sudan

Jamhuryat es-Sudan Al Democratia

The term 'Sudan' was once used to describe all of Africa below the Sahara. It referred to the meeting point of Arab and Negro cultures. Today it usually refers to the Democratic Republic of the Sudan – the largest country in Africa, which borders no less than eight other countries as well as the Red Sea.

Sudan has always been a land of fascination to the peoples of Europe, because it is the land of the River Nile. The White Nile, running north from Uganda, and the Blue Nile, flowing north-west from Ethiopia, join forces at Khartoum for the final journey through Egypt to the sea.

The river encouraged the establishment of an ancient civilization: the Meroë culture flourished here in the seventh century BC. The Romans reached the region. An Arab kingdom succeeded a Christian one, and the Turks invaded in the 16th century. The Egyptians conquered Sudan in the 19th century, and soon this wild country was mapped by intrepid Victorian explorers, such as Sir Samuel and Lady Florence Baker. In 1881, the Sudanese religious leader, the Mahdi, initiated a successful nationalist struggle against foreign occupation, but his successor, the Khalifa, was finally defeated by modern firepower at the Battle of Omdurman (1898).

The Anglo-Egyptian Sudan finally received independence in 1956. A bitter civil war raged from 1964 until 1972 between the Muslim Arabs of the north and the Negro peoples of the south. **There followed relatively peaceful years under the presidency of Ja'afar al-Nimeiri, but economic problems grew in the 1980s, compounded by famine, an influx of Ethiopian refugees, and a re-**newal of fighting in the south. Nimeiri was overthrown in 1985, and a descendant of the Mahdi, Sadiq al Mahdi, became president.

The north of the country is harsh desert. The capital, Khartoum, is really a conurbation of three cities, Khartoum, Khartoum-North and Omdurman. It is the site of an international airport, and is linked by rail with Wadi Halfa on the Egyptian border, Port Sudan on the Red Sea, and the south-west. As one travels south, the desert landscape gives way to grassy plains, and the vegetation becomes more lush. To the west lies a mountainous region, containing Jebel Marra, and in the central-south the Nile forms a huge swamp. This is the *sudd*, a vast tract of floating vegetation in which one can see hippopotamus, crocodile and magnificent birds. The capital of the southern region is Juba.

Sudanese agriculture relies on irrigation. Cotton, gum arabic and groundnuts are leading crops. Rice, millet, cassava and maize are widely cultivated. Mineral resources include asbestos.

Sudan is an ancient, hospitable and fascinating country. Extensive engineering, agricultural and industrial projects are now being carried out which will bring about the Sudan of the future.

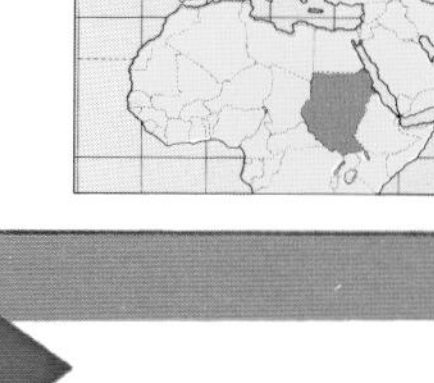

Area:
2,505,813 km²
(967,553 mi²)
Population:
21,440,000
Capital:
Khartoum (pop. 1,000,000)
Other towns:
Omdurman, Khartoum-North, Port Sudan, Wadi Medani, Kassala, El Obeid, Al-Qadarif, Atbara
Currency:
pound

Swaziland

Kingdom of

The Kingdom of Swaziland is a small country in south-eastern Africa, sandwiched between Mozambique and South Africa. The west of the country is mountainous, the centre is hilly, and the east is lowland. Forestry and agriculture are practised; fruits, sugar and cotton being produced. Mineral deposits include asbestos, coal and iron. A rail line crosses the border to join the Mozambique rail network.

The Swazi people first occupied the region in the early 19th century. After the Boer War, Swaziland became a British Protectorate, and achieved full independence in 1968.

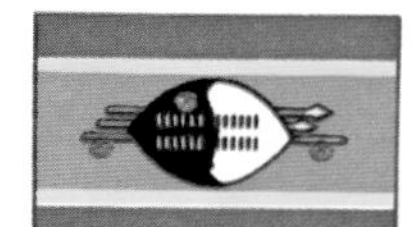

Area:
17,363 km²
(6,704 mi²)
Population:
626,000

Capital:
Mbabane (pop. 25,000)
Other towns:
Manzini
Currency:
lilangeni (plural: emalangeni)

The people of Swaziland keep their traditions and folklore alive. Here Swazi warriors wear their traditional war-dress.

Tanzania
United Republic of

The United Republic of Tanzania is in East Africa, bordering the Indian Ocean. It includes the large mainland territory of Tanganyika, and the offshore islands of Pemba and Zanzibar.

Mainland Tanzania is a hot country, humid on the coast and arid inland. Much of the country is plateau. The north-western border is with Kenya. The north is teeming with wildlife and dominated by the spectacular Kilimanjaro, the highest mountain in Africa. Kilimanjaro is 5,895 metres (19,341 ft) high and despite the fact that it is so near the Equator; it is always covered with snow. The Serengeti National Park and the Ngorongoro Crater are animal reserves on a truly magnificent scale, the scene of huge migrations of wildebeest and other animals. Three large lakes, Victoria in the north, Tanganyika in the west and Nyasa (Malawi) in the south lie on Tanzania's borders. As well as Kenya, Tanzania's neighbours include Uganda, Rwanda, Burundi, Zaire, Zambia, Malawi and Mozambique. The mainland coast is about 800 km (500 mi) long.

The people of Tanzania are divided into some 120 ethnic groupings, including Nyamwezi, Sukuma, Ha, Makonde, Gogo, Masai, Haya, Chagga, Hehe, and small groups of Europeans and Asians. Islam, Christianity and traditional religions are all practised. Among the wide variety of languages spoken in the region, English, and Swahili, the chief language of the East African coast, are commonly used for official purposes.

The early history of Tanzania was dominated by Zanzibar. Occupied by Arabs in the 17th century, a sultanate was established there whose rule eventually took in the mainland coast. The Arabs penetrated the interior to trade, and their main commodity was slaves. Their wretched captives ended up in the slave market in Zanzibar. The plight of the slaves was witnessed by some of the first European explorers to chart the interior, including Sir Richard Burton, John Hanning Speke and the Scottish missionary David Livingstone.

In the later years of the 19th century, the newly united German empire cast its eyes towards East Africa. Its penetration of the interior was fiercely resisted by the peoples of the region. After the First World War, German East Africa was passed to Britain under a League of Nations mandate, and became known as Tanganyika. The British had already declared the Sultanate of Zanzibar a protectorate in 1885.

Mount Kilimanjaro, one of the most beautiful mountains in the world, seen from the Arusha National Park.

After the Second World War, a new generation of Africans looked to a future free of European domination. In 1954 a 32-year-old teacher, Julius Nyerere, founded the Tanganyika African National Union (TANU). When independence finally came in 1961, Julius Nyerere became the president. He set up an economy based upon socialist principles.

After a revolution in 1964, in which the sultan was expelled, the island of Zanzibar united with Tanganyika to form the modern nation of Tanzania. In 1977 TANU joined forces with the Afro-Shirazi Party of Zanzibar to form a party called the Chama cha Mapindozi (CCM).

An attempt to form an East African economic union with Kenya and Uganda in 1967 failed completely, and in 1979 Tanzania invaded Uganda to assist in the overthrow of its ruler General Idi Amin.

The economy of Tanzania is based on agriculture. Coffee is the major crop, and cashew nuts, sisal, tea, oilseed, sugar and tobacco are also produced. Fishing is also important. Industrialization is at a low level, but is growing rapidly. Mineral resources are few, with one important exception – diamonds. The island of Zanzibar is traditionally associated with cloves, and it is still a large producer.

Tanzania has an extensive rail network centred on Dar-es-Salaam, a large town of nearly 800,000 inhabitants. The new capital of Dodoma lies in the centre of the country on a rail link between Dar-es-Salaam and Kigoma. Dar-es-Salaam and Kilimanjaro international airports provide links with the rest of the world.

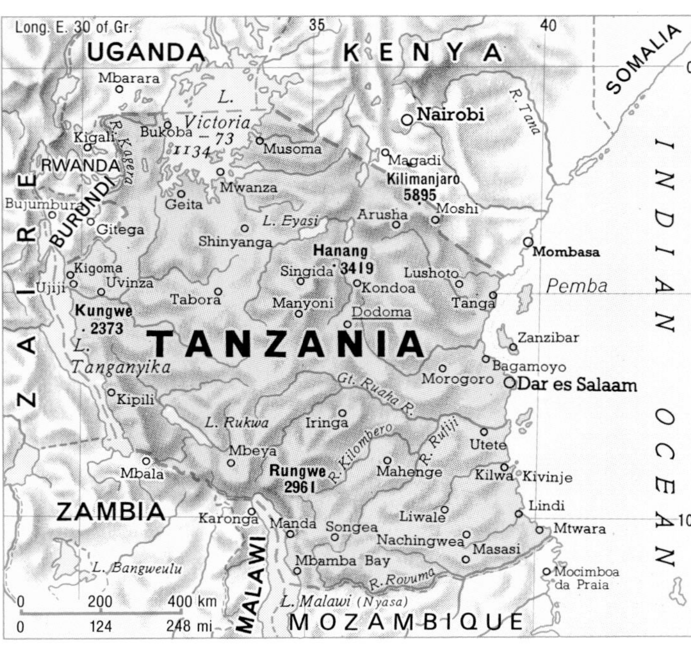

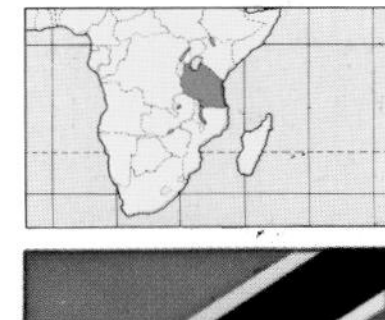

Area: 945,067 km² (364,912 mi²)
Population: 20,000,000
Capital: Dodoma (pop. 46,000)
Other towns: Dar-es-Salaam, Zanzibar, Mwanza, Tanga, Mbeya, Tabora, Morogoro,
Currency: shilling

Togo

République Togolaise

The Republic of Togo is a small West African country sandwiched between Benin and Ghana. Upper Volta lies to the north and there is a short coastline in the south. Togo has a hot tropical climate. Rain forests grow in the Togo mountains, but savannah covers most areas. Farming is the main activity. Cocoa and coffee are grown and phosphates are mined.

About 30 ethnic and language groups are found in Togo, including the Ewe in the south and the Cabrais (Kabre) in the north. Togo was a German protectorate between 1884 and 1914. After the First World War, it was divided between Britain and France. British Togoland was joined to Ghana when that country became independent in 1957. French Togo became independent in 1960. Under the 1980 constitution deputies are elected to the one-party National Assembly every five years.

Area:
56,785 km²
(21,926 mi²)
Population:
2,890,000
Capital:
Lomé (pop. 283,000)
Other towns:
Sokodé, Kpalimé
Currency:
franc CFA

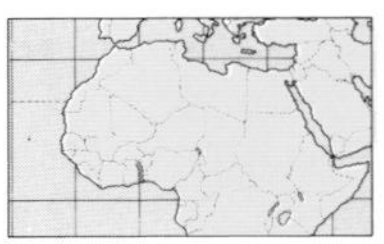

Tunisia

Al-Djoumhouria Attunusia

The smallest of Africa's Mediterranean states, the Republic of Tunisia is bordered by Algeria and Libya. The coastline is about 1,300 kilometres (808 miles) long. It runs eastwards from the Algerian border, taking in Cap Blanc, the northernmost point in Africa. At Cap Ben, the coastline extends in the direction of Sicily before plunging south into the Gulf of Hammamet. Farther south, the Gulf of Gabès is flanked by the Kerkenna Islands in the north and the island of Jerba in the south. The coast below Zarzis takes a turn to the south-east before the Libyan border.

The eastern end of the Saharan Atlas range crosses the border in the north, separating the coastal region from the arid south. The centre of the country is taken up by an area in which *chotts* are the main feature. These are large depressions or salt lakes. As the rainwater they contain evaporates, the *chotts* become encrusted with salt. To the south lies the burning desert of the Sahara. The coastal climate is Mediterranean in type and mild most of the year. Winters in the interior are cold, and, in the desert itself, temperatures are often extremely high, with minimal rainfall.

The Tunisian coast has provided a landfall for traders, raiders and conquerors from the earliest times. The original population was Berber. The ninth century BC saw the foundation of an empire centred on the city of Carthage, near modern Tunis. The settlers were Phoenicians from the kingdom of Tyre, and eventually they dominated large areas of the Mediterranean. Carthage came to rival Rome, and, aided by the tactical genius of their most famous general, Hannibal, the Carthaginians almost succeeded in bringing down their traditional enemy. However, Rome finally destroyed Carthage in 146 BC.

The country became a Roman province, but it was overrun by Vandals after the fall of Rome. The Byzantines then took control, followed by the Arabs in AD 647. Tunisia became converted to Islam, and its new capital, Kairouan, became the seat of the Maghreb emirs and a centre of Arabic culture. Successive Arab dynasties came to rule a huge area of North Africa including parts of Algeria, and the Tripolitanian region of Libya. They even conquered Malta and Sicily. In 1574, the Ottoman Turks captured Tunis, which had replaced Kairouan as the capital. After three centuries of rule by pashas and beys, the French, already established in Algeria, extended their rule eastwards by the Treaties of Le Bardo (1881) and La Marsa (1883).

At the end of the Second World War, the Tunisian National Front became a

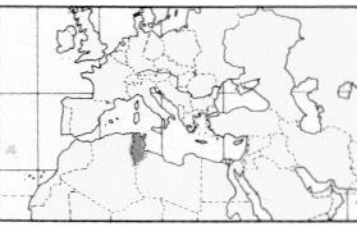

Area:
163,610 km²
(63,174 mi²)
Population:
6,966,000
Capital:
Tunis (pop. 557,000)
Other towns:
Sfax, Nabeul, Kairouan, Bizerte, Jendouba, Médénine, Gabès, Sousse, Béja
Currency:
dinar

focus for the independence movement. Its leader was Habib Bourguiba of the Neo-Destour Party. He was jailed between 1952 and 1954 amid a growing climate of violence and terrorism. Under United Nations pressure, France granted independence to Tunisia in 1956. As prime minister, Bourguiba deposed the monarchy and became president and head of state. Bourguiba retained power in this one-party state. In 1975, he was declared president for life.

About a half of Tunisia is farming or pastoral land. The chief products are typical of Mediterranean Africa, including olive oil, cereals, citrus fruits and wine. Dates grow at oases in the arid south. Sheep and goats are raised extensively in the northern region. Textiles form a significant export. The mining industry is well developed. Tunisia's natural resources include phosphates (a major export), lead, iron-ore and zinc. Oil is present in moderate quantities, and natural gas has also been discovered. Manufacturing and chemical industries are increasingly important to the economy, as is tourism. Tunisia is now one of the more popular holiday resorts of the Mediterranean region. Tunisia is an associate member of the European Economic Community (EEC).

Tunisia is an Islamic country and predominantly Arab in population. Most people of Berber origin live in the interior. There are sizeable minority groups of Jews and Europeans. The old colonial language, French, is still widely used as a language of commerce and education.

The capital, Tunis, is an administrative and industrial centre situated near the ruins of old Carthage. It stands on a picturesque lagoon, separated from the sea by a spit of sand. It is linked by a canal to its port of La Gouletta. Tunis presides over 18 provincial regions. The old capital of Kairouan is regarded as a holy city by the Muslims of Tunisia. Kairouan is famous for its ancient architecture and monuments. Its Great Mosque was built about 1,200 years ago. A high percentage of Tunisians are city dwellers, living in other important centres, such as Sousse and Sfax. Communications between the coastal towns are good, and the north of the country is well served by a road and rail network. There were more than 21,000 kilometres (13,050 miles) of roads, and 2,257 kilometres (1,402 miles) of railways in 1978. There is a major airport at Tunis.

Left: The legacy of rule by Rome: the Capitol at Dougga in the province of Béja, Tunisia.

Uganda

The Uganda region of Africa is fertile. The land attracted such peoples as the Acholi and Lango, who migrated here from the north to join the Bantu-speaking population. By the 19th century, several kingdoms had grown up in the region, the most important of which was Buganda. In 1862, the English explorer John Hanning Speke, arriving at the Bugandan capital of King Mutesa I (near modern-day Kampala), found a powerful and fearsome leader who ruled over a court dominated by elaborate social rituals. In Buganda, the king, or *kabaka,* had absolute power. However, he was advised by a special council known as a *lukiko.*

In 1893 Buganda became a British protectorate, with the *kabaka* retaining power as long as he recognized the authority of the British. By the First World War, the whole of Uganda was under British control. A railway was built, and the use of Asian labourers to build it resulted in the establishment of an Asian minority within the country.

Independence came in 1962, with Dr Apolo Milton Obote, founder of the Uganda People's Congress, as prime minister. The presidency went to the *kabaka* of Buganda, Mutesa II, in order to appease the people of Buganda, the largest of the 40 ethnic and language groups. But the *kabaka* was deposed by Obote in 1966. Obote assumed the presidency, and in 1967 Uganda became a republic within the Commonwealth. In 1971 Major-General Idi Amin seized power. His oppressive eight-year military dictatorship alienated Uganda's neighbours in Africa, and dismayed world opinion. Asians were expelled from the country, all opposition was suppressed, and torture was widespread. Intervention by Tanzanian troops assisted in Amin's downfall.

Dr Obote returned to office for a second time in 1980, but was again ousted in the coup of 1985.

Above: Many modern buildings are being erected in Kampala, Uganda's capital.

The years of unrest greatly damaged the Ugandan economy. Farming is the main activity and coffee is the most vital cash crop. Other traditional exports include tobacco, sugar, tea and cotton. Plantains, bananas, grain crops, sweet potatoes and cassava provide food for home consumption, and the lakes provide fish. Hardwood timber is supplied by extensive forests, and cattle are reared in open country. Tin, copper and tungsten form the country's mineral resources. Industrialization is fairly widespread, but Uganda desperately needs a period of political stability in which to recover her industrial strength. Power is provided by

Area: 236,860 km² (91,343 mi²)
Population: 13,990,000
Capital: Kampala (pop. 332,000)
Other towns: Jinja, Mbale, Entebbe
Currency: shilling

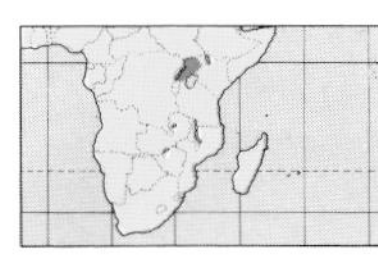

the Owen Falls hydro-electric scheme, which supplies some electricity to Kenya.

The communications network within Uganda is good, although this has also suffered during the turmoil of the 1970s. There are airfields around the country, and an international airport at Entebbe. Most main roads are surfaced. A railway links the capital, Kampala, with the Kenyan port of Mombasa, and with the other regions of Uganda.

The regions within Uganda vary a great deal. The Nile runs across the border with Sudan, and passes through Lake Mobutu Sésé Seko (formerly known as Lake Albert). The north-central region is made up of rolling plains. To the east, along the border with Kenya, the land becomes mountainous. Mount Elgon is 4,322 metres (14,180 ft) high. The south borders Lake Victoria, which has an area of 68,100 km² (26,295 mi²). The frontiers of Uganda, Tanzania and Kenya cut this huge stretch of water into three sections. To the south-west, along the border with Zaire, lie the Ruwenzori Mountains, of which the highest peak, Mount Margherita, reaches 5,119 metres (16,795 ft). These snow-capped peaks are also known as the Mountains of the Moon. In AD 150, the great Egyptian geographer Ptolemy drew a map showing that the source of the Nile lay in the *Lunae Montes*, or Mountains of the Moon. His evidence came from the account of a Greek traveller who 100 years earlier had travelled inland from the East African coast and seen a snow-capped peak. Whether this was Mount Kilimanjaro, Mount Kenya or part of the Ruwenzori remains unclear. On the misty slopes of the Ruwenzori range lives the most remarkable of the giant apes, the rare mountain gorilla.

Uganda is fairly high above sea-level, and so the temperature is rarely excessive, even though the Equator passes through the country just south of Kampala. The rainfall is mostly high, especially in the highlands and around Lake Victoria.

Below: A Ugandan market keeper spreads her wares. The Ugandan economy has been disrupted by the country's recent troubled history.

Burkina Faso (Upper Volta)

Burkina Faso was previously known as Upper Volta, taking its name from the reaches of the Volta River which divide this plateau in western Africa. The region consists of a dry, semi-desert landscape, and the three main branches of the river are known as Red (Rouge), White (Blanc) and Black (Noir) Voltas.

To the north lies the Sahara, and the whole country is subject to terrible droughts. From 1966 to 1973, Burkina Faso had practically no rainfall. Because livestock and agriculture are the mainstays of the economy, the effects of such weather on life in the region are extreme, causing great hardship. Burkina Faso has some limited, mainly undeveloped, mineral resources, but many workers make their living abroad, in neighbouring Ghana or Ivory Coast.

The largest ethnic group in Burkina Faso is formed by the Mossi, who have dominated the region since the 14th century. Their leader is known as the Moro Naba. Other peoples include the Peul (Fulani), Senoufo and Dyula.

French is the official language of the country, because this area was administered by France from 1896 until 1960. The first president of the independent republic was Maurice Yaméogo, who kept the country within the influence of France. A number of *coups d'état* followed independence, bringing a series of military governments.

Area:
274,200 km²
(105,875 mi²)
Population:
6,700,000
Capital:
Ouagadougou
(pop. 286,000)
Other towns:
Bobo-Dioulassou,
Koudougou,
Ouahigouya
Currency:
franc CFA

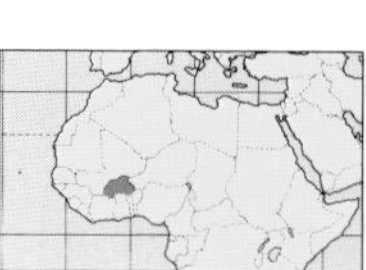

Zaire

République du

The Republic of Zaire is the second largest country in Africa, after Sudan. It lies at the heart of the continent, a huge area of rain forest, savannah, grassland and mountain. The tropical rains swell the waters of the great Zaire (Congo) River. This river rises in Shaba, in the south-east, and sweeps round in a great bend north and then west, reaching the Atlantic Ocean at Boma. Its tributaries form a network of rivers right across the map of Zaire. The country is divided into eight regions: Bas-Zaire, Haut-Zaire, Bandundu, Equateur, Kivu, East Kasai, West Kasai and Shaba. Forests occupy much of central Zaire. Mountains run the length of the eastern border, from the Ruwenzori and the Virunga National Park in the north, to the long Mitumba chain in the south.

Zaire contains a bewildering number of ethnic and language groups. Leading groups include the Mongo-Kundo, Luba, Kongo and Kwango-Kwila. A few pygmies live in the great rain forests. Characterized by their short, slight physique, these people live by hunting and gathering, and by trading with villagers at the forest edge. Their traditional way of life has in most places been changed radically by the modern world, but in the north-east of Zaire the Mbuti pygmies still eke out a living from what nature can provide: they call themselves *bamiki ba'ndura* – the children of the forest.

It is only in this century that communications have opened up the African continent. For most of their history, the various peoples and cultures have been separated by mountains and deserts, impenetrable swamps and forests. It is,

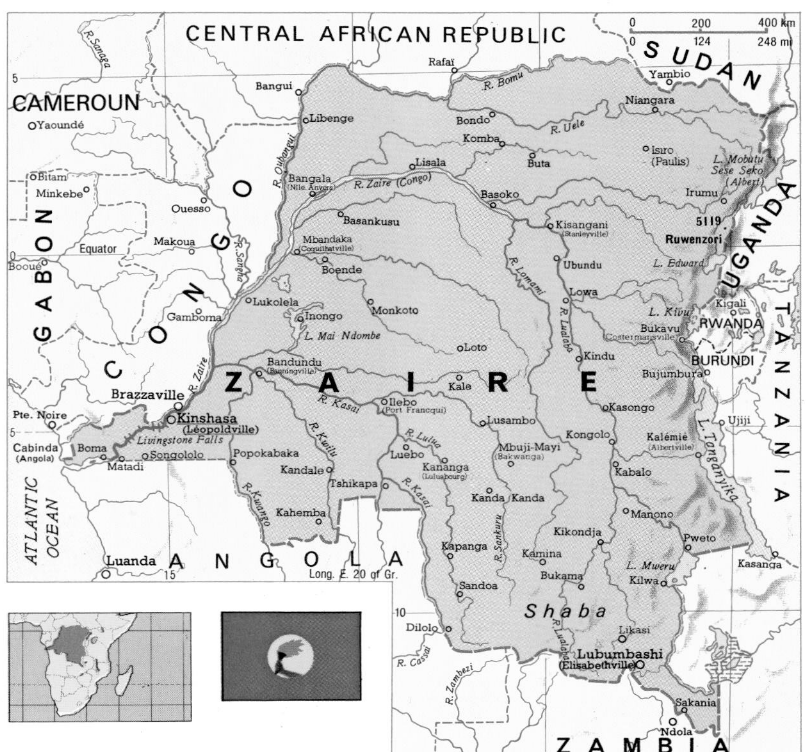

Above: The Zaire river is a natural source of food for the villages along its banks. Here local boys and girls are fishing near Kisangani.

Area:
2,345,409 km²
(905,617 mi²)
Population:
31,940,000
Capital:
Kinshasa (pop. 2,500,000
Other towns:
Kananga, Lubumbashi, Kisangani, Bukavu, Kikwit, Matadi
Currency:
zaire

therefore, hardly surprising that so many languages survive. There are more than 150 languages or dialects within Zaire. Official languages are French, Swahili, and Lingala, which is a Bantu language derived from Bobangi.

The European penetration of the interior in the 19th century was led by the Welsh-born explorer and journalist Henry Morton Stanley. His harrowing accounts of travel in the forests and on the rivers of Zaire were avidly read by the outside world. In 1884 the region was declared to be the Congo Free State, which became the personal possession of King Léopold II of Belgium. Few areas of Africa were to suffer so much during the imperialist era. Atrocities and exploitation were so rife in the Congo Free State that, in 1908, international opinion forced the Belgium government to take over the administration.

Independence came in 1960, when the Democratic Republic of the Congo was founded, with Joseph Kasavubu as president and Patrice Lumumba as prime minister. The new state was plagued with troubles from the start. Belgian troops soon returned, fighting rebel army units, while the province of Katanga (Shaba) attempted to secede, under the politician Moise Tshombe. Lumumba was dismissed. Katanga was occupied by United Nations troops. The UN Secretary-general Dag Hammarskjöld was killed in an air-crash while trying to solve the crisis. After prolonged fighting and political upheaval, General Joseph-Désiré Mobutu, later known as Mobutu Sésé Seko, assumed presidential office in 1965. In 1971 the country was renamed the Republic of Zaire. Regional revolts continued, and in 1977 and 1978 Shaba, as Katanga was now known, was temporarily invaded by mercenary forces.

Zaire is a one-party state, ruled by the Mouvement Populaire de la Révolution (MPR). The 1967 constitution was extensively revised in 1978. A feature of President Mobutu Sésé Seko's government has been to combat the legacy of the colonial period.

The economy of Zaire depends heavily on mining. The rich mineral deposits of the Shaba province explain why this disputed region has been so strategically important since independence. The Kasai provinces are also rich in minerals. Copper, cobalt and diamonds are the most important deposits. Uranium, zinc, gold and manganese are also found. Most of the work force is employed on the land. Coffee and palm-oil are the most valuable products.

Zambia

Zambia is a mining country. Copper accounts for 90 per cent or more of the exports, and mineral production finances the country. Lead, silver, zinc, coal and cobalt are also extracted. The copperbelt straddles the north of the country, near the Zaire border. The chief mining towns are Luanshya, Chingola, Kalulushi, Kitwe, Chililabombwe and Mufulira.

The soil is rather less productive for the farmers of Zambia. Most agriculture is for home consumption. Maize, millet, cassava, groundnuts, vegetables and fruit are cultivated, and cotton and tobacco are also grown as cash crops.

Zambia is a tropical country, but because it occupies high plateau country, the climate is not too extreme. The land is mostly covered by savannah. The north-eastern tongue of territory which extends towards Lake Tanganyika is hilly, and dominated by the Muchinga Mountains. The southern border of the country runs along the Zambezi River, from which the country takes its modern name. Here the famous Kariba Dam has created a huge artificial lake. Power from this hydro-electric scheme, which Zambia shares with Zimbabwe, is supplemented by another on the River Kafue.

Zambia is surrounded on all sides by land. To the south lie Mozambique, Zimbabwe, Botswana and Namibia; to the west lies Angola; to the north Zaire and Tanzania; to the east Malawi. Being landlocked can be an economic drawback. But this has been alleviated to some extent by the construction of a railway linking the copperbelt to Dar-es-Salaam in Tanzania. Built with Chinese aid, this railway provides access to the Indian Ocean. Other routes pass through Zimbabwe, Mozambique and South Africa. An oil pipeline from Dar es Salaam provides another vital link.

The capital of Zambia is Lusaka, in Central Province. This city is the seat of government and administration, and is a thriving centre of business and education. It has an international airport. The city of Maramba (Livingstone) is in the south, by the Zimbabwe border. Its English name comes from the Scottish missionary Dr David Livingstone who explored this region in the 1850s. He was the first European to set eyes on one of the wonders of Africa, called Mose-la-Tunya (the 'smoke that thunders') or the Victoria Falls. At this point on the Zambia-Zimbabwe border, the River Zambezi plunges 108 metres (355 feet), sending up a huge cloud of fine spray. Many other waterfalls are higher, but in terms of volume this is the third biggest in the world, and the largest in Africa. It is 1·6 kilometres (1 mile) across.

An idea of the Africa that Livingstone would have seen may be gleaned from a visit to the Luangwa National Park. Here protection is given to a wide range of wild animals, many of whose habitats are threatened in modern Africa. Species include rhinoceros, hippopotamus, zebra, giraffe, antelope, lion and many others. Wildlife is also protected in the Kafue National Park, a huge area of forest and grassland. Tourism is increasing.

The people of Zambia are divided into six main language and many dialect groups. The Bemba are the largest group of people in the north-east of the country. Their language, along with Nyanja and English, is widely spoken. The Tonga are the major group in the south. Minority populations of Europeans and Asians also live in the country.

The Bemba people settled in Zambia in the 17th century, when the region was dominated by the Lunda empire. When Europeans first came to this part of Africa in the 19th century, Zambia was named

Northern Rhodesia, after Cecil Rhodes, diamond king, politician and managing director of the British South African Company. This commercial organization was given a Royal Charter, allowing it to govern the region, until a British Protectorate was declared in 1911. In the ensuing years a large number of white settlers arrived in the region, attracted by the mining industry. In 1953, Northern Rhodesia was drawn into a federation with Southern Rhodesia (now Zimbabwe) and Nyasaland (now Malawi). This broke up 10 years later.

Zambia became an independent republic within the Commonwealth in 1964. The first president was Dr Kenneth Kaunda, leader of the United National Independent party (UNIP). The multiparty system was abolished in 1972, and the new constitution of the following year allowed for a one-party democracy. Dr Kaunda has retained office since independence.

As an important member of the Organization of African Unity (OAU), Zambia has been a strong opponent of those countries in southern Africa still ruled by white minorities. Zambia lent supprt to guerrillas fighting against the regime of Ian Smith in pre-independence Zimbabwe, and has consistently attacked the policies of the Republic of South Africa. In common with many other African countries, independent Zambia has limited the extent of operations by foreign companies, in this case by insisting on a majority holding in such companies, and by nationalization.

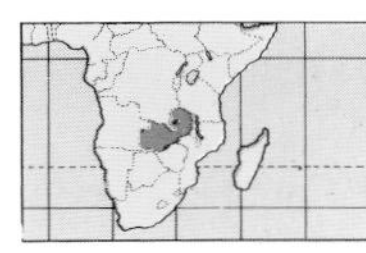

Area:
752,614 km² (290,602 mi²)
Population:
7,539,000
Capital:
Lusaka (pop. 641,000)
Other towns:
Kitwe, Ndola, Chingola, Mufulira, Luanshya, Kabwe (Broken Hill)
Currency:
kwacha

Above: The magnificent Victoria Falls between Zambia and Zimbabwe.
Far left: The Kafue dam, Zambia.

Zimbabwe

Republic of

Zimbabwe is the home of the Shona and the Ndebele (Matabele) peoples, and also has smaller groups of Sotho, Tonga, Hlengwe, Sena and Venda peoples. There are also sizeable minority groups of European and Asian settlers. The history of the country is an ancient one, dominated by the interaction between these ethnic divisions.

To the south-east of Masvingo (Fort Victoria) stand the ruined citadel and temple of Zimbabwe, from which the modern state takes its name. The architecture of these stone buildings shows that an impressive culture once flourished here. Their date is uncertain, but they probably have their origins in either the late Dark Ages or the early Middle Ages. We do know that the Shona people ruled the area for some 700 years, from about 1100. During this period, the Portuguese made incursions into the region. In the early 19th century, the Ndebele, under Mzilikazi, fled north from the troubles in Zulu territory in what is now South Africa. Many of them settled in the west of the region.

In the 19th century, the mineral wealth of southern Africa attracted European interest. The British South Africa Company of Cecil Rhodes (after whom the country was named Southern Rhodesia) sought mining concessions from the Ndebele king, Lobengula. Soon British settlers were pouring in, to prospect or to farm. In 1891, the Ndebele (Matabele) Rebellion signalled the start of desperate resistance to the white invaders, but both Ndebele and Shona lacked modern weaponry and stood little chance.

The whites were now in control of the country, and in 1923 Southern Rhodesia became a British colony governed by the white settlers. In 1952 a federation was formed with the territories of Nyasaland (Malawi) and Northern Rhodesia (Zambia). When this federation collapsed 10 years later, independence was granted to the other two partners. But the whites of Southern Rhodesia could not come to terms with the British. In 1965, they broke away to form an illegal regime under the prime minister Ian Smith. The British sought United Nations support for economic sanctions against the Smith regime, but these proved to be of limited effect. A campaign of guerrilla warfare was waged by African factions hostile to the regime.

British rule was eventually restored in 1979, and after elections in 1980 the country finally became the independent Republic of Zimbabwe and a member of the Commonwealth. Power was now in the hands of the majority. Of the two principal African political leaders, Joshua Nkomo and Robert Mugabe, the latter succeeded in being elected prime minister. He consolidated his powers and was re-elected to office in 1985. Despite difficulties, the new government maintains stability. One priority has been to expand the educational programme for black Africans, which was neglected under white rule.

As with neighbouring Zambia, Zimbabwe's wealth is heavily dependent on its mineral deposits. Copper, nickel, chrome, asbestos and coal are mined. Industry is quite highly developed, and the huge Kariba Dam on the border with Zambia harnesses the power of the Zambezi River for the benefit of both countries. Tobacco, fruits, sugar and cotton are grown for the export market,

Harare, capital of Zimbabwe.

Area:
390,580 km² (150,812 mi²)
Population:
7,878,000
Capital:
Harare (formerly Salisbury) pop. 656,000)
Other towns:
Bulawayo, Mutare (Umtali), Gweru (Gwelo), Kwekwe (Que Que), Kadoma (Gatooma), Hwange (Wankie), Masvingo (Fort Victoria)
Currency:
dollar

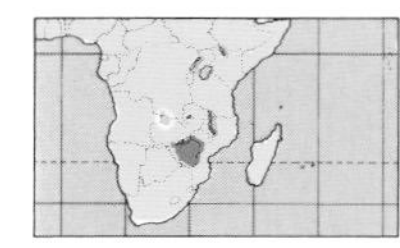

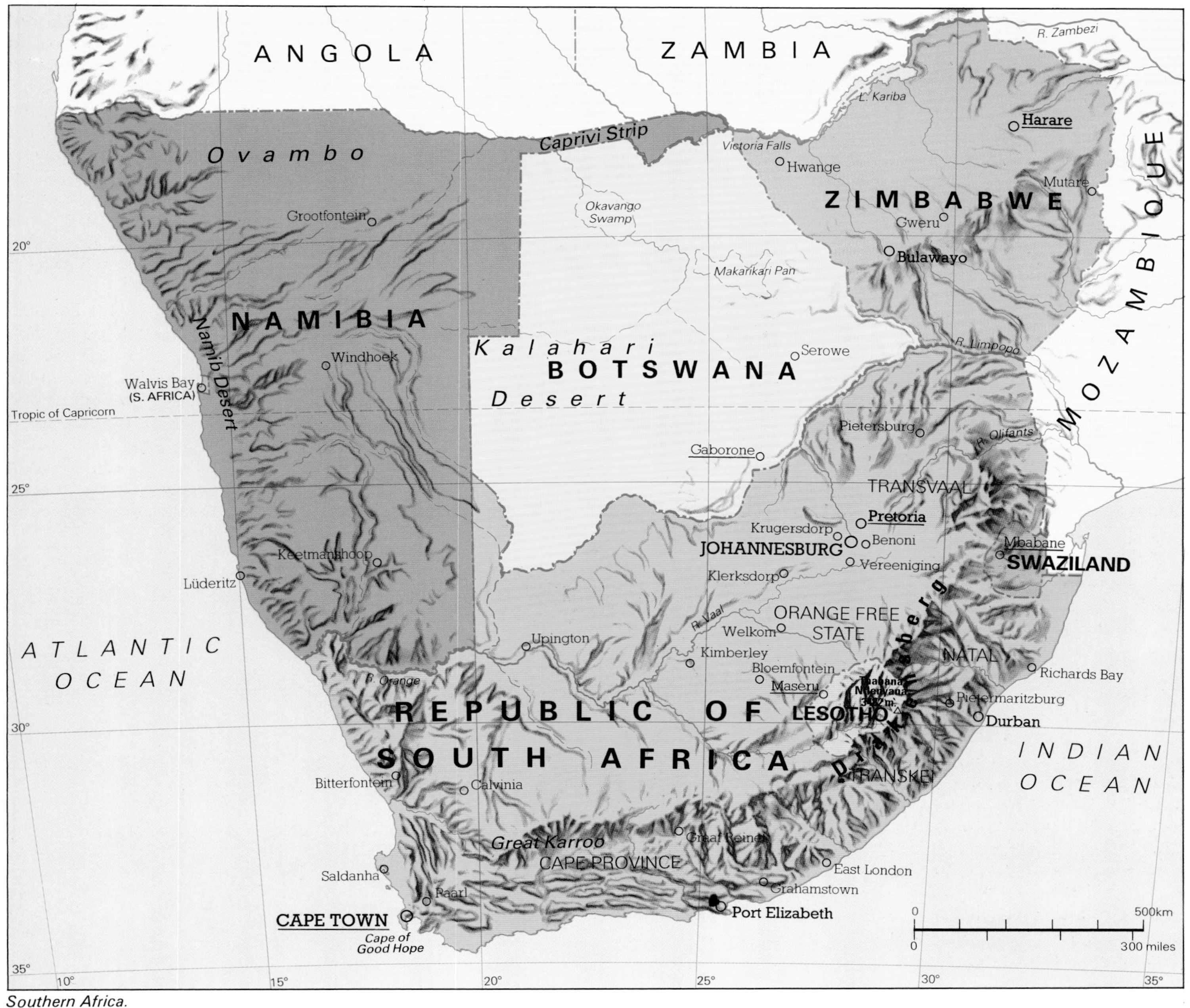

Southern Africa.

and grain crops provide food at home. Cattle farming is also important.

Zimbabwe, like Zambia, is surrounded by land on all sides. It shares borders with Botswana, the Republic of South Africa, Mozambique and Zambia. A railway provides a link between the capital Harare (Salisbury) and the Indian Ocean port of Beira in nearby Mozambique. Communications within Zimbabwe are good. There is an extensive rail network linking the capital, Harare, with other important centres such as Gweru (Gwelo), Bulawayo, and Mutare (Umtali). Harare and Bulawayo both have major airports.

The country is mostly savannah, lying on a high plateau between the valleys of the Limpopo and Zambezi Rivers. The temperature is relatively mild, and the rainfall is variable – high in the east of the country and low in the south. The plains of the west take in Hwange (Wankie) National Park, a tract of bush and forest set aside for the protection of wildlife, and the home of a great variety of species – buffalo, elephant, lion, leopard, cheetah, ostrich, baboon and sable antelope. Such creatures never fail to impress visitors from other continents. Africa is the last region upon Earth to support such large and extraordinary creatures. But their future is by no means assured. The animal reserves provide some chance of survival, but even then every man-made disaster, such as war, and every natural disaster, such as drought, imperils the maintenance of animal protection. Also, hunger and commercial interests encourage hunters to poach game.

Another popular tourist attraction lies on the Zambezi, between Zimbabwe and Zambia. North-west of Hwange (Wankie) are the Victoria Falls, a splendid wonder of the natural world.

The clouds of spray and the deafening roar of the Falls fully justify its descriptive African name *Mose-la-Tunya*, which means 'the Smoke that thunders'. The cloud of spray is sometimes seen 40 kilometres (25 miles) away.

The Americas

The two continents of North America and South America stretch from one end of the Earth to the other – from the pack ice of the Arctic Ocean to the stormy waters of Drake Passage, off Cape Horn. Within these two great land masses, joined by the isthmus of Panama, can be found almost every kind of climate and vegetation from tundra to rain forest, and from desert to savannah. The Americas lie between the world's two greatest oceans, the Atlantic, which includes the Gulf of Mexico and the tropical Caribbean Sea, with its many islands, and the Pacific.

North America ranges from the bare frozen wilderness of the north, through to forest, temperate farmland and grassy plains. Burning deserts occur in the south-western USA and humid swamps in the south-east. The continent is divided by the Rocky Mountains, a range which runs from north to south down the western side. Other mountain ranges extend down the Pacific coast, including the Coast Range, while the east contains the Appalachians. The north is a land of lakes and rivers, many of which drain into the Hudson Bay, a huge inlet of the sea which almost cuts Canada in two. To the west of the large island of Newfoundland lies the Gulf of St Lawrence. The St Lawrence Seaway, flowing from Lake Ontario, forms part of the border between Canada and the USA, along with four other Great Lakes: Erie, Huron, Michigan and Superior. Superior is the largest freshwater lake in the world, having an area of 82,409 square kilometres (31,820 square miles). The central United States is dominated by the Mississippi-Missouri river system, the world's third largest, which drains into the Gulf of Mexico. To the west, in Arizona, the Colorado River flows through the world's largest gorge, the famous Grand Canyon.

To the south of the Rio Grande lie Mexico and Central America. The most western part of the Mexican mainland is a long peninsula called Baja California. The mainland proper, which tapers as it turns south-east, is also dominated by mountains, notably the Western Sierra Madre and the Eastern Sierra Madre. Plateaux, active volcanoes and lakes are a feature of much of the interior, but the Gulf coast and the Yucatán peninsula are low-lying. As the land mass narrows towards the isthmus of Panama, it consists of a highland spine rising behind flat coastlands. The southern and the northern sections of the Americas are separated by human intervention, namely

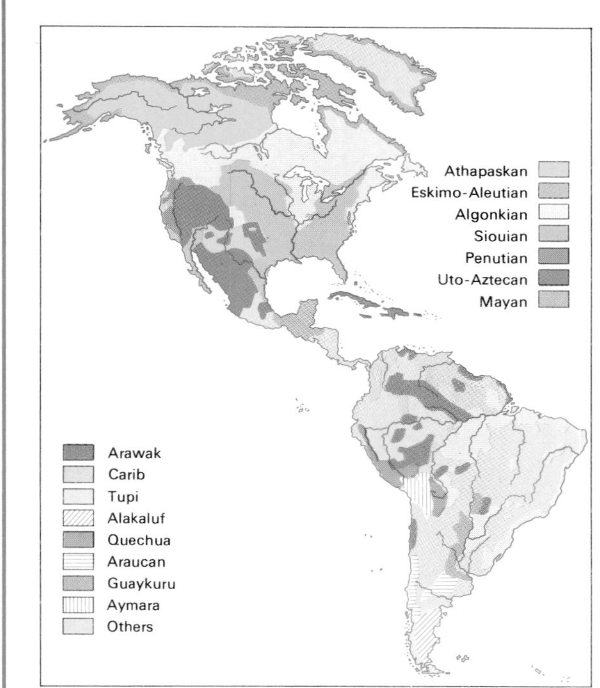

INDIGENOUS LANGUAGES OF THE AMERICAS

When Europeans discovered the Americas, more than 150 languages and about 900 dialects were spoken there. The map, left, shows only the most important language groups and the regions where they were spoken. The Eskimo language of the far north is similar to the languages of northern Siberia. Farther south are the languages of the great Indian nations of North America, and in Central America those of the Aztecs and Mayas. In South America one finds the language of the Incas. Gradually the old languages yielded to those of the European settlers: English and French in the north, and Spanish and Portuguese in central and southern America.

Left: From the Arctic wastes of Alaska (top) to the desolate mountains of Tierra del Fuego, near the Antarctic Circle (bottom) the New World is a land of marvels. Alongside natural wonders are remarkable human achievements. On the island of Manhattan, at the heart of New York City (centre), people have overcome geographical limitations by building upwards into the sky. Below: The famous monument at Mount Rushmore, in South Dakota, in the USA, consists of giant sculptures cut out of the mountainside. The sculpture shows four of the country's most important presidents: George Washington, Thomas Jefferson, Theodore Roosevelt, and Abraham Lincoln. Below right: The Golden Gate Bridge welcomes visitors to the beautiful city of San Francisco, on the west coast of the United States.

the Panama Canal. This waterway, 82 kilometres (51 miles) long, provides a vital shipping link between the Atlantic and the Pacific, and it is the world's busiest canal. To the east lie the islands of the Caribbean, which can be divided into four major groups: the Bahamas; the Greater Antilles (Cuba, Hispaniola, Jamaica and Puerto Rico); the Lesser Antilles (the Leeward and Windward Islands); and Trinidad and Tobago.

Just as the Rockies run down the western side of North America, so the Andes run down the length of South America, providing a high barrier to the west. Mount Aconcagua, which is 6,959 metres (22,835 feet) above sea level, is the highest point in the Americas. The Amazon is the world's second largest river at 6,437 kilometres (4,000 miles). The Amazon basin, which covers an area of about 7,045,000 square kilometres (2,720,000 square miles), is a vast area of rain forest. A crucial region for the world's ecology, the rain forest is being cleared at an alarming rate. On the River Carrao in Venezuela is Salto Angel, which at 979 metres (3,212 feet) is the world's highest waterfall. Major rivers to the south include the Paraná and the Uruguay, which flow into the River Plate (Rio de la Plata). The *pampas* or grassy plains of southern South America support huge herds of cattle. In the far south lie the thinly populated, windswept plateaux of Patagonia, and across the Straits of Magellan, the icy wastes of the Tierra del Fuego archipelago.

The Americas have been known for centuries as the 'New World', because their existence remained unknown to Europeans until fairly recently. During the last phase of the great Pleistocene Ice Age, Asia and North America were joined across the Bering Strait. The original inhabitants of the Americas were Mongoloid peoples who crossed from Siberia and gradually spread southwards to form the many Amerindian groups. Great civilizations grew up in central and southern America, notably those of the Mayas, the Aztecs and the Incas. Agriculture spread over large areas. But in other regions, hunting and gathering remained the traditional way of life, as in the Arctic which was populated by Eskimos, who are also a Mongoloid people.

Just when the first Europeans made landfall in America is uncertain. The Vikings established a colony in Greenland in the late 10th century and explored the North American coast. Leif Ericson

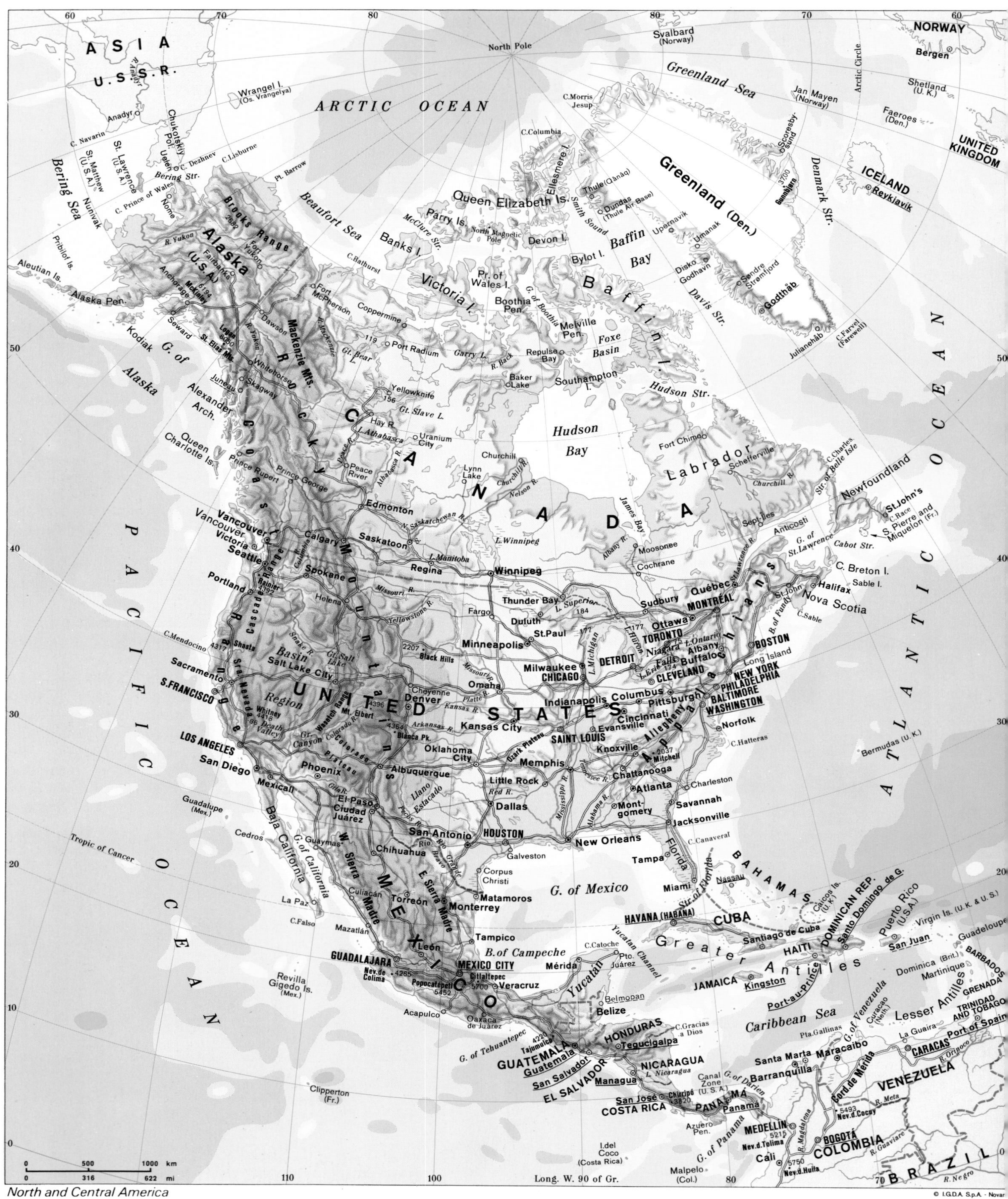

North and Central America

South America

Three views of South America. Top: Part of the River Amazon in Brazil, which drains the world's greatest river basin, a vast region of dense rain forest. Centre: An estancia, *or large ranch, stands on a sheltered site on Tierra del Fuego, at the Americas' southernmost extremity. Right: The Temple of the Sun was built by the Mayas at Palenque in Mexico. The Mayan civilization reached its peak in the 10th century* AD, *but it had already begun to decline before the arrival of the Spanish invaders.*

named part of the north-eastern coast of North America Vinland around AD 1000. Other legends persist in Europe, such as that of the medieval prince of North Wales, Madog, who is said to have taken a fleet across the Atlantic to settle a distant land. But there can be no doubt about the events of the year 1492. Christopher Columbus (Colombo or Colón), a Genoese navigator in the commission of the Spanish throne, set foot in the Bahamas. Columbus had been seeking a route to India by sailing westwards. Thinking mistakenly that he had reached Asia, he called the inhabitants of the Americas Indians, and, as a result, the Caribbean islands are still known as the West Indies. However, the distinctive term Amerindian is now more widely used for the indigenous population of the Americas. The advent of the Europeans was to have a cataclysmic effect on the peoples of America.

In 1499 the South American coastline was charted by Amerigo Vespucci (hence 'America'), and, in 1500, Brazil was discovered by Pedro Cabral. In 1521 Mexico fell to Hernando Cortés. The Dutch, British and French were more active in the northern hemisphere. In the 17th century, colonies grew up along the eastern seaboard of North America. Religious refugees from England, known as the 'Pilgrim Fathers', settled in New England in 1620. Slaves from Africa were sold into the plantations of Virginia and the West Indies. Throughout North and South America, the settlers stole the lands of the Amerindians, who were cheated, harassed, enslaved, murdered and deprived of their rights. European settlement expanded westwards across North America – at the expense of such nations as the Sioux (Dakota), the Ojibwa, the Nez Perces, the Cheyenne, the Iroquois, the Navajo and the Apache. By 1886, the surviving Amerindians of the United States were confined to reservations.

The potential of the European colonies in the Americas was so great that in many places the colonists fought for their independence. The United States broke away from Britain in 1783. The 1787 constitution of the new country was a revolutionary document for humanity. Its concern for human rights inspired the French Revolution and encouraged the reform of oppressive monarchies throughout the Old World. Argentina broke from Spain between 1810–16; Chile in 1818; Colombia in 1819 and Mexico in 1821. Brazil became independent from Portugal in 1822. The United States expanded rapidly, by settlement and purchase of territory. When the rift of

Above: The Grand Canyon, one of the world's most magnificent natural wonders. Left and below: Examples of New World fauna. The llama (far left) is a domesticated animal originating from the Andes. The anaconda (left) is found in the Amazonian rain forests. It has been known to measure as much as 12 metres (39 feet) in length. The bison (below left) was once king of the American prairie, but it has been hunted almost to extinction. The anteater (below) lives in the savannah regions of South America.

the Civil War (1861–65) eventually healed, the United States came to dominate the Americas, and, in the 20th century, the world.

Settled by the poor and oppressed from every land in Europe, North America became the home of Irish and Scottish, of Germans and Poles, Jews and Ukrainians, Armenians, Italians, Greeks, and many other nationalities. The black descendants of African slaves achieved their freedom, but it took many years for that freedom to be recognized in terms of civil rights and social opportunities. The United States, with its tremendous natural resources, has become an industrial giant and a massive agricultural producer, with a standard of living envied by the rest of the world.

In Central and South America, development was less rapid. Formidable problems existed. Only in recent times have cohesive nations emerged, with the capacity to exploit their abundant resources. But political instability and a disregard of human rights has marred progress in places. Nevertheless, the potential of such countries as Brazil and Argentina is immense. These two nations could be super-powers in the 21st century. The major Caribbean islands have only recently shaken off colonialism, but they are also rapidly developing their own identity. In both Central and South America, the priority for the future must be to tackle poverty, a problem made more difficult by the current population explosion.

The governmental systems to be found in the Americas are varied. Canada is a democracy within the Commonwealth. It is divided into 12 provinces and territories: Alberta, British Columbia, Manitoba, New Brunswick, Newfoundland and Labrador, Nova Scotia, Ontario, Prince Edward Island, Québec, Saskatchewan, Yukon Territory, and the Northwest Territories. To the north-east, Greenland is an overseas territory of Denmark, and Alaska, in the far northwest, is part of the United States. The United States is a federal republic, consisting of 50 states and a federal district – the national flag, the 'stars and stripes', contains one star for each of the states. The most recent state to join the union was Hawaii, the Pacific island chain. The individual states retain considerable legislative powers. Federal executive power is held by the president, who is elected every four years. Federal legislative power resides in the two houses of government: the Senate and the House of Representatives. Mexico also has a presidential and bicameral system of democracy, in which the president is

Major Rivers

Amazon (Brazil), 6,437 km (4,000 mi), flows into Atlantic; **Mississippi-Missouri-Red Rock** (USA), 6,231 km (3,872 mi), flows to Atlantic; **Plate-Paraná** (Argentina), 4,700 km (2,920 mi), flows to Atlantic; **Mackenzie** (Canada), 4,241 km (2,635 mi), flows to Arctic Ocean; **Madeira-Mamoré** (tributary of Amazon), 3,200 km (1,988 mi); **St Lawrence** (Canada), 3,058 km (1,900 mi), flows to Atlantic; **Rio Grande-Rio Bravo** (USA-Mexico), 3,034 km (1,885 mi), flows to Atlantic.

Major Lakes

Superior (USA-Canada), 82,409 km² (31,820 mi²); **Huron** (USA-Canada), 61,797 km² (23,861 mi²); **Michigan** (USA), 58,016 km² (22,401 mi²); **Great Bear Lake** (Canada), 31,792 km² (12,276 mi²); **Great Slave Lake** (Canada), 28,438 mi² (10,981 mi²); **Erie** (USA-Canada), 25,612 km² (9,889 mi²); **Winnipeg** (Canada), 24,514 km² (9,465 mi²); **Ontario** (USA-Canada), 18,941 km² (7,314 mi²); **Maracaibo** (Venezuela), 14,243 km² (5,500 mi²); **Nicaragua** (Nicaragua), 8,430 km² (3,255 mi²).

Major Mountains

Aconcagua (Argentina), 6,959 m (22,835 ft); **Ojos del Salado** (Chile-Argentina), 6,880 m (22,572 ft); **Tupungato** (Chile-Argentina), 6,800 m (22,310 ft); **Mercedario** (Argentina), 6,770 m (22,211 ft); **Huascarán** (Peru), 6,768 m (22,205 ft); **Llullaillaco** (Chile-Argentina), 6,723 m (22,057 ft); **Galán** (Argentina), 6,600 m (21,654 ft); **Sajama** (Bolivia), 6,544 m (21,470 ft); **Coropuna** (Peru), 6,425 m (21,079 ft); **Illampu** (Bolivia), 6,421 m (21,066 ft); **Chimborazo** (Ecuador), 6,267 m (20,561 ft); **McKinley** (Alaska), 6,194 m (20,322 ft).

Major Islands

Islands in the Arctic and in Canada: **Greenland,** 2,175,600 km² (840,050 mi²); **Baffin,** 476,065 km² (183,820 mi²); **Ellesmere,** 212,687 km² (82,123 mi²); **Victoria,** 212,198 km² (81,935 mi²); **Newfoundland,** 112,300 km² (43,362 mi²); **Banks,** 60,165 km² (23,231 mi²); **Devon,** 54,030 km² (20,862 mi²); **Melville,** 42,396 km² (16,370 mi²). *West Indies:* **Cuba,** 105,007 km² (40,546 mi²); **Hispaniola,** 76,200 km² (29,423 mi²); **Jamaica,** 10,962 km² (4,233 mi²); **Puerto Rico,** 8.897 km² (3,435 mi²). *South Atlantic:* **Tierra del Fuego,** 47,000 km² (18,148 mi²).

elected every six years, and there is a Senate and a Chamber of Deputies.

In Central America, Guatemala is a presidential republic, divided into 22 departments. Belize is a member of the Commonwealth, having obtained independence from Britain in 1981. Honduras, Nicaragua, El Salvador, Costa Rica and Panama are independent republics. In Nicaragua, a war between left-wing 'Sandanista' guerrillas and the troops of the president, General Anastasio Somoza, led to the victory of the former in 1979. A similar guerrilla campaign in El Salvador led to many deaths in the early 1980s, but right-wing governments, enjoying the support of the United States, continued to control the country. The Panama Canal Zone was controlled by the USA until 1979, when it came under the control of the Republic of Panama. The canal itself remained under US control.

Cuba, the largest island in the Caribbean, has been a Communist republic since 1959, when Fidel Castro wrested power from the regime of General Batista. Haiti was an hereditary dictatorship and the neighbouring Dominican Republic is a presidential republic. Puerto Rico is a democratic commonwealth in association with the United States. The Bahamas received independence from Britain in 1973, but it remained within the Commonwealth, as did Trinidad and Tobago, Jamaica, Barbados, and other smaller island nations.

On the South American mainland, Colombia is a presidential republic, beset by a history of political instability. To the east, Venezuela is a republic consisting of 20 states, 2 federal territories and a federal district. Guyana is a Co-operative Republic within the Commonwealth, having achieved independence from Britain in 1966. Surinam received independence from the Netherlands in 1975, but French Guiana *(Guyane Française)* remains an Overseas Department of France. Ecuador has been an independent republic since 1822. Its rule extends over the Galapagos Island in the Pacific.

Brazil is the giant of South America. A Federative Republic since 1889, it is ruled by a military government. For many years, Peru was also ruled by the military, but in 1980 it became a democratic republic. Its new Constitution allows for a Senate and a Chamber of Deputies. Bolivia is another independent republic, freed from Spanish rule in 1825. Chile too is a republic. Its government, led by General Augusto Pinochet, seized power from the democratically elected Marxist government of Salvador Allende in 1973. A military coup brought General Alfredo Stroessner to power in Paraguay in 1954; there is now a parliament with a Senate and a Chamber of Deputies. In the 19 departments of neighbouring Uruguay, the military has also become involved in politics, but it has been faced with guerrilla resistance. Argentina's military junta fell after the 1982 war with Britain. Democracy was restored under Raúl Alfonsin's Radical Civil Union.

Not only did the arrival of European settlers prove to be disastrous for the Amerindian peoples of the Americas, but it also caused several ecological disasters. Many Amerindians were hunters. They lived in harmony with their environment, killing only sufficient wild animals for their own needs. But the modern firearms of the Whites caused wholesale destruction. The great herds of buffalo,

North and Central America

Flag	Nation	Capital	Area	Population	Economic Resources
	Canada	Ottawa	9,976,139 km² (3,852,019 mi²)	25,360,000	Asbestos, many metals, oil and natural gas, uranium. Cereals, livestock, fishing. Manufactures.
	Costa Rica	San José	50,700 km² (19,576 mi²)	2,624,000	Coffee, bananas, cocoa, sugar, tobacco, rice. Fishing. Cattle, dairy products.
	Cuba	Havana	114,524 km² (44,220 mi²)	10,344,000	Iron ore, copper, chromite, nickel, oil. Sugar and sugar products, tobacco. Fishing.
	Dominican Republic	Santo Domingo	48,734 km² (18,817 mi²)	6,300,000	Sugar, cocoa, coffee, tobacco. Bauxite, nickel, gold, silver. Fishing. Tourism.
	El Salvador	San Salvador	21,041 km² (8,124 mi²)	5,300,000	Coffee, cotton, maize, rubber cattle. Balsam, dye woods, timber. Fishing. Manufacturing.
	Guatemala	Guatemala	108,889 km² (42,045 mi²)	7,714,000	Nickel, lead, zinc. Coffee, bananas, cotton, sugar, beef, chicle gum, mahogany.
	Haiti	Port-au-Prince	27,750 km² (10,715 mi²)	5,220,000	Coffee, sugar, sisal, cotton, rice, maize. Bauxite. Cattle, pigs, horses.
	Honduras	Tegucigalpa	112,088 km² (43,280 mi²)	4,240,000	Bananas, coffee, sugar, tobacco, cotton, timber. Lead, silver, zinc. Manufactures.
	Jamaica	Kingston	10,991 km² (4,244 mi²)	2,310,000	Bauxite, alumina. Bananas, sugar and sugar products, fruit. Manufactures. Tourism.
	Mexico	Mexico City	1,972,547 km² (761,646 mi²)	76,790,000	Oil, many metals, coal. Textiles. Steel. Coffee, cotton, maize, sugar. Tourism.
	Nicaragua	Managua	130,000 km² (50,196 mi²)	3,200,000	Coffee, cotton, meat, sugar-cane. Gold, silver, copper. Hardwoods. Fishing.
	Panama	Panama	75,650 km² (29,210 mi²)	2,072,000	Bananas, rice, sugar-cane, maize. Copper. Timber. The Panama Canal. Some manufacturing.
	United States of America	Washington DC	9,363,123 km² (3,615,319 mi²)	235,100,000	Manufacturing. Many minerals, oil and natural gas, uranium. Cereals, cotton, fruit, livestock, fish.

Other American Nations

Other independent American nations, not listed in the tables, are **Antigua, Bahamas, Barbados, Belize, Dominica, Grenada, St Lucia,** and **St Vincent** and the **Grenadines.** Dependent territories are **Anguilla** (UK), **Bermuda** (UK Colony, representative government), **Cayman Is** (UK), **Montserrat** (UK), **Netherlands Antilles, Puerto Rico** (USA), **St Kitts-Nevis** (UK), **St Pierre & Miquelon** (France), **Turks and Caicos Is** (UK), **Virgin Is** (UK), and **Virgin Is** (USA). The Americas cover an area of 42,082,000 square kilometres (16,249,000 square miles) with a population of 603,000,000 in 1979.

South America

Flag	Nation	Capital	Area	Population	Economic Resources
	Argentina	Buenos Aires	2,766,889 km² (1,068,360 mi²)	27,950,000	Cattle, sheep, horses, dairy products, cereals. Oil and gas. Fishing. Manufacturing.
	Bolivia	La Paz, Sucre	1,098,581 km² (424,188 mi²)	6,252,000	Tin, antimony, copper, lead, oil, gas, silver, wolfram. Cotton, rice, sugar-cane.
	Brazil	Brasilia	8,511,965 km² (3,286,668 mi²)	135,500,000	Many minerals. Manufactures. Bananas, cocoa, coffee, maize, meat, sugar-cane, tobacco.
	Chile	Santiago	756,945 km² (292,274 mi²)	11,700,000	Copper, nitrates, iron ore, oil and gas, other minerals. Timber. Cereals, fruit. Fishing.
	Colombia	Bogotá	1,138,914 km² (439,761 mi²)	28,240,000	Coffee, meat, sugar, hides and skins. Emeralds, gold, other minerals. Fishing. Manufactures.
	Ecuador	Quito	283,561 km² (109,489 mi²)	8,893,000	Oil. Bananas, cocoa, coffee, rice, potatoes, wheat, maize, cattle, sheep. Fishing.
	Guyana	Georgetown	214,969 km² (83,005 mi²)	965,000	Bauxite, alumina, diamonds, gold, manganese. Sugar-cane, rice, fruit, vegetables, timber.
	Paraguay	Asunción	406,752 km² (157,056 mi²)	3,480,000	Cotton, soya beans, timber, tobacco, fruit, tannin, yerba maté, cattle. Food processing.
	Peru	Lima	1,285,216 km² (496,252 mi²)	18,790,000	Many minerals, oil. Timber. Fishing, Cattle, sheep, coffee, cereals, fruit, cotton.
	Surinam	Paramaribo	163,265 km² (63,040 mi²)	410,000	Bauxite, alumina, gold. Rice, citrus fruits, sugar-cane, bananas, timber.
	Trinidad & Tobago	Port of Spain	5,130 km² (1,981 mi²)	1,168,000	Oil, asphalt. Citrus fruits, cocoa, coffee, sugar-cane, coconuts, timber.
	Uruguay	Montevideo	176,215 km² (68,041 mi²)	2,990,000	Cattle, sheep, other domesticated animals, rice, other cereals, fruit, sugar.
	Venezuela	Caracas	912,050 km² (352,164 mi²)	17,257,000	Oil, bauxite, diamonds, iron ore, other metals. Coffee, cocoa, timber. Fishing.

The heights of Point de Açucas tower over the city of Rio de Janeiro, the former capital of Brazil. Today it remains a huge city of over 5 million inhabitants, and the cultural centre of the nation.

which grazed the plains of North America, were slaughtered until they were almost extinct. The passenger pigeon, once one of the most common birds in the United States, did become extinct in the 19th century, within the space of a few decades. Even more destructive to the wildlife of the Americas has been industrialization and pollution, and deforestation, leading to extensive soil erosion. And the habitats of many wonderful creatures have simply disappeared.

But today there is a growing awareness of the need for conservation, and many magnificent wildlife parks and reserves provide a home for the species that remain. Canada's Wood Buffalo National Park is the world's largest, with an area of 45,480 square kilometres (17,560 square miles). In the north of the continent are the beautiful polar bears of the Arctic, and the Kodiak bear (a cousin of the grizzly), which is the largest four-legged carnivore, while the Alaskan moose is the biggest deer in the world. The prairies to the south are the home of the coyote and the prairie dog. Alligators infest the swamps of Florida, while other reptiles of the southern United States include the rattlesnake and the Gila monster. The Southern Hemisphere also abounds in extraordinary birds, mammals and insects. The anteater is a long-nosed mammal which eats termites, and noisy howler monkeys use their tails as an extra limb as they pass through the treetops of the forests. The high Andes mountains are the home of the extraordinary llama, and its relatives the alpaca, guanaco and vicuña.

The New World is truly a land of superlatives. As if nature had not already provided a full complement of natural wonders, humans have provided a catalogue of marvels just as incredible, from the towering skyscrapers of New York City or Brasilia, to the oil pipeline of frozen Alaska, or the rocket launching gantries of Cape Canaveral. But it is also a land of great contrasts, of great wealth and abject poverty.

Opposite: The docks at Buenos Aires, one of the World's major ports.

Argentina
República

Traditionally, the Argentine Republic has been known as cattle country. The vast tracts of grassland known as the *pampas* are the home of huge herds, which are rounded up by the *gaúchos* or cowboys. The *gauchos* are expert horsemen, skilled with the lasso and the *bolas,* a tackle of rope and metal balls used for bringing down wild cattle. The ranches of Argentina provide beef for many countries. Argentina's cattle and its horses, too, are descended from the handful of animals brought to South America by the Spanish *conquistadores.* Crops also play a significant role in Argentinian farming. Sugar-cane, cotton, cereals, oilseeds, fruit, alfalfa and soya are all important.

Increasingly, however, Argentina is becoming an industrial power, and by 1980 82 per cent of the people were city-dwellers. The processing of meat and other foodstuffs is still important, but industries have been developed, producing steel, plastics, textiles, engineering industries and vehicle manufacture. The most important mineral resource is oil, and natural gas reserves are also exploited. There are reserves of coal, iron-ore, lead, salt and zinc.

Argentina, South America's second largest nation, stretches from the Gran Chaco in the north to the wilderness of Tierra del Fuego in the south, which is separated from Antarctica by the Scotia Sea. Stretching north to south along the Chilean border are the Andes, which at Mount Aconcagua reach 6,960 metres (22,835 feet) above sea level. This is the highest point in the Americas. To the north-east the land is drained by the River Paraná, which joins with the River Uruguay to form the River Plate (Rio de la Plata). On the southern bank of the Plate is Argentina's capital, Buenos Aires. The central *pampas* (plains) contain the most fertile land and they form the most densely populated region. In the south lie the bleak plateaux of the Patagonia region.

The history of Argentina is one typical of Latin America. The Amerindian peoples suffered terribly from the advent of European settlers. The Spanish came in the 16th century and governed the country for three centuries. A war of independence was led by General José de San Martín, whose struggle was finally successful in 1816. Throughout its history, in colonial and post-colonial periods, immigrant peoples have come to live in Argentina: Blacks (originally brought here as slaves); Spaniards; Italians; Central Europeans; people of mixed race from neighbouring countries; and people from Wales. Welsh is still spoken in the Chubut region of Patagonia, where the descendants of 19th-century settlers still maintain the traditions of their homeland. Spanish is the official language of this predominantly Roman Catholic country.

Buenos Aires is one of America's major cities, a busy port with a population of 2,908,000 and more than six million more people live in its suburbs. It is the centre of an extensive communications network. There are 40,854 kilometres (25,386 miles) of railway track in the country, and 37,304 kilometres (23,180 miles) of surfaced roads. There are around 183,170 kilometres (113,820 miles) of unmetalled roads. Although there are internal and international air links, the southern and eastern parts of the country are still very sparsely populated.

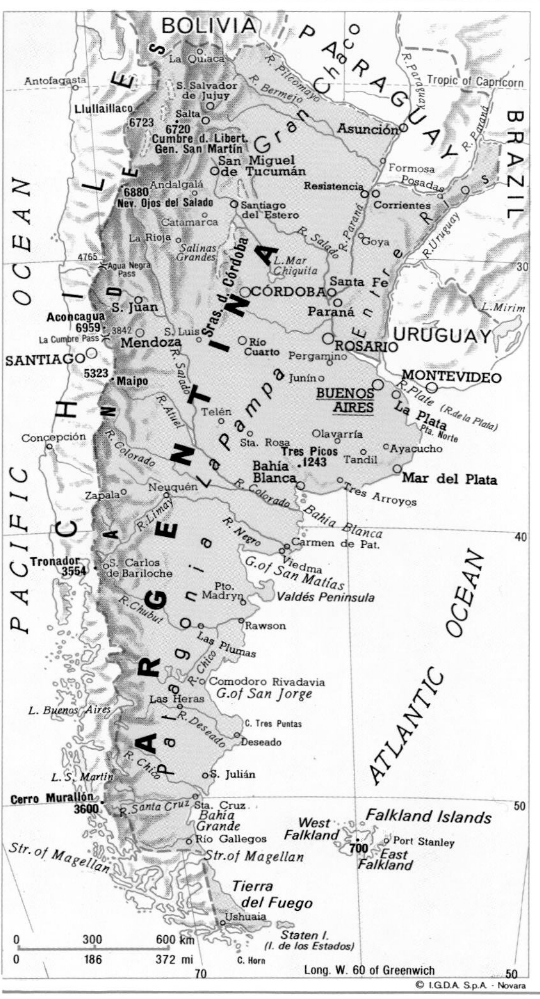

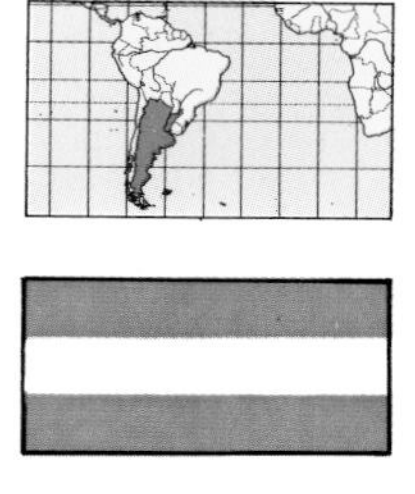

Area:
2,766,889 km²
(1,068,360 mi²)
Population:
27,950,000
Capital:
Buenos Aires (pop. with suburbs 10,865,000)
Other towns:
Córdoba, Rosario, Mendoza, La Plata, San Miguel de Tucumán, Mar del Plata, Santa Fé
Currency:
peso

Belize

República de

A small nation on the Gulf of Honduras, Belize is bordered by Mexico and Guatemala. Guatemala's territorial claim to Belize led to a dispute with Britain, which ruled Belize as a colony from 1862 to 1981. Belize, which was once known as British Honduras, is now an independent member of the Commonwealth.

The country has a humid tropical climate, with large areas of swamp. The southern part of the country is occupied by the Maya Mountains, which reach an altitude of 990 metres (3,248 feet). Dense forest covers much of the land. Sugar-cane, rice and fruit flourish in this climate, and the forests provide valuable timber. The population is made up of Creoles, Blacks, Europeans, and Amerindians. English is the official language.

Area:
22,965 km² (8,867 mi²)
Population:
160,000
Capital:
Belmopan (pop. 4,000)
Other towns:
Belize City
Currency:
dollar

Bolivia

The Republic of Bolivia is a poor, landlocked country, although well provided with natural resources, notably copper, lead, tin (the leading export), silver and wolfram. Natural gas is exported, and oil production is being increased, providing desperately needed revenue. Cereals, cocoa, cotton, nuts, rice, rubber and vegetables are all cultivated.

Bolivia lies in central South America, and shares borders with Chile, Peru, Brazil, Paraguay and Argentina. The northern part of the country lies within the Amazonian basin. It is a hot, humid region covered by rain forest and crossed by many rivers. To the west and southwest are the lofty peaks of the Andes, which reach heights of more than 6,500 metres (21,325 feet) above sea level near Lake Titicaca, the world's highest navigable lake. In the south-east is arid bush. Most of the Bolivian people live on the central plateau, the Altiplano.

The population is predominantly American Indian, speaking Quechua and Aymara. The remainder are of mixed descent or European origin, speaking Spanish, the official language. With the collapse of the Inca empire in the 16th century, the whole of the region came under Spanish rule. Bolivia achieved independence as the result of a war of liberation led by national hero Simón Bolívar after whom the new country was named in 1825.

There are 3,540 kilometres (2,200 miles) of railways in modern Bolivia, and a limited road network. Internal air links are important, and La Paz has an airport for international travel. While La Paz is the seat of government and the largest city, the legal capital is at Sucre. La Paz is the highest major city in the world.

Area:
1,098,581 km² (424,188 mi²)
Population:
6,252,000
Capitals:
Sucre (pop. 80,000, legal capital)
La Paz (pop. 880,000, seat of government)
Other towns:
Santa Cruz, Cochabamba, Oruro, Potosí, Tarija
Currency:
peso

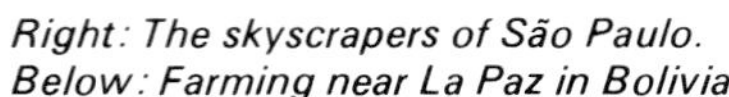

Right: The skyscrapers of São Paulo.
Below: Farming near La Paz in Bolivia.

Brazil

República Federativa do Brasil

Like many of the countries of the Americas, Europeans discovered Brazil by accident. In March 1500, a fleet of 13 caravels left Lisbon under the command of the Portuguese navigator Pedro Alvares Cabral. His destination was the East Indies, following the Cape of Good Hope route established two years previously by Vasco da Gama. However, while making a wide westward sweep through the South Atlantic Ocean, his sailors sighted an unknown land at about 18 degrees of latitude south of the equator.

They landed, claimed the territory for the kingdom of Portugal, and met the Amerindian people of the region. The sailors wondered at these people who wore no clothes, had no weapons of metal, slept on hammocks of liana and lived in thatched huts. Cabral's fleet then sailed eastwards to Mozambique in Africa and Calicut in India. He named his South American discovery Santa Cruz or Vera Cruz, but subsequent Portuguese settlers named it Brazil, after the dye extracted from a tree called brazilwood *(Caesalpina echinata),* which grew widely in the region.

At the end of the 15th century, rivalry between the two great maritime powers, Portugal and Spain, had led Pope Alexander VII to 'share out' the New World

between two countries. In this way Brazil remained a Portuguese colony for three centuries, and Portuguese remains the country's official language. The original inhabitants of the region, the Amerindians, were persecuted and murdered by rapacious colonists, or else they died of European diseases unknown in the Americas, to which they had no immunity. This sad story continues today. Surviving Amerindian peoples include the Atroari, Bororo, Shavante, Surui, Xingu and Yanomamo.

The country's rich mineral reserves and fertile lands attracted European settlers in their thousands and the majority of the people are of European ancestry. There are also descendants of Black slaves introduced to work European plantations and Brazil also has many people of mixed origin. Brazil became an independent empire in 1822 under Pedro I. From 1831 until 1889, the country was ruled by his son Pedro II, who established constitutional government and abolished slavery in 1888. When Brazil became a republic in 1889, it followed a presidential system of government. The Federative Republic of Brazil is the fifth largest country in the world, consisting of 22 states, four territories and a federal district (Brasilia). Four-fifths of the population live on the Atlantic coast, where the towns are densely populated. São Paulo has more than eight million inhabitants, and Rio de Janeiro, the former capital, 5 million. Brasilia, the capital since 1960, is a purpose-built city on the Goias plateau. It was designed by the architect Lucio Costa.

The northern part of Brazil is taken up by the *selvas,* the great rain forest, whose clearance is a source of concern to world ecologists. Through this runs the Amazon, which, at 6,437 kilometres (4,000 miles), is the world's second largest river. It is fed by innumerable tributaries. To the south of this are grassy plateaux, with ridges and fertile valleys. In the southeast are various highland regions, including the Serra do Espinhaco and the Serra da Mantiqueira. The principal river of the south is the Paraná.

The varied climate and huge area of Brazil enable it to be one of the world's leading agricultural producers. It is the world's top producer of bananas, coffee, and sugar-cane. It is also a major producer of cocoa, cotton, rice and other cereals, sisal, tobacco, fruit and vegetables. Cattle are also farmed. Mineral resources include iron-ore, asbestos, diamonds, bauxite, gold, lead, nickel and tungsten. Brazil is the leading industrial power of South America, producing steel and cement.

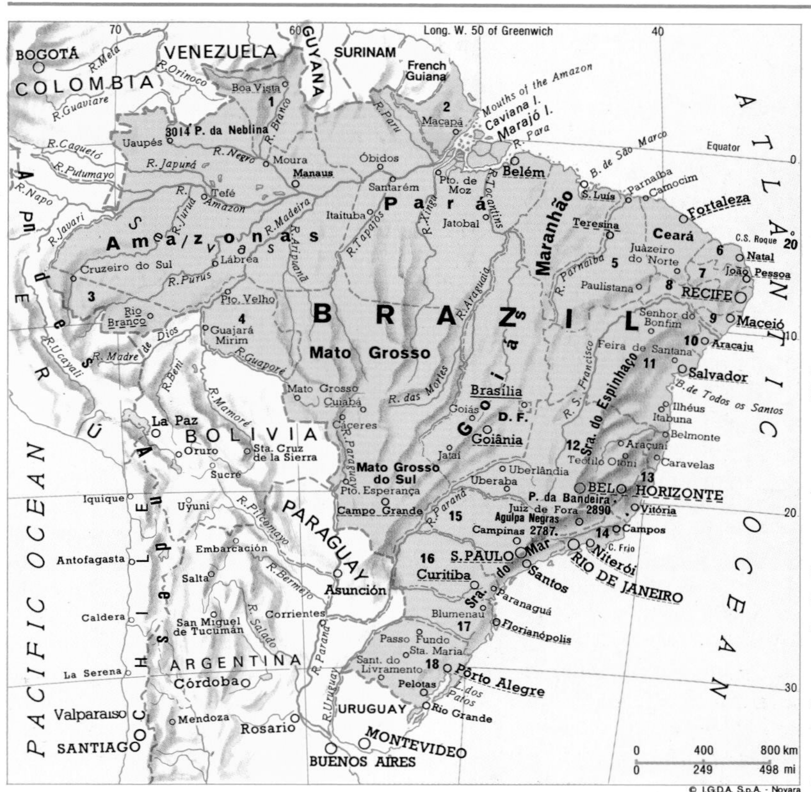

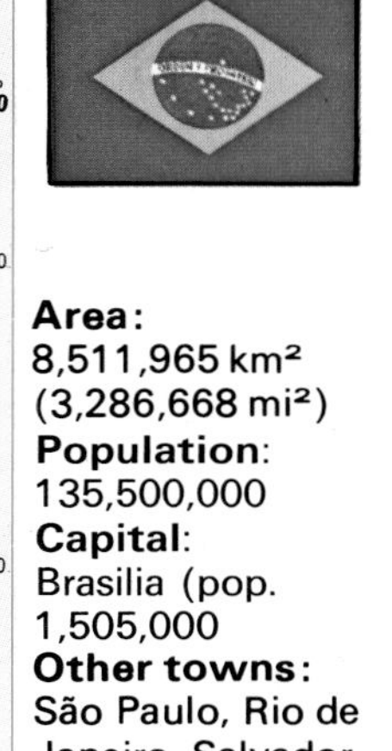

Area: 8,511,965 km² (3,286,668 mi²)
Population: 135,500,000
Capital: Brasilia (pop. 1,505,000
Other towns: São Paulo, Rio de Janeiro, Salvador, Belo Horizonte, Recife, Porto Alegre, Curitiba, Belém, Goiânia
Currency: cruzeiro

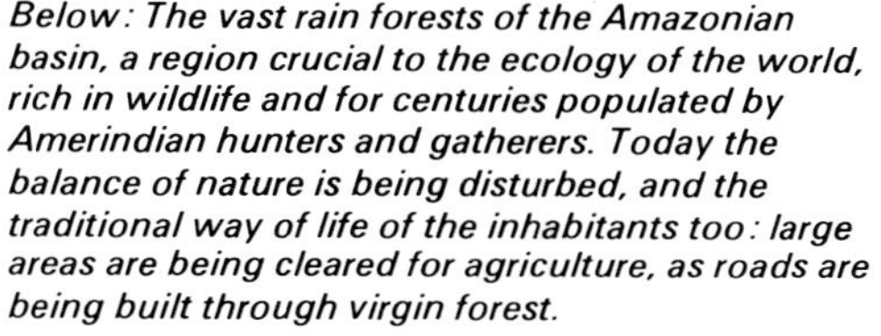
Below: The vast rain forests of the Amazonian basin, a region crucial to the ecology of the world, rich in wildlife and for centuries populated by Amerindian hunters and gatherers. Today the balance of nature is being disturbed, and the traditional way of life of the inhabitants too: large areas are being cleared for agriculture, as roads are being built through virgin forest.

The numbers on the map refer to the States of Brazil as follows:

1 Roraima
2 Amapá
3 Acre
4 Rondônia
5 Piauí
6 Rio Grande do Norte
7 Paraíba
8 Pernambuco
9 Alagoas
10 Sergipe
11 Bahia
12 Minas Gerais
13 Espírito Santo
14 Rio de Janerio
15 São Paulo
16 Paranå
17 Santa Catarina
18 Rio Grande do Sul

Canada

The national emblem of Canada, the maple leaf, appears on its flag. It is a symbol of the huge forests which cover more than one-third of this great country – conifers, silver birch and maple. One can travel long distances through the forests of Canada without ever finding a town. Canada is the second largest country in the world, after the USSR. It occupies the northern part of the American continent, with the exception of Alaska in the north-west, which is part of the United States. Its eastern coastline is with the Atlantic Ocean, its northern coastline is on the Arctic Ocean, and its western coast borders the Pacific Ocean.

For all its great area, Canada is sparsely inhabited. Only 25 million people live in the country, less than half of the population of the United Kingdom. Most Canadians live in the southern part of the country, near the United States border. This narrow belt contains the major towns, industrial centres and ports. The reason for this is simple. The climate of the north is bitterly cold and the Arctic Circle runs across the Northwest Territories. Even the south, which has a continental climate, endures long, freezing winters, although summers are warm.

Western Canada is dominated by the Rocky Mountains, a giant of a range which stretches from the Yukon in the north, through British Columbia and Alberta, and the Coast Mountains. The Rockies cross into the United States and extend southwards down the length of the North American continent. The highest point in Canada, Mount Logan, is situated in the Saint Elias Mountains, near the Alaskan border: Mount Logan is 6,050 metres (19,849 feet) above sea level. In the far south-west, the waters of the Pacific Ocean ensure a milder climate, which partly explains the growth of the large city of Vancouver.

Northern Canada is an Arctic wasteland of islands and ice pack (floating ice). Little grows in this empty wilderness. The traditional hunting grounds of the Eskimos, or Inuit, this region is populated by polar bears, seal, and fish. The treeless tundra regions support mosses and lichens, and some plants which flower only in the brief Arctic summer. To the south, the tundra merges into a land of coniferous forests and lakes. This is the home of the moose (a large deer with huge antlers) and the beaver, a rodent whose skills as an engineer are legendary.

In the Mid-West, the rolling prairies are a continuation of those to the south in the United States. The winters in Canada are longer than those in the

Below: Canada is a land of lakes and mountains, and fascinating wild animals.

Above left: The elk (cervus canadensis). *Above: A grizzly bear* (Ursus arctos horribilis), *an expert fisherman.*

USA, but the farmers of the Canadian prairies have developed a type of wheat which ripens quickly. Today Canada is one of the world's largest grain exporters. Its combine harvesters cover incredibly large areas each summer, the harvesting operation being supervised from the air. In the region of the Great Lakes and the Saint Lawrence and Ottawa rivers, Canada's most densely populated region, are four major cities: Québec, Montréal, Ottawa and Toronto. The Saint Lawrence Seaway provides an outlet from Lake Ontario to the Atlantic, and the Trans-Canada Highway and two trans-continental railway systems provide land links between east and west. The capital is at Ottawa, but Toronto is the largest conurbation and chief business centre.

Cattle and grain from the prairies and timber and pelts from the forests are not the only reason for Canada's wealth. The land is rich in mineral resources, including asbestos, copper, gold, gypsum, iron-ore, lead, molybdenum, potash, silver, uranium, and zinc. Canada also has reserves of oil and natural gas. Service and manufacturing industries thrive in urban areas where 80 per cent of the population lives. The United States is by far Canada's leading export market and source of imports. Japan, Britain and West Germany are also important trading partners.

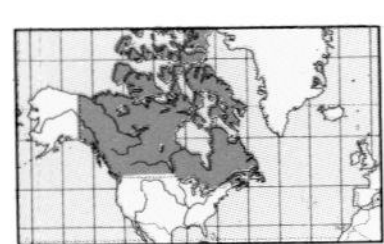

Area:
9,976,139 km²
(3,852,019 mi²)
Population:
25,360,000
Capital:
Ottawa (pop. 718,000)
Other towns:
Toronto (2,999,000)
Montreal (2,828,000)
Vancouver (1,268,000)
Winnipeg, Edmonton, Québec, Hamilton, Calgary, St Catherines-Niagara, Kitchener
Currency: dollar

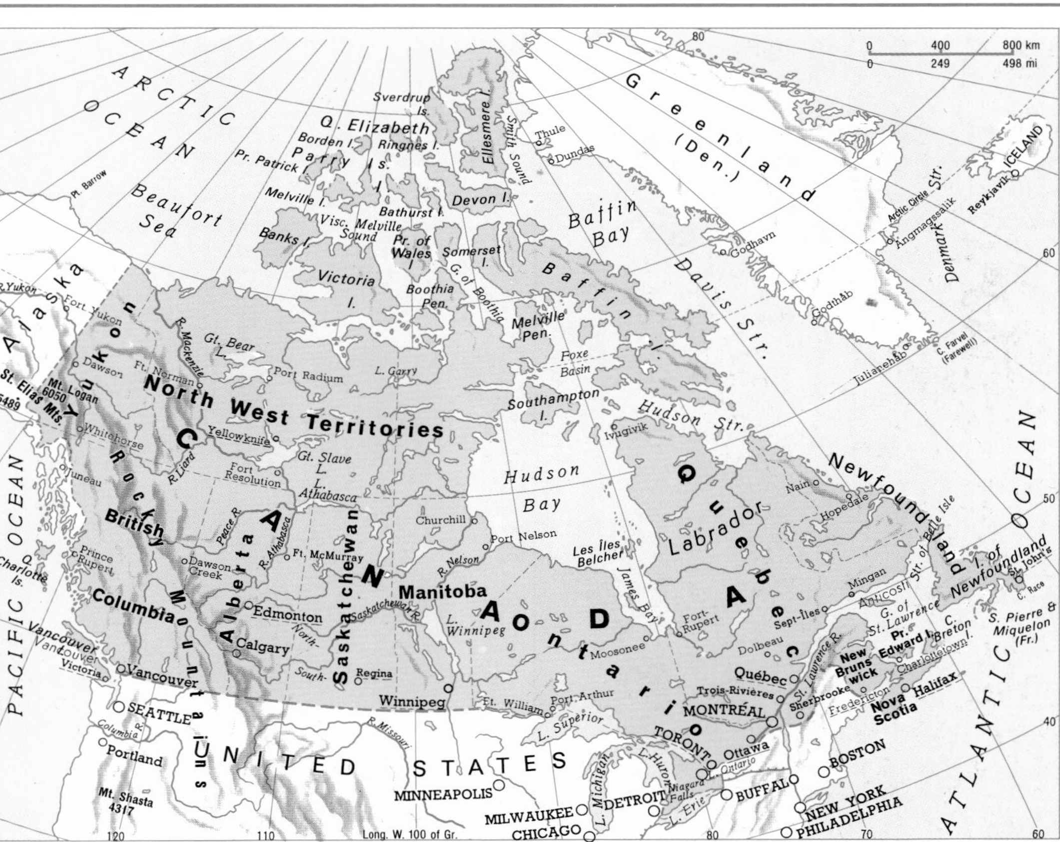

Canada has two official languages: French, which is spoken particularly in the eastern province of Québec, and English. The original inhabitants of Canada were Amerindian peoples who crossed over the Bering Strait from Asia. However, such famous nations as the Cree, Ojibwa (Chippewa) and Chipewyans succumbed to European firepower, European diseases, and confinement in reservations. The Eskimos (Inuit) of the Arctic arrived later. Their way of life, which has long fascinated the rest of the world, has also been changed radically in modern times. Today only one per cent of Canadians are Amerindians or Eskimos.

The Vikings were probably the first Europeans to reach Canada, in the late 10th century. In 1497 John Cabot (Giovanni Caboto), a Genoese in the service of King Henry VII of England, reached Cape Breton Island and Nova Scotia. In 1604–07, the Frenchman Samuel de Champlain explored the Canadian coast and founded Québec. Fur trappers and hunters explored the interior. In a long struggle for regional supremacy, Britain finally emerged the victor when French forces at Québec were defeated by the British troops of General James Wolfe in 1759. The French colonists maintained their individual identity during Canada's subsequent history, and separatism and autonomy for the province of Québec remain vital issues today.

During the American Revolution, many British loyalists fled northwards to Canada and, in the 19th century, immigrants from Europe also arrived. Some, including many Scots, came to escape poverty and maltreatment at home. Others, such as the Hutterites, a religious sect from central Europe, sought freedom of worship, while others came in search of gold. Adventurers from all over the world sought their fortune in Yukon Territory in 1897, braving terrible hardships in order to pan dirt from the rivers, looking for the tell-tale glint of gold. These were rough, wild days, recorded in the popular verse of Robert Service and in the annals of the Royal Canadian Mounted Police – the well-known 'Mounties'.

As early as 1867, Canada achieved self-government as a Dominion within the British Empire. Today the federation has extended to include 10 provinces and two territories. The original members were New Brunswick, Nova Scotia, Ontario and Québec. Alberta, British Columbia, Manitoba, Northwest Territory, Yukon Territory, Prince Edward Island, Saskatchewan and Newfoundland joined subsequently, the latter as recently as 1949. Modern Canada has a bicameral system of government, with a Senate and a House of Commons. Canada remains an important member of the Commonwealth and, in the 20th

century, it was involved in both World Wars. Increasing prosperity has been accompanied by a desire to establish a Canadian identity separate from that of the United Kingdom or that of the United States, whose influence remains great.

The chief domestic issue has remained that of French Canadian separatism. The *Québec Libre* movement which grew up in the 1950s and 1960s received widespread support in the east. However, in a referendum on the issue in 1980, separatism was rejected by the majority of the people in Québec. The ethnic diversity of the Canadian population, which includes Germans, Dutch, Italians and Ukrainians among its number, and the differing ways of life practised in such a vast country, result in some differences in the policies of the individual provinces. Nevertheless, the federation of Canada is a powerful and respected member of the international community.

The awareness of a Canadian identity has perhaps been most apparent in cultural matters. Canadian theatre, film and literature is of international significance. The ethnic art of the Eskimo people, which is typified by small stone carvings, is greatly admired, and its traditions encouraged. In sport, too, Canada has made its mark. The national sport of ice-hockey has a large following.

The inhospitable nature of the terrain has in fact made Canada a unique country, a wide-open land of self-sufficient agricultural communities. Perhaps today the pioneering spirit is reflected in the towering sky-scrapers of such big cities as Toronto as much as in the tranquil backwoods.

Opposite page: Toronto, Canada's largest city, a centre of business with 2,999,000 inhabitants. It is situated on Lake Ontario, in the south-east of the country. Its large port and its closeness to the United States, Canada's major trading partner, have contributed to its growth. The CN Tower (far left) is the world's tallest self-supporting structure, at 553 metres (1,814 feet).

Above: Symbols of a changing nation. The architecture of Vancouver and Montréal contrasts with totems carved by Canada's first inhabitants, the Amerindian peoples (left). Today there are only about 300,000 people of Amerindian or Eskimo origin still living in Canada.

Caribbean Region

Christopher Columbus was the first European to sail in the Caribbean Sea. On 12 October 1492, he landed on Watling Island (San Salvador) in the Bahamas. His fleet of caravels then sailed on to Cuba and Hispaniola, and his logbook records the explorers' amazement at the coasts of these islands, at their beautiful birds, at their lush vegetation and tropical fruits. Columbus thought he was in Japan or the East Indies. But the inhabitants of the islands were not Japanese or Indians. They were Amerindians of the Carib, Arawak and Tanala peoples. And the islands themselves were the outposts of a 'New World' – the Americas.

Running from Florida to the delta of the Orinoco in Venezuela, the islands form a great chain, separating the Caribbean Sea and the Gulf of Mexico from the Atlantic Ocean. The largest islands are those of the Greater Antilles: Cuba, Hispaniola (Haiti and the Dominican Republic), Jamaica and Puerto Rico. The Lesser Antilles, to the south and west, may be divided into two groups. The Leeward Islands include Montserrat, Barbuda, St Kitts-Nevis, Anguilla, Antigua, Guadeloupe, and the Virgin Islands. The Windward Islands take in Grenada, Barbados, St Vincent, St Lucia, Martinique and Dominica. Lying off the coast of Venezuela is the independent island nation of Trinidad and Tobago, and the Netherlands Antilles, including Curaçao and Aruba. Between the Straits of Florida and Hispaniola lies the long archipelago of the Bahamas, including Grand Bahama, Great Abaco, Eleuthera, Andros, and others.

Columbus's discovery was soon followed by European colonization. The Amerindian inhabitants were decimated, and plantations were established, worked by Black slaves, transported from West Africa under conditions of extreme cruelty. The galleons of Spain and other powers, bringing the treasures of the Americas back to Europe, were plundered by ruthless pirates, who found it easy to evade capture among the maze of tiny islands.

Today most West Indians are of Black or mixed descent. The colonizers were Spanish, Dutch, French, Danish and British. A forerunner of the independence struggle was the Black Haitian slave Toussaint l'Ouverture (1746-1803). Inspired by the French Revolution, he joined a revolt against colonial rule in 1791 and soon became its leader. However, when the ideals of the revolution were forgotten by its instigators, Napoleon Bonaparte had Toussaint, who had

Top: Fishermen cast their nets into a tranquil sea off Haiti.

Above: Cricket, lovely cricket. The West Indies play England at Sabina Park, Jamaica.

Caribbean Islands

Flag	Country	Capital	Area	Population
	Anguilla	The Valley (500)	90 km² (35 mi²)	7,000
	Antigua	St. John's (25,000)	442 km² (171 mi²)	79,500
	Bahamas	Nassau (135,000)	13,935 km² (5,381 mi²)	228,000
	Barbados	Bridgetown (88,000)	431 km² (166 mi²)	257,000
	Cayman Islands	George Town (8,000)	259 km² (100 mi²)	19,000
	Cuba	Havana (1,925,000)	114,524 km² (44,220 mi²)	10,344,000
	Dominica	Roseau (20,000)	751 km² 290 mi²)	82,000
	Dominican Republic	Santo Domingo 1,551,000	48,734 km² (18,817 mi²)	6,300,000
	Grenada	St George's (31,000)	344 km² (133 mi²)	115,000
	Guadeloupe	Basse-Terre (15,000)	1,779 km² (687 mi²)	332,000
	Haiti	Port-au Prince (1,000,000)	27,750 km² (10,715 mi²)	6,000,000
	Jamaica	Kingston (663,000)	10,991 km² (4,244 mi²)	2,301,000
	Martinique	Fort-de-France (100,000)	1,102 km² (426 mi²)	330,000
	Montserrat	Plymouth (3,000)	98 km² (38 mi²)	12,000
	Puerto Rico	San Juan (519,000)	8,897 km² (3,435 mi²)	3,666,000
	St Christopher (St Kitts-Nevis)	Basseterre (15,000)	262 km² (101 mi²)	51,000
	St Lucia	Castries (50,000)	616 km² (238 mi²)	134,000
	St Vincent and the Grenadines	Kingstown (34,000)	388 km² (150 mi²)	125,000
	Trinidad and Tobago	Port-of-Spain (63,000)	5,130 km² (1,981 mi²)	1,193,000
	Turks and Caicos Islands	Grand Turk (3,000)	430 km² (166 mi²)	7,500
	Virgin Islands (UK)	Road Town (3,500)	153 km² (59 mi²)	11,500
	Virgin Islands (US)	Charlotte Amalie (15,000)	344 km² (133 mi²)	119,000

become ruler of Haiti in 1799, imprisoned, and slavery was reintroduced. Independence came to most of the Caribbean region in the 1960s and 1970s, but many tiny dependencies still remain, whose small size or isolation pose problems of viability. In the Caribbean region today, just about every kind of political system imaginable is practised, and the generally severe economic problems put them to the test.

Largest of the Greater Antilles is **Cuba,** the giant of the region. A long claw of an island, it contains low-lying and swampy coastal plains. But highlands, mountains and fertile plains lie in the interior. The island was occupied in 1510 by Diego Velázquez de Cuéllar, in the name of the Spanish crown. As a Spanish captain-generalcy, Cuba controlled many of the islands of the region. The struggle for independence was long and hard. Only after the intervention of the United States and the Spanish-American war of 1898 did Spain finally withdraw. But democratic rule was tenuous, and the USA reserved the right to intervene in Cuba's internal affairs until 1934.

Under Fulgencio Batista y Zalvidar, the island came under a corrupt dictatorship. However, in November 1956, a group of revolutionaries landed in Cuba. Led by Fidel Castro, the group fought a three-year guerrilla war against government forces. The revolutionaries swore not to shave until the liberation of Cuba, and so were known as the *barbudos,* or 'bearded men'. Havana fell to Castro in 1959, and his regime is still in power today. Cuba is an ally of the USSR, an alignment which has created problems in its relations with its powerful neighbour to the north, the United States. In recent years, Cuban forces have aided governments or guerillas in several African countries.

The Cuban economy relies on sugar-cane and tobacco, and its Havana cigars are known throughout the world. Coffee, vegetables, and fruits are also grown, and there is a fishing industry. Copper, nickel, chrome, and manganese are mined, and there are reserves of oil. The USSR is Cuba's main trading partner.

Haiti occupies the western corner of the island of Hispaniola, east of Cuba. Haiti is a region of mountainous forests and fertile plains. Sugar-cane, coffee, sisal, cotton and cocoa are grown, but there is severe poverty. Dr François Duvalier ruled from 1957–71, when he was succeeded by his son Jean-Claude (deposed in 1986). The neighbouring **Dominican Republic** also has a history of dictatorial government, but since 1965 has favoured a democratic system. Agricultural produce includes cocoa, coffee, sugar and tobacco. Gold and nickel are mined and the light industrial sector is expanding.

To the south of Cuba, **Jamaica** is a mountainous island of great natural beauty. The highest point is Blue Mountain Peak, at 2,256 metres (7,402 feet) above sea level. Sugar-cane, coffee, bananas and citrus fruit are cultivated, and Jamaican rum has long been famous. Gypsum and bauxite are mined, Jamaica being one of the world's leading producers of the latter. Jamaica is a former British colony, having achieved independence in 1962.

Another of Columbus's discoveries was **Puerto Rico.** This is a United States commonwealth – the USA took over the island in 1898, as a result of the Spanish-American War. Since 1952 it has been self-governing, while retaining strong links with the US political structure. It is a beautiful tropical island, producing sugar-cane, coffee and tobacco. Tourism is important. Many of its citizens live and work in the United States.

The **Bahamas** are also a popular holiday centre for Americans and Europeans. These many islands were a British colony from 1717 until 1973, when they achieved independence within the Commonwealth. The capital, Nassau, is on the island of New Providence. The **Turks and Caicos** Islands to the south-east of the Bahamas remain a British colony.

East of Puerto Rico, the **Virgin Islands** come partly within the sphere of the United States, and partly within that of Britain. Both territories rely on tourism for income. To the south-east lies the **St Christopher-Nevis** became independent in 1983. **Anguilla** had seceded from this

Above: Haitian architecture, an echo of the Old World.
Below: Oil refineries on Trinidad.

group in 1980 and has since been governed separately. The **Antigua** group, which includes the island of Barbuda, is a former British colony, now a member of the Commonwealth. **Montserrat** remains a British colony, but **Dominica** has been independent since 1978. **Guadeloupe** and **Martinique** are Overseas Departments of France, producing rum, sugar-cane and bananas. **St Lucia, St Vincent, Grenada** and **Barbados** are all independent nations within the Commonwealth, relying on tourism and tropical produce.

The largest island off the Venezuelan coast is **Trinidad,** which with **Tobago** forms an independent republic within the Commonwealth. A former British colony, Trinidad includes a wide ethnic mixture within its population. It is a beautiful island, with considerable oil and natural gas reserves. Although **Surinam** (formerly Dutch Guiana) received full independence in 1975, the **Netherlands Antilles** remained under Dutch covereignty, with internal autonomy. Chief of these islands are Curaçao, and Bonaire.

Right: Paradise Island, Nassau, Bahamas.
Below: The Caribbean region.

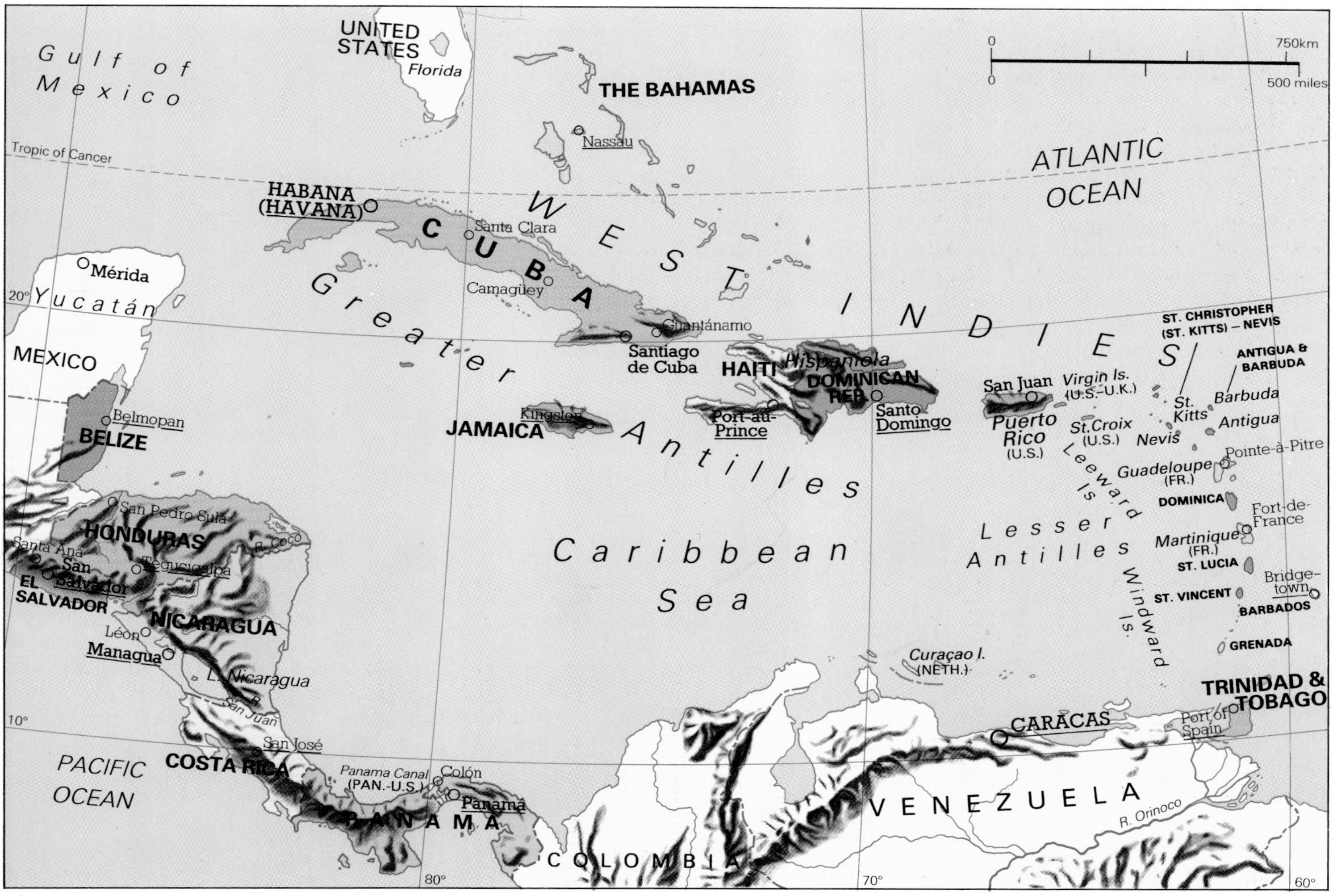

Chile

República de

The word 'Chile' derives from an expression used by the Araucanian Indians of the region, meaning 'the best on Earth'. They were referring to the fertile Aconcagua region of the country. However, not all the land is fertile. The Republic of Chile is in fact the 'longest' country in the world, comprising a strip of land 150 to 200 kilometres (93-124 miles) in width. It is about 4,300 kilometres (2,672 miles) long, spanning about 38 degrees of latitude. The strange shape of this country is determined by the Andes mountains, which stretch down western South America forming a natural barrier with Argentina. Chile is the land between the Andes and the Pacific Ocean. Because it covers such a large section of the Southern Hemisphere, there are considerable differences in climate, terrain, agriculture and ways of life.

In the north of the country, the climate is hot and arid. This is the site of the Atacama desert, one of the most desolate places on Earth. Although it has little vegetation, its soil is rich in minerals: copper, iron ore and nitrate. In central Chile, the climate is more temperate, being of the Mediterranean variety. As a result, cereal crops, vines and fruit are cultivated. The capital, Santiago, is situated in central Chile. It is a large, beautiful city, which is linked by road and rail to the port of Valparaiso on the Pacific coast. Central Chile is the country's most densely populated region.

In the cool, rainy south, the land is mountainous and forested. The coastline breaks up into a maze of islands and fjords, extending down to the icy wilderness of Tierra del Fuego, across the Straits of Magellan. This island is divided between Chile and Argentina. This southern region, known as Magellanes, has reserves of oil and natural gas. Chilean territory also takes in the Pacific islands of Juan Fernandez. It was on one of these 'desert islands' that the Scottish sailor Alexander Selkirk was put ashore in 1704, thereby supposedly inspiring the writer Daniel Defoe to write the story of *Robinson Crusoe.*

The Chilean economy relies on agriculture, fishing, forestry and mining, particularly copper which provides the country's major source of revenue. Consumer goods and steel are produced and oil is refined at San Vicente and Concon.

In such a long, extended country communications are of vital importance. Of the 7,000 kilometres (4,350 miles) of roads only about eight per cent are metalled. The cities of central Chile are linked by rail to Iquique in the north and Puerto Montt to the south. Other lines provide access to Argentina, Brazil and the Atlantic. Shipping plays an important role in internal and international trade, and in the large fishing industry. There are airfields in many of the remoter areas of the country, and large airports at Antofagasta and Santiago.

It was more than 40 years after the European discovery of the South American continent before the Spaniards managed to settle this land beyond the Andes. In 1541 an expedition led by Pedro de Valdivia reached Chile and founded its capital, naming it Santiago de la Nueva Extremadura after a region of his native Spain. The Amerindian inhabitants of the region – the Mapuche – put up a bitter resistance to the settlers, and prevented the southern expansion of the colony for many years. Indeed, it was only during the last 60 years of Spanish rule that Chile consolidated its control of the territories to the south. Mapuche resistance continued until the late 19th century, and the Mapuche still maintain an independent spirit.

In 1810 a great movement of liberation spread through Latin America, as the descendants of the colonists sought to sever their links with Spain. In Chile an eight-year war with Spain took place, in which two leading figures emerged – José de San Martín, the Argentine general, and Bernardo O'Higgins. Born at Chillán, O'Higgins was the son of the Irish-born Viceroy of Chile and Peru,

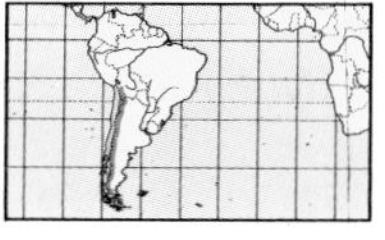

Area: 756,945 km² (292,274 mi²)
Population: 11,700,000
Capital: Santiago (pop. 4,132,000)
Other towns: Valparaiso, Concepción, Viña del Mar, Talcahuano, Antofagasta, Temuco, Talca, Chillán, Valdivia, Osorno, Iquique
Currency: peso

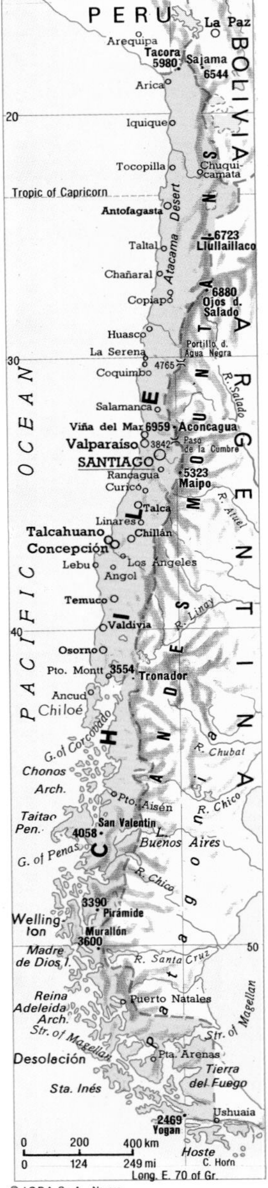

Left: The plain of San Pedro, in the Atacama Desert of northern Chile, one of the driest places on earth.

Ambrosio O'Higgins. When independence finally came after the Battle of Maipu in 1818, Bernardo became Chile's first president.

Further wars tormented this new country in the 19th century. There was a conflict with Spain (1865–66) and another with the united Bolivia and Peru (1879–83). As a result of the latter war, Chile was guaranteed the provinces of Atacama, Arica, Antofagasta and Tarapaca.

In the 20th century, however, Chile avoided the two major World Wars, except for a brief operation against Germany at the end of the Second World War. In 1945, Chile became one of the founder members of the United Nations Organization.

The modern Chilean population is mostly made up of mixed European and Amerindian stock. About 30 per cent are of European descent, while the original people of Chile, the Amerindians, account for only about two per cent of the population. Of the Fuegian Indians, whose way of life so fascinated Charles Darwin in his survey of Tierra del Fuego in the 19th century, only a handful remain, settled at Puerto Eden. Spanish is Chile's official language, and the majority of Chileans follow the Roman Catholic faith.

Right: Puerto Natales, Chile. Below left: Palm trees fill the square in Antofagasta, one of the most important ports on Chile's north coast. Below right: The peak of Cerro Tronador in the Andes, reaching 3,554 metres (11,660 feet).

Colombia

República de

The Republic of Colombia occupies the north-western corner of South America, being joined to Central America by the isthmus of Panama. It has coastlines on both the Pacific and Atlantic oceans. The country is named after Christopher Columbus, who landed on the Atlantic coast in 1502. The Indian peoples of the region came under Spanish rule between 1536 and 1819, when the revolutionary Simón Bolívar founded an independent union of north-western states.

Today Colombia is a Roman Catholic country where Spanish is the official language. The Amerindian peoples of the region include the Guahibo, Tikuna, Banura and Cuiva. There are also people of Black and European descent. The majority of Colombians are of mixed origin.

The physical features of Colombia include a variety of terrains. In the east lie tropical grasslands, which merge into tropical rain forest of the Amazon and Orinoco river basins. The coastal regions consist of humid lowland. But running north to south across the country is part of the northern Andes range, which splits into three great barriers: the Eastern, Western and Central Cordilleras. Most Colombians live in high, fertile valleys in the Andes.

The varied climate enables a wide range of agricultural produce to be cultivated. Important crops include bananas, cereals, cocoa, coffee (the chief export), cotton, rice and sugar-cane. Precious metals, emeralds, copper and iron are mined, and fuel reserves include coal and oil. The latter industry has generated valuable revenue, but is now contracting.

Area:
1,138,914 km²
(439,761 mi²)
Population:
28,240,000
Capital:
Bogotá (pop. 5,000,000)
Other towns:
Medellín, Cali, Barranquilla, Cartagena, Bucaramanga, Cúcuta
Currency:
peso

Right: Most Colombians are of the Roman Catholic faith. This wood-built mission church is decorated for Palm Sunday.

Costa Rica

República de

The Republic of Costa Rica occupies the narrow arm of land between Nicaragua and Panama, having both Pacific and Atlantic Ocean coastlines. The coast is low-lying, but the land rises to fertile, high plateaux and volcanic peaks in the interior. Mount Chirripo reaches a height of 3,820 metres (12,533 feet).

Agricultural products include coffee, the chief cash crop, bananas, sugarcane and rice. Industry is being developed and the economy is sound. Spanish is the official language, the country having been a colony of Spain for three centuries prior to independence in 1821. The people are mostly of European origin.

Area:
50,700 km²
(19,576 mi²)
Population:
2,624,000
Capital:
San José (pop. 271,873)
Other towns:
Alajuela, Limón, Puntarenas, Heredia, Cartago
Currency:
colón

Ecuador

República del

The Republic of Ecuador is a small equatorial country on the north-western coast of South America, between Colombia and Peru. The southern part of the country surrounds the Gulf of Guayaquil. Ecuador also includes the Pacific Galapagos Islands, which are noted for their unique wildlife, in particular the giant tortoise which can weigh up to 181 kilograms (399 pounds). Mainland Ecuador is dominated by the Cordillera Real section of the Andes. Famous peaks include Chimborazo, which reaches 6,267 metres (20,561 feet), and Cotopaxi, which is 5,896 metres (19,343 feet) above sea level. The east is hot and humid lowland. The coastal strip west of the mountains also has an extremely hot climate.

The Amerindian peoples, who make up more than half of the population, include the Jivaro, and the Otavaro – Quechua-speakers famous for their weaving skills. The population includes Europeans, Blacks and people of mixed descent. The kingdom of Quito came under Inca rule in the 15th century AD. In 1533, the great Inca empire fell to the brutal *conquistadores* of Spain, led by Francisco Pizarro. Ecuador became part of the Spanish territory of Peru, but gained independence in 1822, as the result of the campaigns of Simón Bolívar. Spanish is still the official language.

Bananas, cocoa, coffee, sugar and rice are the products of the hot lowlands. Potatoes and cereals are grown in the higher, cooler regions. Balsa wood is extensively forested. Oil reserves in the east are being exploited and oil is the chief export. The capital Quito is linked by road and rail with Guayaquil, the chief port, and has an international airport.

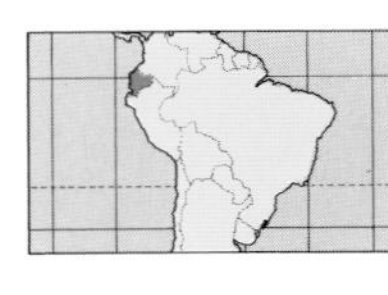

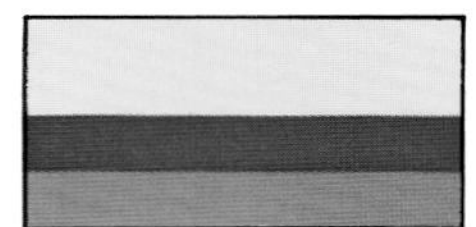

Area:
283,561 km²
(109,489 mi²)
Population:
8,893,000
Capital:
Quito (pop. 1,110,000)
Other towns:
Guayaquil, Cuenca
Currency:
sucre

Far right: The north-west of South America.

Left: the church of San Francisco in Quito, capital of Ecuador.

French Guiana

Guyane Française

France retains possession of several territories in the Caribbean-Atlantic region, which are administered as overseas departments of France. These are Guadeloupe, Martinique, and *Guyane Française* (French Guiana). French Guiana includes l'Île du Diable (Devil's Island), notorious as a penal settlement until 1945. French Guiana is mostly covered by rain forest. The humid, tropical climate is suitable for the cultivation of rice and bananas. Mineral resources include bauxite. The population is of Creole and Amerindian descent.

Area:
91,000 km²
(35,137 mi²)
Population:
79,000
Capital:
Cayenne (pop. 38,000)
Currency:
franc

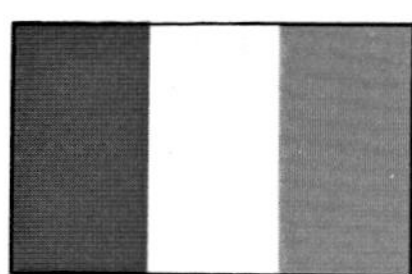

El Salvador

República de

The Republic of El Salvador lies on the Pacific coast of Central America, bounded by Guatemala and Honduras. It is a mountainous land, and densely populated. Most of the population is of mixed Amerindian and European origin. Once part of the Spanish vice royalty of Guatemala, it became an independent country in 1821.

The chief crops are sugar-cane, coffee and cotton. Industrial output concentrates upon steel, textiles and cement. Development has been hindered by political instability, by social problems – there is a high illiteracy rate – and by such natural disasters as earthquakes.

Area:
21,041 km²
(8,124 mi²)
Population:
5,300,000
Capital:
San Salvador (pop. 884,000)
Currency:
colón

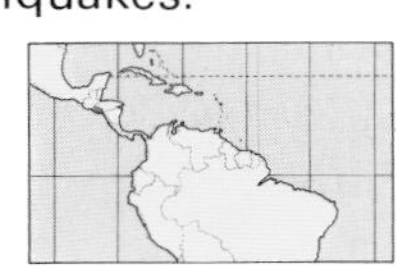

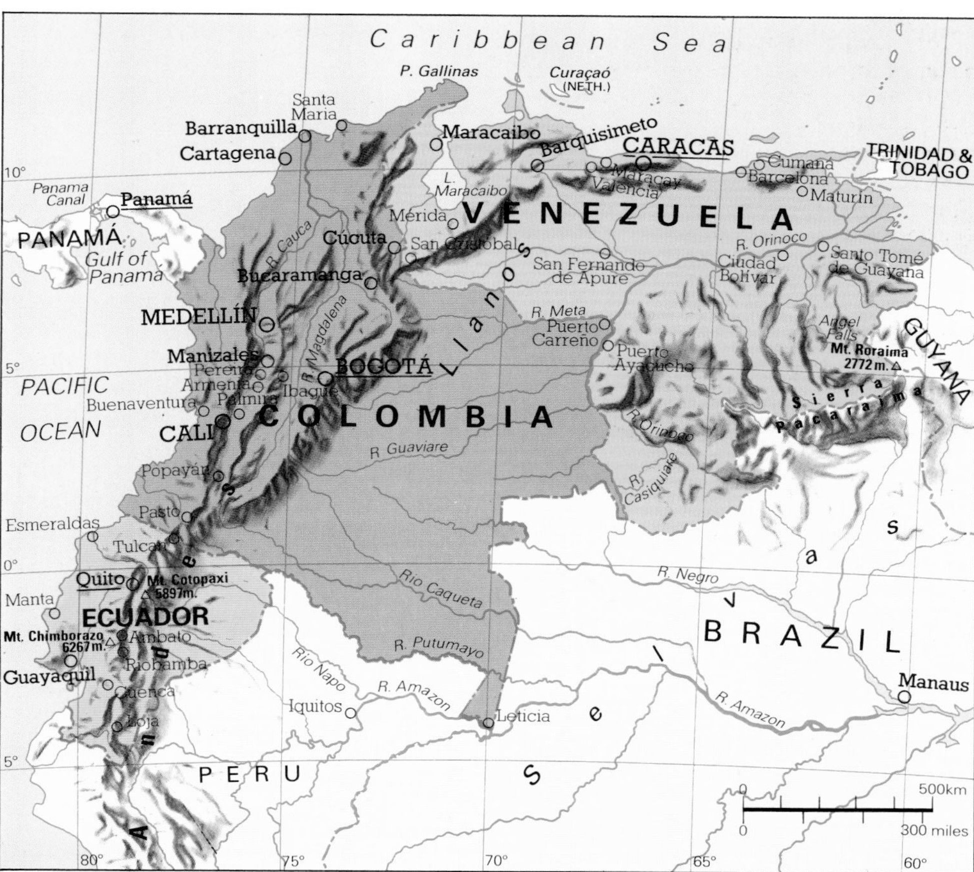

Guatemala

República de

Bridging Central America between the Pacific Ocean and the Gulf of Honduras on the Atlantic is the Republic of Guatemala. Guatemala is bordered by Mexico to the north, Belize to the north-east and Honduras and El Salvador to the south. The central part of the country is taken up by highlands. These are the home of Amerindian peoples who trace their descent from the ancient Mayan civilization. They include the Man, Quichi, Ketchi and Cakchiquel. Guatemala was under Spanish rule for three centuries, and today much of the population is of European and Indian origin. Spanish remains the official language, and Roman Catholicism the religion.

Military intervention in politics has marked the history of Guatemala. The economy depends upon coffee, farming and mineral resources, notably nickel.

Area:
108,889 km²
(42,045 mi²)
Population:
7,714,000
Capital:
Guatemala (pop. 1,500,000)

Other towns:
Quezaltenango, Cobán, Puerto Barrios, Mazatenango, Zacapa
Currency:
quetzal

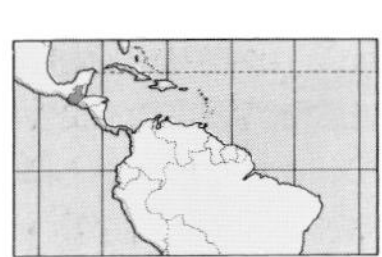

Below: Sugar cane is Guyana's chief crop. It is transported from the fields by barge.

Guyana

The Co-operative Republic of Guyana on the Atlantic coast of north-eastern South America is a former British colony. It became an independent member of the Commonwealth in 1966. A previous Dutch presence in the region is revealed in the existence of such place names as New Amsterdam, and by canals cut through the coastal lowlands. The interior is forested, rising to the Pakaraima Mountains in the west, and the Kanuku Mountains in the south. The principal river is the Essequibo, and the country possesses some spectacular waterfalls, such as the Horse Shoe and the Kaieteur. Rice and sugar are grown in Guyana. The Demerara region of the country gave its name to the brown crystal sugar exported from the Caribbean. The population is of Asian, Black and Amerindian descent, with many of mixed origin. English is the official language.

Area:
214,969 km²
(83,005 mi²)
Population:
965,000

Capital:
Georgetown (pop. 188,000)
Currency:
dollar

Honduras

República de

The Republic of Honduras lies between the Atlantic and the Pacific oceans, in Central America. The Mosquitia region on the Caribbean is low-lying with lagoons. But inland there are mountains and high plateaux, crossed by such rivers as the Patuca and the Ulua. The country has extensive forests. Bananas and coffee are the leading crops, but sugar-cane, cotton, rice and fruit are also cultivated.

Once a Spanish colony, most of the people of Honduras are now of mixed European and Indian origin.

Area:
112,088 km²
(43,280 mi²)
Population:
4,240,000

Capital:
Tegucigalpa (pop. 534,000)
Currency:
lempira

Mexico

Estados Unidos Mexicanos

On 8 November 1519, a group of Spanish *conquistadores* stood spellbound in front of a remarkable sight. They could hardly believe their eyes. In front of them lay the city of Tenochtitlán, standing in the middle of Lake Texcoco and joined to the mainland by three large roads. They could see golden temples, palaces filled with mosaics, lush gardens and wide canals. This was the capital of the great Aztec empire, a city of about 300,000 inhabitants.

Central America was a centre of civilization as remarkable as that of Europe, and just as ancient. In about 1200 BC, the Olmecs had flourished in the Yucatán region, and built great stone sculptures and pyramids.

The Mayan civilization lasted from the fourth to the tenth century AD. The Maya built fine roads, pyramids and magnificent cities, such as Tikal, Tulum, Copán, Palenque, and Uaxactún. They were expert mathematicians and astronomers. The Mayans were followed by the Toltecs and Mixtecs, and then by the Aztecs who reached the height of their power in the late Middle Ages. They were brilliant craftsmen, with a highly developed society centred upon religious ritual. Their rites included human sacrifice. The priests cut the beating hearts out of their live victims and ate their flesh, in order to appease their gods.

When the Spaniards first arrived on the Mexican coast, they were welcomed as gods. Having fought a battle with the Tlaxcalan people, the Spanish leader Hernando Cortés made them his allies Proceeding to Tenochtitlán, the Spaniards extracted a ransom and an oath of fealty from the Aztec king, Montezuma. But gradually they provoked the Aztec population into desperate resistance. The Spanish force was small, eventually consisting of about 1,000 foot soldiers and 46 horses. In the early hours of 1 July 1520, this force had to flee Tenochtitlán, and were almost exterminated in this *noche triste* ('sad night'). Cortés escaped, however, and regrouped his forces. A year later, supported by 10,000 Amerindian allies, Cortés captured the city and razed it to the ground. The modern capital, Mexico City, stands on its ruins.

The last Aztec leader, the young Guatimozino, is today a national hero of Mexico. In the capital, where there are many relics of Spanish rule, there are no monuments to Cortés. But in the Square of the Three Cultures, today there is a monument to this proud Aztec sovereign. The defeated nation became a colony of Spain, and later a viceroyalty. Its great mineral wealth, particularly gold, silver and copper, poured back to Europe. Whilst free in theory, the descendants of the once-proud Maya and Aztecs were virtual slaves, working the land for Spanish masters and perishing in their thousands.

As Mexico grew richer over the years, its borders widened. It came to embrace New Mexico, Texas, Arizona and California, and, for a short time, the distant Philippines. Mexican society took on a strictly hierarchical structure. At the top were Spaniards from Europe. Next came Mexican-born people of Spanish origin, and below them came *mestizos* (people of mixed Amerindian and European stock) and favoured Amerindians. At the bottom were the masses of Amerindian peasants.

At the beginning of the 19th century, Mexico produced half of the world's silver, exported a large quantity of cotton, and had a thriving agriculture. However, wealth was confined to the elite. Popular dissent was fuelled by the American Revolution to the north and by Napoleon's invasion of Spain. In 1810, the Mexican masses revolted, but it was not until the Mexican-born Spanish people joined them that the revolution was successful. In 1821, the last Spanish viceroy stood down and Mexico became independent.

But Mexico's problems were not over. A *mestizo* general, Augustín de Iturbide, was proclaimed emperor, but his despotic rule lasted only a year. He was succeeded by another general, Antonio López de Santa Anna, who became president when a republic was proclaimed in 1823. The emergence of the United States as a major power, however, was marked by its annexation of Texas, Arizona, California and New Mexico in the 1840s.

Under the presidency of the liberal Benito Juárez, conservatives invited the Grand Duke Maximilian of Austria to become emperor. Civil war ensued and Maximilian was captured and shot in 1867. Juarez again became president. He introduced land reform and a fight against illiteracy, but this initiative was lost under the repressive dictatorship of his successor, Porfirio Díaz. Mexico opened itself to foreign capital, and North Americans, or *gringos,* moved into the mines and plantations.

Exploitation of the peasants continued until 1911, when a popular revolution broke out. The *peones,* or peasants, rose led by Emiliano Zapata, assisted by the bandit Pancho Villa, the intellectual Francisco Madero, and others. Despite the death of all the leaders, a new, more liberal Constitution was eventually established in 1917. The 1934 government of Lázaro Cárdenas laid the foundations of a modern, democratic state. Foreign firms were nationalized and

Above: The semi-arid scenery of Mexico's central highlands.

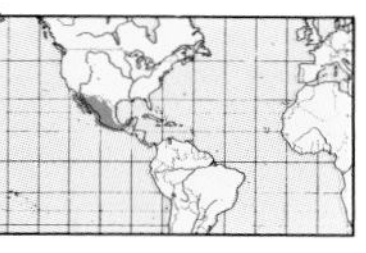

Area:
1,972,547 km²
(761,646 mi²)
Population:
76,790,000
Capital:
Mexico City (pop. 16,000,000)

Other towns:
Guadalajara, Monterrey, Puebla de Zaragoza, Ciudad Juárez, Léon de los Aldamas, Tijuana, Acapulco de Juárez, Chihuahua, Mexicali
Currency:
peso

agriculture was reformed. Today, Mexico has a Senate and a Chamber of Deputies. Presidents are elected for a single term of six years. There are four political parties, the largest of which is the Partido Revolucinario Institucional (PRI). There is still great poverty in the Mexican countryside.

About half the population of modern Mexico is *mestizo*. Europeans and Amerindians account for the remainder. The Amerindians include Mixtec, Zapotec, Tarascan, Taramuhara, Yaqui, Huastec, Huichol, Nahua, Lacandón, and Tzotzil. Spanish is the official language, and Roman Catholicism is the common religion. Amerindian traditions are evident in many Roman Catholic festivals.

Mexico today is an industrial power. Wealth has been generated by exploitation of oil and natural gas reserves and vast new oilfields have recently been discovered. Development of the textile industry, chemical and mechanical engineering, and iron and steel production is taking place. Mineral resources include coal, copper, gold, mercury, lead, silver, sulphur and uranium. Nearly 40 per cent of Mexicans work on the land. The principal crops are beans (a staple food), cocoa, coffee, cotton, fruits, maize, rice, sugar-cane, tobacco and vegetables. Cattle and other livestock are raised. The forests provide timber and the cacti of the desert are used to make the celebrated alcoholic drinks of Mexico – tequila and mescal.

Despite the loss of its historical territories to the United States, Mexico remains a large country, about eight times the size of Britain. The country is divided into 31 states and a federal territory, hence its formal title – *Estados Unidos Mexicanos* (United States of Mexico).

To the west, a long arid peninsula extends below the border with the United States. This is Baja California, which is separated from the mainland by the Gulf of California. The main part of the country is mountainous, dominated by the twin ranges of the eastern and western Sierra Madre. Between the two lies the volcanic region of the central plateaux, surrounding Mexico City. This is the site of the famous twin volcanoes: Popacatapetl, which is 5,452 metres (17,887 feet) above sea level, and Ixtacihuatl, 5,286 metres (17,343 feet) high. To the south-west is Mexico's highest peak, Citlaltépetl, which reaches 5,760 metres (18,898 feet). At the southern end of the central plateaux, the two Sierras merge into a single range, the Sierra Madre del Sud. This range narrows to form the isthmus of Tehuantepec, where the Pacific and Atlantic Oceans are separated by less than 250 kilometres (155 miles). To the north lies the wide, flat peninsula of Yucatán which extends beyond the Guatemalan and Belizian borders. Mexico's principal rivers are the Rio Grande del Norte, the Rio Grande de Santiago, the Balsas and the Papaloapan.

The climate of Mexico varies considerably with the altitude. As the altitude increases, so the humid, tropical heat of the lowlands gives way to a temperate zone, and eventually to extreme cold at the highest levels. Much of the northern part of the country is arid.

Mexico enjoys a developed system of communications with road, rail and air transportation networks. Mexico City, successor to the old Aztec capital which so amazed Cortés, is now one of the world's largest, and most polluted, cities. To the north-west, Guadalajara is a fine town with a population of 2,245,000, and Monterrey, near the Texan border, has nearly two million inhabitants. Mexico is a spectacularly beautiful country, and many tourists visit the beaches, lured by such resorts as Acapulco and Mazatlán. For others the real attraction is the glimpse into the past afforded by such antiquities as Chichén-Itzá, the ruined city of the Maya and the Toltecs.

Above: The fountains of Mexico City, the capital built on the ruins of the old Aztec capital of Tenochtitlán.

Below left: Ancient and modern Mexico are brought together in the work of Diego Rivera (1886–1957) one of the country's leading painters. This example of his mural work, shows the influence of Aztec themes in his work.

Nicaragua

República de

The Republic of Nicaragua was visited by Christopher Columbus in 1502, and ruled by Spanish captain-generals from 1519 until 1821. The right-wing government of General Anastasio Somoza was overthrown by left-wing Sandinista guerrillas in 1979. Sandinista rule was confirmed by democratic elections in 1984, but was met with active hostility by the United States of America.

The country lies at the heart of the Americas. To the east, on the Caribbean, is the humid Mosquito Coast. On the Pacific coast to the west are other, narrower lowlands. The centre of the country is highland, rising to the Cordillera Isabella in the north. Two great lakes lie in the western region, Managua and Nicaragua. The northern border is with Honduras, the southern with Costa Rica.

The Nicaraguan economy depends largely on farming. Coffee, cotton, sugar-cane, bananas and rice are grown, and cattle and timber are also important. There are resources of copper, gold and silver. The capital of the country is Managua, on the lake of the same name. The city was devastated by an earthquake in 1972. Managua is linked by road to the northern and southern borders, to the port of Bluefields on the Atlantic and to the western port of Corinto.

The Amerindian peoples of Nicaragua include the Mosquito, the Monimbo and the Subtavia. Other racial groups include Blacks and Europeans, but the vast majority of Nicaraguans are of mixed European and Indian origin, and Spanish is the official language.

Area: 130,000 km² (50,196 mi²)
Population: 3,200,000
Capital: Managua (pop. 615,000)
Other towns: León, Granada, Masaya, Chinandega
Currency: córdoba

Panama

República de Panamá

The Republic of Panama consists of a narrow thread of land connecting the two great continents of North and South America. This isthmus is only 82 kilometres (51 miles) wide at the point where it is crossed by the Panama Canal. Opened to shipping in 1914, this artery of international trade is controlled by the United States, but it reverts to Panamanian sovereignty at the end of this century. The United States returned the surrounding Canal Zone to Panama in 1979.

Panama is a tropical country. The terrain rises in the interior, with a central highland region. The highest point is Mount Chiriqui at 3,374 metres (11,070 feet) above sea level. Panamanian territory includes a number of offshore islands, such as Coiba and the Las Perlas Archipelago. The principal crops produced are typical of the region, including bananas, sugar-cane, rice, coffee and coconuts. Fishing and mining are significant, and tourism is being developed.

The people of Panama are mostly of mixed European and Amerindian origin, although there are still some peoples of pure Amerindian origin, including the Cuna and the Guaymi. The official language is Spanish and the chief religion is Roman Catholicism. Panama was originally a Spanish colony, becoming independent in 1819 as part of Colombia. In 1903 it seceded and declared itself a separate independent nation. A military government ruled from 1968, and General Omar Torrijos became the effective ruler. But he withdrew in 1978 and in 1980 elections were held for a National Legislative Council.

Area: 75,650 km² (29,210 mi²)
Population: 2,072,000
Capital: Panama City (pop. 467,000)
Other towns: San Miguelito, Colón
Currency: balboa

Below: The Panama Canal forms a vital link between the Atlantic and Pacific Oceans, and is a valuable source of wealth for Panama.

Paraguay

República del Paraguay

The Republic of Paraguay takes its name from the River Paraguay, a tributary of the Paraná. The country lies at the centre of South America, surrounded on all sides by land. To the south is Argentina, and to the east and north is Brazil. The north-western border is with Bolivia. The country is crossed by a network of tributaries of the River Paraguay. In the east is an area of fertile plains and hills. In the south is an area of marsh and lakes, and to the west, between the River Pilcomayo and the Bolivian border, is the Chaco Boreal. This is an arid plain, part of which has been improved by control of water flow. The climate is subtropical, and much of the land is covered by forests, which are a valuable source of timber.

The economy is essentially agricultural. Tobacco, soya beans, maize, fruit and cotton grow well, and there are many cattle ranches. Hydro-electric power is provided by the Aracay scheme, and further schemes are being developed at Yacyreta and Itaipú. Industry is mostly devoted to food processing.

Paraguay has been independent since 1811. Previously it had been ruled by Spain, whose colonists arrived in 1535. Today most people in Paraguay are of mixed European and Amerindian origin. Pure Amerindians make up three per cent of the population. They include Chulupi and Guyakí, and the Guaraní language is more widely spoken than Spanish, the official language. About one-fifth of the population are the descendants of European settlers. Paraguay has a bicameral parliament, with a Senate and a Chamber of Deputies.

The capital of the country is Asunción, which is sited on a bend of the River Paraguay, about 1,610 kilometres (1,000 miles) upriver from the Argentinian capital of Buenos Aires. A network of metalled roads links Asunción with neighbouring countries, but on many of the unmetalled roads transport is at the mercy of adverse weather and floods. A railway runs south into Argentina.

Area:
406,752 km² (157,056 mi²)
Population:
3,480,000
Capital:
Asunción (pop. 708,000)
Other towns:
Caaguazú
Currency:
guaraní

Peru

República del Perú

When the Europeans first began to invade South America in the early 16th century, they heard rumours of a fabulous land in the interior, containing gold and riches beyond all dreams. Spanish *conquistadores* lusted for the wealth of this *Eldorado*. There was in fact a rich territory in the west, the Inca empire. This empire stretched over a huge area, occupying much of Ecuador, Bolivia, northern Chile and the Republic of Peru. In 1531, the Spanish captain-general Francisco Pizarro launched an expedition of conquest from Panama. He took Cajamarca the following year, and extracted a huge ransom from the Inca ruler Atahualpa, who was then treacherously killed. Peru was ruled by Spain from 1533 until 1824 when the country was liberated by revolutionary hero Simón Bolívar. A few traces of the fabulous Inca empire remain, in the ancient ruins of Peru and in the traditions of the Quechua-speaking Indians.

Today about half the Peruvian population is of true Amerindian stock, mostly Quechua and Aymara speakers. There are Jivaro, Campa, Tikuna and Amahuaca Indians in the interior. The remaining population is of mixed blood, that is part European, part Amerindian. There are some Europeans and Blacks. The official languages are Spanish and Quechua. Modern Peru has had a history of military rule, but is currently governed by a democratic parliamentary system.

Peru is an agricultural country, industry being concentrated upon the coast. Coffee, cereals, rice, fruit, cotton, potatoes and sugar are cultivated, and the raising of livestock, notably sheep, cattle and llamas, is important. Peru's fishing industry is now contracting, but a decade ago it was beating world records. In the early 1970s, Peru was the world's leading fishing nation according to the value of the catch, which was mostly used for processing into fishmeal. The country's mineral resources include copper, iron-ore, lead, silver and zinc. Oil is found east of the Andes, and the extensive rain forests provide timber.

Peru lies just below the equator, but its Pacific coast is cooled by the Humboldt current. The low-lying coastal strip is the most populous region, the site of Lima, the capital. Behind the coast are the snowy peaks of the Andes, the highest of

which is Huascarán, at 6,768 metres (22,205 feet) above sea level. The Andes, which contain fertile valleys, run across the Bolivian border at Lake Titicaca, the world's highest lake open to navigation. Highland slopes are cultivated mostly by Indians, who are benefiting from recent agricultural reform. East of the Andes lies the *selva,* a region of tropical forest. Here are the headwaters of the River Amazon, which begins its 6,437-kilometre (4,000-mile) journey to the Atlantic Ocean in Peru, before crossing Brazil.

Area:
1,285,216 km²
(496,252 mi²)
Population:
18,790,000
Capital:
Lima (pop. 5,259,000)
Other towns:
Arequipa, Trujillo, Chiclayo, Chimbote
Currency:
sol nuevo

Below left: Barren mountains rise from the valley of Ayacubo.
Below: The Quechua people keep alive the ancient traditions of the Incas.

Surinam

The Republic of Surinam lies on the north-eastern coast of South America, between Guyana and French Guiana. It was a British colony from 1650 until 1667 when it passed from British to Dutch control, being known as Dutch Guiana. It achieved internal self-government in 1954 and full independence followed in 1975.

The colonial history of this region has resulted in it having an extraordinary mixture of races. Surinam contains Creoles, descendants of runaway slaves called 'Bush Negroes' (Boni), Amerindians (Trio and Coastal Caribs), Chinese, Javanese, Europeans and peoples of mixed origin. The religions of the country reflect the population's diverse ethnic origins, with Christians, Muslims and Hindus all following their own religions. Both Dutch and English are spoken. A Surinamese minority has now settled in the Netherlands.

Surinam's main export is bauxite, the ore from which aluminium is extracted. Sugar-cane and fruit are widely grown on the coast, and rice is the staple food. The hills of the interior are covered by tropical rain forest, which provides timber for export. In the interior are the highlands of the Wilhelmina, Kayser, Eilerts de Haan and Oranje ranges. From these a number of rivers flow into the Atlantic – the Nickerie, Coppename, Saramacca, Suriname and Tapanahani (a tributary of the Maroni, which forms the border with French Guiana).

Area:
163,265 km²
(63,040 mi²)
Population:
410,000
Capital:
Paramaribo (pop. 152,000)
Currency:
guilder

Below: Colonial architecture in Paramaribo, capital of Surinam.

United States of America

The modern history of the United States is illustrated in its flag – the 50 white stars represent the 50 states, while the 13 white and red stripes symbolize the 13 British colonies which proclaimed their independence on 4 July 1776.

But the history of the United States really began much earlier. During the final stages of the last Ice Age, people from Asia crossed the Bering Strait and started a southward migration. These people were the ancestors of the modern Amerindians. The first European settlers were probably Norsemen, who arrived from Greenland nearly 1,000 years ago, but their stay was short-lived.

America was re-discovered in 1492 when Christopher Columbus, seeking a westward route to Asia, landed in the West Indies. Wrongly believing that he was in Asia, he named the indigenous people Indians, a confusion that has persisted to this day.

The first European explorer in North America after the Norsemen was John Cabot who discovered Newfoundland in 1497, claiming it for England. At first, the most active explorers in North America were the Spaniards, who first landed in Florida in 1513, although they did not found their first permanent settlement, St Augustine, until 1565. The French were also soon interested in North America, particularly Canada, the Great Lakes and the Mississippi valley region, which was proclaimed French in the 1680s.

However, it was the English who were the most effective colonizers. In 1584, the English soldier Sir Walter Raleigh explored the North Carolina coast and claimed for England the entire Atlantic seaboard, which was named Virginia after the unmarried status of Elizabeth I. But Raleigh's attempts to found a settlement failed and it was not until 1607 that the first permanent British settlement was founded, at Jamestown, Virginia. The colony was backed by a company of London merchants, which had been granted a charter by James I. Even more well-known was the landing of the Plymouth Fathers at Plymouth, Massachusetts in 1620, who laid the foundations for the colonization of New England.

Despite hardships and clashes with the Amerindians, the British settlements expanded and spread down the eastern seaboard. In 1644, the British ousted the Dutch from their settlement of New Amsterdam on Manhattan Island and renamed it New York after the Duke of York (later James II). By 1760, the 13 British colonies (New Hampshire, Massachusetts, Rhode Island, Connecticut, New Jersey, New York, Pennsylvania, Delaware, Maryland, Virginia, North Carolina, South Carolina and Georgia) formed a continuous strip of land in the east with a population of about $1\frac{1}{2}$ million. Britons formed the majority, but there were also people from Ireland, Germany and France, as well as Black slaves brought from Africa to work the plantations.

The colonists increasingly resented British interference in their affairs, especially 'taxation without representation'. The famous Boston Tea Party heralded the War of Independence (1775–81). At first, the colonists' struggle was based on righting specific grievances, but on 2 July 1776 the Continental Congress, which had been founded by the colonies in 1774 to resist British laws called the Intolerable Acts, which had been introduced by George III's government, voted for independence. On 4 July, it went further and adopted the Declaration of Independence.

Under General George Washington, the small army of the colonists defeated the British forces, creating the new United States of America, whose Constitution was drafted in 1787. This Constitution, which has been amended but which is still substantially in force today, was promulgated in the name of the people and is based on the principle of equality and sovereignty of the people. George

Opposite page: Manhattan by night. New York was the birthplace of the skyscraper.

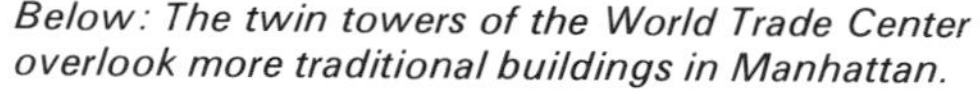

Below: The twin towers of the World Trade Center overlook more traditional buildings in Manhattan.

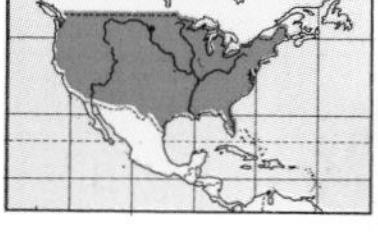

Area: 9,363, 123 km² (3,615,319 mi²)
Population: 235,100,000
Capital: Washington DC (pop. 756,000)
Currency: dollar
States and state capitals: Alabama (Ala), Montgomery; Alaska (Alas), Juneau; Arizona (Ariz), Phoenix; Arkansas (Ark), Little Rock; California (Cal), Sacramento; Colorado (Col), Denver; Connecticut (Conn), Hartford; Delaware (Del), Dover; Florida (Fla), Tallahassee; Georgia (Ga), Atlanta; Hawaii (Ha), Honolulu; Idaho (Ida), Boise; Illinois (Ill), Springfield; Indiana (Ind), Indianapolis; Iowa (Ia), Des Moines; Kansas (Kan), Topeka; Kentucky (Ky), Frankfort; Louisiana (La), Baton Rouge; Maine (Me), Augusta; Maryland (Md), Annapolis; Massachusetts (Mass), Boston; Michigan (Mich), Lansing; Minnesota (Minn), St Paul; Mississippi (Miss), Jackson; Missouri (Mo), Jefferson City; Montana (Mon), Helena; Nebraska (Neb), Lincoln; Nevada (Nev), Carson City; New Hampshire (NH), Concord; New Jersey (NJ), Trenton; New Mexico (NM), Santa Fé; New York (NY), Albany; North Carolina (NC), Raleigh; North Dakota (ND), Bismarck; Ohio (Oh), Columbus; Oklahoma (Okla), Oklahoma City; Oregon (Ore), Salem; Pennsylvania (Pa), Harrisburg; Rhode Island (RI), Providence; South Carolina (SC), Columbia; South Dakota (SD), Pierre; Tennessee (Tenn), Nashville; Texas (Tex), Austin; Utah (Ut), Salt Lake City; Vermont (Vt), Montpelier; Virginia (Va), Richmond; Washington (Wash), Olympia; West Virginia (WVa), **Charleston, Wisconsin (Wis),** Madison; Wyoming (Wy), Cheyenne. The District of Columbia, including the capital, is not a state; it is administered by Congress.

Washington became the first president in 1789, and his name was later given to the Federal Capital founded on the banks of the Potomac River in 1800. (The original capital had been New York City.)

The new, vigorous nation began to expand and, with the Louisiana Purchase accomplished by the third president Thomas Jefferson, the area of the country doubled. Louisiana, a huge region extending far beyond modern Louisiana, was sold by France, under Napoleon, for US $15 million. The same method of purchase subsequently resulted in the acquisition of Florida from Spain (1819) and Alaska from Russia (1867). Other territories gained by military operations were Texas, New Mexico and most of the South-West, including California, which were gained as a result of the US-Mexican War of 1846–48.

In the early 19th century, much of North America was unexplored; the first overland crossing by Meriwether Lewis and William Clark did not take place until 1804–06. But immigration caused a thirst for land that turned more and more people westwards. The colonization of the West was characterized by the courage of those who undertook arduous journeys in covered wagons and often by great heroism. However, the advance of the settlers meant ruin and destruction for the Amerindians. Whites seized Indian lands and by relegating the Indian nations to reservations, prevented them from making use of their seasonal hunting system. This factor, combined with the use of firearms, led to the extermination of wildlife in many areas. By mixing with Europeans, the Amerindians discovered alcohol and contracted unfamiliar European diseases, which either killed or weakened them.

Between 1823 and 1841, the federal government endeavoured to eliminate all friction by creating a permanent Indian frontier to the west of the Mississippi. Tribes from the east were moved to this region along the 'trail of tears' which left many dead in its wake. But further conflict occurred when even these Indian lands were demanded by settlers. The fate of the Amerindians had been decided. The last battle took place at Wounded Knee. Today, the descendants of the proud warriors of the past live on reservations which are little more than tourist attractions. Before the conquest of the West, probably more than two million Indians lived in the USA. There are now about 800,000.

Another problem facing the United States in the mid-19th century was the preservation of national unity, because there was intense rivalry between the

Above: Crater Lake, Oregon, is the deepest stretch of crater in the USA. Below left: America is a land of huge distances, and highways such as this one near Logan, Utah, provide vital links.

Right: The Wild West – the incredible rock formations of Canyon de Chelly National Monument, Arizona. Below left: Angel Arch in Canyonlands National Park, Utah, another example of the effects of erosion.
Below right: The White Sands National Monument, New Mexico – a dazzling, arid landscape.

The federal capital of the USA is at Washington DC. Above: The Capitol, construction of which started in 1793. Above left: The Lincoln Memorial was built at the beginning of the 20th century. Left: A well-turned-out parade at America's most prestigious military academy, West Point (NY).

industrialized states of the North and the agricultural, cotton-growing states of the South. The conflict was brought to a head by the issue of slavery and the demands of the abolitionists that the four million slaves in the South be freed. The South, believing slavery essential for their economy, seceded from the Union, and an independent Confederate States of America was founded in 1861, with its capital in Richmond, Virginia. War broke out in April 1861 and continued for four years, causing more than 600,000 deaths. The South finally surrendered. The Union was reformed and the emancipation of slaves, ratified by President Abraham Lincoln in 1863, was enforced throughout the land. However, the bitter wounds of war healed slowly. The South's economy felt the effects of the war for many years and, despite the acknowledgement of their civil rights, the Blacks did not achieve complete integration into society until quite recently.

The Civil War was followed by a period of reconstruction. Trains could now travel from one end of the country to the other, and this helped to strengthen national unity. The east-west rail link was completed in 1869. Before then, the trip was made by stage coach and took at best 24 days between Missouri and California.

Waves of emigrants followed each other closely, including people from Ireland, Germany, Scandinavia, Poland, Italy, besides Jews from many nations. More than 5,000,000 immigrants entered the country between 1880 and 1890, and almost 9,000,000 more between 1900 and 1910. They came in a spirit of optimism, seeking a better life in a New World.

The country's expansion had by this time reached its peak. The Spanish-American War over Cuba (1898) led to the annexation of Hawaii, the Philippines, Puerto Rico and Guam, in Micronesia. The Samoan islands in Polynesia were occupied in 1899. Later, in 1904, the USA took over a section of the isthmus of Panama where a canal linking the Atlantic Ocean with the Pacific Ocean was opened after ten years' work. This act was important for commercial and strategic reasons. The Panama Canal Zone was returned to Panama in 1979, but the United States will continue to control the Canal itself until the end of the century.

On the world scene, the United States at first played a secondary role compared to the great powers of the day, namely, Britain, Russia and Germany. Faithful to the doctrine expressed by President James Monroe in 1823, of America for the Americans, they rejected European attempts to interfere and refused to become involved in rivalries of the Old World. However, during the First World War, the United States emerged from its isolation. Its assistance to the Allied armies in 1917–18 in their war against the Central Powers was probably decisive and represented an irreversible step in the country's history.

At the end of the war, President Thomas Woodrow Wilson launched the idea of a League of Nations, an organization aimed at achieving world peace and supra-national authority; it was the predecessor of the United Nations Organization. The failure of the League of Nations was one of the causes of the Second World War in which the USA became embroiled after the Japanese attack on Pearl Harbor on 7 December 1941. America's military and economic might played a significant role in the Allied victory.

After the Second World War, the United States emerged as a world superpower, not only because of the decline of the European powers, but also because of its nuclear weapons, which the USA was the first to build and use against Japan in August 1945. The USA emerged as the leader of one of two opposed power blocs – the North Atlantic Treaty Organization (NATO), set up in 1949 between the western democracies. In opposition are the countries of the Warsaw Pact (signed in 1955). These are the socialist nations of eastern Europe, led by the world's other superpower, the USSR. The coexistence of the two blocs has proved difficult and has involved a great deal of friction, engendering fears for world peace.

In terms of population the United States is the fourth largest nation in the world (after China, India and the USSR). (It is also fourth largest in area.) Of the 50 states, 48 form a contiguous unit in North America, sharing borders with Canada in the north, and Mexico in the south, with the Atlantic Ocean in the east and the Pacific in the west. Two states are separated from this huge land mass. They were the last two to join the Union – Alaska in the far north-west of the American continent, and the Hawaiian Islands, which are 5,000 kilometres (3,107 miles) away in the Pacific Ocean.

With these two exceptions, the whole of the United States territory is situated in the temperate zone, although the North has cold winters, which are particularly severe in the heart of the continent, while the South is hot and humid, particularly along the Gulf coast. The rainfall generally decreases from east to west and several hot desert regions occur in the south-west. Both in the eastern and western United States are long mountain ranges roughly parallel to the coasts. On the Atlantic side are the Appalachians. Along the Pacific coast are the Coast Range, backed by the Cascade Range and the Sierra Nevada, beyond which there is a third range consisting of the Rocky Mountains. Between the Rocky Mountains and the Appalachians there is a vast tract of flat plateaux and plains drained by the Mississippi-Missouri river system.

In the USA, everything is gigantic and the statistics incredible. The Great Lakes in the north, along the border with Canada, cover an area as large as Italy. The width of Europe between the tip of Portugal and the edge of Turkey just about equals that of the Mississippi basin. This river system, whose name is of Amerindian origin and means 'the great father of waters', is with its tributaries 6,231 kilometres (3,872 miles) long. This makes it the third largest river system in the world, after the Nile and the Amazon.

The countryside is rich in natural resources and agriculture is one of the mainstays of its economy. Agriculture has become highly mechanized, with a minimum use of labour (barely two per cent of the working population) and maximum use of fertilizers and agricultural machinery. Its main characteristic is its specialization, whereby, depending on the type of soil and climate, one crop is grown over a wide area. In this way, there are huge strips of land, known as 'belts', which are devoted to a single crop, such as wheat, maize, or cotton. Large areas of land are devoted to the grazing of cattle. The cultivation of tobacco is also significant, and the United States provides one-sixth of the world's supply. Vegetables and fruits are widely grown. The United States is the top world producer of beef and the second producer of pork. It comes second for milk and timber.

Industrial performance is just as impressive. It is supported by exploitation of mineral resources, in particular fossil fuels. Coal production is more than a quarter of the world total; with oil and natural gas the USA is the third and first world producer respectively. Metals extracted include iron-ore, zinc, copper, sulphur, lead, gold, silver, tungsten and uranium. This great wealth, together with increasingly more sophisticated technical and scientific back-up, has encouraged the development of huge industrial complexes. Small and medium-sized factories have almost disappeared in the United States, because they have been taken over by giants. Of the 11 largest industrial complexes in the world, ten are American.

The United States was the first to

In the United States leisure activities have become major industries with large turnovers. Huge entertainment centres have been built where everyone can enjoy themselves in fantastic, fairytale worlds. The most famous centre is Disneyland, above, built near Los Angeles in 1954 by Walt Disney, the brilliant film animator and creator of the immortal cartoon character Mickey Mouse. Disneyland is divided into four sections: Fantasyland, Frontierland, Adventureland and Tomorrowland, and a visit there is a must for any visitor to Los Angeles, adult or child, as also is the famous suburb of Hollywood.

discover, at the end of the 19th century, the advantages of mass-production. One of the pioneers was Henry Ford (1863–1947), the car manufacturer. He invented the concept of the assembly line at the beginning of the 20th century. Industrial giants are found in all sectors, from the iron and steel and engineering industries (traditionally based in the North-East, which is rich in coal and iron) to the chemical, textile and oil industries (based in the East and South). The food processing industry is centred upon California (preserved food, fruit and fish) and Chicago (meat and sausages). The more futuristic sectors (microelectronics, space technology) have their stronghold in Texas and California.

Within this civilization where so much is mass-produced, towns, too, are often similar, with groups of skyscrapers in the business sections, and large suburbs consisting of one-family houses. Traces of the past are few and scarce, but some large cities, such as San Francisco and New Orleans, do retain an old-world charm. The history of the country is often reflected in the names of cities. There are Amerindian names, like Chicago, Milwaukee and Saratoga; French names, such as Saint Louis, Des Moines and Baton Rouge; Spanish names, like San Antonio, Santa Fé and Albuquerque; and a host of others borrowed from the Old World, including Plymouth, Birmingham, Paris, London, Milan and Rome.

About half of the population lives in centres of more than 500,000 inhabitants. More than seven million are in New York City, the most important conurbation of the United States. It is situated at the estuary of the Hudson River; its port is the sixth largest in the world as regards volume of trade; there are more than 560 kilometres (350 miles) of wharves.

Other important North American cities include Chicago on Lake Michigan, the world's most important lake port; Los Angeles, in California, an immense conurbation which includes among its suburbs Hollywood, the film capital of the world; Boston and Philadelphia, old centres of cultural tradition; Detroit, the centre of a huge car manufacturing industry; and New Orleans on the Gulf of Mexico, the birthplace of jazz.

Compared to these huge towns, the federal capital of Washington DC may appear somewhat small, since it has only 756,000 inhabitants. Its skyline is dominated not by skyscrapers but by neoclassical buildings with beautiful clear lines, such as the Capitol, with its impressive dome. This is where Congress meets. Here too is the White House, which is the President's official residence. Even though Washington was built on Virginian land, it is not part of Virginia. The town and its periphery form the District of Columbia, which falls under the jurisdiction of none of the individual states. It is the seat of federal government. Within the federal system, every state has its own governor and legislature, thereby allowing a great deal of regional independence. The federal government is headed by the President who is elected every four years and who is also head of the executive. Legislative power is in the hands of Congress, which is made up of the House of Representatives and the Senate.

The President, who must be at least 35 years old, can serve only two 4-year terms. He is also Commander-in-Chief of the Army, Navy and Air Force. In the event of the President's death, the Vice-President serves as President for the remainder of the term.

Below left: Chicago is sited on the southern shore of Lake Michigan. It is the second largest town in the USA. Below: The futuristic financial centre of San Francisco, one of the most beautiful cities in the USA.

Uruguay

República Oriental del

Sandwiched between the giants of Argentina and Brazil in south-eastern South America is a small country officially called The Eastern Republic of the Uruguay. Uruguay is situated on the northern bank of the River Plate (Rio de la Plata) estuary, and bounded in the west by the River Uruguay, the Plate's tributary. Uruguay is cattle-rearing country, and sheep are also important. Cereals, fruits, oilseeds and sugar are cultivated. Industry includes textile manufacture, oil refining, cement, glass, chemicals and food processing.

Most of Uruguay consists of rolling grassy plains, ideal for cattle-ranching. There are ranges of low hills, notably the Cuchilla del Haedo and the Cuchilla Grande. The principal river draining central Uruguay is the Rio Negro, a tributary of the River Uruguay. On the coast are a number of lagoons. One lagoon, Lake Mirim, straddles the border with Brazil.

Uruguay has been independent since 1828, after the area had been fought over between Spain and Portugal, and by Uruguay's newly independent neighbours. At the turn of the 19th century, waves of European immigrants settled the country.

Most people today are of European origin, while the original inhabitants, the Amerindians, form a small minority. Spanish is the official language, and Roman Catholicism is the principal religion.

In recent years, guerrilla resistance to the government has led to military intervention and instability.

The capital of Uruguay is Montevideo, a large port on the estuary of the River Plate, from which vast quantities of meat products are exported.

Area:
176,215 km²
(68,041 mi²)
Population:
2,990,000
Capital:
Montevideo (pop. 1,355,000)
Other towns:
Salto, Paysandú, Mercedes
Currency:
peso

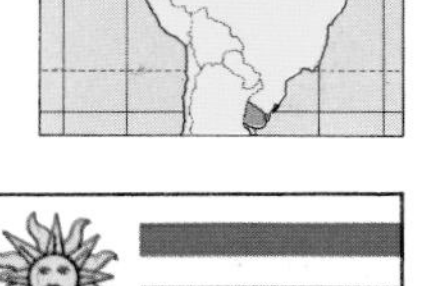

Venezuela

República de

Bordering the Caribbean Sea between Colombia, Brazil and Guyana is the Republic of Venezuela. The west of the country is dominated by the oil-rich Lake Maracaibo, off the Gulf of Venezuela, and by a northern extension of the Andes range – the Cordillera de Mérida. Central Venezuela consists of the basin of the River Orinoco. This forms a giant delta where it reaches the Atlantic. To the south-east, the ground rises to the Guiana Highlands. On the River Carrao are the Angel Falls (Cherun-Meru). At 979 metres (3,212 feet), the Angel Falls are the world's highest. In the far south lies a small part of the Amazon basin. Venezuelan territory includes a number of Caribbean islands, including Margarita and the Nueva Esparta group, Los Roques, Las Aves and La Blanquilla.

Venezuela was a Spanish colony for three centuries, beoming independent in 1821. The people of Venezuela are mostly of mixed European and Amerindian origin. There are also Amerindian peoples (Guahibo, Warrau, Baniwa, Matilones, Gunjiro, Yanomamo and Panare), Europeans, Blacks and Mulattos. Spanish is the official language. The majority of people live in the crowded cities of the north.

Venezuela is one of the world's leading producers of oil, and revenues from this provide much of the country's wealth. Bauxite is another important resource, and iron ore, gold and asbestos are also mined. Industry is developing. Agricultural produce includes cocoa, coffee, rice, groundnuts, sisal, sugar-cane and tobacco. The forests provide timber and gum, and cattle are raised on the plains.

Area:
912,050 km²
(352,164 mi²)
Population:
17,257,000
Capital:
Caracas (pop. 3,508,000)
Other towns:
Maracaibo, Barquisimeto, Valencia, Maracay, San Cristóbal, Ciudad Guyana
Currency:
bolivar

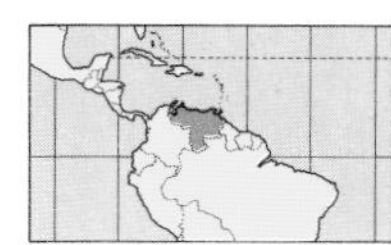

Below: The foothills of the mountains of Venezuela, a northerly extension of the Andes.

Asia

Asia contains 39 independent nations. The largest single continent, Asia is also the most populous region on Earth. It is a fascinating cultural mixture, the birthplace of many ancient civilizations which have determined the course of world history. It was in Asia that many of the world's great religions and philosophies arose, including Hinduism, Buddhism, Judaism, Christianity, Confucianism, Taoism and Islam. Asia contains every kind of human society, from simple hunting and gathering societies to pastoral nomadism, from small agricultural settlements to great industrial cities. It has seen tribalism and rule by warlords, kingdoms and great empires, dictatorship and democracy, and colonialism and revolutionary socialism. Today it includes some of the world's poorest countries, and some of the wealthiest.

Europeans have always found Asia a mysterious, exotic region, but have rarely understood its way of life. Similarly, many Asians have thought that the western way of life seemed to be based on misguided priorities. Today it is important for the peaceful future of humanity that the rest of the world should reach a mutual understanding with the many and vastly different peoples of Asia.

The cultural diversity of the continent is matched by and related to its vast differences in climate and terrain. Asia is, in fact, part of Eurasia, that is, it forms part of the same land mass as Europe. The western border of the continent extends southwards from the Kara Sea along the Ural Mountains, and around the Kazakhstan region of the USSR to the Caspian Sea. Most of Turkey is in Asia, the dividing line with Europe being the Bosporus. The Mediterranean forms its south-western border, and it includes all the countries east of Egypt. Asia's

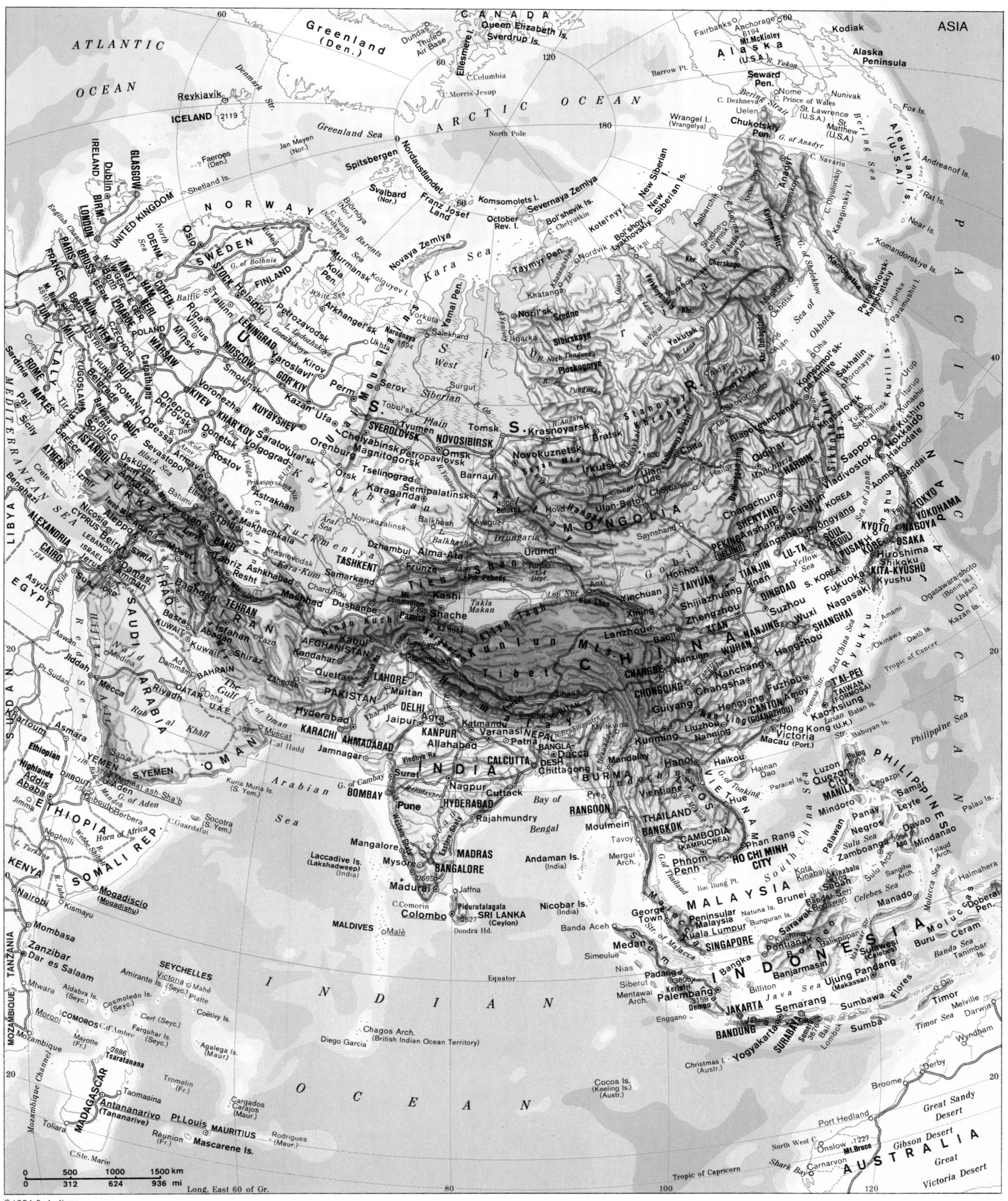
ASIA
ATLANTIC OCEAN
ARCTIC OCEAN
North Pole
Greenland (Den.)
CANADA
Queen Elizabeth Is.
Sverdrup Is.
Ellesmere I.
Alaska (U.S.A.)
Mt.McKinley
Fairbanks
Anchorage
Kodiak
Alaska Peninsula
Seward Pen.
Nome
Bering Strait
Chukotskiy Pen.
Wrangel I. (Vrangelya)
Aleutian Is. (U.S.A.)
Bering Sea
ICELAND
Reykjavik
Greenland Sea
Jan Mayen (Nor.)
Faeroes (Den.)
Shetland Is.
Spitsbergen
Svalbard (Nor.)
Nordaustlandet
Franz Josef Land
Komsomolets I.
Severnaya Zemlya
October Rev. I.
Bol'shevik Is.
New Siberian Is.
Novaya Zemlya
Barents Sea
Kara Sea
NORWAY
SWEDEN
FINLAND
UNITED KINGDOM
IRELAND
Dublin
GLASGOW
LONDON
PARIS
FRANCE
Oslo
Helsinki
Murmansk
Kola Pen.
Arkhangel'sk
LENINGRAD
MOSCOW
Yaroslavl'
Taymyr Pen.
Noril'sk
Yakutsk
Verkhoyansk
Okhotsk
Sea of Okhotsk
Kamchatka
Petropavlovsk-Kamchatskiy
Sakhalin
Kuril Is.
ITALY
ROME
NAPLES
Sicily
Sardinia
MEDITERRANEAN SEA
Crete
LIBYA
EGYPT
CAIRO
ALEXANDRIA
KIYEV
Odessa
Black Sea
Caspian Sea
Volgograd
Astrakhan
SVERDLOVSK
Chelyabinsk
Magnitogorsk
Omsk
NOVOSIBIRSK
Tomsk
Krasnoyarsk
Bratsk
Irkutsk
Ulan-Ude
Chita
Khabarovsk
Vladivostok
HARBIN
West Siberian Plain
Tselinograd
Karaganda
Semipalatinsk
Kazakhstan
Aral Sea
Balkhash
Alma-Ata
TASHKENT
Samarkand
Dushanbe
Kabul
AFGHANISTAN
TEHRAN
IRAN
Baghdad
IRAQ
SYRIA
TURKEY
Istanbul
Ankara
Nicosia
CYPRUS
Beirut
ISRAEL
Jerusalem
SAUDI ARABIA
Riyadh
Mecca
Jiddah
Medina
Red Sea
KUWAIT
BAHRAIN
QATAR
U.A.E.
OMAN
Muscat
YEMEN
S.YEMEN
Aden
Gulf of Aden
Socotra (S. Yem.)
SUDAN
Khartoum
Asmara
ETHIOPIA
Addis Ababa
Djibouti
SOMALI REP.
Mogadiscio
KENYA
Nairobi
Mombasa
TANZANIA
Zanzibar
Dar es Salaam
MOZAMBIQUE
Mozambique Channel
MADAGASCAR
Antananarivo (Tananarive)
MAURITIUS
Port Louis
Réunion (Fr.)
SEYCHELLES
COMOROS
MONGOLIA
Ulan-Bator
Gobi
Ürümqi
Tien Shan
Takla Makan
Kunlun Mts.
Tibet
Lhasa
Himalaya
Karakoram
Hindu Kush
PAKISTAN
Karachi
LAHORE
Multan
Quetta
Hyderabad
DELHI
Jaipur
Agra
Kanpur
Allahabad
Varanasi
Patna
Katmandu
NEPAL
BANGLADESH
Dacca
Chittagong
CALCUTTA
INDIA
AHMADABAD
BOMBAY
Pune
Nagpur
HYDERABAD
MADRAS
BANGALORE
Mangalore
Mysore
Madurai
Arabian Sea
Bay of Bengal
Laccadive Is. (Lakshadweep) (India)
MALDIVES
Malé
SRI LANKA (Ceylon)
Colombo
Jaffna
Andaman Is. (India)
Nicobar Is. (India)
BURMA
Mandalay
RANGOON
Moulmein
THAILAND
BANGKOK
CAMBODIA (KAMPUCHEA)
Phnom Penh
HO CHI MINH CITY
VIETNAM
Hanoi
Hue
LAOS
Vientiane
CHINA
PEKING (BEIJING)
TIANJIN
SHENYANG
Changchun
Lanzhou
Xi'an
Chengdu
CHONGQING
WUHAN
NANJING
SHANGHAI
Hangzhou
Guiyang
Kunming
Nanning
CANTON (GUANGZHOU)
Hong Kong (U.K.)
Macau (Port.)
TAI-PEI
TAIWAN (FORMOSA)
N. KOREA
Pyongyang
SEOUL
S. KOREA
PUSAN
JAPAN
TOKYO
YOKOHAMA
OSAKA
NAGOYA
KYOTO
Sapporo
Hokkaido
Honshu
Shikoku
Kyushu
Sea of Japan
East China Sea
Ryukyu Is.
PACIFIC OCEAN
Philippine Sea
PHILIPPINES
MANILA
Quezon City
Luzon
Mindanao
South China Sea
MALAYSIA
Kuala Lumpur
SINGAPORE
Brunei
Sarawak
Sabah
Borneo
INDONESIA
Sumatra
Medan
Padang
Palembang
JAKARTA
BANDUNG
Semarang
SURABAYA
Yogyakarta
Java Sea
Sulawesi (Celebes)
Ujung Pandang (Makassar)
Banjarmasin
Pontianak
Celebes Sea
Moluccas
Timor
Timor Sea
INDIAN OCEAN
Equator
Tropic of Cancer
Tropic of Capricorn
Chagos Arch. (British Indian Ocean Territory)
Diego Garcia
Christmas I. (Austr.)
Cocos Is. (Keeling Is.) (Austr.)
AUSTRALIA
Great Sandy Desert
Gibson Desert
Great Victoria Desert
Port Hedland
Broome
Darwin
Long. East 60 of Gr.
0 500 1000 1500 km
0 312 624 936 mi

Above: A nomadic encampment in Mongolia. Their large round tents are made of felt, and known as yurts. Today collectivization is tending to result in more permanent settlements.

The highest mountains

Everest (Nepal/China), 8,848 m (29,029 ft); **Godwin Austen, K2** (Pakistan/India), 8,611 m (28,251 ft); **Kanchenjunga** (Nepal/Sikkim), 8,579 m (28,146 ft); **Lhotse** (Nepal), 8,501 m (27,890 ft); **Makalu** (Nepal/China) 8,470 m (27,789 ft); **Dhaulagiri** (Nepal), 8,172 m (26,811 ft); **Cho Oyu** (Nepal/China), 8,153 m (26,749 ft); **Nanga Parbat** (Pakistan/India), 8,126 m (26,660 ft); **Manaslu** (Nepal), 8,125 m (26,657 ft); **Annapurna** (Nepal), 8,075 m (26,493 ft); **Gasherbrum** (Pakistan/India), 8,068 m (26,470 ft).

remaining boundaries are its coasts: the Red Sea and Indian Ocean in the south, the Pacific Ocean in the east, and the Arctic Ocean in the north.

The entire northern part of the Asian continent is taken up by Soviet Asia, much of which lies north of the Arctic Circle. This is a region of snow, ice pack, and tundra – a treeless wasteland which can support little life apart from mosses, lichens and a few flowering plants which bloom during the short summer. The great rivers of northern Asia have their outlets on this northern coast. The Ob and Yenisey drain into the Kara Sea, and the Lena into the Laptev Sea. South of the tundra belt lies a region of coniferous forest, called taiga. To the south, the forest gradually gives way to the open steppes.

Much of Siberia is low-lying, but the land rises towards the east. The land between the Urals and the River Yenisey is particularly flat. To the east, the plains merge into plateaux, while farther east, a series of mountain ranges surround and extend from the Sea of Okhotsk. Southern Siberia is also bordered by mountains, such as the Altay range on the Mongolian border. Lake Baykal is the world's deepest lake, with a maximum depth of 1,940 metres (6,365 feet).

South of the 50th parallel, in the far west, is the world's largest lake – the Caspian Sea (Kaspiskoye More or Daryaye-Khazar). It has an area of 371,800 square kilometres (143,560 square miles). It lies 29 metres (95 feet) below sea level, and is surrounded by a large depression. East of the Caspian Sea lies a region of steppes and deserts. Much of Mongolia is taken up by the Gobi Desert, a vast tract of wilderness suffering climatic extremes. To the east lies the Manchurian region of China.

The 40th parallel crosses Turkey in the west. Western Turkey enjoys a Mediterranean climate, but inland the climate becomes more continental. To the south and east are harsh deserts, relieved only by the fertile basin of the rivers Tigris and Euphrates, a region known since ancient times as Mesopotamia. Iran, stretching from the Caspian to the Persian Gulf, is a land of mountains and deserts.

In Afghanistan and Pakistan, the mountains rise up dramatically. The Hindu Kush and the Karakoram range lead into the great chain of the Himalayas. Numbered among these snowy summits are the world's highest peaks, including Everest (Sagarmatha) at 8,848 metres (29,029 feet), Godwin Austen, Kanchenjunga, Makalu, Dhaulagiri,

The longest rivers

Chang Jiang or **Yangtze Kiang,** 5,800 km (3,604 mi) into S. China Sea; **Ob-Irtysh** 5,410 km (3,362 mi) into Kara Sea; **Huang He** 4,845 km (3,010 mi) into Hwang Hai; **Mekong** 4,500 km (2,796 mi) into S. China Sea; **Amur** 4,416 km (2,744 mi) into Sea of Okhotsk; **Lena** 4,400 km (2,734 mi) into Laptev Sea; **Yenisey** 4,092 km (2,543 mi) into Kara Sea; **Indus** 3,180 km (1,976 mi) into Arabian Sea; **Brahmaputra** 2,900 km (1,802 mi) into the Bay of Bengal; **Salween** 2,820 km (1,752 mi) into the Gulf of Martaban.

The greatest lakes

Caspian Sea (USSR/Iran), 371,800 km² (143,560 mi²); **Aral Sea** (USSR), 66,500 km² (25,677 mi²); **Baykal** (USSR), 31,500 km² (12,163 mi²); **Balkhash** (USSR), 18,200 km² (7,027 mi²); **Tonlé Sap** (Cambodia), 10,000 km² (3,861 mi²); **Issyk-Kul'** (USSR), 6,280 km² (2,425 mi²); **Urmia** (Iran), 5,800 km² (2,240 mi²); **Poyang Hu** (China), 5,050 km² (1,950 mi²); **Taymyr** (USSR), 4,560 km² (1,761 mi²); **Khanka** (USSR/China), 4,000 km² (1,544 mi²); **Dongting Hu** (China), 3,915 km² (1,512 mi²).

The chief islands

Borneo (Malaysia/Indonesia/Brunei), 736,000 km² (284,187 mi²); **Honshū** (Japan), 227,414 km² (87,810 mi²); **Sulawesi** (Indonesia), 172,000 km² (66,413 mi²); **Luzon** (Philippines), 104,687 km² (40,422 mi²); **Mindanao** (Philippines), 94,360 km² (36,435 mi²); **Hokkaidō** (Japan), 78,000 km² (30,118 mi²); **Sakhalin** (USSR), 76,400 km² (29,500 mi²); **Kyushu** (Japan), 36,554 km² (14,114 mi²); **Taiwan** (Taiwan), 35,854 km² (13,844 mi²); **Sumatra** (Indonesia), 420,000 km² (162,172 mi²).

Asia is the home of a remarkable range of wildlife and domestic animals. The tiger, opposite, is now an endangered species. Yaks, above, still provide butter and other daily necessities for the Tibetans. The cobra, left, is a deadly poisonous snake. Asian elephants, right, are often adorned and used in parades and religious festivals.

Flag	Country	Capital	Area	Population	Resources, products
	Afghanistan	Kabul	647,497 km² (250,014 mi²)	17,150,000	Natural gas, cotton, lapis lazuli, sheep, textiles, carpets.
	Bahrain	Manama	622 km² (240 mi²)	467,000	Oil, dates, rice, pearls, fish, food processing, refinery.
	Bangladesh	Dacca (Dhaka)	143,998 km² (55,601 mi²)	96,000,000	Jute, tobacco, sugar, rice, tea, coal, textiles.
	Bhutan	Thimphu	47,000 km² (18,148 mi²)	1,400,000	Rice, fruit, timber.
	Burma	Rangoon	676,552 km² (261,232 mi²)	35,310,000	Oil, natural gas, lead, silver, teak, jute, rubber.
	Cambodia (Kampuchea)	Phnom Penh	181,035 km² (69,902 mi²)	6,700,000	Rice, rubber, tobacco, fish, food processing.
	China	Peking (Beijing)	9,596,961 km² (3,705,610 mi²)	1,024,950,000	Coal, oil, tungsten, tin, iron ore, tea, cotton, rice, tobacco, livestock, engineering.
	Cyprus	Nicosia	9,251 km² (3,572 mi²)	655,000	Fruit, vegetables, olive oil, wine, tobacco, copper.
	India	Delhi	3,287,590 km² (1,269,415 mi²)	685,184,000	Textiles, jute, tea, rice, cotton, sugar, coffee, rubber, coal, iron ore.
	Indonesia	Jakarta	2,027,087 km² (782,705 mi²)	158,000,000	Oil, bauxite, tin, rice, soya, sugar, tea, tobacco, fish, rubber, coffee.
	Iran	Tehran	1,648,000 km² (636,331 mi²)	43,830,000	Oil, natural gas, iron ore, cotton, rice, fruit, tobacco.
	Iraq	Baghdad	434,924 km² (167,934 mi²)	14,000,000	Oil, cereals, tobacco, dates, cotton, textiles, iron ore, copper.
	Israel	Jerusalem	20,770 km² (8,020 mi²)	4,150,000	Oil, iron ore, fruit, olive oil, tobacco, chemicals.
	Japan	Tōkyō	372,313 km² (143,759 mi²)	120,055,000	Coal, lead, iron ore, sugar fish, rice, micro-electronics engineering.
	Jordan	Amman	97,740 km² (37,740 mi²)	3,500,000	Phosphates, olives, fruit, vegetables, sheep, goats.
	Korea (North)	Pyŏngyang	120,538 km² (46,543 mi²)	20,000,000	Iron ore, coal, lignite, rice, vegetables, cotton, tobacco, manufactures.
	Korea (South)	Sŏul (Seoul)	98,484 km² (38,027 mi²)	42,000,000	Tungsten, rice, vegetables, textiles, chemicals, consumer goods.
	Kuwait	Kuwait	17,818 km² (6,880 mi²)	1,910,000	Oil, natural gas, fishery, cement, fertilizers.
	Laos	Vientiane	236,800 km² (91,434 mi²)	3,938,000	Rice, timber, fruit, tobacco, maize, coffee, cotton, fishing.
	Lebanon	Beirut	10,400 km² (4,016 mi²)	3,500,000	Iron, salt, precious stones, olives, fruit, textiles.
	Malaysia	Kuala Lumpur	329,749 km² (127,324 mi²)	15,070,000	Tin, iron, bauxite, rice, rubber, timber, palm-oil.

Nanga-Parbat, and Annapurna. Between the Himalayas and Kunlun Shan lies the high plateau region of Tibet – the rooftop of the world'. This windswept plateau is an inaccessible region, enclosed by high mountains and deep valleys. Tibet is an autonomous region of China.

Eastwards, the land descends towards the coast of the Yellow Sea (Hwang Hai). Central China is a more temperate, rainy region, dominated by the meandering course of the Yellow River, or Huang He. Beyond the Yellow Sea, North and South Korea form a mountainous peninsula extending southwards towards Japan. The populous Japanese archipelago has a monsoon climate. Its highest mountain is Fujiyama, which reaches 3,776 metres (12,388 feet) on the principal island of Honshū.

South-western Asia contains large burning deserts. This region is inhospitable to most living things, but is rich in oil reserves. To the east across the Arabian Sea lies the Indian subcontinent. The lofty mountains to the north feed the waters of several major rivers, notably the Indus, whose fertile valley occupies much of Pakistan, and the Ganges (Ganga), the holy river of the Hindu religion, which with the Brahmaputra, flows into the Bay of Bengal. The plains of northern India are fertile. The south of the country is occupied by the plateau of the Deccan, bounded by the Vindhya range to the north, the Western Ghats and the Eastern Ghats. Off the southern tip of India lies the large tropical island of Sri Lanka (formerly Ceylon).

South China is dominated by the basin of the Chang Jiang (Yangtze Kiang), and bordered by the South and East China Seas. To the south lies a region once called Indo-China, a land of forest and paddy fields, punctuated by mountainous areas. A number of great rivers rise in the mountains to the north of this region. The Irrawaddy and the Salween run south into the Andaman Sea; the Chao Phraya into the Gulf of Siam; and the Mekong into the South China Sea. Extending southwards from Thailand, a narrow isthmus leads to peninsular Malaysia. Malaysia, Indonesia and the Philippines form the southern extremity of the Asian continent. Asia's diversity is exemplified by the fact that it includes the equatorial forests of Borneo and the icy wastes of the New Siberian Islands, far to the north of the Arctic Circle.

The history of Asia contains many highlights in the story of humanity. In China and in Java, remains have been found of our early ancestors. It was in Asia that the world's first cities evolved.

Flag	Country	Capital	Area	Population	Resources, products
	Maldives	Malé	298 km² (115 mi²)	168,000	Coconuts, coir, copra, fruit, fishing, tourism.
	Mongolian P. R.	Ulan Bator	1,565,000 km² (604,283 mi²)	1,866,000	Coal, salt, cattle, horses, wool, cereals, cement.
	Nepal	Katmandu	140,797 km² (54,365 mi²)	16,100,000	Rice, maize, vegetables, timber, cattle.
	Oman	Muscat	212,457 km² (82,035 mi²)	1,500,000	Oil, dates, tobacco, limes, fishing, frankincense.
	Pakistan	Islamabad	803,943 km² (301,421 mi²)	88,000,000	Coal, cotton, sugar, tobacco, wheat, rice, textiles, carpets.
	Philippines	Manila	300,000 km² (115,837 mi²)	54,400,000	Copper, iron ore, rice, maize, coconuts, timber, textiles.
	Qatar	Doha	11,000 km² (4,247 mi²)	294,000	Oil, natural gas, dates, fishing, refinery.
	Saudi Arabia	Riyadh	2,149,690 km² (830,450 mi²)	10,443,000	Oil, dates and other fruits, water melons, sorghum, wheat, cattle, sheep, goats.
	Singapore	Singapore	581 km² (224 mi²)	2,502,000	Rubber, rice, petro-chemicals, steel, shipping, textiles.
	Sri Lanka	Colombo	65,610 km² (25,334 mi²)	15,398,000	Graphite, precious stones, tea, rubber, coffee, coconuts.
	Syria	Damascus	185,180 km² (71,502 mi²)	10,500,000	Oil, asphalt, olives, cotton, cereals, livestock.
	Taiwan	T'ai-pei	35,961 km² (13,885 mi²)	17,100,000	Coal, rice, sugar, fruit, cotton, textiles, engineering plastics.
	Thailand	Bangkok	514,000 km² (198,467 mi²)	50,583,000	Tin, rice, tobacco, tapioca, rubber, maize.
	Turkey	Ankara	780,576 km² (301,399 mi²)	51,420,000	Iron ore, coal, lignite, chromium, cotton, cereals, fruits, textiles.
	United Arab Emirates	Abu Dhabi	83,600 km² (32,280 mi²)	1,622,000	Oil, natural gas, fruit, pearls, fishing.
	Vietnam	Hanoi	329,556 km² (127,249 mi²)	60,000,000	Coal, lignite, iron ore, rice, livestock, fishing, cotton, manufacturing.
	Yemen (Arab Republic)	San'a	195,000 km² (75,294 mi²)	9,273,000	Oil, fish, cotton, rice, salt.
	Yemen (PDR)	Aden	332,968 km² (128,567 mi²)	2,500,000	Refined oil, cotton, fish, coffee, dates, bananas.

This table includes the major countries of Asia. Although the bulk of the USSR lies within the Asian continent, its capital is in Europe. Part of Turkey lies in Europe. Small territories not included are Brunei and Hong Kong. The first is a former British territory, now independent. The second is a British Crown Colony, scheduled to reunite with the People's Republic of China in 1997. Macau comes under the jurisdiction of Portugal. Asia has a total area of about 44,387,000 km² (17,139,000 mi²) and a population of about 2,693,000,000. Cyprus (see page 180) is at the crossroads between Asia and Europe. Geographically it is included in Asia although culturally it is often thought to be European.

The Sumerian civilization which grew up along the banks of the Rivers Tigris and Euphrates in the fourth millennium BC was the first to make use of a system of writing, and the first to use wheels for transport. This region remained in the forefront of progress under the Babylonian and the Assyrian Empires. Another Asian river basin was the centre of a great civilization more than 4,000 years ago. This was the Indus valley civilization, where highly advanced cities, such as Harappa and Mohenjo-Daro, were built.

Many great civilizations also arose in the ancient world, including those of the Hittites, the Persians and the Hebrews. The Huang He saw the start of a culture that eventually spread over the whole of China, where successive dynasties presided over a remarkable series of technological advances and artistic achievements that continued over the centuries. In India, the religions of Hinduism and Buddhism provided the foundation of a cultural tradition that still thrives today. Another great civilization was that of the Khmers, in Cambodia, to which the magnificent ruins of Angkor Wat bear witness. In the Near East, the Arabs, inspired by the Islamic faith, spread their civilization into North Africa and Europe. Their scholarship, literature, and scientific skill, which thrived during Europe's Dark Ages, had a considerable effect on European culture, contributing much to the Renaissance. At the other extremity of the Asian continent, the Japanese developed a culture every bit as remarkable.

Most people in Europe share a common linguistic heritage with many of the people in Asia because the Indo-European family of languages spans the continents, demonstrating early racial links between them. Aryan peoples invaded and settled India about 1500 BC, and in classical times, the Macedonian-Greek Empire of Alexander the Great (356–323 BC) stretched from Egypt to India. But the real beginnings of modern contacts between Europe and Asia began with the journeys of the Venetian Marco Polo, who reached the Chinese court of Kublai Khan in 1275. Trading caravans of the Middle Ages brought silks and spices out of the mysterious East. The desire for this lucrative trade led the Portuguese to seek a sea route to India around the Cape of Good Hope. Vasco da Gama reached the Indian city of Calicut in 1498, while Columbus, looking for a shorter westward route to the Indies, accidentally discovered the Americas. Trading stations were soon founded in many parts of Asia, but initially they had little effect on the

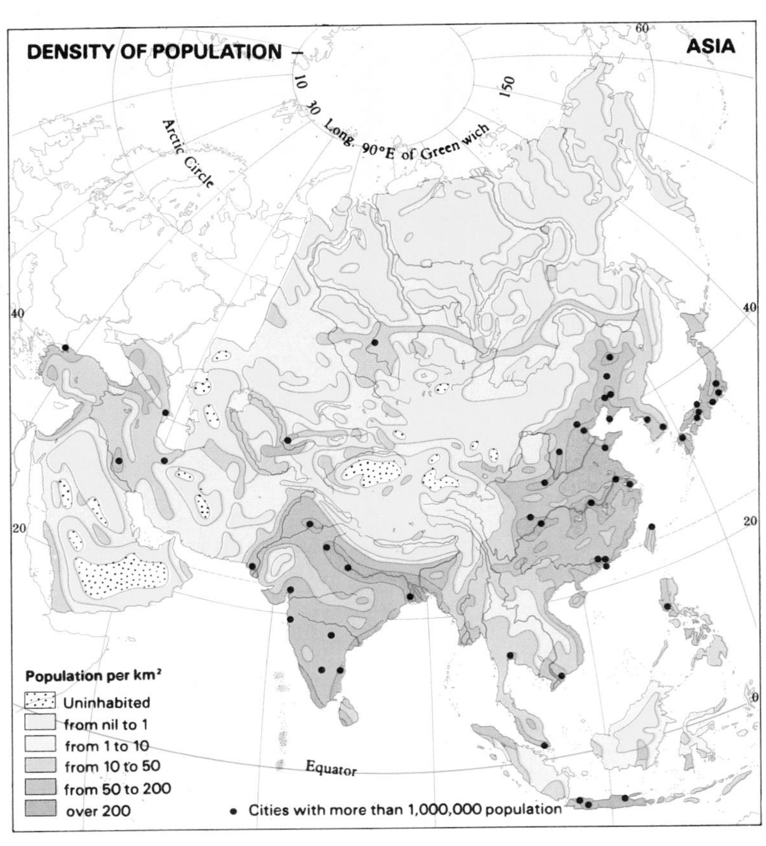

Above: The population map of Asia reveals areas of particularly high density in Bangladesh, China, India, Indonesia and Japan.

About 90 per cent of Asians live in the southern part of the continent, where the population explosion is a serious problem. In China alone, the population increases by 15 million every year. Above: Communist Chinese demonstrate in Peking (Beijing). Above right: Tokyo is capital of Japan and the world's largest city. Right and opposite: Benares (Varanasi) in India. This is a holy city of the Hindu faith, whose adherents come here to purify themselves by bathing in the River Ganges or to die there and be cremated on its banks.

indigenous cultures. Before long, however, intense rivalry between the nations of Europe led to colonization and military intervention. Following the Industrial Revolution, Europe had a technological advantage over the traditional cultures of Asia, and used it to create great empires. The subject nations provided cheap labour and a ready market for mass-produced goods.

This period came to an end in the 20th century. Foreign traders relinquished their hold on China, the British abandoned their empire in India, and the nations of Indo-China and the islands of Indonesia and Malaysia became independent. Today much of Asia has its destiny in its own hands once again, even if it is beset by economic problems.

Both in former colonies and in countries which never lost their independence, the 20th century has meant a large cultural upheaval. In Soviet Asia, the hunters and reindeer herders of the Arctic Circle have seen the collectivization of their livelihood, as have the nomadic herdsmen of Mongolia. The revolutionaries in China have sought to modernize their most traditional of lands, while capitalism and high technology have made Japan Asia's most industrialized nation. In the Arab countries of the Near East, oil has brought political power and great wealth to sheikhdoms which were, until recently, poverty-stricken. But despite all these changes, the cultural foundations of Asia are strong. Changes which appear to be fundamental often prove to be superficial, because they are adaptations of traditional values to the modern world.

Perhaps the most outstanding problem faced by Asia today is one of over-population. Much of the land mass is uninhabitable or at the best inhospitable. But in other areas, fertile regions have encouraged settlement from the earliest times, such as the fertile river basins in which many great civilizations arose. Today the plains of India, Bangladesh and China have experienced a population explosion that threatens the economic future of these lands. The islands of Java and Japan are also greatly overcrowded.

These regions often suffer natural disasters, such as drought, flooding or earthquakes, which result in widespread hardship and famine. Faced with starvation on the land, many peasants abandon their villages for an uncertain existence in the shanty towns of the big cities. The slums of Bombay and Calcutta pose a moral problem not just to Asia but to the whole world.

Afghanistan

Democratic Republic of

The Democratic Republic of Afghanistan lies in south-western Asia, and is the meeting point for a variety of cultural traditions, because it is surrounded by Iran, the USSR, China and Pakistan.

It is a land of arid desert and inaccessible mountain valleys, of great heat and extreme cold. The mountains of the Hindu Kush occupy the centre and north-east of the country. The terrain is difficult and the main highway runs in a 'U', from the ancient city of Herat in the west, to Kandahar in the south, and then back up to Kabul, the capital, in the east. From Kabul, roads run to Mazar-i-Sharif in the north, and Jalalabad and the Khyber Pass in the extreme east. The chief rivers are the Kabul and the Helmand.

Top: Whilst the cities of Afghanistan are in the control of Soviet and government forces, the remote mountains are still controlled by partisans. Left: A group of Kirghiz crossing a mountain pass in Afghanistan. Opposite: Bangladeshi workers soaking and washing jute, which will then be made into rope and cloth. Bottom right: The reclining Buddha at Rangoon is awe-inspiring in scale.

The geographical position of Afghanistan has given it great strategic importance over the centuries. This was as true in the days of Alexander the Great (356–323 BC) who incorporated the region in his empire, as it was in the days of the British Empire, when British troops fought Afghani guerrillas in order to secure India's North-west Frontier. The country was a monarchy until 1973, when it became a republic. In 1979 Soviet troops intervened to protect the Afghani government from guerrillas opposed to its rule. After a long war, the Soviet troops began to withdraw in May 1988.

The people of Afghanistan are from a number of ethnic backgrounds: they include Pashtuns, Hazara, Baluchis, Nuristanis, Uzbeks and Turkomen. The chief languages are Pushtu, Dari and Farsi. The country follows strict Islamic beliefs. For example, most women still wear veils. The country is sparsely populated, and about 12 per cent of the population is nomadic. Traditions are strong in Afghanistan. Some tribes claim descent from the army of Genghis Khan. They are certainly a proud, feuding, warlike people, who, at the same time, are warm and hospitable. The artistic traditions of the region are exemplified by fine carpets and textiles.

Afghanistan is a poor land, and most people scrape a living from raising sheep and goats. Wheat is used to make unleavened bread, which is eaten along with rice and meat or lentils. Sweet black tea is drunk on all occasions. Fruit is grown in the warm south-west. Mineral resources include silver, lapis lazuli, iron and coal.

Area:
647,497 km²
(250,014 mi²)
Population:
17,150,000
Capital:
Kabul (pop. 2,000,000)
Other towns:
Kandahar, Herat, Kunduz, Charikar, Mazar-i-Sharif
Currency:
afghani

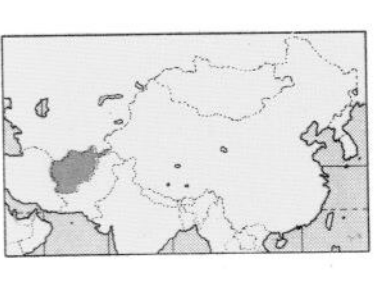

Bangladesh

People's Republic of

When Britain withdrew from India in 1947, bitter conflict occurred between the Muslim and the Hindu sections of the population. The principally Muslim parts of the Indian Empire were separated to become the Republic of Pakistan. Pakistan comprised two regions: West Pakistan and East Pakistan, which were separated by some 1,600 km (1,000 mi). West Pakistan dominated the partnership, and in 1971 the eastern part seceded after a war which involved India. It became known as the People's Republic of Bangladesh.

The people of Bangladesh are Bengalis, as are the inhabitants of the neighbouring Indian province of West Bengal. Their history dates back thousands of years, to the time when farming settlements first grew up on the fertile plains of the Rivers Ganges (Ganga), Jamuna (Brahmaputra) and Meghna. Their land was invaded by Aryan peoples, and later by the Moghuls and the British. But the people have retained a unique culture and language.

The country occupies a delta region, and the coast on the Bay of Bengal is a maze of islands and waterways. The climate is hot, with a dry winter season and a monsoon season. The area is subject to severe flooding, which can cause widespread loss of life. War, flooding and famine have all caused great hardship in recent years.

The chief cash crop is jute, and rice, tea and sugar-cane are also produced on a large scale.

The capital is Dacca (Dhaka), a large city in the centre of this densely populated country. The chief port is Chittagong, in the east. Bangladesh is served by a road and rail network and Dacca has an international airport.

Area:
143,998 km²
(55,601 mi²)
Population:
96,000,000
Capital:
Dacca (Dhaka)
(pop. 4,023,000)
Other towns:
Chittagong, Khulna, Narayanganj, Rajshahi, Barisal
Currency:
taka

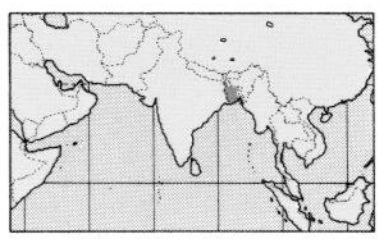

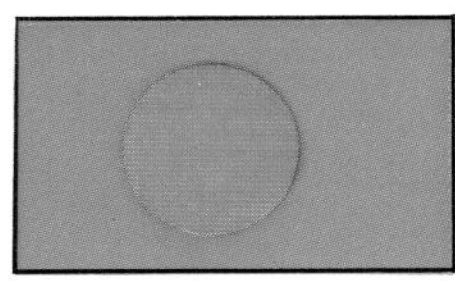

Bhutan

Druk-yul

Bhutan is a mountainous, independent kingdom in the Himalayas. It shares borders with Tibet (now an Autonomous Region of China), and with India. Sikkim, to the west, is now part of India, and India is also involved in the direction of Bhutan's foreign policy. The economy is based on agriculture, and timber, wheat and rice are exported. Most of the people of Bhutan, who speak Dzongkha, are Buddhists, but some are Hindus.

Area:
47,000 km²
(18,148 mi²)
Population:
1,400,000
Capital:
Thimphu
Currency:
ngultrum

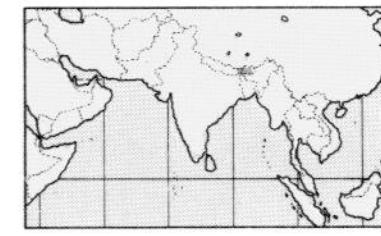

Brunei

The island of Borneo lies between the Philippines and the islands of Sumatra and Java. It is separated from the Asian mainland by the South China Sea. The south of the island forms part of Indonesia. The north of the island is occupied by the Malaysian provinces of Sabah and Sarawak, but a small section of the north comes under the rule of the Muslim Sultanate of Brunei.

The chief colonial powers in this part of the world were the Dutch, the French and the British. In 1963 Brunei decided not to join the new Federation of Malaysia, choosing instead to remain a British protectorate as it had been since 1888. However on 31 December 1983 this tiny state finally became independent. Links with Britain remain close.

The climate of Brunei is damp and hot. The forests and plantations of the region provide a variety of products. Rubber is extensively grown; the East Indian acacia tree provides catechu, a substance used in dyeing and tanning; and the starchy pith of various palms provides the food sago. The chief resource is oil.

The people of Brunei are mostly of Malay or Chinese extraction. Some still live in water dwellings built on stilts. The chief centre of population is the capital Bandar Seri Begawan.

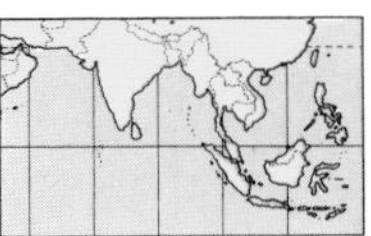

Area:
5,765 km²
(2,226 mi²)
Population:
214,400
Capital:
Bandar Seri Begawan (pop. 58,000)
Currency:
dollar

Burma

Pyidaungsu Socialist Thammada Myanma Naingngandaw

'For the temple bells are callin', and it's
there that I would be —
By the old Moulmein Pagoda, looking
lazy at the sea.'

This was the dream of a British soldier described by the writer Rudyard Kipling (1865–1936) in his famous poem *Mandalay*. Burma was part of the British Indian Empire, until its soldiers finally withdrew in 1948. However, upon independence, Burma did not become part of the Commonwealth. In 1962, an army *coup d'état* ousted the parliamentary government and established the Socialist Republic of the Union of Burma. Military rule ended in 1974 and U Ne Win became president. In 1981, U San Yu was elected Head of State.

The Burmese people are divided into a number of ethnic and language groups, including Burmans, Shan, Chin, Karen, Thai and Kachin, as well as Indians, Bengalis and Chinese. Burmese is the official language. Burma is a predominantly Buddhist country. Magnificent shrines, temples, and pagodas, such as the Shwe Dagon with its beautiful golden roofs, are a testament to the religious traditions of the Burmese people.

Burma is situated on the Bay of Bengal and is surrounded to the north, east and west by mountains. The highest peak is Hkakabo Razi, at 6,077 metres (19,938 ft). The principal rivers are the Chindwin, the Salween and the Irrawaddy. The capital, Rangoon, is on the Rangoon River above the Gulf of Martaban.

Burma is an agricultural land. The fertile river valleys are suitable for growing rice, which is the staple diet and an important export. Tobacco, tea, cotton, jute and rubber are also cultivated. Burma possesses valuable mineral deposits, and there are important oilfields and refineries. The rivers provide hydro-electric power. With the help of foreign aid, a number of industrial schemes have been successfully set up. But for the many Burmese who live in small villages and work the land all day, life has not changed in centuries. It is taken up by labour and religious devotions and is much as it must have been when British troops first entered the region.

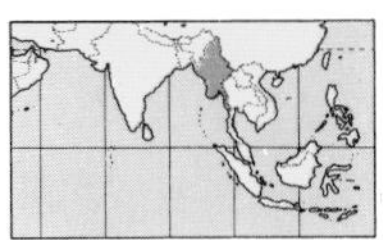

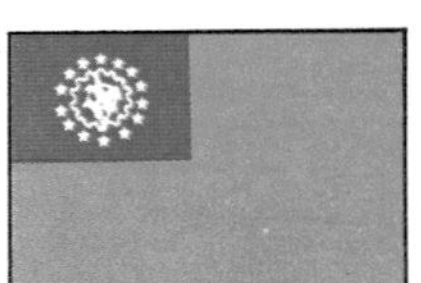

Area:
676,552 km²
(261,232 mi²)
Population:
35,310,000
Capital:
Rangoon (pop. 2,459,000)
Other towns:
Mandalay, Bassein, Henzada, Pegu, Myingyan, Moulmein
Currency:
kyat

Below: A distant view of the picturesque Ananda temple in Burma.

Cambodia

Democratic Kampuchea

South-east Asia has had more than its fair share of tragedy this century, and the ancient land of Cambodia, or Democratic Kampuchea, is no exception. Seven hundred years ago, this was the centre of a powerful empire, but in 1863 it became part of French Indo-China. Independence was finally achieved during the years 1949–53. The Kingdom of Cambodia became the Khmer Republic in 1970, when Prince Norodom Sihanouk was deposed. In neighbouring Vietnam, the fighting between communist forces and the USA and their allies had already spilt over into Cambodian territory. Soon a terrible civil war was being waged between Republican troops (supported by the USA) and Khmer Rouge troops (supported by North Vietnam).

The latter took the capital Phnom Penh in 1975, and the following year Pol Pot came to power. He attempted to reorganize Cambodian society by forcing people to work in rural areas. This action led to widespread chaos and reports of atrocities. Three years later Vietnamese troops invaded Cambodia and enabled the United National Front to take power, although this government was not recognized by China or the western alliance. Khmer Rouge resistance to the government continues in parts of the country. Democratic Kampuchea, as it is now officially called by the United Nations, is a country of refugees and victims of war.

The Khmer people have lived in the region of the Mekong and Tonlé Sap rivers for centuries. In the north-west, the ruined city of Angkor and its splendid temple of Angkor Wat are a record of the achievement of Khmer culture. The people are traditionally Buddhists of the Theravada sect, and their religion has played an important part in their history. The official language is Khmer.

The most prominent features of Cambodia's physical geography are the Mekong and the Tonlé Sap. The latter river forms a vast lake in the centre of the country. The flood plains of the rivers are cultivated for rice, but much of the land is covered by rain forest. This is a flat country, but a series of hills does stretch down the western side, notably the Cardamom and the Elephant ranges.

A highland region also exists to the east, across the borders with Laos and Vietnam, and is the home of hill tribes.

The tropical, wet climate means that rice is the principal export crop as well as being the staple food of the region. Bananas, tobacco, rubber, maize and soya beans are also grown, as is kapok, a tree whose fluffy seeds are processed to make stuffing for fabrics and insulation fibre.

Industrial progress has been hindered by the years of war, as have communications. There is a network of roads, and railways link the capital, Phnom Penh, with the coast, and with Bangkok, the capital of Thailand. The chief sea port is Kompong Som, on the Gulf of Thailand. In a country of waterways, it is hardly surprising that they provide a useful means of transportation; the chief rivers are easily navigable.

Above: Workers in the paddy fields. Rice is Cambodia's principal crop. Below: These mighty statues stand in the ruined city of Angkor, once the capital of the powerful Khmer Empire.

Area: 181,035 km² (69,902 mi²)
Population: 6,700,000
Capital: Phnom Penh (pop. 500,000)
Currency: khmer

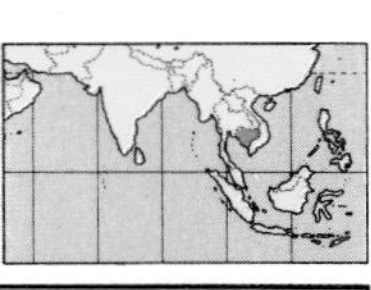

China
People's Republic of

The People's Republic of China, the world's third largest country, occupies a large part of the Asian continent. It covers an area of almost the same size as Europe, including European Russia. It is the world's largest country in terms of population, and is the home of more than one-fifth of the world's population. It shares borders with Korea, the USSR, Mongolia, Afghanistan, India, Nepal, Bhutan, Burma, Laos and Vietnam. Even within its own boundaries, there are people of several ethnic and cultural backgrounds, including Tibetans, Mongols, Uighurs, Manchus, Cantonese, Hakka, Tai and many others.

Its regions vary greatly in climate, produce, demography, and development. Broadly, the country can be divided into two main regions. The eastern half of the country is a region of great plains crossed by rivers, intensely cultivated and highly populated. The western part of the country is largely occupied by barren mountains, plateaux or desert.

The north-eastern part of China is known as Manchuria. This is a large plain surrounded on three sides by mountains, with the sea in the south. The north is covered by thick forests which provide timber for building and wood-pulp for paper making – a technology invented in China under the Han emperors of the second century AD. Central Manchuria is open, pastoral country, devoted to cattle rearing. In southern Manchuria, around the River Liao, there is extensive cultivation of cereals, soya beans, and sugar-beet. There are also deposits of iron and coal. Manchurian steel production is sufficient to meet the requirements of the whole country. Here too are textile industries and engineering, and large-scale hydro-electric schemes. The economic potential of Manchuria is tremendous.

To the south-west of Manchuria lies the capital, Beijing (Peking) a city of nearly nine million people. Farther south still is the basin of the Huang He or Yellow River. 'Yellow' refers to the golden-brown colour of the soil of the region, called loess, which has been deposited by winds and ancient floods. This alluvial plain is extremely fertile, allowing the cultivation of cereals, hemp, cotton and soya beans.

The Qin Ling chain of mountains separates this region from the more southerly basin of the Chang Jiang or the River Yangzi. Here the climate is warmer and more humid, and the river is like a great arm of the sea that pushes inland. Tides are noticeable as far as 600 kilometres (373 miles) upstream, and the river is navigable as far as Yichang. This region is irrigated not only by the great river, but also by its tributaries, by lakes and canals. This allows for two crops to be grown in a year. Rice, grain and cotton are cultivated. Large cities have arisen in this area, including Wuhan, Huangshi, Jiujiang, Nanchang, Wuhu, Nanjing (Nanking) and, on the coast of the East China Sea, the port of Shanghai, which with 11,320,000 inhabitants is the world's second largest city.

South China is dominated by uplands. The Sui Jiang (Si Kiang) descends through the uplands to a wide delta to the South China Sea. Typical crops of this region include tea and sugar-beet in the hills, and rice on the coastal plains. There are deposits of coal, tin and uranium. The major cities of this region include the trading centre of southern China, Guangzhou or Canton. Two foreign enclaves remain on this coast, the Portuguese territory of Macau and the British colony of Hong Kong.

To the west, the land rises steeply to Qing Zang: this is the Tibetan plateau,

Below: Some traditional Chinese dancers.

which lies between Kunlun Shan and the mighty Himalayas, which rise to Mount Everest on the border with Nepal. The Tibetan plateau is a barren, sparsely populated region with a unique cultural heritage. For much of the 20th century, this outpost was regarded as an independent country, presided over by Buddhist priests, or lamas. The Chinese invaded the region in 1950, and the ruler, the Dalai Lama, fled the country in 1959. Today Tibet, with its capital at the holy city of Lhasa, is an Autonomous Region of the People's Republic of China.

The north-west of China is occupied by another huge, barren plateau, Xinjiang or Sinkiang. This Autonomous Region was, until recently, undeveloped. Today it has been transformed by the discovery of oil and uranium deposits. Scientists flock to Xinjiang and nuclear installations are being developed.

To the east of Xinjiang is the Gobi desert, which straddles the border with Mongolia. This is another wilderness that has proved to have mineral resources. Along the southern border of the Chinese Autonomous Region of Inner Mongolia is one of the wonders of the world, the Great Wall of China. This wall is 3,460 kilometres (2,150 miles) long, with an additional 2,860 kilometres (1,777 miles) of wall branching off it. The world's largest wall, it was built in the third century BC against barbarian invders. It protected a splendid civilization which was unknown in Europe at the time.

The Chinese civilization is one of the world's most ancient. Its origins date back to the 20th century BC, when a society developed along the Huang He, or Yellow River. As ruling dynasties came and went, the ancient Chinese developed a culture unique in its achievements. Calligraphy, papermaking, woodenblock printing, porcelain-manufacture and sericulture (the cultivation of silkworms for textile production) were all skills at which the Chinese excelled. Another Chinese invention, gunpowder, had a less beneficial effect on humanity.

The first European to bring back news of this extraordinary world was a Venetian, Marco Polo, who in AD 1271, at the age of 17, left for the east in the company of his father and uncle, both merchants. Pope Gregory had entrusted them with messages and gifts for the ruler of China, the Great Khan. During this period, China was controlled by a dynasty of Mongol extraction. When Marco Polo made his journey, Kublai Khan (a grandson of Genghis Khan) was emperor. The Mongols were barbarians if they are compared with the Sung dynasty that they

Above: The Taoist temple of Lun Men reflects peace and serenity. Chinese architectural styles have had considerable influence in other Asian countries. Below: This rocky part of Yunnan province is known as Shillin, or the 'stone forest'.

A section of the Great Wall of China. Built in the third century BC, as a defence against warring tribes, it has a total length of 6,320 kilometres (3,927 miles) and still stands firm today. One-third of the country's workforce was employed to build it, It is the longest structure of its kind in the world, and is visible from the Moon.

supplanted. But they rapidly adopted the civilized ways of the Chinese. The Polos were received with courtesy, and Marco remained with this court for 17 years, familiarizing himself with the country, which he called Cathay. Eventually he returned to Europe and told his incredible story.

The rule of the Mongol Khans did not last long. By 1368, the Ming dynasty was in control of China. The emperors were the 'enlightened ones', under whom culture and art reached new splendours. It was under their rule, which continued until 1644, that contact with Europeans began to increase. The Portuguese obtained a commercial foothold at Macau in this period, and Jesuits arrived in the land. The country was surveyed and mapped, and the first Chinese dictionary produced. In the 17th century, the Ming were replaced by the Manchus, China's last dynasty.

In Europe, interest in China was growing. Chinese art was discovered and imitated, and splendid silks and porcelains were imported. But European cultural interest was accompanied by economic interest, which soon turned to interference in Chinese affairs. In 1839, the Chinese government forbade the import of the drug opium from British India. Britain used this act as a spurious excuse to start a morally indefensible war against China. Easily beaten in this Opium War (1840–42), the Chinese were compelled to pay an indemnity, cede the territory of Hong Kong, and open their doors to British commerce. France, Germany and Russia soon made demands similar to those of Britain, as, later, did Japan and the United States. China's economy thus fell into the hands of foreign powers.

The foreign presence inspired some popular resentment, which flared up into a major uprising in 1900. The Boxer Rebellion, so called after a terrorist group, was suppressed by a joint European force. However, an awareness of nationhood was growing, and in February 1912 imperial rule at long last came to an end, when the six-year-old empress, Pi-Yu, was forced to abdicate. A republic was proclaimed.

The focus of the nationalist movement was the Kuomintang (Party of National Unity) under the leadership of Sun Yat-Sen (1866–1925). This great modern politician, the son of peasants, was driven by a desire to create a democratic, nationalist and socialist state. But the task was not an easy one. The first decades of republican China were troubled by conflict between the southern part of the country, a Kuomintang stronghold, and the northern part, ruled by warlords. The Japanese profited from the chaos to lead repeated attacks and invasions.

Eight years of war with Japan came to an end with that country's defeat at the end of the Second World War in 1945. But peace was still not at hand. The Kuomintang had been allied with the Red Army of the Chinese Communist Party in their struggle against Japan. Now the two forces fought each other to determine the country's future. The leader of the nationalist Kuomintang was Chiang Kai-Shek, the successor of Sun Yat-Sen. The leader of the Communists was the war veteran Mao Tse-Tung, who had led the revolutionary army on an incredible, arduous trek to Manchuria, known as the 'long march', ten years earlier.

The civil war lasted until 1949. Chiang Kai-Shek was finally expelled from the mainland with the remnants of his forces. He sought refuge on the island of Formosa, now known as Taiwan. This island, 35,854 square kilometres (13,844 square miles) in area, is now all that remains of the Kuomintang. The People's Republic of China, established on the mainland, still claims the territory of this island. At first, the Nationalists represented the whole of China in the United Nations, but the mainland Republic of China was admitted to UN membership in 1971.

The revolution in the Soviet Union had relied on the industrialized working classes. In China, 90 per cent of the population were peasants, working the land. Mao Tse-Tung understood this, and his undeniable achievement was the improvement of the peasant's life. In the old China, between five and six million Chinese sometimes died of starvation in a single year, and this was considered to be a phenomenon as natural as a sandstorm or a flood. Desperate families in rural areas were often reduced to selling baby girls, who were regarded as useless mouths to feed, because males were needed to labour in the fields. A sack of rice was an acceptable price for a baby girl. These degrading social conditions are now a thing of the past. But the

Area:
9,596,961 km²
(3,705,610 mi²)
Population:
1,024,950,000
Capital:
Peking (Beijing)
(pop. 9,230,000)
Other towns:
Shanghai, Tianjin, Chongqing, Guangzhou, Shenyang, Wuhan, Harbin, Lüda, Nanjing, Xián, Chengdu, Qingdao, Taiyuan, Fushun
Currency:
(renminbi)
yuan

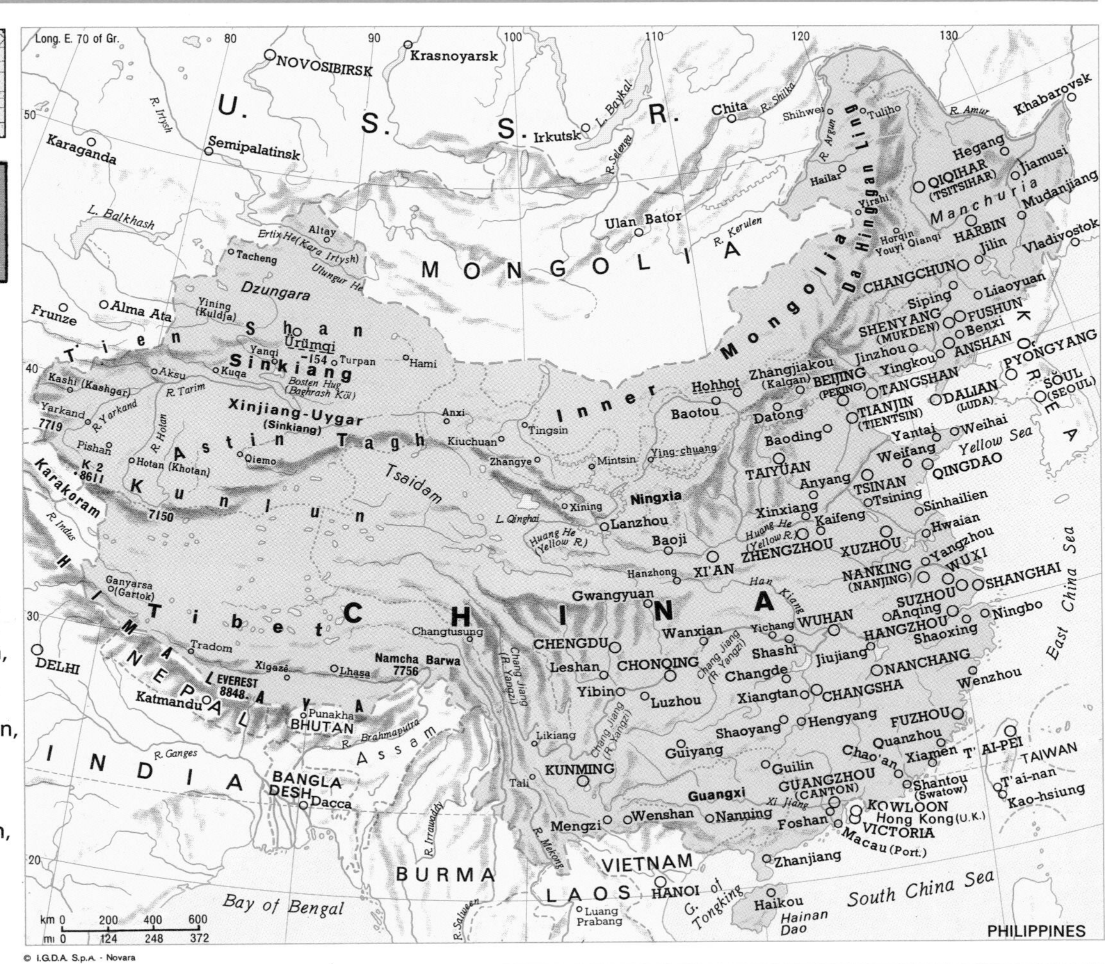

sacrifices made by the people to achieve change have often been hard.

The first years of the new regime were difficult. Between 1958 and 1961, the Communist leaders planned a 'Great Leap Forward' in the economy. This collective effort was designed to carry China forward to parity with more developed societies, but it nearly ended in disaster. Lack of capital, the wear and tear upon machinery, lack of careful preparation and the reappearance of Asia's perennial scourges, drought and flood, led in 1961 to the prospect of famine. Only massive acquisition of foreign food supplies averted the threat.

In political matters, it was clear that even if China was a poor country, it was one of the world's superpowers. It had tested its own atomic weapons and had a huge army. But under Mao, China was aligned not only against the capitalist United States, but also against a former ally, the Soviet Union. A number of border incidents in the 1960s fuelled the disagreement between the two countries. Internally China was torn by strife from 1966 onwards by the 'Cultural Revolution', which consisted of a series of ideological purges. Mao Tse-Tung died in 1976, and, subsequently, China adopted a more pragmatic approach to both internal and external politics.

In 1982 a new constitution was introduced, which stressed modernisation and economic change at the expense of ideology. Relations with the West improved dramatically, and the country became more open to international influence. Trade and technical cooperation with the outside world flourished. Potentially contentious issues such as the return of the British territory of Hong Kong to China in 1997 were settled amicably.

A feature of life in Communist China is the commune. All the farms in a single district are grouped together, and the resources are pooled. At one time, family life was excluded. The children were raised in kindergartens and all private property was forbidden. Today, however, the nuclear family has re-formed, and the economic rules have been relaxed.

Industry has been greatly developed in China in recent years, based on its considerable mineral reserves. But agriculture employs over three-fifths of the people and must remain in the forefront of economic activity, because China has many mouths to feed. China is among the world's top three producers of cotton, groundnuts, maize, millet, rice, sorghum, soya beans, tea and wheat.

The continual increase in population is probably the country's most pressing problem. The population is now more than 1,000 million and is growing at the rate of about 13 million a year. However much productivity improves, there is always the population explosion to compensate for it. The way of life for the Chinese people, therefore, remains austere with a modest standard of living – the streets of the cities are filled with bicycles rather than cars. The government takes all the measures it can to tackle the population problem. There is active propaganda against getting married too young, and couples who exceed the maximum of three children can be fined.

Education in China has grown steadily at all levels, interrupted only by the Cultural Revolution. One particular problem has been the Chinese use of ideograms when writing. The symbols do not represent sounds, as in our alphabet, but ideas. The world of ideas is virtually infinite, and some 40,000 major signs are

Above: The world's second largest city, Shanghai. Right: Three portraits of the Chinese people, who form more than one-fifth of the world's population. Birth control is a major priority in China.

included. After six years at school, a child could write about 2,000 ideograms and read about twice that number. In the 1950s, it was decided to rationalize the old system as an educational priority. Some 230 simplified symbols were introduced and there are now more than 2,000 in use. Printed texts now read left to right horizontally instead of right to left in vertical columns. In primary school, a basic Roman alphabet of 30 characters *(pinyin)* is used as an introduction to literacy, before the full range of ideograms is tackled at about eight years of age. The Chinese language has a great many dialects, which vary considerably. The most widespread is *Putonghua,* or Mandarin. Others include Cantonese, Amoy, Hakka, Wu and Fuzhou.

For all its planning for the future, revolutionary China has taken scrupulous care in the uncovering of its past. Archaeological excavations in the vicinity of Anyang and Zhengzhou have revealed much about the Shang civilization of 3,500 years ago, and digs near Peking have uncovered the tombs of the Ming emperors. China remains a land where civilization has flourished and continues to flourish. The traditions of Buddhism, and the philosophies of Taoism (drawn up by Lao-Tse in the seventh century BC) and Confucianism (drawn up by K'ung Fu-Tse a century later) may no longer enjoy official approval, but the same spirit of practical wisdom remains a feature of modern China. Since 1949, China has been through social upheaval and catastrophe. But the miseries of the Manchu dynasty are now far away, and life for the Chinese peasant has never been as secure as today.

However the real test for the People's Republic of China lies in the future. The aim of the Cultural Revolution of 1966–68 was to perpetuate the revolutionary fervour of the early days by attacking bureaucracy and opportunism. Today many of those ousted in the 1960s are back in favour. A pragmatic approach to internal and international politics has become the order of the day.

The admission of the People's Republic to the United Nations Organization in 1971, and the subsequent thaw in relations with many countries of the West, has resulted in a great renewal of interest in the Chinese way of life. Historically the Chinese always regarded Westerners as barbarians, and the misunderstanding was reciprocated. It is to be hoped that increased contact will today lead to mutual understanding.

Hong Kong

When the British Empire finally broke up in the mid-20th century, a number of colonies and other associate states remained in British hands. Some were strategic centres, such as Gibraltar, while others were commercial centres, such as the Crown Colony of Hong Kong. This colony consists of a section of the Chinese mainland (Kowloon and the New Territories) and several offshore islands in the South China Sea, the chief of which is Hong Kong. These were acquired by treaties made with China in the mid-19th century. **Britain has agreed to return the colony to China in 1997 when the lease on the New Territories expires.**

The colony occupies hilly land, the highest point being Tai Mo Shan, which reaches 942 metres (3,091 ft) in the New Territories. These territories are on a peninsula which extends from the Guangdong (Kwantung) province of the People's Republic of China, some 130 kilometres (81 miles) south-west of Guangzhou (Canton). Some 65 kilometres (40 miles) to the west lies another remnant of the colonial era – the Portuguese territory of Macau.

Mainland China has been a communist country since 1949 and its austerity contrasts sharply with the neon lights and skyscrapers of capitalist Hong Kong. The people of Hong Kong, packed into the crowded back streets or living in sampans in the harbour, are mostly Chinese who speak Cantonese, although Mandarin and some other dialects are also heard.

The capital is Victoria, on Hong Kong island, which is linked to Kowloon by road tunnel, underground railway and ferry. The teeming city streets of Victoria are lined with banks, bars, office blocks and night clubs. Hong Kong owes its origins to a magnificent natural harbour, which is one of the Far East's most important ports of call. There is an international airport at Kai Tak.

The wealth of Hong Kong comes from a number of sources. Banks, insurance companies and other big business concerns provide much of it. Dock yards and freight transit are also important. Hong Kong's light industry is geared to microelectronics for calculators and similar items, clothing manufacture, and consumer goods for the household. Having first made its name with the manufacture of cheap toys and plastic goods, Hong Kong is now the producer of reliable clocks, watches and cameras. The tiny colony has to export to survive. Its main customers are the member countries of the European Economic Community (EEC), in particular West Germany and the United Kingdom, the Commonwealth countries, the USA and Japan.

Economic success has brought a high standard of living to the colony, although problems inevitably abound in such an artificial enclave, notably overcrowding and crime.

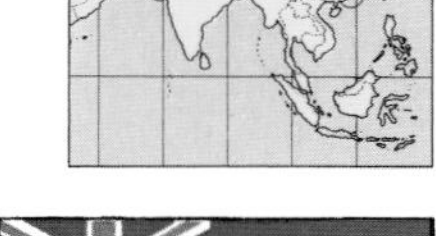

Area:
1,045 km² (403 mi²)
Population:
5,398,000
Capital:
Victoria (pop. 767,000)
Other towns:
Kowloon
Currency:
dollar

Below: Hong Kong's busy streets will become part of the People's Republic of China in 1997.

India

Bharat

The Republic of India is a vast country, the world's seventh largest by area and the second largest by population. Its territory occupies most of the Indian subcontinent, a great triangle of land that extends southwards into the Indian Ocean. India is bounded to the west by the Arabian Sea and to the east by the Bay of Bengal. It shares land frontiers with Pakistan, Nepal, Bhutan, China, Burma and Bangladesh. It is a land of great beauty and variety, of huge mountains, of great rivers and dusty plains, of dense forest and deserts, of peaceful villages and crowded cities. India contains four main physical regions: the Himalayas, the Deccan plateau, the river basin of the Ganges (Ganga) and Brahmaputra, part of which is in Bangladesh, and the Indus River basin, most of which is in Pakistan.

India's northern border is marked by the Himalayas, the world's most formidable range of mountains. The central section of the range is occupied by the independent nations of Nepal and Bhutan, but the eastern and western sections belong to India, the latter culminating in the peak of Nanda Devi, which at 7,817 metres (25,646 feet) is India's highest point. North-west of Nanda Devi, below the Karakoram Range, lie the valleys and rivers of Kashmir. This spectacularly beautiful region is the subject of disputed territorial claims between India and Pakistan. The far north-east of India is occupied by Assam. This is the region of the Brahmaputra basin, wedged between the Himalayas and the mountains of the Burmese border.

In north-western India, straddling the border with Pakistan around the 30th parallel, is the Punjab. 'Punjab' means 'land of the five rivers', and it is the five tributaries of the Indus, the Jhelum, Chenab, Ravi, Sutlej and Beas, which prevent drought in the region. Farther south lie the sandy stretches of the Thar Desert, and, on the Tropic of Cancer, the swampy lowland region of the Kutch.

The most fertile region of India is the immense plain drained by the Ganges. This great river is fed by Himalayan snows, and crosses the northern part of India before reaching the sea in Bangladesh, a journey of some 2,500 kilometres (1,553 miles). This is a region of green farmland, of villages and of ancient cities such as Benares (Varanasi), a place of pilgrimage for Hindus. The Ganges is prone to massive flooding.

Above: A miniature of the Moghul period represents the god Krishna, who is dancing while holding a lotus flower. Right: The Golden Temple of Amritsar, a centre of the Sikh religion, was founded in about 1500 by the Guru Nanak. It was the centre of a bitter battle between Sikh separatists and government forces in 1984. Below: Fishing boats line the harbour at Bombay, the major port of the Arabian Sea.

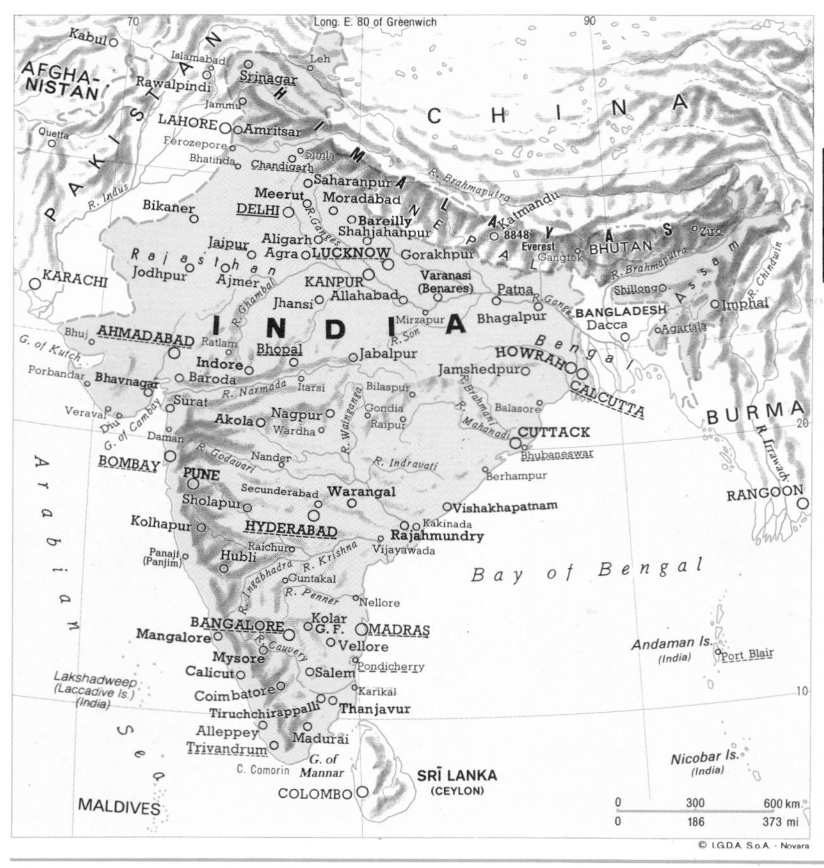

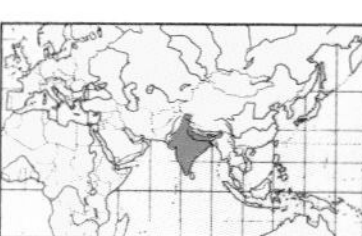

Area:
3,287,590 km² (1,269,415 mi²)
Population:
685,184,000
Capital:
Delhi (6,222,000)
Other towns:
Calcutta, Bombay, Madras, Hyderabad, Ahmadabad, Bangalore, Kanpur, Poona (Pune), Nagpur, Lucknow, Howrah, Jaipur
Currency:
rupee

The main part of India below the Vindhya range is taken up by the Deccan. This huge plateau rises to the west. It is bordered on both sides by mountains, namely the Western Ghats and the Eastern Ghats (*ghat* means step). The central part of the Deccan is hot and often suffers from drought.

Varied climatic conditions exist in India, giving rise to greatly varying ways of life. In the north, the climate is affected by altitude, with harsh, freezing winters and cool summers, although the valleys of Kashmir have a rather milder climate. Elsewhere in India, the climate is conditioned by the monsoons. The monsoons are winds that change direction with the seasons, in accordance with differences in temperature and pressure that occur between the land mass of southern Asia and the waters of the Indian and Pacific Oceans.

From October to March, winds blow across India from a high air pressure system over the interior of the continent to the sea. These are cool, dry winds, giving a pleasant climate. The weather in Delhi in January is rather like that of a warm spring day in west-central Europe. But from March to May, temperatures rise and the weather becomes more oppressive every day. As the hot air rises, a low pressure system is created and masses of cool air from the ocean are sucked on to the land. Around June, the first sea breezes herald the arrival of the summer monsoons, which last until October. As the winds carry rain inland, they encounter the barriers of the mountain ranges. As they rise, they shed their moisture in torrential downpours. The Western Ghats are the first to receive the monsoons, from the Arabian Sea. The rains then reach eastern India, in Assam, and Bangladesh. Regions not affected by the monsoons, such as the central part of the Deccan and the Thar Desert, suffer from perennial drought.

The pattern of the monsoons is irregular. There are some years when little rain falls and drought and famine afflict many areas. In other years, the storms are so violent that they wreak havoc with widespread flooding. The rains are eagerly awaited, but also feared, although India depends on the monsoons for its survival.

India is a land with an ancient culture, a land with a brilliant record of continuous civilization, and a cradle of people and religions. Remains of *Ramapithecus,* perhaps one of our earliest ancestors, have been unearthed in the Siwalik Hills. Agriculture reached India in about 5000 BC, and, by 2300 BC, the sub-continent's first great civilization had arisen, in the Indus valley of modern Pakistan. The original Indians were those of the Dravidian group, with dark skins.

In about 1800 BC, fair-skinned Aryans began invading the sub-continent. Originating in the Caspian area, these Aryans were an Indo-European people related to the Hellenic, Latin, Germanic and Celtic peoples. Their language was Sanskrit, a distant relative of the principal tongues of Europe, which still forms the basis of most of the 15 languages and 800 or so dialects of modern India. The Aryan charioteers and archers drove the Dravidians to the south of India.

The subsequent history of India represents a mixture of the Aryan and Dravidian cultures. One of the most salient aspects of Indian cultural tradition is an interest in religious meditation, from which arose two of the world's greatest faiths, Hinduism and Buddhism. Buddhism is now practised primarily in eastern and south-eastern Asia, whilst Hinduism remains the principal religion of India. Other religions of modern India include Islam, Parseeism, Jainism, Sikhism, and Christianity.

One aspect of the Hindu faith, which has had a profound effect on social development in India, is the division of society into exclusive sections, or 'castes'. There are four principal castes and thousands of sub-castes: the Brahmins (priests); the Kshatriyas (warriors and rulers); the Vaisyas (merchants and farmers); and the Sudras (workers and peasants). Below these are the outcastes, or Untouchables, who are now, in a more enlightened age, referred to as the Harijan, 'the children of god'. Caste distinction is now officially abolished, but its effects linger on, being responsible for many social injustices.

Another religious doctrine with social repercussions has been that of the 'transmigration of souls'. This is the belief that, after death, each individual is re-born in the form of superior or inferior beings, such as animals, according to his or her conduct in the previous life. This doctrine results in a profound respect for all living things. Cows are sacred and may not be killed – an important consideration in a land so regularly stricken by famine.

The Macedonian general Alexander the Great crossed the Indus in 326 BC and defeated King Porus and his formidable array of 200 elephants on the Jhelum, or Hydaspes. But his troops turned back westward, and India was left alone. A number of powerful kingdoms thrived in India during the classical period. The Mauryan king of the third century BC, Ashoka, made Buddhism the official religion and established the rule of law. His statutes were carved upon a pillar that today has become the emblem of India. The same region flourished once again under the Gupta dynasty (AD 320–500). Hinduism flourished under Gupta rule. Many of the great cultural and artistic achievements of this dynasty survive today.

The next wave of invaders from the north had more impact than Alexander. Inspired by the new faith of Islam, Arabs poured in in the eighth century. By the 13th century, they had established the Sultanate of Delhi, which fell in 1526, to Babur (Zahir ud-Din Mohammed), a descendant of the Mongol conqueror Tamburlaine. He established Moghul rule in India and presided over a glittering court. Moghul miniature painting and craft work is unsurpassed in its intricacy and delicacy.

Stories of the wealth of India aroused European interest in the region. Merchant caravans brought back stories of jewels and peacocks along with the spices and textiles that they traded. Portugal was the first to find a sea route to this promised land, when Vasco da Gama made landfall at Calicut on 20 May 1498. The Portuguese, Dutch, French and English secured bases on the Indian coast.

The East India Company, founded by the English in 1600, secured a commercial monopoly, and profited from the decline of the Moghul Empire to achieve military and political rule over most of the region. Rivalry with the French led to war. The Company was abolished in the 19th century, following a mutiny of Indian troops, or *sepoys* in 1857. On the death of the last Moghul emperor, power passed to the British crown, which ruled by a viceroy, while allowing *rajahs* and *maharajahs,* the regional rulers, to retain their authority – a power more nominal than actual. In 1877, Queen Victoria assumed the title of Empress of India.

The British government carried out many much needed public works in India. An extensive rail network was built which, today, is the country's principal transportation system. Western technology was introduced. An educational system was started, and a civil service established. But Britain failed to come to terms with many of India's essential problems, and grew rich at the expense of the poverty-stricken masses. Currents of nationalist feeling became evident, which found a spokesman of great moral standing in Mohandas Karamchand Gandhi (1869–1948). This much-loved patriot became known to his countrymen and the world as *Mahatma* ('great soul'). Gandhi was a great advocate of non-violent protest as the chief weapon of the struggle for independence. He believed that the future of India should develop from its traditional centre, the village, and encouraged the practice of self-sufficient cottage industries, such as spinning. Gandhi's activities contributed significantly to the final withdrawal by the British, which occurred in 1947.

Unfortunately, the achievement of independence was marred by consider-

Below: The extremely beautiful, peaceful valleys of Kashmir are bordered by the snowy peaks of the Himalayas. They are grazed by domesticated animals. The soft undercoat of Kashmir goats provides a wool of the highest quality, famous throughout the world.

India is a land of dazzling colours. Left: Wreaths of marigolds are sold in the main square of Jaipur. Below: A seller of incense and brilliant vegetable dyes exhibits his wares. Right: The mysterious East is exemplified by a snake charmer mesmerizing a swaying cobra. The wildlife of the Indian sub-continent is prolific, including many species of snake, deer and the increasingly rare tiger. Below right: Needles for cleaning the ear are part of the equipment of a street masseur. India is famous for its traditional medicines and its techniques of yoga.

able strife and bloodshed as Muslims and Hindus clashed over the vexed question of partition. The predominantly Islamic areas of the country in the north-east and north-west became the separate state of Pakistan, although the north-eastern region eventually broke away to become Bangladesh. India's relations with Pakistan remained strained, sometimes escalating into armed conflict. The chief architect of the new India was a follower of Gandhi's, Jawaharlal Nehru, known as *Pandit* or 'sage'. His daughter, Indira Gandhi, later became Prime Minister. A skilful international diplomat, her domestic policies caused frequent unrest. She was assassinated by Sikh separatists in 1984, and succeeded by her son Rajiv.

Today the Republic of India is a Union of States within the Commonwealth made up of 21 states and 9 Union territories. It has retained a democratic system of government with two houses of parliament. Official languages are Hindi and English. Recognized languages are Bengali, Gujarati, Assamese, Punjabi, Tamil, Urdu, Telegu, Sindhi, Sanskrit, Marathi, Malayalam, Kannanda, Kashmiri and Oriya.

The tasks that confront India today are immense. A sequence of five-year economic plans was initiated by Nehru. Great progress has been made. The amount of irrigated land had been virtually doubled, as has the production of cereals and pulses. India is the world's largest producer of groundnuts, jute, millet and tea and one of the world's top four producers of coconuts, rice, sorghum, sugar-cane, tobacco and wheat. Mineral resources include coal (of which India is the world's sixth largest producer); iron; manganese; bauxite, and oil (still in modest proportions).

Energy sources have been developed to power industry. Iron and steel have a primary place, and there is a considerable engineering industry. Textiles are one of India's chief exports, cotton having played a crucial role in India's economy throughout its history. Paradoxically in this traditional, predominantly agricultural country, the nuclear industry is one of the most advanced in the world. Although unable to feed its own inhabitants adequately, India may have a nuclear bomb.

The great economic advances India has made will, however, be in vain if the population continues to grow at its present alarming rate of 2·5 per cent per year (1971–81). It already totals nearly seven hundred million and was increasing by about 18 million every year in the late 1970s. As a result, the struggle against poverty and unemployment becomes ever more difficult. Stricken by famine and starvation, the poor crowd into such great cities as Calcutta and Bombay. There they eke out a wretched existence in squalid slums and shanty towns. Many simply make their homes on the streets, where they live and die. In an attempt to curb the population explosion, the government has instituted a number

Top: The minarets and domes of the city of Hyderabad reveal that it was an ancient centre of Islamic culture. It was founded in 1589 in the heart of the Deccan plateau. Today it is an important centre of communications. Above: Bicycles, scooters, oxcarts, and rickshaws jam the streets of India's capital, Delhi. New Delhi is India's seat of government.

of vigorous campaigns for birth control and voluntary sterilization. Modernization of agriculture must also be a priority if India is to feed its teeming millions.

The capital of India is Delhi, in the north, a city of more than four million inhabitants. It is an administrative and business centre and the seat of government. Old Delhi consists of a bustling area of commerce and bazaars, while New Delhi is an elegant city of Edwardian architecture, laid out by the British. India's largest city is Calcutta, on the Bay of Bengal, with more than seven million people. Bombay, the great port on the Arabian Sea, has a population of nearly six million.

The growth of population, the modernization of agriculture and industrialization pose a threat to one of India's greatest assets – its unique wildlife. The world of Rudyard Kipling's *Jungle Book* has already all but disappeared. The magnificent tiger is now an endangered species, and receives protection in special reserves. The tough hide of the Indian rhinoceros, a massive creature with a single horn, protects it effectively from other animals, but not from man's destruction of its habitat. India is famous for its snakes, many of which are venomous. Mongooses have long been used in India to attack cobras. Other animals domesticated in India include the Asian or Indian elephant, a more docile beast than its African cousin. No ceremonial parade is complete without an elephant dressed in all its finery.

India is a land of great contrasts. It is a land of priceless architectural treasures, such as the Taj Mahal, and a land of slums and poverty. At the sacred city of Benares, the religious tradition of purification by pilgrims in the waters of the Ganges has remained unchanged over the centuries. But India is also host to modern engineering and technology. It is a land of social turmoil, still practised in the civilized skills of courtesy and hospitality. More than any other country, India seems to symbolize the traditions, problems and aspirations of the Asian continent.

The Indian way of life has spread to many other parts of the world. In ancient times Hindu kingdoms grew up in parts of South-east Asia, and in more recent times India's colonial history resulted in Indian communities being established in the West Indies and in African countries such as Kenya, Uganda, Tanzania, Zimbabwe and South Africa: Gandhi himself, the father of modern India, was trained as a lawyer in South Africa. Many people of Indian origins live in Britain, where Sikh temples are now a common sight and where Indian cuisine is now as familiar to the British palate as fish and chips. Many other Indians live in Canada, and study in the USA. But the centre of Indian culture remains in the Asian subcontinent – an extraordinary, fascinating country. In this land of paradoxes, two-thirds of the people are illiterate, and yet India is a centre of philosophy and religion, which continues to attract people tired of Western materialism.

Indonesia

Republik

Lying on the equator in South-East Asia is the world's largest archipelago. No less than 13,677 islands make up the Republic of Indonesia, and about half of these islands are inhabited. The islands lie scattered across a number of small seas, including the Java Sea, Flores Sea, Banda Sea and the Arafura Sea. To the north is the South China Sea and to the west lies the Indian Ocean.

The climate in this part of the world is warm and humid. The maximum annual temperature is about 33°C (91°F). The monsoon lasts from December to March, and the dry season from May to September. The principal islands of Indonesia are Sumatra, Java, Sulawesi (Celebes), Kalimantan (the large southern section of the island of Borneo), and Irian Jaya (the western half of the island of New Guinea). Much of the archipelago is mountainous, and there are many active volcanoes. One of the most violent eruptions in history occurred on the island of Krakatau (Krakatoa) in 1883. The highest peak is Puncak Jaya, which reaches 5,200 metres (17,060 ft), in Irian Jaya.

The archipelago has been inhabited since the dawn of time. It was in Java that remains of some of our earliest ancestors were discovered – fossils of *Homo erectus* that date back some 500,000 years. The aboriginal peoples of the region became mixed with migrating peoples from the East Asian mainland in the third millennium BC, and from India in the first millennium BC. Today the peoples of the region form a bewilder-

Right: A small Indonesian boy engages the services of the local barber.

Above: In northern Sumatra's hilly country local farmers use the traditional method of terracing hillsides to acquire the maximum area of rich agricultural land.

ing array of ethnic groupings. There are Chinese, Acehnese, Menangkabau, Bataks, Sundanese, Javanese, Balinese, Dayaks, Iban, Wajaks, Ambonese, Iria-nese and many others. Over 200 languages are spoken in Indonesia. The official language, based upon Malay, is known as Bahasa Indonesia. The majority of people are Muslims, but there are also Hindus, Buddhists, Christians and followers of local religious traditions.

Indonesia's position on the Indian Ocean resulted in an influx of settlers from the Indian sub-continent during the European Dark Ages and the medieval period. A succession of Hindu kingdoms were established in the region, and Buddhists from China and India also visited the archipelago. The culmination of the Hindu era was the establishment of the Majapahit Empire, based upon Java. This finally collapsed in the 16th century, and the region became predominantly Muslim.

European interest in the islands began with the Venetian traveller Marco Polo's visit in 1292. The Portuguese and the Spanish soon entered the region in search of spices. Pepper, cloves and nutmeg were rare exotic commodities in Europe 500 years ago, and the trade in them was lucrative. The Dutch followed in the Moluccas and in Java, and the British in Sumatra. Trade prospered, but was accompanied by bitter rivalry between the European traders and harsh repression of the local peoples. Much of Indonesia remained in Dutch hands throughout the colonial era.

An independence movement led by Dr Mohammed Hatta and Achmad Soekarno began to grow up in the 1920s. The region was invaded by Japan during the Second World War. After the war, independence was finally achieved following a further struggle with the Dutch. The Republic of Indonesia was formally established in 1949 under President Soekarno. Irian Jaya was added to its territory in 1963. Soekarno pursued a policy of confrontation with the new state of Malaysia to the north, and fell from effective power after a communist coup failed in 1965. He was succeeded in 1967 by Major-General Soeharto. Soeharto was re-elected for five-year terms in 1968, 1973, 1978 and 1983. The principal parliamentary body is the People's Consultative Assembly.

The traditional way of life in Indonesia revolves around farming. Rice and maize are produced, the former being the staple diet of the region. Spices, including pepper, nutmeg and cloves, are still much in demand. Other food crops include coffee, tea, coconuts, sugar-cane, soya beans, cassava and palm-oil. Timber is widely cultivated or felled in the extensive forests. Tobacco and rubber are also grown.

Mineral resources include coal, tin, copper, nickel and bauxite, but by far the most important for the Indonesian economy is oil. Many areas contain both island and offshore rigs, and there is a refining industry. Oil has funded industrialization. Important sectors include pesticides, fertilizers, paper, textiles, tobacco, food processing, mechanical and chemical engineering, and shipbuilding.

Tourism is a growing industry and such delightful spots as Bali are currently being discovered by tourists from Australia and North America.

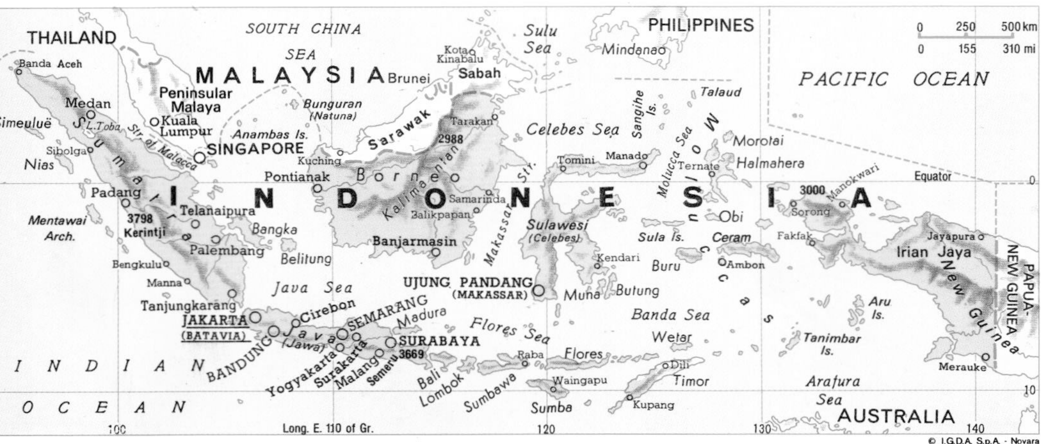

Area:
2,027,087 km²
(782,705 mi²)
Population:
158,000,000
Capital:
Jakarta (pop. 6,506,000)
Other towns:
Surabaya, Bandung, Semarang, Medan, Palembang, Ujung, Pandang (Makassar), Malang, Surakarta
Currency:
rupiah

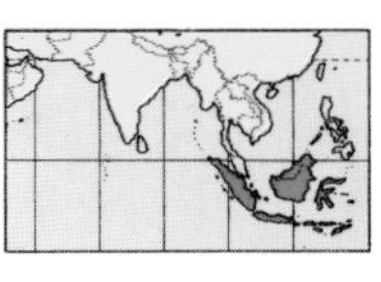

Iran

Until 1935, the Islamic Republic of Iran was still called Persia, linking it to the civilization which had flourished in the region in ancient times. The name Iran had been a geographical rather than a political term, referring to the vast area lying between the Tigris and Indus rivers, the Caspian Sea and the Persian Gulf, including Armeniya, Afghanistan and Uzbekistan. But because Persia occupied the greatest part of this region, the two names had long been synonymous.

The modern nation of Iran has a roughly rectangular shape. The northern frontier is with the USSR, running along the borders of Armeniya, Azerbaydzhan, the Caspian Sea (Daryaye-Khazar) and Turkmeniya. The eastern frontier is with Afghanistan and Pakistan, and the southern coast runs along the Gulf of Oman and the Persian (Arabian) Gulf. The western frontier is with Iraq and Turkey. Iran, therefore, occupies an important strategic position in the modern world, which is made more significant by its great reserves of oil.

Iran is a land of deserts and mountains. To the north of the capital, Tehran, and south of the fertile Caspian shore, is the extended crescent of the Elburz Mountains, reaching a height of 5,671 metres (18,606 feet) above sea level at Mount Damavand, Iran's highest peak. To the south-west lies the Zagros range. In the interior are the desert regions of Dasht-e-Kavir (Great Salt Desert) and Dasht-e-Lut (Great Sand Desert).

The ancient civilization of Persia began in the sixth century BC, with the founding of the Achaemenid dynasty of Cyrus I. The empire rapidly expanded to take in Babylonia, Egypt and Asia Minor. A great flowering of civilization accompanied the conquests, and fine cities and roads were built. Persepolis, the capital founded by Darius I, included magnificent palaces and sculptures. But the Greeks proved harder to conquer. Xerxes I of Persia was the victor at Thermopylae in 480 BC, but was subsequently defeated in a naval battle at Salamis. The Persian Empire finally fell to the Macedonian-Greek army of Alexander the Great, who defeated Darius III at Issus in 333 BC.

Islamic Persia dates from AD 641, when the Arabs conquered the region and spread the new faith, making Persia a leading centre of the arts and sciences. Today most Iranians are still Muslims, mainly of the Shia sect. Turks and Mongols also invaded the country. By the end of the 19th century, Iran was a remote and backward country ruled by the oppressive Shahs of the Qajar dynasty, but falling under the influence of the great powers of the day – the British, Russians and French.

A nationalist movement developed

Iran today and yesterday. Above: An oilfield in the south-western Khuzestan region. Right: The glories of ancient Persia survive today in this bas-relief, which represents Xerxes, son and successor of Darius I, who built Persepolis in about 518 BC.

and the former military officer and prime minister Reza Khan seized power in 1921. In 1925, he was elected Shah by the constituent assembly. He was succeeded in 1941 by his son, Mohammed Reza Shah Pahlavi. Under the Pahlavi dynasty, which claimed the ancient civilization of Persia as its common heritage, the country was modernized. The army was restructured, education made more widely available, and land ownership reformed. The country began to industrialize rapidly, deriving huge revenues from its oil. The West wanted it as an ally because of its strategic importance. However, most people of Iran had little taste for the increasing westernization. Even less to their liking was the corruption of the ruling classes and the government's suppression of all opposition. Particularly hated was the ruthless secret police, Savak.

Rioting in 1979 led to the exile of the Shah, and to the recall of a religious leader, the Ayatollah Ruholla Khomeini, who had lived in exile since 1964. Iran became a fundamentalist Islamic Republic governed by strict religious laws. In 1980, a long war began with neighbouring Iraq.

The problems of modern Iran are immense. Although farming still provides the only means of earning a living for 40 per cent of the workforce, only 10 per cent of the land is cultivated, the greater part of the land being too mountainous or too arid for farming. Crops which are grown include cotton, fruit, rice, sugarbeet, tobacco, vegetables and wheat. Domesticated animals, principally sheep and goats, are reared. There were also 7·6 million cattle in 1980. A typical Iranian meal consists of mutton kebab with rice or unleavened bread.

Industries include fertilizers, plastics, cement, food processing and textiles. Persian rugs have been famous throughout the world for centuries, and the ancient craft of carpet-making continues today. But the lynchpin of the Iranian economy is oil, which accounted for more than half of the gross domestic product in 1978. Iran's huge oilfields are in the south-west of the country and, in 1981, Iran was the second largest oil producer in south-western Asia after Saudi Arabia. However, in the two years following the 1979 revolution, production dropped by about two-fifths. The entire oil industry is now nationalized.

The official language of Iran is Farsi, or Persian. The Iranian people are Aryan in origin. Minorities within the country include the Kurds, whose territories straddle the borders of Turkey, Iraq, Iran and the USSR. The Kurds have long been involved in a struggle for the formation of an independent Kurdish state. In the far south-east, across the border with Pakistan, is the homeland of the Baluchis. About 2,000,000 Iranians are nomads, who move their camels and tents with the seasons in search of pasture for their herds.

About half of the population lives in urban areas. Iran's capital, Tehran, is its largest city, with nearly $4\frac{1}{2}$ million inhabitants. It is situated in the north on the main route between Tabriz and Mashhad, a holy city famous for its mosque. Shirāz in the south-west is near the site of the ancient capital of the Achaemenid dynasty, Persopolis, whose ruins are a tourist attraction, particularly the Throne Hall of Xerxes, and the Palace of Darius I.

Above: A minaret in Esfahan.

Below: Iranian girls strolling in the streets of Esfahan wear the traditional chador. *Esfahan is one of Iran's most beautiful cities, famous for its magnificent carpets and its mosque.*

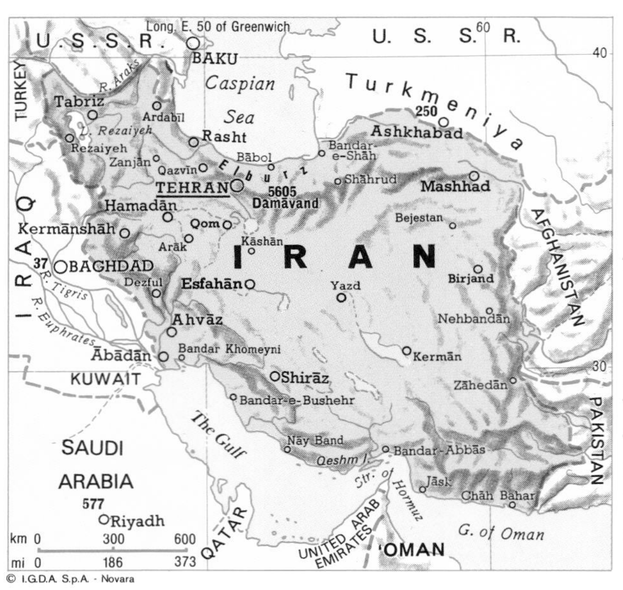

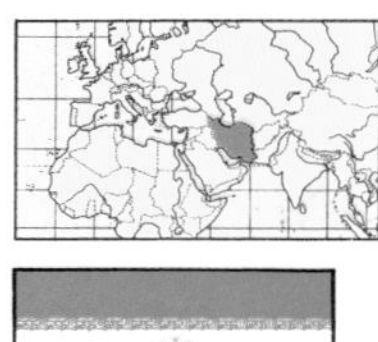

Area:
1,648,000 km²
(636,331 mi²)

Population:
43,830,000

Capital:
Tehran (pop. 4,496,000)

Other towns:
Esfahān, Mashhad, Tabriz, Shirāz, Ahvāz

Currency:
rial

Iraq

al Jumhouriya al'Iraqia

The earliest civilizations we know of grew up along the great rivers of the Middle East. The ancient land of Mesopotamia (the eastern part of the Republic of Iraq) saw the rise of the great Sumerian civilization along the rivers Tigris and Euphrates about 5000 BC. This fertile land gave rise to the Biblical story of a 'Garden of Eden'. Mesopotamia was the site of Ur of the Chaldees, of Babylon and of Nineveh, capital of the powerful Assyrian Empire.

By the early seventh century AD, the whole of this region was invaded by Arabs. With them came the new faith of Islam. The Caliphate of Baghdad became the centre of the Islamic world, and, under such renowned rulers as Haroun Al-Raschid (763–809), it became a famous centre of culture and learning. Later invaders were the Mongols and Turks. Until 1923, Iraq was part of the Turkish Ottoman Empire.

Iraq then became an independent monarchy. But upon the assassination of King Feisal II in 1958, the country became a republic, with a succession of military rulers. In 1980, under President Saddam Hussein, Iraq became involved in a war with Iran.

Most people in modern Iraq are Arabic in origin, although there is a large minority of Kurds in the north. The Kurdish people live across the borders of five countries. In Iraq, as elsewhere, they have struggled for autonomy for many years and there was fighting in the 1960s and early 1970s.

Much of Iraq is desert. The western borders with Syria and Jordan and the southern borders with Saudi Arabia take in a great sweep of empty desert. To the north and east, along the Turkish and Iranian borders, Iraq is hemmed in by mountains. To the south is a large area of marshland and waterways. But running down the centre of the country is the great fertile plain of ancient Mesopotamia, watered by the Tigris and Euphrates.

Irrigation is used to aid agriculture, and this enables the cultivation of cereal crops, rice and dates. Livestock production provides wool and skins for export. Industry in modern Iraq is growing apace. Both farming and factories are subsidized by the chief source of the country's income, oil. There are oilfields at Basra, Khanaqin and Kirkuk. A petrochemical industry is being developed.

Baghdad is the capital of Iraq, situated on the River Tigris in the central Mesopotamian region. It is linked by railway and road to the cities of Mosul in the north of the country and to Basra in the south. An oil pipeline runs westwards into Syria, and a railway runs from Mosul along the Turkish-Syrian border to Aleppo.

Above: An old bridge across the Euphrates reminds us of the remarkable history of Iraq.
Below: A ruined palace at Samarra.

Area:
434,924 km²
(167,934 mi²)
Population:
14,000,000

Capital:
Baghdad (pop. 3,206,000)
Other towns:
Basra, Mosul, Kirkuk
Currency:
dinar

Israel

Medinat Israel

The State of Israel (Medinat Israel) is a Middle Eastern nation on the Mediterranean Sea. It includes most of what was once called Palestine and it shares frontiers with Egypt, Jordan, Syria and Lebanon. The coast of Israel consists of a low-lying plain, the site of such large cities as Tel Aviv-Yafo and Haifa. Inland the terrain rises to the hill country of Galilee, Judea and Samaria. Har Meron to the north of Lake Tiberias is Israel's highest peak, at 1,208 metres (3,963 feet) above sea level. To the east, the land drops abruptly to the valley of the Jordan. Included within Israeli territory to the south-west of Jerusalem, the capital, is a corner of the Dead Sea. This extraordinary lake lies 392 metres (1,286 feet) below sea level. The Jordan is the chief of the rivers which flow into it, but evaporation is so intense that no water flows out of it. Its water is saturated with mineral salts. The southern part of Israel is wedge-shaped, and consists of the Negev Desert, a burning hot wasteland of sand. The borders converge at Elat (Eilat), a port and tourist resort on the Gulf of Aqaba.

Jerusalem is the holy city of three faiths – Judaism, Christianity and Islam. To many people, this region has been known variously as the 'Promised Land' or the 'Holy Land'. It has always been held in special respect, and its religious significance has, over the ages, resulted in a history of strife and bloodshed, as well as in the fruits of civilization.

The story of the region in ancient times has been made familiar by the books of the Old Testament. The Hebrew people (also known as Israelites or Jews) fled slavery under the Egyptian pharaohs and, in about 1200 BC, settled the hills to the west of the Jordan River, a land that they believed had been promised them by God. There were 12 tribes of Israel, and eventually they divided to form two separate kingdoms, Israel and Judea. The Kingdom of Israel was destroyed by Assyria in 721 BC, but Judea survived, albeit under successive overlords: the Babylonians, the Persians, the Greeks, and the Romans.

Jesus Christ lived at a time when Israel was under the rule of Rome. Revered by his followers as the Son of God, he was never accepted as such by the priests of his homeland, and they encouraged the authorities to have him put to death as a political agitator. Christianity became one of the great faiths of the world. Rebellion against Rome came in AD 66, but the rising was drowned in blood within four years. The Jewish nation was destroyed and its people scattered or enslaved. After the death of the Prophet Mohammed in AD 632, the Arabs, a Semitic people like the Jews, brought the Islamic faith to the region. During the Middle Ages, the Christian lands of Europe repeatedly attempted to expel the Muslims from what they regarded as the 'Holy Land'. The Crusaders met with some success. But, in the end, the region remained Islamic, and became part of the Turkish Ottoman Empire.

Palestine, as this region had become known, had been largely an Arab country for more than 1,000 years when the first Jewish settlers began to return at the end of the 19th century, fleeing persecution in Russia and elsewhere. They were inspired by Zionism, the aim of which was to establish once again a homeland for the Jews. The settlers were at first received without hostility by the Palestinian Arabs. This was partly because the economy benefited by the Jewish immigration. The new arrivals were well provided with money and technical expertise and they made regions flourish which had for centuries remained uncultivated.

In the First World War, Turkey joined with the other Central Powers against the Allies. However, British forces with Arab support overthrew Turkish authority in Palestine, and the region came under a British mandate. In 1917 the British foreign secretary Lord Balfour made a declaration which promised the Zionists a homeland in Palestine. The influx of refugees increased following the terrible persecution of the Jews unleashed in Nazi Germany in the 1930s. When the Second World War ended, the full horror of this holocaust was realized. Survivors of the concentration camps began to struggle into Palestine. In 1948 the British mandate ended. After a Jewish terrorist campaign, the Republic of Israel was proclaimed on 14 May.

By now the number of Jews was greater than that of the Palestinian Arabs, and tension between the two communities escalated into open conflict. The Arab countries surrounding the new nation came to the support of the Palestinian Arabs, but Israel managed to survive. Further wars were fought against the Arabs in 1956, 1967 and 1973. In 1979 President Anwar-as-Sadat of Egypt and Prime Minister Menachem Begin of Israel signed a peace agreement. But in 1982 an Israeli offensive against Palestinian camps in Lebanon transpired to be a major invasion of that country, and the city of Beirut was devastated. It was three years before the Israelis began to withdraw from Lebanon, leaving absolute chaos behind them.

Israel does not have well-defined borders with her Arab neighbours, but rather lines of demarcation which roughly correspond with ceasefire lines. Occupied territory includes a strip of strategic Syrian territory, the Golan Heights, and Jordanian land on the West Bank of the River Jordan. The problem of Palestinian refugees is today more pressing than ever. While the Israelis have built themselves a nation, the Palestinian Arabs feel dispossessed, without a homeland. For more than 30 years, the Palestinians have been compelled to seek refuge in neighbouring Arab states, living in large camps, and fighting for recognition of their right to self-determination. Their efforts have in the past ranged from terrorism to international diplomacy.

Opposite: The Mount of Olives in Jerusalem. The political and cultural centre of Israel, Jerusalem was declared the capital in 1950, although is not internationally recognized as such. Right: The town of Nazareth, where Jesus Christ spent his boyhood.

Despite this explosive situation, Israel is a prosperous and developed country. Since the founding of the nation, agriculture has made extraordinary progress. A large amount of land has been brought under cultivation and desert regions have been reclaimed. Cereals, citrus fruits, cotton, olives, tobacco and vegetables are grown. Cattle, poultry and fish farming are also practised. Farming co-operatives, known as *kibbutzim,* have been established. In these co-operatives, agricultural equipment and the organizing of the sale of produce are shared. The industrial sector of the economy is technologically advanced, with diamonds, textiles, food processing and **fertilizers playing an important role. Inflation proved to be a major problem in the 1980s.**

The urban centres are in a state of constant growth, and the population is boosted by continual waves of immigrants. Any Jew wishing to settle in Israel is welcomed. In 1940 the Jewish population of Israel was half a million. Today it has increased by more than six times. The most important city is Tel Aviv, founded in 1909 beside the port of Yafo (Jaffa), with which it has now merged. The capital is at Jerusalem, although this status is not recognized by the United Nations Organization (UNO). The major port is in the north, at Haifa, a major industrial centre.

The state of Israel is a republic. The parliament has one chamber, known as the *Knesset.*

The Knesset has 120 members. They are elected by universal suffrage, for a four-year term. The country is headed by a President, who is elected by the Knesset, for a five-year term.

An extraordinarily high portion of the population, 89 per cent in 1980, lives in urban areas. In 1979 Israel had 141 hospitals and highly developed social services; the life expectancy at birth is 72 years. The high rate of population increase, 2·3 per cent a year, is caused partly by continuing immigration.

Below: The city of Tel Aviv-Yafo (Jaffa). This great conurbation on the Mediterranean shore is an important commercial centre.

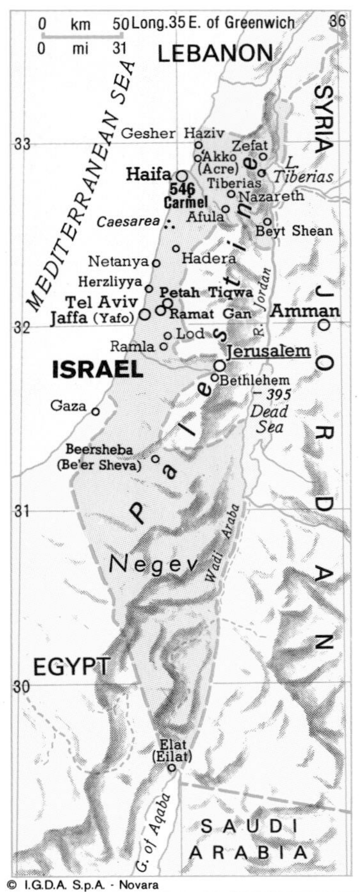

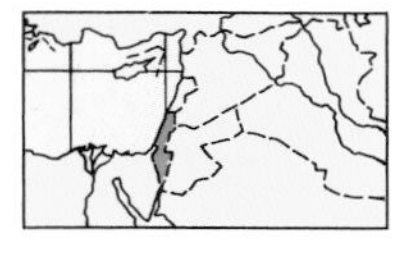

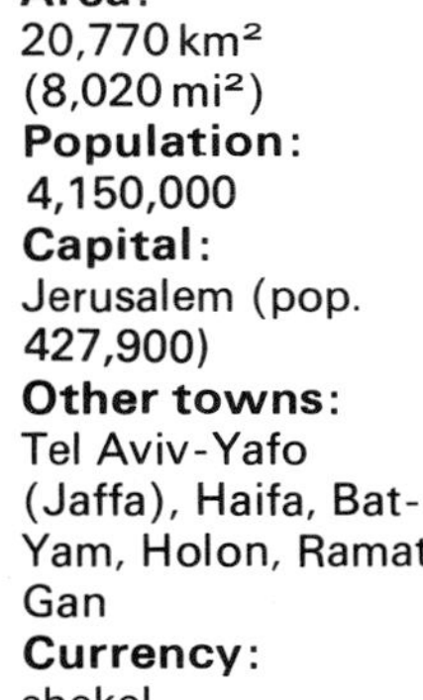

Area: 20,770 km² (8,020 mi²)
Population: 4,150,000
Capital: Jerusalem (pop. 427,900)
Other towns: Tel Aviv-Yafo (Jaffa), Haifa, Bat-Yam, Holon, Ramat Gan
Currency: shekel

Japan

Nippon

The first European to travel in the Far East was the Venetian Marco Polo, who visited China in the 13th century. He refers to islands east of China as Cipangu. The Chinese name was *Jih-pen-kuo,* or 'land of the rising sun'. Today the Japanese use this same name, *Nihon Koku* in Japanese, for their country. This poetic name is reflected in the country's flag, which shows a bright red sun on a white background.

The Japanese archipelago stretches in a bow shape from the island of Sakhalin (which belongs to the USSR) to the Korea Strait. To the east, Japan faces the open ocean of the Pacific. To the west, its picturesque coastline encloses the Sea of Japan. There are four main islands, the largest of which is Honshū. To the north is Hokkaidō. To the south-west are Shikoku and Kyūshū. There are some 3,000 small islands.

The archipelago is mountainous. The only flat area of any size is on the eastern coast of Honshū, the site of Tōkyō, Japan's capital. Japan is studded with volcanoes, which number 165, about 59 of which are active. The most famous is Fujiyama, or Mount Fuji, which is sacred to Japanese Buddhists. It is Japan's highest mountain, at 3,776 metres (12,388 feet), and its immense crater measures about 22 kilometres (14 miles) across. The volcanoes lend a unique beauty to the Japanese landscape, but they also present a continual threat, as do earthquakes, which are common. The eastern coast particularly is subject to tidal waves (*tsunami*) and typhoons. Japan is a stormy country with a rainy, monsoon climate, and it has had a stormy history.

The first emperor of Japan is said to have been Jimmu, who came to power in 660 BC. Excavations at Toro, near Shizuoka, have revealed an advanced agricultural settlement of the Yayoi period, probably belonging to the first century AD. The people of Toro worked in the paddy fields, and life in Japan continued to revolve around the rice harvest throughout much of its history. The Shinto religion of early Japan centred upon belief in nature spirits and ancestor worship. Buddhism arrived from China in the sixth century AD, and brought with it an influx of Chinese culture. In AD 794, the imperial capital was established at Kyōtō. As in Europe, society developed along feudal lines, with powerful families of the nobility perpetually vying for power.

Above: The sacred Mount Fuji, a volcanic peak of 3,776 metres (12,388 feet) above sea level.

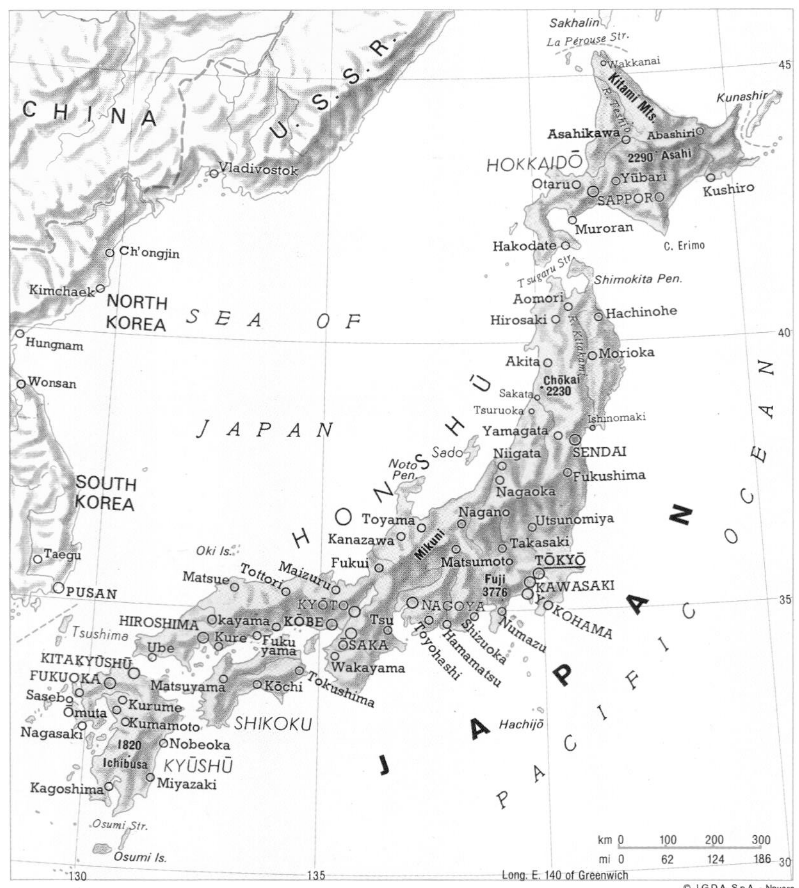

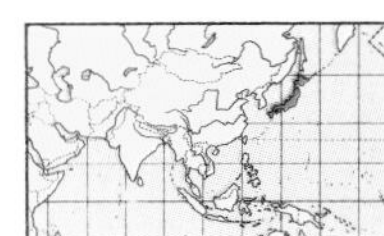

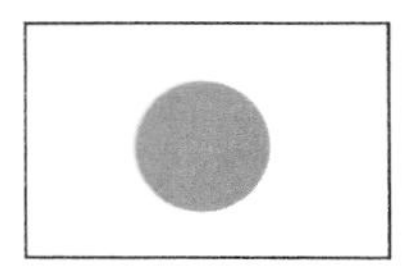

Area:
372,313 km² (143,759 mi²)
Population:
120,055,000
Capital:
Tokyo (pop. 11,807,000)
Other towns:
Yokohama, Ōsaka, Nagoya, Kyōtō, Sapporo, Kōbe, Kita-Kyūshū, Kawasaki, Fukuoka, Hiroshima, Sakai, Chiba, Sendai, Okayama, Amagasaki, Higashiosaka
Currency:
yen

These feudal lords, belonging to 260 clans in all, were known as *daimyo*. Next in the feudal hierarchy were the retainers or *samurai*, who held land or other allowances in fief. The *samurai* formed the military class. Their magnificent armour and weapons can be seen in museums throughout the world. The rest of the population consisted of craftsmen, peasants and merchants, who lived in a state of total subjection to the omnipotent *daimyo*. Japanese society was strict and harsh, with a rigid code of honour. By the 17th century, painting, literature, calligraphy and ceramics were all flourishing.

Japan remained free of European contact until the Portuguese arrived in the 16th century, and started to spread the Christian gospel. But the excessive zeal of the Jesuit missionaries sparked off resentment. In 1638, all foreigners were expelled, and Japan remained a closed society until the mid-19th century when the major powers sought to open up trade with Japan.

In 1868, the young emperor Mutsuhito curbed the power of the feudal lords, and earned the support of the middle classes and intellectuals. There began a period of reform and modernization. To emphasise the break with the past, the capital was transferred from Kyōtō to Edo, which was renamed Tōkyō. The first railway was built in 1872, between Tōkyō and Yokohama. In 1889, the emperor granted a Constitution and summoned a parliament. However, he retained the 'divine' nature with which he was traditionally acclaimed. For the first time, young Japanese left the country to study abroad. Westernization was rapid. In a few decades, Japan's society changed in ways so fundamental that they would have taken centuries elsewhere.

The new outward-looking, powerful Japan soon felt tempted to expand its territories. In 1894, Japanese penetration of Korea led to a war with China, as a result of which Japan acquired large territorial gains. The European powers began to be alarmed by Japanese intentions. Tsarist Russia felt its control of Manchuria to be under threat. War broke out in 1904, and again, in spite of the obvious disproportions in strength, Japan shocked the world. The Japanese beat the Russians on land at Mukden and on sea at Tsushima.

Japan annexed Korea in 1910. In the First World War, Japan sided with the Allies against the Central Powers. In the 1930s, Japan again turned its attention to China, which was torn apart by internal conflict and was virtually undefended against external attack. Despite the con-

Top: The city of Hiroshima today. Devastated by the first atomic bomb in 1945, the town has been completely rebuilt. Above: The Olympic stadium in Tōkyō, designed by the architect Kenzo Tange. Left: Japanese architecture of a previous age. This Buddhist temple was built in 1053 in the old Japanese capital of Kyōtō,

demnation of the League of Nations (the predecessor of the United Nations Organization), Japan annexed Manchuria and part of Mongolia. In 1937 Japanese soldiers in Manchuria launched a major invasion of China.

In the Second World War, Japan found allies in Italy and Germany, totalitarian nations which shared its aggressive and provocative aims. Before declaring war and in breach of international law, Japan attacked the United States fleet at Pearl Harbor, on 7 December 1941, so involving the USA in a protracted war in the Pacific. Japan rapidly advanced through eastern Asia, occupying the Malayan peninsula, Burma, the Dutch East Indies and the Philippines. But gradually the Allied counter-offensive reversed the situation. In July 1945, after the fall of Nazi Germany, the victors invited Japan to surrender. They were met with a refusal.

In response, the Allies took a step which was to change the course of world history. The Americans had developed a terrible new weapon, the atomic bomb. On 6 August 1945, the first of these bombs was dropped on Hiroshima. Three days later a second was dropped on Nagasaki. The cities were gutted and whole populations annihilated. A terrible firestorm swept across the sky. The survivors of these attacks could not be described as lucky, because many died long, slow deaths caused by radiation sickness. The atomic age had arrived. Japanese surrender followed rapidly.

Surrender found Japan reduced to its present size, having lost all its overseas territories. It was disarmed, occupied, and scarred by its experiences. Under US supervision, the fanatical militarists gave way to democratic government. The emperor Hirohito remained as a symbol of the state, but he had no governing powers and was no longer considered 'divine'. Instead, he presided over a new Japan with a democratic Constitution. From 1947 onwards, this Constitution allowed for free elections, with the legislative power belonging to the Diet. The Diet is made up of a House of Representatives, and a House of Councillors. Executive power is entrusted to a cabinet of ministers.

Most of the political life in post-war Japan has been dominated by the conservatives of the Liberal Democratic Party. Other parties represented today

Top: Contestants line up for a bout of Sumo wrestling, a traditional sport of Japan. Centre: A jizo *group in the Kyomizu Deva temple at Kyōto. These are protective deities devoted to children. Right: The traditional transport of the Far East, the rickshaw, is still to be seen.*

include Japan Socialists, Democratic Socialists, Komeito, Communists, and New Liberals. The rebirth of Japan from the ashes of the Second World War began with the support of the USA, who saw the country as the most effective bulwark against the Communist regime in China. The importance of Japan to the USA was confirmed during the Korean War (1950–53). When the American occupying forces withdrew in 1952, the economic revival of the country was already under way. Since then it has progressed dramatically.

Economic recovery was accompanied by political recognition. Treaties were signed in the 1950s with India and South Korea, and peace was made with the Soviet Union, although there remained territorial disagreements with the latter over the Kurile Islands. In 1968 the USA returned to Japan the Bonin Islands, the Marcus Islands and Volcano Islands. Ten years later a treaty of friendship was signed between Japan and the People's Republic of China, Japan's old enemy.

Today Japan shares third place with West Germany in the world economic league, after the USA and the USSR. It is the most industrialized and successful country in Asia. The extraordinarily energetic Japanese have once again proved their ability to adapt rapidly to change. The industrial development seems even more astounding when the scarcity of natural resources is considered. Japan has small quantities of coal, lead, sulphur and zinc, but hardly enough to meet demand, and so raw materials must be imported. Industrial success has been based principally upon a spirit of initiative and an abundant supply of cheap labour. In Japan, the large companies are powerful, paternalistic organizations which the individual is expected to serve with complete loyalty. The extensive introduction of automation and new technology has enabled Japan to make goods at competitive prices and so to conquer markets throughout the world. Japanese industry is particularly successful in the fields of micro-electronics, household electrical goods, including television sets, cars and motor cycles, and shipbuilding. The textile and chemical industries are also important. Japan's economic expansion has in recent years led to some concern among its

Top: Skyscrapers dominate the skyline of Ōsaka, a rapidly developing town with more than $2\frac{1}{2}$ million inhabitants. Japanese women have in the past played a rather subservient role in society. Today they are as likely to be working in a factory, far left, as performing the ancient ritual of the tea ceremony, left, but even so traditions remain strong in modern Japan.

Above: This magnificent painted and gilded figure is the guardian of the temple at a Buddhist sanctuary in the town of Nikko. Left: A painting on silk by the great Masanobu (1434–1530), who founded the Kanō school. Right: A kabuki *actor.* Kabuki *is a form of theatre popular in Japan since the 17th century.*

western allies, who are anxious about Japan's import policies and its erosion of their traditional markets. But despite minor differences, Japan continues to be respected for its determination and versatility, and its remarkable economic recovery.

Only one-seventh of Japan's land area is cultivated, because much of the countryside is mountainous. The forests, which cover nearly 70 per cent of Japan, provide timber and lacquer. Farming is of an intense kind, using fertilizers and machinery to exploit the soil's resources to the maximum. The main crop is rice, which has always been the country's staple food. Cereals, fruit, potatoes and tobacco are cultivated. Tea is the national drink, and is widely grown. The drinking of tea is often turned into an elaborate and ancient ritual, the tea ceremony. Cattle and pigs are important and about 2,000,000 Japanese are engaged in the fishing industry, which provides another major source of food. However, Japan has to import food.

Agriculture. including fishing, employed 12 per cent of the workforce in 1980, as compared with 33 per cent in 1960. This rapid change is an indication of how fast Japan has been changing because of continuing industrialization. In consequence, agriculture now accounts for only 4 per cent of the gross national product.

Tōkyō, Japan's capital, is one of the world's largest cities, with more than 11 million inhabitants. A vigorous birth control campaign and economic success has reduced the birth rate dramatically in the last 30 years, but even so Japan remains a densely populated country. And the extensive industrialization has caused ecological problems, such as pollution. In the neighbourhood of Tōkyō are two other major cities, with more than 5,000,000 inhabitants between them: Yokohama and Kawasaki. Most of Japan's major cities are on Honshū island, and another major centre of population is around Ōsaka and Kōbe. Japan is linked by a modern communications network, and was the pioneer of high-speed rail travel.

Despite its modern faces, Japan remains in many ways a traditional country, still fond of tradition and ceremony. The Shinto and Buddhist religions are still practised. The Japanese mostly belong to a single Mongoloid ethnic group, but in the north are the Caucasoid Ainu people, who have lived in this region for at least 7,000 years. The Japanese language belongs to the Uro-Altaic group, and its characters derive from the Chinese.

Jordan

The Hashemite Kingdom of

The Hashemite Kingdom of the Jordan is an Arab state in the Middle East, bordered by Syria, Iraq, Saudi Arabia and Israel. Jordanian territory on the west bank of the River Jordan has been occupied by Israel since 1967. The west of the country, including the Jordan valley and the surrounding hills, is fertile, producing grain, vegetables, fruit and olives. New irrigation projects have extended the areas of cultivation. But to the east lie the sandy and stony wastes of the desert, crossed only by a few nomadic Bedouin. Most Jordanians are Arabs. Jordan has few mineral resources, but a phosphate industry is being developed and there is an oil refinery at Zarqa. Phosphates are the chief export.

This largely inhospitable region has been inhabited since ancient times. Following the era of the Old Testament, the region was occupied by Greece and Rome, and then by Arabs upon the rise of Islam in the seventh century AD. The Ottoman Empire of the Turks then controlled the region until the end of the First World War. In 1921 the region came under British mandate. In 1946, Transjordan, as the kingdom was at first called, became independent and the present name was adopted in 1949, three years before King Hussein acceded to the throne.

The years of independence have been marked by hostility towards the new nation of Israel, by the tragic series of wars which have destroyed the peace of the Middle East since 1948, and by the problems created by the Palestinian refugees.

The capital of Jordan is Amman, which is linked by road and rail to Zarqa and Mafraq in the north, and the port and tourist resort of Aqaba in the south. The country is crossed by an oil pipeline which runs from Saudi Arabia to the Lebanese coast.

Area:
97,740 km² (37,740 mi²)
Population:
3,500,000
Capital:
Amman (pop. 1,238,000)
Other towns:
Zarqa, Irbid
Currency:
dinar

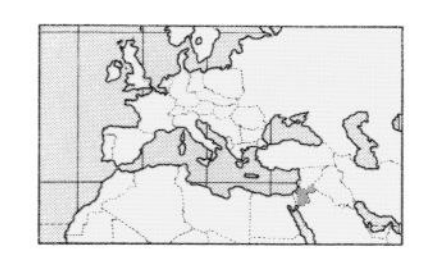

Right: In many parts of Jordan, life is much the same as it was two thousand years ago, at the time of Christ.

Korea

North and South

The Korean peninsula stretches southwards towards Japan from the mainland of northern China, near the Soviet border. The eastern coastline is on the Sea of Japan, and the intricate, fragmented coastline of the south and west are on the Korea Strait and the Huang Hai (Yellow Sea) respectively. The peninsula is mountainous, particularly in the cold, forested region of the north.

The peoples of Korea are descended from Chinese and Mongoloid stock, and speak an Ural-Altaic language. The region was once a centre of Buddhism, but the doctrines of the Chinese philosopher Confucius (K'ung Fu-tse) spread under the Yi dynasty, whose rule lasted from the Middle Ages until 1910, when the country came under the rule of the emperor of Japan.

Upon the defeat of Japan in the Second World War, the peninsula was occupied by the USA and the USSR. Allies in the war, these countries had contrasting plans for the region. The Americans occupied the south below the 38th parallel, and the Russians the north. When North Korean troops crossed this border in 1950, United Nations forces, including British and American troops, came to the aid of the South. After a three-year war, the 1953 ceasefire line became the boundary between North and South.

In the southern Republic of Korea, the traditional cultivation of rice, soya, barley and maize continues as ever, but is accompanied by a rapidly expanding industrial sector. Chief exports are textiles, iron and steel, microelectronics and consumer goods. The southern capital is at Sŏul (Seoul). A coup in 1961 ousted Syngman Rhee as president, in favour of Park Chung Hee. In 1979 he was assassinated and succeeded in turn by Choi Kyu Hah and Chun Doo-Hwan. The decision to hold the 1988 Olympic Games in Sŏul was accompanied by civil unrest and demands for greater democracy in government, but the Games were peaceful.

In North Korea (officially the Democratic People's Republic of Korea), the Communist party is headed by General-Secretary Kim Il Sung. Industry is the main activity and the mining industry has been developed. Agriculture has been collectivized. The capital of the north is Pyŏngyang.

Area of North and South Korea:
220,277 km² (85,054 mi²)
Population:
62,000,000 (20,000,000 North Korea; 42,000,000 South Korea)

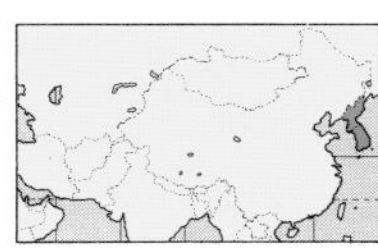

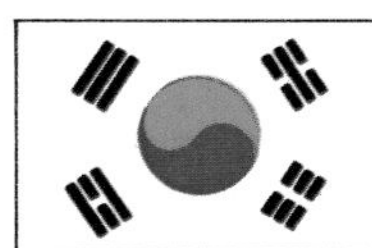

Capitals:
Pyŏngyang (North Korea) (pop. 1,500,000)
Sŏul (Seoul) (South Korea) (pop. 8,367,000)
Currency:
won (North Korea)
won (South Korea)

Kuwait

Dowlat al

At the top of the Persian Gulf, sandwiched between Saudi Arabia and Iraq, lies the Emirate of Kuwait. This small emirate, like others in this hot, barren region, occupies territory that historically seemed to have little to offer. Less than one per cent of the land can be farmed. But Kuwait's great secret, oil, lay underground. This 'black gold' has, since 1946, transformed this sleepy little state, which formerly depended on trading, fishing and animal husbandry, into a busy centre of international activity, with the finances available to fund a rapid development of social amenities, such as schools and hospitals. Kuwait is one of the world's wealthiest nations and its resources now finance one of the world's most elaborate welfare systems.

The Kuwaitis are Arabs and like other people around the Gulf follow the Islamic faith. But the oilfields have brought in an influx of outsiders to the region, including Europeans, Americans, Pakistanis and Indians. From 1899 until 1961, Kuwait was bound by treaty to Great Britain. Upon full independence, Iraq laid claim to the territory, but this claim was dropped two years later. The Kuwaiti stake in its own resources has been increased by the progressive nationalization of foreign interests in its oil industry.

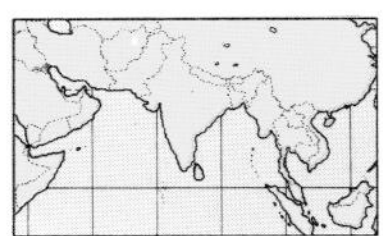

Area:
17,818 km²
(6,880 mi²)
Population:
1,910,000
Capital:
Kuwait City (pop. 400,000)
Currency:
dinar

Kuwait is a land of great contrasts. Below: A goatherd with his flock. Bottom: The modern port of Kuwait.

Laos

In the heart of what was once called Indo-China, there is a long strip of a country which shares borders with Vietnam, Cambodia (Kampuchea), Thailand, Burma and China. This is the Lao People's Democratic Republic, or Laos, and its capital is Vientiane on the Mekong River, which forms the south-western border of its territory. The former royal capital of Luang Prabang is on the upper reaches of the Mekong in the centre of the northern region, to the east of the Plain of Jars. Laos is a mountainous land, and most of its people live in the fertile region along the Mekong. Laos is in the monsoon belt, and the summer rains fill the paddy fields of the farmers. Rice is the staple food of the region, and maize and fish are also eaten. Agriculture is the chief activity and tin is the only important mineral.

There are people of Chinese and Vietnamese origin in Laos, but the native population is Lao. They are Buddhists or followers of local religious traditions. In the late Middle Ages, Laos was united under a powerful central kingdom, which later divided into three: Luang Prabang, Vientiane and Champarrac. Laos became part of French Indo-China in 1893, as a protected state. Despite Japanese intervention in 1941, Laos achieved independence as a single kingdom in 1949.

Unfortunately, the whole of this region became embroiled in disastrous civil war, as different factions struggled for power. The communist Pathet Lao, supported by North Vietnam, led a long fight against government forces. A coalition government was established in 1973, but by 1975 Pathet Lao controlled the whole country. With the Americans finally defeated in Vietnam, the king abdicated and the way was open for the communists to establish the People's Democratic Republic of Laos.

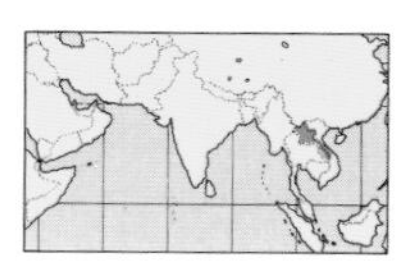

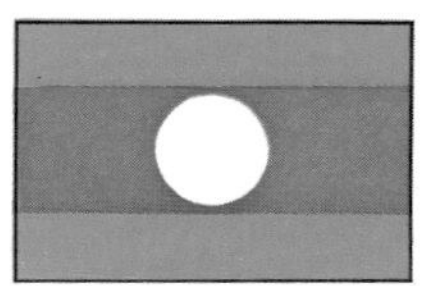

Area:
236,800 km²
(91,434 mi²)
Population:
3,938,000
Capital:
Vientiane (pop. 120,000)
Other towns:
Savannakhet, Luang Prabang, Pakse
Currency:
kip

Above right: Pineapples and spring onions are amongst the produce being sold in a market in Vientiane. Right: A ferry on the Mekong River

Lebanon

al-Jumhouriya al-Lubnaniya

The flag of Lebanon features a cedar tree. In Biblical times, the cedars of Lebanon provided timber for the merchant fleet of the Phoenicians and were famous throughout the known world. Today the few remaining cedars are venerated as relics of a bygone age.

Lebanon is a Middle Eastern republic, with a coastline on the Mediterranean Sea. It is bordered by Syria to the north and east. Its southern frontier is with Israel. Jebel Liban, or the Lebanon mountains, runs down the centre of the country from north to south, reaching 3,086 metres (10,125 feet) at Qornet es Saouda. The border with Syria runs along the Anti-Lebanon range, whose highest point is Talat Musa at 2,659 metres (8,723 feet). Between the two lie the fertile Beqa'a depression and the 'Asi and Litani rivers. The climate is Mediterranean, and favours the cultivation of citrus fruits, grapes and cereal crops.

In the fourth millennium BC, Lebanon was the homeland of the Phoenicians. Great traders and settlers, they were never organized in a centralized state. The region of the Lebanon later came under a long series of external rulers: the Egyptians, Assyrians, Babylonians and Persians. It came under the Macedonian-Greek Empire of Alexander the Great (356–323 BC), and then it was incorporated within the Roman Empire. In the seventh century AD, the Arabs conquered the region. In the 16th century, Lebanon became part of the vast empire of the Ottoman Turks. Although ruled by Muslims, the Christian Maronite sect continued to flourish. In 1860 the Druzes, who held emirates from the Turkish overlords, attacked the Maronites. France then intervened. After the First World War, and the final collapse of the Ottoman Empire, Lebanon was assigned to French rule. In 1946, it became fully independent for the first time.

Lebanon still contained the seeds of conflict, because the population was still bitterly divided between Christian and Muslim. The tension increased with the formation of the state of Israel on its southern border in 1948. One section of the populace supported the Arab front that was set up to oppose Israel, while the Maronites were inclined to join in western support for the new nation.

Palestinian refugees fled into Lebanon, and an anti-Israeli guerrilla movement grew up in their camps. The Israelis started to strike at guerrilla bases within Lebanon, and in 1969 bombarded the capital, Beirut. In 1975 the anti-Palestinian movement within Lebanon, organized into an extreme right-wing movement known as the Phalange, attempted to rout their leftist enemies. The result was a bitter civil war, with the country divided into two hostile camps.

In 1982 Israel invaded Lebanon, and did not begin to withdraw until three years later. By 1987 the government of Amin Gemayel was powerless, presiding over a country of rival armed militias. Shiite Moslems were prominent in campaigns of terror and kidnapping. Syrian troops were called in to restore order to parts of Beirut.

Lebanon's communications are centred upon Beirut. A highway and railway join the capital with the ancient Mediterranean ports of Tyr (Tyre or Sour) and Saïda (Sidon) leading to the Israeli border in the south, and with the port of Tripoli and the Syrian border in the north. A road eastwards links Beirut with Damascus in Syria, and there is a road and rail link along the Beqa'a to Homs.

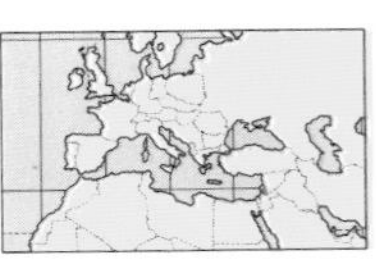

Area: 10,400 km² (4,016 mi²)
Population: 3,500,000
Capital: Beirut (pop. 940,000)
Currency: pound

Malaysia

The Federation of Malaysia lies between the Indian Ocean and the South China Sea. It is made up of two main parts: the Asian mainland below Thailand on the Malay Peninsula; and the northern part of Borneo, which is divided into the provinces of Sarawak and Sabah. Sabah is separated from the Philippines by the Balabac Strait. The climate is equatorial and humid, with heavy monsoon rain supporting large areas of rain forest.

Peninsular Malaysia consists of a highland region in the centre and north, with lowland and swamp on the coast and in the south. The capital is at Kuala Lumpur in the west. A railway and road links Kuala Lumpur to the Thai border in the north and the island of Singapore in the south, which forms a separate nation.

In Sarawak, the Sultanate of Brunei forms an independent state. The rest of the province consists of a mountainous interior and a lowland region in the west, the site of the principal town, Kuching. The chief town of the Sabah province is Kota Kinabalu, formerly known as Jesselton. Sabah is also a mountainous province.

The people of Malaysia probably originate from the Indo-China region, and are mixed with successive settlements of Indians and Chinese. Ethnic groups within the country also include Sakai (Temiar), Jajun, Dusun, Iban and Dayak. The main and official religion is Islam, which has over the years become modified by local beliefs in spirits and traditional rituals. The official language is Malay.

Malaysia is the world's largest producer of rubber. This natural substance, as remarkable as any modern synthetic plastic, is produced from the trunk of the rubber tree. On the plantations, workers cut into the bark every few days. A sticky substance known as latex seeps out into a pail. It is collected and chemically processed to make the rubber we use in such things as car tyres and erasers. Other products from the country's plantations and forests include teak and other hardwoods, palm-oil, and copra from the coconut palm. Tea, pepper and pineapples are also cultivated, and rice is the staple food of the country. Fishing provides another valuable source of protein.

The Malaysian economy relies on its extensive mineral resources as well as agriculture. The country is the world's major producer of tin, which is produced by opencast mining. Some oil is also extracted. Industrialization is taking place rapidly. Malaysia's chief trading partners are Japan, the member countries of the European Economic Community, Singapore and Australia.

Malaysia is a federation, and its history is one of a number of small separate states. Singapore and the various states on the Malay Peninsula, together with Penang and Malacca, were under British rule during the colonial era. After the Japanese invasion in the Second World War, independence came to the Malay states in 1957. Power reverted to individual rulers, but under a single Constitution and having a supreme head of state, who is one of the rulers of the Malay states. In 1963 Singapore joined the federation, together with Sarawak and British North Borneo, which became known as Sabah. Singapore, however, left to form an independent republic in 1965. The early 1960s were marked by a state of conflict with Malaysia's southern neighbour, Indonesia, then under the rule of President Soekarno. This dispute was not settled until 1966, when Major-General Soeharto took power in Indonesia. Malaysia remains a member of the Commonwealth.

The Federation of Malaysia is a parliamentary democracy, with a Senate and a House of Representatives. In addition, each of the 13 states within the federation has its own constitution and a degree of autonomy.

The traditional way of life on the Malay Peninsula has changed considerably with the industrialization of modern times. Factories have gone up around Kuala Lumpur, the capital, which has a population of nearly a million. In the countryside, tin mines gouge out swathes of landscape. But despite this, the ancient way of life continues with few changes in the villages and paddy fields. In eastern Malaysia, the economy is less developed. Much of the island of Borneo is still sparsely inhabited and covered by dense forest. It is the home of a wide variety of wild animals and plants.

Area:
329,749 km² (127,324 mi²)
Population:
15,070,000
Capital:
Kuala Lumpur (pop. 938,000)
Other towns:
George Town, Ipoh, Johore Bahru, Kuching, Kota Kinabalu (Jesselton)
Currency:
dollar

Below: The traditional way of life in Malaysia survives despite the rapidly increasing industrialization of the towns.

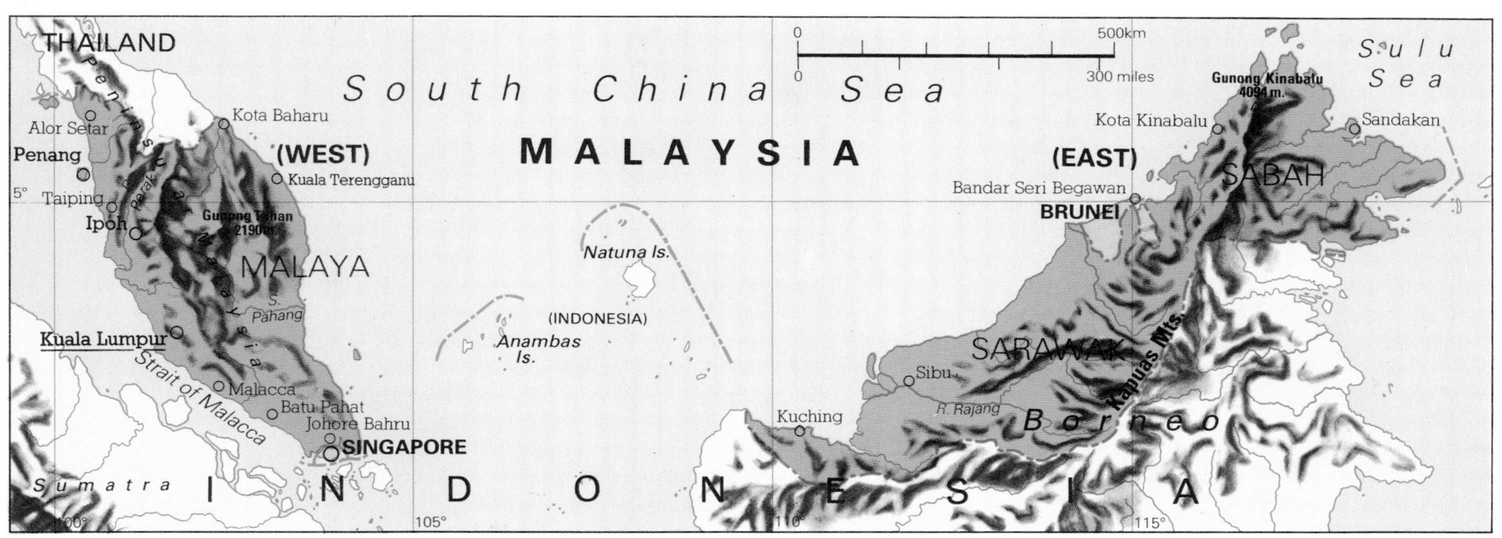

Maldives

Republic of

South of the Indian subcontinent, a long low-lying chain of coral islands stretches out into the ocean. Groups of coral islands are called atolls: the tiny creatures which make up coral together form huge reefs, or horseshoe islands surrounding a lagoon. North of Eight Degree Channel the atolls form the Laccadive Islands (Lakshadweep) which belong to India. To the south, they form the Republic of Maldives, an independent nation, although the islands were under British protection from 1887 to 1965.

There are more than 2,000 Maldive islands, but less than 10 per cent of them are large enough for habitation. The people who live on these islands are traditionally traders and fishermen, by reason of their central position in the Indian Ocean. The islands have great strategic value and until recently Gan, in Addu Atoll, was the site of a British air base. The Maldive islanders are Muslims. Their republic is governed by a representative assembly. The capital and administrative centre is at Malé in the centre of the coral island chain.

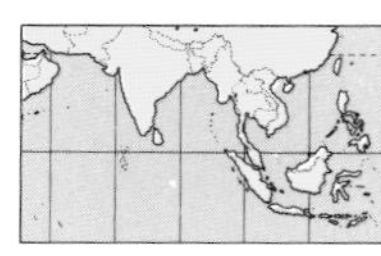

Area:
298 km² (115 mi²)
Population:
168,000
Capital:
Malé (pop. 40,000)
Currency:
rupee

Below: There are more than 2,000 Maldive Islands, but less than 10 per cent of them are inhabited.

Mongolian People's Republic

Lying on high plateau land between China and the Soviet Union is the Mongolian People's Republic. The south of the country is taken up by the arid wilderness of the Gobi Desert and by regions of steppe. Encircling the country in the north-west are the high mountains of the Altay range. In the east is the Hangayn range. The chief rivers are the Kerulen and the Selenge.

Traditionally, the people of Mongolia are nomadic herdsmen, living in large felt tents known as yurts. They are expert horsemen. In the 13th century, they conquered much of Asia, streaming westwards to strike fear into the heart of Russia. The conquests of Temujin, known as Genghis Khan (1162–1227), stretched as far as the Black Sea. Mongolia later became a province of China. In 1912, it became an autonomous kingdom, but fighting from the civil war that took place in Russia after the revolution of 1917 spilled across its borders, and in 1924 the Mongolian People's Republic was founded.

Many changes have been introduced under communism. Power has been removed from the nobles and from the Buddhist priests. Agriculture, including livestock production, has been collectivized and many nomads have now settled. Industry is being developed, based upon coal and other minerals. The country is a member of Comecon (the communist Council for Mutual Economic Aid). The principal industrial centre is Ulan Bator, the capital, which is linked by railway track to the Soviet border and to the region of Inner Mongolia, which lies over the border in China.

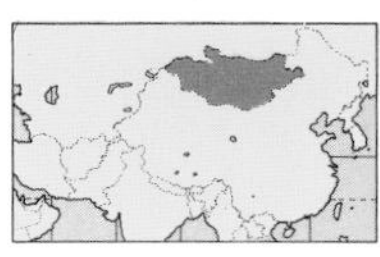

Area:
1,565,000 km²
(604,283 mi²)
Population:
1,866,000
Capital:
Ulan Bator (pop. 480,000)
Other towns:
Darkhan, Erdenet
Currency:
tugrik

Below: Traditional Mongolia: horsemen lead Bactrian camels past a yurt encampment.

Nepal

The highest mountain in the world is Everest (Sagarmatha), which towers to a height of 8,848 metres (29,029 ft). It is part of the mighty Himalayan range, and rises on the China-Nepal border. The Kingdom of Nepal lies between the Tibetan Autonomous Region of China, and the great dusty plains of northern India. The north of Nepal is taken up by a great wall of mountains, many of which are as impressive as Everest itself. The snows of these peaks swell the waters of the River Ganges on its way to the sea. The peaks descend towards the centre of the country, a land of snowy, rhododendron-covered ridges, and of green valleys with terraced cultivation. Along the southern border extends the Terai, a strip of humid forest, which provides a home for the tiger and other rare species.

Culturally, Nepal is a mixture of Indian and Tibetan influences, of Hinduism and Buddhism. It was the birthplace of Gautama Buddha in about 568 BC. Today Nepal contains several language groups, including the Gurkhas, and the Sherpas. Historically, they occupied a number of tribal homelands and small kingdoms or city-states. They were united under one monarchy in the 18th century.

Nepal exports jute, rice, timber, cattle, ghee (liquified butter) and cereals. Road building, air travel and foreign aid have opened up Nepal to the outside world.

Area:
140,797 km²
(54,365 mi²)
Population:
16,100,000
Capital:
Katmandu (pop. 235,000)
Currency:
rupee

Pakistan

Islamic Republic of

To the north-west of India, bounded by Iran and Afghanistan, is the Islamic Republic of Pakistan. To the north-east lies the disputed territory of Kashmir and the beginnings of the great Karakoram-Himalayan range of mountains. In the north-west, the Khyber Pass provides a route to Kabul through wild hill country. The Sulaiman and Kirthar ranges extend southwards to the coast, and to the west of these mountains is the Baluchistan plateau. But running down the centre of the country is the great fertile valley of the River Indus, which is fed by a number of tributaries, notably the Sutlej, the Ravi, the Chenab, the Jhelum and the Beas.

The Indus valley was the site of a great civilization as early as the third millennium BC, as excavations of such sites as Mohenjo-Daro have revealed. Waves of invaders and settlers came to the region over the ages, including Aryans, Persians, Greeks (Alexander the Great crossed the Indus in 326 BC), Pushtu, Baluchi, Moghul and British.

The Pakistan region was incorporated into the British Empire in the 19th century. It was part of British India. But when India received independence in 1947, the predominantly Muslim areas of territory to the north-west and north-east of the subcontinent were partitioned off into a separate state known as Pakistan, amid general violence and unrest. The Kashmir region was bitterly fought over and was itself partitioned. The newly independent state of Pakistan became a republic in 1956. In 1971 a civil war broke out between the two widely separated parts of the country, West Pakistan and East Pakistan. India came to the support of East Pakistan, which seceded to become a separate nation, Bangladesh, a year later. Unlike India, Pakistan has not always maintained parliamentary democracy, and the army was in control from 1977 to 1988. Pakistan left the Commonwealth in 1972.

Pakistan is still an agricultural country, as it was 4,000 years ago. The chief crops are rice, which is the staple food, and cotton. Sugar-cane and cereal crops are also cultivated and livestock are reared

Below: Pakistan is an Islamic country. These mosques are at Lahore, near the Indian border.

for their wool and skins which are exported.

Extremes of climate and infertile terrain pose serious problems for the farmers of Pakistan. The climate can be extremely hot between March and May, and quite cool during the winter. Monsoon winds blow during June and October. But agriculture is now aided by a system of irrigation, which has considerably extended the fertile area.

Industry is being developed in Pakistan, exploiting hydro-electric power. Industrial products include cement, sugar, textiles, paper, electrical engineering goods and fertilizers. Natural resources include gas in large quantities, and deposits of rock salt.

Modern Pakistan is divided into four main provinces: the Punjab, the Sind, the North-west Frontier and Baluchistan. In addition, there are Tribal Areas and the Islamabad Capital Territory. The principal languages spoken in the country include Punjabi, Sindi, Pushtu and Baluchi. The official language is Urdu. Islam came to this part of the world about 1,200 years ago. Today most Pakistanis are Muslims, and religion plays an important role in the lives of the people, in the organization of society and in the organization of the legal system.

The capital of Pakistan and the seat of government is at Islamabad in the north. Islamabad, however, is a relatively small city, and the major centres of population are elsewhere. Lahore, on the Indian border, has nearly 3,000,000 inhabitants, and is a centre of business and trade. Karachi, a port on the Arabian Sea coast, has about 5,103,000 inhabitants, which makes it the largest city in this densely populated country. It has an important international airport. Pakistan has a good rail and road network linking the chief towns.

Area:
803,943 km²
(310,421 mi²)
Population:
88,000,000
Capital:
Islamabad (pop. 250,000)
Other towns:
Karachi, Lahore, Faisalabad, Hyderabad, Rawalpindi, Multan
Currency:
rupee

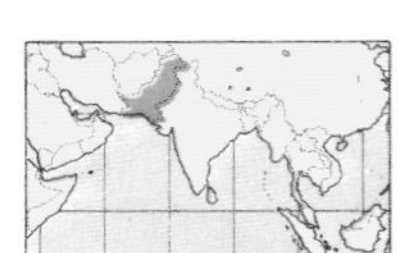

Right: The upper valleys of Pakistan are terraced to give a larger agricultural area.

Philippines

Republic of the

The Republic of the Philippines is a group of islands in South-East Asia. They are separated from the continental mainland by the South China Sea. There are literally thousands of islands, ranging from tiny coral atolls to large islands of volcanic rock. The two biggest are Luzon, which covers 104,687 square kilometres (40,422 sq mi), and Mindanao, 94,360 square kilometres (36,435 sq mi). The other major islands are Samar, Negros, Palawan, Panay and Mindoro. The climate is tropical and humid, but cooler at higher altitudes: the islands are mountainous. On Luzon, the Cordillera Central rises to 2,929 metres (9,610 ft) and on Mindanao Mount Apo is 2,954 metres (9,692 ft). Both islands also have low-lying areas of swamp, and large lakes. Several seas are enclosed within the various island groups, including the Sulu Sea, the Mindanao Sea, the Visayan Sea and the Sibuyan Sea.

The Filipino people are mostly of Malayan origin, mixed with Chinese and Spanish stock. Official languages are English and Pilipino. Most of the people are Roman Catholics. The first European landfall on the islands was an unfortunate one, because the Portuguese explorer Ferdinand Magellan (Magalhães) was killed here in 1521. Spain secured rule over the islands 44 years later. After the Spanish-American War, in 1898, the islands came under the control of the United States. Full independence came in 1946, following liberation from Japanese occupation in the Second World War. Years of unrest and resistance to the government led to the imposition of martial law in 1972. Opposition to the regime of President Marcos grew with a guerrilla war being fought by the New People's Army (N P A), and with the 1986 Presidential challenge by Mrs Corazon Aquino. Civil order broke down after this election, with accusations of malpractice and intimidation. Mrs Aquino was elected President in February 1986, and ex-President Marcos left the country.

The Philippines have fertile agricultural land. Rice and maize are the principal crops, and fruit, coconuts, sugarcane and tobacco are also grown.

There are valuable mineral deposits in the Philippines, notably copper, iron-ore and chromium. Hydro-electric power has been developed and industries include food processing, textiles and engineering. Tourism is a major source of revenue, and the United States an important trading partner.

The capital, Manila, is the major port. Founded in 1571, it is on the island of Luzon. There is a road and rail network, but because of the geographical nature of the Philippines much travel is done by boat or light aircraft.

Area:
300,000 km²
(115,837 mi²)
Population:
54,400,000
Capital:
Manila
(metropolitan pop. 5,926,000)
Other towns:
Quezon City,
Davao,
Iloilo
Currency:
peso

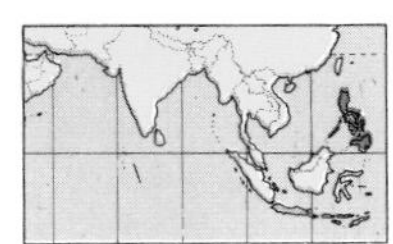

Above left: The street life of Manila is often hectic and confused. Below left: Colourful religious processions are often seen in the Philippines.

Saudi Arabia and the Arabian Peninsula

al-Mamlaka al-'Arabiya as-Sa'udiya

The Arabian peninsula is a large area of land bordered by the Red Sea in the west, by the Gulf of Aden and the Arabian Sea in the south, and by the Gulf of Oman and the Persian (or Arabian) Gulf in the east. To the north lie the countries of Jordan, Iraq and Kuwait, which have separate entries in this atlas.

Saudi Arabia is the giant of the region. It is a land of deserts and burning heat. Behind the coastal strip along the Red Sea, rise the highland regions of Hijaz and Asir, which slope gently to the east into a plateau region. The central area is called the Najd. To the south lies the formidable desert of Rub al Khali, the appropriately named 'Empty Quarter' which is largely devoid of moisture. To the east is the desert of Ad Dahnā and to the north is another desert, An Nafūd. The land drops down eastwards towards the low-lying Gulf coast.

This desert land has long been the home of nomadic peoples and traversed by caravans of camels. It was at Mecca that the Prophet Mohammed was born in about AD 570, and the holy cities of Mecca and Medina still attract Muslim pilgrims from all over the world. The region became part of the Ottoman Empire of the Turks in 1517, and 400 years passed before Abdulaziz ibn Saud ended Turkish rule. By 1927, Saudi Arabia was unified under his kingship. In 1938, a discovery was made which transformed Saudi Arabia from pauper to prince. The treasure of Saudi Arabia was oil, in massive quantities. Saudi Arabia is now the world's third largest oil producer.

The south-western corner of the Arabian peninsula is occupied by the **Yemen Arab Republic,** of which the capital, San'a, is in the central highlands. This country is now a republic, its monarchy having been overthrown in 1962. Its economy depends upon cotton, coffee and skins.

Its neighbour, **South Yemen,** (officially the **Yemen People's Democratic Republic**) is much larger, but more sparsely populated. Here the southern highlands of Hadhramaut give way to empty desert in the interior. The port of Aden occupies a strategic position at the entry to the Red Sea, and was under British rule until 1967. The National Liberation Front came to power after a bitter struggle with British troops.

To the east is the independent sultanate of **Oman.** Oman is another oil producer and its economy has benefited accordingly. South of Muscat and Matrah on the Gulf of Oman lies Jebel al Akhdur, a mountainous region with fertile valleys. In the Dhufar region of the south is another fertile highland. The interior is arid desert.

Beyond the Strait of Hormuz is the Persian or Arabian Gulf. On its southern shore are the **United Arab Emirates,** an independent federation of seven emirates: Abu Dhabi, Dubai, Ajman, Sharjah, Umm al Qaiwain, Fujairah, and Ras al Khaimah. These were formerly the Trucial States, and they were bound by treaty to Britain until 1971. Oil has brought wealth to the Gulf, and the UAE have been transformed by this single product. Two other independent nations to the north – **Qatar**, an emirate on a peninsula in the Gulf, and **Bahrain**, an island sheikhdom – have had a similar history, both having become fully independent in 1971. Oil dominates the economies of both countries.

Flag	Country	Area	Population	Capital	Currency
	Bahrain	622 km² (240 mi²)	467,000	Manama (122,000)	dinar
	Oman	212,457 km² (82,035 mi²)	1,500,000	Muscat (30,000)	rial Omani
	Qatar	11,000 km² (4,247 mi²)	294,000	Doha (200,000)	Qatar riyal
	Saudi Arabia	2,149,690 km² (830,045 mi²)	10,443,000	Riyadh (669,000)	riyal
	United Arab Emirates	83,600 km² (32,280 mi²)	1,622,000	Abu Dhabi (516,000)	dirham
	Yemen Arab Republic	195,000 km² (75,294 mi²)	9,273,000	San'a (448,000)	riyal
	Yemen People's Democratic Rep. (South Yemen)	332,968 km² (128,567 mi²)	2,500,000	Aden (270,000)	dinar

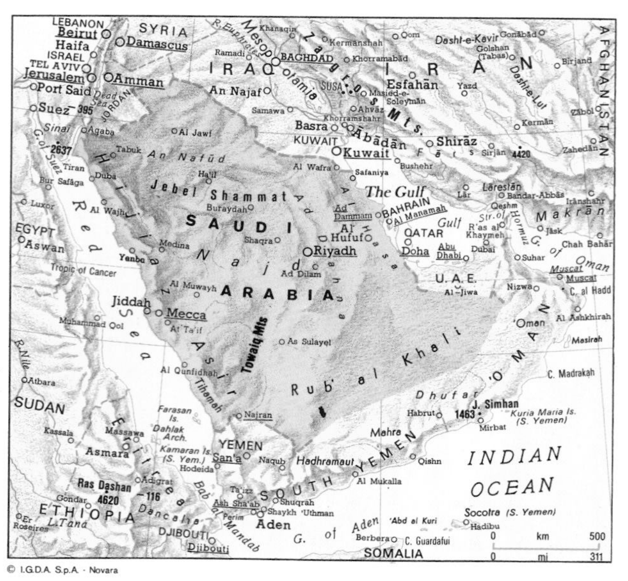

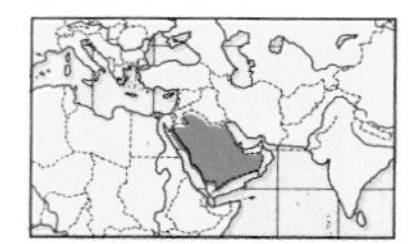

Area: 2,149,690 km²
(830,045 mi²)
Population: 10,443,000
Capital: Riyadh (pop. 1,000,000)
Other towns: Medina, Mecca
Currency:

These ruins stand in Diriyah the home town of the Saudi Royal family.

Singapore
Republic of

At the foot of the Malay Peninsula are 55 small islands which make up the Republic of Singapore. Singapore is also the name of the largest island, which is joined to the mainland by a causeway across the Straits of Johor. Singapore is a humid country, just north of the equator. The average rainfall is 2,440 mm (96 in) a year and temperatures average 24°C to 31°C (75°–88°F) throughout the year.

The settlement at Singapore was originally founded by Sir Thomas Stamford Raffles in 1819. Its position on the Strait of Malacca made it an ideal centre for trade, and Singapore became part of the British Straits Settlements. In the Second World War, it was occupied by Japanese troops. In 1959, Britain granted Singapore a degree of autonomy. It became part of the newly independent Federation of Malaysia in 1963, but withdrew two years later to become an independent republic. It retained its links with the Commonwealth. Singapore has a parliamentary system and has enjoyed stable government.

Singapore still lives from its trade, being one of the world's great ports. It is also an important centre of business and of industry, producing micro-electronics, consumer goods and textiles. Only two per cent of the people work on the land. They produce rubber, coconuts and market produce.

The people of Singapore belong to several ethnic groups. The majority are Chinese. There are also Malays, Indians, Europeans and people of mixed descent. The official languages are Malay, Mandarin Chinese, Tamil and English.

Area:
581 km² (224 mi²)
Population:
2,502,000
Capital:
Singapore
Currency:
dollar

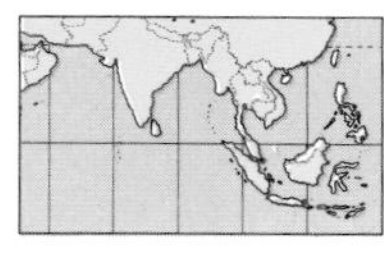

Above: A versatile undertaker in the streets of Singapore. Below: The product for which Sri Lanka is best known is tea. It is picked by hand, below right, and shipped out of Colombo, below left.

Sri Lanka Democratic Socialist Republic

Separated from southern India by the Gulf of Mannar and the Palk Strait is the Democratic Socialist Republic of Sri Lanka, formerly known as Ceylon. The coast and the northern sector of this tropical island consist of fertile plains, but the centre of the southern sector is highland, rising to such mountainous peaks as Pidurutalagala, which is 2,524 metres (8,281 ft) above sea level. Much of the island is forested.

The warm rainy climate is ideal for the cultivation of rice, which is the staple food, and rubber. Tea, sugar-cane and copra are also produced in quantity. Manufactured goods include textiles, paper and fertilizers. The tourist industry is being encouraged.

Sri Lanka is a fascinating island. In the town of Kandy, the annual Esala Perahera festival provides a glittering cavalcade of elephants, drummers and dancers. There are many such festivals celebrating the religious and historical traditions of the island.

The original inhabitants of the island were the Vedda. The Aryan Sinhalese people invaded the island about 2,500 years ago. Later invaders and settlers included the Dravidian Tamils, Arabs, Portuguese, Dutch and British. Today, the bulk of the population are Sinhalese Buddhists, with a large minority of Tamils who follow the Hindu faith. There is continuing conflict between these two communities. Sri Lanka also contains people of Arab, Malay and European descent. The official language is Sinhalese.

Sri Lanka became independent after more than 100 years of British rule in 1948. It became a republic in 1972. The Sinhalese-Tamil conflict escalated in the 1980s. In 1987 an agreement between the Sri Lankan and Indian governments called in the Indian Army to restore order.

Area:
65,610 km²
(25,334 mi²)
Population:
15,398,000
Capital:
Colombo (pop. 624,000)
Other towns:
Dehiwela-Mount Lavinia, Moratuwa, Jaffna, Kotte, Kandy
Currency:
rupee

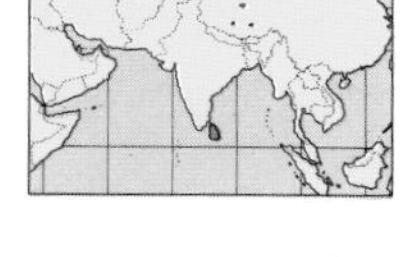

Syria

al-Jamhouriya al Arabia as-Souriya

The Syrian Arab Republic is part of the Levant. This is the name given to those Middle Eastern lands which form the eastern limit of the Mediterranean. Syria's northern border is with Turkey. To the east lies Iraq, and to the south-west lie Israel and Lebanon. Since the Six-Day War of 1967, a narrow but strategic section of the country, the Golan Heights, has been occupied by Israel.

Syria is an arid country, broken by a few mountainous areas. Only two rivers have water all the year round: the Orontes, which flows across the Turkish border into the Mediterranean, and the Euphrates, which crosses the Turkish border at Jerablus and flows south-east into Iraq. The coastal strip is a fertile zone, as are the oasis regions around Aleppo and Damascus. The north-eastern section of the country has been made fertile by large-scale irrigation from the Tabqa dam.

It might seem that such a harsh, inhospitable land has little to offer. But Syria was the home of ancient civilizations, and has a history stretching back thousands of years. Populated in Biblical times by people of Aramaic descent, Syria was ruled in turn by the Assyrians, the Egyptians, the Persians and the Macedonians. When the empire of Alexander the Great (356–323 BC) broke up, the region passed to the dynasty founded by one of his generals, Seleucus I. The Seleucids were followed by the Romans, and they were succeeded by the Byzantines, who fought with the Persians for the region. Syria was finally conquered by the Arabs in AD 636 and became the centre of a great Islamic empire, the Caliphate of Damascus. In the ninth century, it came under Turkish rule.

During the great medieval wars of religion, the Crusades, various Christian principalities were founded in the region. But these were, in turn, replaced by rule of the Egyptian Mamelukes and the Ottoman Turks. With the fall of the Ottoman Empire in 1918, Syria was placed under a French mandate. It became independent during the Second World War, although foreign troops did not finally leave until 1946.

In 1958 Syria joined with Egypt to form a United Arab Republic, but withdrew only three and a half years later. The 1973 Constitution describes the country as a 'democratic, popular, socialist state'. The 1970s and 1980s posed a series of political problems for Syria, as the Middle Eastern region was rocked by serious crises, notably the war with Israel in 1973 and the Israeli invasion of Lebanon in 1982.

Modern Syria is mainly populated by Arabs, with minority groups of Kurds, Turkmen, and Druzes. It is an Islamic country, although there are some Christian sects, such as that of the Maronites.

Agriculture is important to the economy. In the fertile areas, cereals, citrus fruits, vines, olives, tobacco and cotton are all cultivated. Textiles are widely produced and we still use the term 'damask' to describe a certain kind of weave. The name comes from Damascus, Syria's capital, now a city of more than 2,000,000 people. The country is fast becoming industrialized, and oil wells provide much needed wealth. An important source of income lies in the oil pipelines which transport crude oil from Iraq and Saudi Arabia. Syria has refineries at Baniyas and Homs. Other natural resources include natural gas, phosphates and metals.

© I.G.D.A. S.p.A. - Novara

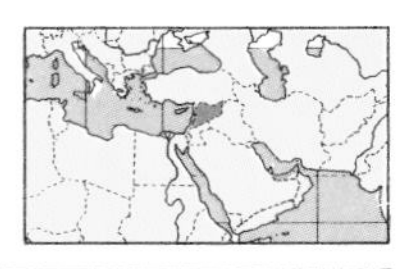

Area: 185,180 km² (71,502 mi²)
Population: 10,500,000
Capital: Damascus (pop. 2,250,000)
Currency: pound

Below: The skyline of the capital, Damascus.

Taiwan

The island of Taiwan, once known as Formosa, lies between the East and South China Seas, and is separated by the Formosa Strait from mainland China. Japan ruled Taiwan from 1895 until the end of the Second World War. When Communist forces established control of the Chinese mainland in 1949, the Nationalist leader General Chiang Kai-Shek withdrew to this island. For many years, Chiang Kai-Shek's government on Taiwan, which was called the Republic of China, was recognized as the voice of China at the United Nations. But inevitably the mainland People's Republic of China finally received recognition by the UN and was admitted in 1971. Taiwan withdrew. Aid from the USA has been used to develop manufacturing industries. Crops include rice, the staple diet, tea and sugar, but manufactures are the chief exports.

Area: 35,961 km² (13,885 mi²)
Population: 17,100,000
Capital: T'ai-pei (pop. 3,050,000)
Other towns: Kao-hsiung
Currency: dollar

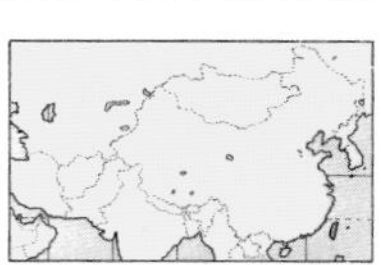

Thailand

Prathes Thai

The Thais are a traditionally Buddhist people spread over a large area of South-East Asia. The Kingdom of Thailand, which was once known as Siam, is centred on the basin of the Chao Phraya river, which runs southwards into the Bight of Bangkok on the Gulf of Thailand. The long border with Burma is highland country, becoming mountainous in the north-west. The eastern region is a large plateau, divided from the neighbouring state of Laos by the Mekong river. The south-eastern border is with Cambodia (Kampuchea) and a long tongue of territory extends to the south-west, bordering upon Peninsular Malaysia.

While neighbouring countries fell under British and French rule during the colonial era, Thailand retained its ancient independence. The absolute powers of the monarch were limited about 50 years ago. Today, the king, Bhumibol Adulyadej, appoints the Senate, but the people elect the National Assembly. Since the Second World War, in which Thailand was an ally of Japan, there has been a succession of *coups d'état*. Elections took place in April 1983. Thailand continues to be a centre of Theravada Buddhism and contains many splendid temples and shrines which bear witness to the culture and religious traditions of the Thai people.

The Chao Phraya basin is fertile, and most Thai people are farmers. Because of the tropical climate, rice is cultivated as the major crop. There are also many thriving rubber plantations. The forests provide teak, a hardwood used in cabinet-making and boat-building. Elephants are still used to haul logs in the lumber camps. Thailand is a producer of tin and lignite, and is developing the exploitation of its offshore reserves of natural gas. Industrialization is increasing rapidly.

The capital of Thailand is Bangkok, a major port on the Menam river. It is a huge, crowded city, a centre of commerce, education, entertainment and administration.

Area:
514,000 km²
(198,467 mi²)
Population:
50,583,000
Capital:
Bangkok (pop. 5,468,000)
Other towns:
Chiang Mai, Nakhon Ratchasima (Korat), Kaen, Udon Thani, Pitsanulok
Currency:
baht

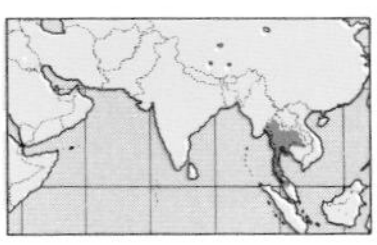

Below: Buddhist monks on a Thai farm. Rice, maize and tapioca are cultivated.

Turkey

Türkiye Cumhuriyeti

Turkey is a halfway house between Asia and Europe. Geographically, the territory to the west of the Bosporus is in Europe, but the vast eastern mass of the country, including the capital Ankara, is in Asia. Historically, Turkey is a meeting point of eastern and western cultures, having been crossed in both directions by invading armies.

It was the site of the ancient city of Troy, whose destruction by the Greeks in the 12th century BC was related by the poet Homer in the *Iliad*. Turkey was also the site of ancient Greek settlements, of Roman occupation, and of New Testament evangelization. In AD 330, the Roman emperor Constantine the Great built the city of Constantinople (now Istanbul) on the ancient site of Byzantium. This became the capital of the eastern empire and the centre of Christendom.

In the Middle Ages, waves of fierce Seljuk Turks, an Asian people related to the Huns, swept westwards and, in the 11th century, they occupied the land that now bears their name. They were followed by Ottoman Turks in the late 13th century. Constantinople fell to the Ottoman Turks in 1453, and the Ottoman Empire was founded. Under the Ottoman sultans, Islamic culture flourished. A visit to their impressive palace of Topkapi, which still stands in Istanbul, reveals their mastery of textile crafts, calligraphy and weaponry. The Ottoman Empire spread south to Arabia and Egypt, westwards into North Africa, and north-west into the Balkan region of Europe. In 1529, the Turks besieged Vienna itself.

The empire finally disappeared after the First World War. But between the wars, the energetic modernization programme of the national hero Mustafa Kemal (called 'Atatürk') regenerated the country. Since 1960, Turkey has been beset by political troubles with periods of military rule and clashes between the left wing and the extreme right. Traditional hostility with Greece continued and Turkey invaded part of Cyprus in 1974. As a member of the North Atlantic Treaty Organization (NATO), Turkey maintains a defended border against the USSR.

The European part of Turkey is a fertile plain bordered by Greece and Bulgaria, the Black Sea and the Sea of Marmara. The Aegean coast of Asian Turkey, stretching south from the Dardanelles, enjoys a Mediterranean climate. The southern coast north of the island of Cyprus is lined by the Toros mountains,

while the Anadolu range is near the Black Sea coast in the north. In the east, along the borders with Iran and the USSR, there are high mountains – notably the peak of Bügük Ağri, which reaches 5,165 metres (16,946 ft). This mountain is better known as Mount Ararat, where Noah's Ark is said to have come to rest in the Bible story. The major lakes are Tuz in the west and Van in the east. In eastern Turkey, the climate is one of extremes.

Crops include grain, citrus fruit, figs, grapes, tobacco and cotton. Livestock production is also important. Mineral resources include coal, lignite, chromite, copper and iron-ore. Industries produce textiles, cement, paper, iron, steel and other items. Craft industries, such as carpet-making, still thrive.

The capital of the country is Ankara, which is linked by road and rail to the other chief cities. The Asian and European sections of Turkey are now linked by a suspension bridge across the Bosporus.

Above left: The old city of Afyonkarahisar. Above: The dome and minaret of the palace built by Ishak Pasha of Dogubayazit. Below: These strange rock formations are to be found in Cappadocia.

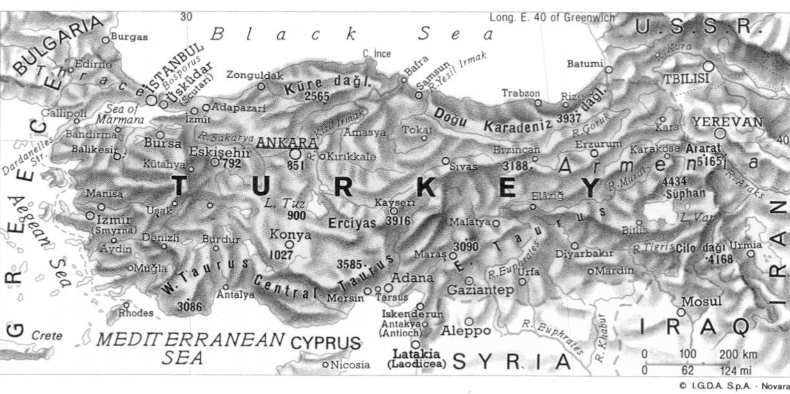

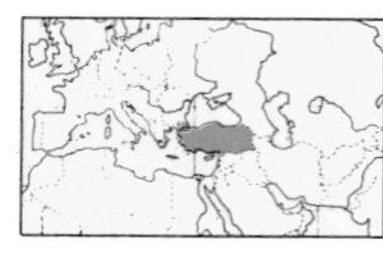

Area:
780,576 km²
(301,399 mi²)
Population:
51,420,000
Capital:
Ankara (pop. 3,196,000)

Other towns:
Istanbul, Izmir, Adana, Bursa, Gaziantep, Konya, Eskişehir
Currency:
lira

UNION OF SOVIET SOCIALIST REPUBLICS—

Whilst the greater part of the USSR lies in the continent of Asia, its capital, Moscow, is in Europe. See p. 233

Vietnam

Socialist Republic of

An old Vietnamese adage refers to the country as 'two baskets of rice tied to a staff'. The two 'baskets of rice' are the populated regions of Tonkin (Tongking) in the far north and Cochin-China (Cochin-Chine) in the far south. The 'staff' is the long, thin strip of land which links the two. The Socialist Republic of Vietnam lies in a region once called Indo-China on the South China Sea. China lies on its northern border and Laos and Cambodia are to the west.

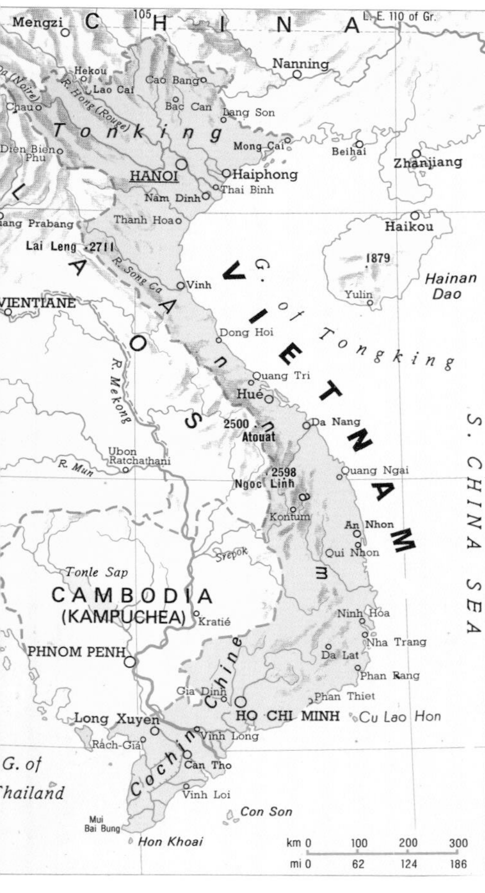

Area:
329,556 km²
(127,249 mi²)
Population:
60,000,000
Capital:
Hanoi (pop. 2,571,000)

Other towns:
Ho Chi Minh, Haiphong, Da Nang, Nha Trang, Qui Nhon, Hué, Can Tho, My Tho
Currency:
dong

The capital of the country is Hanoi, in Tonkin. This region is dominated by the course of two major rivers, the Hong (Fleuve Rouge or Red River) and the Da (the Noire or Black River). The Hong forms a large delta on the Gulf of Tonkin, whose chief port is Haiphong. The central 'staff' is occupied by the long chain of the Annam mountains and a narrow coastal plain. The Cochin-China region is fertile, thanks to the River Mekong, which here divides into a delta on its 4,500-kilometre (2,796-mile) journey from China to the sea. The principal town of the south is Ho Chi Minh City, formerly known as Saigon.

Vietnam is a wet, humid country, and rice is the staple crop. Sugar-cane and maize are cultivated, and livestock and fishing also provide food. Mineral resources include coal and iron-ore. The people of Vietnam are mostly of Annamese stock. Other ethnic groups include Thais, Chinese, Muong and Montagnards. The predominant religion is Buddhism.

Between 1959 and 1975, the country became a symbol throughout the world of all the horrors of modern warfare. To the Vietnamese, it was the latest chapter in a 2,000-year saga of guerrilla warfare. This region, with its unique and ancient culture, fell under foreign rule as early as 112 BC. The Chinese ruled Vietnam despite continual revolts until AD 907. There followed a number of Vietnamese dynasties, power eventually being consolidated in the north by the Trinh clan and in the south by the Nguyen. In 1771 both were swept away by a revolt. But, by 1802, a representative of the Nguyen, Nguyen Anh, had regained power, and proclaimed himself emperor under the name Gia-long. The new empire did not last long. By 1887, the whole of Vietnam was under French rule, and with Cambodia and Laos became part of French Indo-China.

In 1930 the Indo-Chinese Communist Party was formed, under the leadership of Ho Chi Minh (1892–1969). In 1941, the party became known as the Vietminh. During the Second World War, Vietnam was occupied by the Japanese. When the French returned to their former territory in 1945, they were faced by a protracted war against the Vietminh. They finally withdrew in 1954, after their defeat at Dien Bien Phu. A conference at Geneva decided to divide Vietnam into two zones pending elections. But the treaty was not ratified by the United States, and the elections were never held. The country was partitioned. The North became a Communist nation, while the South took the opposite road. War broke out again. Communist guerrillas in the South, the Vietcong, were supported by North Vietnam and by aid from the Communist world. The southern government and army received assistance from the United States, and this gradually became a massive military commitment. The war spilled over the borders of Vietnam and almost engulfed the whole of South-East Asia. The people suffered greatly. In 1973, American forces withdrew from South Vietnam. The war continued, but victory finally went to the Vietcong, who on 30 April 1975 entered Saigon, which was renamed Ho Chi Minh City. The country was re-unified as the Socialist Republic of Vietnam.

The new country faced immense problems caused particularly by the devastation of the South. In foreign relations, Vietnam has been pro-Soviet. Vietnamese forces invaded Cambodia in 1978. This action was followed by a border conflict with China in 1979.

Left: The Da Nang region of Vietnam is an important agricultural area. The principal crops are rice, cotton and tobacco. Industries include textiles and food-processing.

Australasia

Australasia is the smallest of the world's seven continents and, disregarding Antarctica, it is also the most sparsely populated. Its overall area of 8·51 million square kilometres (3·29 million square miles) is about four-fifths of that of Europe. But its total population of about 22·5 million in 1979 was only one-thirtieth of the population of Europe. One factor that has contributed to the low population density is that Australasia was explored only recently and that the first European settlement in Australia, for example, was not established until 1788. Australasia is, therefore, a new continent, even compared with the New World of the Americas.

Apart from the islands of Micronesia, Australasia is situated mostly south of the equator and is surrounded on most sides by the Pacific Ocean, which accounts for its alternative name of Oceania. Australasia includes Australia, which some regard as a continent in its own right, two major island nations, namely Papua New Guinea and New Zealand, and groups of islands and archipelagos scattered throughout much of the Pacific. This impressive complex of islands (excluding Tasmania, which is federated with Australia, and New Guinea and New Zealand) makes up a land area of about 140,000 square kilometres (54,000 square miles). This does not include Taiwan or the island groups that form Japan, the Philippines and Indonesia, which are all part of Asia. Geographers have divided the Pacific Islands into three main groups: Micronesia, Melanesia and Polynesia. These island groups contain separate archipelagos, some of which form broad, curving arcs, while others are arranged in nearly straight lines.

The Physical Setting

The geographical differences between the Australian landmass and the island groups are marked. The Australian landmass is ancient, with peaks of moderate height, because the highlands have been worn down by millions of years of incessant erosion. The islands are of much more recent origin. Their lofty peaks, volcanoes and continuing volcanic activity, manifested in geysers, hot springs and fumaroles, testify that they are geologically 'young'. Particularly in Micronesia and Polynesia, many islands are composed of coral. They were formed from the accumulation of calcareous material produced by massive colonies of extremely small animals called coral polyps. These islands often appear in a ring or horseshoe shape. Such islands, called atolls, enclose lagoons. Atolls owe their unusual shape to polyp colonies that have built up layer upon layer of coral on the rims of submerged volcanic cones over thousands of years. The coral now forms low islands surrounding a lagoon that occupies the old crater.

Coral polyps can live only in warm water, and most of the Australian islands lie in the tropics. However, the climate varies. For example, the mountainous volcanic islands generally have more rain than low coral islands or the vast desert interior of Australia. The amount of rain and the nature of the soil affect the vegetation, which ranges from the desert steppes of western Australia to the

luxuriant tropical forests of Papua New Guinea, palm-tree and mangrove-swamp-lined islands, and the temperate woodlands of south-eastern Australia, Tasmania and New Zealand.

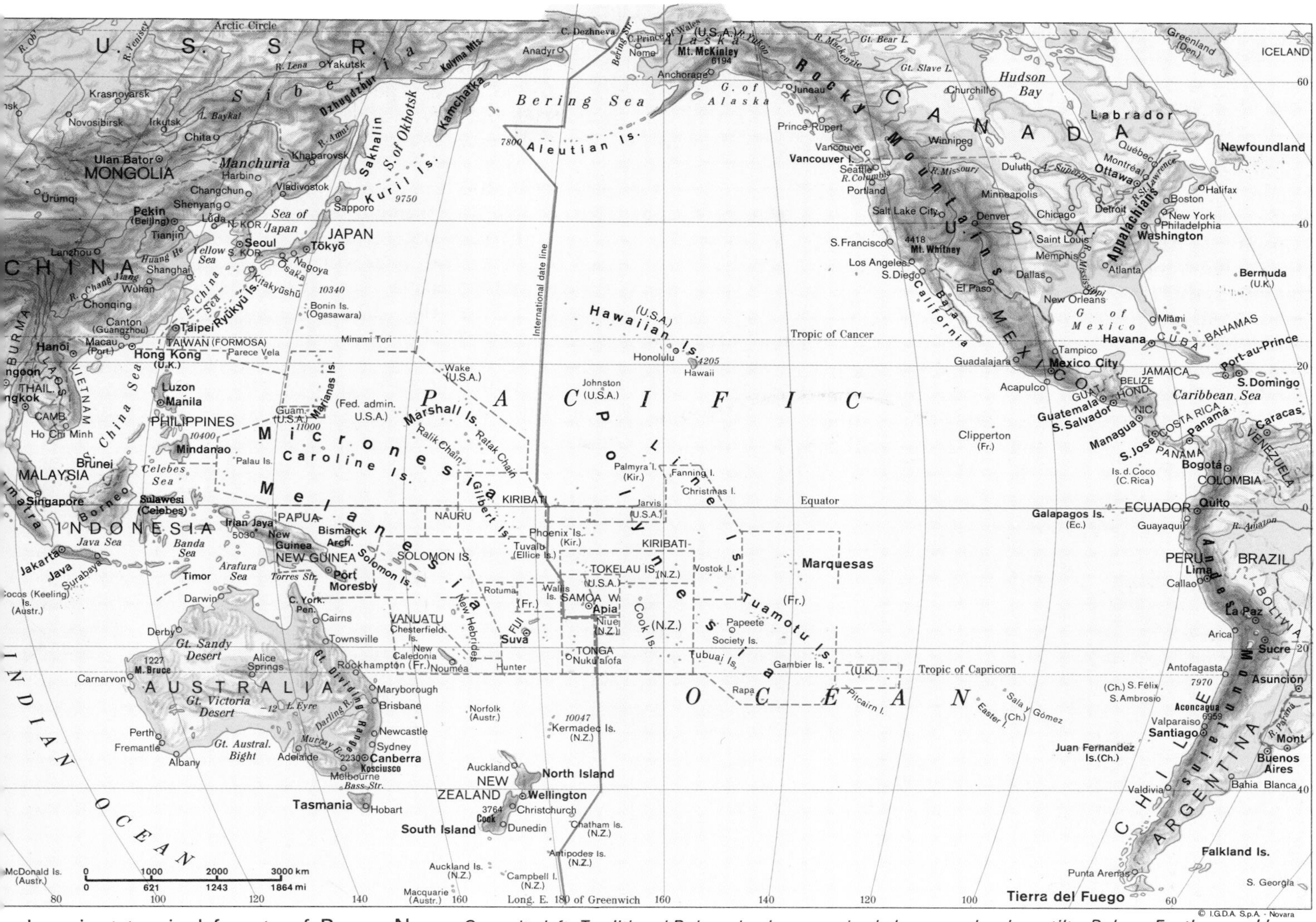

The arrival of European settlers in Australasia has had a marked effect on the region's landscapes. In the early days of exploration, many islands were covered with vegetation while the seas abounded with seals and whales. The destruction of the precious timber and the hunting of marine animals has greatly reduced these natural resources. The fertile land, however, continues to support the plants from which the islanders have always obtained nourishment, notably coconut palms, banana and pineapple plants, breadfruit trees, sweet potatoes and sago. These products form the basic foods on many islands. The Europeans introduced plantation agriculture and the cultivation of cocoa, coffee, cotton and hemp, various fruits, rice, spices, sugar-cane and rubber. Another particularly important European innovation was the introduction of stock-rearing, especially in Australia and New Zealand.

Opposite left: Traditional Polynesian houses raised above sea-level on stilts. Below: Feathers and leaves adorn these Papuan warriors at a tribal ceremony.

The Population: Human and Animal

In Australia and New Zealand, most people are of British or Irish descent and English is the official and most widely spoken language. The Australian Aborigines, the first inhabitants of Australia, have declined by two-thirds since the first European settlement was established in 1788. Today, about 100,000 survive, but many are of mixed blood. The Maoris of New Zealand were also depleted, but their numbers have recovered to about 270,000 in the late 1970s.

The indigenous population of the many Pacific islands is divided into three main ethnic groups. The short or medium-sized Melanesians, also called Australoids, are dark-skinned, and have Negroid features, with frizzy black hair. The Micronesians, by contrast, are Mongoloid in type, while the Polynesians are ethnically mixed, but predominantly Caucasoid, with olive complexions and straight or wavy hair. The proud Maoris of New Zealand are Polynesians.

Australasia possesses some animal species which are unknown or extinct elsewhere. Such animals include the marsupials, such as the kangaroos, possums and koalas, which carry their young in pouches. There are also the monotremes, primitive mammals that lay eggs rather than bear live young. One of these is the duck-billed platypus. In addition, Australasia has a large number of mice and bats. Some birds are unusual or of great beauty. For example, the emu or the Australian ostrich and the cassowary are large flightless birds. The male lyrebird has a magnificent tail and lyrebirds are remarkable mimics of other birds and human sounds. And the birds of paradise in Papua New Guinea possess dazzlingly vivid plumage.

A Lost Paradise

Of the three major island groups, Melanesia in the south-west includes Papua New Guinea, the Solomon Islands, the Vanuatu Republic (formerly the New Hebrides), New Caledonia and Fiji. Many Melanesian islands are mountainous and dotted with volcanoes. Because of the humid tropical climate, vast forests flourish on some wet windward slopes, with luxuriant savannah on the drier leeward slopes. Excluding the western part of New Guinea, which belongs to Indonesia, Melanesia contains a land area of about 540,000 square kilometres (208,500 square miles).

Micronesia lies north of Melanesia. The Micronesian islands range in size from small to extremely small. The Mariana Islands extend in a nearly straight line from north to south. Most of these islands, together with the Caroline Islands and the Marshall Islands, form part of the American Trust Territory of the Pacific Islands, while the independent Kiribati Republic contains the former Gilbert Islands. Micronesia has a land area of about 3,500 square kilometres (1,350 square miles).

In Polynesia, the islands are scattered over a vast part of the Pacific Ocean, east of Micronesia and Melanesia. The main island groups include Tonga (also called the Friendly Islands); Tuvalu (formerly the Ellice Islands); Western Samoa; French Polynesia, including the Tuamotu Archipelago, the Marquesas Islands and the Society Islands which contain the exquisite Tahiti; and Hawaii, the island chain that became the 50th state of the United States in 1959. Most Polynesian islands have a tropical oceanic climate and lush vegetation where the soils are deep enough to support plants. Food-producing plants include sago-palms, banana and bread-fruit trees and taro, and plantation agriculture, introduced by European settlers to produce export crops, is flourishing. Turtles are found on many islands and they are also exported on a large scale. Many Polynesian islands have provided havens for writers and

Above left: Makapuu beach, on Oahu Island in Hawaii.
Left: Forests border a lagoon on the Palau Islands, in Micronesia.

Flag	State	Capital	Area	Population	Economic Resources
	Australia	Canberra	7,686,848 km^2 (2,968,071 mi^2)	15,450,000	Gold, silver iron ore, lead, zinc, bauxite, oil, wheat, sheep, cattle, fishing and other industry.
	Fiji	Suva	18,274 km^2 (7,056 mi^2)	677,000	Gold, manganese, sugar-cane, rice, fishing, food and cement industry.
	Kiribati	Tarawa	886 km^2 (342 mi^2)	64,000	Coconuts, copra, fishing.
	Nauru	Nauru	21 km^2 (8 mi^2)	8,000	Phosphates, fishing.
	New Zealand	Wellington	268,676 km^2 (103,742 mi^2)	3,279,000	Coal, lignite, cereals, tobacco, sheep, cattle, fishing, chemical and textile industry.
	Papua New Guinea	Port Moresby	461,691 km^2 (178,270 mi^2)	3,260,000	Copper, gold, silver, rice, sweet potatoes, coconuts, bananas, coffee, cocoa, timber, fishing.
	Solomon Islands	Honiara	28,446 km^2 (10,984 mi^2)	258,000	Copra, cocoa, coconuts, sweet potatoes, fishing, timber.
	Tonga	Nuku'alofa	699 km^2 (270 mi^2)	98,000	Bananas, sweet potatoes, citrus fruits, copra, livestock, fishing.
	Tuvalu	Funafuti	24 km^2 (9 mi^2)	8,000	Coconuts, copra, fishing.
	Vanuatu	Vila	14,763 km^2 (5,700 mi^2)	117,000	Manganese, coconuts, copra, cocoa, fishing, timber.
	Western Samoa	Apia	2,842 km^2 (1,097 mi^2)	158,000	Bananas, coconuts, cocoa, livestock, fishing, timber.

The Nations of Australasia

The table, left, lists all the independent nations of Australasia. In addition, New Zealand controls many islands, including the **Kermadec Islands,** the **Tokelau** group, the **Cook Islands** and **Niue;** Britain has responsibility for **Pitcairn Island;** France rules **New Caledonia, French Polynesia** and the **Wallis and Futuna Islands** as Overseas Territories; **Easter Island** is part of Chile; and the USA controls **Guam, Midway Islands, Johnston Attol, Wake Island, American Samoa** and the **Trust Territory of the Pacific Islands.** Australasia covers 8,510,000 km^2 (3,285,909 mi^2). The population is about 24 million and so there are 2·8 people per km^2 (7·3 per mi^2).

Above: The Maoris of New Zealand are of Polynesian origin.
Below left: Boats compete in a race off Tahiti.

artists, such as Robert Louis Stevenson, Herman Melville and Paul Gauguin, who sought a 'lost paradise' where life was spontaneous, happy and natural. These same islands are now much frequented by tourists, for whom the Polynesians revive old traditions, although it must be said that little remains of their original culture.

Politically, 11 Australasian countries enjoy independence: Australia, New Zealand, Papua New Guinea (including the eastern half of the island of New Guinea), Fiji, the Kiribati Republic, Nauru, the Solomon Islands, Western Samoa, Tonga, Tuvalu and Vanuatu. Many islands are still ruled by France, New Zealand and the United States, although some are so sparsely inhabited that independence is scarcely viable in economic terms. Such islands remain dependent on foreign aid, although many have been granted a considerable degree of self-government.

Australia

Australia is the world's sixth largest country. It is also the largest and the most economically important part of the continent of Australasia. However, it is thinly populated, because two-thirds of the country is made up of the western plateau region, which is largely desert or semi-desert territory, including some vast, normally dry salt lakes, such as Lake Eyre in South Australia. The western plateau averages 300 metres (984 feet) above sea level, although the mostly flat landscape is occasionally broken by low mountain ranges. Between the plateau and the eastern highlands lie the central lowlands which extend from the Gulf of Carpentaria in the north to the Great Australian Bight in the south. The central lowlands average about 150 metres (492 feet) above sea level. Much of this region is arid, but the Great Artesian Basin, which covers about 1,735,000 square kilometres (670,000 square miles), is used for rearing livestock, because it has a regular water supply from artesian wells. These wells tap water that originated as rainfall in the eastern highlands. There, it seeped into the ground and percolated through layers of porous rock, called aquifers, that underlie the Great Artesian Basin.

The headwaters of Australia's longest rivers, the Murray and its tributary the Darling, rise in the eastern highlands. The Murray is 2,575 kilometres (1,600 miles) long, while the Darling is 165 kilometres (103 miles) longer. The waters of both rivers are utilized in irrigation projects.

The eastern highlands are often called the Great Dividing Range, because they form a watershed. The range reaches a maximum height of only 2,230 metres (7,316 feet) at Mount Kosciusko, in the Australian Alps in the south-east. (The Australian Alps is the name for a scenic section of the Great Dividing Range.) Australia's subdued relief is a consequence of the fact that, geologically, it is an extremely ancient landmass that has been planed down to monotonously level surfaces by natural erosion. East and south of the Great Dividing Range lies a mostly narrow, but fertile coastal plain which contains some of Australia's main cities.

One of Australia's most famous tourist attractions is the Great Barrier Reef along the coast of Queensland. This is the world's largest coral reef, measuring 2,027 kilometres (1,260 miles) in length.

Northern Australia lies in the tropics and has summer monsoon rain in November to April. By contrast, southern Australia has a warm temperate climate, with cooler winters. However, only about one-third of the country has enough rainfall for farming. The best watered areas are the northern, eastern and south-eastern coasts, the Great Dividing Range, and an area in the south-west, around Perth, which has a Mediterranean-type climate, with hot dry summers and cool moist winters. Northern Australia contains tropical forests and extensive savannah. Eucalyptus trees, which Australians call gum trees, are the country's most important native trees. Forests of eucalyptus flourish in the south-east, while eucalyptus and beech forests grow in the cool temperate island of Tasmania, which, structurally, is an extension of the Great Dividing Range on the mainland. However, Tasmania is now separated from south-eastern Australia by the Bass Strait.

Above: The kangaroos of Australia are marsupials; their young develop in the mother's pouch. Left: Two Australian Aborigines light a fire in the traditional way. The Aborigines are descended from people who came from Asia about 30,000 years ago, crossing from island to island on primitive boats and rafts.. Right: The arid landscape of Murchison Gorge, Western Australia.

Strange Animals

Because of its long isolation from other continents, a number of unusual animals have evolved in Australia. Many of the mammals of Australia are marsupials. These creatures do not have a placenta like their counterparts in other continents, but instead have a pouch that functions as an incubator for new-born young. Scientifically, marsupials are divided into three groups. The dasyurids include marsupial mice, the almost extinct Tasmanian wolves, together with

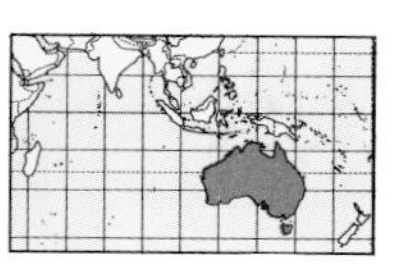

Area:
7,686,848 km²
(2,968,071 mi²)
Population:
15,450,000
Capital:
Canberra (pop. 256,000)
Other cities:
Sydney, Melbourne, Brisbane, Adelaide, Perth, Newcastle, Wollongong, Hobart, Gold Coast, Geelong
Currency:
dollar

fierce nocturnal Tasmanian devils. Small burrowing animals called bandicoots form the second marsupial group. The third and largest group, the phalangeroids, includes the kangaroos, a family of animals which contains a wide range of species, ranging from tiny rat kangaroos to somewhat larger wallabies and the true kangaroos. The true kangaroos include the largest species, the red kangaroo which may be 1·4 metres ($4\frac{1}{2}$ feet) tall when it is seated erect. Red kangaroos live on the inland plains of Australia. Large burrowing marsupials called wombats are also phalangeroids, as are the many species of possums. All the possums have tails except for the beautiful, tree-living koala, which feeds exclusively on eucalyptus leaves and shoots.

Australia and New Guinea are also the home of primitive mammals called monotremes. These include spiny anteaters (or echidnas) and platypuses. The Australian platypus is one of the world's strangest animals. It has webbed feet and a duck-like bill, and it lays eggs like a hen. But it suckles its young, although not from nipples but from mammary glands in the mother's pouch.

Non-marsupial mammals in Australia include bats and rodents. The famous wild dog, or dingo, is the only large carnivore on the grasslands. It was introduced by the Aborigines perhaps 12,000 years ago and it subsequently reverted to the wild. Another mammal, now regarded as a pest, is the rabbit which was first brought to Australia in 1858. It became so abundant that the disease myxomatosis was introduced in the early 1950s. Millions of rabbits died as a result.

Australia has about 650 species of native birds. There are about 60 kinds of parrots, the world's only black swans, the kookaburra bird, also called the laughing jackass because of its braying call, the lyrebird, and the flightless emu and cassowary.

A Prosperous Nation

Australia is one of the world's richest nations. Its wealth is traditionally based on agriculture, and farm products still account for one-third of the exports. However, farming is highly efficient and only six per cent of the workforce is employed on the land. Australia has about 133 million sheep and leads the world in wool production. Most of the wool comes from the hardy Merino sheep, which have a high quality, heavy fleece. New South Wales is the leading sheep state, followed by Western Australia and Victoria. The country also has 25 million cattle, and beef and dairy products are important.

Below: The magnificent Sydney Opera House, symbol of the new Australia. Above: Ayers Rock, sacred to Australia's Aborigines, and a spectacular sight.

Major crops include wheat, which is grown in the south-east and south-west, sugar-cane, which flourishes on the tropical coastlands of Queensland and northern New South Wales, and a great variety of fruits. However, only two per cent of the country is cultivated.

During the 19th century, mining became important when gold rushes attracted large numbers of hopeful prospectors and adventurers. Today, Australia is among the world's top 12 producers of bauxite, copper, gold, iron-ore, lead, lignite, manganese, nickel, salt, silver, tin, tungsten, uranium and zinc. In 1980, Australia also produced most of the coal it needed and nearly 70 per cent of its oil requirements. There are several major mining areas in the eastern highlands, but the most spectacular finds since the Second World War have been in Western Australia.

Mining and manufacturing are now the most important sectors of the economy. In 1978, they accounted for 32 per cent of the gross domestic product, compared with 5 per cent from agriculture and 63 per cent from service industries. Britain was once Australia's leading trading partner. But following Britain's entry into the European Economic Community, the relative importance of trade with Britain has declined. By the early 1980s, Japan and the United States were Australia's leading trading partners. The main exports from Australia are metals and metal ores, cereals, coal and coke, textiles, meat and meat preparations, petroleum and petroleum products, and sugar and honey.

Australia is now a highly urbanized nation. By 1980, 89 per cent of the people lived in urban areas (compared with 81 per cent in 1960) and, surprisingly, 54 per cent of the population lived in the four largest cities, namely Sydney (population with suburbs, 3,333,000), Melbourne (2,865,000), Brisbane (1,138,000) and Adelaide (969,000).

Living standards are generally high and nearly all families own their own homes. The average life expectancy at birth is 73 years. Because of the warm climate, most Australians enjoy outdoor activities and sports. The ancestors of most Australians came from the British Isles and English is the official language. But Australia has developed its own distinctive culture.

A New Continent

The first inhabitants of Australia were probably the Tasmanian Aborigines, who were displaced and driven southwards to the island of Tasmania by later arrivals, the ancestors of the Australian Aborigines who reached the country from Asia about 16,000 years ago. At that time, the sea level was lower than it is today, with the result that a land bridge linked New Guinea to the Australian landmass. The Aborigines were a nomadic, food-gathering people, who lived by hunting, fishing, and collecting plants and insects. They were extremely well adapted to life in the harsh interior of Australia and their complex religious beliefs were expressed in their fascinating art, including carvings, paintings, legends, songs, dance and ritual.

Although Portuguese navigators may have visited Australia in the 16th century, the first certain sighting was made by a Dutch navigator, Willem Jansz, in 1606. And, 10 years later, another Dutchman, Dirk Hartog, landed in western Australia. A third Dutchman, Abel Janszoon Tasman, circumnavigated Australia in 1642–43, but he sailed so far from the coast that he never sighted the Australian mainland. He did, however, discover Tasmania, which he called Van Diemen's Land after the governor of the Dutch East India Company, Anthony van Diemen. However, the island was renamed Tasmania in 1856. Tasman also discovered New Zealand before turning north and returning to Batavia (now Jakarta) in Java. The Dutch East India Company was primarily interested in trade, not exploration. The sight of Australia's barren coasts and their hostile inhabitants, the Aborigines, soon made the Dutch lose interest.

In 1770, Australia was rediscovered by the British navigator Captain James Cook, who charted Australia's pleasant eastern coast, which the Dutch had not seen, claiming it for Britain. However, the coast had few landing places and, in addition, the Great Barrier Reef in the north-east made sailing hazardous. But after the loss of its American colonies, Britain wanted to find new places for penal settlements. In 1788, a convict settlement was founded by Captain Arthur Phillip on the site suggested by Captain Cook, now the site of Sydney. In 1793, the first free men arrived, although transportation of convicts continued until 1852 in the east and 1868 in the west.

The early settlements were confined to the coast, because the Great Dividing Range formed a natural barrier to inland exploration. However, an expedition crossed the mountains in 1813 and discovered the rich plains that lay to the west – plains that could support the Merino sheep which had been introduced in 1797. Exploration of the interior continued throughout the 19th century and the first south-north crossing was made in 1860-61. Immigration increased after the discovery of gold in various places in the 1850s and 1890s. The comparatively late exploration and colonization of Australia makes it a new continent, even compared with the Americas.

The Aboriginal population declined rapidly when it came into contact with the Europeans. Early settlers treated the Tasmanian Aborigines in a brutal manner and exposure to unfamiliar diseases and a new diet weakened them. By 1876, they were extinct. The Australian Aborigines numbered perhaps 300,000 when the first settlement was established at Sydney in 1788. Today, only about 40,000 full-blooded Aborigines remain, living mostly on inland reservations in Northern Territory, Queensland and Western Australia, although there are another 60,000 people of mixed blood.

In 1901, the Australian states united to form the Commonwealth of Australia and its first parliament met in May 1901. Australian soldiers served with much distinction with the Allies in the First and Second World Wars. Ties with Britain were close, but after the Second World War a substantial number of immigrants from European countries other than Britain and Ireland were admitted into Australia. Further, Britain's reorientation of its trade within western Europe weakened traditional ties between Britain and Australia. Increasingly, Australians see their country as a Pacific Ocean nation. Its natural allies, therefore, are the non-Communist countries of South-East Asia, the United States and Japan, a major market for its minerals.

Australia is a federation of six states and two territories. The states are New South Wales which has an area of 801,428 square kilometres (309,450 square miles) and a population of 5,378,000 (1980). Queensland has an area of 1,727,522 square kilometres (667,036 square miles) and 2,488,000 people. South Australia covers 984,377 square kilometres (380,091 square miles) and has a population of 1,347,000. Tasmania has an area of 68,322 square kilometres (26,381 square miles) and 435,000 people. Victoria covers 227,618 square kilometres (87,889 square miles) and has a population of 4,053,000 and Western Australia sprawls over 2,527,621 square kilometres (975,973 square miles) and has 1,374,000 people. The capitals of the six states are respectively Sydney, Brisbane, Adelaide, Hobart, Melbourne and Perth. Northern Territory covers 1,347,519 square kilometres (520,308 square miles). It has a population of only 137,000 and its capital is Darwin.

The Australian Capital Territory includes the federal capital Canberra, the capital city since 1927. The Capital Territory covers 2,432 square kilometres (939 square miles) and has 256,000 people.

Australia is a monarchy within the Commonwealth. The British monarch is the Head of State, represented in Australia by a Governor-General. However, real power is exercised by the federal parliament, including a House of Representatives and a Senate, and the government. Each of the six states has its own parliament, although their powers are limited by the Commonwealth federal government. In 1988 Australians marked 200 years of European settlement with bicentennial celebrations.

Above: The koala, an Australian marsupial, is an appealing little creature that lives in eucalyptus trees. Below: The scarlet flowers of Sturt's desert pea.

New Zealand

New Zealand is a beautiful island nation in the south-western Pacific Ocean, whose superb scenery is attracting an increasing number of tourists. It lies about 2,000 kilometres (1,243 miles) south-east of Australia, from which it is separated by the Tasman Sea. Its eastern coasts face the vast Pacific.

North Island, where more than 70 per cent of the people live, has extremely varied scenery. It is a geologically young island, with fold mountains in the east and a central volcanic plateau, with active volcanoes, hot springs and geysers. The three active volcanoes are Ruapehu, which is 2,796 metres (9,173 feet) above sea level, Ngauruhoe, 2,290 metres (7,513 feet) high, and Tongariro, 1,968 metres (6,457 feet) high. Lake Taupo, which covers 616 square kilometres (238 square miles) on the central plateau occupies the crater of an extinct volcano. North of Lake Taupo, the hot springs are harnessed to produce electricity. North Island also has fertile plains and busy cities. It covers an area of 114,681 square kilometres (44,281 square miles).

The other main island, South Island, is larger, with an area of 150,452 square kilometres (58,093 square miles). The scenery of South Island is dominated by the magnificent Southern Alps, a range of fold mountains that reach a maximum height of 3,764 metres (12,349 feet) at Mount Cook. The Southern Alps contain long glaciers, which once reached the sea in the south-west, gouging out spectacular, steep-sided fiords, or sounds, in what is now Fiordland National Park. The eastern side of South Island contains fertile lowlands, such as the Canterbury Plains, and the Otago Plateau in the south-east.

Stewart Island, the third largest island, is situated to the south of South Island. It covers only 1,735 square kilometres (670 square miles). New Zealand also includes a number of other small islands, including the Chatham Islands, about 850 kilometres (528 miles) to the east, and various tiny uninhabited islets.

Much of New Zealand's wildlife has been introduced by Europeans and such species as rabbits and red deer have become pests. The only native mammals are bats, but New Zealand has several unusual birds, including the flightless kiwi, takahe and weka. The large flightless moa was hunted to extinction by the Maoris in the 17th century.

New Zealand has a cool temperate climate with generally ample rainfall. Summers are pleasant and winters mild, except in the mountains. Most of the people are of British origin and British traditions are strong. But eight per cent are Maoris and one per cent, other Pacific islanders. Nearly all of the Polynesian population is bilingual and speaks English, the official language.

Exploration and Colonization

Not long ago, New Zealand was a natural paradise. It was settled by the Maoris, according to their traditions, in the 14th century, although there is evidence to suggest that there were Polynesian settlements in New Zealand by AD 1000 or even earlier.

New Zealand's location, far to the south of the busy shipping routes to the East Indies, caused it to remain unexplored by Europeans until the 17th century. The first Europeans to reach it were Dutch, as the country's name bears witness – Zeeland is one of the provinces of the Netherlands.

The Dutch navigator Abel Janszoon Tasman discovered the islands in December 1642, after having sailed eastwards from the island that now bears his name, Tasmania. Tasman made the first European contacts with the Maoris, a dark-haired, slender people with light brown complexions, whose hair was held together at the neck with white pins. But the fierce and menacing appearance of most of the Maoris he encountered made Tasman decide to continue his voyage. He therefore failed to realize that New Zealand consisted of two islands, because he mistook the 26-kilometre (16-mile) wide Cook Strait between North and South Island for a deep inlet. The Dutch kept their discovery of New

Below: Geysers and hot springs abound in the area around Rotorua, on North Island, New Zealand.

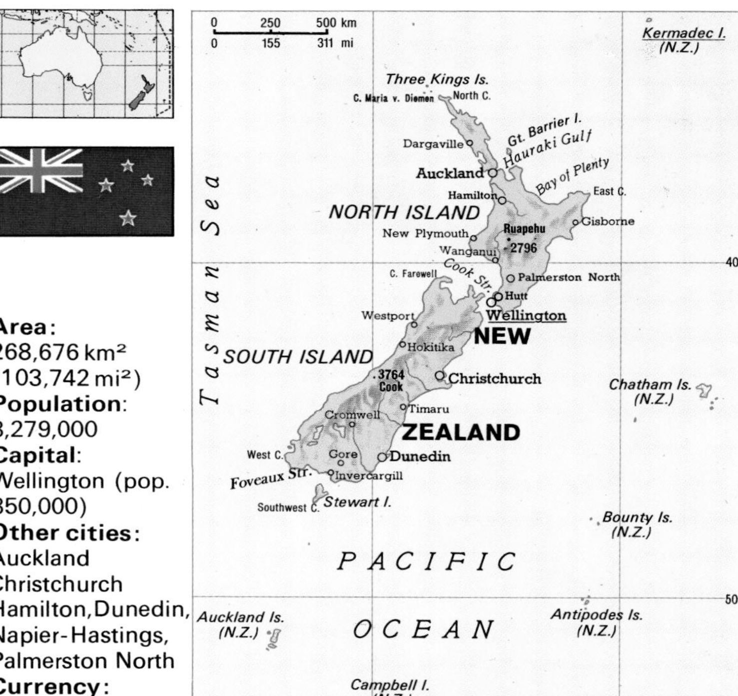

Area:
268,676 km² (103,742 mi²)
Population:
3,279,000
Capital:
Wellington (pop. 350,000)
Other cities:
Auckland
Christchurch
Hamilton, Dunedin,
Napier-Hastings,
Palmerston North
Currency:
dollar

Zealand a secret and, for more than a hundred years, it was forgotten by Europeans. In 1769, however, it was rediscovered by the great British navigator Captain James Cook.

Cook made three voyages to the area. He explored Cook Strait, which was named after him, drew detailed maps and gathered important information about the flora, fauna and the indigenous population. At first, as Tasman before him, he found that the Maoris were hostile, but he eventually established friendly relations. He observed that the Maoris practised cannibalism during tribal wars, but his reports did not deter western sea captains from seeing the islands for themselves. At first, they hunted seals and whales and made landings to cut down the karri, a tree similar to the eucalyptus which provided them with excellent timber for building masts for their sailing ships. Soon, escaped convicts from Australia and other adventurers also visited the coasts, which acquired a reputation for lawlessness.

In the first half of the 19th century, missionaries, scientists and naturalists, most of them British, began to arrive. Appalled by the lawlessness in the coastal settlements, the missionaries pressed Britain to colonize the islands. The first settlers arrived in 1839 and founded Wellington on North Island, which is now the nation's capital. British immigration continued and New Zealand was made part of the colony of New South Wales in Australia.

In 1852, however, New Zealand was granted the status of a self-governing British colony.

There was a major influx of immigrants in 1861 when gold was discovered near Dunedin. But the early years of colonization were marred by a series of wars with the Maoris concerning land ownership. The Maori fighting lances tipped with sharks' teeth could not counter firearms. Like the North American Indians, the Maoris were doomed, and exposure to unfamiliar diseases brought in by the Europeans further sapped their ability to fight on. By 1870, the Maoris numbered no more than 42,000. But after peace came in 1881, they gradually revived in numbers, reaching more than 270,000 in the late 1970s.

In 1907, New Zealand became a dominion of the British Empire. In the First World War, New Zealand forces fought alongside Allied troops in Europe, while in the Second World War, New Zealanders fought in both Europe and the Pacific. Today, New Zealand is an independent nation in the Commonwealth. The British monarch, represented by a Governor-General, is the Head of State. Executive power lies with a cabinet and a prime minister. Legislative power is entrusted to a House of Representatives with 92 elected members.

Riches from Livestock

New Zealand is a wealthy country, with highly developed social welfare and public health services. The chief source of its wealth comes from its pastoral industry. In 1980, New Zealand had 68 million sheep and 8 million cattle. Two-thirds of the country is suitable for either pasture or arable land. New Zealand is the world's third largest wool producer, after Australia and the USSR, and it also exports meat, dairy products and skins. New Zealand is the world's second largest producer of lamb and mutton and it ranks eighth in butter production.

Arable farming is less important than pastoralism, but cereals, fruits, tobacco and vegetables are grown. Agriculture is highly efficient and it now employs only 10 per cent of the workforce as compared with 35 per cent in industry, which now accounts for about one-third of the gross domestic product. Some 85 per cent of the population lives in urban areas and many people work in factories which process the various products obtained from livestock. New Zealand also has some minerals, including coal, iron ore and a little gold, and both light and heavy industries have been developed. New Zealand has abundant hydro-electric power and nearly 90 per cent of its electricity now comes from hydro-electric stations. Most hydro-electric power stations are on South Island, and power lines transmit energy from South Island to North Island, where industrial concentration and population density are highest.

New Zealand's forests cover about 7 million hectares (17 million acres). They contain some high quality indigenous hardwoods and introduced conifers, including the valuable radiata pine. There is a sizeable and expanding wood pulp and paper industry. Fishing by local and foreign vessels is another major activity in the fish-rich seas that encircle New Zealand.

Before the Second World War, New Zealand sold four-fifths of its exports to Britain. However, since Britain joined the European Economic Community, New Zealand has diversified its trade. By 1981, the USA, Australia and Japan were each almost as important export markets as Britain. Major exports include meat, especially lamb, beef and mutton, wool, dairy products, aluminium, fish, and pulp and waste paper. Petroleum and petroleum products, machinery and transport equipment are particularly important imports.

Centre left: Lake Wakatipu, surrounded by the beautiful peaks of New Zealand's Southern Alps. The lake is 77 km (48 miles) long and covers an area of 293 km (113 miles). Below left: A farm at Rotorua. Below: A view of Wellington, New Zealand's capital since 1865. It is situated in the far south of North Island.

Pacific Islands

The islands of the Pacific Ocean, which form part of Australasia, or Oceania (as opposed to those of Asia, which are covered in the section on Asia in this book) are divided into three main groups according to their original inhabitants, namely Micronesia, Melanesia and Polynesia. The islands themselves are either of volcanic origin or they are low-lying coral atolls.

Micronesia

Micronesia, which literally means 'small islands', covers an area of about eight million square kilometres (three million square miles) in the western Pacific Ocean. The Micronesians are a muscular Mongoloid people with copper-coloured skins, straight black hair and dark eyes. Nearly all Micronesians are Christians, although old beliefs linger on in places. The Micronesian island groups include three American territories and the independent republics of Kiribati and Nauru.

The **Trust Territory of the Pacific Islands** has been American since 1944. It includes the Mariana Islands (excluding Guam), the Marshall Islands, the Federated States of Micronesia (Kosrae, Ponape, Truk and Yap), and the Republic of Belau. Each of these now has its own constitution and local government. Nine languages are spoken. Tourism, fishing and farming are the main activities.

Area:
1,779 km² (687 mi²)
Population:
133,000
Capital:
Saipon (in the northern Marianas)

Guam is an 'unincorporated territory' of the USA. It is the largest island in the Mariana Archipelago and it has rugged volcanic mountains and coral reefs along its shores. Fishing and farming are the main activities, and tourism is increasing. Bananas, cassava, coconuts, fruits, maize, sugar-cane, sweet potatoes and taro are the leading products. Discovered in 1521, Guam was Spanish until 1898 when it was ceded to the USA. It was occupied by Japan during the Second World War, but liberated in 1944. The people were granted full US citizenship in 1950.

Area:
549 km² (212 mi²)
Population:
116,000
Capital:
Agaña

Wake Island consists of three small islands, 3,700 kilometres (2,300 miles) west of Hawaii, which form another unincorporated US territory. The islands cover only eight square kilometres (three square miles), with a population of about 1,000.

The Republic of Kiribati (pronounced Kiribas) includes Ocean (or Banaba) Island, the 16 Gilbert Islands, 8 of the Line Islands (the rest are uninhabited US dependencies), and the Phoenix Islands. Kiribati, which became fully independent in 1979, exports copra. Kiribati is a member of the Commonwealth.

Area:
886 km² (342 mi²)
Population:
64,000
Capital:
Tarawa (pop. 24,000)
Currency:
Australian dollar

Nauru, near the equator, is a coral island with high-quality phosphate deposits on which the economy depends. However, these reserves are expected to become exhausted by 1993. Nauru became an independent republic in 1968. It has a special relationship with the Commonwealth.

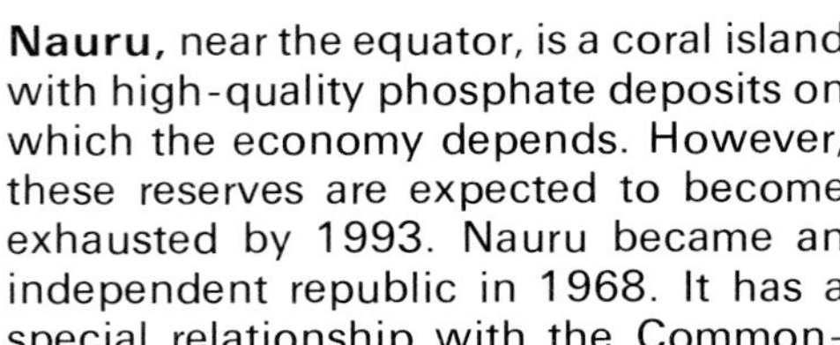

Area:
21 km² (8 mi²)
Population:
8,000
Capital:
Nauru
Currency:
Australian dollar

Melanesia

Melanesia lies south of Micronesia in the south-western Pacific. The name Melanesia means, literally, 'black islands', and most Melanesians are stocky people with Negroid features and black, frizzy hair. Old local religions are more important in Melanesia than in Micronesia, although about half of the people in the region are Christians. Melanesia includes the French New Caledonia, and four independent island nations: Fiji, Papua New Guinea, the Solomon Islands, and Vanuatu.

New Caledonia has been French since 1853 and a French Overseas Territory since 1958. It includes the large island of New Caledonia and various small island groups, including the Loyalty Islands and the Bélep Archipelago. The territory is rich in minerals, such as chrome and iron-ore, manganese and nickel, while coconuts, coffee and meat are the chief farm products. Captain James Cook discovered New Caledonia in 1744.

Area:
19,058 km² (7,359 mi²)
Population:
145,000
Capital:
Nouméa (pop. 74,000)
Currency:
franc CPA

Fiji contains two large volcanic islands Viti Levu and Vanua Levu and 320 small ones. Agriculture and tourism are the main activities on these fertile tropical islands. An Indian-dominated government was overthrown in a military coup in 1987. Fiji became British in 1874 and achieved independence within the Commonwealth in 1970. Indians now make up 48 per cent of the population and Melanesians only 44 per cent.

Area:
18,274 km² (7,056 mi²)
Population:
677,000
Capital:
Suva (pop. 71,000)
Currency:
dollar

Papua New Guinea is Australasia's second largest nation. It includes the eastern part of New Guinea, the Bismarck Archipelago, New Britain and New Ireland, the D'Entrecasteaux Islands, the Louisiade Archipelago, the Trobriand Islands, Bougainville and Buka in the northern Solomon Islands, and about

600 other small islands. About 700 languages are spoken by the predominantly Melanesian population. A few remote groups have never come into contact with western civilization, and tribal warfare breaks out periodically. Mainland Papua New Guinea contains mountain ranges swathed in tropical forest, about 40 active volcanoes, and hot, swampy valleys. Cocoa, coffee, copra, fish and timber are important products, but the most valuable resource is copper, which is mined on the island of Bougainville. Australia governed the mainland from 1914 until 1975, when Papua New Guinea became an independent member of the Commonwealth.

Area:
461,691 km²
(178,270 mi²)
Population:
3,260,000
Capital:
Port Moresby
(pop. 139,000)
Currency:
kina

The **Solomon Islands** were British from the 1890s until 1978, when they achieved full independence within the Commonwealth, although Bougainville and Buka in the north had joined Papua New Guinea. Most of the islands have a rainy tropical climate, and copra, palm-oil and timber are exported. Fishing is important.

Area:
28,446 km²
(10,984 mi²)
Population:
258,000
Capital:
Honiara (on Guadalcanal, pop. 23,500)
Currency:
dollar

The **Republic of Vanuatu** was governed jointly by Britain and France from 1906. In 1980, however, it became fully independent. This new nation contains about 80 mountainous islands, with three active volcanoes. The largest island is Espiritu Santo. Copra and fish are the leading products of these tropical islands. Tourism is increasing.

Area: 14,763 km²
(5,700 mi²)
Population:
117,000
Capital:
Vila (pop. 15,000)
Currency:
vatu

Above: A nickel smelting factory at Doniambo, New Caledonia.

Below: A richly adorned war canoe from the Solomon Islands.

Polynesia

Above: A Polynesian atoll. An atoll is a ring of coral, which has formed an island.

Polynesia, a word meaning literally 'many islands', covers a vast area bounded roughly by New Zealand, Hawaii and Easter Island. The Polynesians are generally taller than the other Pacific islanders, and they have light brown skins, and black hair that may be curly or straight. Most Polynesians are, at least nominally, Christians, although pre-Christian beliefs survive in isolated areas.

The Maoris of New Zealand are Polynesians, but New Zealand is covered by a separate section on pages 151–153. The Hawaiians are another important Polynesian group. The beautiful Hawaiian volcanic island chain became the 50th state of the United States in March 1959 and is dealt with in this book in the section on that country.

Polynesia includes other islands ruled by the USA, France, New Zealand, Britain and Chile. There are also three independent nations: Tonga, Tuvalu, and Western Samoa.

Johnston Atoll, which has an area of about two square kilometres (less than one square mile), and **Midway Islands,** which cover about five square kilometres (two square miles), are both 'unincorporated territories' of the USA.

American Samoa, which has been under US rule since 1900, is a sizeable group of eight islands, about 1,050 kilometres (652 miles) north-east of Fiji. The largest island is Tutuila. These tropical islands produce copra and fish. American Samoa is another unincorporated US territory under the US Department of the Interior.

Area:
197 km² (76 mi²)
Population:
35,000
Capital:
Pago Pago (pop. 1,250)
Currency:
US dollar

France controls two Overseas Territories in Polynesia. The first, called **French Polynesia,** has had the status of an Overseas Territory since 1958. It contains about 130 islands spread across a vast area of ocean. There are five main archipelagos: the Windward Islands (Îles du Vent), including Moorea and the famous scenic island of Tahiti, much beloved of artists; the Leeward Islands (Îles sous le Vent); the Tuamotu Archipelago, including 78 atolls, and the Gambier Islands; the Austral or Tubuai Islands; and the Marquesas Islands north of the Tuamotu Archipelago. The Windward and Leeward Islands are together also called the Society Islands. Discovered in 1767, they were so named after the British Royal Society. The islands became a French protectorate in 1843. Tourism is the main source of income, while copra is the chief product. The High Commissioner of French Polynesia is also responsible for the uninhabited Clipperton Islands, which are about 1,000 kilometres (621 miles) from the coast of Mexico.

Area:
4,000 km² (1,544 mi²)
Population:
172,000
Capital:
Papeete (pop. 63,000)
Currency:
franc CPA

The **Wallis and Futuna Islands,** a French Overseas Territory since 1961, lie about 400 kilometres (249 miles) west of Samoa. It contains two archipelagos: the Wallis Archipelago, the main island of which is Uvea; and the Îles de Horn. Bananas, copra, taro and yams are leading products. The Wallis Archipelago became French in 1842, and the entire territory became a French protectorate in 1887.

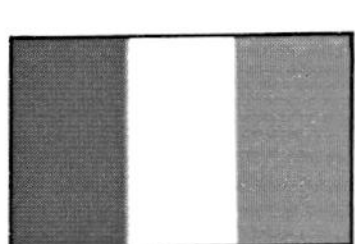

Area:
200 km² (77 mi²)
Population:
13,000
Capital:
Mata-Utu (pop. 6,000)
Currency:
franc CPA

New Zealand's possessions in Polynesia include various small islands, such as the Kermadec Islands, the overseas territory of Tokelau, and two self-governing territories: the Cook Islands and Niue.

Six of the **Cook Islands** are volcanic, while the rest are atolls. Exports, mainly to New Zealand, include copra and fruit. The islands became British in 1880 and New Zealand took over in 1901. Internal self-government came into effect in 1965.

Area:
236 km² (91 mi²)
Population:
18,000
Capital:
Rarotongo

Niue has enjoyed internal self-government since 1974, having been ruled by New Zealand from 1901. This coral island produces copra, honey, limes and passion fruit.

Area:
259 km² (100 mi²)
Population:
3,000
Capital:
Alofi

Pitcairn Island is a small British possession in the south-eastern Pacific, which became famous as the refuge of the mutineers from the *Bounty.* **Easter Island,** between Pitcairn Island and South America, belongs to Chile. Easter Island, which covers 166 square kilometres (64 square miles), is known for its huge stone statues.

Tonga, or the **Friendly Islands,** became an independent monarchy in the Commonwealth in 1970. It contains 169 islands and islets which form three main groups: Vava'u in the north; Ha'apai in the centre; and Tongatapu in the south. Discovered by the Dutch seaman Abel Tasman in 1643, Tonga became a British protectorate in 1900. Leading products are bananas, coconuts and copra.

Area:
699 km² (270 mi²)
Population:
98,000
Capital:
Nuku'alofa (pop. 21,000)
Currency:
pa'anga

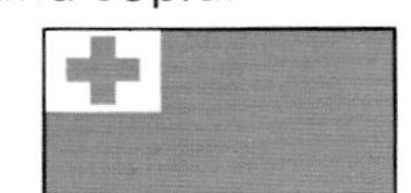

Tuvalu was formerly called the Ellice Islands, and was ruled with the Gilbert Islands (which are now part of the Republic of Kiribati). Most of the islands are low-lying, and coconuts and copra are the chief products. Tuvalu achieved full independence within the Commonwealth in 1978 after 86 years of British rule.

Area:
24 km² (9 mi²)
Population:
8,000
Capital:
Funafuti
Currency:
Australian dollar

Western Samoa, 960 kilometres (597 miles) north-east of Fiji, contains two large volcanic islands, Savai'i and Upolu, two other small islands, and various islets. Before the First World War, Germany ruled the islands, but New Zealand took over after the war. Western Samoa became an independent monarchy in 1962 and a member of the Commonwealth in 1970. Bananas, cocoa and coconuts are leading products.

Area:
2,842 km²
(1,097 mi²)
Population:
158,000
Capital:
Apia (pop. 33,000)
Currency:
tala

Below: Although independent of Britain many Pacific islands like Tonga retain British customs, such as the game of cricket.

Antarctica

The name Antarctica immediately brings to mind a picture of an icy region lost in the seas of the Southern Hemisphere, possibly because it was the last land area to be explored. Today, however, it does not seem to be quite as remote. We know that aircraft and ships regularly supply the scientific stations that various countries have set up on Antarctica. And the ruthless hunt for seals and whales has focused our attention on the need to protect the region's wildlife and natural resources. Apart from seeming to be less distant, Antarctica has also become less mysterious. Aerial surveys and explorations on sleds have produced much detailed information about the physical structure of Antarctica. We now know that the ice sheet of Antarctica conceals a true continent, with lofty mountain ranges, peninsulas and coasts.

Antarctica is the fifth largest continent, with an area of 13,209,000 square kilometres (5,100,000 square miles). This makes it larger than either Europe or Australasia, although it has no permanent population. Around the continent are many islands, large and small. The ice sheet of Antarctica is the world's largest body of ice. It reaches a maximum depth of 4,776 metres (15,669 feet) in Wilkes Land. In places, high mountain peaks jut through the ice. The highest mountain is the Vinson Massif, which rises 5,140 metres (16,864 feet) above sea level. Mount Erebus is Antarctica's only active volcano. It rises 3,794 metres (12,448 feet). In many places, the ice extends to the coast, joining islands to the mainland and extending out to sea in massive ice shelves. The icebergs that break off from Antarctica are generally flat-topped, unlike the icebergs of Greenland. The largest iceberg ever recorded came from Antarctica and was of the flat-topped type. It was sighted in the South Pacific Ocean in 1956 and covered an area larger than that of Belgium.

The Antarctic ice sheet cools the Southern Hemisphere and so affects its climate. For example, the island of South Georgia is about the same distance from the South Pole as northern England is from the North Pole. But ice and snow cover South Georgia for most of the year, while northern England has a temperate climate. And Tierra del Fuego, at the southern tip of South America, the populated region that is closest to Antarctica, is rainy and chilled by icy winds that blow from the south.

A Deserted Land

A study of the rocks of Antarctica has revealed that it once belonged to a much larger continent called Gondwanaland. This landmass also included Africa, India, Australia and South America. About 180 million years ago, Gondwanaland began to break up and the fragments slowly drifted apart, carried by currents in the Earth's semi-molten upper mantle. Consequently, Antarctica became isolated from the rest of the world. It remained empty of people until quite recently, but it was no great loss to mankind. Because of the climate, human settlement is not possible except in artificial habitats, like the underground homes built for scientists who must get all their supplies from the outside world. Inland, at Vostok Station, the world's lowest screen temperature of −88·3°C (−126·9°F) was

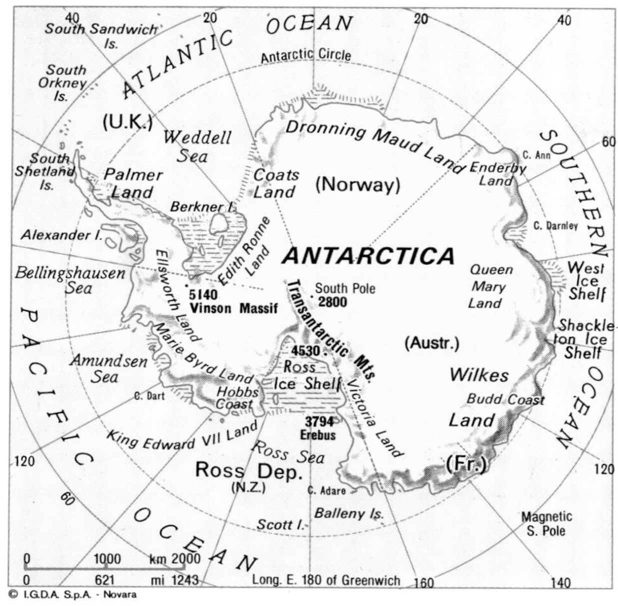

Below opposite: The rather comic appearance of penguins when on land is transformed when they are in their element – they are magnificent swimmers. Below: An Australian scientific survey on Mount Hansen. The continent is divided into 'spheres of influence', in which a number of countries undertake scientific research. Bottom: A flat-topped iceberg awash in the Ross Sea.

recorded in the most severe winter month of August. But even on the fringes of Antarctica in mid-summer, temperatures seldom rise above freezing point. Life is made doubly unpleasant by fierce blizzards, in which winds reach speeds of more than 300 kilometres per hour (186 mph).

In these conditions, the vegetation in Antarctica consists mainly of mosses and lichens which grow only on small patches of bare rock in the warmest months. The vegetation is confined mostly to the coasts where the sea moderates the climate. In summer, in the warmer air, various tiny insects are found. However, if the continent is barren, the sea, by contrast, teems with life. Large stretches of green-brown or blood-red water reveal the presence of abundant plankton. Plankton, formed by millions of microscopic plants and animals, constitutes the basic food for most aquatic animals, from fish to whales, that live around Antarctica. The many sea-birds, such as petrels, sea-gulls and cormorants, also eat plankton. Searching for food, they plunge into the icy water, being protected by their impermeable feathers and body fat. Birds are the most familiar inhabitants of Antarctica, and penguins are the most familiar of the birds. Penguins are confined to the Southern Hemisphere. They cannot fly and, when walking upright, often in dense, noisy groups, they look rather awkward. But they are superb swimmers, able to stay underwater for some time. Penguins are so well adapted to the polar climate that certain species, such as the Emperor penguin that weighs up to 40 kilograms (88 pounds), lay their egg or eggs on the ice in mid-winter. The male helps to

hatch the egg by keeping it warm under its feathered abdomen. By the time that the egg hatches, the male will have lost half of its weight. The male Emperor penguin also helps to care for the helpless young birds. The most common penguin is the Adélie penguin, which weighs only about 7 kilograms (15 pounds).

The mammals of Antarctica are aquatic animals. They include enormous sperm whales, killer whales, dolphins and seals, which sail around on rafts of ice as if they were boats. Periodically they dive from the ice to catch fish. From the 19th century, many of these animals have been over-hunted. Some species, such as blue whale calves, which have been slaughtered with explosive harpoons, are almost extinct. Recent conservation laws are intended to ban military experiments and the dumping of radio-active wastes.

Seal hunters discovered a Continent

In 1773, the British Captain James Cook became the first explorer to cross the Antarctic Circle (latitude 66½° South), and took his sailing ship into the ice pack. A Russian expedition in 1819–21 circumnavigated Antarctica. The first certain landing did not take place until 1831, although bold seal hunters may have landed long before then. At the start of the 20th century, one of the main objectives of explorers was the South Pole. In 1901–04, the British explorer Robert Falcon Scott got within 925 kilometres (575 miles) of the pole and, in 1908, an Irishman, Ernest Shackleton, got within 156 kilometres (97 miles).

The final race for the South Pole took place in 1911. The first to arrive was the Norwegian Roald Amundsen who reached the pole, with four companions, on 14 December, 1911. His rival, Robert Falcon Scott, on his second expedition, reached the pole on 18 January, 1912. But Scott and all his companions tragically lost their lives on the return journey, when only 10 km (6 miles) from safety.

Top: An exciting moment as a sno-cat endeavours to bridge a crevasse. Above: The Astrolabe *and the* Zélée, *ships of the French Antarctic expedition of 1837–40. The expedition was led by the explorer Dumont d'Urville, who discovered Adelaide Island, which he named after his wife, and the island of Joinville, close to the Southern Shetlands. Today ice-breakers are used to penetrate the ice pack. Right: Eskimos of Baffin Island; unlike the Antarctic, parts of the Arctic are inhabited.*

The Arctic

The region known as the Arctic consists of the Arctic Ocean, in the centre of which is the North Pole, and the northernmost parts of the continents that surround this icy sea. The Arctic extends southwards to the Arctic Circle, latitude 66½° North. Within this boundary lie northern Alaska, Canada, including many bleak islands, Norway, Sweden, Finland and the USSR, as well as most of the island of Greenland.

The climate of the Arctic is severe. Polar ice pack (floating ice) covers the Arctic Ocean for the greater part of the year, the ice cover being permanent around the North Pole, and most of Greenland is buried by a huge ice sheet, the world's second largest after Antarctica. But the southern parts of the Arctic have short, warm summers when the snow melts and mosses, lichens, some flowering plants and low shrubs spring to life. This is the typical treeless tundra. In summer, it forms a monotonous and boggy landscape which attracts the great northern herbivores, including the Canadian musk ox, caribou and reindeer. These animals graze on the tundra and, in a few weeks, accumulate the fat reserves they need to survive the long winter. Many other smaller herbivorous mammals live in the tundra region, including Arctic hares, lemmings, voles, muskrats and marmots. Such animals procreate rapidly when the weather is mild and food abundant. To maintain the biological equilibrium, the tundra also has its carnivores, all of which are dangerous hunters. These include the brown bears of Alaska, the black bears of Europe and Siberia, coyotes, ermines, foxes, lynxes, martens, minks, otters and wolves. Many of these animals have beautiful furs and are, therefore, the victims and prey of human hunters.

The waters of the Arctic are cold. When the surface is covered by ice, the temperature is below freezing and, even in **summer, the temperature hardly rises** higher than –1·5°C (29°F), the freezing point of this salty ocean. The centre of the Arctic Ocean is always blanketed by floating ice, with a thickness of 2–3 metres (7–10 feet). In the coldest months, the pack ice extends southwards, only to break up in the spring. Huge icebergs also drift southwards in the North Atlantic and Pacific oceans. These jagged islands of ice have broken away from land glaciers and ice sheets.

The Arctic Ocean is rich in plankton, which supports a great variety of fauna – not only fish, but also mammals. There are the cetacean mammals, such as dolphins and whales, including the sperm whale and the dangerous killer whale. Other marine carnivores include sea lions, seals and walruses. Finally, there is the king of the ice – the massive polar bear which hunts its prey around the edges of the ice pack.

The Peoples of the North

The people of the Arctic include the Lapps of northern Scandinavia, the Chukchi and Samoyeds of Siberia, and the Eskimos of Alaska, Canada and Greenland. For thousands of years, these hardy people have lived as nomads in the icy Arctic wastes. The Lapps and some of the Siberian peoples depended on the reindeer, from which they obtained not only meat, milk, cheese, skins and leather, but also the bones from which they made many utensils, the tendons and nerves which were used as thread for making clothes and leather boots, and the gut, which when dried and stretched, could be used as transparent windows in their tents. Today, however, fewer and fewer Lapps follow their traditional lifestyle of following the annual migrations of the reindeer.

Change has also come to the Eskimos, who traditionally lived by hunting and fishing using stone or metal-tipped harpoons. The Eskimos were well adapted to their environment. For example, their winter huts were made of blocks of ice, although inside they were warm, being heated by oil lamps and body heat. In summer, the Eskimos lived in tents made

An extraordinary variety of wild life has learned to adapt to the freezing conditions of the Arctic. Below left: The polar bears which can weigh up to 800 kg (1,764 lb). Below right: Seals, traditionally hunted by the Eskimos for their blubber and skins. A bull can weigh a tonne. Bottom: Man also has adapted to life in the Arctic.

from animal skins. In winter, the Eskimos travelled on sleds drawn by teams of dogs. In summer, they hunted in narrow, one-man kayaks. Kayaks are lightweight canoes with a skin cover that makes them watertight even when they capsize.

Today the Arctic is a source of oil and various mineral ores, including iron-ore and copper. To exploit these resources, technicians, scientists and other workers have gone to the Arctic and mixed with the local population. The introduction of new technology has increasingly undermined traditional ways of life and more and more of the Arctic people now live in modern homes and enjoy 20th-century comforts.

Exploration of the Arctic

In the Age of Exploration, the Arctic was of interest because it might have offered a short route from Europe to Asia. There were two possible courses. The first was to sail north of the Canadian mainland, along what came to be known as the North-West Passage. The second route lay to the north of Eurasia – the North-East Passage.

Many explorers lost their lives in vain attempts to find these routes. The North-East Passage was finally sailed by the Swede Nils Nordenskjöld in 1878-79,

Top: Eskimos on Baffin Island. The life of the Eskimos has changed radically this century. Above: An Eskimo igloo, a home made out of blocks of ice for use on hunting expeditions. The entrance is an extension consisting of a short corridor that slopes downwards to prevent warm air from escaping. Right: Tents are widely used during the brief summer months. Formerly they would have been made of skins.

while the voyage through the North-West Passage was completed by the Norwegian Roald Amundsen in 1903–06. But neither passage was, by then, important, because faster and easier ways of ship travel, notably via the Panama and Suez canals, had been established.

The other goal of Arctic explorers was the North Pole. Famous among the unsuccessful attempts to reach it was the expedition of the Norwegian Fridtjof Nansen who, in 1893, became the prisoner of the ice in his ship, the *Fram.* Carried by ocean currents, the ship drifted northwards to latitude 84° North in the winter of 1894–95. Nansen then decided to try to reach the pole on foot. But he encountered enormous difficulties and was forced to turn back when only 438 kilometres (272 miles) from his objective.

The first explorer to reach the pole by land was the American Commander Robert Peary of the US Navy in 1909. Amundsen flew over the pole in an airship in 1926. In 1958 the US atomic submarine *Nautilus,* named after Captain Nemo's submarine in Jules Verne's *20,000 Leagues Under the Sea,* crossed the Arctic Ocean beneath the ice pack via the North Pole.

Europe

The origin of the name 'Europe' is a matter of dispute. Some believe it to derive from *ereb,* a word meaning 'west' in ancient Semitic languages. The term may have been applied to the lands of the Mediterranean, lying to the west of Asia. Others believe the name has a Greek origin. Europa, a well known figure in Greek mythology, was the beautiful daughter of Agenor (or, according to Homer, Phoenix). The god Zeus fell in love with Europa, and having turned into a white bull, he abducted her. They swam westwards from the shore of Asia Minor to the island of Crete, which forms part of the continent that bears her name.

The map of Europe shows that it is an enormous peninsula extending from Asia. In fact, Europe and Asia do form one great, single land mass, sometimes referred to as Eurasia. The border between Europe and Asia is the result of history and culture rather than of any insurmountable natural barrier. It runs from north to south through the USSR, along the Urals. Skirting Kazakhstan, it runs to the Caspian Sea, and then along the Iranian and Turkish borders to the Black Sea. The Bosporus, in Turkey, provides the most famous part of the border between the two continents. Because of this irregular boundary, 5,571,000 km² (2,151,092 mi²) of the USSR, or nearly one-fourth of the total, is in Europe, together with 23,623 km² (9,121 mi²) of Turkey, which constitutes three per cent of Turkey's total area.

The rest of Europe lies open to the ocean, with the Arctic Ocean in the north, and the Atlantic in the west. The ragged coastline and islands of north-western Europe enclose a number of minor seas, including the Irish Sea, the North Sea, the English Channel and the Baltic Sea. In the south, through the narrow gateway from the Atlantic at Gibraltar, is the Mediterranean Sea, which includes a number of minor ones: the Tyrrhenian, the Adriatic, the Ionian and the Aegean Seas. Beyond the Dardanelles lies the Sea of Marmara, and beyond that the Black Sea and the Sea of Azov. Europe has the most intricate coastline of any continent. Since ancient times, this geographical feature has encouraged trade, human contact, migration and maritime skills – all of which have helped in the development of European civilization.

The entire eastern half of Europe is occupied by the vast Sarmatian or Russian Plain, which stretches over approximately 5,000,000 square kilometres (1,931,000 square miles). This is a huge tract of lowland, occasionally broken by modest heights, which rarely exceed 400 metres (1,312 feet), such as the uplands of Central Russia and the Volga, and the Valday hills.

In the west, however, there is great variety. The highest ranges encircle the Mediterranean, forming a crescent from the Strait of Gibraltar to the Bosporus. It begins with the mountains of the Iberian peninsula, which continue into the Pyrenees, between France and Spain, and on

Top left: The ancient village of Lindos on the Greek island of Rhodes. Top right: The green fields and hills of Northern Ireland. Above left: Windmills in the La Mancha region of Spain, made famous by the novel Don Quixote. *Above right: The Hungarian capital Budapest on the River Danube.*
Opposite: A 17th-century map of Europe is illustrated around its borders by national costumes of the day and views of major cities.

into the Alps and the Balkans. Many of these mountains are high and rugged, with glaciers and snowy summits. Most spectacular are the Alps, where Mont Blanc, in France, reaches 4,810 metres (15,781 feet). The highest point in Europe, in the Caucasus range in the far south-eastern corner, is Elbrus at 5,633 metres (18,481 feet). This range extends from the Black Sea to the Caspian. The mountains of northern Europe are considerably less dramatic. The backbone of the Scandinavian peninsula is mountainous; but Gladhöppingen in Norway reaches only 2,472 metres (8,110 feet). The mountains of the British Isles are similarly ancient, and have been greatly eroded. Ben Nevis in Scotland is the highest peak at 1,347 metres (4,419 feet).

The mountains of southern Europe surround some fertile plains, including Andalucia, in Spain; the Po valley, in Italy; the plain of Hungary; and Wallachia, in Romania. Much of northern Europe consists of lowlands or rolling hills and river valleys and about two-fifths of the Netherlands is below sea level.

Eastern Europe has only a few major rivers, but they are long ones with considerable volume and they are mostly navigable for long distances. Chief of these are the Volga and the Danube. The lowlands of Germany and France are also drained by navigable rivers, notably the Rhine. The rivers of the Mediterranean basin tend to be shorter and more rapid, being navigable only in stretches.

The variations in the terrain ensure that the climate varies considerably within the continent. But Europe is fortunate in having fewer extremes than elsewhere in the world. Europe lies largely in the temperate zone and only a small portion of its territory lies north of the Arctic Circle. The Arctic regions suffer the harshest climatic conditions. Here summers are short, and winters severe and long. Snow and ice covers the ground for most of the year, and the vegetation consists of mosses, lichens, and a few flowering plants, but no trees. Eastern Europe is the region least exposed to the moderating influence of the sea, and has a typically continental climate, with long cold winters and mild summers. Here there are extensive forests, and cereals can be cultivated.

North-western Europe on the other hand is affected by the Atlantic, by ocean winds and by the North Atlantic Drift, an extension of the Gulf Stream, a warm current to which Norway owes its ice-free ports and Ireland its lush, green meadows. Winters are mild, and sum-

The Major Rivers

Volga: 3,531 km (2,194 mi), into the Caspian Sea; **Danube**: 2,860 km (1,777 mi), into the Black Sea; **Ural**: 2,428 km (1,509 mi), into the Caspian Sea; **Dnepr**: 2,201 km (1,368 mi), into the Black Sea; **Kama**: 2,032 km (1,263 mi), tributary of the Volga; **Don**: 1,870 km (1,162 mi), into the Sea of Azov; **Pechora**: 1,809 km (1,124 mi), into the Barents Sea; **Dnestr**: 1,352 km (840 mi), into the Black Sea; **Rhine**: 1,326 km (824 mi) into the North Sea.

The Main Lakes

Ladoga (USSR), 18,400 km² (7,105 mi²); **Onega** (USSR), 9,610 km² (3,711 mi²); **Vänern** (Sweden), 5,585 km² (2,156 mi²); **Saimaa** (Finland), 4,400 km² (1,699 mi²); **Rybinsk** (USSR), 4,100 km² (1,583 mi²); **Chudskoye** (USSR), 3,550 km² (1,371 mi²); **Ilmen** (USSR), 2,200 km² (849 mi²); **Vättern** (Sweden), 1,912 km² (738 mi²); **Mälaren** (Sweden), 1,140 km² (440 mi²); **Päijänne** (Finland), 1,090 km² (421 mi²); **Inarijarvi** (Finland), 1,000 km² (386 mi²).

The Main Islands

Great Britain, 229,885 km² (88,764 mi²) between North Sea and Atlantic Ocean; **Iceland,** 102,820 km² (39,701 mi²) in Atlantic Ocean; **Ireland,** 84,420 km² (32,597 mi²) in Atlantic Ocean; **North Novaya Zemlya,** 48,904 km² (18,883 mi²) between Barents Sea and Kara Sea; **Spitsbergen,** 39,435 km² (15,227 mi²) in Arctic Ocean; **South Novaya Zemlya,** 33,275 km² (12,848 mi²) between Barents Sea and Kara Sea.

High Mountains

Mt Elbrus (USSR), 5,633 m (18,481 ft); **Mont Blanc** (between Italy, France and Switzerland), 4,810 m (15,781 ft); **Monte Rosa** (between Italy and Switzerland), 4,634 m (15,203 ft); **Weisshorn** (Switzerland), 4,505 m (14,780 ft); **Matterhorn** (between Italy and Switzerland), 4,478 m (14,692 ft); **Gross Combin** (Switzerland), 4,314 m (14,154 ft); **Finsteraarhorn** (Switzerland), 4,274 m (14,022 ft); **Aletschhorn** (Switzerland), 4,195 m (13,763 ft); **Jungfrau** (Switzerland), 4,158 m (13,642 ft); **Pelvoux** (France), 4,103 m (13,461 ft); **Gran Paradiso** (Italy), 4,061 m (13,323 ft); **Bernina** (between Italy and Switzerland), 4,050 m (13,287 ft); **Monviso** (Italy), 3,841 m (12,602 ft).

Left: Vineyards in the Alsace region of France. Below: The Tromsø fjord in Norway. Bottom: The Engadine valley in Switzerland.

Opposite top: Mosses grow on a lava field in Iceland. Opposite centre: The town of Mariehamn lies amid the woods of Åland Island, in Finland. Opposite below: Dairy products and tulips are important products of the Dutch countryside.

mers are cool, and there is a moderate rainfall in all seasons. Here there are deciduous woods of beech, oak and birch. Cereals, fruit and vegetables are cultivated, and there is rich pasture for dairy herds. In the Mediterranean region the climate is milder in winter and warmer in summer. The warmth of the sea moderates the short, wet winters and tempers the heat of the long, dry summers. Olive trees and vines flourish in this climate, and citrus fruits, cereals and tobacco are also grown. There is extensive scrubland, and wooded slopes.

The temperate climate of Europe has facilitated change and development. There is no desert, and the land is mostly fertile. There is a wide variety of mineral resources. The land area, 10,531,000 square kilometres (4,066,000 square miles) in all, supports some 695,000,000 people – about one-sixth of the world's population. Europe is the most densely populated continent, particularly in the countries of the industrial north-west – Belgium, the Netherlands, Germany and Britain. From ancient times, the continent has seen great migrations of peoples, often pushing westwards from central Asia in search of fertile lands or territory.

Most of the population speaks languages of the Indo-European family. There are three main groups: the Romance group, the Balto-Slavic group and the Germanic and Scandinavian groups. The Romance languages originate from the Mediterranean basin. They include languages derived from the Latin tongue of ancient Rome – Italian, French, Spanish, Catalan, Portuguese, Romanian and Ladin. Generally, the Mediterranean people are of average height, with olive complexions, dark hair and brown eyes. The Germanic and Scandinavian peoples are often taller, with a fair complexion, blue eyes and blond hair. These include Germans, Austrians, some Swiss, Dutch, Flemish, English, Danes, Norwegians, Swedes and Icelanders. The Balto-Slavs, who settled the eastern part of Europe, include Russians, Ukrainians, Poles, Czechs, Slovaks, Lithuanians, Latvians, Serbians, Croats and Slovenians. They are often characterized by a solid physique, high cheek bones, strong features and almond-shaped eyes. However, the physical characteristics are blurred in many places by inter-breeding.

Other groups include the Celts, who settled much of western Europe before being driven westwards by Germanic tribes, or being assimilated by such conquering peoples as the Romans. These include the Scots, the Irish, the Manx, the Welsh, the Cornish, the Bretons and some Spanish. Five Celtic

Europe

languages are still spoken. At the other end of Europe are the Hellenes, or Greeks, the founders of European culture, and the Albanians. Other groups include the Jews, who were dispersed across much of Europe from their homeland in south-western Asia in the first century AD. Many Hungarians claim descent from Mongol invaders, as do the Bulgarians, but in their case their language and culture is now Slavic. Other European groups of Asian origin include the Turks, the Tartars, the Kazakhs, the Finns and the Laplanders.

Modern history has added a further cosmopolitan dimension to the cities of Europe. Refugees have arrived to escape wars of political persecution elsewhere. The citizens of former colonies have settled in their adopted homelands. And economic forces have driven workers of less developed countries to the industrial centres of north-western Europe. It has been from just such a mingling of cultures that European civilization has in the past developed.

Politically, Europe is a complex mosaic of nations. On the one hand, there is the vast expanse of the USSR, and sizeable territories, such as France and Poland. On the other hand, there are such tiny states as Andorra, Liechtenstein, Monaco, San Marino and Vatican City.

The Yalta conference: the fate of Europe is decided

On 4 February 1945, the three great war leaders, Josef Stalin of the USSR, Franklin D. Roosevelt of the USA and Winston Churchill of the United Kingdom, met for an eight-day conference in Yalta, a small town in the Soviet Union. The Second World War was not yet over (Germany surrendered in May of that year and Japan in August), but the Allied troops had already launched the last, decisive offensive on the European front. In Yalta the immediate post-war problems were discussed.

As far as Germany was concerned, it was decided to divide the country into four occupation zones which later developed into two independent nations, the Federal Republic of Germany (West Germany) and the German Democratic Republic (East Germany). Berlin was also divided into four occupied zones: the American, Soviet, British and French.

The new boundaries of Poland were determined and the government of Poland agreed. It was also decided that free elections should be announced in those eastern European countries which had been freed from the Germans. Finally, the Soviet Union undertook to attack Japan in order to expedite the end of this terrible war, which for six years had shattered Europe and torn apart the rest of the world.

But even these tiny countries have played their part in European history. Today the great cultural diversity of the past is disappearing. Europeans travel in each others' countries, eat each others' food and watch the same television programmes. National costume is only worn on special or ceremonial occasions. A street in Birmingham or Rotterdam, Düsseldorf or Milan looks much the same. But even so traditional cultures and national temperaments do survive. In a relatively small physical area, Europe offers considerable variety.

European civilization was born in the Aegean. The Minoans, on the island of Crete, were using bronze weapons by about 3000 BC. Between 2000 and 1400 BC, the Minoans had built fabulous palaces at Phaistos, Mallia and Knossos. On the Greek mainland, the city of Mycenae was another centre of civilization. These powers were superseded by the iron-using Dorian Greeks in about 1000 BC. Within 500 years, Greece was the centre of a civilization which was to determine the future of Europe. Ancient Greece was a collection of city-states rather than a unified empire, a society dependent on slaves and given to internal warring. But it was the centre of the first discussions on political theory and philosophy, the place where laws were codified and drama and poetry thrived, and the site of fine buildings which still astound us today. To the north of Greece lay the kingdom of Macedon. In 338 BC, the Greek states fell to Philip II of Macedon, and his son Alexander the Great founded a Greek-Macedonian empire that stretched to India.

Meanwhile, in Italy, a number of city-states had been founded by the Etruscans. One of their cities, Rome, broke away from Etruscan rule in 509 BC. The Roman Empire set the course of subsequent European history. Their magnificent culture was heavily influenced by that of Greece. But their success was the result of military efficiency, organization, and technological expertise. The Roman Empire was to surround the Mediterranean Sea and cover most of western Europe, as Celtic and Germanic tribes were subjugated. The relics of Rome survive today. Physically, the heritage of Rome is manifested in innumerable monuments, aqueducts and fortifications. Also, in the world of ideas, it is evident in law, philosophy and literature. Rome was sacked in AD 455 and finally collapsed in 476. Its eastern offshoot of Constantinople (now Istanbul) was a centre of culture, but it was no great imperial power. Nevertheless, long after the empire had crumbled, the memory of strong, centralized government and the 'Roman peace' lingered on as an ideal.

The age of Rome was followed by the so-called Dark Ages, which were characterized by conquests, disruption and lack of central authority. But kingdoms which were by no means 'barbarian' were soon established. The first great empire to arise was that of Charlemagne, king of the Franks, who was crowned Holy Roman Emperor in AD 800. His authority stretched from the Pyrenees to eastern Europe, and provided the foundations of medieval Europe. It was during the Middle Ages that the political map of Europe began to take its present shape. The Holy Roman Empire survived in the German-speaking lands as a federation of states and principalities. In the west, great kingdoms arose, including those of France, England, Scotland, Aragon, Castile and Portugal. Medieval Europe was feudal in character. This meant that society was organized as a pyramid, at the top of which was the pope, who held authority from God. Next came the monarchs, then the nobles, retainers and serfs. The superior provided protection for the inferior, in return for service on the land or in battle.

This social structure began to collapse with the rise of the merchant class, whose control of the finances of the kingdom gave them power. Kings needed money to fight wars, and if they did not have it, they had to borrow it. The rise of capitalism saw the rise of the middle classes, and of a banking system based initially in Italy. Italy had remained a collection of small city-states and kingdoms, and it was here that a great rebirth, or 'Renaissance' of culture took place. A growing interest in all aspects of learning occurred, particularly in the arts of classical Greece and Rome. The result was an outpouring of genius into painting, sculpture, architecture, literature, music, engineering and metalwork. Medieval works of art had, on the whole, expressed conformity with the prevailing social structure. Renaissance works of art, however, displayed an exuberant individuality which was without precedence. In northern Europe, this change of spirit was marked by the Reformation. Inspired by the teachings of such men as Martin Luther (1483–1546), northern states broke away from the papacy. The 'Christendom' of medieval Europe had become a collection of individual, competitive nation states.

The new, self-confident Europe expanded rapidly. Its exploration of the world soon led to the founding of overseas colonies in Asia and in the newly discovered world of the Americas. Exploitation and plunder led to great material wealth, for nations and for individuals.

The monarchies of Europe seemed secure. In France Louis XIV (1638–1715) presided over a glittering court and wielded absolute power. But 1649 had seen the execution of another king who tended towards autocratic rule. This was Charles I of England. And the 18th century saw the first great revolution of modern times, when the French people, starved and ground down by injustice, arose against the tyranny of the Bourbon dynasty. Both the English and French revolutions were short-lived. Out of the bloodbath of the latter arose Napoleon Bonaparte (1769–1821). A brilliant soldier, his conquests made France the dominant power in Europe at the outset of the 19th century. No republican – he had himself crowned emperor in 1804 – he rationalized social administration and law. Having failed in his bid to invade Russia, Napoleon was finally defeated by the British and Prussians at Waterloo, in 1815.

The European countries were now overlords of much of the world. Even though Britain had lost its American colonies, this small country came to rule India and much of Africa and the Far East. In the 18th century, rapid development of technological and engineering skills occurred in Britain. In the 19th century, this resulted in full-scale industrialization. Huge new cities and factories were built, and railways crossed the countryside. The social effects were devastating. Wages and living conditions for the working classes were appalling. As industrialization spread through France, Germany and other parts of Europe, many people sought ways of counteracting social injustices. The proposed remedies varied from the social reform of Lord Shaftesbury (1801–85), or the co-operative experiments of Robert Owen (1771–1858), to the more radical solutions advanced by the German Communist Karl Marx (1818–83) or by the Russian anarchist Mikhail Bakunin (1814–76).

The First World War broke out in 1914 between the Allies and the Central Powers, which included the major new power of a united German empire. For the first time, the full horrors of a modern war were revealed, with prolonged carnage. New weapons appeared, such as poison gas and tanks. In 1917, one of the participants, Russia, experienced a revolution at home. Russia had for years been a great power, but it was backward and crippled by the autocratic rule of the tsars. The revolution, led by the Marxist Vladimir Ilyich Lenin (1870–1924) brought the USSR, as it became known, to the forefront of the world stage.

In the 1920s and 1930s, a new threat to Europe arose from the German fascist, Adolf Hitler (1889–1945). A totalitarian and a racist, Hitler rebuilt Germany into a military machine designed to subjugate the rest of Europe. Hitler found allies in the Italian fascist Benito Mussolini, and the militarist empire of Japan. German tanks rolled across the borders of Europe to the east and west. Jews and dissidents were systematically murdered in concentration camps. Hitler was finally defeated by the Allies in 1945.

After this Second World War, Europe was exhausted and shattered. The post-war years saw Europe divided into two mutually hostile camps. The socialist countries of eastern Europe, allied with the USSR, formed one bloc, while the

Europe has some of the world's most delightful capital cities, bustling with activity and full of history. Top, from left to right: Brussels, Amsterdam and Vienna; centre left: London's Tower Bridge; centre right: The Sacré Coeur in Paris; bottom left: Rome; bottom right: Moscow.

The Countries

The tables list the major European nations, but note that the USSR includes both the European part (24·87 per cent of the area) and the Asian part of that country. Minor territories include the **Faeroe Islands,** 1,399 km² (540 mi²), belonging to Denmark; **Gibraltar,** 6 km² (2·3 mi²), belonging to the UK; **Isle of Man,** 588 km² (227 mi²) and the **Channel Islands,** 195 km² (75 mi²), which are subject to the British Crown, although technically not part of the UK; **Monaco,** 1·9 km² (0·7 mi²); **San Marino,** 61 km² (24 mi²); **Turkey,** 23,623 km² (9,121 mi²) in Europe, the rest being in Asia; and **Vatican City** (Holy See), 0·44 km² (0·17 mi²). The total area of Europe is 10,531,000 km² (4,066,000 mi²), and the population is approximately 695,000,000.

Above: Gold ingots are weighed in a foundry in the canton of Ticino, Switzerland. Although it lacks mineral resources, Switzerland has developed thriving manufacturing industries based on superb workmanship. It is also a centre of banking and international finance.

Flag	Country	Capital	Area	Population	Resources and Products
	Albania	Tiranë	28,748 km² (11,100 mi²)	2,752,000	Oil, wheat, maize, sugar, olives, tobacco, timber, industry, metal ores.
	Andorra	Andorra la Vella	453 km² (175 mi²)	42,000	Tobacco, timber, sheep, hydroelectricity, tourism.
	Austria	Vienna (Wien)	83,849 km² (32,376 mi²)	7,560,000	Lignite, iron, graphite, wheat, barley, potatoes, sugar, timber, industry.
	Belgium	Brussels (Bruxelles)	30,513 km² (11,782 mi²)	9,889,000	Coal, wheat, vegetables, sugar, livestock, engineering, textiles, chemicals.
	Bulgaria	Sofia (Sofiya)	110,912 km² (42,826 mi²)	8,930,000	Lignite, coal, iron, cereals, sunflowers, tobacco, livestock, timber, textiles, machinery.
	Czechoslovakia	Prague (Praha)	127,869 km² (49,373 mi²)	15,556,000	Coal, lignite, metal ores, cereals, vegetables, timber, textiles, mechanical engineering, beer.
	Denmark	Copenhagen (København)	43,069 km² (16,630 mi²)	5,112,000	Barley, sugar, wheat, potatoes, fishing, livestock, engineering, chemicals.
	Finland	Helsinki	337,032 km² (130,136 mi²)	4,872,000	Iron, oats, barley, timber, livestock, shipyards, wood and paper industry.
	France	Paris	547,026 km² (211,219 mi²)	54,832,000	Coal, iron, cereals, grapes, potatoes, sugar, fishing, livestock, industry, tourism.
	Germany, East (German Democratic Republic)	East Berlin	108,178 km² (41,770 mi²)	16,765,000	Lignite, coal, potash, wheat, potatoes, livestock, chemicals, engineering, precision instruments.
	Germany, West (Federal Republic of Germany)	Bonn	248,577 km² (95,981 mi²)	61,421,000	Coal, lignite, wheat, potatoes, sugar-beet, livestock, fishing, chemicals, consumer goods, engineering.
	Greece	Athens (Athinai)	131,944 km² (50,947 mi²)	9,740,000	Lignite, marble, wheat, olives, tobacco, grapes, fruit, livestock, fishing, chemicals, tourism.
	Hungary	Budapest	93,030 km² (35,921 mi²)	10,710,000	Bauxite, lignite, wheat, maize, vines, sunflowers, timber, livestock, industry.
	Iceland	Reykjavik	103,000 km² (39,771 mi²)	242,000	Hot springs, sheep, furs, fishing, fish processing.
	Ireland, Republic of	Dublin	70,283 km² (27,138 mi²)	3,443,000	Cereals, potatoes, sugar-beet, livestock, beer, textiles, cement, chemicals.

Right: Duisberg in the Ruhr district of West Germany, the industrial heartland of Europe. Opposite: Oil tankers off Milford Haven in Wales. Britain has large oil deposits in the North Sea.

Flag	Country	Capital	Area	Population	Resources and Products
	Italy	Rome (Roma)	301,225 km² (116,310 mi²)	58,085,000	Natural gas, rock salt, cereals, grapes, olives, vegetables, fishing, industry, tourism.
	Liechtenstein	Vaduz	157 km² (61 mi²)	26,000	Cereals, potatoes, timber, livestock, textiles, tourism.
	Luxembourg	Luxembourg	2,586 km² (998 mi²)	366,000	Iron, oats, wheat, barley, potatoes, timber, iron, beer.
	Malta	Valletta	316 km² (122 mi²)	341,000	Potatoes, tomatoes, wheat, grapes, fishing, tobacco, shipyards, tourism.
	Netherlands	Amsterdam, Den Haag	40,844 km² (15,771 mi²)	14,529,000	Natural gas, oil, wheat, potatoes, flowers and bulbs, fishing, dairy products, chemicals, engineering, textiles.
	Norway	Oslo	324,219 km² (125,188 mi²)	4,146,000	Oil, iron, barley, oats, reindeer, fur, fishing, industry.
	Poland	Warsaw (Warszawa)	312,677 km² (120,732 mi²)	37,340,000	Coal, rock salt, natural gas, rye, potatoes, sugar, timber, fishing, engineering, textiles.
	Portugal	Lisbon	92,082 km² (35,555 mi²)	10,129,000	Pyrites, tungsten, grapes, olives, apples, peaches, citrus fruits, timber, fishing, tourism, industry.
	Romania	Bucharest (Bucuresti)	237,500 km² (91,704 mi²)	22,653,000	Oil, natural gas, lignite, cereals, potatoes, fruit, timber, livestock, industry.
	Spain	Madrid	504,782 km² (194,908 mi²)	38,671,000	Coal, iron, sulphur, lead, cereals, grapes, olives, citrus fruits, livestock, fishing, industry.
	Sweden	Stockholm	449,964 km² (173,742 mi²)	8,359,000	Iron, pyrites, zinc, barley, wheat, sugar-beet, timber, paper, engineering.
	Switzerland	Bern	41,288 km² (15,942 mi²)	6,482,000	Dairy produce, wheat, mechanical engineering, precision instruments, pharmaceuticals, watches.
	United Kingdom of Great Britain and Northern Ireland	London	244,046 km² (94,232 mi²)	55,780,000	Coal, oil, iron-ore, cereals, vegetables, livestock, fishing, engineering, textiles, chemicals, plastics.
	USSR (Union of Soviet Socialist Republics)	Moscow (Moskva)	22,402,200 km² (8,650,010 mi²)	278,719,000	Oil, natural gas, iron, gold, cereals, livestock, cotton, fishing, engineering paper.
	Yugoslavia	Belgrade (Beograd)	255,804 km² (98,772 mi²)	22,850,000	Coal, bauxite, chromite, oil, iron-ore, maize, wheat, timber, fishing, engineering, chemicals.

capitalist countries of the west, allied with the USA, formed the other. Both developed formidable arsenals of nuclear weapons. Relations between the western countries of the North Atlantic Treaty Organization and the eastern countries of the Warsaw Pact have varied over the years. But Europe remains ideologically divided.

Reconstruction after the war was a difficult problem for both East and West and both blocs established economic schemes to assist development. Perhaps the most interesting development in Europe for a long period has been the creation of a European Economic Community (EEC). Its origins go back to 1951, when six countries – France, West Germany, Italy, the Netherlands, Belgium and Luxembourg – formed the European Coal and Steel Community (ECSC), with the object of creating a single market for products that are essential for industrial development. This was remarkable in that it was the first supranational body of this kind within Europe.

In 1957 Euratom was formed as an agency to co-ordinate the development of nuclear research. And in the same year the Treaty of Rome was signed by the original ECSC members. Its objective was the gradual fusion of the individual national markets into a single 'common market', and to allow the circulation of all products without tariff barriers. In 1973, membership was extended to Britain, Ireland and Denmark, with Greece becoming a member in 1981. Spain and Portugal also joined the EEC in 1986.

Non-EEC members have a separate economic organization, the European Free Trade Association (EFTA). This is a less formal organization which includes Austria, Iceland, Norway, Sweden and Switzerland. It was established in 1960. Denmark, Portugal and the United Kingdom were formerly members, but they left to join the EEC. Finland remains an associate member of EFTA.

The EEC's activities are covered by the Commission of the European Communities, the Council of Ministers, the European Parliament, and the European Court of Justice. Many people consider that the extension of EEC activities into other areas than the purely economic is a first stage towards a united, federal Europe. But critics of the EEC see it as a costly bureaucracy, others as a threat to national sovereignty, and some as a political irrelevance. But few would dispute that it is better to see the nations of Europe sitting down round a table to discuss mutual problems, than continuing the endless succession of wars which have dominated its history.

Albania

Republika Popullore Socialiste e Shqipërisë

The Socialist People's Republic of Albania is one of the smallest, poorest and least known countries in Europe. And yet Albania occupies a strategic position on the Adriatic Sea, separated from the heel of Italy only by the Strait of Otranto. It is bordered by Yugoslavia to the north and east, and by Greece to the south, and the Greek island of Corfu (Kerkyra) lies only a few miles off Albania's coast.

Albania is a wooded, mountainous country. Its territory stretches some 120 kilometres (75 miles) inland from the coast, rising to peaks of over 2,300 metres (7,546 ft) high. The major rivers are the Drin, which brings the waters of the mountains and of Lake Ohridsko to the sea, and the Vijöse, which runs north-west from the Greek border. The warm climate is similar to that of southern Yugoslavia, and staple crops include maize and wheat.

Albania is sparsely populated. It is not much smaller than Belgium, and yet has only one-quarter as many inhabitants. However, Albania has an extremely high birth rate. This feature may relate to the fact that for the first time in its history, Albania is not being invaded or fought over. Over the centuries, its strategic position between Italy and the Balkans has made it little more than a bridgehead for invading troops, or a poor country ready for plundering by richer ones. It has been occupied by a bewildering succession of invaders. The ancient Greeks were here, as were the Romans, the Byzantines, the Venetians, the Slavs and the Turks.

Independence achieved in 1913 was short-lived as the First World War ruled out any hope of peace. A Republic was attempted in 1920, but the president Ahmed ben Zog proclaimed himself king in 1928 amid growing instability. Italy, under the control of Mussolini's fascists, took advantage of the country's instability and occupied the country. Italy suffered a major defeat here in 1943 during the Second World War, after which an independent republic was set up. Power now lay in the hands of the Communist Labour Party led by Enver Hoxha. Although, in common with other countries in eastern Europe after the war, its policies were Marxist-Leninist, Albania kept much to itself. The USSR was condemned as much as the USA, and Albania turned to China as an ally, but differences with China ended the special relationship in 1977. Hoxha died in 1985.

The problems of postwar Albania were huge. Eight out of ten people were illiterate, the people lived on the land scratching a living from the soil, and there was no railway. Recent years have seen rapid industrialization financed by the country's mineral resources (coal, chromium, copper and oil), and the creation of collective farms. Schools and hospitals have been built, and industrial centres, such as Tiranë and Durrës, are growing fast. Nevertheless, the problems remain formidable.

The Albanian language is unique in that it bears little relation to its neighbours, although it is an Indo-European tongue. It would suggest that the Albanians are descended from the ancient Illyrians, with later Slavic admixtures. Religions traditional to the country are Islam and Christianity (Roman Catholicism and Greek Orthodox), but religions are not favoured by the government. Since 1967, Albania's constitution has declared the country to be officially atheist.

Above: Lake Skadarsko near the town of Shkodër in north-western Albania. The lake straddles the border with Yugoslavia.

Left: A typical Albanian folk dance. The costumes and music reflect the legacy of more than 400 years of Turkish rule.

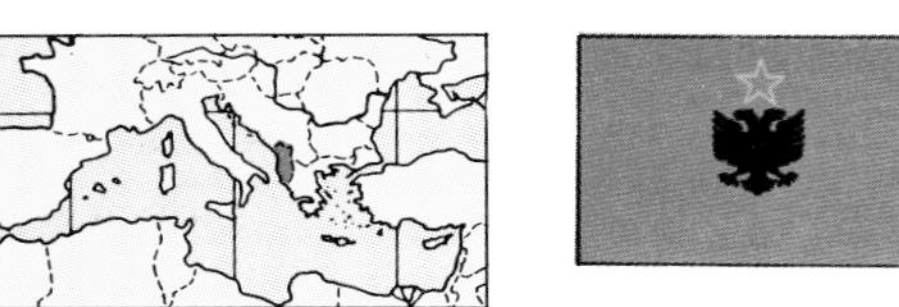

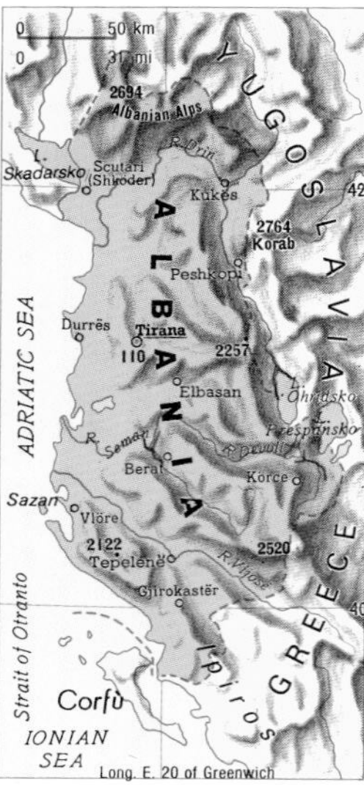

Area: 28,748 km² (11,000 mi²)
Population: 2,752,000
Capital: Tiranë (pop. 200,000)
Other towns: Shköder, Durrës, Vlöre, Körce, Elbasan, Berat, Gjirokastër, Kukës
Currency: lek

Austria

Republik Österreich

The Republic of Austria lies at the heart of Europe. The Austrians have a saying that 'the Balkans begin at the Kärntnerstrasse', Vienna's main street, because the country is a bridge between eastern and western Europe. It shares borders with Yugoslavia, Hungary, Czechoslovakia, West Germany, Switzerland, the tiny principality of Liechtenstein and Italy. Its strategic position made it, for much of its history, the centre of a great empire, occupying large areas of its neighbouring territories. But even within the reduced borders of the 20th century, Austria is an impressive country. It is a land of green meadows, fast rivers and snowy mountains, of elegant palaces and castles, of baroque churches and cheerful villages.

Above: Salzburg on the River Salzach is a major Austrian tourist centre, known for its annual music festival and as the birthplace of Wolfgang Amadeus Mozart in 1756. Right: Vienna, one of Europe's most beautiful cities, is famous for its architecture. The Burgtheater (State Theatre) is built in neo-Renaissance style. Franz Schubert, Johann Strauss and Arnold Schönberg were all born in Vienna.

The northern part of the country is dominated by the valley of the great River Danube (Donau), which crosses the German border below Passau, and winds its way to the capital, Vienna (Wien) before crossing the Czech border near Bratislava. In the south-east is the River Mur. Crossing the Tirol region and running along the north-western border is the River Inn. Austria is mostly a land of high mountains, belonging to the great European chain of the Alps. In the Tirol, along the Italian border, are some of Europe's highest peaks, such as the Wildspitze at 3,774 metres (12,382 feet) above sea level. The Ötztaler, Stubaier and Zillertaler Alps lead into the Hohe Tauern range, where the Gross Glockner peak reaches 3,797 metres (12,457 feet), and the Niedere Tauern range, which points a long finger into the central region of Steiermark. Major cities of the north include Vienna, Linz and Salzburg. Innsbruck is in the west, and Klagenfurt and Graz are in the south.

Austria is an industrial country. Its mineral resources include iron ore, magnesite, zinc, lead, lignite, gypsum and salt. Energy production is considerable, despite a 1978 referendum which

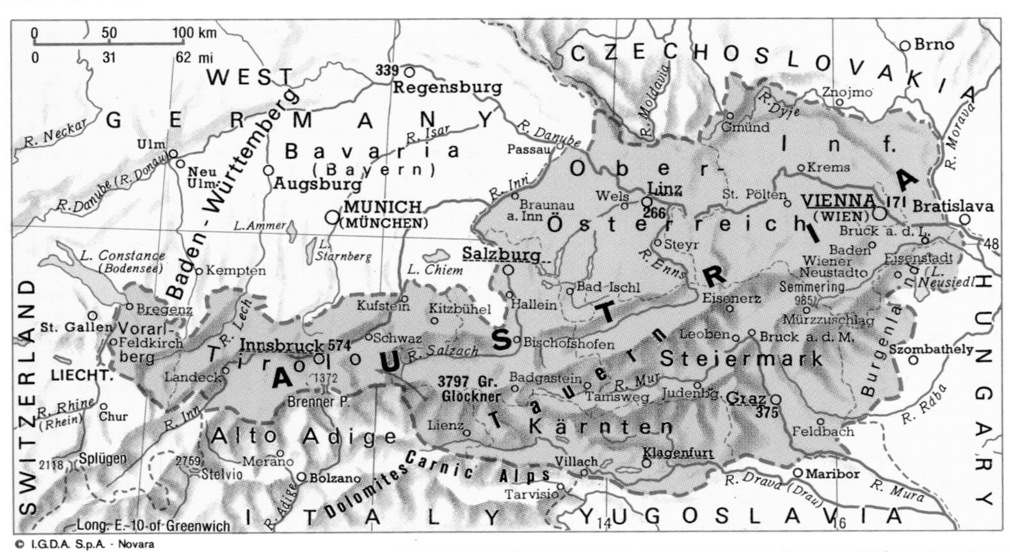

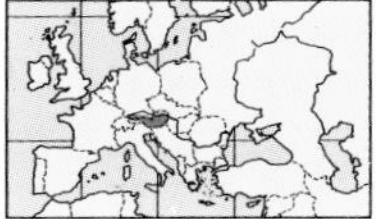

Area:
83,849 km²
(32,376 mi²)
Population:
7,560,000
Capital:
Vienna (Wien) (pop. 1,615,000)
Other towns:
Graz, Linz, Salzburg, Innsbruck, Klagenfurt, Villach, St Pölten, Wels, Steyr, Dornbirn, Leoben, Wolfsberg, Kapfenberg, Bregenz, Feldkirch, Klosterneuberg, Baden
Currency:
schilling

Right: Austria is famous for the beautiful and ancient castles scattered throughout its forests. This is the castle of Hochöster-witz in Kärnten (Carinthia).

Above: The white Lippizaner horses perform ceremonial exercises to music at the Spanish Riding School in Vienna. The splendour of these displays recalls the glittering days of the Hapsburgs.

rejected the introduction of nuclear power. (Hydro-electricity accounts for two-thirds of Austria's electrical energy.) Iron and steel, engineering and paper are the leading industries. Austria's forested slopes provide timber. Dairy farming is important in the Alps, but most agricultural activity is in the low-lying north, around the Danube. Cereal crops and vegetables are cultivated, and the climate favours vineyards and orchards.

Austria is a major tourist centre, for both summer holiday makers and for winter sports enthusiasts. Skiing is becoming a popular sport even for people who have little winter snow sports tradition.

Austria is a German-speaking land, with small minorities speaking Slovene and Croat. Most people are Roman Catholics. The history of Austria really began in 803 when the Frankish king Charlemagne, who had become Holy Roman Emperor in AD 800, took the region from the Avars, a people of Asiatic origin who had settled there about 200 years earlier. The new territory became the eastern marches (frontier territory) of the empire, called the *Ostmark*. When the Holy Roman Empire was reduced to its eastern provinces, Austria came to dominate this federation.

The Hapsburg dynasty ruled Austria from 1278 until 1918. For most of this period, the rulers also held the post of Holy Roman Emperor. It was Friedrich III (1415–83) who chose the vowels 'AEIOU' as his motto: *Austriae Est Imperare Orbo Universo,* or 'It is for Austria to rule the whole world.' Austrian possessions spread into Bohemia and eastern Europe. The Hapsburgs also controlled much of Germany and Italy, and, by an astute policy of marriage rather than war, acquired Spain, with its vast territories in the New World, and the Netherlands.

In the 16th and 17th centuries, Austria clashed with the Turks, rulers of the Balkans, who nearly took Vienna. It was Napoleon who finally cut the Holy Roman Empire down to size, because he did not want another large empire challenging his control of Europe. From 1806, the Hapsburgs were rulers of the Austrian Empire, not of the Holy Roman Empire. The final collapse of Hapsburg Austria came in the First World War, which was in fact sparked off by the assassination of the Austrian Archduke, Franz Ferdinand, in 1914. Austria was defeated and demoralized. In 1938, the country was annexed by Germany, and defeat in the Second World War led to occupation by the victors. For ten years, the country was occupied by British, American, French and Soviet troops. But in 1955, it became an independent, democratic federal republic (with nine federal states), and it had a strict policy of neutrality.

For all its chequered history, Austria has made an important contribution to European culture, particularly in the fields of opera, music, theatre and painting. Austrian culture has always been of a popular kind, light, witty and elegant. The great days of Vienna are still recalled in the exuberant waltzes of Austrian composer Johann Strauss (1825–99).

Belgium

Royaume de Belgique

The Kingdom of Belgium is a constitutional monarchy, bounded to the southwest by France, to the east by Luxembourg and Germany, and to the northeast by the Netherlands. Its sandy, low-lying coastline borders the North Sea. The coastal region includes reclaimed land or 'polders' protected by a system of dykes. Most of the land is low and flat, serving agriculture or industry. In the south is the forested plateau of the Ardennes. Belgium's principal rivers are the Schelde (Escaut or Scheldt), the Meuse (Maas) and the Sambre.

The name Belgium is extremely old, deriving from the Belgae, a Celtic people who lived in north-eastern Gaul at the time of the Roman empire. They inhabited a territory bounded by the Rhine, the highlands of the Vosges, the Marne, the Seine and the North Sea. The modern kingdom of Belgium, however, dates only from 1830.

The region was settled by Rome after 57 BC, when Julius Caesar conquered the Belgic confederation. The descendants of these Romanized Gauls still inhabit the south of the country, and are known as Walloons. They retained the old Latin dialect of the Gauls, which became French. However, during the great barbarian invasions which swept Europe during the Dark Ages, the northern part of the region was settled by the Franks, a Germanic people who came from the country between the Rhine and the Weser. From this stock came the Flemings of today, whose language is closely related to Dutch. Even today, the linguistic frontier runs along a line parallel to the old Roman road to Cologne (Köln). The division between the two ethnic and linguistic groups in modern Belgium is sometimes uneasy, but both languages are official.

The medieval period was equally important in determining the future of this region. The Frankish king Charlemagne, who was crowned Holy Roman Emperor in 800, included this territory in his vast empire, which stretched from Spain into eastern Europe. It later became subject to a series of feudal lords, including the Counts of Flanders, the Dukes of Brabant, the Princes of Liège (Luik). This was the age of chivalry, and the Flemish nobles became renowned for their valour in the Crusades. Baldwin IX, Count of Flanders, was elected Emperor of Constantinople. Under the Dukes of Burgundy, the region became consolidated with all other territories between the Somme, the Moselle (Mosel) and the Zuider Zee (Ijsselmeer). In effect, this was the area of modern Belgium and the Netherlands, and the area became known in English by rather vague terms such as the 'Low Countries' – hence the name Netherlands. Medieval Flanders was the centre of a thriving textile trade, for which Britain supplied the wool. Many Flemish weavers settled in Britain.

In the 16th century, the region passed into the hands of Charles V, the all-powerful Hapsburg emperor who had in fact been born at Ghent (Gand). Charles was attached to his birthplace, and could speak Flemish. But when control passed to the Spanish branch of the family, trouble broke out. The Dutch were ardent Protestants, and did not take kindly to the suppression of their religion. After a long struggle, they succeeded in gaining independence. The Flemings and Walloons, however, were Roman Catholics and they remained under Spanish rule, despite efforts by the French kings to appropriate the territory for themselves.

The strategic position of these lands and their prosperity involved them in many of the major European wars of the 17th and 18th centuries. In 1713, the region passed to Austria, and in 1794 to revolutionary France. It was near the Belgian village of Waterloo in 1815 that the British and Prussians finally defeated Napoleon in one of the most famous battles of all time. The Congress of Vienna, which attempted to rearrange Europe after the fall of Napoleon, brought the Dutch, Flemings and Walloons together again. But the Flemings and Walloons rebelled against this Kingdom of the Netherlands, and declared their independence in 1830. The following year, the crown of the new kingdom of Belgium was offered to a German prince, Leopold of Coburg. He was the great-great-grandfather of the present

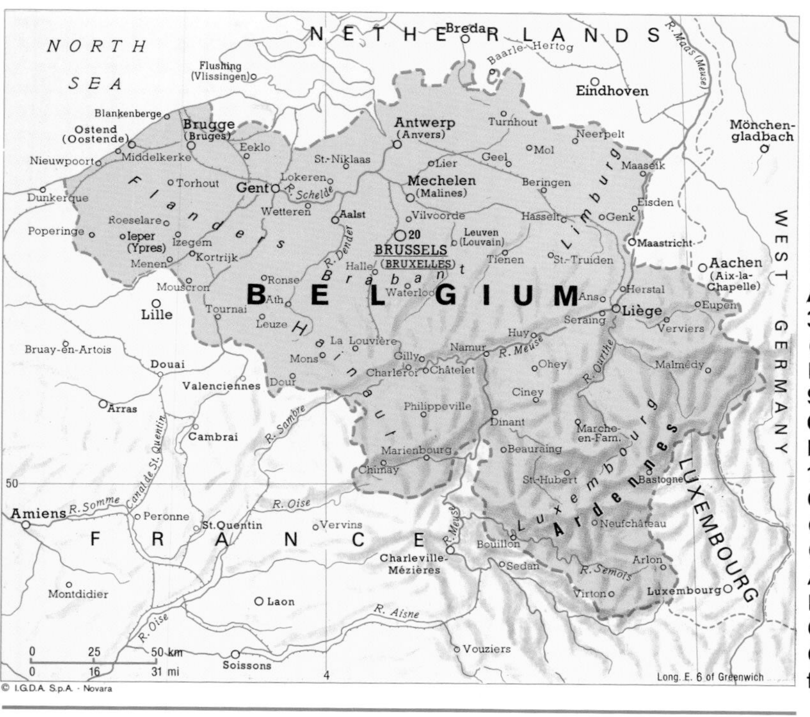

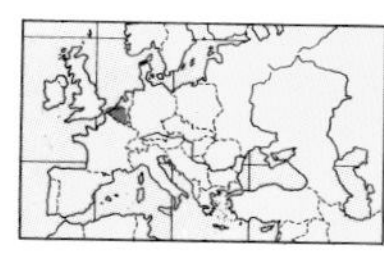

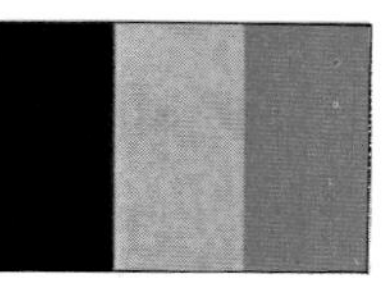

Area:
30,513 km² (11,782 mi²)
Population:
9,889,000
Capital:
Brussels (pop. 100,000)
Other towns:
Ghent (Gand, Gent) Charleroi, Liège, Antwerp, Bruges, Namur, Mons, Ostende (Ostend)
Currency:
franc

Below: Belgium contains a complex network of canals. Large ships can use some of them, including the Albert Canal, linking Antwerp with Liège. This canal was built in 1939.

king, Baudouin.

Under the House of Coburg, Belgium thrived and became a prosperous country. Belgium became a colonial power in the African continent in 1908 when the Congo Free State, which had been the personal property of Léopold II since 1884, passed under government control. The exploitation and excesses which had occurred in this region (now Zaire) had earned the criticism of the civilized world. Industrial development at home was tragically interrupted in the 20th century by two invasions by Germany. The first occasion, in 1914, brought Britain into the First World War. The second resulted in the occupation of the country by Nazi troops from 1940–44. Once again, Belgium was in the centre of a European battlefield. Recovery was quick, despite the loss of the Congo, which became independent in 1960.

Modern Belgium is an affluent country. It is densely populated, with nearly 10 million people living in an area less than half the size of Scotland. Personal incomes are among the highest in the world. While farming flourishes, it occupies only three per cent of the labour force on a full-time basis. The great strength of Belgium lies in its industrial capacity. This was initially based on coal, the mining of which is now declining. But steelworks, mechanical and chemical engineering works, food processing plants, glass works and potteries employ a large amount of labour and generate considerable wealth. Textiles are still produced at Ghent (Gand), Bruges (Brugge) and other centres.

Commerce is aided by an excellent communications system. Like the Netherlands, Belgium makes considerable use of its chief asset, water. A network of rivers and canals has been used for centuries, and the town of Antwerp (Antwerpen or Anvers) on the estuary of the Schelde (Scheldt, Escaut) is a major European port. The main canals open to shipping include the Ghent-Terneuzen, the Willebroek Rupel-Brussels, the Brugge-Zeebrugge, and the Albert, which joins Liège (Luik) with Antwerp.

Belgium was a founder member of the European Coal and Steel Community in 1950, and of its successor, the European Economic Community (EEC) in 1958. Belgium's capital, Brussels, is the centre of many EEC offices, including that of the Commission and the Council of Ministers.

The country is divided administratively into nine large provinces. The capital is Brussels (Bruxelles, Brussel), a large centre of industry and commerce situated in the centre of the northern part of the country.

Belgium's contribution to the arts has been considerable, notably in the field of painting. Left: Peasant life was the favoured subject of Pieter Breughel the Elder (c. 1520–69). Below: Splendid public buildings line the Grand' Place in Brussels, capital of Belgium. Brussels, a centre of business and trade, is the meeting place of the country's two cultures, Flemish and Walloon.

Bulgaria

Narodna Republika

Industrialization has changed the face of Europe in the last 200 years. But for many years, such countries as the People's Republic of Bulgaria remained under-developed. The traditional role of market gardener, assigned to Bulgaria by the more powerful countries of Europe, ensured that for a long time the country remained a rural backwater. Of course, farming remains important to the Bulgarian economy. Bulgaria's position on the Balkan peninsula, lying between Yugoslavia, Romania, Greece, Turkey and the Black Sea offers a temperate climate, with sunny, Mediterranean-type weather in the south. There is no shortage of fertile arable land, which provides low-priced agricultural produce for export.

But since the Second World War, things have changed. Industrial capacity has expanded rapidly. Two-thirds of Bulgaria's exports now derive from engineering, and there is a steel and a petro-chemical industry. The agricultural industry itself, now largely reorganized on a co-operative basis, is fast being mechanized and brought up to date. The chief crops are wheat, maize, tobacco (of which Bulgaria is the largest European producer), fruit, vegetables, oilseed, flowers and cotton.

Bulgaria is divided into two by the Balkan Mountains (Stara Planina) which run across the country from east to west. To the north of them, extending as far as the valley of the River Danube (Dunav), there are fertile plateaux, with a climate typical of eastern Europe. It is here that cereals are cultivated.

South of the mountains lies a plain where the climate is warmer, and more suited to fruit and vegetable farming, and to vineyards. This extends south as far as the Rodopi (Rhodope) range of mountains, whose snowy, forested slopes rise to a height of 3,000 metres (9,843 ft). The Balkan range is rather more hospitable, containing sheltered, fertile valleys which are densely populated. The capital, Sofiya (Sofia), a major industrial centre, lies beneath these mountains. One valley in particular has become famous for its roses, which are grown under glass or in the open air, gathered and processed to make attar of roses for perfumes and cosmetics.

The people of Bulgaria are Slavic, part of the waves of peoples who in ancient times migrated westwards from the Russian steppes and from Asia. The Bulgarian language is part of the South Slavic linguistic group. Hence it is closely related to the Serbo-Croat tongue of Yugoslavia and it is allied to Russian. The alphabet is Cyrillic, so-called after Cyril, the Greek monk who in the ninth century translated the Bible into the ancient Slav tongue.

The Bulgarians believe deeply that they belong to the Slav world and its traditions. To the south, the country lies strategically open to Turkey, and for 500 years Bulgaria was a part of the Turkish empire. And yet its people refused to accept the Islamic faith, remaining faithful to the Orthodox Church. In 1878, by the Treaty of Berlin, Bulgaria became an independent kingdom, within the German sphere of influence. In the First World War, Bulgaria was allied with Germany. In the Second World War, the Germans occupied the Bulgarian ports on the Black Sea. Bulgaria was forced to join the Allies in September 1944. After the war, the 1946 referendum abolished the monarchy, and gave birth to the People's Republic of Bulgaria, a Socialist country which has close economic and political links with the USSR.

Bulgaria has an extensive rail network which links the capital, Sofiya, with Istanbul and with the Black Sea ports of Burgas and Varna. It takes only a few hours to sail to the Soviet port of Odessa.

Top left: Rose petals, which provide attar of roses which is used to make perfume, are harvested in Balkan mountains. Top right: The cathedral of Sofiya, Bulgaria's capital, is dedicated to the memory of Russian soldiers killed in a war with Turkey in 1877–78. This war led to Bulgarian independence.

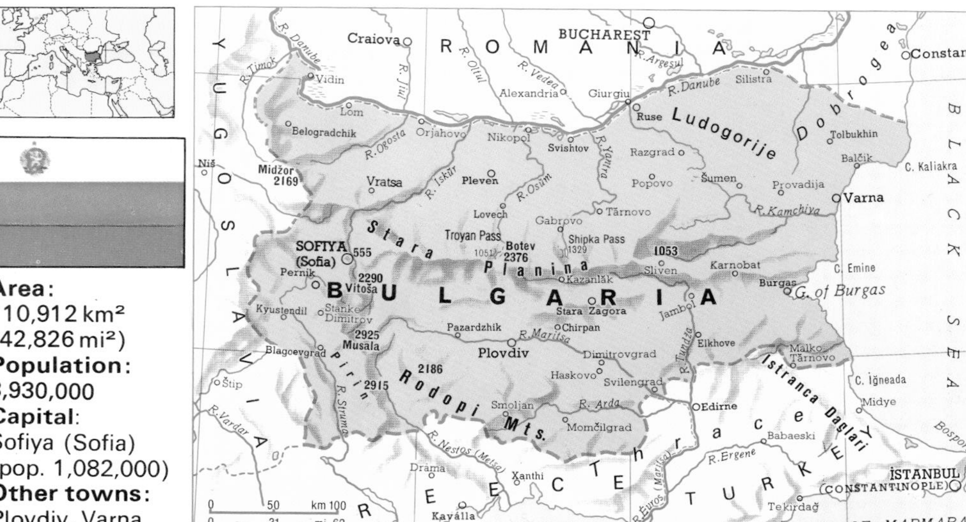

Area:
110,912 km² (42,826 mi²)
Population:
8,930,000
Capital:
Sofiya (Sofia) (pop. 1,082,000)
Other towns:
Plovdiv, Varna
Currency: lev

Cyprus

Kypriaki Dimokratia

In the north-eastern corner of the Mediterranean Sea, about 70 kilometres (43 miles) off the Turkish coast and 80 kilometres (50 miles) off the Syrian coast, lies the island Republic of Cyprus. Its name derives from the Latin *cuprum*, which means 'copper' and this metal can still be found on the island. Politically, the island is part of Europe, but geologically it is connected to Asia, because the mountains of Cyprus belong to the same formation as the Taurus range on the coast of Turkey.

There are two mountain ranges in Cyprus. The northern chain is scarcely 1,000 metres (3,281 ft) high, descending abruptly to the sea. But to the south, the volcanic mass of Troödos reaches 2,000 metres (6,562 ft). Its slopes descend gently, covered in vineyards.

Between the two ridges lies the central plain of Mesaoria, a fertile region crossed by a single river, the Pediaios. This is the most populated region of the country. It is also the site of the capital, Nicosia.

The climate of Cyprus is of the Mediterranean type, hot and dry in summer and mild and moist in winter. Cyprus is famous for its strong, sweet wine and its raisins. Grapes, along with citrus fruits, olives and tobacco are the chief cash crops.

Cereals and vegetables are grown for domestic consumption. Flocks of sheep and goats graze the hills.

Cyprus has had a turbulent history. The Phoenicians, Egyptians and Romans came and went. After the Third Crusade, in 1195, the island became an independent Christian principality. Then, for more than a century, it came under the Republic of Venice, and was a centre of trade. In 1571, Cyprus was conquered by the Turks, who remained there for 300 years. Under their rule, minarets appeared on the skyline and churches were turned into mosques. Even so, the Christian tradition did stay alive.

It was when the Ottoman Empire declined at the end of the 19th century, that Cyprus came under British administration, and became a crown colony. As such, it was in a valuable strategic position, controlling approaches to the Suez Canal, and oil routes from the Middle East.

The people of Cyprus come from different ethnic backgrounds, and this has led to considerable strife since 1955. The two main communities are of Greeks and Turks; there are also minorities of Armenians and Maronites. A Greek organization (EOKA), dedicated to union with Greece, or *enosis*, waged an armed campaign against the British.

Britain, Greece and Turkey finally reached agreement with the Cypriot population and provided for independence as a republic in 1960. Trouble between the Turkish and the Greek communities soon broke out, and the United Nations intervened.

In 1967 the government was overthrown by the military in mainland Greece, and in 1974 this led to a *coup d'état* in Cyprus, which overthrew President Makarios. Turkey invaded the north of the island and occupied the area inhabited by the Turkish section of the population. In 1975 the Turkish section was declared to be the 'Turkish Cypriot Federated State', but it was not internationally recognized as such.

The 1974 invasion disrupted the island's chief asset – its tourist potential. Its fine beaches and warm climate make it an ideal resort for international tourism, which provides a major source of revenue. There are in addition ruins of several famous towns of ancient times, for example Citium and Paphos. British people also know Cyprus for its connections with Richard I who captured it during the Third Crusade in 1191.

Archbishop Makarios, the first president and founder of independent Cyprus, died in 1977. His successor, Spiros Kiprianou, was proclaimed president by the Greek House of Representatives in 1977. He was elected to serve for 5-year terms in 1978 and 1983. Legislative power is vested in the House of Representatives whose 50 members were divided ethnically into 35 from the Greek community and 15 from the Turkish community. However no Turkish members have attended the House since December 1963. From 1976 the Turkish Cypriot leader Rauf Denktash served as president of the Turkish Cypriot Federated State. In 1983 Denktash made a unilateral declaration of independence, claiming to found a Turkish Republic of Northern Cyprus.

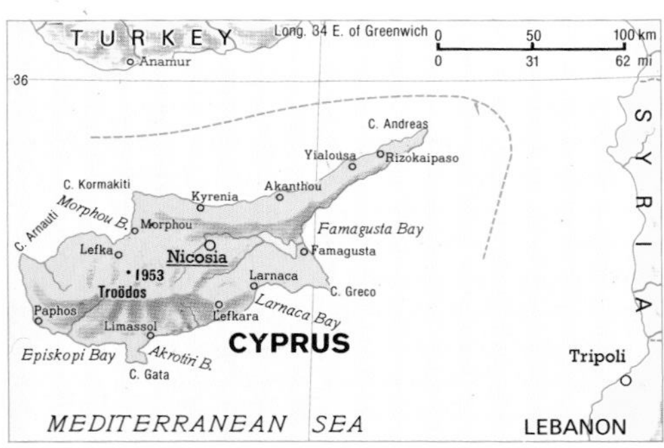

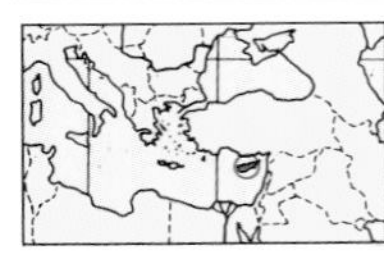

Area:
9,251 km² (3,572 mi²)
Population:
655,000
Capital: Nicosia (pop. 234,000)
Other towns:
Limassol, Famagusta, Larnaca
Currency: pound

Below left: The minarets of the Selimiye mosque in the Turkish sector of the capital, Nicosia, a testament to the Islamic faith of the Turkish Cypriot population, which forms 18 per cent of the total.

Below right: The church of Saint Lazarus in Larnaca. The Greek population, 78 per cent of the total, are Christians of the Greek Orthodox persuasion. Attempts are now being made to resolve the differences between the two communities, which have caused so much bloodshed in recent years.

Czechoslovakia

Československá Socialistická Republika

The Czechoslovak Socialist Republic lies in central Europe. It is landlocked and shares borders with East and West Germany, Austria, Hungary, the USSR and Poland. It is populated mostly by two Slavic peoples, the Czechs and the Slovaks, each with their own language. Czechoslovakia has been an independent republic only since 1918, but it has an ancient history.

In the fifth and sixth centuries AD, Slavic peoples settled in the region. The Czechs (now the most numerous of the two) took the north of the region, and the Slovaks the south. Since then, the two peoples have shared the same history. They were both converted to Christianity at the same time. And, while both have experienced domination by their Germanic neighbours, they have maintained a common Slavic culture. When, in 1945, Europe was recreated out of the ruins of German occupation, both Czechs and Slovaks were united in their wish to recreate the combined nation that had been founded at the end of the First World War.

The history of Czechoslovakia has always been centred on its magnificent capital, Prague (Praha). Inhabited since the first Slavic settlement of the Bohemia region, it was the seat of the first royal house of Bohemia. Christianity was encouraged in the region by Duke Wenceslaus (*c*.903-935), the patron saint of Czechoslovakia and the 'good king' of the Christmas carol. Prague became the capital of a renowned medieval kingdom under the Holy Roman Emperor Charles IV (1316-78). In 1348 he founded in Prague the first German and Czech language university. German cultural in-

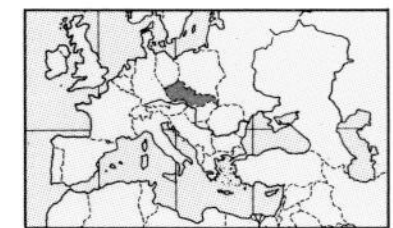

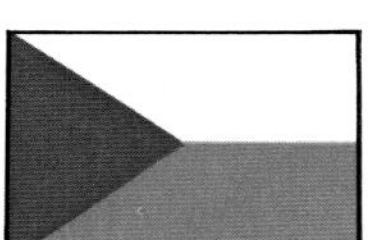

Area:
127,869 km²
(49,373 mi²)
Population:
15,556,000
Capital:
Prague (Praha)
(pop. 1,191,000)

Other towns:
Bratislava, Brno, Ostrava, Košice, Plzeň, Olomouc, Havířov, Hradec Králové, Pardubice, České Budějovice
Currency:
koruna

Of the three main regions of Czechoslovakia, Bohemia has long been the most developed. It has a thriving agriculture, top, and advanced industrial development with such traditional craft industries as the manufacture of glassware. Prague, above, is the ancient capital of Bohemia on the River Vltava.

fluence and settlement increased. It was from Prague that the popular reformer John Huss, a precursor of the Reformation, preached his sermons. Huss's condemnation to death as a heretic in 1415 sparked off a series of wars. As part of the Holy Roman Empire, Czechoslovakia fell under the domination of the Austrian Hapsburg dynasty. Nevertheless, it retained a national identity. It was a Bohemian claim for independence that began the terrible Thirty Years' War, which tore Europe apart between 1618 and 1648.

When Austria and the Central Powers were defeated in the First World War, Czechoslovakia became an independent nation. But peace was not to last. Hitler's ambitions reached eastwards, and a year after the annexation of Austria in 1938, Czechoslovakia was occupied by Germany. After the eventual defeat of Germany, a socialist republic was founded in 1948. Today, like its eastern European neighbours, Czechoslovakia is a member of COMECON and of the Warsaw Pact. Relations with the USSR are close.

Czechoslovakia has been industrialized since the 19th century, having large reserves of coal and lignite. Chemical and mechanical engineering, textiles, leather and food-processing are important industries. Traditional craft industries still thrive, such as the Karlovy Vary ceramics and the beautiful glassware of Bohemia. Industry is nationalized, and agriculture is organized on a state-owned or collective basis. Rye and potatoes are grown on the Bohemian plateau, and cattle are raised. The richest farmland is in Moravia, where cereals, vegetables and sugar-beet are cultivated. Slovakia contains vineyards and orchards, and mixed forests provide timber.

The physical geography of Czechoslovakia helps to explain the history and the economies of the various regions. The Bohemian plateau lies in the north-west. It is crossed by the River Vltava (Moldau), on which Prague stands. Bohemia has always been a major crossroads of Europe, thereby enjoying cultural and trading contacts with the rest of Europe. Its accessibility also made it an area of settlement. But at the same time, it was open to attack and invasion. The central region, Moravia, is the chief flat area of the country. Enclosed by mountains, it is drained by the River Morava, a tributary of the Danube (Dunaj), which forms part of the border with Hungary in the south. Moravia has always been an important link between northern and southern Europe, even in Roman times. Slovakia, however, has always been less accessible, being a mostly highland region. The Tatry (Tatra) range of mountains (which takes in a wonderful national park) reach 2,663 metres (8,737 feet) at Gerlachovsky, near the northern border with Poland. This region has avoided the urbanization of the [illegible] Southern Slovakia also includes a [illegible] of lowland.

Because Czechoslovakia lies far from the moderating influence of the sea, its climate is typically continental, with cold winters and mild summers. Average annual temperatures vary between about −7°C and 20°C. The rainfall is normally between 500 mm (20 in) and 1,000 mm (39 in) in a year.

Below: St Wenceslaus, an early Prince of Bohemia and now the country's patron saint, watches over the main square of modern Prague. This square is the bustling centre of the city.

Denmark

Kongeriget Danmark

One of the most famous landmarks in Copenhagen, the capital of the Kingdom of Denmark, is the bronze statue of a little girl, a mermaid, whose body ends in a fish's tail, thoughtfully watching the waves along the shore. She is the heroine of a fairy tale by Hans Christian Andersen, the famous Danish story-teller, who told of a mermaid, in love with a prince of the land, but homesick for the depths of the sea. In a way, the mermaid might be taken as a symbol of Denmark, which is a country almost entirely surrounded by the sea, although it owes its prosperity to its fertile land.

The continental part of Denmark, the Jylland (Jutland) peninsula looks rather like a clenched fist extended towards Scandinavia. On the western side of Jylland, the islands are few and small, but on the eastern side there is a large archipelago, with four major islands: [illegible]ælland, Lolland, and Falster; and a h[illegible] minor ones.

[illegible]mark's only land border is the [illegible]ern one, with West Germany, which cuts across the base of Jylland. All the other borders are maritime. To the east is the Baltic Sea. To the west is the North Sea. To the north, Denmark is separated from the Scandinavian peninsula by the Skagerrak and Kattegat, two arms of the North Sea.

The climate is typically maritime, with cool summers and mild winters. Denmark has a moderate rainfall in both summer and winter. The land is flat and low-lying: if it was just 50 metres (164 feet) lower, the sea would cover more than half of it. It is an ideal country for cycling, and the bicycle is the Danes' favourite vehicle. These flat, green lands, assailed by strong sea winds, are farmed under one of the most organized and rational systems of farming in the world. The percentage of arable land is about 62 per cent, and its wheat yield per hectare is the highest in Europe. More than half the land is given over to the cultivation of cereals. The remainder is occupied by meadows and pasture. Fodder crops are widely grown, because livestock rearing is extremely important. Butter, lard, bacon and eggs are the most important exports. The fishing industry, with its ancient traditions, also plays a significant part in the economy. There are numerous ports on the south-eastern side of Jylland and around the coasts of the islands. On the biggest island, Sjælland, is the capital, Copenhagen, one of the most important ports in Europe.

Industry (shipping, cars, chemicals, rubber, cement and pottery) has progressed steadily over the last 30 years. But farming remains extremely important.

This prosperous country with its mechanized farming and modern industry has not had a peaceful history. Its origins are lost in the Dark Ages, when the Jutes, a people of Germanic extraction, established themselves there. It is from the Jutes that the Danish peninsula got the name of Jutland or Jylland. In the tenth century, these fierce tribes were converted to Christianity through the work of a missionary, St Anscarius. At the same time King Gorm the Old united the principalities of Jylland under his rule. The work of unification was completed by one of his successors with the name of Harold Bluetooth.

At that time the Danes successfully dedicated themselves to piracy and raiding. They crossed the sea in light longships, with a single sail and two teams of oarsmen. These were the famous Vikings, who spread terror through northern Europe. They attacked the Engl[illegible] the Franks, and even raided [illegible]ne Mediterranean. The ocean was th[illegible] of Swans', on which they roam [illegible] search of adventure and booty. 'The fury of the storm helps the arm of the seaman', went one of their war songs, 'the winds serve us by bringing us to our destination; the pirate must sleep on his shield and the blue of the open sky will serve as a curtain'.

The successors of Harold II, Svend and Canute the Great, brought England and

Above left: The bronze statue of the Little Mermaid in Copenhagen reminds us of the heroine of a tale by Denmark's most famous writer, Hans Christian Andersen (1805–75), above right.

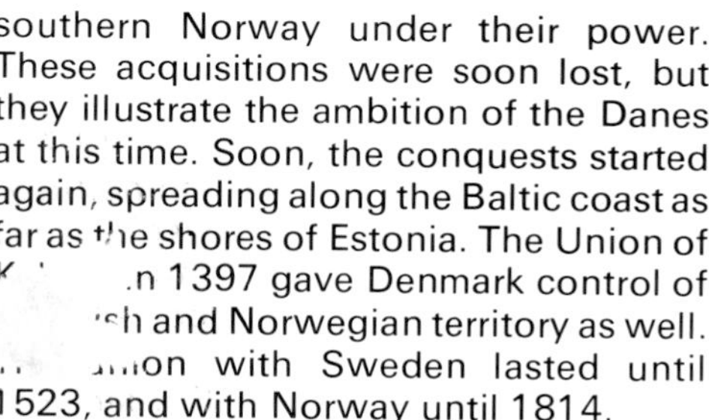

southern Norway under their power. These acquisitions were soon lost, but they illustrate the ambition of the Danes at this time. Soon, the conquests started again, spreading along the Baltic coast as far as the shores of Estonia. The Union of K[illegible]n 1397 gave Denmark control of [illegible]h and Norwegian territory as well. [illegible]on with Sweden lasted until 1523, and with Norway until 1814.

At the end of the Middle Ages, the power of the nobility declined and the absolutist nature of the monarchy asserted itself. After the Thirty Years' War (1618-48), the country gradually desisted from military adventures. Farming and commerce found a new impulse, and progress gained momentum with the reforms of a minister, Count Bernstorff, who in 1788, abolished serfdom, the system surviving from the Middle Ages by which peasants were bound to the land.

At the beginning of the 19th century, involved against its will in the Napoleonic wars, Denmark endured English occupation, the ruin of her commerce and finances and, finally, separation from Norway, although Denmark was allowed

Above: The remains of an ancient Viking longship, or drakar, may be seen today in the museum at Roskilde, a port near Copenhagen. Right: Sightseeing boats in the old port of Copenhagen.

Greenland has been self-governing since 1979, but is still a part of Denmark.

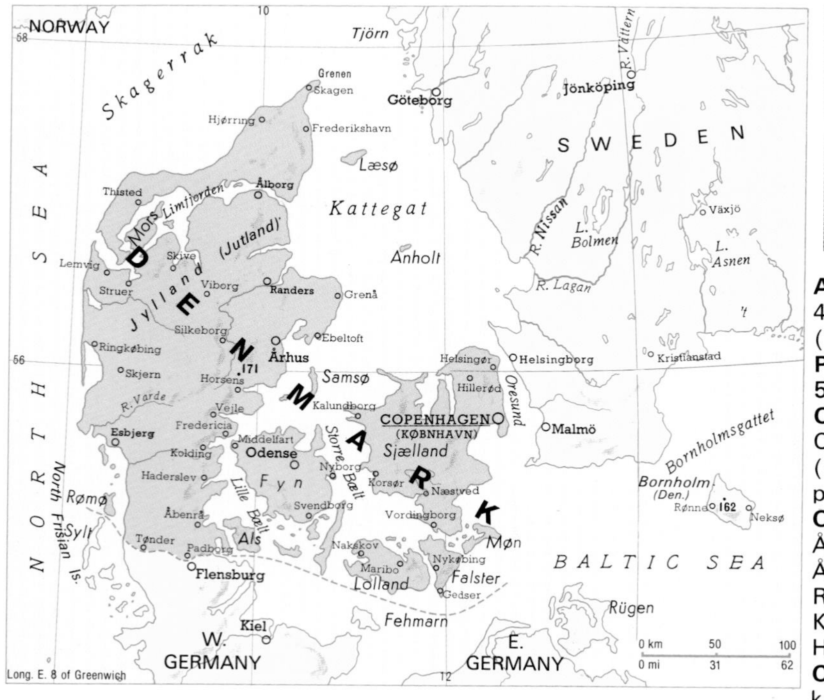

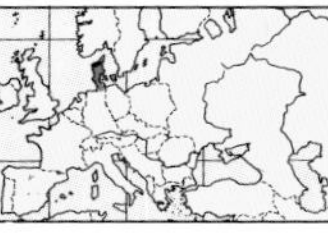

Area:
43,069 km² (16,630 mi²)
Population:
5,112,000
Capital:
Copenhagen (København, pop. 1,366,000)
Other towns:
Århus, Odense, Ålborg, Esbjerg, Randers, Helsingør, Kolding, Herning, Horsens
Currency:
krone

to retain Greenland, which had become a Danish colony in 1721. Other misfortunes of war in the 19th century included the loss of Schleswig, Holstein and Lauenburg, which were absorbed into neighbouring Prussia. Part of Schleswig was recovered by a plebiscite after the First World War, in which Denmark had observed strict neutrality. The same neutrality was declared in the Second World War, but this did not protect Denmark from the Germans, who suddenly attacked the country on 9 April 1940.

After the war, political life in Denmark was resumed along the lines of a traditional democracy. The country is a constitutional monarchy, and the legislative power lies with the *Folketing*, or parliament. Denmark joined the EEC in 1973. The former colony of Greenland, together with the Faeroe Islands, are still a part of Denmark, although Greenland has been self-governing since 1979.

Finland

Suomen Tasavalta – Republiken Finland

In the far north of Europe is a land of lakes and dark forests, whose folklore has given rise to tales of trolls and fairies. The Republic of Finland straddles the Arctic Circle, with coasts on the Baltic Sea and the Gulf of Bothnia. Its territory borders Sweden in the north-west, Norway in the north, and the USSR in the east.

Finland is geologically one of the oldest parts of the European continent, and its physical characteristics have been determined by intense glaciation. Ice erosion and deposition have created a great maze of lakes (55,000 in all), a low-lying relief, and a ragged coastline dotted with islands. The climate is marked by long, hard winters, heavy snowfall and brief summers.

The first inhabitants of Finland were probably Lapps, some of whom still live in the far north. The Finns, a people of Mongol extraction, reached the country that now bears their name around the fourth century AD, and settled in the more hospitable south.

From 1157, when the Finns were converted to Christianity, the region fell under Swedish influence. In 1809, however, Finland fell into the hands of Tsar Alexander I of Russia.

Following the Russian Revolution in 1917, civil war broke out in Finland. The Finnish Communists were defeated by General Carl Gustaf Mannerheim who, in 1919, was elected first president of the independent Finnish republic. A conflict with USSR in 1939 led to a loss of territory. In the Second World War, Finland sided with Germany until 1944 and, as a result, lost further territory. Today Finland maintains a delicate balance between the great powers.

Traditionally, Finland has an agricultural economy, relying on the cultivation of cereal crops, vegetables and the raising of livestock, mostly in the far south. Fishing has always been important, and the great forests of pine, spruce and birch remain the country's most valuable asset. Industrialization has, however, been rapid in this century. The timber industry is today supported by metalworking, mechanical and chemical engineering, shipbuilding, electronics, textiles, glass and furniture manufacture. Industry is concentrated around the capital, Helsinki, which was founded by the Swedes in the 16th century. Other big cities are Turku, which was the capital until 1812, and Tampere, the largest city in the interior.

Above: The Unioninkatu, one of the main streets in Helsinki.

Most Finns are Lutheran Christians. Both Finnish and Swedish are recognized as official languages. Proportionately, over 90 per cent of the population speak Finnish, and only six per cent Swedish.

Below: Vast quantities of timber float on the waters of Lake Saimaa.

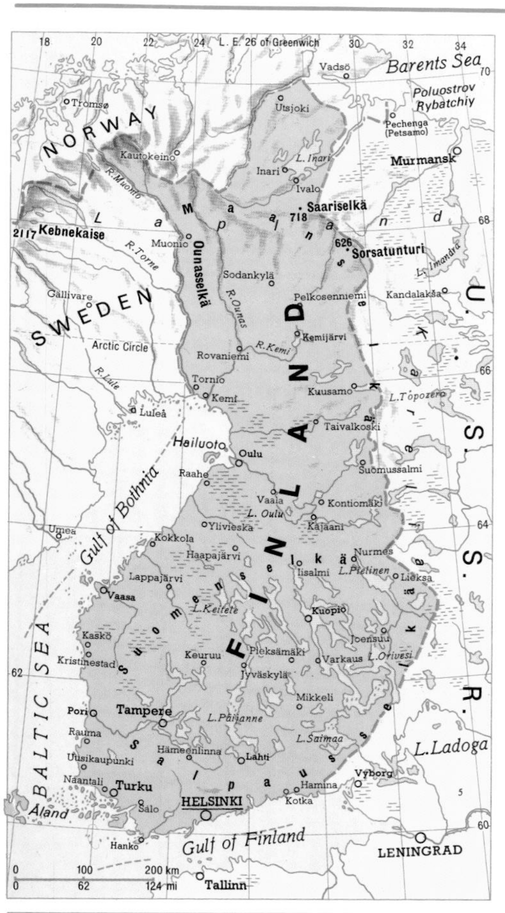

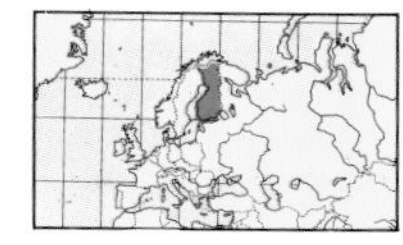

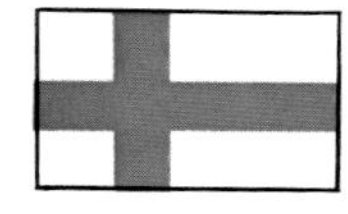

Area:
337,032 km² (130,136 mi²)
Population:
4,872,000
Capital:
Helsinki (pop. 932,000)
Other towns:
Tampere, Turku, Espoo, Vantaa, Lahti, Oulu, Pori, Kuopio, Jyväskäla, Kotka
Currency:
markka

France

République Française

In the Middle Ages, French poets liked to write about their national hero, Charlemagne, and about the glorious days when his empire was founded. They described their homeland as *douce France*, meaning 'sweet France'. It is an apt description, even today. The French Republic is a land of beautiful scenery, with a pleasant climate, a fascinating history, and a long cultural tradition. Its geographical position in western Europe has made it the meeting point of two of the great civilizations which have left their imprint on the continent: that of the Latin peoples and that of the Germanic peoples. France is the only European country to have both a North Sea and a Mediterranean coastline. It also has a coast on the Atlantic Ocean. France is roughly hexagonal in shape. Its southern side borders the Mediterranean Sea and Spain. The Atlantic coastline forms the western side. To the north is the English Channel, and beyond the Strait of Dover, the point closest to England, is the North Sea. On the north-eastern side are land boundaries with Belgium, Luxembourg and West Germany, where the border turns abruptly to the south, past Switzerland and Italy. On the one hand, France is closely linked to the lands of the warm south. On the other, it is surrounded by the traditions of northern Europe.

In ancient times France was called Gallia, or 'land of the Gauls'. This was the name given to its then inhabitants, various Celtic tribes, by the Romans. It was conquered by Julius Caesar in a series of campaigns between 58 and 51 BC, and became a province of the Roman Empire. Today, particularly in southern France, one can still see impressive monuments which are the legacy of five centuries of Roman presence. The Celtic languages of the Gauls disappeared without trace. Modern French is derived directly from the Latin which was spoken all over Gaul, modified over the centuries and including a few additional words of Germanic origin which appeared at the time of the barbarian invasions. A settlement of the Brittany region by Celts from the British Isles resulted in the Breton language, which can still be heard in this part of France today.

In the fourth and fifth centuries AD, successive waves of peoples from central and eastern Europe profited from the decline of Rome and established themselves by force in the territory of the romanized Gauls, and intermixed with them. To the north were the Franks, to the east, the Alemanni and Burgundians, and to the south and west, the Visigoths. In the ninth century, the Normans, of Scandinavian origin, settled in the region which later took their name, Normandy. Of the early invaders, the Franks soon asserted their supremacy. The greatest of their sovereigns, Charlemagne (AD 742-814) united central and eastern Europe in one vast dominion which covered about one-quarter of the area of the old Roman Empire. The kingdom of France was created when Charlemagne's Empire broke up, after his death. It is here that the history of modern France begins.

In AD 987, after an initial period of ineffective rulers, a man with an iron fist came to the throne. This was Hugh Capet, Count of Paris, who founded a dynasty whose various branches were destined to rule the kingdom of France for 800 years. This strong and centralized monarchy was to play an important part in creating national unity.

Below: France's ancient capital, Paris, stands on the River Seine. It is the commercial, administrative and cultural centre of the country.

At the outset, the sovereignty of the Capets was virtually limited to the area around Paris and Orléans. Like all medieval sovereigns, they had to contend with the arrogance of the feudal lords who, as absolute masters over their own lands, represented a continual threat to central authority. One of the feudal lords was the King of England, who still owned vast possessions on French soil, inherited from his ancestors. The tension broke out into protracted warfare in the 14th century when the English King Edward III, son of a French princess, claimed the crown of France.

This war, which was to be called the Hundred Years War, in fact lasted for more than a century, from 1337 to 1453, with periods of peace alternating with the campaigns. On several occasions, France stood on the verge of disaster, invaded on all sides and exhausted by disagreements between the feudal lords, some of whom, including the Dukes of Burgundy, supported the English. In 1431, the English boy-king Henry VI was ceremoniously crowned in Paris. That same year, Joan of Arc, taken prisoner by her enemies, died at the stake. A warrior and a religious mystic, she had personified the French spirit of liberation and had inflicted major defeats on the invaders. Her example was not, however, wasted. The war of liberation continued and, in the end, the English were forced to evacuate the occupied territories and leave the country.

The monarchy came out of this long war strengthened, with a standing army, equipped with the new weapons, cannons, which were to dominate the battlefields of the future. From that time, its policy was one of consolidation. After subduing the rebellious nobles and absorbing the larger feudal domains by a series of annexations, wars of conquest began. The prestige of France increased all the time.

This was largely due to the splendour of the court, the vitality of its culture and the flourishing of the arts. Italian masters, from Leonardo da Vinci to Benvenuto Cellini, were called upon to work for the sovereigns of France, and they filled the royal palaces with masterpieces. The great rebirth of culture in Italy, the Renaissance, came to France. It prepared the ground for the great achievements of the 17th century, the golden age of French literature and the arts.

This century was dominated by the figure of one man, Louis XIV. Under his long reign (1643-1715) France became the major power in Europe, taking the place of Spain, which was on the decline, and even pushing into the background the great empire of the Austrian Hapsburgs. During the rule of this 'Sun King', as Louis was called by poets and by his courtiers, all was not light. Futile wars, terrible famines, religious intolerance, and social injustices abounded. Nevertheless, the achievements of Louis XIV cannot be denied. France not only reached its present north-eastern boundaries and laid the basis of a colonial empire in North America, but it also presented to its contemporaries the most prestigious model of civilization which had appeared in the world since classical times.

For a whole century, Europe lived, thought and reasoned according to the French example. The courts tried to imitate that established by the 'Sun King' at Versailles, in a setting of fabulous splendour. French replaced Latin in political, diplomatic and intellectual circles. French fashion, interior decoration and cooking became predominant among the European aristocracy. The ideas of the enlightenment, the rationalist philosophy which influenced European

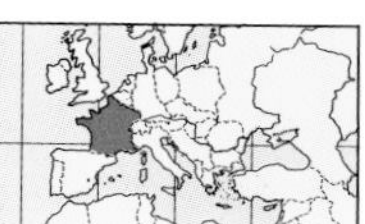

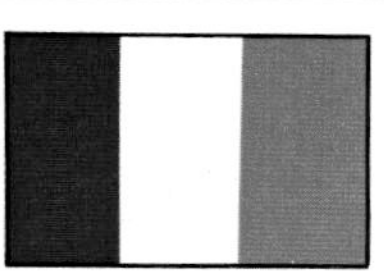

Area:
547,026 km² (211,219 mi²)
Population:
54,832,000
Capital:
Paris (pop. 8,707,000)
Other cities:
Lyons (Lyon), Marseilles (Marseille), Lille, Bordeaux, Toulouse, Nantes, Nice, Grenoble, Rouen, Toulon, Strasbourg, Valenciennes, St-Étienne, Lens, Nancy, Clermont-Ferrand, Tours, Rennes, Mulhouse, Montpellier, Douai, Orléans, Dijon, Reims, Le Mans, Brest, Angers, Dunkerque, Caen, Metz, Limoges, Avignon, Mantes-la-Jolie, Amiens, Béthune
Currency:
franc

The French Republic is divided into 96 *départements* (departments), grouped into 22 administrative regions. It also includes the Overseas Departments of French Guiana, Guadeloupe, Martinique, Mayotte, Réunion and St Pierre and Miquelon, and the Overseas Territories of French Polynesia, New Caledonia and Wallis and Futuna.

Above: A scenic stretch of coastline in the department of Côtes-du-Nord, in Brittany, a region with a typically mild maritime climate. Left: Rolling hills dominate the Puy-de-Dôme region in the northern part of the Massif Central in central France. Right: The Canigou massif in the eastern Pyrenees, near France's border with Spain.

thought in the 18th century, were spread by French intellectuals. One can, then, understand the enormous shock wave that passed through Europe as a result of the French Revolution.

This Revolution took place in 1789 and was initially aimed at modernizing a nation in which the monarchy and nobility still enjoyed medieval privileges. But reform turned to violent revolution. The monarchy was overthrown, Louis XVI and his queen, Marie Antoinette, were sent to the guillotine, together with many representatives of the *ancien régime*. From the ruins of the past, arose a republic, governed by a Constitution based on the rights of man and guaranteeing liberty. The new ideas spread through Europe like wildfire, and were to form an inspiration for all the democratic movements of the 19th century.

Meanwhile, in France, the Republic was short-lived. It was succeeded by the dictatorship of Napoleon Bonaparte, appointed Consul for life in 1802 and Emperor in 1804. His military campaigns did, however, herald new times for the whole continent. The true greatness of Napoleon, the brilliant general who placed France at the centre of an empire greater than that of Charlemagne, did not arise so much from his spectacular victories, as from his putting an end to the remains of feudalism throughout Europe. Perhaps his greatest achievement was the introduction of a progressive and more rational legal system. After the fall of Napoleon, France was torn in the 19th century between attempts to restore the old monarchy and the tremors of revolution. The Second Republic, proclaimed in 1848, was replaced in 1852 by a second Empire headed by a nephew of Bonaparte, called Napoleon III. The years covered by the frivolous, glittering era of the second Empire came to a tragic end in the war against Prussia in 1870, in which France was defeated. France lost its regions of Alsace and Lorraine, which it was to regain after the First World War. Under the Third Republic, established in 1875 and based on universal suffrage, came the rapid industrialization of the country. In Africa and Asia, a vast colonial empire was formed, which had been started as early as 1830 by the conquest of Algeria. The French possessions in North America had been lost, but even so the new overseas empire was second in size only to that of Britain. Made prosperous by a long period of stability, France in the *belle époque* (1870-1914) saw literature and the arts flourishing again. Paris was once again the hub of intellectual activity in Europe.

The two World Wars had a terrible impact on France. The enemy was the same as in 1870, Germany. France was victorious in the First World War, at the price of great sacrifices. But in the Second World War, France had to endure four years of German occupation, until liberation in 1945 by the Allied armies, with the assistance of the French resistance. For the Fourth Republic, times

Right and below: The cultivation of vines and the production of fine wines is of great importance in France. The most productive areas are Champagne, the middle and lower valleys of the Loire, the western part of the country, and the Mediterranean region. These vineyards are in the Cognac region, which together with Armagnac, produces the world's best brandy.

were difficult after the war. These were times of social unrest and growing independence movements throughout the overseas empire from Indo-China to Algeria.

Colonialism was coming to an end, but France at first found it hard to accept this change. Its armed forces sometimes used harsh methods of suppression against rebels. The remains of the colonial empire were finally dismantled by General Charles De Gaulle, who had already been head of the Free French forces during the Second World War. In 1958, he took power and established the Fifth Republic. France became a presidential republic, a country like the United States, where the president is entrusted with great authority. He or she is elected for a seven-year period, directly by the people. The appointment of the prime minister and the cabinet depends on the president, who can even appoint them against the will of the two chambers, the Senate and the National Assembly. It is these two bodies which are responsible for the legislative functions.

In spite of the problems of the 20th century, France still plays an important part in the world. In area, it is the second largest European country after the USSR. The characteristics of its landscape and climate have, since ancient times, encouraged agriculture, which is still a mainstay of the economy. More than two-thirds of France is occupied by fertile plains and low hills. The mountains are mostly along the borders of the country. The Alps on the Italian border include Mont Blanc, the highest point in western Europe, at 4,810 metres (15,781 feet). The Jura straddle the border with Switzerland, the Vosges rise on the west bank of the Rhine near the frontier with West Germany, while the Pyrenees form the border with Spain. The only high ground in the interior is formed by the plateau of the Massif Central.

The rolling countryside is drained by a number of major rivers. In the centre of the country is the Loire, while the Paris region contains the Seine. To the south, the Rhône descends over a distance of 812 kilometres (505 miles) to the Golfe du Lion. In the Aquitaine region, the Garonne and the Dordogne unite near the Atlantic coast and flow through a long estuary called Gironde. On the Franco-German border is the Rhine, with its tributaries the Meuse and Moselle.

All these rivers, connected by navigable canals, form a large network of waterways which are vital for communication and for irrigation. Agriculture is flourishing today, thanks to the application of modern farming techniques. In 1939, France barely produced half the national food requirement. With mechanization, the use of chemical fertilizers, and a programme of rationalization, it is able to export 20 per cent of its output. The main crops are cereals, but sugar-beet, potatoes, vegetables, fruit and grapes are also important. French vineyards include some famous names: Bur-

gundy (Bourgogne), Bordeaux, and Champagne are all areas where wines of the highest quality are produced. Other important sectors are the raising of livestock, dairy farming, fishing and forestry.

France's coal deposits and its abundant iron ore deposits in Lorraine have contributed to the development of industry, especially in the iron and steel and metallurgical sectors. In Provence, near Les Baux, there are deposits of bauxite, the ore from which aluminium is obtained and which has taken its name from the town. The presence of these minerals also means that the engineering industries are active, particularly the car and aeronautics industries. Also important is the chemical industry. There are also textile industries, which follow in an ancient tradition. These are concentrated particularly around Roubaix for wool, Belfort and Lille for cotton and Lyons for silk.

Most businesses and industries are established in the western half of the country. There is an enormous industrial concentration in the Paris area. The vast number of factories and offices poses its own problems. Every day the capital is submerged by a flood of commuters, whose numbers are calculated at four million people. This makes it increasingly urgent to decentralize Paris, or to counteract the excessive crowding of the capital by increasing the development of regional centres. There is an obvious imbalance between the capital and the other cities. Paris now has more than two million inhabitants in the urban centre. The ring of suburbs and satellite towns brings the figure to more than $8\frac{1}{2}$ million. The second most important city in France is Marseilles. Although it is the biggest port on the Mediterranean, it has only a million or so inhabitants. The city of Lyons (Lyon) is about the same size. Only 104 French cities have a population of more than 50,000 inhabitants.

The 96 departments into which France has traditionally been divided have now been grouped into 22 regions, which are responsible for development. This reorganization should ensure that future development will be more controlled and better distributed geographically.

Various centres have been created, consisting of a few cities or groups of cities, which it is proposed to expand until they attract industry and jobs away from the capital. Will this experiment be successful? Whatever happens, many French people will continue to regard Paris, the centre of French civilization for so many years, as their spiritual home.

Top left: Bordeaux, a busy commercial and industrial centre. Top right: Modern buildings now dominate the skyline of Paris. Left: The docks area of Saint-Nazaire, a city which has grown up on the northern bank of the Loire estuary. It is joined to Saint-Brévin-les-Pins on the opposite bank by a 3,356 metre (11,010 ft) long bridge.

German Democratic Republic

Deutsche Demokratische Republik

Federal Republic of Germany

Bundesrepublik Deutschland

For people born after the Second World War, the expression 'the two Germanies' sounds as natural as 'the two Americas' or 'the two poles'. Young people might be forgiven for thinking that there was a clear geographical boundary or natural frontier between the two areas of German territory. In fact, the division is a recent one. It was the result of the defeat suffered by Germany in 1945, when British, American and French forces advanced into Germany from the west, and Russian troops invaded from the east. The line where these troops met marked the boundary between the Allied and the Soviet zones of military occupation. In 1949 these zones became two separate nations. The West became the Federal Republic of Germany, while the East became the German Democratic Republic.

Political division is not, however, something new in German history. The fragmentation of the country goes back a long way – in fact it was recorded in Roman times in the writings of Julius Caesar and Tacitus, who were the first to describe the land.

During the days of the Roman Empire a number of Germanic tribes lived in central Europe, between the Rhine (Rhein), the Danube (Donau) and the Vistula (Wisła) rivers, living from agriculture and animal-rearing. They were of Indo-European origin. The Heruli, Vandals, Goths, Quadi, Marcomanni, Suevians, Bavarians, Alemanni, Franks and many other tribes shared common ancestors and had similar customs, but had never been unified. They elected a king only in times of war, and even then his powers were limited.

After the third and fourth centuries AD, the barbarian peoples, which Rome had not managed either to civilize or subdue, struggled to carve out kingdoms for themselves in western Europe. Each wave of barbarian invaders was followed by another. The most powerful of the kingdoms thus created was that of the

An industrial skyline towers above a café in Dortmund, in West Germany's Ruhr district. West Germany is one of the world's leading industrial powers, but its citizens enjoy pleasant company.

Franks, which between the fifth and ninth centuries began to expand over much of western Europe. The Frankish king Charlemagne was crowned Holy Roman Emperor in AD 800. Under the successors of this great sovereign, two areas began to emerge: a French territory in the west, and a German area in the east. It was the latter, subdivided into counties, marches and dukedoms, which inherited the title of Charlemagne's Holy Roman Empire, a supranational body whose sovereignty extended over not only Germany, but Austria, Bohemia, central and northern Italy, and the Netherlands. But paradoxically the existence of this large empire, which soon became widely known as the Empire 'of the German nation', prevented the Germans from achieving any real and lasting unity.

For more than three centuries, the title of emperor was a prerogative of Germany's reigning dynasties: first Saxony, then Franconia, then Swabia. However, concern with the Italian part of the empire and disputes with the popes dissipated its cohesion. Frederick I, called Barbarossa, (*c*.1123-90), who became emperor in 1152 travelled down into Italy six times. His nephew Frederick II hardly ever set foot in Germany. These continuous absences created a dangerous gap in the emperor's power, allowing free rein to the feudal lords. This prevented the formation of a unified nation, as happened in France, Spain and England, where there were strong centralized monarchies. When, in 1430, the Holy Roman Empire passed permanently to the Hapsburgs of Austria, Germany remained a mosaic of feudal domains, principalities and free cities, without a centralized government.

The Protestant Reformation, sparked off in the 16th century by the teachings of the German monk Martin Luther (1483-1546) aggravated the lack of unity and set many princes against the empire, a bastion of Roman Catholicism. The dispute eventually continued into the Thirty Years' War (1618-1648). This proved to be a disaster not only for the Germans, but also for the whole Holy Roman Empire, which was reduced to little more than a name at the end of the hostilities.

From the 300 or so large and small states into which Germany was divided, the Kingdom of Prussia emerged during the 18th century. Thanks to its powerful, well-organized army and excellent administration, its ruling dynasty, the Hohenzollern, was able to rival the predominance of the Hapsburgs in central Europe. However, not even Prussia was able to stand up to Napoleon. France invaded, occupied Berlin, annexed half the kingdom's territory and became the dominant power in Germany. This defeat ultimately re-awakened the German patriotic spirit. Prussia called upon the German nation to rise up against Napoleon, and it was the Prussians, together with the British, who finally beat the great soldier at Waterloo in 1815. In the same year, the Congress of Vienna reduced the number of small German states to a 'reasonable' 39.

The time was ripe for unification. This was achieved by the efforts of Prussia. Four years after its victory over Austria in 1866, Prussia, assisted by the principal German states, resoundingly beat the France of Napoleon III. At the royal palace of Versailles the German Empire, headed by Kaiser Wilhelm I was proclaimed in January 1871.

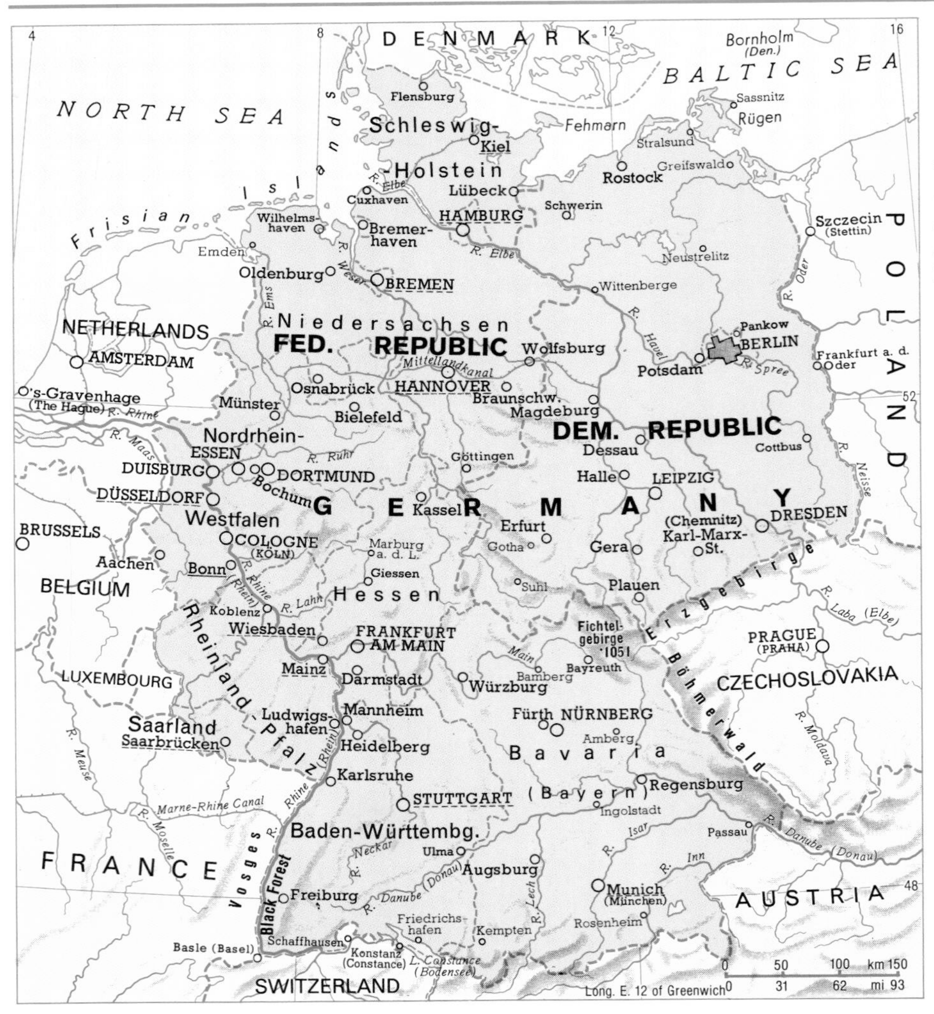

West Germany (Federal Republic of Germany)
Area: 248,577 km² (95,981 mi²)
Population: 61,421,000
Capital: Bonn (pop. 293,000)
Other towns: Berlin (West), Hamburg, Munich (München), Cologne (Köln), Essen, Frankfurt am Main, Dortmund, Düsseldorf, Stuttgart, Duisburg, Bremen, Hannover, Nuremberg (Nürnberg), Bochum, Wuppertal, Bielefeld, Gelsenkirchen, Mannheim, Wiesbaden, Karlsruhe, Münster Braunschweig,
Currency: Deutsche Mark (DM)

East Germany (German Democratic Republic)
Area: 108,178 km² (41,770 mi²)
Population: 16,765,000
Capital: Berlin (East) (pop. 1,186,000)
Other towns: Leipzig, Dresden, Karl-Marx-Stadt, Magdeburg, Halle an der Saale, Rostock, Erfurt, Potsdam, Gera, Zwickau, Schwerin, Cottbus, Jena, Dessau
Currency: Mark of the GDR

Left: This monument in Bremen illustrates a folktale by the brothers Grimm. Above: A beach on the Baltic Sea. Sunbathing is enjoyable, within the shelter of a wickerwork windbreak. Below: The Black Forest (Schwarzwald) and the traditional costume of the region.

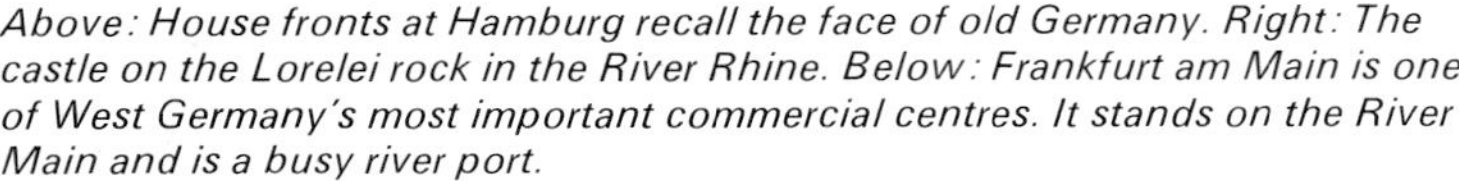

Above: House fronts at Hamburg recall the face of old Germany. Right: The castle on the Lorelei rock in the River Rhine. Below: Frankfurt am Main is one of West Germany's most important commercial centres. It stands on the River Main and is a busy river port.

Before the end of the century, Germany achieved great political and economic power and founded a large overseas empire. The empire, however, did not last long. It collapsed after the disastrous carnage of the First World War, for which the German military elite, headed by Kaiser Wilhelm II was largely responsible. In the bitter years after the war in this vanquished country, which had become a republic, Adolf Hitler's National Socialist (Nazi) party emerged and gained ground. Hitler came to power in 1933. The Nazis preached the superiority of the German race and cultivated dreams of revenge and world domination. Jews and dissidents were exterminated. Hitler initiated a belligerent policy of annexation and invasion which finally induced Britain, the United States and the USSR to take up arms against him. The Second World War, which resulted in an appalling loss of life, ended in unprecedented catastrophe for Germany. The invaded country's economy was shattered and its cities were devastated.

From these ruins, the two Germanies were born in 1949, after four years of military occupation by the victorious powers. First, on 23 May, the Federal Republic of Germany (West Germany) was created by the fusion of the British, Americans and French occupied zones. This was followed, on 7 October, by the establishment of the German Democratic Republic (East Germany) in the territory occupied by the Russians.

The Federal Republic of Germany, as its name indicates, is a confederation of ten states (*Länder*), which enjoy a large measure of autonomy in matters of internal administration, economy, education and justice. Political control and supreme legislative power are the responsibility of the Federal Parliament, composed of a lower house (*Bundestag*), and an upper house (*Bundesrat*), in which the representatives appointed by the *Länder* sit.

East Germany is ruled by a government similar to that of the socialist republics of Eastern Europe. The legislative power is held by the People's Chamber (*Volkskammer*), with 454 members elected every five years. Executive power is held by the State Council, whose president is also Head of State. The Council of Ministers, composed of 24 members, comes under the State Council. East Germany is divided into 14 districts.

The city of Berlin, the former capital of Prussia and then of the unified Germany, is in a unique position. On the eve of the Second World War, Berlin had a population of four and a half million people, and its industrial, economic and political importance was considerable. It was occupied by Soviet troops on 2 May 1945, after terrible destruction, and was then divided by the victorious Allies into four sectors: American, British, French and Russian. This division still remains today, though in a simplified form.

Today there are two Berlins, just as there are two Germanies. In 1961, during a period of particular tension between the eastern and western blocs, the city was physically divided into two parts by the construction of a wall. To the east, in the zone once under Soviet control, is the capital of the German Democratic Republic. West Berlin, on the other hand, consisting of the three sectors occupied by the Western Allies, has joined with the Federal Republic of Germany, although it is isolated from it and surrounded by the territory of East Germany.

The West Germans established the seat of their government in the city of Bonn, on the Rhine (Rhein), which up until 1949 had been known internationally only as the birthplace of Ludwig van Beethoven. It is one of the smallest capital cities in Europe, and it was chosen deliberately to avoid competition between the big, prestigious cities of West Germany, such as Hamburg, Munich (München), Cologne (Köln), Frankfurt, Stuttgart and others, all of which had risen up from the ruins of war.

The German Democratic Republic, although it covers a smaller area, also has great historical centres and artistic traditions, as well as increasing economic growth. Leipzig and Dresden have risen again after having been the victims of terrible bombing.

Above: The central building in the Alexanderplatz in East Berlin, the Haus des Lehrers, *has a 125 metre (410 foot) mosaic across its facade.*

The differences in the economies of the two countries is not only the result of their opposite political paths, but also of the geographical characteristics of the areas they occupy. Germany, as a whole, is divided into three main geographical regions. To the south lie the Alps, formed by secondary ranges of the great European Alpine system. In the centre and south there is a region of horsts, which are uplifted blocks, such as the Black Forest and the Odenwald, between which flow the rivers in downfaulted rift valleys. The uplands in East Germany include the Harz Mountains, the Erzgebirge and the Thüringer Wald. To the north are level plains, largely covered by glacial deposits, reaching as far as the coast. Many of Germany's major rivers are navigable. The Rhine is a major artery of trade, and the Danube, Weser and Elbe have all played an important part in German history. The Oder now lies on the German Democratic Republic's eastern border. The highest point in the whole region is the Zugspitze, which reaches 2,968 metres (9,738 feet) in the Bavarian Alps.

Two different aspects of East Germany: top, Stralsund, opposite the island of Rügen, in the Baltic; below, the Pragerstrasse, in Dresden, the third most important city.

The central region of West Germany is rich in mineral resources, notably coal, lignite, lead, zinc, iron, oil, natural gas, rock salt and potassium salts. This is consequently the most industrialized region, particularly in the Ruhr, a region of iron and steel works and mechanical and chemical engineering plants. This inheritance provided the starting point for a spectacular economic recovery in West Germany, which is now Europe's greatest industrial power after the USSR, and a major producer of consumer goods. West Germany was a founder member of the European Economic Community.

East Germany also had to rebuild after the war. The eastern territory was traditionally agricultural, although it contained large deposits of lignite and potash. Today, 77 per cent of the people live in urban areas and, with Russian assistance, East Germany has become the world's eighth most important industrial power, with iron, steel and chemical industries, although it must still import many raw materials, including petroleum from the USSR. By 1980 industry accounted for 70 per cent of West Germany's gross national product, as compared with 9 per cent from agriculture. The percentage of the workforce engaged in agriculture fell from 18 per cent in 1960 to 10 per cent in 1980, by which time 50 per cent were employed in industry. The government owned 97·6 per cent of all industrial enterprises by 1978. Apart from Berlin, the chief industrial centres are in the south, including Dresden, Erfurt, Karl-Marx-Stadt, Magdeburg and Leipzig. East Germany is a member of COMECON.

Despite the division of the two Germanies in their political and economic paths, both nations share a common cultural heritage and both are aware of Germany's unique contribution to the world of literature, music, painting and philosophy. The German language, which is spoken over the whole region, albeit with differences of dialect, first became a literary medium in the Middle Ages. Printing was invented in Germany in the 15th century, and Luther's translation of the Bible had a strong influence on the development of the language. Major German writers have included Johann Wolfgang von Goethe (1749-1832) and Johann Christoph Friedrich von Schiller (1759-1805). Germans have also played an important part in the visual arts, from the time of Albrecht Dürer (1471-1528) until the Expressionist movement of this century. But probably the most remarkable achievements have been in the world of music: Johann Sebastian Bach (1685-1750); Ludwig van Beethoven (1770-1827); Richard Wagner (1813-1883). The long list of German composers sound like a history of western music itself. Today both Germanies have shared a tragic past. But both have recovered dramatically and today are leading contributors to the cultural and economic development of Europe as a whole.

Right top: Hampton Court on the River Thames was built by Cardinal Wolsey in 1514 and given to Henry VIII in 1529. Bottom right: Eton College, a famous private school, was founded by Henry VI in 1440. Far right: Canterbury Cathedral in Kent. This is the see of the Archbishop of Canterbury, head of the Anglican church throughout the world.

Great Britain and Northern Ireland

United Kingdom of

The British Isles are a group of islands lying between the Atlantic and the North Sea, and separated from the mainland of Europe by the English Channel. They are occupied by two nations – the Republic of Ireland and the United Kingdom of Great Britain and Northern Ireland. The latter is composed of a union of four countries: the Kingdoms of England and Scotland, the Principality of Wales, and the Province of Northern Ireland. The United Kingdom takes in a large number of offshore islands. To the west are Rockall, Saint Kilda, the Hebrides, Anglesey, and the Isles of Scilly. To the south is the Isle of Wight. To the north lie the Orkney and Shetland Islands.

The Channel Islands, off France, come not under the rule of the United Kingdom, but of the Dukedom of Normandy, which in fact belongs in title to the British monarch. The Isle of Man, in the Irish Sea, has its own parliament. The political problems of Northern Ireland have led to a variety of relationships with central government being attempted in recent years. On mainland Britain, England, Wales and Scotland form a single political unit, although the latter has a separate legal and educational system.

The English language is spoken throughout the United Kingdom, but other languages are also spoken regionally. Welsh is widely spoken in Wales, where it is an official language and a medium of instruction. Gaelic has survived in Scotland, and small numbers can still speak Manx in the Isle of Man and French *patois* in the Channel Islands. Use of the ancient Cornish language died out about 200 years ago.

If all this seems a little complicated, it is not surprising. Traditions die hard, and, historically, the British are a mixture of races and cultures. Unity has been achieved by the political domination of its island neighbours by England, a domination which survived, sometimes uneasily, for several centuries. This has

ATLANTIC OCEAN
North Sea
Orkney Is.
Kirkwall
Shetland Is.
Lerwick
Continuation northwards
Wick
Lewis
Outer Hebrides
Inner Hebrides
Skye
North West Highlands
Inverness
Loch Ness
Aberdeen
Cairngorms
Grampian Mts.
Fort William
Ben Nevis 1344m.
R. Tay
Dundee
Perth
SCOTLAND
Dunfermline
R. Forth
Glasgow
Edinburgh
Greenock
Motherwell
R. Clyde
Ayr
Southern Uplands
UNITED KINGDOM
Cheviot Hills
Dumfries
North Channel
Newcastle upon Tyne
R. Tyne
Sunderland
Carlisle
Londonderry
Larne
NORTHERN IRELAND
Belfast
Lough Neagh
Portadown
Lough Erne
Sligo
Cumbrian Mts.
Scafell Pike 978m.
Pennines
Darlington
Teesside
Isle of Man
Lancaster
York
Connacht
Dundalk
Irish Sea
Bradford
Halifax
Leeds
R. Ouse
Hull
Bolton
Huddersfield
REPUBLIC OF IRELAND
Lough Corrib
Galway
Dublin (Baile Átha Cliath)
Dun Laoghaire
Anglesey (Ynys Mon)
Liverpool
Manchester
Sheffield
R. Mersey
Lincoln
Wicklow Mts.
Snowdon 1085m.
Stoke-on-Trent
ENGLAND
The Wash
Lough Derg
Leinster
Derby
Nottingham
R. Trent
Norwich
R. Shannon
Limerick
Wolverhampton
Leicester
R. Ouse
WALES
BIRMINGHAM
Coventry
Aberystwyth
Northampton
Cambridge
Munster
Wexford
Carrantoohill 1041m.
R. Blackwater
Killarney
Cork
Cambrian Mts.
Worcester
R. Wye
R. Avon
Ipswich
St. George's Channel
Fishguard (Abergwaun)
R. Severn
Gloucester
Luton
Oxford
Swansea (Abertawe)
LONDON
Reading
R. Thames
Bristol
Cardiff (Caerdydd)
Bristol Channel
Bath
Dover
Southampton
Brighton
Exeter
Bournemouth
Portsmouth
Isle of Wight
Dartmoor
Torquay
Plymouth
Penzance
English Channel
Isles of Scilly
FRANCE
Channel Is.
0 100km
0 60 miles
58°
56°
54°
52°
50°
60°
10°
8°
6°
4°
2°
0°
2°

given the English language supremacy. Its use spread around the world with the British Empire, and today English is spoken in North America, Australia, and large sections of the developing world. English is currently a language of international literature, business and communications. It is also one of the official languages of the United Nations Organization and the European Economic Community.

So just who are the British? They are largely descendants of successive migrations of races who long ago pushed westwards across Europe and of subsequent invaders and immigrants. Britain became an island in about 5000 BC, when the Straits of Dover were formed. This narrow stretch of water did not deter waves of new settlers, who sought new hunting lands or who wished to clear farmland from the forests which then covered the region. Stone weapons were succeeded by bronze and iron.

In about 500 BC, a central European people, the Celts, began to move westward into Gaul (modern France). From Gaul, they entered the British Isles. Fierce fighters, the Celts were fine metalworkers and craftsmen of great skill. Successive tribes occupied Scotland, Wales, England, and Ireland. Some later settled the Brittany region of France. The name Great Britain, first used in medieval times, was originally used to distinguish the country from Little Britain, that is, Brittany in France.

Julius Caesar carried out two raids upon Britain, in 55 and 54 BC. But on both occasions, his fleet was hampered by stormy crossings. It was not until the reign of the Emperor Claudius (41–54 AD) that Roman rule was consolidated in the south. After several revolts, the British Celts settled down to life under Roman rule. To the north, however, the Scots and Picts were never really subdued. In the second century, the Emperor Hadrian built a wall of defence against them. Hadrian's Wall ran from the Solway Firth to the mouth of the River Tyne. Its ruins still stand today. The Roman presence in Britain lasted until 409 AD, but with the city of Rome itself threatened by barbarian invaders, the legions withdrew.

The country was now an easy target for invaders. The Irish raided the western coastline, and across the North Sea came a stream of Germanic peoples, including Saxons, Jutes and Angles (from whom the name England is derived). They settled the coasts and swarmed up the river valleys. Eventually they overcame resistance and settled over much of the

Above: The green hills of Skye, an island in the Inner Hebrides off the west coast of Scotland.
Below: Fortifications protect the old town of Pembroke (Penfro) in South Wales.

country, gradually becoming intermixed with those Celtic people who had not fled. They did not penetrate Wales and Scotland. As a result, in these regions, as in Ireland, Celtic culture and autonomy survived.

The Germanic invaders became converted to Christianity, and founded small kingdoms. They were increasingly subjected to fierce raids by the Vikings, freebooting warriors from Scandinavia. From 1017 until 1042, England was ruled by Danish kings. Independence, restored by Edward the Confessor, was short-lived. In 1066, Duke William of Normandy landed near Hastings in Sussex with 50,000 men. Edward's successor, Harold, was killed, and William 'the Conqueror' was crowned King of England. England has not been successfully invaded since 1066. Powerful castles were built all over the country, and Norman power spread beyond England's borders into Wales and Ireland.

In the 12th century, the English crown was inherited by the Angevin house of Plantagenet. This family retained vast possessions in France, and a bid to unite the crowns of the two countries led to the so-called Hundred Years' War (1338–1453). In 1429, Henry VI of England was crowned king in Paris, but only 24 years later all English possessions in France had been relinquished except for Calais.

The Plantagenets were more successful on their western border. Llywelyn, the last independent Welsh Prince of Wales, was killed in 1282, and Edward I gave the title to his son. An iron ring of castles was built, and Wales was compelled to follow the fortunes of England, although a revolt by Owain Glyndŵr at the beginning of the 15th century almost succeeded. In Scotland, the Battle of Bannockburn, won by Robert the Bruce in 1314, secured Scottish independence, which was maintained until the Union under the House of Stuart in 1707.

In medieval England, the system of parliamentary democracy known today had its origins. As early as 1215, barons had forced the king to limit his powers by signing a document known as Magna Carta. In 1264 a quarrel between Simon de Montfort and the king led to the setting up of a rudimentary 'Model Parliament'. And, in 1377, a second chamber representing knights of the shires and citizens of the towns came into being.

From 1455 until 1485, England was torn apart by civil war. Two branches of the royal family, that of York (whose symbol was a white rose), and that of Lancaster (whose symbol was a red rose) fought for control of the country. At the end of the struggle, the victor was Henry Tudor, a Lancastrian who as Henry VII married a Yorkist, and so ended the long strife. He was a Welshman, and he finally united the land. The house of Tudor laid the foundations of the country's power. When Protestant Reformation swept through Europe, his son, Henry VIII, broke with the popes in Rome and declared himself head of the Church of

Above: Horse racing at Ascot is a major event in summer. Formal dress is worn. Right: A line across the courtyard of the Greenwich Observatory in London marks the Prime Meridian, longitude 0°. Centre right: A sign outside a public house commemorates one of Britain's great admirals, Horatio, Lord Nelson (1758–1805). Far right: A piper wears the traditional dress of the Scottish Highlands, namely the kilt and sporran. Traditions still play an important part in British life.

Three aspects of the United Kingdom. Above left: Rows of terraced houses are common sights in industrial towns. Above right: Edinburgh Castle stands on a high rock overlooking Scotland's capital city. Left: The urban sprawl of Birmingham, a great industrial centre.

England, a title still held by the British sovereign. The Tudor period was one of bitter religious battles, but also one of great political and economic achievement.

In England, the most popular sovereign was Elizabeth I, a shrewd and ruthless ruler. During her long reign (1558–1603), England became a great maritime power, vying with Spain, whose invading fleet, or Armada, was repelled in 1588. English ships explored and settled the 'New World' of the Americas, and, in 1577–80, Sir Francis Drake circumnavigated the world.

In 1587, Elizabeth ordered the execution of the Scottish queen, Mary, for alleged conspiracy against the English crown during her captivity in England, to which she had fled from strife at home. But it was her son, James Stuart, who inherited the throne of England. Elizabeth I was unmarried and died without issue, and James was a descendant of the house of Tudor on the female side. As James VI of Scotland and James I of England, Mary's son united the two crowns. Parliamentary union followed 104 years later. Since Ireland had, at least nominally, been under English rule since the 12th century, the British Isles were now united.

The capricious absolutism of the Stuart monarchs led to widespread dissatisfaction, however. Under James's son, Charles I, tension between king and parliament degenerated into civil war. The king, defeated and held prisoner by the parliamentary forces, was tried for treason and then beheaded in front of the Palace of Whitehall in 1649. For 10 years there was a republic, during which the parliamentarian general, Oliver Cromwell, governed the country as Lord Protector. After Cromwell's death, the monarchy was soon restored with Charles II, but the Stuarts continued to make themselves unpopular. With the 'Glorious Revolution' of 1688, no blood was shed but James II was forced to leave the country.

James II's successor was William of Orange, who ruled jointly with his wife, James's daughter Mary. She died in 1694, and he died eight years later. They were followed by Anne, the second daughter of James II, and the last Stuart sovereign. From 1714, the country was ruled by the German house of Hanover. The first sovereign, George I, was a direct descendant of James I. Two subsequent attempts to restore the Stuarts led to armed uprisings in Scotland, in 1715 and 1745, which were suppressed with great brutality.

Britain prospered under the Hanoverians. They recognized the power of Parliament, and their constitutional role. Competing with France, British colonial interests spread around the world. The loss of the American colonies in 1789 was a major setback, but the foundations were already laid for Britain's role as the leading world power in the 19th century. The French Revolution followed the American, and soon Napoleon Bonaparte was stunning the world with his brilliant military campaigns. But he was finally defeated by the British and Prussians at the Battle of Waterloo in 1815. Under the long rule of Queen Victoria (1837–1901), Britain became the centre of a vast empire.

During this period, Britain changed from an agricultural country to an industrial one. Exploitation of coal resources had spearheaded a host of technological innovations which were to change the face of Europe. Railways spread across the country, and in such new cities as Manchester large textile mills processed cotton from the colonies. In 1877, Victoria was proclaimed Empress of India. By the 20th century, the British empire covered one-fourth of the world. The cost was considerable in social terms, both at home and abroad. In the factories of northern England, conditions were appalling, and the struggle for a better life was long and hard.

The First World War (1914–18) changed the face of Britain permanently. In this war against the ever-increasing power of Germany, a whole generation was killed or maimed amid the horrors of trench warfare. After the Second World War (1939–45), in which Britain, the USA and the USSR defeated fascist Germany, Italy and Japan, the face of modern Britain finally appeared. The colonial era was soon over. The empire was dismantled piece by piece, and in a world dominated by the USA and the USSR, the United Kingdom looked more and more for co-operation with its neighbours – and traditional enemies – in Europe. Most of Ireland had withdrawn from the United Kingdom after years of struggle in 1921. The Irish Free State became the Republic of Ireland in 1948. The Province of Ulster, however, remained a part of the United Kingdom, in accordance with the wishes of the Protestant majority. The desire of the Roman Catholic minority for union with the Republic of Ireland led to a bitter and still unresolved conflict. Despite division at home and loss of power abroad, the United Kingdom nevertheless remains a strong force in world politics. It is a member of the Commonwealth, the union of nations which emerged from the dismemberment of the British Empire, and since 1973 it has been a member of the European Economic Community (EEC). The United Kingdom was also a founder member of the North Atlantic Treaty Organization (NATO), a military alliance of the USA and other western nations.

At home, social change has been rapid, while many ancient traditions have continued unchanged. After the Second World War, a programme of social welfare ('the Welfare State') was inaugurated, and certain industries, such as coal mining, were nationalized. The multiparty parliamentary system continued. Both the Conservative and Labour parties succeeded in forming governments, while the smaller Liberal party remained influential. Scottish and Welsh nationalism began to revive as a political force in the 1960s.

Traditionally, the strength of the country's economy relies on coal, steel, engineering and the manufacturing industries. Postwar recovery and industrial modernization were slower than in some other European countries, but world recession speeded up the search for new markets, and the development of new fields, such as microelectronics. At the same time, such traditional industries as mining were rapidly modernized. In agriculture, too, technical advances improved efficiency dramatically. The discovery of extensive oil fields in the North Sea has provided a valuable boost for British industry in recent years.

The landscapes of the United Kingdom vary greatly in character. The south of England is dominated by the River Thames and its valley, across which sprawls one of the largest cities in the world. This is the capital, London. A conurbation of the ancient cities of London and Westminster, it has now spread far into the surrounding countryside. Greater London covers 1,795 square kilometres (693 square miles). The City of Westminster is the seat of government, and the City of London is one of the world's leading financial and business centres. London is a cosmopolitan city in which traditions mingle with new fashions and styles. It is also a centre for the arts and for culture.

South of London lies the agricultural land of the Weald, bordered by chalk downs to the north and south. Here stands the ancient city of Canterbury, the ecclesiastical centre of the Anglican church. Central-southern England is occupied by rich farmland and the open country of Salisbury Plain. To the west, the landscape is more hilly. The rocky coasts of Devon and Cornwall surround a number of bleak uplands – Dartmoor, Exmoor and Bodmin Moor. Tourism, china clay mining, dairy farming and some tin mining and fishery are the chief economic activities of the south-west. Along the Channel coast are three major ports: Portsmouth and Southampton in the centre, and Plymouth to the west.

To the west of London are two chains of hills, the Chilterns and the Cotswolds. Between them in a clay vale is Oxford, a centre of the automobile industry and, together with Cambridge, one of Britain's oldest university towns. Farther west, the port of Bristol lies on the River Avon.

North-east of London, between the Thames and the Wash, lies a huge area of

Above: Fishing trawlers line the quay at Peel on the Isle of Man.

flat land. East Anglia, as this region is called, is mostly farmland, devoted to sheep raising and cereal production. The English Midlands surround the cities of Birmingham, Coventry, Leicester and Nottingham. This is an industrial region, with coalfields, automobile manufacture and engineering industries.

The north of England is split down the centre by the Pennine Chain, a range of low mountains running northwards from the River Trent. To the east of the Pennines lies Hull, England's chief fishing port, and the Ridings of Yorkshire. This is agricultural land punctuated by the industrial areas around the large towns of Leeds and Sheffield. Travelling northwards to Durham and Northumberland, one enters a landscape of moors and dales, and then a major coal-producing region. The Rivers Tyne, Tees and Wear support heavy industry and shipbuilding. The principal towns are Newcastle upon Tyne, Gateshead and Sunderland.

On the western side of the Pennines, the town of Stoke-on-Trent lies at the centre of Staffordshire, a region famous for its potteries. The principal river of the north-west is the Mersey, upon which lies the great port of Liverpool. Joined to the Mersey estuary by a canal is another large residential area – the manufacturing centre of Manchester. North of Manchester the country becomes rural, with the picturesque landscape of lakes and the Cambrian mountains.

The capital of Wales (in Welsh, Cymru) is at Cardiff (Caerdydd) on the Bristol Channel. Heavy industry is concentrated on the southern coast between Cardiff and Swansea (Abertawe), with steelworks, and coal mining in the valleys of the hinterland. The rest of the country is devoted to farming, especially the raising of sheep, and to tourism. It is a mountainous land, culminating in the splendid peaks of Snowdonia (Eryri). Ferries to the Republic of Ireland sail from Swansea, Fishguard (Abergwaun) and Holyhead (Caergybi).

The Scottish border is formed by the Cheviots, and the country continues to be hilly south of the Firths of Clyde and Forth. The capital is at Edinburgh, the site of an imposing castle on a towering rock. This elegant town is the site of an annual international arts festival. The largest town in Scotland is Glasgow, a major industrial centre. The River Clyde has in its day been shipyard to the world. To the north-east of Dundee, on the River Tay, lie the Grampian mountains. The Highlands of Scotland are an area of great scenic beauty, attracting many tourists. The highest mountain in the British Isles is Ben Nevis, which reaches 1,347 metres (4,419 ft). Lying between the hills are deep stretches of inland water, called lochs. On the east coast, the fishing port of Aberdeen has in recent years become a service centre for the oil and natural gas fields of the North Sea. The same industry is also changing the traditional way of life on the Orkney and Shetland islands. In the Hebrides, crofting and hand weaving are still carried out.

Separated from Scotland by the North Channel, the Province of Northern Ireland occupies six counties of the old Irish province of Ulster. Belfast is the chief town and a centre of manufacture and shipbuilding. The second city is Londonderry, on Lough Foyle. The interior is largely hilly, with the exception of the valley of the River Bann. This flows from Lough Neagh, the largest lake in the British Isles, to Coleraine and the coast.

The climate of the United Kingdom is temperate with few extremes. The country is warmed by an extension of the Gulf Stream on its Atlantic Coast. The west coast tends to be warm and wet, while the east coast is drier and colder. The highest rainfall is in the mountains of Scotland and Wales.

The climate ensures a varied flora, and the coastline attracts a large bird population. Mammals and reptiles are less well represented. There are 10 national parks, covering a total area of 13,608 square kilometres (5,254 square miles).

Many of the so-called 'Stately Homes' are open to the public for the greater part of the year, and some combine a 'Safari Park' where wild animals are allowed to roam relatively freely. Thus it is possible to see them more in their natural state.

Above: London's Oxford Street, a busy shopping centre.

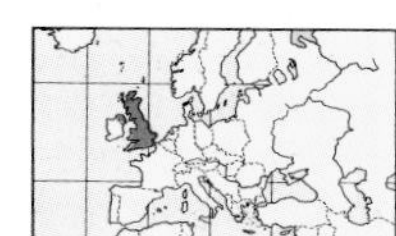

Area:
244,046 km² (94,232 mi²)
Population:
55,780,000
Capital:
London (pop. 6,755,000)
Other towns:
Birmingham, Leeds, Sheffield, Liverpool, Bradford, Manchester, Bristol, Kirklees, Dudley, Doncaster (England); Glasgow, Edinburgh (Scotland); Cardiff, Swansea (Wales); Belfast (Northern Ireland)
Currency:
pound sterling

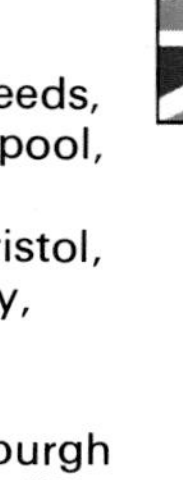

Greece

Elliniki Dimokratia

Greece, officially the Hellenic Republic, is the birthplace of European civilization. It is an enchanting country of beautiful coasts and wooded hills, of tiny islands set in deep blue seas. It occupies part of the Balkan peninsula, extending southwards into the Mediterranean. It shares borders to the north with Albania, Yugoslavia, and Bulgaria, and to the east with Turkey.

Most of mainland Greece is made up of three smaller peninsulas: the main body of land including the regions of Macedonia, Thessaly and Attica; the Chalcidice (Khalkidhiki), which extends three long fingers from the north-east; and the Peloponnese, a large region stretching southwards from the isthmus of Corinth, which is today cut by the Corinth Canal. Between Macedonia and the Turkish border lies the region of Thrace (Thraki).

To the west of Greece lies the Ionian Sea and its islands. To the east lies the Aegean Sea, and the island groups of the Cyclades (Kikladhes) and the Dodecanese (Sporadhes). To the south lies the large island of Crete. Much of Greece is mountainous. The Pindhos (Pindus) range stretches north to south, and in the east is Olympus (Ólimbos), which at 2,917 metres (9,570 feet) is Greece's highest point. It was revered in ancient times as the home of the gods. The highest point on Crete is Mount Ida (Ídhi Óros) at 2,456 metres (8,058 feet).

Both sea and mountains have played their part in determining Greek history. The mountains have acted as a barrier to communications, resulting in the emergence of regional differences. But the coastline and many islands ensured that from the earliest times the Greeks were seafarers and traders, a fact which encouraged the emergence of their unique civilizations.

The first great empire to arise in this region was the Minoan civilization of Crete. From 1950-1400 BC the fabulous palace at Knossos was the centre of Mediterranean civilization. On the mainland, the people of the Mycenae region became powerful during this period, and when Crete finally fell – possibly destroyed by an earthquake or a tsunami (tidal wave) generated by a volcanic eruption, possibly as a result of invasion – the Mycenaeans came into their own. Warriors of the Bronze Age, they conquered much of southern Greece and, in about 1193 BC, destroyed the city of Troy in Asia Minor. But within a century or so, Mycenae fell to the Dorian Greeks, who were northerners using iron weapons.

By the time of Greece's golden age, Dorians were concentrated in the Peloponnese, Crete and Rhodes; the Aeolians were scattered over the centre of the country, some Aegean islands and Asia Minor; and the Ionians were in Attica, the Cyclades and also in part of Asia Minor. These groups spoke various Greek dialects and each had its own culture. But certainly by the fifth century BC, the Greek peoples saw themselves as part of a common Hellenic culture, quite separate from the surrounding 'barbarians'. The barren soil of their homeland led to Greeks founding settlements throughout the Mediterranean region.

The city-states gradually evolved a number of systems of government. Some were ruled by 'tyrants', who were popular, or not so popular dictators. Others tried experimenting with 'democracy', or rule by the people, although this did not extend to the slaves who maintained the fabric of their society. Others were 'oligarchies', ruled by an elite. Sparta remained a traditional monarchy, and was famous for its harsh military discipline. The predominant states of ancient Greece were Athens, Sparta, Thebes and Corinth. The region was almost conquered by Xerxes I of Persia in 479 BC, but his armies were finally defeated at Plataea. The city-states were perpetually at war with each other, but despite the strife, this was a golden age. Ancient Greece was a centre of learning and scientific enquiry. Its architecture, literature, philosophy, sculpture and social innovations have survived 2,500 years and more, and they still astound us today.

The northern kingdom of Macedonia came to the fore about 359 BC, and its king, Philip II, made the south a part of his empire in 338 BC. His son, Alexander the Great (356-323 BC), established a Macedonian-Greek Empire that stretched from Egypt to India. Upon Alexander's death his empire was divided. Macedonia and Greece were formally united, but when the Romans conquered Macedonia in 197 BC, the Greeks were declared free. Within 50 years, Greece was also reduced to a province of Rome, with the name Achaea. Although Greece was no longer a political power, its culture was absorbed by the Romans and spread by them throughout the lands of the empire.

Rome was eventually shattered by barbarian invasions in the fifth century AD. However, in AD 330, a new eastern empire had been founded, centred upon Constantinople (formerly Byzantium, now Istanbul). This Christian empire survived, and it was permeated by Greek language, culture and customs. In the ninth century AD, the Christians of Con-

Area:
131,944 km²
(50,947 mi²)
Population:
9,740,000
Capital:
Athens (Athinai, **pop. 3,027,000,** including Piraeus)
Other towns:
Thessaloníki, Pátrai, Lárisa, Iráklion, Vólos, Kavalla, Sérrai, Khaniá, Tríkkala, Ioánnina
Currency:
drachma

stantinople broke away from the popes of Rome, and this Eastern Orthodox sect became the most widespread religion in Greece and eastern Europe, and remains so today. In the Middle Ages, Greece was divided between various western European powers, notably Venice.

In 1453, Constantinople fell to the Muslim Turks, and before long the whole of Greece was part of the Turkish Empire. The Greeks suffered considerable oppression under the Turks. Resistance came to a head in a War of Independence which began in 1821. The Greek nationalist cause was supported by many European idealists, such as the British poet Lord George Byron. Independence was ratified by the Congress of London in 1830 and Greece became a monarchy.

Greece was occupied again in the 20th century – by Germany in the Second World War. It was a disastrous period, and 300,000 Greeks died of famine in the winter of 1941-42. A resistance movement arose once again, and after the defeat of the Germans in 1944, guerrillas continued to fight the Greek regular army, with the intention of making Greece a Communist republic. This civil war lasted until 1949, but Greece remained a constitutional monarchy. Postwar problems and unstable governments culminated in a military dictatorship led by army colonels (1967-74). This regime was at first supported and then disowned by King Constantine II, who fled the country. When the oppressive regime finally fell, democratic liberties were restored, and a republic was founded. The 1975 Constitution entrusts legislative power to a parliament of 300 members elected by universal suffrage. They in turn elect the president, who chooses the cabinet.

Above left: The tholos, *a circular central cell surrounded by a colonnade, from the sanctuary of Athena Pronaia at Delphi. Above right: The skylight in the palace of Knossos, in Crete.*

Below right: The Parthenon in Athens.

In spite of the better prospects offered by democracy, including membership of the European Economic Community on 1 January 1980, Greece is still a poor country, suffering the aftermath of years of oppression. Some 37 per cent of the workforce is employed on the land, either in the raising of livestock, mostly sheep and goats, or in the cultivation of crops, including olives, vines, fruit, tobacco and wheat. Fishing is important, and sponges are collected from the seabed. Industrial development is hampered by the lack of energy resources, but is growing in the regions of Athens and Salonika (Thessaloniki). Piraeus, which is now part of Greater Athens, is a major European port and the Greek merchant navy is one of the largest in the world.

The country is certainly more prosperous than it was 20 years ago, and one of the reasons is the growth in tourism. Its sunny climate, beautiful beaches and fascinating archaeological sites and ruins attract visitors from all over the world. Greece remains a country in harmony with its ancient origins, with a seafaring people with a long cultural tradition.

Hungary

Magyar Népköztársaság

The People's Republic of Hungary's fine capital city of Budapest, on the Danube, has a famous monument showing a group of proud warriors on horseback. It was erected to mark the thousandth anniversary of the country being settled by the Magyars in AD 896. This region had once constituted the Roman province of Pannonia. But with the fall of Rome, it was invaded by a number of barbarian tribes, including the Vandals, Huns and Langobards. But the Magyars, horsemen from the Volga region, found the vast plains of Hungary to their liking, and they settled permanently.

The Magyar chiefs were brought within a single kingdom and converted to Christianity during the reign of King Stephen I (*c.* AD 975–1038). Perhaps the most famous medieval king was Matthias Corvinus (*c.* 1443–90), who obtained the crown of Bohemia and fought off a Turkish invasion. However, the country was eventually torn apart by the Turks and by the Hapsburgs of Austria. From 1699 onwards, Hungary was under Hapsburg rule.

In 1848, a revolution against Austrian rule occurred, led by Lajos Kossuth, but independence was short-lived. Not until 1918 was Hungarian independence re-established. The Communist experiment of Bela Kun was suppressed, and a regency was established under Nikolaus Horthy, who in the Second World War supported Germany until 1944, when German forces invaded Hungary. Soviet troops occupied Hungary after the war, and a Communist government came to power three years later. Despite an up-

Above: The Danube and the Parliament Buildings in Budapest. Below: A traditional Hungarian dance.

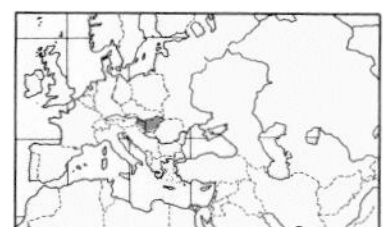

Area:
93,030 km² (35,921 mi²)
Population:
10,710,000
Capital:
Budapest (pop. 2,093,000)

Other towns:
Miskolc, Debrecen, Szeged, Pécs, Györ, Nyíregháza, Székesfehérvár, Kecskemét, Szombathely, Szolnok
Currency:
forint

rising in 1956, Hungary today remains a Communist country, a member of COMECON and of the Warsaw Pact.

The economy of Hungary is now heavily industrialized, with iron and steel production, mechanical and chemical engineering, food processing and textile manufacture. Natural resources include lignite, bauxite and natural gas, but many minerals must be imported. Agriculture is rapidly being mechanized. Organized on a collective basis, the chief crops are cereals and vegetables. There are also many orchards, and vineyards producing famous wines. The raising of livestock is important and horsebreeding has been an obsession since the Magyars first settled the region.

Most of Hungary is made up of a great lowland plain, crossed by the River Danube (Duna) and its tributary, the Tisza. In the central-western region lies Balaton, central Europe's largest lake, with an area of 591 square kilometres (228 square miles). Northern Hungary contains the wooded Felföld region, where there are hills. Highest of these is Mt Kékes which reaches 1,015 metres (3,330 feet). To the west is the Alföld, a vast level area. This was once the open steppeland of the *Puszta,* but it is increasingly being cultivated. The Pannonian region (Dunántul) contains low hills, culminating in the ridge of the Bakony Forest. The climate is continental, with cold winters and hot summers. The rainfall is adequate for farming.

Budapest is the main centre of population, a city of more than 2,000,000 inhabitants. The official language is Hungarian, which reflects the unusual racial origins of the Magyars in that it belongs to the Finno-Ugric group of languages.

Iceland

Ísland

In AD 874, a group of Vikings colonized an island which lay in the North Atlantic Ocean, just south of the Arctic Circle. No one had ever lived there before, although monks from Ireland, who thought that it must lie at the gates of hell itself, had once visited it. The appearance of the island was like nowhere else on Earth. It was a landscape of empty rock and mossy heathland, of glaciers, volcanoes and hot springs, truly a land of ice and fire.

The Republic of Iceland is separated from Greenland by the Denmark Strait. The northern regions of the country have an Arctic climate, with bitter winters, short summers and little rain. But the warm ocean currents of the North Atlantic Drift warm the island's south-western shore, and this affects the climate favourably in the south, where Reykjavík, the capital and only large city, is situated.

The rest of the island is a strange world, a lunar landscape. It contains some of Europe's most impressive glaciers. Vatnajökull, in the south-east, covers an area of 8,500 square kilometres (3,282 square miles). The island is covered with volcanoes, many of which are still active. A spectacular eruption in 1963 actually created a new offshore island, Surtsey.

Geysers, which gush up from the depths of the earth, and hot springs, are also found in Iceland. These are sufficient to provide an exploitable source of thermal energy, the hot water being used for central heating. There are many rivers on the island, the largest of which is the Thjórsa. These include some remarkable waterfalls, such as the Gullfoss, on the River Hvítá near Reykjavík.

The Vikings who founded the colony were from Norway. They divided the island into cantons, and set up a legislative assembly known as the *Althing.* This is the world's oldest surviving parliament.

Above: This geyser in Iceland is a hot spring which periodically shoots upwards. Hot springs are harnessed to heat homes and produce energy.

The Icelanders have had to struggle with a hostile landscape from the earliest days. In order to survive, they had to adapt to the environment. The measure of their success may be gauged by the fact that today their standard of living is high, comparable to the Scandinavian countries themselves. Less than 0·1 per cent of the land is suitable for agriculture, and Iceland has few mineral resources of any value. But there are other assets, notably hydro-electric and geothermal energy. Ingenuity has enabled glasshouse cultivation to become significant. But Iceland's chief resource is all around in the sea. Iceland has a large fishing fleet, and fish, together with such by-products as fishmeal and oil, provide the country's major export.

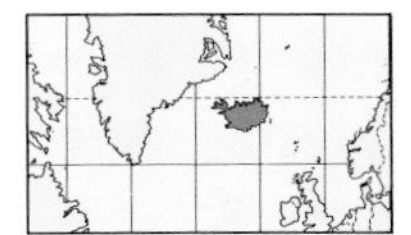

Area:
103,000 km² (39,771 mi²)
Population:
242,000
Capital:
Reykjavik (pop. 89,000)

Other towns:
Kópavogur, Akureyri, Hafnarfjördur, Keflavík, Akranes
Currency:
krona

Ireland – Éire

Republic of

Ireland is the second largest island of the British Isles. It lies on the western edge of Europe, facing the open ocean of the Atlantic on one side, and Great Britain, across the Irish Sea, on the other. The approaches to the Irish Sea are St George's Channel and North Channel. About four-fifths of the island is occupied by the Republic of Ireland. The six counties of Ulster province which form Northern Ireland are part of the United Kingdom. Although republicans on both sides of this border wish to see a united Ireland, the majority of people in Northern Ireland are Protestants, and reject a merger with the predominantly Roman Catholic south. The Republic of Ireland includes the provinces of Munster, Leinster, Connacht and three counties of Ulster province.

The Republic of Ireland has a wet, mild climate. Temperatures are moderated by the warm Atlantic currents of the Gulf Stream. Most of the land is low-lying, forming a great central plain. Ancient mountain ranges are today little more than hills. The highest point in Ireland is Carrauntoohill, in Macgillicuddy's Reeks, which reaches 1,042 metres (3,419 feet). Major lakes include Loughs Derg, Corrib, Mask, Ree, Conn and Allen.

The central plain is crossed by the River Shannon, which at 386 kilometres (240 miles) is the longest river in the British Isles. It rises in the north, and to the west of Limerick (Luimneach) opens into a broad estuary, emerging into the Atlantic between Loop Head and Kerry Head. The west coast of Ireland has a ragged outline, and is pounded by the breakers of the Atlantic. It is characterized by *rias* (submerged river valleys) and bays, such as Donegal, Clew, Galway, Dingle and Bantry, and by islands, such as the Aran group. The east coast is relatively straight. Here the chief river is the Liffey, on whose banks stands the capital, Dublin (Baile Átha Cliath).

The Irish people are mostly of Celtic origin. Although English is the common tongue, Irish Gaelic is still spoken and is an official language. The Irish name for the country is Éire. Gaelic Celts invaded the country around the fifth century BC, part of the great movement of Celtic tribes who swept westwards across Europe. The Irish are Gaels, like the Scots and Manx, and cousins of the Brythonic Celts (Welsh, Cornish and Bretons).

Below left: The Dingle Peninsula, in County Kerry. Right top: The port of Cobh, in County Cork, is dominated by St Colman's Cathedral; below right: County Wicklow has many fine beaches, like this at Greystones, four miles from Bray.

Christianity came to Ireland in AD 432, preached by St Patrick, a Welsh-born missionary who is now revered as the patron saint of Ireland. Christianity was to thrive in Ireland, and during the European Dark Ages the country was a centre of learning and of civilization. Irish monks travelled throughout Europe, and the ancient Celtic delight in ornamentation and metalwork found its expression in magnificent works of art, such as finely wrought chalices and the illuminated manuscripts of the Book of Kells and the Book of Durrow. From the eighth century, Ireland was the object of fierce attacks by Viking raiders, who founded the town of Dublin and settled the east coast.

Medieval Ireland did not have a strong centralized monarchy like England and France. There was continual strife between the kings of the various provinces and the High King. In 1152, the King of Leinster, Dermot MacMurrough, sought the assistance of the Norman English in his struggle against the High King, Rory O'Connor. Some 20 years later, Henry II of England himself took Dublin, and in the feudal tradition granted lands to his lords, who soon carved out their private empires. English political authority did not extend beyond the Dublin region ('the Pale'), and the barons, a law unto themselves, became an integral part of the Irish social structure.

The English crown did not reassert its power over the whole of Ireland until the time of Henry VIII. By now England was of the Protestant faith, while Ireland was Roman Catholic, and the religious differences fuelled a hatred that was over the centuries to become a bitter and protracted tragedy. In the 17th century, Irish land was seized by English and Scottish Protestant settlers. Subsequent rebellions by the Irish people were put down with great brutality. The Irish patriot Wolfe Tone (1763-98) persuaded the French revolutionary government to support a rebellion, but like all other attempts it failed, and repression continued. The 19th century was disastrous for the Irish people. A potato blight resulted in repeated crop failures, and peasants died of starvation in their thousands. The large estates were owned by English landlords, many of whom

rarely set foot in Ireland. Thousands of people emigrated to seek a better life. To this day, there is a large Irish population in the United States. A champion of the Irish cause was Charles Stewart Parnell (1846-91) who made Home Rule for Ireland a major issue in British politics.

In 1916 the years of nationalist frustration culminated in a major rising. British troops, along with many Irishmen, were at this time involved in the seemingly endless struggle of the First World War. At Easter, on April 24, a group of armed rebels including Eamon de Valéra (1882-1975) and Michael Collins (1890-1922) seized the post office in Dublin. Resistance was crushed within a week, but the seeds were sown. The First World War came to an end, and, from 1919-21, a full-scale war broke out between the forces of Sinn Féin (the Irish nationalist movement) and the British. The ruthless and provocative actions of the British special auxiliary forces, known as the 'Black and Tans', became the focus of Irish hatred. Ireland received dominion status in 1921 as the Irish Free State, while Northern Ireland remained part of the United Kingdom. This solution was unacceptable to the Irish Republican Army (IRA) who continued their struggle. Neutral in the Second World War, Ireland finally became a fully independent republic in 1949. But the partition of Ireland remained a vexed issue. In the 1960s, Northern Ireland erupted into violence, which continues.

The Head of State of the Republic of Ireland is the president, elected every seven years. There is a bicameral legislature, consisting of a Senate (Seanad) and a House of Representatives (Dáil). Executive power is vested in the Taoiseach, or head of government. The principal political parties are Fianna Fáil, Fine Gael, and Labour. A general election must be held at least once every five years.

Since 1973, the Republic has been a member of the European Economic Community (EEC). The Irish economy depends to a great extent upon agriculture, the country's chief resource being its green pastures. Cattle, pigs, and sheep are raised, and dairy farming is of the greatest importance. Crops include barley, oats and wheat, potatoes and sugar-beet. Fishing is carried out around the coasts. Ireland has few mineral resources, although coal is mined. The main industries are concerned with processing farm products and brewing. Manufacturing industry is mostly based on Dublin and Cork, but must rely largely on imported raw materials. A major source of income is tourism. Visitors are attracted by the beautiful scenery, by the ancient buildings and monuments, by fishing and other outdoor activities, but above all by the hospitality and friendliness of the Irish people, which has survived Ireland's long history of hardship and suffering.

Area:
70,283 km²
(27,138 mi²)
Population:
3,443,000
Capital:
Dublin (pop. 915,000)
Other towns:
Cork (Corcaigh), Limerick (Luimneach)
Currency:
pound

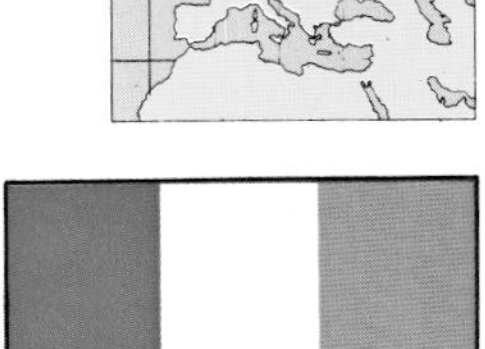

Killarney in County Kerry, is deservedly one of the most popular beauty spots in Ireland.

Italy

Repubblica Italiana

Of all the countries in Europe, the Italian Republic has the most distinctive outline on the map. It is a long, thin peninsula, shaped rather like a boot, aiming a kick at the island of Sicily (Sicilia). To the west, Italian territory includes the island of Sardinia (Sardegna). Its northern borders are with France, Switzerland, Austria and Yugoslavia. Italy stretches southwards into the Mediterranean. Its eastern shore is on the Adriatic, its southern shore is on the Ionian Sea, while its western shores are on the Ligurian and Tyrrhenian seas.

The country is mostly made up of mountains and hills, which occupy three-quarters of its area. The highest peaks are to be found within three major systems. The mighty range of the Alps in the north culminate in Mt Rosa. At 4,634 metres (15,203 feet), it is the highest point in Italy. The Apennines (Appenninos), which form the backbone of the Italian peninsula, reappear in the mountains of Sicily. Their highest point is Monte Corno in Abruzzi, which is 2,912 metres (9,554 feet) high. The Apennines contain many fertile valleys and basins. The third mountain system, the Sardinian-Corsican, forms the heart of the two Mediterranean islands, Sardinia and Corsica, which belongs to France.

Low-lying plains account for the remainder of the Italian landscape. The largest is the great Po valley, in the north. The remaining plains are coastal, and bounded by foothills of the mountains. On the Tyrrhenian coast are the Maremma region facing Corsica, the Roman plain, the Pontine marshes, the Campania plain around Naples, and the region between the Sele River and the Gulf of Gioia in the toe of Italy. The Adriatic coast contains the Terra d'Otranto in the south. Sicily has the plain of Catania and Sardinia the fertile Campidano plain.

The varied relief of the country affects the character of Italy's many rivers. Those descending from the Alps generally start their journey as torrents in full spate. When they reach the plains, they slow down, widen out and often form lakes. Their waters are sometimes diverted into canals and irrigation networks. Italy's longest river is the Po, which flows into the Gulf of Venice. It is 652 kilometres (405 miles) long. Most of the rivers rising in the Apennines are short and remain swift and torrential for most of their length. They contain little water in summer, but form swollen rapids in spring

Above: Italy, from an atlas 'Theatrum Orbis Terrarum' *of 1570. Right: A typical view in the Valle d'Aosta.*

and autumn. The principal Apennine rivers include the Arno on which Florence (Firenze) stands, and the Tiber (Tevere), on which Rome (Roma) is situated.

Italy is famous for its lakes, particularly those in the Alps. At altitudes of more than 2,000 metres (6,562 feet), these beautiful, peaceful stretches of wâter have a backdrop of majestic peaks. Principal lakes are Garda, Maggiore and Como. Many of the lakes of central Italy, such as Bolsena and Bracciano north of Rome, occupy the craters of extinct volcanoes. Lake Trasimeno, near Perugia, is an exception. This formerly huge lake is now shrinking.

Four volcanoes are still active in southern Italy. Mount Vesuvius, which devastated Pompeii and Herculaneum in AD 79, dominates the Bay of Naples, while Etna, Europe's highest volcano, towers over the Catania plain in Sicily. Stromboli and Vulcano are volcanoes in the Lipari Islands north of Sicily. Periodically these erupt, with fire and great streams of lava. In many parts of Italy, volcanic activity is also demonstrated by hot springs, by fumaroles giving off sulphurous fumes, as at Pozzuoli, or by mofettes, holes in the ground from which carbon dioxide is emitted, as in Campania, Sicily and the Po valley. Southern Italy is also subject to earthquakes.

The coastline of Italy, including its many islands, is 7,456 kilometres (4,633 miles) long. Italy is a maritime country. Even in the broad northern region, no point is farther than 250 kilometres (155 miles) from the sea. The coasts include areas of great scenic beauty, as well as busy ports and centres of population. The Ligurian coast is dominated by Genoa (Genova), a port which handles the largest volume of trade in Italy. The northern part of the Tyrrhenian coast (Maremma) was once marshy, but it has now been drained, and is low and sandy. The southern part of the Tyrrhenian coast is rocky and sheer, with especially beautiful sections, such as the Amalfi coast. The major port is Naples (Napoli), which is sited on a spectacular bay. The Ionian coast is divided by the Sila promontory into two wide gulfs, the Gulf of Squillace and the Gulf of Taranto. Between the ports of Brindisi and Rimini, the Adriatic coastline is rocky, but to the north it is low and sandy. There are several large lagoons, including the Valli di Comacchio, and a maze of islands around Venice. To the north-east lies the Gulf of Trieste. Italy's islands include the Tuscan archipelago, chief of which is Elba; the Ponziane islands off the Gulf of Gaeta; the Lipari or Aeolian Islands; Ischia and Capri in the Bay of Naples, Pantelleria between Sicily and Tunisia; and the large islands of Sicily and Sardinia.

The seas of Italy have a considerable effect on its climate, which is typically Mediterranean, except in the more continental northern interior. Flowers start blooming in Sicily as early as January. The Apennines act as a barrier to westerly winds, as a result of which the west coast is wetter than the east. Italy was once covered in large forests, but today these only survive in the Alpine region. Elsewhere centuries of agriculture have left their mark, as evidenced by vast tracts of olive groves and vineyards.

Italy's central position in the Mediterranean region ensured it a crucial role in European history. Italy was already densely populated in the prehistoric era, and continued to attract settlement over the ages. The ancient Greeks founded colonies here, the most notable of which was Syracuse (Siracusa) in Sicily. The first great native civilization was that of the Etruscans, which flourished in the Tuscany region between the eighth and third centuries BC. It derived much from Greek culture, but had its own unique character. Surviving examples of metalwork, pottery and sculpture are of the highest order. There were 12 Etruscan city-states. One of them, Rome, became an independent republic in 509 BC, having overthrown the king, Tarquinius Superbus. By 391 BC, Rome had conquered the rest of Etruria.

By AD 117, under Emperor Trajan, the Roman Empire had expanded to include much of the known world: Britain, Gaul, Spain, western Germany, south-central Europe and the Balkans, the Black Sea coast, Asia Minor, the Middle East and the Levant, Egypt and the North African coast – a truly remarkable achievement that was to determine the course of European civilization. In cultural matters, the Romans borrowed from the Greeks, but their own achievements in literature, philosophy and the arts were extraordinary. Military supremacy was the result of brilliant strategy and tactics, of technological innovation and of ruthless efficiency. The empire was held together by the rule of law. Roman skill at engin-

Top: The valley of Funes (in the Alto Adige) dominated by the Odle, part of the Dolomite range. Right: Torcello, an island in the Venetian lagoon.

SWITZERLAND
FRANCE
HUNGARY
YUGOSLAVIA
ALGERIA
TUNISIA
LIGURIAN SEA
ADRIATIC SEA
TYRRHENIAN SEA
MEDITERRANEAN SEA
IONIAN SEA
Sicilian Channel
G. of Genoa
G. of Venice
G. of Taranto
G. of Squillace
G. of Manfredonia
Alto Adige
Trentino-
Friuli-
Ven. Giulia
Lombardy
Piemonte
Veneto
Liguria
Emilia Romagna
Tuscany
Umbria
Marche
Lazio
Abruzzi
Molise
Campania
Apulia
Basilicata
Calabria
Sicily
Sardinia (It.)
Corsica (Fr.)
Milan
Turin
Genoa
Venice (Venezia)
Bologna
Florence (Firenze)
VATICAN CITY
Rome
Naples
Bari
Palermo
Messina
Catania
Cagliari
Trieste
Zagreb
Ljubljana
Budapest
Tunis
Pelagie Is.
Linosa
Lampione
Lampedusa
E. 12 of Gr.
Long. E. 12 of Greenwich
0 50 100 km
0 31 62 mi

eering resulted in a network of towns linked by roads spreading across Europe for the first time. Many magnificent examples of Roman architecture survive today.

Roman dominance of the known world was assured by their final defeat of the rival Mediterranean power of Carthage in 149 BC. But at home, the early egalitarian ideals of the republic soon gave way to a society dominated by a wealthy elite. Dictators came to power, and after the murder of the brilliant conqueror of Europe Julius Caesar (100-44 BC), a succession of emperors ruled over Rome. Most were ruthless intriguers. Some were enlightened and just, and a few, such as Caligula (AD 12-41), were insane megalomaniacs. Christianity became established in Rome under the reign of Constantine I (*c.*AD 274-337) who founded an empire in the east at Constantinople (now Istanbul). Rome itself was sacked by barbarian Vandals in AD 455, and the last Roman emperor in the west, Romulus Augustus, was of such little import that he was pensioned off in 476.

During the Dark Ages, Italy was subjected to waves of invasion by Goths and Langobards, and the country was devastated by wars. The Middle Ages may be said to begin with the coronation of the Frankish king Charlemagne as the Holy Roman Emperor in 800. But the domain of this empire was soon reduced to the states of Germany and northern Italy. Southern Italy had a succession of foreign rulers, including Arabs, Normans, Suevians, Angevins and Aragon Spaniards. Rome, the Holy See of the papacy, was the centre of a large church state which ensured the popes' independence from ambitious monarchs, and it was the focus of all the Christian world. With such powerful divisions, it is hardly surprising that Italy failed to become a centralized monarchy like England or France. Instead, it fragmented into a number of small states.

But during the 15th and 16th centuries, there arose among the small states of Italy an incredible explosion and flowering of the arts, combined with curiosity about the learning of the classical world. This was the Renaissance, and its magnificent works of art reflect a self-assurance and technical skill hitherto

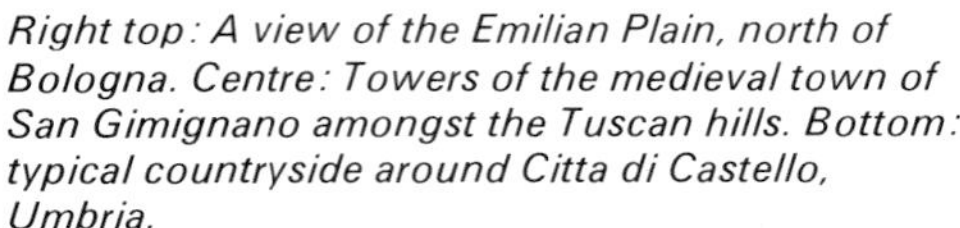

Right top: A view of the Emilian Plain, north of Bologna. Centre: Towers of the medieval town of San Gimignano amongst the Tuscan hills. Bottom: typical countryside around Citta di Castello, Umbria.

unseen in Europe. The same period saw Italy become a battleground between the armies of France and Spain. By 1559, Spain ruled Lombardy, Naples and the islands, and its supremacy also extended over northern Italy. During the course of the 18th century, the Austrians replaced the Spanish in Lombardy; Sardinia passed to the house of Savoy, already ruling Piedmont; and Naples and the south (the Kingdom of the Two Sicilies) became a feudal backwater under the Bourbons.

The rise of Napoleon Bonaparte in the early 19th century aroused great hopes for Italy, because his rapid conquests led to the creation of a Kingdom of Italy. This was in effect merely a puppet state under French control, and, upon Napoleon's downfall in 1815, Italy was once again divided. But the seeds of liberation had been sown, and a 50-year struggle for independence began, called the *risorgimento*. It was a long, hard struggle, and featured such national heroes as the military leader Guiseppe Garibaldi (1807–82), who fought for the cause of freedom all over Italy. In 1861, Victor Emmanuel II of Sardinia was declared king of all Italy. Nine years later, Rome itself was seized from Pope Pius IX, and Italy became a truly independent nation.

The climax of the kingdom was reached at the end of the First World War, with the Italians among the victors against the Central Powers. But as in Germany, the 1920s saw the rise of an ugly new political creed – fascism. Benito Mussolini (1883-1945) marched on Rome in 1922 and made himself dictator. Arrogant and overbearing, Mussolini invaded Abyssinia (now Ethiopia) and Albania, and formed an alliance with Nazi Germany. But entry into the Second World War proved to be a disaster. Amid an Allied invasion of Italy, Italian anti-fascists took up arms against their compatriots. Mussolini was killed. With the war over, the Italian people went to the polls in June 1946, and voted in favour of the abolition of the monarchy. Italy became a parliamentary republic, with two elected chambers: the Senate and the Chamber of Deputies. Today Italy is a leading member of the European Economic Community (EEC) and of the North Atlantic Treaty Organization (NATO).

A transformation of the Italian economy has made the country an industrialized nation. This has been accompanied by a flood of population into the big industrial cities of the north, and by the depopulation of the rural south, which, by European standards, remains poverty-stricken. Industrial development has been concentrated in a large triangle formed by the northern cities of Milan (Milano), Genoa (Genova) and Turin (Torino). Italy is poor in mineral resources and relies largely on the import of raw materials, although it has considerable hydro-electric potential. Major industries include iron and steel, mechanical engineering, motor vehicles, textiles, chemicals, and shipbuilding. Food processing is important, and of the manufactured goods, Italian leather and garments have long been admired throughout the world. However, the agricultural sector still continues its ancient traditions. Crops include cereals, olives, grapes – Italian wines are among the best in the world – citrus fruits and vegetables. Livestock and fishing are also of economic importance.

Italy is a popular attraction for tourists from all over the world. The capital, Rome (Roma), is full of reminders of the classical age. Whether in Rome, or in Italy's medieval villages, or among the Renaissance splendours of Venice (Venezia) or Florence (Firenze), tourists are aware of a continuing cultural tradition which has spanned the centuries, a tradition that has provided a foundation stone for European civilization.

Rome remains the world centre of the Roman Catholic faith. The area around St Peter's Basilica is a special enclave with the status of an independent nation, **Vatican City.** It is the world's smallest country, with an area of 44 hectares (108·7 acres) and a population of about 1,000, but it is an area of special significance to many Christians. Vatican City has played a greater part in European history than many larger nations.

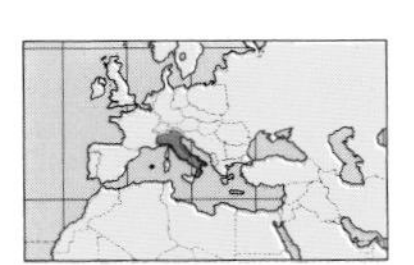

Area:
301,225 km² (116,310 mi²)
Population:
58,085,000
Capital:
Rome (pop. 2,831,000
Other cities:
Milan, Naples, Turin, Genoa, Palermo, Bologna, Florence, Catania, Bari, Venice, Messina, Verona, Trieste
Currency:
lira

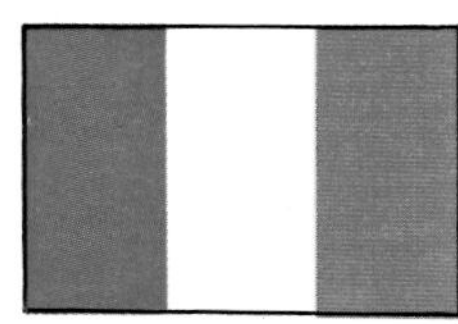

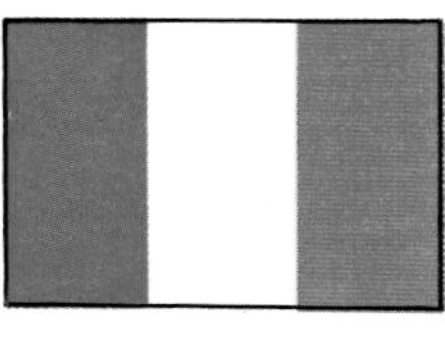

Vatican City

Area:
44 hectares (109 acres)
Population: 1,000

Above: Brienno, a village on the romantic Lake Como.

Liechtenstein

This small country, between Austria and Switzerland, is a constitutional monarchy ruled by princes of the House of Liechtenstein. Its history dates back to 1342. For centuries largely unchanged, the country is now rapidly becoming industrialized. There is a wide variety of light industry, particularly manufacture of precision instruments and textiles. Tourism is also important. It forms a narrow strip of lowland, along the banks of the Rhine.

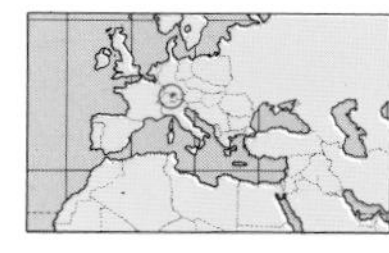

Area:
157 km² (61 mi²)
Population:
26,000
Capital:
Vaduz (pop. 4,500)
Currency:
Swiss franc

Luxembourg

Grand-Duché de

One of the smallest states in Europe, the Grand Duchy of Luxembourg occupies an area only one-eighth of the size of Wales. It lies between Germany, Belgium and France.

The forested plateau of the Ardennes crosses the northern border, so the northern region consists mostly of wooded hills and is a home for deer and wild boar. The climate is less mild than in the south, but the scenery is beautiful, with medieval castles standing above the valleys. The rest of the country is occupied by fertile rolling plains and picturesque river valleys. The capital, Luxembourg, lies in one of these, on the River Alzette. The south is the most populated area of the country.

Luxembourg was originally one of the many small feudal states of medieval Europe. Founded in 963 by Count Siegfried I, the family of Luxembourg was powerful and influential, numbering Holy Roman Emperors among its members. In 1354, it became a Duchy, which passed to the Dukes of Burgundy in 1441. Under their rule, Luxembourg followed the fortunes of the southern Netherlands, being passed back and forth between the Spanish and Austrian branches of the Habsburg dynasty, and France. Under Napoleon it became a department of France, and then in 1815 it became a Grand-Duchy under the sovereignty of the Netherlands.

When rebellion against the Dutch led to the formation of the nation of Belgium, part of Luxembourg was included in the new nation. The rest forms modern Luxembourg. The little country's neutrality was recognized by the Treaty of London in 1867, but after this had twice been violated by Germany this century, Luxembourg opted for a more partisan stance, joining NATO in 1949.

The Grand-Duchy boasts one of the highest standards of living in the world. It is rich in iron ore and about one-quarter of the national income comes from the steel industry. A close economic partner of Belgium since 1921, Luxembourg became part of the Benelux customs union in 1944 together with Belgium and the Netherlands.

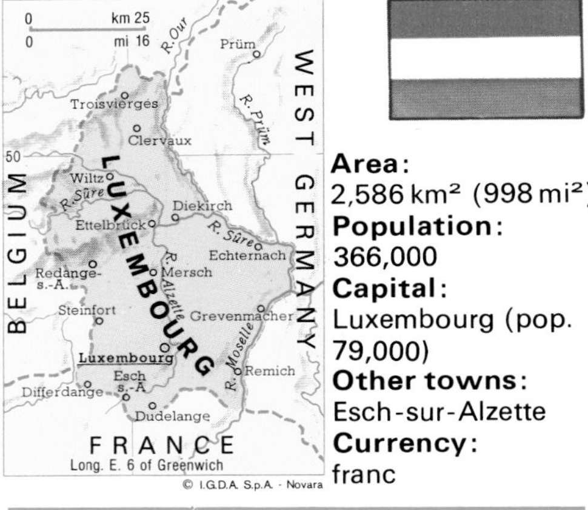

Area: 2,586 km² (998 mi²)
Population: 366,000
Capital: Luxembourg (pop. 79,000)
Other towns: Esch-sur-Alzette
Currency: franc

Top: The town of Wormeldange, which stands on the banks of the Moselle. Below: The docks in Grand Harbour, the area formed by Valletta and its suburbs.

Malta

Repubblika Ta'Malta

The Republic of Malta consists of a cluster of islands that lie about 90 kilometres (56 miles) south of Sicily. The largest of them are Malta, Gozo and Comino. The coastline of the main island of Malta is high and rocky, with deep inlets. The interior is flat, broken by occasional hills. It is an arid landscape.

Malta has a subsoil poor in minerals, and has few other assets, although its warm climate has made it a tourist haven in recent years. But over the centuries it has been fought over time and time again. The reason is its strategic importance, because its position in the Mediterranean Sea gives it control of the shipping lanes.

Malta achieved independence within the Commonwealth in 1964, and became a republic ten years later. English is still an official language, along with Maltese. Maltese is an Arabic dialect which has borrowed from the Sicilian dialect. It is written in the Roman alphabet.

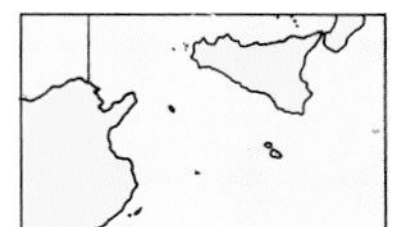

Area: 316 km² (122 m²)
Population: 341,000
Capital: Valletta (pop. 14,000)
Currency: pound

Monaco

The Principality of Monaco is one of the smallest countries in the world, and one of the best-known, not only for its favourable position on the south-east coast of France, with a very high tourist rating, but also for its international banking facilities, and for its world-famous Casino.

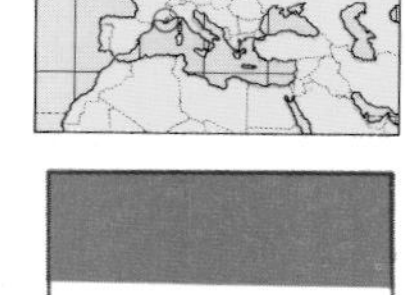

Area:
190 hectares (467 acres)
Population:
28,000
Capital:
Monaco
Currency:
French franc

Right: The harbour at Monte Carlo.

The Netherlands

Koninkrijk der Nederlanden

The Kingdom of the Netherlands (Nederlanden) is the official name of the country which is usually and inaccurately called Holland. In fact, Holland represents just one region of the Netherlands. The provinces of Noord Holland and Zuid Holland extend along the North Sea coast from Friesland to Zeeland, and it is in this area that the most important cities, such as Amsterdam, are situated. However, there are another nine provinces: Groningen, Friesland, Drenthe, Overijssel, Gelderland, Utrecht, Zeeland, Noord-Brabant and Limburg. The north and the west of the Netherlands have a coastline on the North Sea. In the east, the country borders the Federal Republic of Germany, while Belgium lies to the south. For the past 150 years, the country's frontiers have remained unchanged. Considering the troubled history of this part of Europe, that is quite remarkable in itself. The Netherlands has, of course, suffered foreign domination and invasion in the course of its history. But the truly epic battle has not been against human enemies, but against the forces of nature, and the sea.

The country's name describes its topography. Nederland literally means 'low land', and much of Dutch territory does lie below sea level. During centuries of hard work, this land was reclaimed from the sea. The waters were driven back, and vast stretches of land called polders were made suitable for agriculture. From the start of the Middle Ages, the people learned to build dykes (sea walls) to act as barriers against the sea and canals to regulate the water flow. Some of the oldest and most famous Dutch cities, such as Amsterdam and Rotterdam, have names that end in 'dam' which means 'dyke'. The most incredible reclamation project has been the Zuider Zee (Ijsselmeer) reclamation project, which was begun in 1920. In reality, this was an inland sea covering 3,600 square kilometres (1,390 square miles), but with a depth of barely 4 metres (13 feet). This stretch of water was formed between the 11th and the 14th centuries in the area between Friesland and Noord Holland, the result of coastal flooding. The reclamation started with the construction of an impressive barrage 7·5 metres (25 feet) high. This steep-sided dyke has a road running along the top. The reclaimed land was then freed of salt and turned into pasture. Subsequently, locks and canals were built for irrigation purposes, and the land became suitable for agriculture. Although this has been a major project, it is just one example of the struggle that the Dutch have always waged against unfavourable natural conditions. More than 2,500 kilometres (1,553 miles) of dyke has been constructed over the years in order to cope with the waves and the tides. The coastline has had to be strengthened partly because of the effects of the outflow of two major rivers, the Maas and the Rhine (Rijn).

For the Dutch, the sea is not only an enemy, but also a source of wealth. Since the early days, navigation, trading and sailing were natural vocations for the Dutch, as well as the basis for an enviable prosperity, which the country's resources alone would never have been able to provide.

It was towards the end of the Middle Ages that this region first became wealthy. Before then, it had been extremely poor and desolate. It had been

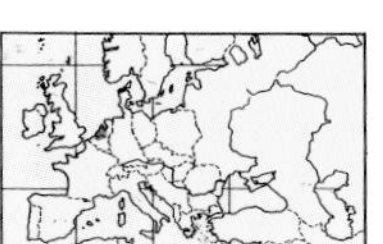

Area:
40,844 km² (15,771 mi²)
Population:
14,529,000
Capital:
Amsterdam (pop. 994,000)
Seat of government:
The Hague (Den Haag) (pop. 672,000)
Other towns:
Rotterdam, Utrecht, Eindhoven, Arnhem,
Currency:
guilder

Left: Rotterdam is the chief port in the Netherlands and the busiest in the world.

occupied by Batavian tribes, and afterwards by the Frisians, both peoples of Germanic origin. During the rule of Charlemagne (AD 742-814), it was brought under imperial control. When his empire crumbled, a feudal system was established with several earldoms and duchies ruled by the local nobles. But soon the industrious citizens had laid the foundations for a mercantile and urban civilization, which was destined to prevail over the feudal system. Initially, the neighbouring region of Flanders (presently part of Belgium) was supreme and the centre of the European textile industry. At the beginning of the 17th century, however, Holland and Zeeland took the lead, followed by the other provinces. Towns became established which were famous for textile manufacture, printing, and the production of brass and ceramics. All goods from northern and central Europe were conveyed to Dutch ports and the money-market of Amsterdam acquired international importance. At the end of the 17th century, the Dutch fleet was superior to any other European navy. Economic growth was helped by political independence which had, however, been achieved only with great difficulty.

At the end of the Middle Ages, the Netherlands, together with Flanders, were ruled by the Dukes of Burgundy and later, through marriage, by the Spanish branch of the Hapsburg family. Spanish domination proved oppressive, especially because the majority of the Dutch had become Protestants with the Reformation. Political oppression was linked to religious persecution. This resulted in a period of conflict during which the patriots found a leader of great esteem in William the Silent (1533-84), Prince of Orange and ancestor of the presently ruling house. Under his rule, the Netherlands finally achieved its independence, by separating itself from Flanders which, as a Roman Catholic region, remained loyal to Spain. William the Silent is buried in the cathedral of Delft. Included in his funeral monument is his dog, which died of grief when the prince was assassinated by a fanatic.

Independence was itself accompanied by colonial expansion. Dutch navigators were among the greatest to have explored distant continents. This resulted in a vast colonial empire extending from South America to Indonesia and as far as Australasia. The country's wealth inevitably aroused the envy of neighbouring powers in Europe, particularly France. First Louis XIV and later Napoleon threatened to invade. The attempts made by Napoleon had a brief success. In 1806, Napoleon's brother Louis became king, but of a Holland that was controlled by the French empire. When this crumbled, however, the Congress of Vienna in 1815 restored the old dynasty in the country and added territories of Belgium and Luxembourg, giving it the collective name of the Netherlands. The Belgians, who were separated from the Dutch because of their difference in religion, soon broke away from the union and in 1830 formed their own kingdom. Luxembourg had to wait until 1890 to obtain its independence.

The old overseas empire, the source of so much wealth and strength for the Dutch, is today little more than a memory. But even after the tragic events of the Second World War, when the country was invaded by the Germans, the Dutch were able to adjust to their new situation with that practical sense which is one of their most remarkable qualities. At the same time, they managed to maintain a leading role in Europe's economy.

It is today a crowded country, especially on the coast. The population density is 350 people per square kilometre (908 per square mile). Rotterdam, on the mouth of the Rhine, has in its Europoort, the world's chief port as far as volume of trade is concerned, with approximately 265 million tonnes of goods per year. From here eastwards many of the towns merge into each other, forming one big conurbation in the shape of a horse-shoe. This area extends over 180 kilometres (112 miles) and, with more than four million inhabitants, it accommodates one-third of the overall population. The most well-known centres of this region are Rotterdam, Delft, The Hague, or Den Haag, the seat of government, Haarlem, Amsterdam (capital of the Netherlands and famous for its beautiful canals), and Utrecht.

Industry is highly developed, although the country has few minerals apart from some oil and natural gas. The metallurgical, mechanical engineering, chemical, textile and electronics industries are all important. Also of considerable significance is the food industry, while the shipyards and diamond-cutting factories are famous. The farming industry is among the most advanced and successful in Europe. It employs some six per cent of the work-force. Cereals, potatoes, sugar-beet, vegetables, fruit and flowers are cultivated; Dutch tulips are famous the world over. Dairy farming is of the greatest importance. The Netherlands is the world's greatest exporter of cheese, and the third greatest exporter of butter.

Norway

Kongeriket Norge

The word 'Norway' means 'the road to the north'. And that seems an apt description of a country, of which a good part is situated north of the Arctic Circle, and which contains in Cape North (Nordkapp) the northernmost point of the European continent. Here the long polar night reigns in winter, while in summer the day never ends, and the 'midnight sun' never sets. The Kingdom of Norway is bordered in the east by Sweden, Finland and the USSR. Its northern, western and southern coasts face, respectively, the Arctic Ocean, the Norwegian Sea, the North Sea and the Skagerrak. The character and history of the country has, therefore, been determined by two factors: its northerly location, and the seas which surround it.

With a lengthy coastline, much of it formed by islands and fjords, Norway has found in the sea a means of escaping the isolation to which its inhospitable territory might well have condemned it. The sea has also brought prosperity to its inhabitants. The sea is Norway's past, which belongs to the Vikings who lived there. It is also its present, which belongs to its merchant navy, the world's fifth largest in tonneage, and to its fishing fleet. In particular, the offshore rigs in the sea now give Norway its future, and they have supplied vast quantities of oil and natural gas since 1971.

The Norwegian economy has in the past been based on fishing. Only 2·5 per cent of the land is suitable for cultivation, the major crops being barley, oats, potatoes and wheat. Its economy is now strongly influenced by the energy derived from the North Sea. This supplements the existing hydro-electric projects. In relation to the number of inhabitants, Norway is the world's largest producer of electrical energy. As a result, industry is expanding rapidly, particularly in the field of metallurgy, which relies principally on imported ore. Apart from oil, Norway has few natural resources. Also important is the steel industry, and the engineering and shipbuilding industries. Norway has developed particular expertise in the building of oil platforms. Traditional industries still thrive as well, notably timber and its by-products, and the processing of fish.

Physically, Norway can be divided into three regions. In the north is Finnmark. Here the edges of coastal plateaux form four large peninsulas, surrounded by numerous little islands and deeply gouged-out fjords. To the south of Mount Kistefiellet, the land becomes narrow. Here the Swedish border is only some 10 kilometres (6 miles) from the Norwegian Sea. The central part of Norway is characterized by a ragged coast-line and many islands. Two fjords are particularly broad, the Ofotfjorden and the Vestfjorden. Inland there are mountains covered in forests, inter-

Below: The city of Bergen in south-western Norway has been a leading commercial city since it was founded in 1070.

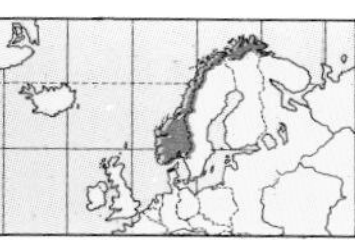

Area:
324,219 km²
(125,188 mi²)
Population:
4,146,000
Capital:
Oslo (pop. 449,000)
Other towns:
Bergen, Trondheim, Stavanger, Kristiansand, Drammen, Skien, Tromsø
Currency:
krone

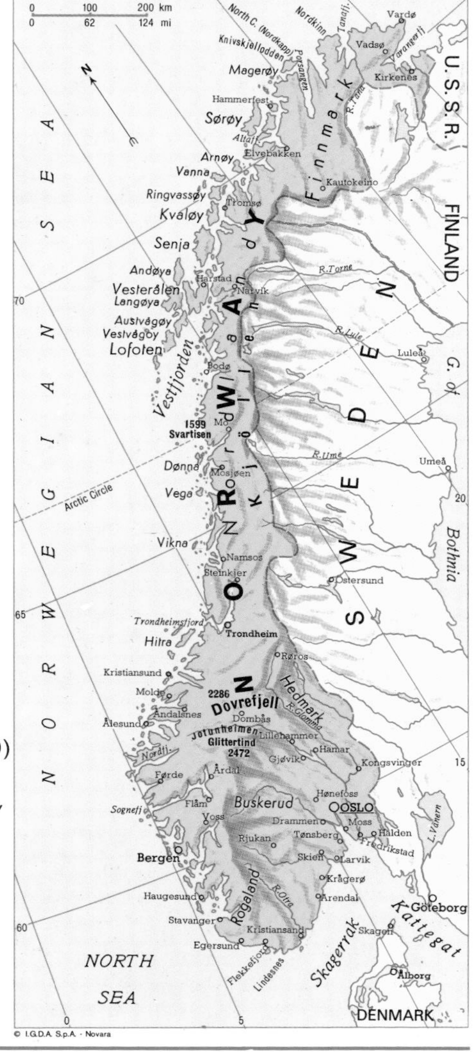

spersed with valleys and plains. To the north-west of the Vestfjorden is the large archipelago of the Lofoten and Vesteralen Islands. Thanks to the North Atlantic Drift (an extension of the Gulf Stream), the temperatures are relatively mild, although the region is well to the north of the Arctic Circle. And the ports remain open throughout the year, because the warm current prevents freezing.

The great Trondheimsfjord marks the beginning of Norway's southern region. The scenery is rather reminiscent of the Alps, with high, snowy peaks and beautiful U-shaped valleys. The chief difference is that these mountains are surrounded by arms of the sea. These fjords, the result of glaciation, include the longest in the country. For example, the Sognefjorden is both Norway's longest at 204 kilometres (127 miles), and also the deepest at 1,244 metres (4,081 feet).

The immense glacier of Jostedalsbreen cuts a giant swathe through this region. But the south also has the highest density of the population, and the large cities, including Kristiansand, Ålesund, Bergen and Oslo, the capital, which is sited at the head of yet another big fjord, the Oslofjorden.

In addition to Scandinavian Norway, there are a number of distant territories which are also, politically, part of Norway. One is the island of Jan Mayen in the Greenland Sea, on which the Norwegians set up a weather station in 1921. Other islands make up the Svalbard archipelago, about 500 kilometres (311 miles) from the northern coast of Norway. These islands have officially belonged to Norway since 1925. Bouvet Island in the South Atlantic, and Peter Island in the Antarctic Ocean are also part of Norwegian territory.

Norway seems to have been inhabited since the eighth millennium BC. But it only really entered the history of the European peoples in the eighth century AD, at the time of the Vikings, the intrepid sailors and warriors who were feared throughout Europe. At the end of the ninth century AD, the Norwegian Vikings were united for the first time under one king, Harold I Haarfagr, or Fair-haired. But the definitive unification of the kingdom came only with Olaf II, the Saint, who reigned from 1015 to 1030 and introduced Christianity. In the following centuries, the struggles between the ruling dynasty and the other powerful families led to a weakening of the country, which eventually fell within the sphere of influence of neighbouring Sweden and Denmark. In 1397, as the result of a series of marriages between the sovereigns, the Union of Kalmar marked the integration of the three states. But while Sweden finally broke away in 1523, Norway remained with Denmark. It was by no means a peaceful union. There were violent revolts, such as that of the Norwegian peasants in 1435. But in 1537, the Danish Constitution removed all autonomy from Norway.

Norway remained under Denmark for centuries, until Denmark fought against Britain in the Napoleonic Wars. After Denmark's defeat, the Treaty of Kiel in 1814, resulted in a brief period of independence followed by union with Sweden. Independence came only in 1905. Following the refusal of the Swedish king Oscar II to allow an autonomous Norwegian Ministry of Foreign Affairs, the Norwegian parliament declared the union dissolved and the Swedes accepted the *fait accompli*. The Norwegian population offered the throne of their kingdom to Prince Karl of Denmark who, under the name of Haakon VII ruled until 1957, when he was succeeded by his son, Olaf V. Under Haakon VII Norway was neutral in the First World War, but, in the Second, it was occupied by Germany.

Although Norway, abandoning neutrality in the period after the Second World War, joined the North Atlantic Treaty Organization (NATO) and the United Nations Organization (UNO), it remains a peaceable country. It is one of the most unspoilt countries in Europe, with a beautiful countryside and protected wildlife. The Norwegians love festivals, like the 'day of the sun', which, on 21 January celebrates the first 'victory' of the Sun over the polar night. They also like skiing, and boating on the fjords. There is a widespread concern for peace and social justice. Of the five Nobel prizes, four are awarded by the Academy of Science in Stockholm, but the fifth, the Peace Prize, is awarded by five Norwegian citizens chosen by the Storting. The Storting is the parliament in Oslo, which was the first parliament in the world to be elected entirely by universal suffrage, without any distinctions of wealth or sex.

Norway is a constitutional monarchy and legislative power is vested in the Storting which sits between October and June. The Storting is elected by universal adult suffrage, the voting age being 18. When it assembles, the Storting divides itself into the Lagting, comprising one-fourth of the Storting's members, and the Odelsting, including the others. Legislation is considered by both the Lagting and Odelsting. Should they disagree, the Bill is then considered by the full Storting. Executive power is vested in the king, who exercises his power through a Council of State (cabinet), consisting of the prime minister and other ministers. For local government, Norway is divided into 19 counties, including Oslo, an urban district. The counties are further divided into 47 urban districts and 407 rural districts. Conscription is compulsory in Norway, the training period being one year. Compulsory service after the initial training is 50 hours a year up to the age of 44.

Left: The coastline of Norway is indented by fjords, long arms of the sea which were worn out by glaciers.

Poland

Polska Rzeczpospolita Ludowa

Poland is probably unique in that its position on the map has actually shifted sideways in this century. The present borders of the Polish People's Republic were decided at the end of the Second World War. Poland then ceded a large amount of territory to the USSR in the east, but gained part of the Prussian region of Germany in the west. This 'move' was possible only because Poland lacks any natural borders. It is not surrounded by great chains of mountains or by major rivers, and the Oder-Neisse rivers were only adopted as its western border in 1945.

Poland consists largely of a vast plain facing the Baltic Sea in the north. To the west this blends with the lowlands of Germany, and to the east with the immense expanse of the USSR. To the south, however, the land rises to a plateau, and the border with Czechoslovakia is better defined, by the Sudety mountains and the Beskidy Zachodnie. The climate is continental.

The lack of distinct frontiers has left Poland without natural lines of defence, and this has resulted in a history of conquest and partition. The Poles are a Slavic people. Poland became an independent kingdom in 1024 and, during the Middle Ages, it became a major European power. But its fortunes declined. During the 18th century, it was partitioned between Russia, Austria and the militaristic state of Prussia. By 1795, it had disappeared off the map altogether. The Polish people then had to wait until 1918 and the collapse of the Central Powers, defeated in the First World War, before they achieved independence. But the worst of Poland's trouble was yet to come. In the Second World War, Poland was caught between the might of Germany and the USSR. As well as becoming a major theatre of war, Poland witnessed the terrible persecution of the Jews by the Nazis, and their setting up of such concentration camps as Auschwitz (Oświecim). After the war, a Communist government came to power. Today Poland is a member of COMECON (the Council for Mutual Economic Aid) and of the Warsaw Pact. Most of the people are devout Roman Catholics. Legislative power is exercised by the Sejm (or parliament), and executive power lies with the Council of Ministers. There have been occasional periods of unrest in postwar Poland, notably in 1956, 1970 and 1980, which saw the birth of Solidarity, an independent trade union movement led by Lech Walesa. Solidarity was subsequently outlawed.

Industrialization has been rapid in Poland, having been greatly helped by the acquisition of the Silesian coalfields after the Second World War. The textile industry, based in Łódź, has always been important. Today steel and iron are produced, and chemical, electrical and mechanical engineering are important. Other mineral resources include lead, zinc and sulphur. The chief agricultural produce includes flax, potatoes, rye, sugar-beet and tobacco. Poland's extensive forests provide timber.

Most of Poland consists of a low-lying plain. The only highlands are in the far south along the border with Czechoslovakia. These highlands include the Sudety range, the Beskidy Zachodnie, and the Tatry, above. The highest point in Poland is Rysy Peak, situated among the beautiful lakes and forests of the Tatry. It is 2,503 metres (8,212 feet) above sea level.

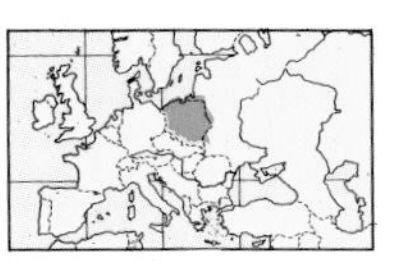

Area:
312,677 km² (120,732 mi²)
Population:
37,340,000
Capital:
Warsaw (Warszawa) (pop. 1,628,000)
Other towns:
Łodz, Krakow, Wrocław, Poznán,
Currency:
zloty

Portugal

República Portuguesa

The Republic of Portugal is situated on the western edge of Europe. To the north and east is Spain, but to the west and south the 830-kilometre (516-mile) coastline is pounded by the breakers of the Atlantic Ocean. The Atlantic islands of the Azores (Açores) and Madeira also form part of the country.

Early invaders of the region included the Romans, the Visigoths and the Arabs. The Portuguese language is a Romance tongue which has been influenced by Arabic. With a powerful neighbour to the rear and limited resources at home, it is hardly surprising that the Portuguese turned outward to the ocean in the late Middle Ages, becoming a nation of sailors and explorers. Prince Henry the Navigator (1394–1460), son of King João I, built an observatory at Sagres and founded the world's first school of navigation. He sponsored many exploratory missions. Bartolomeu Diaz returned from the Cape of Good Hope in 1488. Vasco da Gama reached India 10 years later. And in 1500, Pedro Alvarez Cabral reached Brazil.

The explorers were followed by colonists and Portugal soon acquired extensive territories in South America, Africa and Asia. Wealth flowed back to Portugal, but her power later declined and from 1580 until 1640 the country became a Spanish viceroyalty. In the Napoleonic Wars, Portugal was the scene of fighting between British and French troops, and in 1821 Brazil broke away from the Portuguese crown. Most of the other colonies did not achieve independence until the mid-1970s. In 1974, the long period of right-wing dictatorship, which had suppressed the monarchy, came to an end. Democratic government was restored to Portugal and decolonization followed quickly.

The Portuguese economy relies chiefly on agriculture and fishery. Cereal crops, vegetables, citrus fruits, olive oil and figs are the main crops. Vineyards produce fine grapes and port wine takes its name from the northern town of Porto (Oporto). Portugal is the world's chief producer of cork, and has large forests. The sea provides sardines, and canning and food-processing are important.

Mineral resources include tin, tungsten, sulphur, copper and iron ore. Industry is still on a modest scale, but is being developed rapidly. **Portugal became a member of the European Economic Community in 1986.**

The terrain is mostly rugged hill country. It is crossed by three major rivers: the Douro, the Tejo (Tagus) and, running south into the Gulf of Cadiz, the Guadiana. The capital is Lisbon (Lisboa).

Top left: Typical Portuguese fisherman's dress.

Top right: A flower lady on the island of Madeira.

Above: The ancient city of Porto (Oporto) has given its name to port wine. It stands on the River Douro in the northern part of Portugal. With its suburbs, it has more than a million people and so it is Portugal's second largest city.

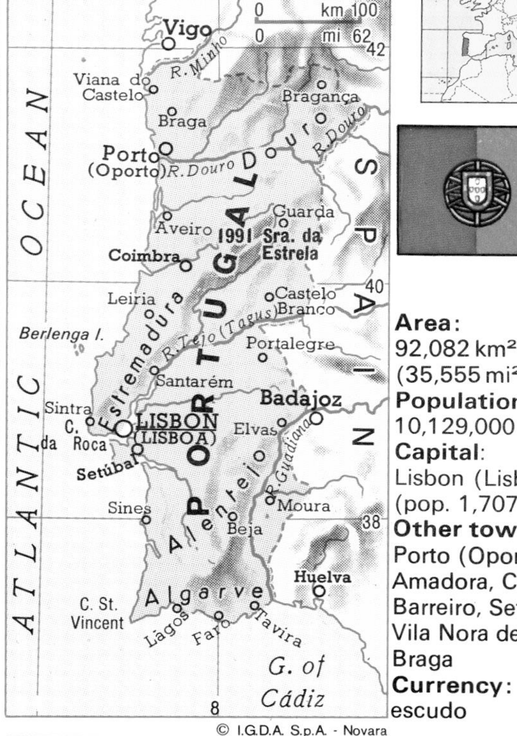

Area: 92,082 km² (35,555 mi²)
Population: 10,129,000
Capital: Lisbon (Lisboa) (pop. 1,707,000)
Other towns: Porto (Oporto), Amadora, Coimbra, Barreiro, Setúbal, Vila Nora de Gaia, Braga
Currency: escudo

Romania

Republica Socialistă România

With its position on the Black Sea coast, and with borders with the Soviet Union to the north, Hungary and Yugoslavia to the west, and Bulgaria to the south, the Romanian Socialist Republic is, geographically speaking, very much an East European state. But, as the name of the country suggests, the culture and language are, in fact, Latin in origin. In ancient times, this region was known as Dacia and Scythia Pontica. It became part of the Roman empire about 106 BC, under the Emperor Trajan.

Despite some mixture with Slavic peoples and culture, the Dacio-Roman culture has survived to this day, and the Romanian language, with its Latin roots, Slavic influences and Turkish and Magyar borrowings, bears witness to the country's history.

The fact that there was such a strong cultural and racial difference between Romania and its neighbours probably explains the strongly independent national spirit which characterizes Romania's history.

In the Middle Ages, two powerful principalities grew up in the region: that of Wallachia, founded in 1247, and that of Moldavia, founded in 1352. In the 15th century, both principalities fell into the hands of the Turks.

In the following centuries, there was endless fighting for Romanian territory between Turks, Russians and Austrians. The two principalities remained formally in Turkish possession until 1877, although in 1821 the echoes of the French Revolution led to nationalistic stirrings in the region which resulted in a degree of autonomy being granted by the Turks.

The third region of modern Romania, Transylvania, was for a long period under Austrian rule. In 1859, the first steps towards a union of the separate entities took place when, in defiance of the Turks, both principalities elected a single prince, Alexander John I. In 1866, he was deposed and replaced by a German prince, Charles of Hohenzollern-Sigmaringen. It was he who, in 1877, proclaimed full Romanian independence. Four years later, he became the first King of Romania, under the name of Carol I.

At the outbreak of the First World War, Romania declared herself neutral, but then joined the Allies against Austria and Germany. At first the war seemed to be going against her, but by the end of the conflict, the territory was more than doubled by the annexation of Transylvania and other territory. During the Second World War, Romania sided with the Germans, with whom she shared defeat, but signed a separate armistice in 1944. King Michael abdicated in 1947 and the Romanian People's Republic came into being.

Like other countries in eastern Europe, Romania came within the sphere of influence of the Soviet Union, although it has often taken an independent line in policy. The country is now known as the Romanian Socialist Republic, and its president since 1967 has been Nicolae Ceauşescu.

The physical features of Romania are dominated by the great horseshoe of the Carpathians, and the Southern Carpathians, or Transylvanian Alps. These peaks surround the central region of Transylvania, where the memory of the infamous 15th century prince Vlad Tepec 'the Impaler', who is thought to be a model for the legendary Count Dracula, creation of Bram Stoker (1847–1912) and villain in many a contemporary movie, still persists. Wallachia lies to the south, bordered by the River Danube (Dunărea, Dunav).

To the north-east lies Moldavia, along the border with the USSR. The boundary is formed by the River Prut (Prutul). Behind the Black Sea port of Constanţa lies the Dobrogea region and a stretch of plain, upon which the capital, Bucharest (Bucureşti) is situated.

The climate is continental, being hot and dry in summer and cold in winter. The land is, however, good for agriculture and crops include cereals, vegetables and vines. Livestock breeding is of growing importance.

The chief natural resource is oil, which is present in large quantities, and natural gas is also exploited. Coal, lignite, iron-ore, copper and uranium are mined, and there is a rapid growth in industrial output, particularly in the fields of mechanical and chemical engineering.

Romania is noted for its practice of traditional crafts, including excellent leather work, fine carpets with geometrical patterns, and enamel pottery. A feature of the latter is a simple spiral motif which has remained in this form since the Stone Age.

Above: Liberty Square and the Cathedral of Cluj-Napoca. Cluj, which is in Transylvania, is Romania's sixth largest city. It has 274,000 inhabitants.

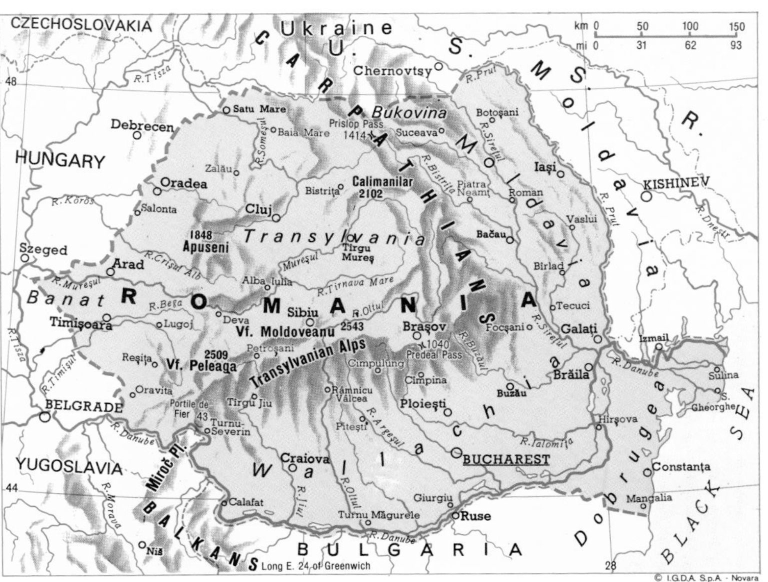

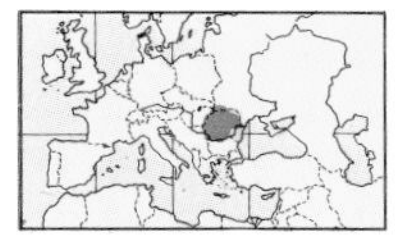

Area:
237,500 km²
(91,704 mi²)
Population:
22,653,000
Capital:
Bucharest (Bucureşti)
(pop. 1,960,000)
Other towns:
Braşov, Timişoara,
Currency:
leu

San Marino

Repubblica di San Marino

The oldest republic in Europe, San Marino stands between Emilia Romagna and the Marches in the central Italian peninsula, not far from Rimini. According to tradition, it was founded in the fourth century by a stone-cutter named Marino. The country has retained its independence since then.

Area:
61 km² (24 mi²)

Population:
22,000

Currency:
lira

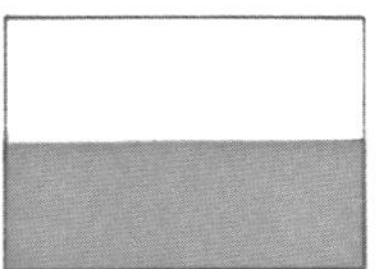

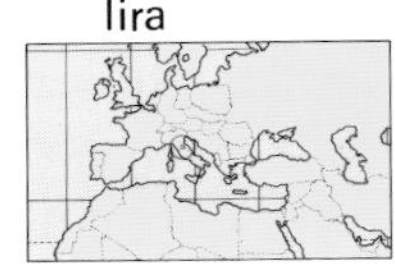

Spain

Estado Español

The Spanish State (Estado Español), as Spain is officially known, occupies most of the Iberian peninsula. Iberia is the westernmost of the three large peninsulas which extend southwards into the Mediterranean. To the north, the north-west and the south-west, Spain faces the Atlantic Ocean. This accounts for the country's strategic position in Europe and its long history as a seafaring nation. In the north-east, the great mountain range of the Pyrenees separates Spain from France. To the west, Spain has a frontier with Portugal. There are no natural frontiers with Portugal, except for a stretch of the River Duero (which the Portugese call the Douro) and parts of the River Guadiana. Otherwise, the Extremadura plateau simply merges with the highlands across the Portuguese border. It is easy to understand how, at one period in their history, the two countries were politically united under a single government.

Spain also borders the tiny **Principality of Andorra,** which covers 453 square kilometres (175 square miles) in the Pyrenees. Andorra has about 42,000 people and tourism is the main industry. At the southern tip of the Iberian peninsula is the rocky promontory of **Gibraltar,** which has belonged to Britain since 1704. Although only 6 square kilometres (2·3 square miles) in area, Gibraltar has great strategic importance, controlling the entrance to the Mediterranean. Close to Gibraltar is Tarifa, the southernmost town in Spain near the Puntas Marroquí, which is only 12 kilometres (7 miles) from Africa. Two well-known groups of islands also belong to Spain. The Balearic Islands, including Majorca and Minorca, are in the Mediterranean. The Canary Islands, including two provinces, Las Palmas and Santa Cruz de Tenerife, are off the Moroccan coast. Also under Spanish jurisdiction are the small enclaves of Ceuta and Melilla in Morocco, and the tiny islands of Chafarinas, Alhucemas and Velez de la Gomera near Morocco.

Spain's land borders extend for 1,945 kilometres (1,209 miles). The coastline of the mainland is almost twice as long at

3,904 kilometres (2,426 miles). The coasts are almost straight, except in the north-western region of Galicia, which faces the Atlantic. This is cut into by the *rias*. These deep, narrow inlets owe their origin to coastal submergence. Spain's otherwise regular coastline is largely unbroken. Because of this, and the fact that coastal mountain ranges act as a barrier, the effects of a maritime climate are not really felt in the interior. In this, the Iberian peninsula differs from southern Europe's other two, the Italian and Balkan peninsulas. The coastal strip is generally flat, but there are some rocky areas, especially to the north of the River Ebro. This coast is backed by impressive ranges of mountains.

There are three principal mountainous and highland regions in Spain. In the north of the country are the Pyrenean range and the Cantabrian Cordillera. In the centre is the vast Meseta, a plateau, while in the south stretching from Gibraltar to the Gulf of Valencia, is a succession of small ranges and massifs. The most impressive of these ranges is the Pyrenees, which Spain shares with France. The highest peaks, such as Pico de Aneto, which is 3,404 metres (11,168 feet) high, are in Spanish territory. Running to the west of the Pyrenees is the Cantabrian Cordillera, which lies parallel to the Atlantic coast. It includes the Picos de Europa, which reach 2,648 metres (8,688 feet). The centre of the country is mostly occupied by the immense Meseta, a Spanish term for 'tableland'. The Meseta is bordered on almost every side by mountainous regions, which isolate it from the coasts and the benefits of sea winds. It is itself broken by a number of ranges and massifs, such as the Sierra de Guadarrama, the Cuenca mountains and the Sierra Morena. Between these run river torrents which are subject to periods of drought. The deep, narrow river valleys are called *cañones*, from which comes the English term 'canyon'. In the south, the mountains include the Sierra Nevada, which contains Spain's highest peak, Mulhacén, which reaches 3,478 metres (11,411 feet) above sea level.

Some major rivers rise in the mountains of Spain. The most important are the Ebro, which rises in the Pyrenees and reaches the Mediterranean after a journey of 910 kilometres (565 miles); the Guadalquivir, which rises in the Sierra de Segura and flows into the Gulf of Cadiz, having crossed the region of Andalucia; and lastly the three great waterways of the Meseta, the Rivers Duero, Tajo (Tagus) and Guadiana, which all flow into the Atlantic, crossing Portugese territory. The longest river is the Tajo, which flows for 1,007 kilometres (626 miles).

Below far left: A farm in fertile Andalucia. Centre below: The north-eastern region of Navarre includes the Basque country. Below: Large flat areas are typical of the Meseta.

The harshness of the terrain and the arid nature of the Meseta mean that, although Spain is almost as large as France, it is sparsely populated. About 39 million inhabitants live in Spain, but the population is distributed unevenly. About one-third of the people occupy one-sixth of the territory. The main concentrations of population are in centres of industrial activity and in the best irrigated and most fertile areas of the countryside. Large areas of the Meseta are inhabited only by shepherds and their herds.

This harsh but fascinating landscape has been the stage for many of the most important steps in European history. Before the rise of the Roman Empire, the Iberian peninsula had been inhabited by peoples of various origins. Some belonged to the Celtic group, and others came from North Africa. Phoenicians, Greeks and then Carthaginians established trading posts and colonies along the coasts. The Roman conquest came in the third century BC, during the Punic or Carthaginian Wars. The conquest was far

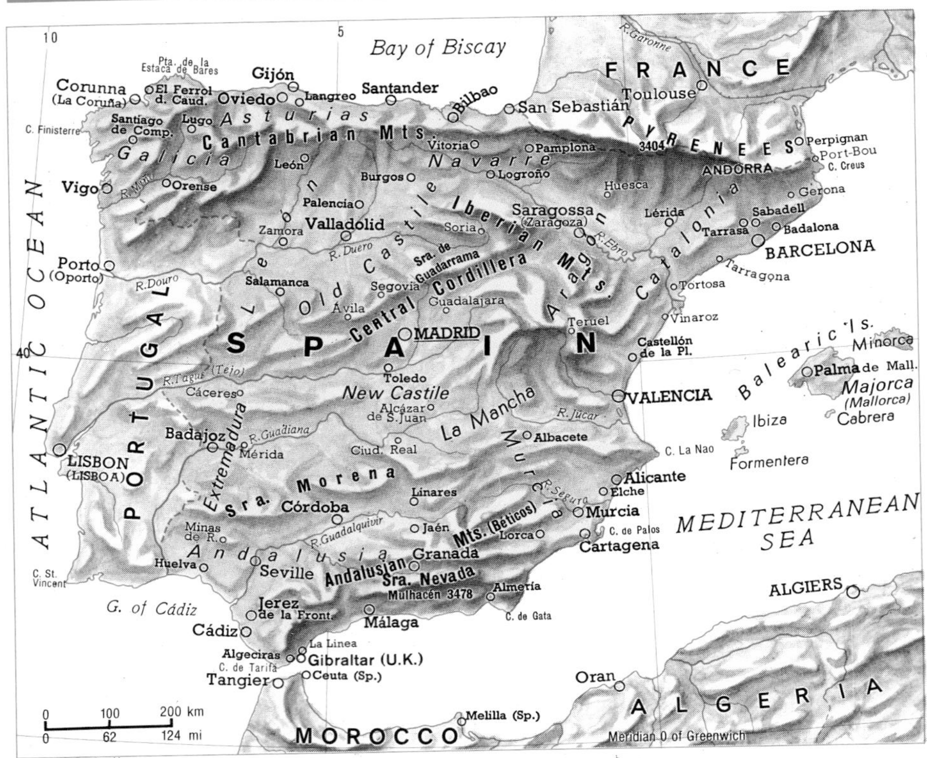

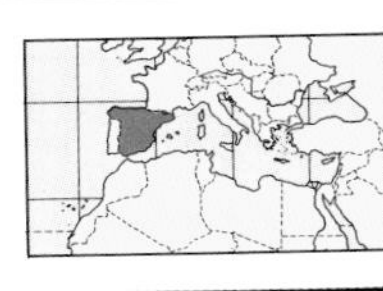

Area: 504,782 km² (194,908 mi²)
Population: 38,671,000
Capital: Madrid (pop. 3,244,000)
Other towns: Barcelona, Valencia, Seville (Sevilla), Saragossa (Zaragoza), Bilbao, Málaga, Las Palmas,
Currency: peseta

from easy, but the result was an integration of the two peoples, Latin and Iberian, which was complete and lasting. The legacy of the Roman Empire is still evident today. Monuments and architectural remains survive from the Roman period, and the Spanish language itself is obviously of Latin origin. This is true not only of Castilian, but also of Galician which is spoken in the north-west, and Catalan, which is spoken in the Cataluña (Catalonia) region, around Barcelona. Basque is an exception. It is spoken in the three provinces of the Basque country, situated between the upper Ebro and the Bay of Biscay. The origins of this language are shrouded in mystery, and to this day the Basque people retain a separate identity, expressed in a campaign for political autonomy. Recognition of regional differences has led to some devolution of power. In the early 1980s, regional governments were established for the Basques, Catalans and Galicians.

The period of Roman domination was for Spain an era of prosperity. Two emperors, Trajan and Hadrian, were of Iberian origin, as were many of Rome's leading philosophers and men of letters, such as the philosopher Seneca, the poets Lucan and Martial, and the orator Quintilian. At the time of the fall of the western Roman Empire, in the fifth century AD, the barbarian Visigoths established a kingdom on the Iberian peninsula, with its capital at Toledo. Some 300 years later the faith of Islam arrived in Spain, as Arab invaders flooded across the Strait of Gibraltar in AD 711. The Arabs founded a splendid and highly developed civilization in the country, which reached its climax in the tenth century, under the Caliph of Córdoba. Their magnificent architecture is still visible today, especially in southern Spain.

From the year 1000, the Christian populations of the north, never completely subdued by the Arabs, started to revolt. Out of the ruins of Islamic power, various independent Roman Catholic kingdoms were formed: León, Navarre, Castile and Aragon. By 1260, the small Caliphate of Granada, which occupied the region around this southern city, a jewel of Arab civilization, was all that remained of the ancient conquest. The centre and north of the country belonged to the kings of Castile. The other large Christian kingdom, Aragon, was to expand towards the Mediterranean, and eventually it was to include Sicily, Sardinia and the Kingdom of Naples.

Spain's destiny as a Euroean power was confirmed by the marriage in 1469 of Isabella of Castile with Ferdinand of Aragon. The two countries were united ten years later. These two sovereigns, who would go down in history with the name of *los reyes catolicos*, the Catholic monarchs, not only eliminated the last traces of Arab rule, when Granada fell in 1492, but, by astutely backing the expeditions of Christopher Columbus, opened the horizons to colonial expansion by Spain. Most of the New World was colonized initially by seafarers and *conquistadores* of Spanish origin.

By the 16th century, Charles V, the Hapsburg grandson of the *reyes catolicos* (born of the marriage of their daughter Joanna to Philip, son of the Holy Roman Emperor Maximilian I) could boast that 'on his lands the sun never sets'. Under his rule the central European dominions of the House of Hapsburg were united with the kingdom of Spain, possessions in Italy, and the immense colonial empire of the Americas. Spanish hegemony in Europe lasted for the whole of the 16th century. It was reinforced in 1559 by the treaty of Cateau-Cambrésis (1559) which, in bringing an end to conflict with France, recognized Spanish possession of the Netherlands, Franche Comté, the Duchy of Milan, the Kingdom of Naples and the immense overseas territories. In 1580, the annexation of Portugal was also achieved, and this lasted for 50 years. A major setback occurred in 1588, when a Spanish fleet despatched to invade England, the *armada*, was defeated in the English Channel and scattered by storms. Political power was accompanied by a flourishing of the arts. In the 17th century, painting, literature and the theatre experienced a *siglo de oro*, a golden age.

Political decline started under the last Hapsburg kings, who in 1700 were

Above left: Seville is an elegant city on the River Guadalquivir. Above: The walls of Avila were erected in the late 11th century. Below: A popular fiesta *at Berga, in Catalonia.*

succeeded by the Bourbon dynasty. Impoverished by wars, compelled to renounce its rule of the Netherlands and Portugal, and, in 1714, deprived of all its Italian possessions, Spain found itself pushed to the edge of the European stage. No longer dictating the politics of the continent, Spain was overtaken by events it could not control. In 1808, the country was invaded by the armies of Napoleon. The Spanish and Portuguese people put up a determined resistance to the French, with the assistance of British troops under Sir Arthur Wellesley, who was later created the Duke of Wellington. But after the fall of Napoleon Bonaparte and the restoration of the Bourbons, the decline only gathered speed. In the course of the 19th century, the American colonies all cut their ties with the homeland: the last to depart was Cuba in 1898.

The monarchy was abolished in 1931, but this constitutional change was not enough to open the doors to progress. After five years of political confusion, General Francisco Franco challenged the legitimate government of the day and plunged the country into civil war. The conflict lasted for three years and cost two million lives. Whole areas were devastated. Eventually, the supporters of General Franco, including conservatives, Falangists and monarchists, supported by arms and contingents of volunteers from the fascist countries of Europe, emerged the victors. Many anti-fascist volunteers from other countries fought

on the Republican side, and many were killed during the conflict.

A right-wing dictatorship was established in Spain, destined to last almost 40 years. Spanish citizens were deprived of many freedoms. The hold slackened only in 1975, with the death of Franco. His chosen successor was King Juan Carlos, of the House of Bourbon. Although the monarchy was restored, it has in fact guided the country towards a gradual **return to democratic government. A recurring domestic problem has been terrorism and attempted *coups d'état*. Nevertheless Spain has succeeded in returning to the mainstream of European politics and became a member of the European Economic Community (EEC) in 1986.**

Industrialization has been held back by insufficient energy production, by lack of capital, and by poor communications. The country has iron ore, coal, copper, lead and zinc mines, and it is the world's largest producer of mercury, after the USSR. But its resources are still a long way from being exploited to the full.

Spanish heavy industry (steel and engineering) is concentrated in the north along the Atlantic coast, in the Cataluña region, around Barcelona, which is the second most important city in Spain, and in Madrid. The chemical, textile and food-processing industries are all active. Three-quarters of the population now lives in urban areas, but farming is still important. Farming in the Atlantic coastal regions produces cereals and animal fodder. On the Mediterranean plains the typical agriculture of the region flourishes. Vines, olives, citrus fruit, vegetables and rice are all grown, and Spain is Europe's third largest wine producer. Inland, agriculture is hindered by the arid climate and by lack of modern farming techniques. Much of the region is devoted to sheep-breeding. The fishing industry is important along the coasts. In the Spanish economy, considerable revenue is derived from money earned by its citizens abroad, and remitted home. Many Spaniards have sought work in Germany, Switzerland, France, and Latin America. Tourism is also extremely important. Millions of visitors come to Spain every year to enjoy its sunny beaches and admire the superb cities.

The capital of Spain is Madrid. Built at the command of Philip II in the barren landscape of the Meseta, it possesses one of the most famous museums in the world, the Prado. The cities of Córdoba and Granada, in the Mediterranean hinterland, bear witness to the splendid civilization of the Arabs. Seville, in Andalucia, is an enchanting city, and the largest river port in the country.

Other historical centres include Burgos, Toledo and Salamanca which has been the most prestigious university town in Spain since the Middle Ages. And in Barcelona, the highly original buildings of Antonio Gaudí (1852–1926) are much admired.

Above and below: The bullfight is a spectacle which attracts a large following in Spain. The men of horseback are called picadores. *The centre of attraction is the* matador, *who kills the bull. He is distinguished by his splendid* traje de luces, *a costume which consists of a short jacket and a pair of knee-length breeches, both finely embroidered. The black hat is called a* montera. *It is thrown to the ground when the matador kills the bull.*

Sweden

Konungariket Sverige

A century ago, Sweden was a poor country. Its 3½ million inhabitants lived mostly by farming, struggling against adverse environmental conditions. Today, the population has more than doubled, and it enjoys a higher national income per capita than the United States. Unemployment is practically unknown, and its system of social services is one of the best organized and most progressive in the world.

It all began with the Industrial Revolution, which came to Sweden around the middle of the 19th century. The opening of the first hydro-electric schemes made use of Sweden's chief asset – water. The forests yielded huge amounts of timber, and rich deposits of iron ore were found in the soil. Sweden is still the principal European producer of iron ore outside the Soviet Union. Other mineral resources include uranium, lead, zinc and sulphur. Sweden was one of the first countries to make full development of resources a priority, and traditional industries include paper manufacture, mining and automobile assembly. Today the fastest developing industries are engineering and chemicals.

Agriculture has not been forgotten, although it now chiefly serves the home market. Mechanization has arrived, with the result that today only five per cent of the workforce are employed on the land, or in fishing. The chief crops are cereals (barley, oats, wheat and rye), potatoes and beet.

The choice of crop obviously varies from region to region, because much of the country endures a harsh climate. Sweden occupies the central part of Scandinavia. Together with Norway and Finland, it occupies the extreme north of the European continent, crossed by the Arctic Circle. It is a land which really enjoys only two seasons: summer and winter. This is the 'land of the midnight sun', of short winter days and short summer nights, and deserted tracts of ice and snow. Geographically it can be divided into three distinct areas: from north to south, Norrland, Svealand and Gotland.

Norrland, the 'land of the north', actually occupies two-thirds of the country. Its main feature is plateaux, which stretch from the Norwegian border, where the country's highest peaks are to be found. These include Kebnekaise, which reaches 2,117 metres (6,946 ft), and Sarektjåkko, 2,090 metres (6,857 ft) above sea level. The plateaux descend gently towards the Gulf of Bothnia. Here the sea and lakes are iced over from October to May. Because of this, fishing has never been an important Swedish industry. In the northern winter, motorized vehicles are used to cross stretches of sea, rather than boats.

South of the Norrland lies a transitional region of forests, small lakes and peat bogs. This marks the border between Norrland and Svealand. Svealand is the central-southern region, which is for the most part flat with occasional gentle hills. This is a land of water, and it contains the third largest lake in Europe, Vänern. Some 92 metres (302 ft) in depth, it covers an area of 5,585 square kilometres (2,156 square miles). Thanks to the navigability of the lakes, the milder climate, and the presence of rich mineral deposits, Svealand has always been the most important part of Sweden. It is here that the two largest cities of the country are found: Stockholm, the capital, and Göteborg (Gothenburg), the largest port, situated on the estuary of the Göta. The southern extremity of Sweden is taken up by Gotland, which in turn is divided into Smålånd and Scania. The former is a plateau which stretches from Lake Vättern to the south-east coast, while the latter is a large plain. This is a mild, sunny region, favourable to agriculture and human settlement. Here is Sweden's third city: Malmö, an important centre of trade and communications.

Above: Stockholm has been the capital of Sweden since the end of the 16th century.

Despite the inhospitable nature of much of Sweden's terrain, and the cold climate, it has not deterred settlement. People were certainly living there in Neolithic times. Cave paintings, dwelling places and pottery vases of a characteristic funnel shape bear witness to early habitation.

The Latin writer Tacitus (*c.* AD 55–120) refers to the Svioni people, settled around Uppsala. To the north lay the territory of the Lapponi, and to the south that of the Gauti. At Uppsala there was a great pagan temple, known throughout the lands of the north, and this was the focus for the unification of the whole territory. Between the seventh and tenth centuries, Sweden was the land of the Vikings, daring warriors whose longships

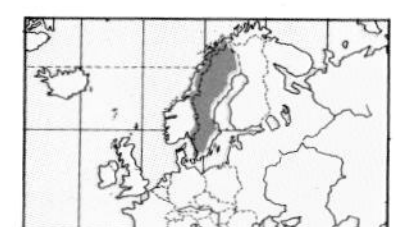

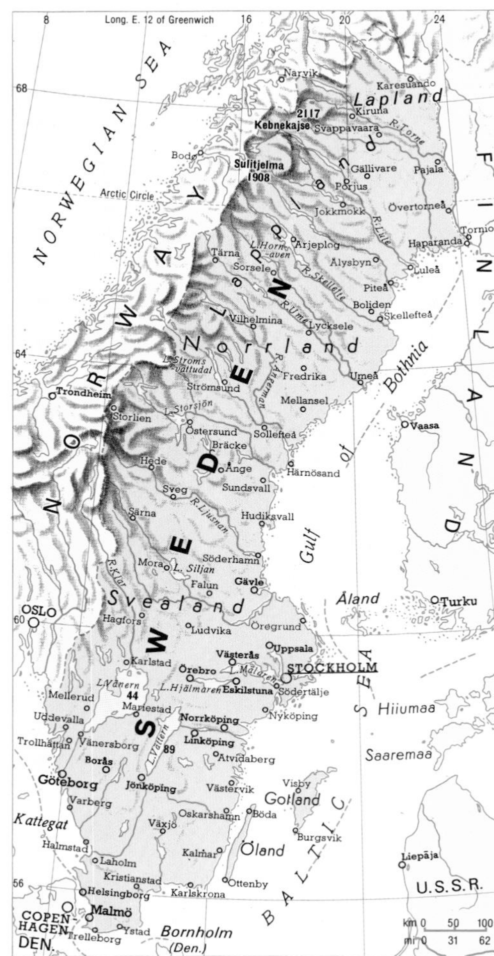

Area:
449,964 km² (173,742 mi²)
Population:
8,359,000
Capital:
Stockholm (pop. 1,551,000)
Other towns:
Göteborg (Gothenburg), Malmö, Uppsala, Norrköping, Västerås, Örebro, Linköping, Jönköping, Borås, Helsingborg
Currency:
krona

Above: Near the capital, is the magnificent castle of Drottingholm, dating from the 17th and 18th centuries.
Right: The beauty of Sweden's forests and lakes is shown in this landscape photograph.

sailed the oceans of the known world. Their raids were feared from Britain to France and from Russia to Constantinople. They established a trade with the Arabs in slaves and precious metals. In about 1000 AD, the Vikings were converted to Christianity and, in 1140, the ancient temple of Uppsala became a great cathedral dedicated to the new religion.

Power in medieval Sweden lay with the aristocracy. When in the 13th century, King Albert attempted to limit the power of the nobles, they enlisted the help of Princess Margaret, already ruler of Norway and Denmark. The three countries were united under one crown by the Union of Kalmar (1397). It was an uneasy alliance. The repressive policies of Christian II of Denmark led to a peasant's revolt, and increased support for the independence movement led by the aristocrat Gustav Vasa, who became King of Sweden as Gustavus I in 1523. It was under his rule that the Swedish people embraced the Lutheran doctrine. Under his successors, the country knew a long period of economic development and territorial expansion. Gustavus II (Adolphus) was the champion of the Protestant cause in the Thirty Years' War. In the 18th century, Russia, Poland and Denmark allied to attack Sweden. The Peace of Nystad (1721) marked the end of this Great Northern War and of Swedish dominance.

In the 19th century, Sweden once again had a foreign sovereign. Charles XIII had no male issue and so named as his heir the French marshal Jean-Baptiste Jules Bernadotte, who came to the throne in 1818 with the name of Charles XIV. With him began an era of peace that has lasted into our own time. Sweden remained neutral in both world wars.

It is perhaps its recent peaceful, neutral existence that has enabled Sweden to devote itself to social and economic reform. In the new apartments and office blocks of the cities, amidst all the contradictions and unhappiness that seem inevitable in an industrial society, it is sometimes hard to remember that not so far away the old Sweden still survives – in the vast forests of fir and birch, which evoke memories of the old Viking sagas, of the spiteful trolls and beautiful *skogsra* of ancient folklore.

Switzerland

Schweiz – Suisse – Svizzera

The great French novelist Victor Hugo once wrote that when the peoples of Europe are united, they will probably look to Switzerland as their mother. If so, it will be a fair judgement, for the independently-minded Swiss were among the first in Europe to discover the value of co-operation, unity and peace. Indeed, Switzerland is already a centre for co-operation on an international scale, being the home of the International Red Cross and of United Nations agencies, such as the World Health Organization.

Switzerland is a confederation of small states, or cantons, which over the centuries have overcome serious religious, cultural and linguistic differences in order to stand together against external rule. The first to stand up for themselves were the cantons of Uri, Schwyz and Unterwalden. On 1 August 1291, they swore to help each other resist the abuses of the Habsburgs, whose dynasty ruled the region from Austria. Over the years, they were joined by other cantons. Today there are 23, three of which are subdivided for administrative purposes.

A look at Switzerland on the map of Europe will show that it stands at a crossroads of cultures. It contains Italian speakers, French speakers and German speakers (who form the majority). A tiny proportion also speak Romansch, which is recognized as a national language. For the sake of simplicity, Switzerland uses Latin on stamps and coins, calling itself Helvetia.

One thing that has held the various groups in Switzerland together is their way of life. They inhabit the most mountainous country in Europe, farming the valleys and raising dairy herds. It is a spectacularly beautiful country, with forests and snowy peaks rising above brimming lakes. The chief mountain range is the Alps, which form one chain along the southern border with France and Italy (with such peaks as the Matterhorn) and another chain to the south of the Berner Oberland, which culminates in the Finsteraarhorn, the Aletschhorn and the Jungfrau. Running north-east along the French border are the Jura mountains. Snow from the Swiss mountains feeds some of Europe's major waterways, such as the Rhône and the Rhine (Rhein). The largest of the lakes are Geneva (Leman), Constance (Bodensee), Neuchâtel, Vierwaldstätter, Thun and Brienz.

Agriculture plays an important part in the Swiss economy, with grain crops, fruit and vegetables being grown in many areas. Dairy produce is a major export, and milk from the Alpine pastures supplies the cheese and chocolate industry. There are few mineral resources in Switzerland, but the hydro-electric potential of its vast bodies of water is one compensation. The best known industry is precision engineering. Switzerland has long had a reputation for fine clocks, watches and optical instruments.

Service industries thrive in Switzerland. The country's neutrality in times of war has provided a stable, long-term security in which banks can prosper. Huge sums of money from all over the world are deposited in Swiss banks, which are renowned for their confidentiality and expertise. Tourism is another industry of great importance. Switzerland's scenery attracts visitors in summer and winter alike.

The government of Switzerland is a federal one, and it is based at the capital,

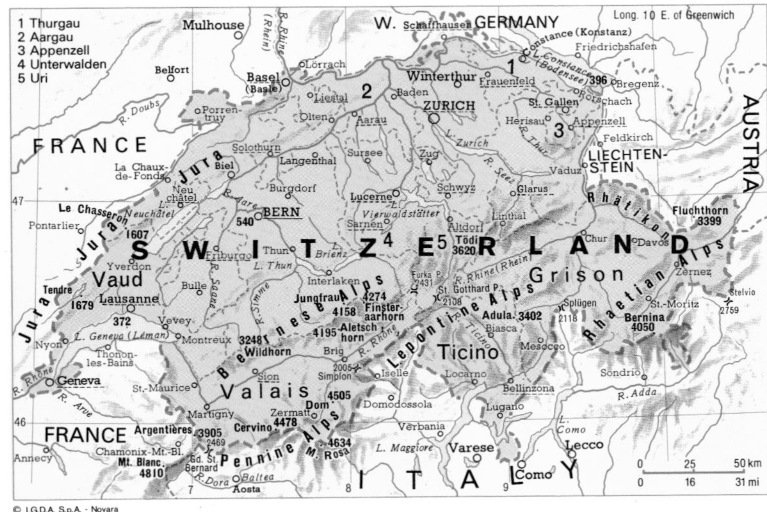

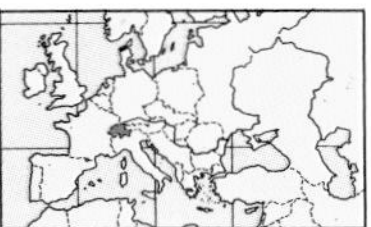

Area: 41,288 km² (15,942 mi²)
Population: 6,482,000
Capital: Bern (Berne) (pop. 301,000)

Other towns: Zürich, Basle (Basel), Geneva (Genève), Lausanne, Winterthur, Saint Gallen, Lucerne, Biel (Bienne)
Currency: franc

Above: The European headquarters of the United Nations Organization at Geneva. Geneva was the headquarters of the League of Nations from 1919 until 1940. Today it is the home of the International Red Cross, which was founded by the Swiss philanthropist Henri Dunant, and of UN agencies, such as the International Labour Organization and the World Health Organization.

Bern. Executive power belongs to the Federal Council of seven members, and each year the Federal Assembly votes in a President and Vice-President of the Council. The Federal Assembly is the legislative arm of government, and is made up of two chambers – the National Council, which has 200 members, and the Council of States, which has 46 members. Switzerland is a democratic republic.

Communications within Switzerland are hampered by the mountainous terrain. Feats of engineering were necessary to establish the rail network. Today there are nearly 5,000 kilometres (3,107 miles) of track, including rack-and-pinion lines which enable locomotives to haul carriages up steep inclines. There is a good road system, which includes dramatic mountain passes. The River Rhine (Rhein), which crosses into Germany below Basle (Basel), forms one of Europe's main arteries of trade, linking Switzerland and the North Sea.

Right: Typical lakeside scenery at the small town of Spiez on Lake Thun in the canton of Bern. Spiez is a centre of tourism and agriculture, two important sectors of the Swiss ecocomy.
Below: The Matterhorn.

TURKEY

While most of Turkey is considered to be part of the Continent of Asia, the territory to the west of the Bosporus is in Europe *(see page 139).*

Union of Soviet Socialist Republics

Soyuz Sovyetskikh Sotsialisticheskikh Respublik

The Union of Soviet Socialist Republics (USSR) is also known as the Soviet Union. It came into being after the November 1917 Revolution, which transformed the ancient Russian empire into the first nation in history to be governed by a Communist regime. Before the revolution, this vast country was called Russia, a name which many people still use, although strictly it refers now only to a part of the USSR, namely the Russian Soviet Federal Republic, which covers 76 per cent of the country. Before the revolution, the country was ruled by a tsar (czar) meaning emperor (from the Latin word *caesar*). His official title was 'Tsar of all the Russias'. And today this enormous land still contains a multitude of cultures.

The USSR, the world's largest nation, is more than twice the size of the USA and it occupies about 15 per cent of the world's total land area. It straddles two continents, 25 per cent being in Europe and 75 per cent in Asia. To appreciate its immensity, we must remember that when night falls on Moscow, the capital, and the red star on the Kremlin lights up, the sun of the next day is already rising in Vladivostok, in the far south-east of the USSR. Soviet territory is crossed by no less than 11 time zones.

In Europe, the USSR shares borders with Norway, Finland, Poland, Czechoslovakia, Hungary and Romania. In Asia, it borders Turkey, Iran, Afghanistan, China, Mongolia and North Korea. The northern coastline borders the frozen seas of the Arctic Ocean, including the Barents, Kara, Leptev and East Siberian seas. In the east are seas belonging to the North Pacific Ocean, namely the Bering and Okhotsk seas and the Sea of Japan. In the south-west are the Black Sea, which is linked to the Mediterranean, and the Caspian Sea, which is an immense salty lake. The Bering Strait separates the USSR from Alaska, and hence it forms the boundary between Asia and North America. Between the last Soviet island and the first belonging to Alaska is a stretch of sea only 4 kilometres (2·5 miles) wide.

In spite of a coastline which represents two-thirds of its borders, the USSR has never been a seafaring country. Instead, it has always had more of a continental mentality. The extent of the coastline does not bear comparison with the vastness of the territory, and there is a great shortage of natural harbours. In the north and east, the ports are frozen over for a good part of the year. Most of this immense country is a plain, which stretches from the desolate regions north of the Arctic Circle to the deserts of central Asia. The mountainous areas, with the highest peaks in the Caucasus and the Pamir, skirt the southern borders of the USSR. In the Asian part of the country, mountains stretch from Samarkand to the Sea of Okhotsk, from which a number of ranges radiate. East of Samarkand is the USSR's highest mountain, Communism Peak at 7,495 metres (24,590 feet) above sea level. The Urals cross the country from north to south, and form the divide between Europe and Asia. Much of the eastern part of Siberia forms a plateau. The climate is typically continental, with harsh winters and lots of snow. In northern areas, the temperature can fall as low as −60°C (−76°F), but the central-southern areas have hot summers.

The USSR is a country of great contrasts. It stretches from the frozen wastes of the far north, inhabited by polar bears and reindeer, to the desert steppes of central Asia, where caravans of camels are still seen today. Great stretches of forest, the so-called taiga, occupy about half the territory. This is the home of elks, lynx, wolves, brown bears and, in southern Siberia, even tigers. Proceeding farther south, where the summers are hot with little rain, the trees disappear and the steppes begin. The ground is covered in grass as far as the eye can see. Still farther south, the grass becomes more and more scarce until it disappears in desert, with

Below: Fountains adorn Moscow (Moskva), the capital of the USSR.

scorched expanses of sand or stones, such as the Kara Kum and Kyzyl Kum east of the Caspian Sea. On the shores of the Black Sea, however, and particularly in the Crimea, the climate and scenery are almost Mediterranean, and vines and fruit trees are cultivated.

The USSR is crossed by a number of great rivers. In fact, some of Europe's longest and deepest rivers flow through Soviet territory. The principal rivers are the Volga, revered by Russians for the fertility it brings to the area crossed in its 3,531 kilometre (2,194 mile) journey to the Black Sea; the Ural, the third most important river in Europe (after the Volga and the Danube) at 2,428 kilometres (1,509 miles); the Dnepr, which is 2,201 kilometres (1,368 miles) long; and the Don at 1,870 kilometres (1,162 miles). All these rivers are slow-flowing, broad and have gentle gradients. They are navigable for long stretches, and linked by a wide network of canals. Their alluvial silt has benefited agriculture over the ages, and today the rivers are valuable providers of hydro-electric energy. The Asian part of the country is less well provided with waterways, with the exception of the vast Siberian plain, which is crossed by major rivers, such as the Ob, Yenisey and Lena.

In this land of contrasting landscape and climates, there is a great variety of inhabitants. The population numbers more than 270 million, which places the USSR third in the world league after China and India. These belong to more than 100 ethnic and language groups, from remote nomadic tribes in Asia to the great masses of the Russian people, who constitute more than half the inhabitants of the USSR. The Slavic element is prevalent, with the Russians, the Ukrainians, the Letts and the Lithuanians. Then there are the Finno-Ugrians of Asiatic origin, the Tartars, such as the Kazakhs, Uzbeks, Turkomans, Azerbaydzhanians and Bashkirs. There are also Caucasians, such as Georgians, Circassians, and Armenians, and Mongols, such as Yakuts, Buryats, and Khalkhas. There are Polish and German minorities in the Baltic areas, while Jews live in many parts of the USSR. This is a mosaic of peoples, with varied origins, customs and religions. Newspapers in the USSR are printed in some 120 languages, and radio and television programmes are no less varied.

The USSR is more than a country, it is a separate world. The land is neither truly European nor truly Asian, but it has participated in and drawn from both. Through its long and troubled history, it has been first subject to the influence of one continent, and then the other. At the time of the Roman Empire, Russia was ruled by nomadic tribes of Asian origin. On the edge of the Black Sea, they established trading links with Greek and Roman colonies, providing early contacts between east and west. Russian civilization first became established about the year 1000, with the state of Kiyev (Kiev), founded in the Ukraine by a group of Vikings with a view to monopolizing commerce between northern Europe and the Byzantine Empire. From the name of *Rossiy* by which these warrior-merchants were known, came that of Russia. It was because of them that the Byzantine civilization and the Greek Orthodox religion penetrated the

Slav world, leaving a legacy which survives today.

The break-up of the state of Kiyev occurred in the 12th century. It was the result, on one side, of the pressure of European Crusaders, especially the order of the Teutonic Knights, who were anxious to acquire the fertile Slav lands for themselves, and, on the other, of ferocious Asian tribes, such as the Mongols, who established various principalities in European Russia. Two main Slav cities survived. In the north was Novgorod, which in about the middle of the 13th century, under the leadership of the first national hero, Alexander Nevskiy, drove back the Teutonic Knights. The other was Moscow, site of a small warrior state within the Mongol area of influence. In 1328, Moscow became capital of the principality of Muscovy, and the nucleus of the future Russian nation.

The culture and customs of the Muscovites at this time had a strong Asian flavour. For example, women lived in a completely separate environment called the *terem*. It is not hard to see analogies with the Islamic harem, although polygamy was not practised. The expulsion of the Mongols and the total elimination of the rule by the Crusaders occurred only in the 16th century. In the meantime, despite the struggles of the feudal lords, the centralizing and unifying power of the Tsar asserted itself. The first dynasty was that of the Ruriks, whose line culminated in the notorious figure of Ivan IV, the Terrible.

A decisive change occurred in Russian history between the 17th and 18th centuries, through the work of the Tsar Peter I, the Great, who promoted the Europeanization of the country. He transferred the court and government to a new capital, St Petersburg (present day Leningrad), on the banks of the Neva. Laid out in the French style, this city remained the seat of the tsars until the revolution.

Area:
22,402,200 km² (8,650,010 mi²)
Population:
278,719,000
Capital:
Moscow (pop. 8,537,000)
Republics and their capitals:
Armenia (Yerevan); Azerbaydzhan (Baku); Belorussia (Minsk); Estonia (Tallinn); Georgia (Tbilisi); Kazakhstan (Alma-Ata); Kirghizstan (Frunze); Latvia (Riga); Lithuania (Vilna); Moldavia (Kishinev); Russian Soviet Federal Socialist Republic (Moscow); Tadzhikstan (Dushanbe); Turkmenistan (Ashkhabad); Ukraine (Kiyev); Uzbekhistan (Tashkent)
Largest cities:
Leningrad, Kiyev, Tashkent, Kharkov, Gorkiy, Novosibirsk, Minsk, Sverdlovsk, Kuybyshev
Currency:
rouble

Two great names from Russian history. Top left: Peter the Great (1672–1725) was the tsar who modernized Russia. Top right: Catherine the Great (1729–96) was a ruthless monarch who came to power in 1762 after her husband was dethroned and murdered.

Above: This painting depicts the romantic world of old Russia with its troika, *or three-horse sleigh.*

Moscow, however, retained its importance, and the westernization introduced by Peter the Great remained superficial. At the dawn of the 20th century, the country still had a feudal system, in which the power was shared between the tsar (who exercised it through a rigid military and bureaucratic apparatus), the Orthodox Russian Church, and the large landowners. The bourgeoisie was small and of little importance. There were, on the other hand, large masses of peasants who had been freed from serfdom only in

1861. This was a medieval system whereby peasants were indiscriminately bought and sold together with the land that they worked. The peasants remained deprived of the most elementary rights.

It was in this environment that the seeds of revolution were sown, assisted by intellectuals and rebels who were cruelly persecuted. The most common punishment was deportation to forced labour in Siberia. This bleak territory in northern Asia was first used as a place of confinement in the 18th century, under Catherine the Great, and it was practically colonized by people who had been deported. Lenin himself, the future revolutionary leader whose real name was Vladimir Ilyich Ulyanov, assumed this name in memory of his years of forced labour on the River Lena, in Siberia. The revolutionary movement reached its climax in 1917, while the Russian army was locked in the bitter conflict of the First World War. Within a few months, the last Tsar, Nicholas II, was deposed. Power passed to the Soviets, revolutionary councils of workers, peasants and soldiers founded in 1905, at the time of the first popular risings. And despite a bloody civil war between the revolutionaries and sections of the army faithful to the old regime, the country was, by 1920, under the

Above: A railway track in the region of Lake Baykal. The weather can be bitterly cold here in southern Siberia. Below: Stretching into the distance are the mountains of Turkmenistan in the far south. This region is mostly barren. Below right: A complete contrast, prosperous country like this is also seen.

complete control of the Soviets.

There followed hard years for the USSR, which was isolated by the European powers and involved in a vast programme of reconstruction, industrialization and modernization. Lenin, who died in 1924, was succeeded by another leader, later accused of tyranny and a personality cult. This was the Georgian Joseph Vissarionovich Dzhugashvili, or Stalin (1879–1953). However, 'this man of steel' (which is what his name means) personified the spirit of the resistance by the Soviet people to Nazi aggression, from 1941 to 1945, during the Second World War.

Russia had already suffered invasion twice by European leaders seeking territorial gain, namely by Charles XII of Sweden in the 18th century, and Napoleon at the beginning of the 19th century. In both cases, the country was defended, not only by its people, but also by the appalling climate. The long march through ice and snow defeated even Napoleon. The weather was also an important ally in the fight against the German armies. But the immense human effort cost the country more than 20 million dead.

At the end of the war, the victorious Soviet army entered Berlin, and since then the USSR has been recognized as a world superpower, together with the United States. Since the 1950s, the two countries have been in competition with each other in the conquest of space. The USA is able to boast the first landing on the Moon (1969), but the first man in space was a Soviet citizen, the cosmonaut Yuri Alexeivich Gagarin in 1961, as was the first woman, Valentina Tereshkova in 1963. The rivalry between the two superpowers is not, however, limited to flights in space. It conditions world politics, which have in recent history alternated between periods of cold war and periods of détente. On their agreement depends world peace. The USA is a member of the North Atlantic Treaty Organization (NATO), while the USSR plays a leading role in the Warsaw Pact, a military alliance of other European Communist countries, established on the Soviet model after the Second World War. The USSR is also a member of an economic union with the same countries, COMECON.

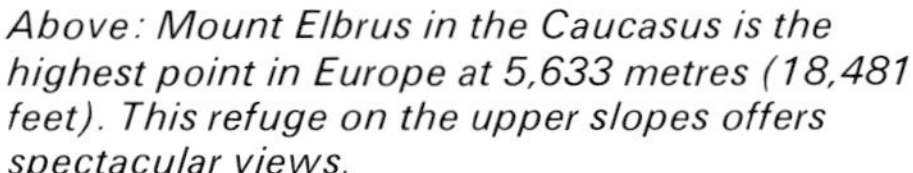

Above: Mount Elbrus in the Caucasus is the highest point in Europe at 5,633 metres (18,481 feet). This refuge on the upper slopes offers spectacular views.

The USSR is a federal state, composed of 15 autonomous republics. Each of these republics has its own government, its own laws and representative assemblies, called soviets. Of these, six are in Europe: one, the Russian Soviet Federal Republic (RSFSR) includes the Siberian region in Asia and a large part of the USSR in Europe. The principal legislative body of the USSR is the Supreme Soviet, which is elected every four years and is made up of two chambers. During the periods when it is not sitting, it delegates its functions to the Presidium, a committee of 33 members, whose president is, in effect, the Head of State. Executive power belongs to a Council of Ministers, nominated by the Supreme Soviet. The Communist party is the only party allowed.

The political and social changes which have occurred in the country since 1917 have had profound repercussions in the economic field. On the eve of the revolution, Russia still had an economy based largely on farming. Today it is the world's second greatest industrial power. This change was made possible by years of hard sacrifices, faced by the whole population, and by the programming of

Right: St Basil's Cathedral in Moscow was built between 1555 and 1560 in the reign of Ivan the Terrible. It contains an elaborate assortment of domes in the oriental style. Centre and bottom: Industrialization since the 1917 Revolution has made the USSR the world's second largest industrial power.

the economy through a series of five-year plans. These plans set out the priorities and objectives of the economy in a forthcoming five-year period.

The USSR is rich in natural resources. Coal reserves are immense, there are large numbers of hydro-electricity stations and the country leads the world in oil production. This has allowed rapid industrial development, especially in the fields of steel production, chemical and mechanical engineering, and textiles. The USSR today produces one-fifth of the world's steel supply, and has a primary position in the field of engineering. The nuclear and space industries have also been in the forefront of modern technological development.

Despite such massive industrial activity, about 14 per cent of the work-force is still employed in agriculture. Farming has been extensively reformed since the revolution, with nationalization and collectivization. The *sovchoz* farms belong to the government; the *kolchos* are large co-operatives formed by the farmers of one or more villages, who pool together their machinery in the common interest. Mechanization is still far from complete. The chief crops are cereals. The USSR is the world's biggest producer of wheat, rye, oats and barley, and the seventh biggest of maize. The cultivation of sugar-beet is also growing in importance. The USSR is the world's largest cultivator of flax, for the production of linen textiles. The cultivation of hemp and cotton is also widespread. The country's other sources of wealth include forestry, cattle-breeding and fishing. The latter includes both fresh water fishing, and sea fishing in the Black Sea, the Sea of Azov, the Caspian Sea, the Baltic Sea, and the Pacific Ocean.

Large numbers of cities have grown up in both the European and Asian parts of the USSR. Those cities destroyed in the Second World War have been reconstructed with scrupulous respect for traditional styles. Moscow, the capital, with more than eight million inhabitants, has nine railway stations, six airports, an elaborate underground rail system, and a university. The second city of the country and its principal port is the old capital of the tsars, St Petersburg, today known as Leningrad. Its historical centre includes one of the greatest museums of art in the world: the Hermitage, a former palace of Catherine the Great. The third city of the USSR in importance is Kiyev (Kiev), capital of the Ukraine. It was founded in AD 862 on the River Dnepr. Other major centres are Kazan, the old capital of the Tartars; and Odessa, a port on the Black Sea.

Yugoslavia

Socijalistička Federativna Republika Jogoslavija

The Yugoslavs are a people proud of their own identity and of their national unity. And yet the Socialist Federal Republic of Yugoslavia is really a cultural mosaic, inhabited by a population with greatly varying languages, traditions and history. The country is in fact composed of six republics: Bosnia (Bosna) and Hercegovina; Croatia (Hrvatska); Macedonia (Makedonija); Montenegro (Crna Gora); Serbia (Srbija); and Slovenia (Slovenìja). The population is mostly of Slav origin. There are also small groups of Hungarians, Turks, Magyars and Italians. Religious faiths also vary. There are Orthodox Christians, Roman Catholics, Protestants, Muslims and Jews. There are three official languages: Serbo-Croat, Slovenian and Macedonian. National unity has been maintained only by allowing each republic a great deal of autonomy and by respecting the very real important regional differences and needs.

Between the sixth and seventh centuries AD, three peoples from eastern Europe, the Slovenians, the Croatians and the Serbs, began to settle in the region of present-day Yugoslavia. The Slovenians established themselves in the north, but later came under Austrian rule. The Croatians, who established themselves farther south, voluntarily offered their crown to Hungary when their own monarchy died out, later becoming part of the Hapsburg empire. The Serbs managed to remain independent rather longer. In the 14th century, theirs was an important kingdom which, under the great emperor Stephen Dushan, extended to Albania, Montenegro, Macedonia, Thessaly and Epirus. But in 1354, the Turks began to invade the Balkan area, and took southern Serbia in 1389. By 1459, the Yugoslavian peoples were mostly subjects of the Ottoman Empire, although Croatia and Slovenia remained under Hapsburg rule. In 1878, Serbia and Montenegro became fully independent kingdoms, although Macedonia was retained by Turkey.

The assassination of Austrian archduke Franz Ferdinand at Sarajevo in 1914, and Austria's subsequent declaration of war against Serbia, sparked off the First World War. The realization of their dream was delayed. It was only at the end of the war, in 1918, that the Kingdom of the Serbs, Croats and Slovenes could finally be established. The country was renamed Yugoslavia in 1929. But internal disputes continued, partly arising from the suspicion that the Serbs planned to dominate the other regions.

Germany and Italy attacked Yugoslavia in 1941 and compelled it to surrender in 12 days. Serbia went to the Germans, Macedonia to the Bulgarians, Montenegro and Croatia formed 'independent' states, while Germany and Italy divided Slovenia between them. The invading troops were especially merciless to Serbia, and it was here that resistance began. Josip Broz, the future Marshal Tito (1892–1980) led an army of Communist partisans and, with the help of the Allies, liberated the whole country in 1945. On 31 January 1946, the Federal People's Republic of Yugoslavia was born. Ideological differences emerged with the USSR. Partial reconciliation came in 1962, but Yugoslavia continued to maintain an independent line.

One of the reasons that so many contrasting cultures remained intact in this region over the ages was the great variety in terrain.

The Alpine area lies in the north-western corner of the country, that is Slovenia and part of Croatia. Its main feature is an extensive mountain region which culminates in Triglav, the highest point in Yugoslavia, at 2,863 metres (9,393 feet) above sea level. Here are green forests, and innumerable caves, such as the splendid examples at Postumia. The Dalmatian coast faces the Adriatic Sea, with its myriad islands created by coastal submergence. This is Mediterranean Yugoslavia, separated from the interior by a mountainous border formed by the Velebit, the Dinaric Alps and by the uplands of Montenegro.

Beyond this barrier, the scenery changes once again. The climate becomes continental and the karst (limestone) plateaux and narrow valleys of the

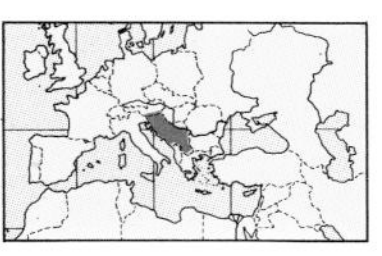

Area: 255,804 km² (98,722 mi²)
Population: 22,850,000
Capital: Belgrade (Beograd, pop. 1,455,000) 1,407,000)
Other towns: Zagreb, Skopje, Sarajevo, Lubljana, Novi Sad, Split,
Currency: dinar

Below: Cetinje in the Montenegro region.

Dinaric region begin. It is one of the most inaccessible areas of the country and corresponds, more or less, with Bosnia and Hercegovina, and the south-western part of Croatia. To the south lies Montenegro, and, on the Albanian border, the waters of Lake Skadarsko (Scutari). To the east, between the Rivers Sava and Danube (Dunav), stretches the flat plain of Sirmio, characterized by a continental climate and steppe-like terrain. In the east is the most important region of Yugoslavia: Serbia. This is dominated by the hills of Sumadija, where the capital, Belgrade (Beograd) is situated. Finally, to the south of Serbia and stretching as far as the Greek border, are the broad valleys and tall mountains of Macedonia.

The regional differences in climate and landscape are reflected in Yugoslavia's agriculture. Maize, wheat, barley and oats, as well as plums, apples, olives and grapes are grown mainly in Croatia, Slovenia and Serbia, that is, in the less mountainous regions. In Croatia and Slovenia, cattle are also reared, while Macedonia offers pasture for flocks of sheep. The Dalmatian coast is the most important fishing area in the Mediterranean, especially for sardines, pilchards and tuna. The most important fishing centres are Pula, Zadar and Split.

Although rich in mineral resources, which include lignite, bauxite, copper, iron-ore, zinc and mercury, Yugoslavia had to wait until the period after the Second World War before it could compete with the other industrialized countries. Today, great progress is being made, especially in the area of engineering (cars, lorries and tractors) and chemical industries (plastics and phosphates). Shipbuilding, textiles, particularly carpets, and food-processing (sugar refineries and distilleries) are also important, as is the long-established timber and wood-pulp industry.

Above left: Dubrovnik is a beautiful old port on the Dalmatian coast.
Above: Mostar on the River Neretva, in Hercegovina.
Below: Korcula, from the road to Lumbarda.

Supplementary Material

Index

Acknowledgments

World Physical Relief Map

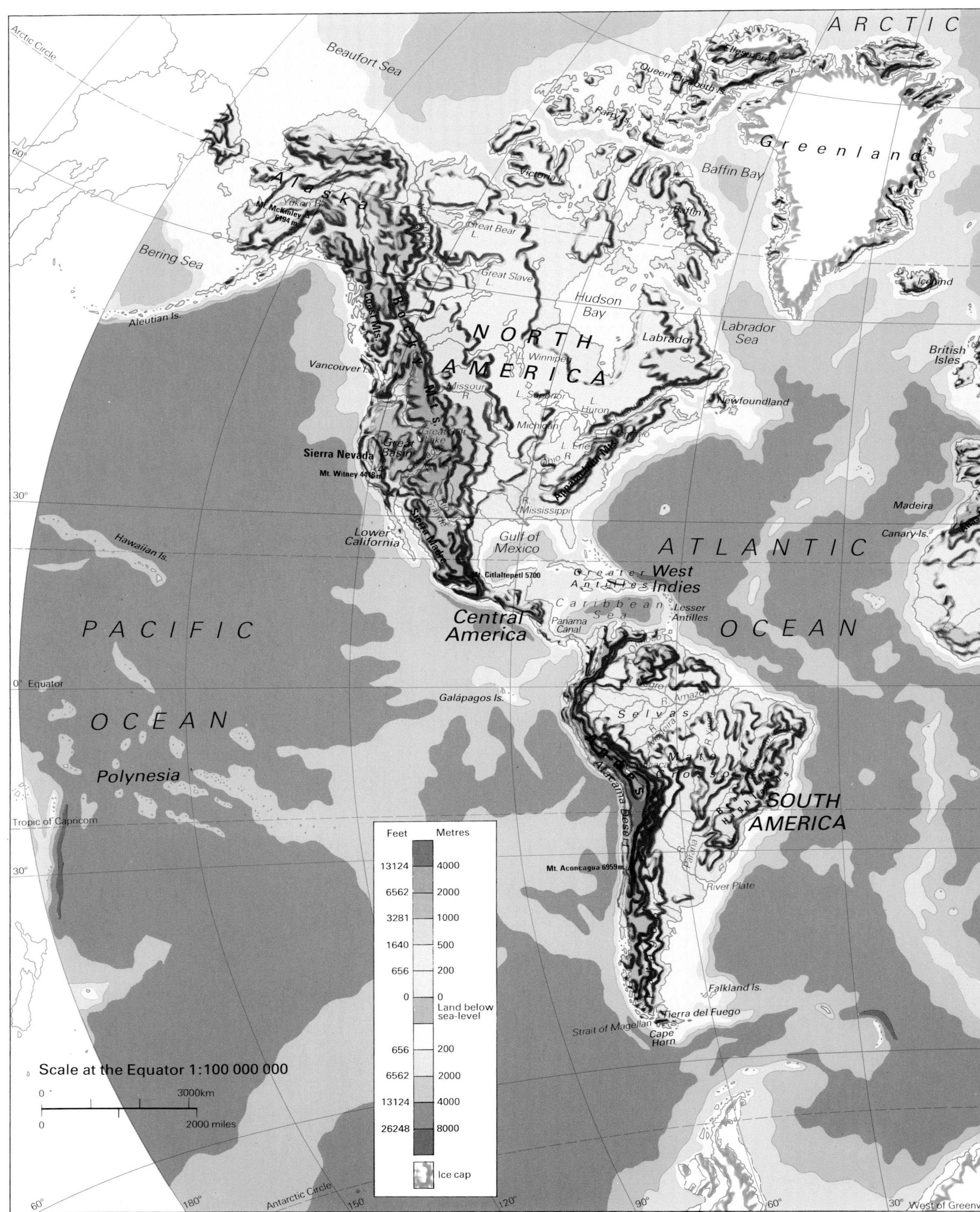

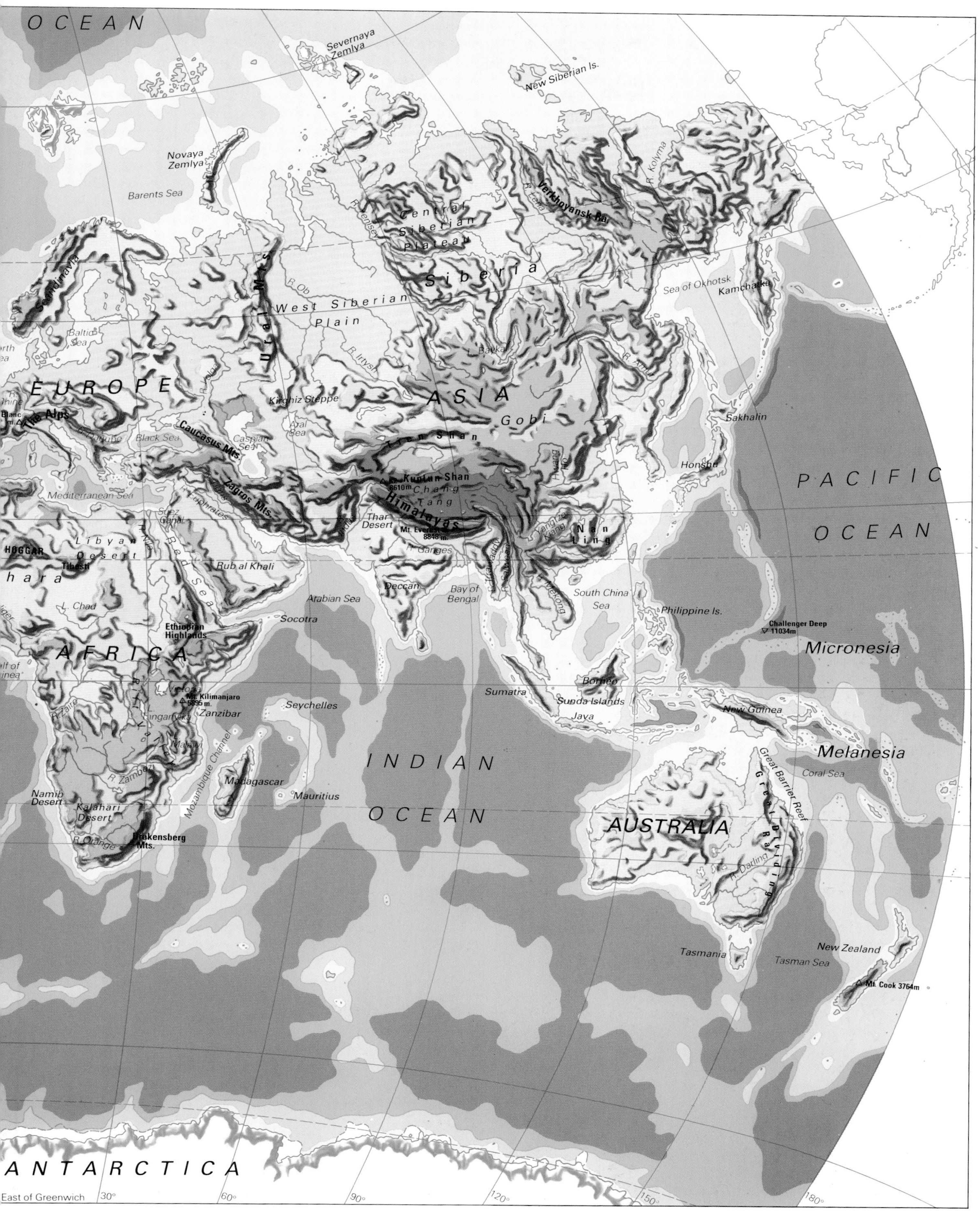
OCEAN
Severnaya Zemlya
New Siberian Is.
Novaya Zemlya
Barents Sea
Verkhoyansk Ra.
Central Siberian Plateau
Siberia
Sea of Okhotsk
Kamchatka
West Siberian Plain
Baltic Sea
EUROPE
The Alps
Ural Mts.
Kirghiz Steppe
ASIA
Gobi
Sakhalin
Caucasus Mts.
Black Sea
Caspian Sea
Aral Sea
Tien Shan
Kunlun Shan
Chang Tang
Himalayas
Honshu
PACIFIC
OCEAN
Mediterranean Sea
Zagros Mts.
Suez Canal
Thar Desert
Mt. Everest 8848 m.
Nan Ling
Libyan Desert
HOGGAR
Tibesti
Sahara
Rub al Khali
Red Sea
Deccan
Bay of Bengal
Arabian Sea
South China Sea
Philippine Is.
L. Chad
Ethiopian Highlands
Socotra
Challenger Deep 11034m
Micronesia
AFRICA
Mt. Kilimanjaro 5895 m.
Zanzibar
Seychelles
Sumatra
Borneo
Sunda Islands
Java
New Guinea
INDIAN
OCEAN
Melanesia
Coral Sea
Madagascar
Mauritius
Mozambique Channel
Namib Desert
Kalahari Desert
Drakensberg Mts.
AUSTRALIA
Great Barrier Reef
Great Dividing Range
Tasmania
New Zealand
Tasman Sea
Mt. Cook 3764m
ANTARCTICA
East of Greenwich
30°
60°
90°
120°
150°
180°

World Political Map

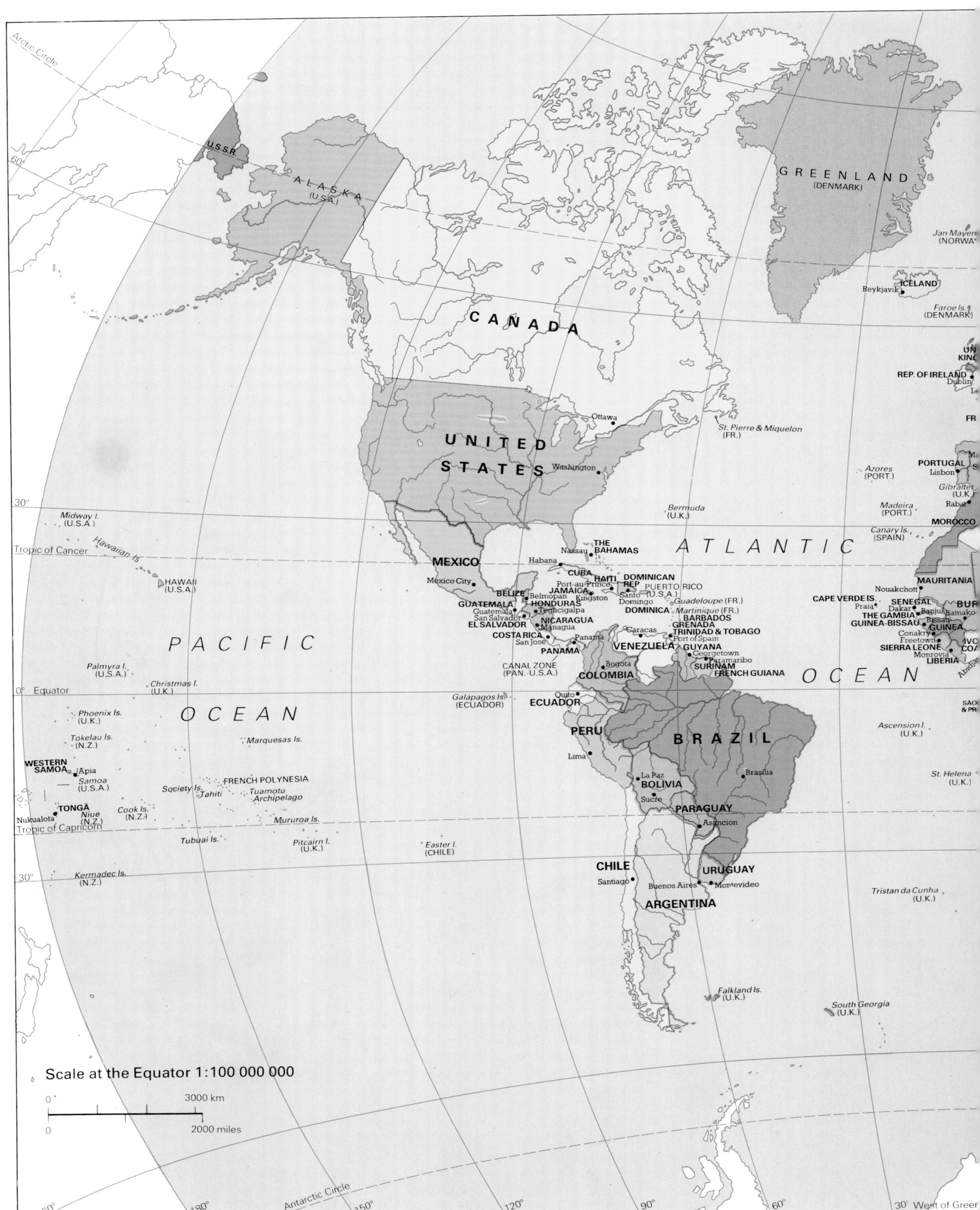

UNION OF SOVIET SOCIALIST REPUBLICS
Moscow
SWEDEN
FINLAND
Helsinki
Oslo
Stockholm
POLAND
Berlin
Warsaw
GERMANY
Prague
CZECH
Vienna
Budapest
AUSTRIA
HUNGARY
Belgrade
ROMANIA
Bucharest
YUGOSLAVIA
Sofia
BULGARIA
ITALY
Rome
Tirana
ALBANIA
Ankara
TURKEY
GREECE
Athens
Tunis
MALTA
TUNISIA
Tripoli
CYPRUS
Nicosia
LEB
SYRIA
Beirut
Damascus
ISRAEL
Jerusalem
Amman
JORDAN
Baghdad
IRAQ
Tehran
IRAN
KUWAIT
LIBYA
Cairo
EGYPT
SAUDI ARABIA
Riyadh
BAHRAIN
QATAR
Abu Dhabi
Muscat
OMAN
UNITED ARAB EMIRATES
YEMEN
Sana
SOUTH YEMEN
Aden
DJIBOUTI
Kabul
AFGHANISTAN
Islamabad
PAKISTAN
Delhi
NEPAL
Katmandu
Thimbu
BHUTAN
Dacca
BANGLADESH
INDIA
SRI LANKA
Colombo
MALDIVES
Male
MONGOLIA
Ulan Bator
CHINA
Beijing
N KOREA
Pyongyang
Seoul
S KOREA
JAPAN
Tokyo
Taipei
TAIWAN
MACAO (PORT.)
HONG KONG (U.K.)
Hanoi
BURMA
Rangoon
LAOS
Vientiane
THAILAND
VIETNAM
Bangkok
CAMBODIA
Phnom Penh
Manila
PHILIPPINES
BRUNEI
Kuala Lumpur
MALAYSIA
SINGAPORE
INDONESIA
Djakarta
PAPUA NEW GUINEA
Port Moresby
SOLOMON IS.
Honiara
NAURU
KIRIBATI
Tarawa
TUVALU
Funafuti
Wallis & Futuna Is. (FR.)
New Hebrides
VANUATU
Vila
Suva
FIJI
New Caledonia (FR.)
AUSTRALIA
Canberra
NEW ZEALAND
Wellington
PACIFIC OCEAN
Ryukyu Is. (JAPAN)
Bonin Is. (JAPAN)
Marcus I. (JAPAN)
Wake I. (U.S.A.)
Mariana Is. (U.S.A.)
Guam I. (U.S.A.)
PACIFIC ISLANDS TRUST TERRITORY (U.S.A./U.N.)
Marshall Is.
Palau Is.
Caroline Is.
NIGER
CHAD
N Djamena
Khartoum
SUDAN
NIGERIA
Lagos
CENTRAL AFRICAN REP.
Bangui
Yaounde
ETHIOPIA
Addis Ababa
SOMALI REP.
Mogadishu
UGANDA
Kampala
KENYA
Nairobi
ZAIRE
Libreville
GABON
CONGO
Brazzaville
RWANDA
Kigali
BURUNDI
Bujumbura
Kinshasa
CABINDA (ANG.)
Dodoma
TANZANIA
Luanda
ANGOLA
ZAMBIA
Lusaka
MALAWI
Lilongwe
MOZAMBIQUE
Harare
ZIMBABWE
NAMIBIA
WALVIS BAY (S. AFR.)
BOTSWANA
Gaborone
Pretoria
Maputo
Mbabane
SWAZILAND
Maseru
LESOTHO
REP. OF SOUTH AFRICA
Cape Town
SEYCHELLES
Victoria
COMORO IS.
Moroni
Tananarive
MADAGASCAR
MAURITIUS
Port Louis
Réunion (FR.)
INDIAN OCEAN
Cocos Is. (AUSTRALIA)
Amsterdam I. (FR.)
Prince Edward Is. (S. AFRICA)
Kerguelen I. (FR.)
Antarctica
East of Greenwich
30°
60°
90°
120°
150°
180°

World Facts

The Continents

	Area km²	Area mi²	Population	Highest point
Asia	44,387,000	17,139,000	2,693,000,000	Everest, 8,848 m (29,029 ft)
Africa	30,330,000	11,711,000	521,000,000	Kilimanjaro, 5,895 m (19,341 ft)
North America	21,515,000	8,307,000	252,000,000	Mt McKinley, 6,194 m (20,322 ft)
Latin America*	20,566,000	7,941,000	393,000,000	Aconcagua, 6,960 m (22,835 ft)
Antarctica	13,209,000	5,100,000	—	Vinson Massif, 5,140 m (16,864 ft)
Europe	10,531,000	4,066,000	695,000,000	Mt Elbrus, 5,633 m (18,481 ft)
Australasia	8,510,000	3,285,000	24,000,000	Mt Wilhelm, 4,694 m (15,400 ft)

**including Mexico, Central America and the Caribbean*

Canyons: *largest,* Grand Canyon, north-central Arizona, USA, 349 km (217 mi) long; 6–20 km (4–13 mi) wide; up to 2,133 m (7,000 ft) deep.

Caves: *largest cave system,* Mammoth Cave National Park, Kentucky, USA, mapped passageways cover 345 km (214 mi); *deepest caves,* Réseau du Foillis, France, 1,402 m (4,600 ft); *largest cavern,* Sarawak Chamber in Gunung Mulu National Park, Sarawak, Malaysia, 700 m (2,297 ft) long, 300 m (984 ft) wide, 70 m (230 ft) lowest height.

Deltas: *largest,* Ganges-Brahmaputra in Bangladesh, 75,000 km² (29,000 mi²).

Depressions: *deepest point on land,* shoreline of the Dead Sea (Israel/Jordan), 392 m (1,286 ft) below sea level; *largest,* Caspian Sea basin (USSR/Iran).

Deserts: *largest,* Sahara, North Africa, about 8,400,000 km² (3,243,000 mi²).

Earthquakes: *most destructive in human life,* 1556 in Shensi province, China, killed an estimated 800,000 people; *most destructive of property,* 1923 earthquake in Sagami Bay, Japan, led to destruction of 570,000 houses in Tokyo/Yokohama, cost of damage estimated at £1,000 million (now more than four times that figure); *most intense,* Concepción, Chile, 9.5 on Richter scale.

Glaciers: *longest,* Lambert Glacier in Australian Antarctic Territory, up to 64 km (40 mi) wide, with Fish Glacier limb it forms an ice mass of more than 510 km (317 mi).

Ice sheets: *largest,* Antarctica, containing more than seven times as much ice as the next largest ice sheet of Greenland.

Islands: *largest,*	Area km²	Area mi²
Greenland	2,175,600	840,050
New Guinea	789,903	305,000
Borneo	736,000	284,187
Madagascar	587,041	226,670
Baffin Land	476,065	183,820
Sumatra	420,000	162,172
Honshū	227,414	87,810
Great Britain	229,885	88,764
Ellesmere	212,687	82,123
Victoria	212,198	81,935

Lakes: *largest,*	Area km²	Area mi²
Caspian Sea	371,800	143,560
Superior	82,409	31,820
Victoria Nyanza	68,100	26,295
Aral Sea	66,500	25,677
Huron	61,797	23,861
Michigan	58,016	22,401
Tanganyika	32,893	12,701
Great Bear	31,792	12,276
Baykal	31,500	12,163
Great Slave	28,438	10,981

deepest, Lake Baykal, 1,940 m (6,365 ft), or 1,485 m (4,872 ft) below sea level.

Mountains: *largest range,* Himalaya-Karakoram, which contains 96 of the world's 109 peaks that are over 7,315 m (24,000 ft). For list of peaks, see the article on Asia.

Peninsula: *largest,* the Arabian peninsula, about 3,250,000 km² (1,255,000 mi²).

Rivers: *longest,*	kilometres	miles
Nile	6,671	4,145
Amazon	6,437	4,000
Mississippi–Missouri–Red Rock	6,231	3,872
Chang Jiang (Yangtze)	5,800	3,604
Ob-Irtysh	5,410	3,362
Huang He (Hwang Ho)	4,845	3,010
Plate-Paraná	4,700	2,920
Mekong	4,500	2,796
Amur	4,416	2,744
Lena	4,400	2,734

largest river basin, Amazon, 7,045,000 km² (2,720,000 mi²); *greatest flow,* Amazon, average discharge, 120,000 m³sec (4,200,000 cusecs).

Volcanoes: *highest active,* Antofalla, Argentina, 6,450 m (21,161 ft); *largest crater,* Mt Aso, Japan, circumference 114 km (71 mi); *greatest eruption,* Santorini (Thira) in the Aegean Sea in about 1470 BC, 62 km³ (15 mi³) of rock removed by eruption.

Waterfalls: *highest,* Salto Angel, Venezuela, 979 m (3,212 ft).

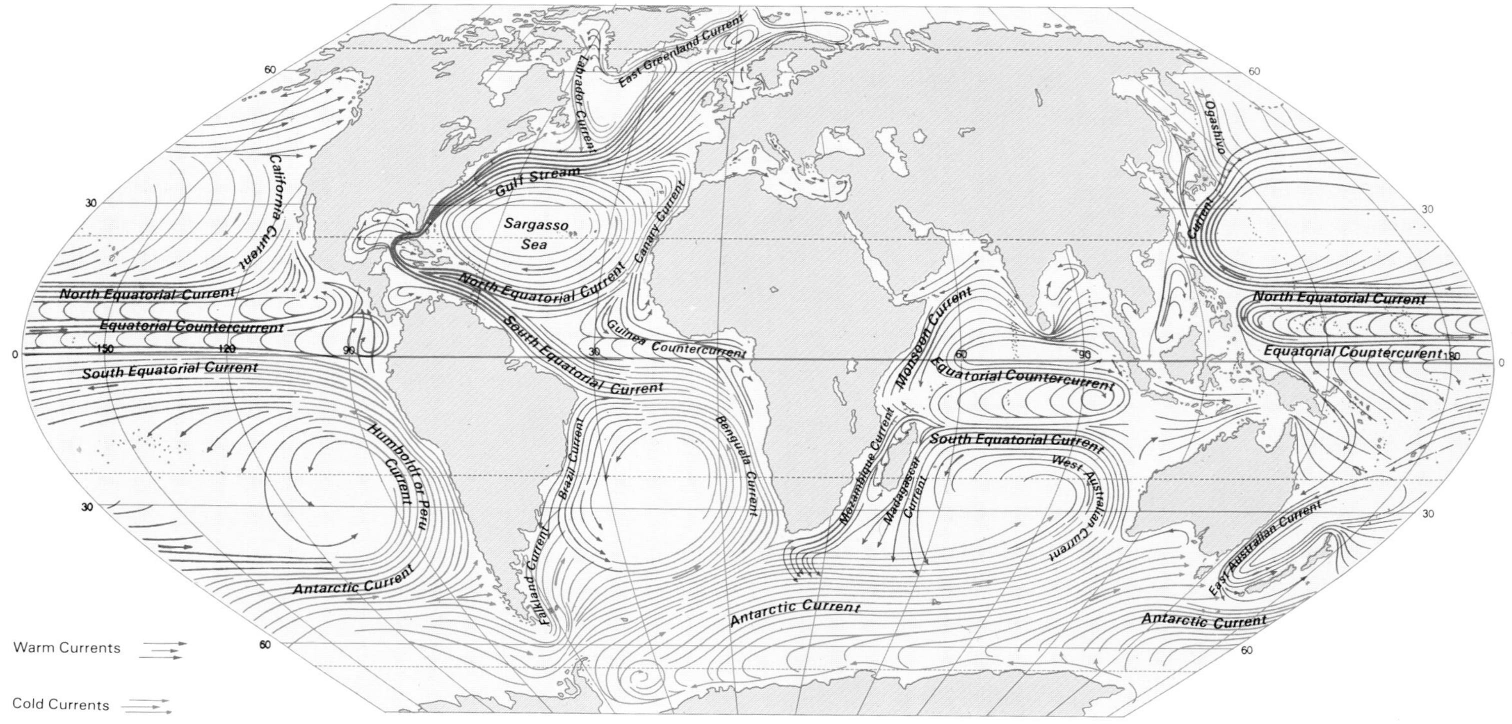

Below: Ocean currents follow distinct paths, which are related to the world's prevailing winds and to temperature and salinity differences. Ocean currents help to redistribute heat between the tropical and polar regions.

The Earth's Identity Card

Volume: 1,083,208,840,000 km³ (259,875,620,000 mi³).
Density (specific gravity): average, 5·41 g/cm³; continental crust, 2·7; oceanic crust, 3·0; upper mantle, 3·4; outer core, 10; centre of Earth, about 13·6.
Mass: 5,974 million million million tonnes (5,880 million million million tons).
Radius: 6,378 km (3,963 mi, equatorial radius); 6,357 km (3,950 mi, polar radius).
Circumference: 40,077 km (24,903 mi, equatorial); 40,009 km (24,861 mi, polar).
Surface area: 510,100,000 km² (196,961,460 mi²); dry land, 149,400,000 km² (57,686,820 mi²), or 29·3%; surface of oceans, 360,700,000 km² (139,274,640 mi²), or 70·7%.
Crust: oceanic crust averages 6 km (4 mi) in thickness; the maximum thickness of the continental crust is about 70 km (43 mi).

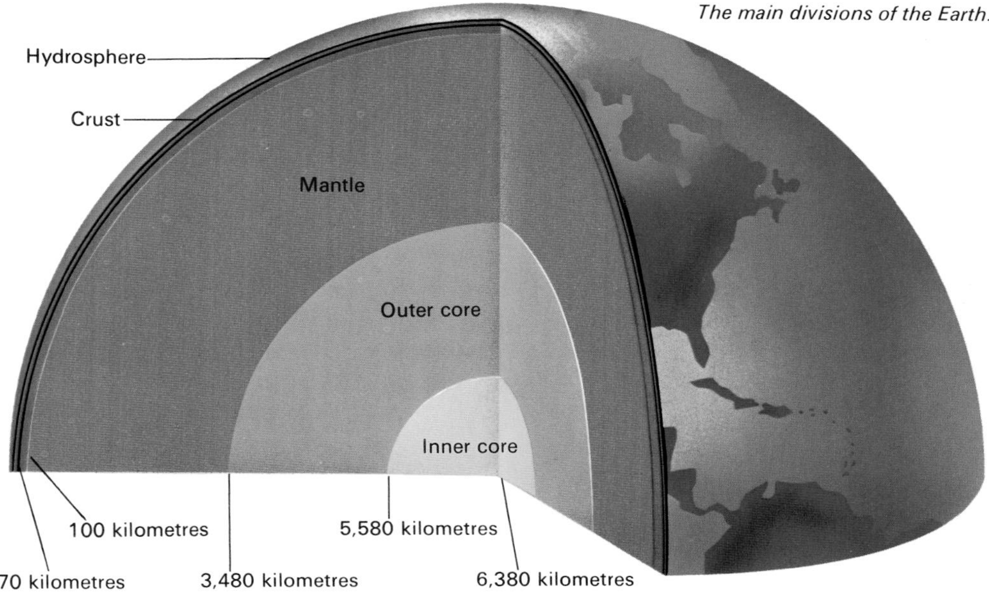

The main divisions of the Earth.

The Earth formed about 4,600 million years ago. At first, it may have been a huge ball of gas with a small rocky core, not unlike the modern planet Saturn. From this gaseous mass, our present rocky planet began to form into a solid molten mass.

For a long time, the Earth's blazing surface was no place for living organisms. But volcanic action released water vapour from the rocks into the atmosphere. As the Earth cooled, the water vapour condensed into clouds from which rain fell. Rainwater filled hollows on the surface, creating environments in which the first life forms, probably bacteria, could evolve.

For millions of years, the atmosphere around the Earth was probably poisonous, consisting mainly of nitrogen, sulphur dioxide and carbon dioxide, and all early life forms had to live in water to escape the burning ultraviolet rays from the Sun. About 1,900 million years ago, however, the first advanced oxygen-producing plants evolved. These plants had two main effects. First, through photosynthesis, they began to increase the amount of oxygen in the atmosphere. Second, some of the oxygen was converted into a layer of ozone in the stratosphere between 10 and 80 kilometres (6–50 miles) above the surface. This ozone layer absorbs and so blocks out much of the Sun's dangerous ultraviolet radiation. Slowly the scene was being set for an explosion of life forms, which occurred at the start of the Palaeozoic ('ancient life') era.

The history of the Earth in the last 600 million years is divided into three eras, which are subdivided into periods. The vast expanse of time before the Cambrian period, the first in the Palaeozoic era, is called the Pre-Cambrian. Pre-Cambrian rocks contain few fossils, probably because all early plants and animals were soft-bodied and decayed rapidly after death. But at the start of the Cambrian period, many organisms had hard parts and consequently stood a far better chance of being fossilized. As a result, Cambrian rocks are rich in fossils.

The geological time scale from the Cambrian period to the present day, with highlights of evolution, is as follows:

Cambrian period (600–500 million years ago): nearly all the main invertebrate animal groups evolved and, close to the end of the period, the first vertebrates, primitive armoured fishes, appeared.

Ordovician period (500–435 million years ago): fishes developed.

Silurian period (435–395 million years ago): the first land plants evolved.

Devonian period (395–345 million years ago): called the age of fishes, the Devonian period was marked by the evolution of amphibians.

Carboniferous period (345–280 million years ago): amphibians increased and the first reptiles evolved; coal was formed from swamp vegetation. In the USA, the Carboniferous period is divided into two periods, the Mississippian period (345–300 million years ago) and the Pennsylvanian period, which continued until 280 million years ago.

Permian period (280–230 million years ago): reptiles increased and amphibians became less important.

The Permian period is the final period of the Palaeozoic era. The following Mesozoic ('middle life') era contains three periods:

Triassic period (230–195 million years ago): the first dinosaurs and large sea reptiles evolved, as did primitive mammals.

Jurassic period (195–141 million years ago): dinosaurs were the dominant land animals; the first bird, *Archaeopteryx*, appeared.

Cretaceous period (141–65 million years ago): dinosaurs continued their reign, but they suffered sudden extinction at the end of the period; flowering plants evolved.

The Cenozoic ('new life') era consists of two periods, the Tertiary and the Quaternary. These periods are divided into shorter epochs. The Tertiary period (65–1·8 million years ago) consists of the following:

Palaeocene epoch (65–55 million years ago): mammals developed quickly.

Eocene epoch (55–38 million years ago): mammal types, including the earliest elephants and horse, increased rapidly; the Himalayas started to rise.

Oligocene epoch (38–22·5 million years ago): early apes evolved; the Alps began to rise near the end of the epoch.

Miocene epoch (22·5–6 million years ago): the number of mammal species began to decline.

Pliocene epoch (6–1·8 million years ago): early forms of people began to evolve alongside ape-like creatures.

The Quaternary period covers the last 1·8 million years. It contains two epochs:

Pleistocene epoch (1·8 million to 10,000 years ago): this epoch was marked by a great Ice Age in the northern hemisphere, animal extinctions and the emergence of *Homo sapiens*.

Holocene or **Recent epoch** (10,000 years ago to the present): the rise of modern Man.

World Population

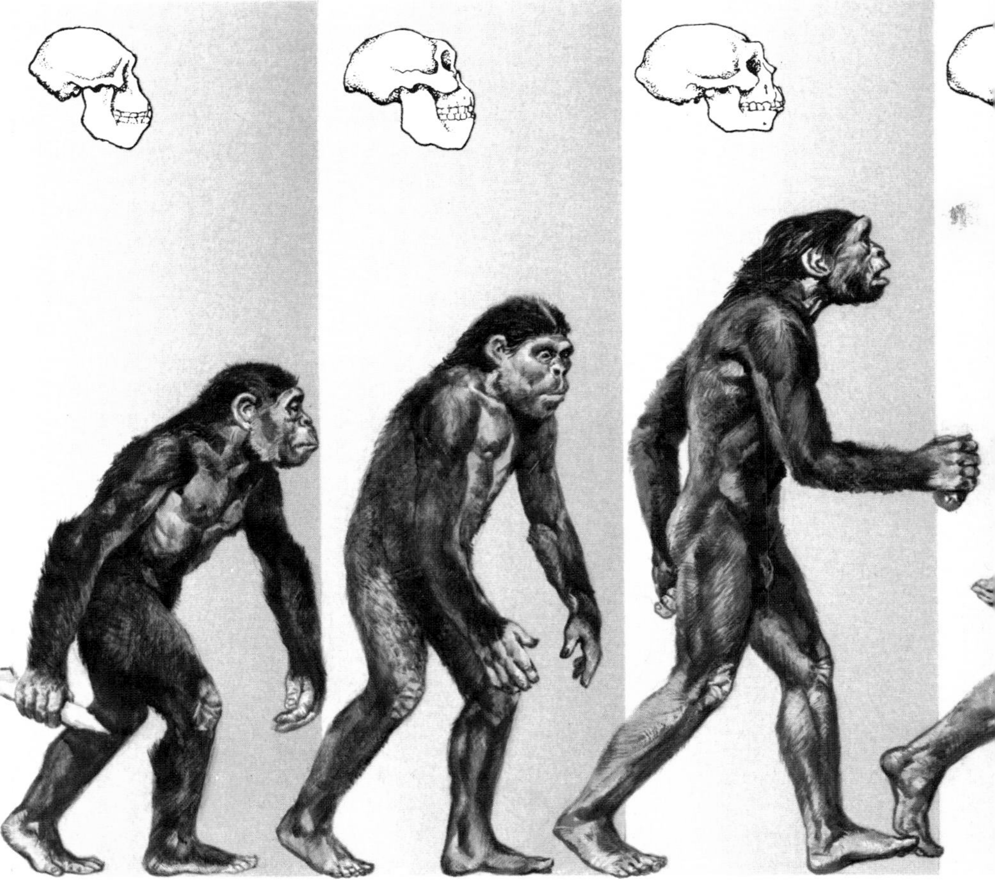

Australopithecus
height: 1·20 m (3·9 ft)

Paranthropus
height: 1·25–1·55 m (4·1–5·1 ft)

Pithecanthropus
height: 1·60 m (5·2 ft)

The world's population is unevenly distributed, with the vast majority crowded on only about 10 per cent of the world's land area. This imbalance is reflected in the tables on this page. For example, the USSR and Canada are the largest countries, but they are thinly populated by comparison with China and India.

The 20th century has been marked by a population explosion, with the world's population doubling in the 50 years between 1925 and 1975. By 1980 it stood at 4,415 million and was increasing by the high rate of 1·8 per cent a year.

The highest rates of increase, as shown in the table on the opposite page, are occurring in the developing continent of Africa, while the lowest rate is in Europe, excluding the USSR. In fact in such European countries as Austria, West Germany, Switzerland and the UK, the rate in 1975–80 was either zero or the population was actually in decline. The relationship between the rate of population growth and the degree of economic development is highlighted by Japan, Asia's only truly industrialized nation, where the rate has been steadily falling. It reached 0·9 per cent a year in 1975–80, the lowest rate in Asia. Most developed countries, with their low birth and death rates, have comparatively balanced population structures, with, for example, roughly similar numbers in each age group, although the proportion of older people is increasing. On the other hand, developing countries, with their high birth rates, have a disproportionately young population – in many countries, 40 to 50 per cent of the population is under 15 years of age. This means that the developing countries which most

Largest Countries by Area

	Area (km²)	Area (mi²)
USSR	22,402,000	8,650,010
Canada	9,976,139	3,852,019
China	9,596,961	3,705,610
United States	9,363,123	3,615,319
Brazil	8,511,965	3,286,668
Australia	7,686,848	2,968,071
India	3,287,590	1,269,415
Argentina	2,766,889	1,068,360
Sudan	2,505,813	967,553
Algeria	2,381,741	919,646
Zaire	2,345,409	905,617
Saudi Arabia	2,149,690	830,045
Indonesia	2,027,087	782,705
Mexico	1,972,547	761,646
Libya	1,759,540	679,399
Iran	1,648,000	636,331
Mongolia	1,565,000	604,283
Peru	1,285,216	496,252
Chad	1,284,000	495,782
Niger	1,267,000	489,218
Angola	1,246,700	481,380
Mali	1,240,000	478,793
Ethiopia	1,221,900	471,804
South Africa	1,221,037	471,471
Colombia	1,138,914	439,761

Largest Countries by Population

China	1,024,950,000
India	685,184,000
USSR	278,719,000
United States	235,100,000
Indonesia	158,000,000
Brazil	135,500,000
Japan	120,055,000
Bangladesh	96,000,000
Nigeria	88,847,000
Pakistan	88,000,000
Mexico	76,790,000
West Germany	61,421,000
Vietnam	60,000,000
Italy	58,085,000
United Kingdom	55,780,000
France	54,832,000
Philippines	54,400,000
Thailand	51,420,000
Turkey	50,583,000
Egypt	48,000,000
Iran	43,830,000
Ethiopia	42,000,000
South Korea	40,000,000
Spain	38,671,000
Poland	37,340,000

Major World Cities

	Population
Mexico City (Mexico)	16,000,000
Shanghai (China)	11,890,000
Tokyo (Japan)	11,807,000
Buenos Aires (Argentina)	10,865,000
Calcutta (India)	9,230,000
Peking (Beijing, China)	9,166,000
Paris (France)	8,707,000
Cairo (Egypt)	8,540,000
Moscow (USSR)	8,537,000
São Paulo (Brazil)	8,490,000
Sŏul (Seoul, South Korea)	8,367,000
Bombay (India)	8,227,000
Tianjin (Tientsin, China)	7,760,000
New York City (USA)	7,071,000
London (UK)	6,755,000
Jakarta (Indonesia)	6,506,000
Chongqing (Chungking, China)	6,000,000
Bangkok (Thailand)	5,468,000
Karachi (Pakistan)	5,103,000
Rio de Janeiro (Brazil)	5,093,000
Bogotà (Colombia)	5,000,000
Guangzhou (Canton, China)	5,000,000
Leningrad (USSR)	4,779,000
Istanbul (Turkey)	4,741,000
Tehran (Iran)	4,496,000
Shenyang (China)	4,400,000

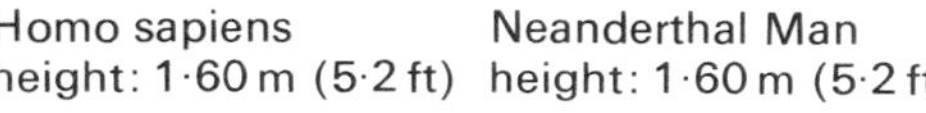

Homo sapiens height: 1·60 m (5·2 ft)
Neanderthal Man height: 1·60 m (5·2 ft)
Cro-Magnon Man height: 1·82 m (6 ft)

Left: The course of human evolution is studied by comparing fossil remains, especially the skulls of man-like primates, although the amount of information available to scientists is still limited and interpretations of that evidence differ. Primates evolved in the Palaeocene epoch and most scientists now agree that people and apes had a common ancestor in a primate named Ramapithecus, *which lived in the Miocene epoch. After* Ramapithecus, *the line of evolution is indistinct, but a man-like ape* Australopithecus *evolved in the Pliocene epoch, more than two million years ago. The Australopithecines included* Paranthropus robustus, *but scientists are not agreed as to whether they are our ancestors or whether another man-like species was living at the same time. On the evolutionary scale, the upright* Pithecanthropus *represents an advance on the* Australopithecines. *The next in line were* Sinanthropus *and* Homo sapiens, *one type of which was Neanderthal Man, who is known scientifically as* Homo sapiens neanderthalensis. *Neanderthal Man lived during the Pleistocene Ice Age and his remains have shown that he was a cave dweller. But Neanderthal Man became extinct, having been supplanted by Cro-Magnon Man, who is scientifically known as* Homo sapiens sapiens, *the same species as Modern Man. In about 8000 BC, at the start of the Holocene epoch, the world contained perhaps eight million people. But following the invention of farming in about 6000 BC and the growth of towns and cities, the rate of population increase accelerated. By AD 100, the human population had risen to 300 million. The 1,000 million mark was passed in the 1800s, the 2,000 million mark in the 1920s and should pass the 6,000 million mark by the year 2000.*

lack financial resources are those that must pay exceptionally large sums to educate and keep healthy a section of the population which contributes nothing to the economy. By contrast, the developed world is faced with the less onerous problem of providing pensions for its older citizens.

Annual Rates of Population Increase

	1975–80
Africa	2·9%
America, North	0·8%
America, Latin	2·7%
Asia, East (inc. China and Japan)	1·3%
Asia, South	2·5%
Europe	0·4%
Oceania (inc. Australia)	1·5%
USSR	0·9%

Life Expectancies

Countries with high average life expectancies at birth (1980) included:

Japan 76; Denmark 75; Netherlands 75; Norway 75; Switzerland 75; Greece 74; Australia 74; Canada 74; France 74; USA 74; Belgium 73; Bulgaria 73; Ireland 73; Italy 73; New Zealand 73; Spain 73; W Germany 73; UK 73.

Countries with low average life expectancies at birth (1980) included:

Afghanistan 37; Upper Volta 39; Ethiopia 40; Chad 41; Angola 42; Burundi 42; Yemen A R 42; Mali 43; Mauritania 43; Niger 43; Senegal 43; Central African Republic 43; Bhutan 44; Nepal 44.

Below: Rush hour crowds stream over London Bridge. London's population has been declining in recent years. This is because many workers have chosen to live outside the city and to commute to their work each day.

Economies

The per capita gross national product (GNP), the total domestic and foreign output of a country divided by its population, is a measure of a country's wealth. On this basis, some of the oil-rich nations of the Middle East were among the world's richest in 1980:

United Arab Emirates (US $ 30,070)
Qatar ($26,080) Kuwait ($22,840)

Among the developed nations, those with high per capita GNPs included:

Switzerland ($16,440)	Iceland ($11,330)
Luxembourg ($14,510)	Austria ($10,230)
West Germany ($13,590)	Canada ($10,130)
Sweden ($13,520)	Japan ($9,890)
Denmark ($12,950)	Australia ($9,820)
Norway ($12,650)	Finland ($9,720)
Belgium ($12,180)	UK ($7,920)
France ($11,730)	East Germany ($7,180)
Netherlands ($11,470)	New Zealand ($7,090)
USA ($11,360)	Italy ($6,480)

At the bottom of the scale, countries with low per capita GNPs included:

Bhutan ($80)	Rwanda ($200)
Bangladesh ($120)	Zaire ($220)
Chad ($120)	Malawi ($230)
Nepal ($140)	India ($240)
Ethiopia ($140)	Gambia ($250)
Guinea-Bissau ($160)	Tanzania ($260)
Burma ($180)	Sierra Leone ($270)
Upper Volta ($190)	Mozambique ($270)
Mali ($190)	Sri Lanka ($270)
Burundi ($200)	Uganda ($280)

Note: No recent figures exist for Afghanistan, Kampuchea, Laos, Somalia and Vietnam.

In most developed countries, agriculture is highly mechanized and only a small proportion of the workforce is employed on the land, with a far higher proportion in industry, including mining and manufacturing, and service industries. The breakdown of the workforce in selected developed economies in 1980 was as follows:

	Agriculture	Industry	Services
UK	2%	42%	56%
USA	2%	32%	66%
Belgium	3%	41%	56%
West Germany	4%	46%	50%
Canada	5%	29%	66%
Sweden	5%	34%	61%
Switzerland	5%	46%	49%
Australia	6%	33%	61%
Netherlands	6%	45%	49%
Norway	7%	37%	56%
Denmark	7%	35%	58%
Israel	7%	36%	57%
France	8%	39%	53%
New Zealand	9%	35%	56%
East Germany	10%	50%	40%
Czechoslovakia	11%	48%	41%
Italy	11%	45%	44%
Japan	12%	39%	49%
USSR	14%	45%	41%

By contrast, an extremely high percentage of the workforce in the poorest developing nations works in agriculture, as follows:

	Agriculture	Industry	Services
Bhutan	93%	2%	5%
Nepal	93%	2%	5%
Rwanda	91%	2%	7%
Niger	91%	3%	6%
Madagascar	90%	3%	7%

Countries which occupy an intermediate position are as follows:

	Agriculture	Industry	Services
Bangladesh	74%	11%	15%
China	71%	17%	12%
India	69%	13%	18%
Philippines	46%	17%	37%
Brazil	30%	24%	46%

The most industrialized countries have the highest proportion of city and town dwellers, although, in many developed nations, urbanization is now proceeding quickly, causing urban unemployment and the mushrooming of squalid shanty towns, because of lack of housing. In 1980, the percentages of people living in urban areas in selected countries were as follows:

UK 91%	Japan 78%	Czechoslovakia 63%
Australia 89%	France 78%	USSR 62%
Israel 89%	USA 77%	Poland 57%
Sweden 87%	E Germany 77%	India 22%
W Germany 85%	Netherlands 76%	China 13%
New Zealand 85%	Brazil 68%	Rwanda 4%
Denmark 84%	Mexico 67%	Burundi 2%
Canada 80%		

The main food crops in any country are determined by the climate, but everywhere the basic foods are cereals. The following table shows the top five countries in the production of four cereal crops in 1980:

Barley	Maize	Rice	Wheat
USSR	USA	China	USSR
France	China	India	USA
Canada	Brazil	Indonesia	China
UK	Romania	Bangladesh	India
W Germany	Mexico	Thailand	France

Leading meat and fish producers in 1980 are listed below:

Beef and Veal	Pork	Mutton and Lamb	Fish
USA	China	USSR	Japan
USSR	USA	New Zealand	USSR
Argentina	USSR	Australia	China
Brazil	W Germany	China	USA
France	France	Turkey	Peru

Beverage crops are important in world trade. Major producers in 1980 were as follows:

Cocoa	Coffee	Tea	Grapes
Ivory Coast	Brazil	India	Italy
Brazil	Colombia	China	France
Ghana	Ivory Coast	Sri Lanka	Spain
Nigeria	Indonesia	USSR	USSR
Cameroun	Mexico	Turkey	USA

Leading producers of vegetable fibres in 1980 were as follows:

Cotton (lint)	Flax	Hemp	Jute
USSR	USSR	USSR	India
China	China	India	China
USA	France	China	Bangladesh
India	Poland	Romania	Thailand
Pakistan	Egypt	Hungary	Burma

Besides agriculture, mining is the other industry supplying raw materials for manufacturing. The top nations producing minerals used to generate energy in 1980 were:

Coal	Petroleum	Natural gas	Uranium
USA	USSR	USA	USA
USSR	Saudi Arabia	USSR	S Africa
China	USA	Netherlands	Canada
Poland	Iraq	Canada	Niger
UK	Venezuela	UK	France

The major producers in 1980 of four basic metallic ores were as follows:

Bauxite	Copper	Iron ore	Zinc
Australia	USA	USSR	Canada
Guinea	USSR	Australia	USSR
Jamaica	Chile	USA	Peru
USSR	Canada	Brazil	Australia
Surinam	Zambia	China	USA

The most industrialized countries of the world are in North America, Europe, including the USSR, and Australasia. The other continents are predominantly in the developing world, although Japan is an obvious exception. The following table shows the major producers of three industrial metals in 1980:

Aluminium	Refined copper	Crude steel
USA	USA	USSR
USSR	USSR	Japan
Japan	Japan	USA
Canada	Chile	W Germany
W Germany	Zambia	China

The leading producers of such consumer goods as radios and television sets in 1980 (with their percentage share of world production) was as follows:

Radios	Television sets
Hong Kong (37%)	Japan (23%)
Japan (17%)	USA (16%)
USA (9%)	USSR (12%)
USSR (8%)	South Korea (8%)
South Korea (4%)	West Germany (7%)

Japan's importance as an industrial and trading power in the modern world is highlighted by its pre-eminence in its production of vehicles and ships

Cars	Commercial vehicles	Merchant vessels
Japan (24%)	Japan (42%)	Japan (52%)
USA (22%)	USA (17%)	S Korea (5%)
W Germany (12%)	USSR (8%)	USA (4%)
France (12%)	Canada (6%)	Spain (4%)
Italy (5%)	Brazil (*)	Poland (3%)

*1980 figure unavailable

Opposite: A Fiat car factory in Italy makes great use of automated machinery. Automation, together with the use of computers and robots, has been revolutionizing industrial production in many countries in recent years.

COMAU
INDUSTRIALE

Climate

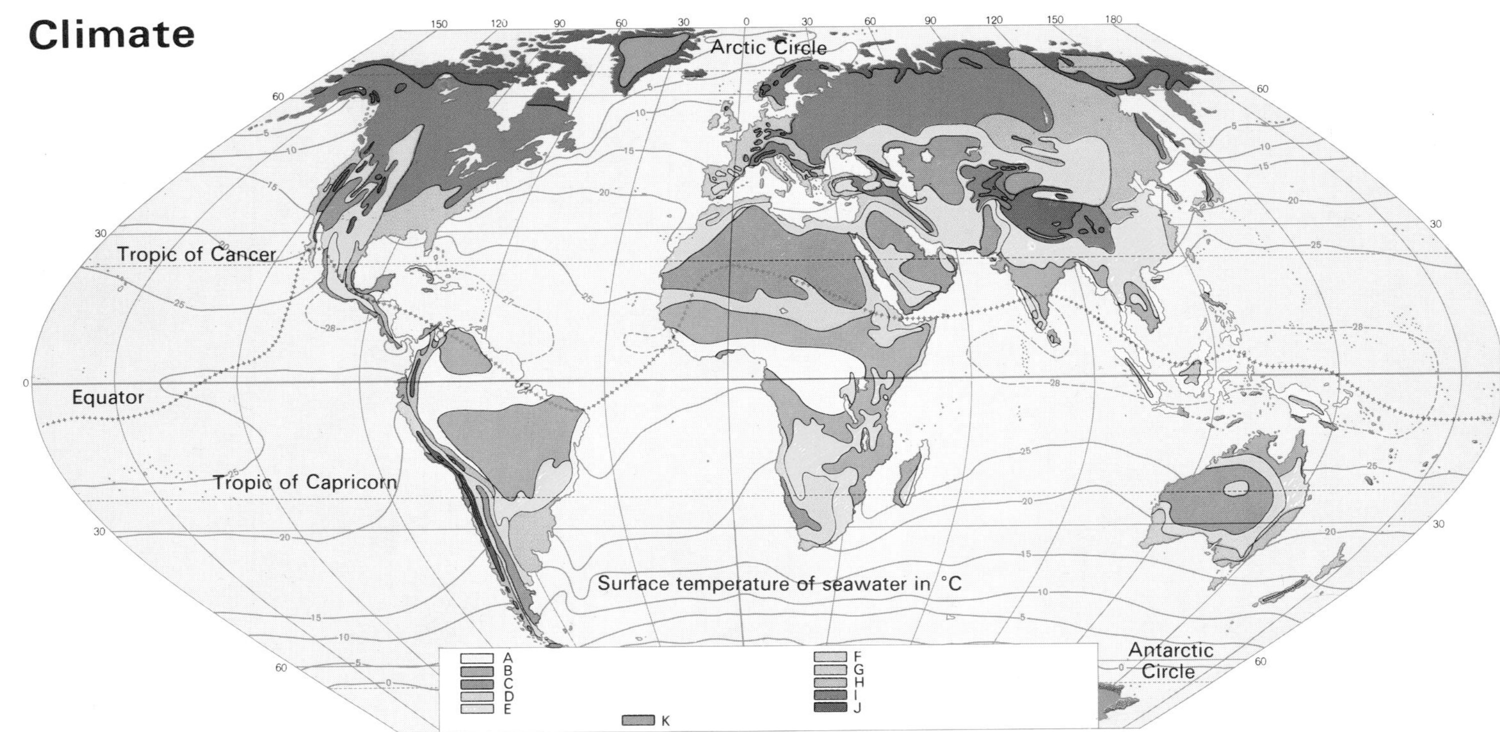

Above: A map of climatic zones. The key is as follows: **A** *is the wet tropical climate with rain in every month (rain forest type);* **B** *is the wet tropical climate with a dry season (savannah);* **C** *is desert;* **D** *is the semi-arid steppe climate;* **E** *is the warm, moist temperature climate, with a dry winter;* **F** *is the warm, moist temperate climate with a dry summer;* **G** *is moist temperate;* **H** *is the cold temperate climate with a dry winter;* **I** *is the cold climate with a wet (snowy) winter (taiga);* **J** *is tundra with a long winter and a brief summer; and* **K** *is the true polar climate.*

While weather is the condition of the air at a particular moment or over a short period of time, climate is the average or usual weather of a place. Any description of climate is, therefore, based on statistics acquired over a long period, usually several decades. In classifying climates, climatologists are concerned not only with absolute values of weather features, such as temperatures and rainfall amounts, but also with the reliability of such features.

Circulation of the Atmosphere

Climate is obviously related to latitude, because the Sun's heating is most intense in the tropics and least effective near the poles. This difference between the cold and dense air of the polar regions and the warm, light air of the tropics is responsible for the general circulation of the atmosphere, with a heat exchange between the tropics and the poles. Winds are the chief mechanism whereby the heat exchange occurs.

At the equator, radiation from the heated surface warms the lower air, which expands and rises, creating a band of low air pressure around the Earth, called the doldrums. The rising air eventually cools and spreads out north and south. It finally sinks back to the surface around latitudes 30° North and 30° South. These latitudinal zones are called the horse latitudes. Here the sinking air creates a high pressure zone, from which air currents (winds) flow outwards both to the north and south.

The winds that flow back towards the doldrums are the north-east trade winds in the northern hemisphere and the south-east trade winds in the southern hemisphere. (Winds do not blow directly north-south, because they are deflected by the Coriolis effect, caused by the rotation of the Earth.) Also flowing from the horse latitudes are the south-westerly winds of the northern hemisphere and the north-westerly winds of the southern

Below: The maps show the main pressure systems that affect climate in January, summer in the southern hemisphere, and July, summer in the northern hemisphere. The July map shows the summer monsoon in India, caused by the creation of an intense low pressure system over Asia.

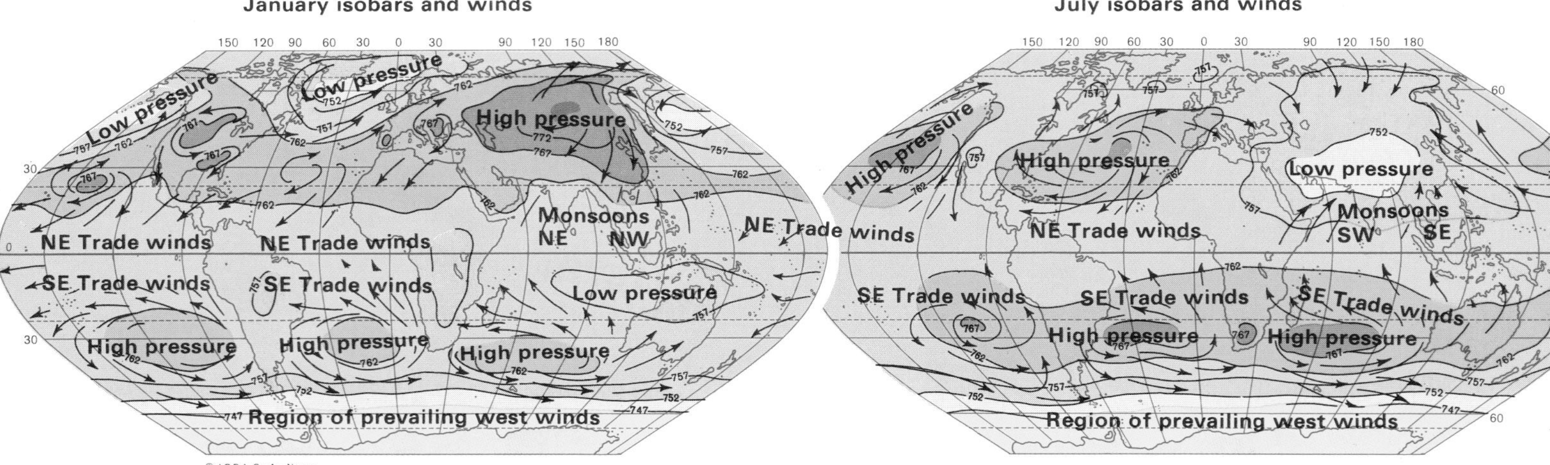

Climatic Extremes

Highest shade temperature: 58°C (136·4°F) at Al-Aziziyah, south of Tripoli in Libya (in the Sahara), 1922.
Maximum average annual temperature: 34·4°C (94°F) at Dallol, in the Danakil depression of eastern Ethiopia.
Lowest screen temperature: −88·3°C (−126·9°F), recorded at the Russian Vostok station in Antarctica, August 1960.
Minimum average annual temperature: −57·8°C (−72°F), at the Pole of Cold in Antarctica (78° South, 96° East).
Sunshine: *maximum*, eastern Sahara, more than 4,300 hours per year (97%); *minimum*, North Pole, nil for 186 days.
Maximum rainfall: *one year*, 26,461 mm (1,041·8in) at Cherrapunji in north-eastern India in 1860–61; *one month*, 9,299 mm (366·1 in) at Cherrapunji, July 1861.
Maximum average annual rainfall: 11,455 mm (451 in) at Mt Wai'ale'ale on Kauai Island in Hawaii.
Driest place: Calama, Atacama desert in Chile, no rain for hundreds of years.
Hailstones: the heaviest single hailstone weighed 0·76 kg (1·67 lb). It was found at Coffeyville, Kansas, USA in 1970.
Most destructive hurricane: Hurricane Betsy in 1965 caused so much damage in the USA that insurance companies had to pay out $715 million in compensation.
Killer storm: an estimated one million people were drowned when a storm in the Bay of Bengal caused floods on islands in the Ganges delta in Bangladesh in 1970.
Worst tornado: 689 people were killed by a tornado in the south-central USA in 1925.
Lightning: a bolt of lightning killed 21 people in a hut in Zimbabwe in 1975.

hemisphere. The westerlies in both hemispheres meet up with cold air from the poles – winds called polar easterlies – along a boundary named the polar front. It is here that the low air pressure depressions, or cyclones, of the middle latitudes form from the intermingling of the polar and tropical air.

Influence of the Terrain

Climatic zones do not occur in parallel latitudinal bands, because several factors complicate this simple pattern. For example, the terrain affects climate, and temperatures fall by 6·5°C for every 1,000 metres (1°F for every 280 feet). In consequence, polar and tundra climates can be found on the equator around the peaks of such high mountains as Kilimanjaro in East Africa.

High mountain ranges also deflect winds, and force them to rise and become turbulent. When warm onshore winds rise over mountain ranges that border coastlines, the ascending air is cooled. Because cold air can hold much less invisible water vapour than warm air, water vapour condenses as the air rises into tiny water droplets or ice crystals. Large quantities of these droplets and crystals form clouds, which bring rain and snow to the windward slopes. Beyond the crest of the mountains, the winds blow down the leeward slopes, generally becoming warmer as they descend. These winds have a drying effect. They tend to pick up moisture by evaporation rather than lose it through precipitation.

Nearness to the Sea

Another factor which profoundly affects climate is proximity to the sea. The sea has a moderating influence on the climate of coastlands. This is because water heats more slowly than land, but it retains heat far longer than the land. By day, therefore, the land in coastal regions heats up swiftly and the lower layers of air are warmed. The warm air rises, creating a temporary low pressure, into which cool air from the sea is drawn. At night, the land cools quickly, and cold air flows from the land towards the sea, because the pressure gradient between land and sea has been reversed.

Water also transports heat, and so warm ocean currents flowing polewards from the tropics temper the winter cold of some coastlands, while cold currents from polar regions chill subtropical and tropical coastlands in summer. For example, the Gulf Stream is a warm current which flows from the Caribbean Sea across the North Atlantic Ocean. Its extension, called the North Atlantic Drift, brings mild conditions to the British Isles and even to northern Norway, where ports north of the Arctic Circle never freeze up in winter. Conversely, the cold Humboldt and Benguela currents chill the west coasts of South America and Africa respectively.

In the hearts of continents, far from the moderating influence of the oceans, climates tend to be extreme. Intense heating of the land in summer results in hot days, unalleviated by cool sea breezes, while temperatures often plummet at night. Cooling in winter in the middle latitudes can lead to the development of large, cold high pressure air masses, which are responsible for prolonged spells of freezing weather.

There are broadly four main types of air masses. The polar continental air masses are cold and dry in winter and warm in summer. They contrast with polar maritime air masses which are moist and relatively warm. Similarly, tropical continental air masses, like that over the Sahara, are warm and dry, compared with tropical maritime air masses which are warm and moist.

Reversals of wind directions, related to changes in the character of air masses

Below: The world maps show the main isotherms in degrees Centigrade for January and July. They reflect the annual migration of the overhead Sun, which is overhead at the Tropic of Capricorn ($23\frac{1}{2}$°S) on December 21, and at the Tropic of Cancer ($23\frac{1}{2}$°N) on June 21.

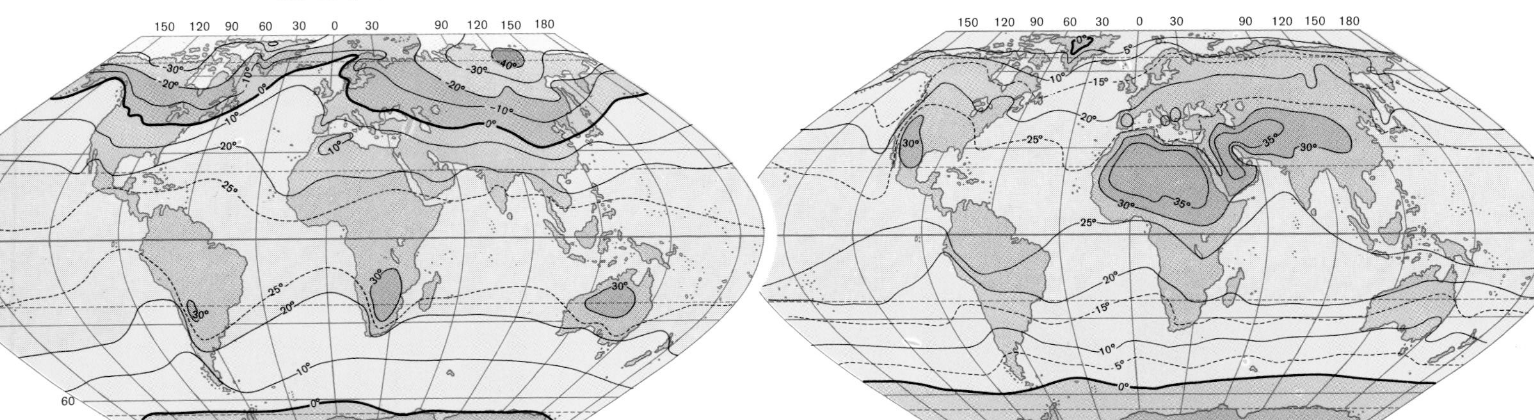

according to the season, are monsoons. The most developed monsoon occurs in southern Asia, where a high pressure air system develops in winter, from which blow the dry north-east trade winds. But rapid heating in spring, which occurs as the overhead Sun moves northwards, causes a marked low pressure air system to develop over northern India. The south-east trade winds are drawn across the equator and into this low pressure system. As they are sucked towards the land, they change direction and become south-west winds. Full of moisture evaporated from the Indian Ocean, they bring the summer rain on which Indian farmers rely for their annual crops.

Climatic Regions

Climatic regions can be defined in various ways, but most classifications are based on two main factors, temperature and rainfall. Such classifications have the advantage of relating to climatic boundaries for particular plants, such as the tree line, a boundary defined on mountain slopes or around the tundra which is the limit of tree growth.

Climate and Soils

Soil is the weathered product of the bedrock in any region. It is composed of inorganic grains of rock and, usually, particles of humus, the decayed, organic remains of dead plants, animals and animal excretions.

The chemical composition of the bedrock and the amount of humus clearly affect the nature of any soil. But even more important is the climate. For example, the main feature of soils in tropical humid climates is that heavy rain leaches (dissolves) many elements from the top layer of the soil, creating red laterites (coloured by iron). By contrast, the red sandy soils so common in hot deserts are often saline, because there is no rain to remove the salts. Semi-arid regions contain typical chestnut-brown soils, which are only slightly leached and are coloured by their humus content, which is derived from dead grasses and shrubs. Dark brown prairie soils are characteristic of rather more humid grasslands, while black earths, or chernozems, contain more humus.

By contrast, the cold northern regions are typified by greyish-white soils called podzols. Although they are often rich in humus, these soils are heavily leached, and the leaching removes many minerals.

Climate and Vegetation

Besides largely determining the character of soils, climate is also the main factor that shapes the vegetation of a region. Classifications of vegetation usually refer to the climax vegetation of an area – that is, the plant life that would prevail given the climate and soils, if the region were undisturbed by human activities.

Around the tropical forests are regions with a marked dry season where forests give way to savannah. In turn, the savannah gives way to scrubland, semi-desert and desert. Temperate regions may be warm, like Mediterranean climates with their hot, dry summers and mild, moist winters. Cool temperate climates are

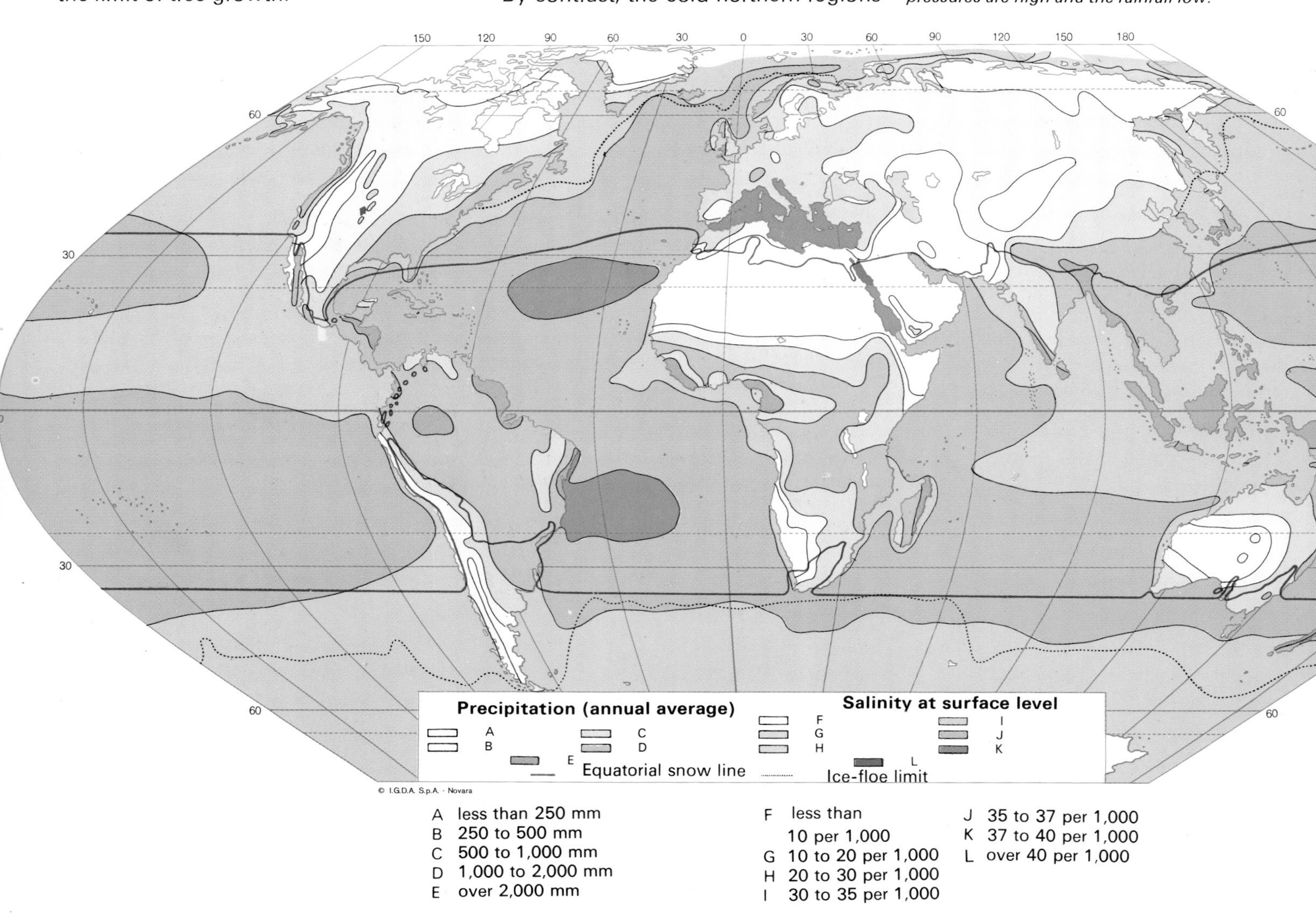

Below: A map of the distribution of precipitation on Earth and the salinity of oceans. The highest salinities in the open oceans conform with the horse latitudes (around 30°N and 30°S) where air pressures are high and the rainfall low.

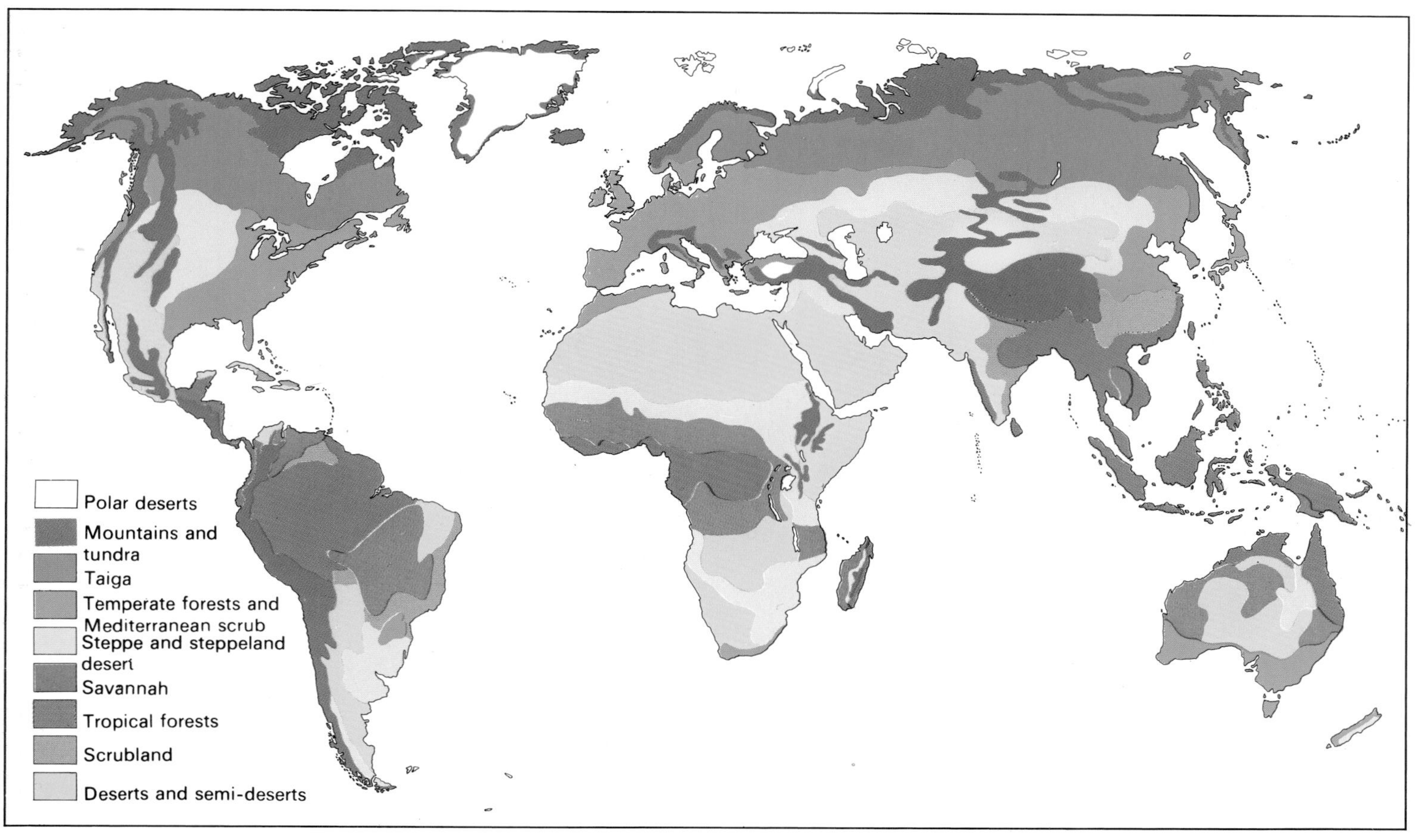

Above: The map shows the world's main vegetation zones. The descriptions of the zones refer to the climax vegetation – that is, the vegetation that would flourish if the region had been undisturbed. For example, the deciduous forests that once represented the climax vegetation of the eastern USA and much of west-central Europe have been cut down.

Land Utilization

Arable land: nearly 10 per cent of the world's land surface.

Meadows and pasture: about 20 per cent of the world's land surface.

Forests: about 27 per cent of the world's land surface, or 4,035 million hectares (10,000 million acres). The coniferous forest (taiga) of the northern USSR is the world's largest forest, covering about 1,100 million hectares (2,718 million acres). This represents 27 per cent of the world's forests. It was estimated in the early 1980s that the world's tropical forests were disappearing by 50ha (124 acres) per minute, which would eliminate them in 40 years.

Deserts: Hot deserts cover about 20 per cent of the world's land surface. They occur mostly in the high air pressure belts between latitudes 10° and 35° North and South.

Ice: Ice covers 10 per cent of the world's land surface, as compared with 30 per cent during the height of the Pleistocene Ice Age. If all the ice melted, the sea level would rise between 60 and 90 metres (197–295 feet), flooding many densely populated lowlands and great cities.

typified by deciduous forest. But most of the original climax vegetation of the cool temperate regions has been destroyed. In the northern hemisphere, the cold snowy climates between the cool temperate lands and the tundra support coniferous forests. This is the taiga, which merges into the tundra, with its brief summer when mosses, lichens and some flowering plants spring to life. Beyond the tundra are the polar wastes blanketed by ice and snow.

Ecosystems

Soils, vegetation and climate combine to create environments, or ecosystems, in which a group of specially adapted plants and animals co-exist, depending on each other for their existence. Providing that an ecosystem remains undisturbed, the number of plants and animals will remain fairly constant.

Disturbance of the balance of nature, however, may have disastrous consequences. For example, the introduction of goats on the South Atlantic island of Saint Helena in the 16th century led to the removal of the island's vegetation cover and the loss of its soil through erosion. By the early 19th century, green hillsides had been transformed into bleak, rocky outcrops.

Goats, which are particularly voracious and destructive animals, were also largely responsible for the destruction of the original coniferous forests of many Mediterranean lands. The maquis, or heathland, of many areas today, is not, therefore, the climax vegetation, but a secondary plant cover.

Climate and Man

Climate obviously has a direct bearing on plant and animal life and, in many ways, it still moulds human activities, limiting the crops that can be grown, the clothes that we must wear, the types of houses that we build to provide protection from the weather, and even the sports we play. This is particularly true in the poorer parts of the world where people's lives are still predominantly shaped by their environment. For example, a long drought can be a matter of life and death to an Indian farmer or an African nomad herding his livestock in the arid Sahel region south of the Sahara.

However, human ingenuity is such that rainless deserts have been made to bloom by irrigation and people can even live in the bleakest of the continents, Antarctica, in heated underground homes, although they must get all their supplies from the outside. Central heating and air conditioning have now made it possible for people to live practically anywhere in comparative comfort.

The Oceans

The three major oceans are the Pacific, Atlantic and Indian. They are interconnected and must not be thought of as separate bodies of water. Around the poles are two large expanses of seawater, which are sometimes called the Arctic and Antarctic oceans. These areas are polar extensions of the three main oceans.

Parts of the oceans are called seas. Definitions of seas and, hence, their areas vary. For instance, the Malayan Sea, consisting of the waters between the Indian and the South Pacific oceans was once rated as the largest sea. But the International Hydrographic Bureau no longer accepts the Malayan Sea as a separate entity. Major seas include:

Sea	**Area km²**	**Area mi²**
South China Sea	2,974,600	1,148,600
Caribbean Sea	2,589,800	1,000,000
Mediterranean Sea	2,512,150	970,000
Bering Sea	2,273,900	878,000
Okhotsk, Sea of	1,507,300	582,000

The Ocean Floor

Until the introduction of echo-sounders in the 1920s, the ocean floor was thought to be featureless. But mapping has revealed many varied features.

The continental shelves, as their name implies, are gently sloping areas around many land masses, the higher parts of which emerge as islands. The shelves extend outwards to a water depth of about 180 m (591 ft). Geologically, the shelves are submerged parts of the continents and their edges, not the coastlines, are the true boundaries of the continents. The continental shelves end where the gradient suddenly changes at the continental slopes. These slopes plunge sharply down to the abyss.

The abyss, which is largely covered by oozes composed of volcanic dust or the remains of marine organisms, does contain some enormous plains, but it also has other interesting features. The deepest parts of the abyss are the ocean trenches, which reach a maximum depth of 11,033 m (36,198 ft) in the Marianas Trench in the Pacific. These trenches are zones of crustal instability, being associated with much earthquake activity.

Many volcanic seamounts rise from the abyss and some of them surface as islands (as in Hawaii). But the most impressive mountains are the long ocean ridges, extending from about 4,000 m (13,123 ft) deep to about 1,000 m (3,281 ft), with occasional peaks (as in Iceland), emerging above the surface.

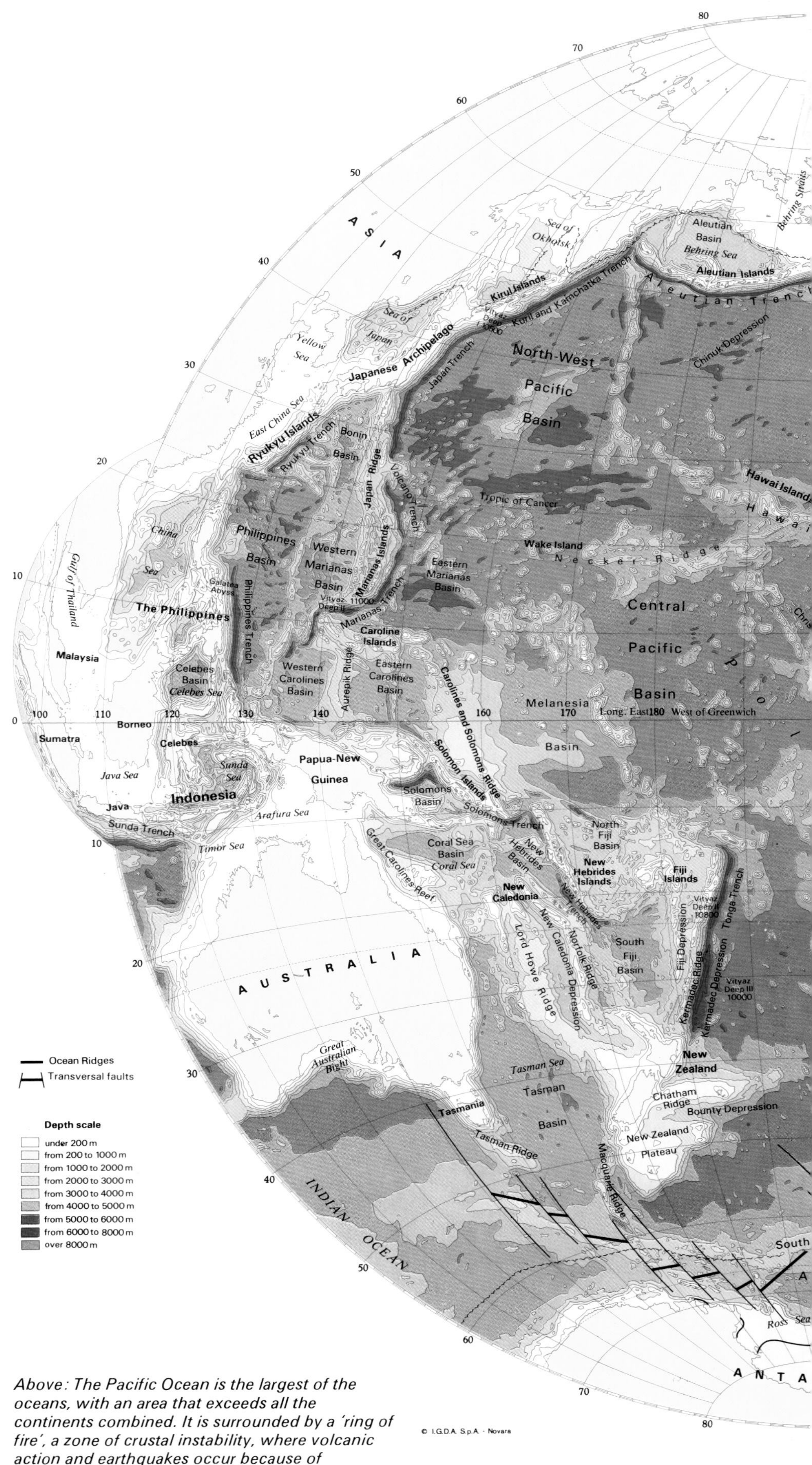

Above: The Pacific Ocean is the largest of the oceans, with an area that exceeds all the continents combined. It is surrounded by a 'ring of fire', a zone of crustal instability, where volcanic action and earthquakes occur because of movements of plates (sections of the crust).

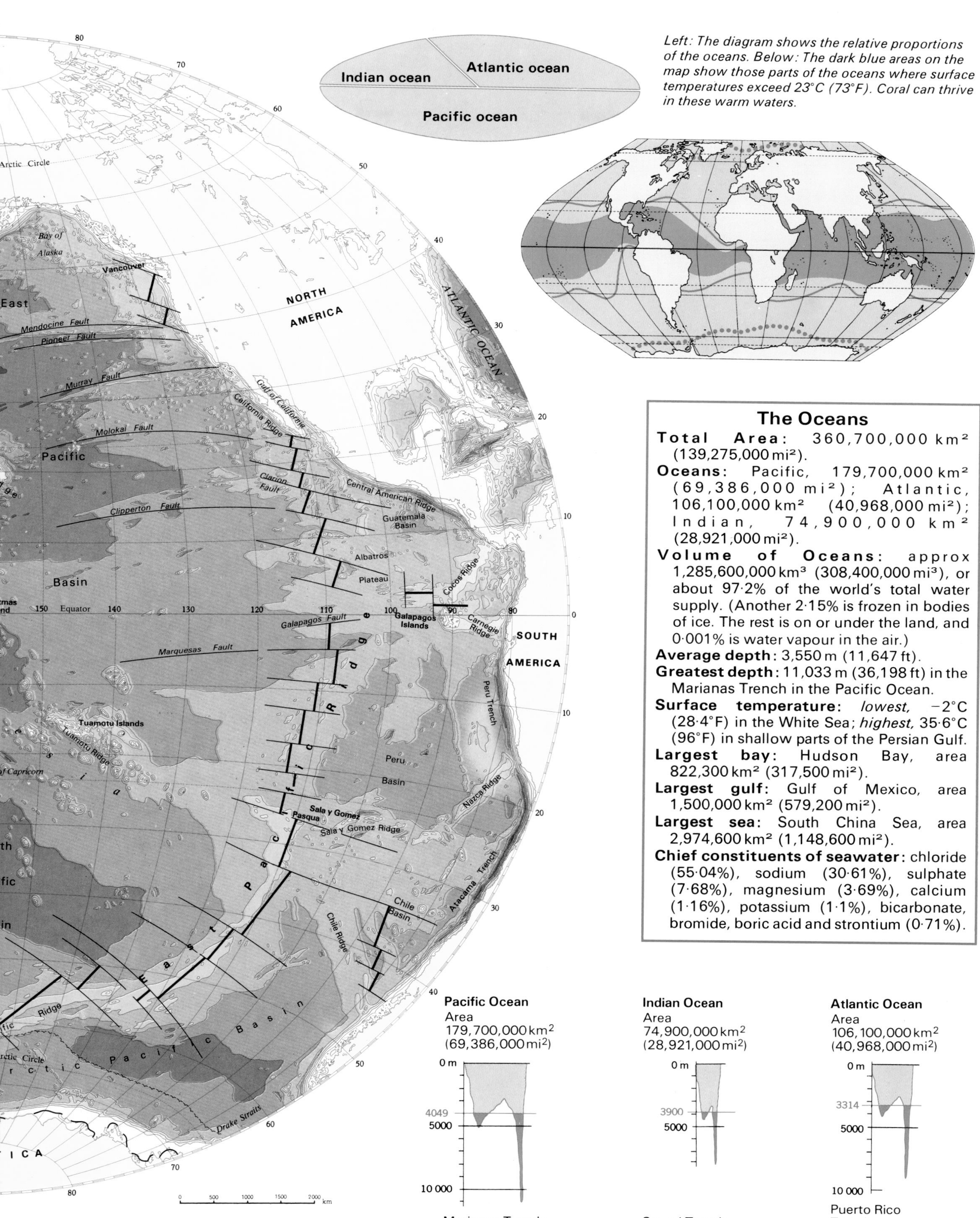

Left: The diagram shows the relative proportions of the oceans. Below: The dark blue areas on the map show those parts of the oceans where surface temperatures exceed 23°C (73°F). Coral can thrive in these warm waters.

The Oceans

Total Area: 360,700,000 km² (139,275,000 mi²).

Oceans: Pacific, 179,700,000 km² (69,386,000 mi²); Atlantic, 106,100,000 km² (40,968,000 mi²); Indian, 74,900,000 km² (28,921,000 mi²).

Volume of Oceans: approx 1,285,600,000 km³ (308,400,000 mi³), or about 97·2% of the world's total water supply. (Another 2·15% is frozen in bodies of ice. The rest is on or under the land, and 0·001% is water vapour in the air.)

Average depth: 3,550 m (11,647 ft).

Greatest depth: 11,033 m (36,198 ft) in the Marianas Trench in the Pacific Ocean.

Surface temperature: *lowest,* −2°C (28·4°F) in the White Sea; *highest,* 35·6°C (96°F) in shallow parts of the Persian Gulf.

Largest bay: Hudson Bay, area 822,300 km² (317,500 mi²).

Largest gulf: Gulf of Mexico, area 1,500,000 km² (579,200 mi²).

Largest sea: South China Sea, area 2,974,600 km² (1,148,600 mi²).

Chief constituents of seawater: chloride (55·04%), sodium (30·61%), sulphate (7·68%), magnesium (3·69%), calcium (1·16%), potassium (1·1%), bicarbonate, bromide, boric acid and strontium (0·71%).

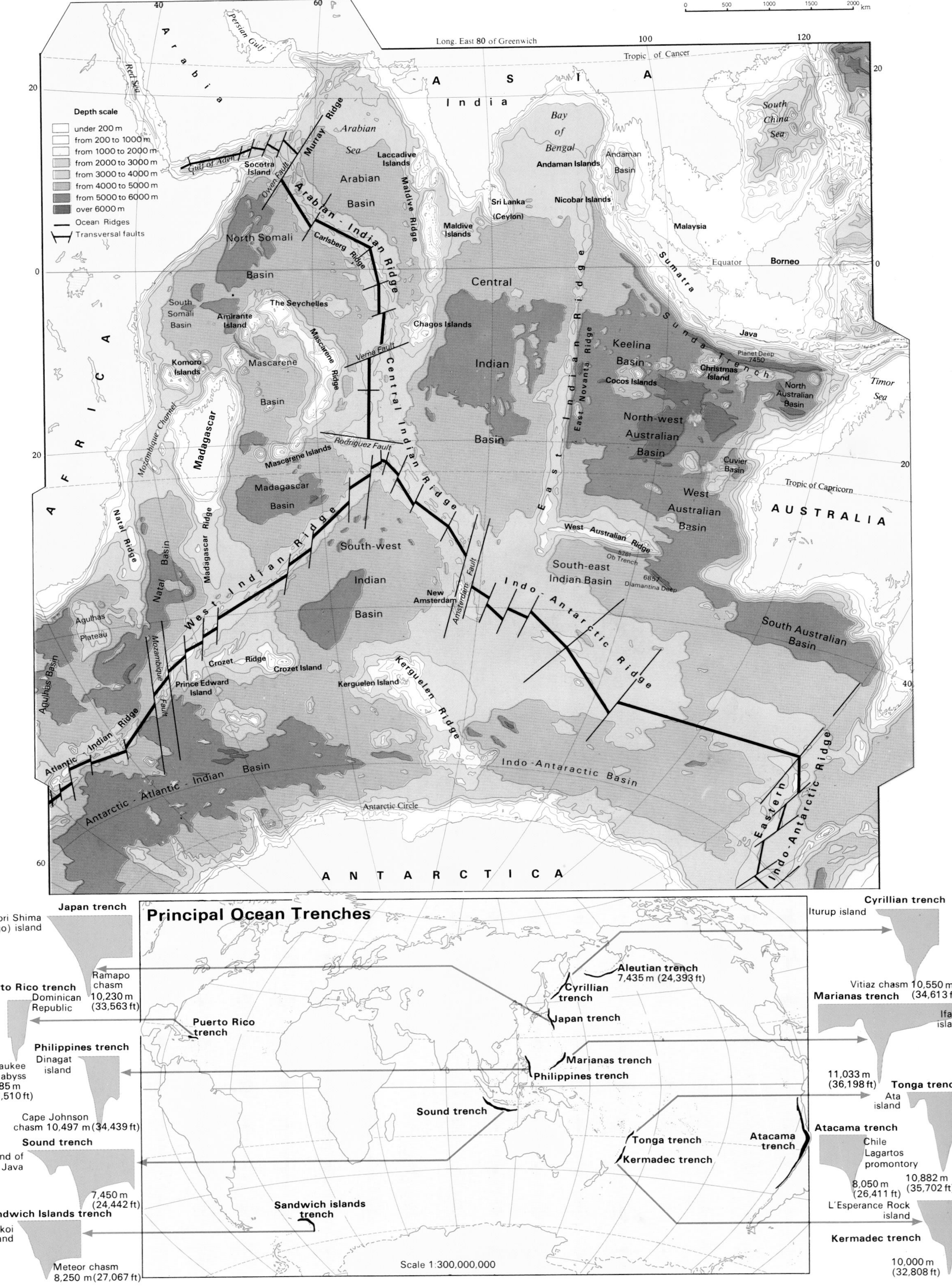

0 500 1000 1500 2000 km
Long. East 80 of Greenwich
40
60
100
120
Tropic of Cancer
Persian Gulf
Arabia
Red Sea
A S I A
India
Depth scale
under 200 m
from 200 to 1000 m
from 1000 to 2000 m
from 2000 to 3000 m
from 3000 to 4000 m
from 4000 to 5000 m
from 5000 to 6000 m
over 6000 m
Ocean Ridges
Transversal faults
Gulf of Aden
Socotra Island
Murray Ridge
Owen Fault
Arabian Sea
Laccadive Islands
Arabian Basin
Arabian - Indian Ridge
Maldive Ridge
Bay of Bengal
Andaman Islands
Andaman Basin
Sri Lanka (Ceylon)
Nicobar Islands
Maldive Islands
Malaysia
South China Sea
North Somali Basin
Carlsberg Ridge
Equator
Borneo
Sumatra
Central Indian Basin
East Indian Ridge
South Somali Basin
Amirante Island
The Seychelles
Chagos Islands
Sunda Trench
Java
Planet Deep 7450
Christmas Island
Keelina Basin
Cocos Islands
East Novanta Ridge
Verne Fault
Mascarene Ridge
Mascarene Basin
Komoro Islands
Central Indian Ridge
North Australian Basin
Timor Sea
Mozambique Channel
Madagascar
AFRICA
North-west Australian Basin
Rodriguez Fault
Mascarene Islands
Cuvier Basin
Tropic of Capricorn
Madagascar Basin
West Australian Basin
AUSTRALIA
Natal Ridge
Natal Basin
Madagascar Ridge
South-west Indian Basin
West Indian Ridge
West Australian Ridge
5261 Ob Trench
South-east Indian Basin
6857 Diamantina Deep
New Amsterdam
Amsterdam Fault
Indo-Antarctic Ridge
Agulhas Plateau
Mozambique Fault
Crozet Ridge
Crozet Island
Prince Edward Island
Kerguelen Island
Kerguelen Ridge
South Australian Basin
Agulhas Basin
Atlantic - Indian Ridge
Antarctic - Atlantic - Indian Basin
Indo-Antaractic Basin
Antarctic Circle
Eastern Indo-Antarctic Ridge
ANTARCTICA
20
0
40
60
Principal Ocean Trenches
Japan trench
Tori Shima (Mitsugo) island
Ramapo chasm 10,230 m (33,563 ft)
Puerto Rico trench
Dominican Republic
Milwaukee abyss 8,385 m (27,510 ft)
Philippines trench
Dinagat island
Cape Johnson chasm 10,497 m (34,439 ft)
Sound trench
Island of Java
7,450 m (24,442 ft)
Sandwich Islands trench
Visokoi island
Meteor chasm 8,250 m (27,067 ft)
Aleutian trench 7,435 m (24,393 ft)
Cyrillian trench
Japan trench
Puerto Rico trench
Marianas trench
Philippines trench
Sound trench
Tonga trench
Kermadec trench
Atacama trench
Sandwich islands trench
Scale 1:300,000,000
Cyrillian trench
Iturup island
Vitiaz chasm 10,550 m
Marianas trench
11,033 m (36,198 ft)
Tonga trench
Ata island
Atacama trench
Chile Lagartos promontory
8,050 m (26,411 ft)
10,882 m (35,702 ft)
L'Esperance Rock island
Kermadec trench
10,000 m (32,808 ft)

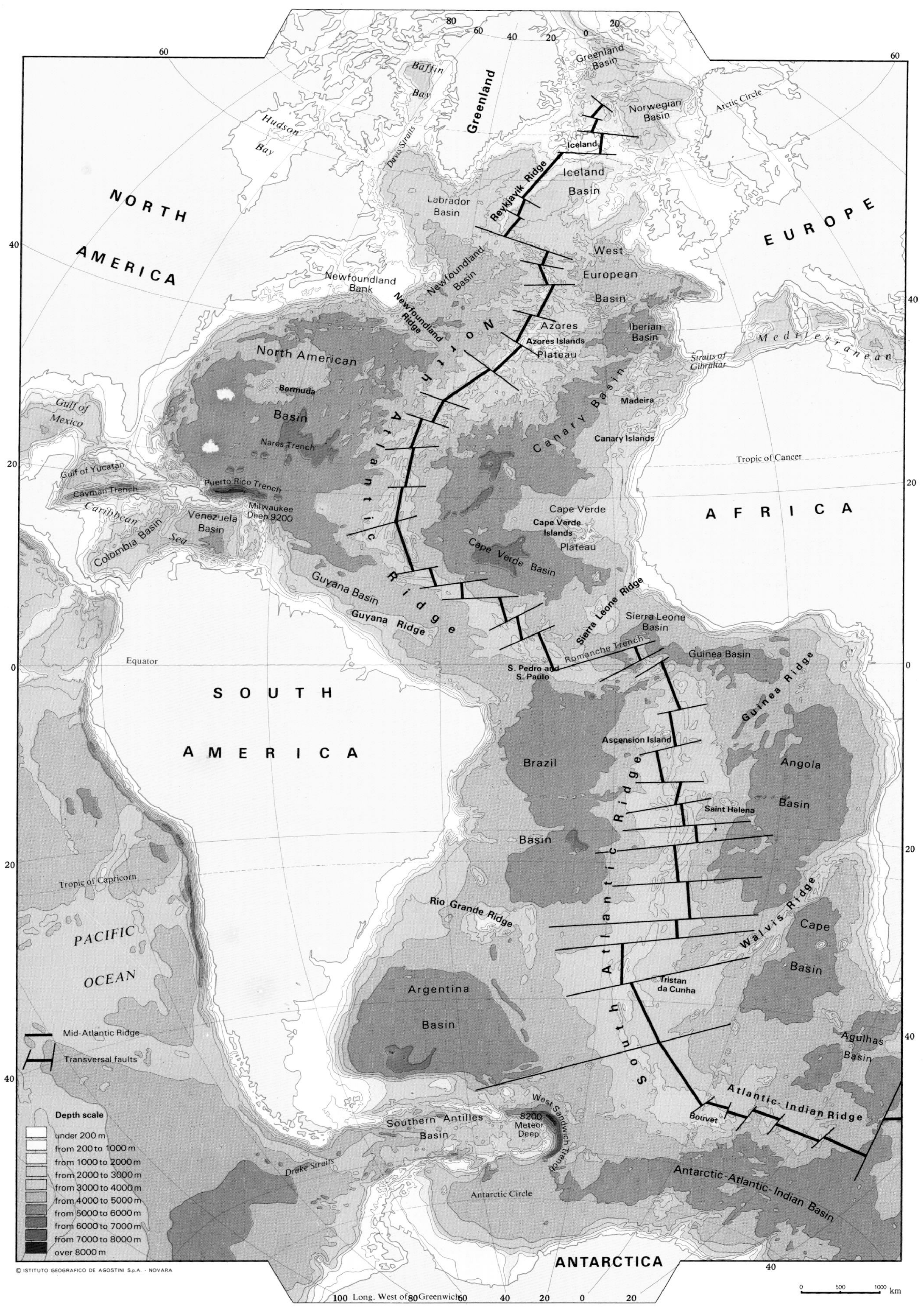
NORTH AMERICA
EUROPE
AFRICA
SOUTH AMERICA
ANTARCTICA
Greenland
Baffin Bay
Hudson Bay
Davis Straits
Greenland Basin
Norwegian Basin
Arctic Circle
Iceland
Iceland Basin
Reykjavik Ridge
Labrador Basin
West European Basin
Newfoundland Bank
Newfoundland Basin
Newfoundland Ridge
North Atlantic Ridge
Azores Plateau
Azores Islands
Iberian Basin
Straits of Gibraltar
Mediterranean
North American Basin
Bermuda
Madeira
Canary Basin
Canary Islands
Gulf of Mexico
Nares Trench
Tropic of Cancer
Gulf of Yucatan
Puerto Rico Trench
Caymian Trench
Caribbean Sea
Milwaukee Deep 9200
Venezuela Basin
Colombia Basin
Cape Verde Plateau
Cape Verde Islands
Cape Verde Basin
Guyana Basin
Guyana Ridge
Sierra Leone Ridge
Sierra Leone Basin
Romanche Trench
Guinea Basin
Equator
S. Pedro and S. Paulo
Guinea Ridge
Ascension Island
Brazil Basin
Angola Basin
Saint Helena
South Atlantic Ridge
Tropic of Capricorn
Rio Grande Ridge
Walvis Ridge
Cape Basin
PACIFIC OCEAN
Tristan da Cunha
Argentina Basin
Agulhas Basin
Mid-Atlantic Ridge
Transversal faults
West Sandwich Trench
Atlantic-Indian Ridge
Bouvet
8200 Meteor Deep
Southern Antilles Basin
Drake Straits
Antarctic Circle
Antarctic-Atlantic-Indian Basin
Depth scale
under 200 m
from 200 to 1000 m
from 1000 to 2000 m
from 2000 to 3000 m
from 3000 to 4000 m
from 4000 to 5000 m
from 5000 to 6000 m
from 6000 to 7000 m
from 7000 to 8000 m
over 8000 m
100 Long. West of 80 Greenwich 60 40 20 0 20
0 500 1000 km

Drifting Plates

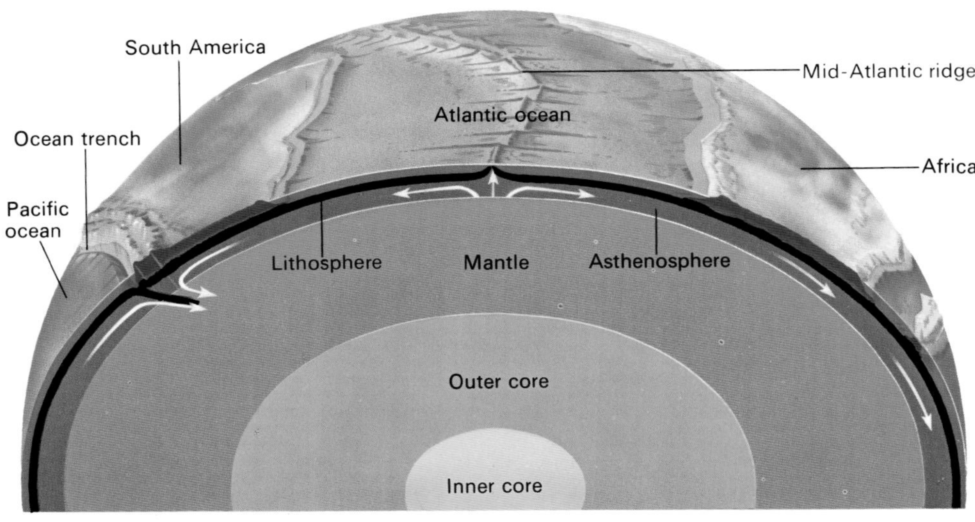

Above: The diagram shows the asthenosphere, a semi-molten layer of the upper mantle. Convention currents in the asthenosphere carry plates, made up of rigid sections of the lithosphere, around. The arrows show the directions of the currents, which pull plates apart in the Atlantic, but push other plates against each other to the west of South America.

Natural landscapes do not seem to change much in one person's lifetime. However, erosion and powerful forces operating within the Earth are constantly shaping and reshaping the land. In addition, the world map itself is also slowly changing.

The similarities between the shapes of the Americas and Europe/Africa were noticed in the early 1900s by the German meteorologist Alfred Wegener (1880–1930), who suggested that the landmasses had once been joined together but that continental drift had pulled them apart. Evidence to support this notion gradually accumulated. Rock structures and fossils in rocks on both sides of the Atlantic were found to match up. For instance, the northern Appalachians and the mountains of eastern Greenland in North America were formed at the same time as the mountains of northern Scotland and the plateaux of western Norway. Was it possible that they were all formed as a single range by the same Caledonian orogeny (period of mountain building), when North America and Europe were joined together? And why should the fossils of *Lystrosaurus* appear in Triassic rocks (formed between 230 and 195 million years ago) in Africa, Antarctica and India? *Lystrosaurus*, a freshwater reptile could not possibly have swum from Africa to Antarctica. Hence, such fossil evidence suggested that the landmasses had once been linked together in a single landmass.

New Evidence

Such arguments were intriguing, but Wegener's theory found little support because no one could suggest a possible mechanism whereby continents could be moved. However, the idea of continental drift was revived after the Second World War during studies of the ocean floor. First, the charting of the continental shelves revealed that the Americas fitted together with Europe and Africa even better than Wegener had thought, by matching the edges of the continental shelves rather than the coastlines.

Second, nearly all of the ocean crust was found to be less than 200 million years old. The oceans were, therefore, far younger features than the continents, where rocks up to 3,800 million years old have been found. Further, the youngest rocks were consistently found in the centres of the ocean ridges. Away from them, on either side, the rocks became progressively older.

Plate Edges

Study of the massive ocean ridges and the deep ocean trenches revealed that they were active zones, where earthquakes were common. Further, volcanic action was frequent along the ridges. For instance, an island outcrop of the mid-Atlantic ridge, Iceland, is a focus of volcanic and seismic activity. This and other evidence suggested that the ridges and trenches represented breaks in the Earth's crust between large, rigid and geologically inactive areas called plates.

A third kind of plate edge was also indentified. Called a transform fault, this plate edge was a long tear in the Earth's lithosphere where horizontal movements take place. One of the best known of such boundaries is the famous San Andreas fault which runs south-eastwards from San Francisco, past the eastern edge of the city of Los Angeles, and on to the Gulf of California.

The Driving Force

Beneath the ocean ridges, the crust was much warmer than elsewhere. In fact, hot, molten material is rising in a semi-molten layer of the upper mantle called the asthenosphere. This material spreads out laterally beneath the crust, only to sink again after it has cooled. The spreading motions of this convection current is the force that pulls the overlying and less dense plates in the lithosphere apart like giant rafts. These movements extend down to a depth of 70 to 100 km (43–62 mi). As they move apart, magma wells up from below to form new crustal rock along the centre of the ridge. This process is called ocean spreading.

Along the ocean trenches, however, crustal rock is being destroyed as one plate is pushed beneath another in what is called a subduction zone. The descending plate melts and forms large

Right: The Atlantic is being widened by an average of 2–3 cm (0·8–1·2 in) per year along the mid-Atlantic ridge (or rise). As a result, the African plate is moving eastwards and the American plate westwards. Beyond South America, the Nazca plate in the south-eastern Pacific, is moving eastwards from the Pacific ocean ridge (or East Pacific rise). Because of the collision of the two plates, the Nazca plate is being forced beneath the South American plate along the ocean trenches that border the west coast of South America. This is a subduction zone, where earthquakes occur as the Nazca plate descends in periodic jerky movements. As the plate descends, the forward edge melts. The resulting magma rises through the continental crust, fuelling the active volcanoes of South and Central America.

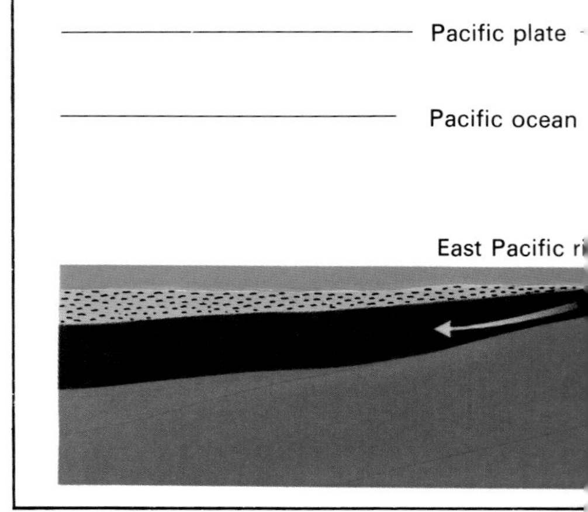

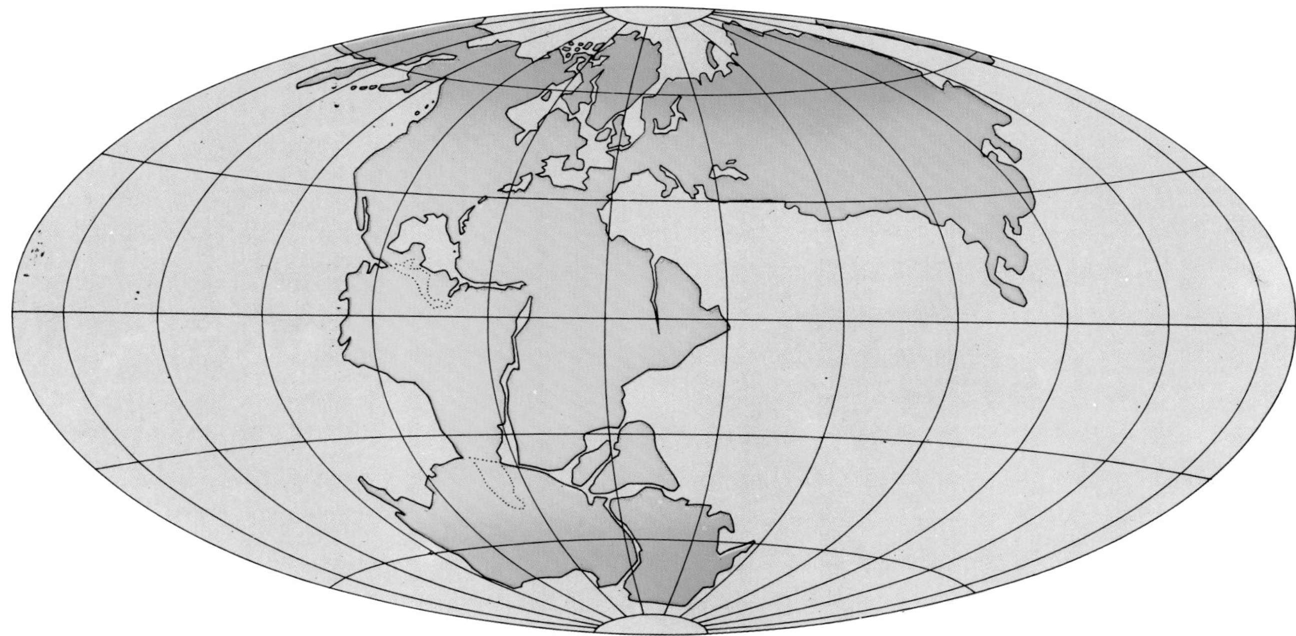

reservoirs of molten magma. Because of its comparatively low density, some of this magma is forced upwards to form new volcanoes.

The movement along transform faults is lateral. For example, in California, the San Andreas fault represents part of the border between the North American and Pacific plates. The Pacific plate is sliding north-westwards carrying Los Angeles with it. However, the edges of the plates are jagged and become jammed together. As a result, the movements are not smooth. Instead the plates lurch forward when tension causes the jams to break. The most violent lurches trigger off major earthquakes. A displacement of 6·4 m (21 ft) was measured at one point on the San Andreas fault during the 1906 earthquake which wrecked the city of San Francisco.

The study of plate tectonics has greatly helped geologists to understand more about the nature and causes of both earthquakes and volcanoes. A study of plate movements over comparatively recent geological time has also shed light on orogenesis (the process of mountain building).

About 180 million years ago, the world's landmasses were grouped together in one supercontinent called Pangaea. At that time, India was not part of Asia; it was wedged between Africa, Antarctica and Australia. However, the plate bearing India broke away and drifted towards the Asian landmass. In the collision zone between the two plates, sediments on an ancient seabed were squeezed together into huge folds. Slowly, these sediments rose to form the Himalayas, where it is now evident that the rocks have been compressed by as much as 650 km (404 mi). This explains why fossils of marine organisms have been found in rocks near the top of the world's highest mountain, Everest.

Above: About 180 million years ago, the Earth's landmasses formed a single supercontinent, called Pangaea. Gradually, North America and Eurasia moved away from South America and Africa. About 136 million years ago, South America began to move away from Africa and, by 100 million years ago, Australia and Antarctica were moving away from Africa. India, which had been part of the southern landmass, broke away and moved northwards. By 50 million years ago, it was pushing against Asia, squeezing up intervening sediments into the majestic Himalayan range.

By inference, geologists now appreciate that such ancient mountain ranges as the Appalachians in North America and the Urals in the USSR are former plate boundaries. Like the Himalayas and the Alps, they were formed when ancient plates collided. However, both ranges are geologically inactive, showing that the former plates were welded together in the process.

Plate movements set up tension in the rock strata near plate edges. Such tension can shear the rocks, causing large faults to develop. Tugging movements create rift valleys and block mountains.

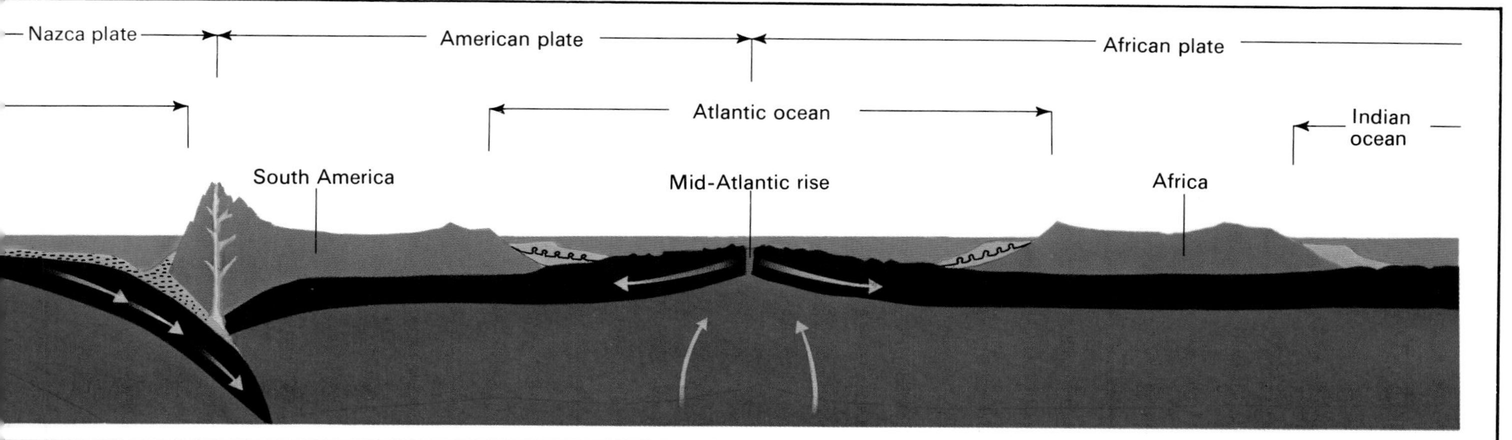

The Earth in Space

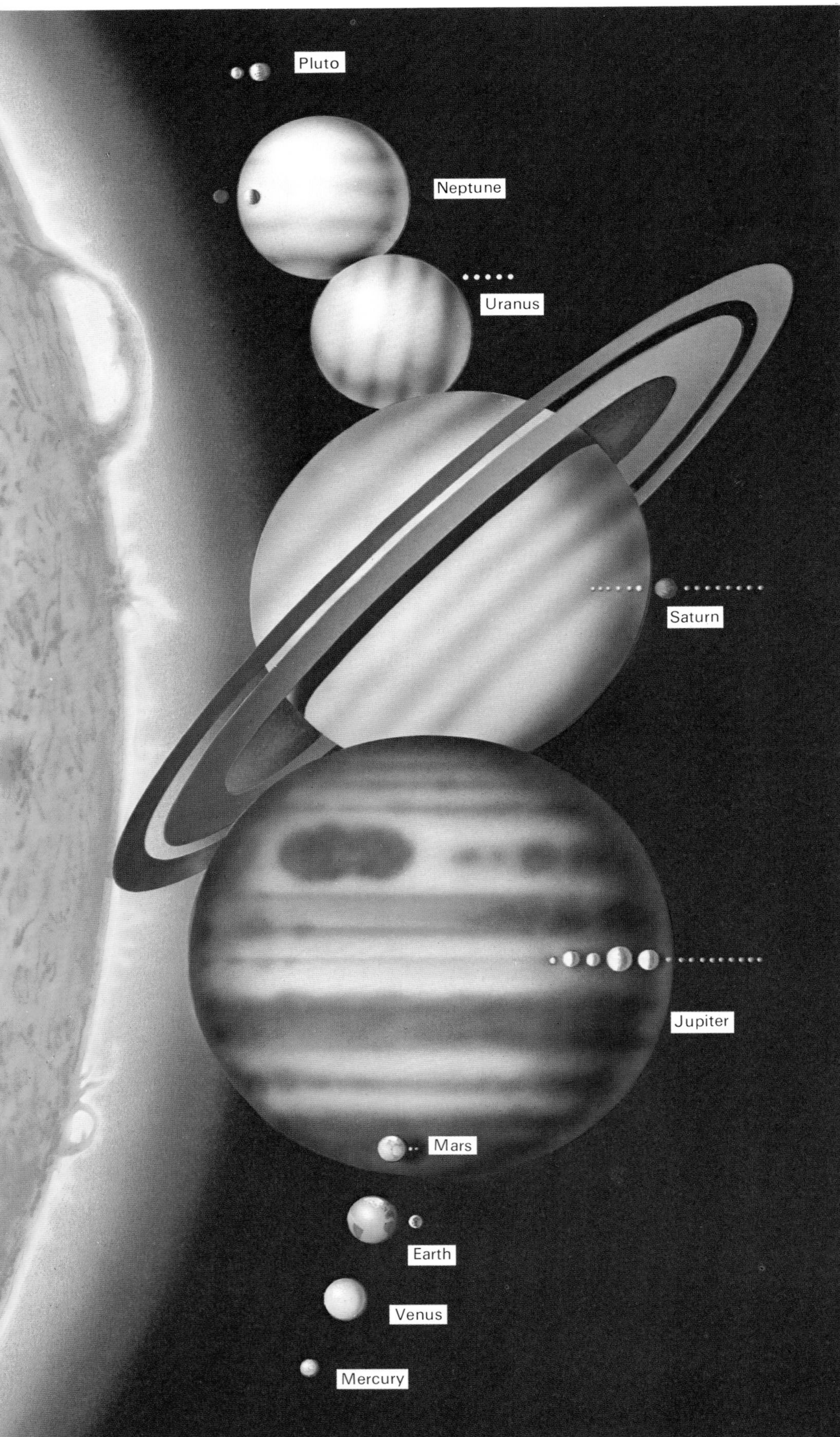

The Earth is the fifth largest of the nine planets. The following table gives the diameters of the planets in kilometres and miles. The third column shows how the volumes of the planets compare with that of Earth (1·0):

Table of diameters and volumes

	(km)	(mi)	(volume)
Mercury	4,878	3,032	0.06
Venus	12,104	7,523	0.86
Earth	12,756	7,928	1.00
Mars	6,794	4,222	0.15
Jupiter	142,800	88,750	1,316
Saturn	120,660	74,990	755
Uranus	52,400	32,570	67
Neptune	48,400	30,080	57
Pluto	3,000?	1,900?	0.01

The planets revolve around the Sun in well-defined orbits. The time required for each planet to complete one orbit is known as the period of revolution. The farther a planet is from the Sun, the longer is its period of revolution:

Table of revolution periods

Mercury	87 days 23 hours
Venus	224 days 17 hours
Earth	365 days 6 hours
Mars	1 year 321 days 17 hours
Jupiter	11 years 314 days 3 hours
Saturn	29 years 168 days 0 hours
Uranus	84 years 3 days 7 hours
Neptune	164 years 288 days 4 hours
Pluto	247 years 246 days 22 hours

The planets also rotate on their axes in what is called a period of rotation. The following table lists these periods:

Table of rotation periods

Mercury	58 days 15 hours 30 minutes
Venus	243 days 3 hours 50 minutes
Earth	23 hours 56 minutes
Mars	24 hours 37 minutes
Jupiter	9 hours 50 minutes
Saturn	10 hours 39 minutes
Uranus	17 hours 18 minutes
Neptune	18 hours 12 minutes
Pluto	6 days 9 hours 17 minutes

Mercury and Venus have no satellites, while Earth has one (the Moon). Mars has two small satellites: Deimos and Phobos. Jupiter has 16 satellites of which four are of considerable size; the largest are Ganymede and Callisto, which are planet-sized with diameters of 5,276 km (3,279 mi) and 4,820 km (2,996 mi) respectively, followed by Io and Europa. Saturn is known for its spectacular rings, though Jupiter, Uranus and Neptune also have rings. Saturn may have as many as 23 moons, including the huge Titan with a diameter of 5,140 km (3,195 mi), Iapetus, Rhea, Tethys, Dione, Enceladus, Mimas, Hyperion and Phoebe. Uranus has 15 satellites, the largest being Titania, Oberon, Ariel, Umbriel and Miranda. Neptune has two, Triton and Nereid, while Pluto has one satellite, Charon.

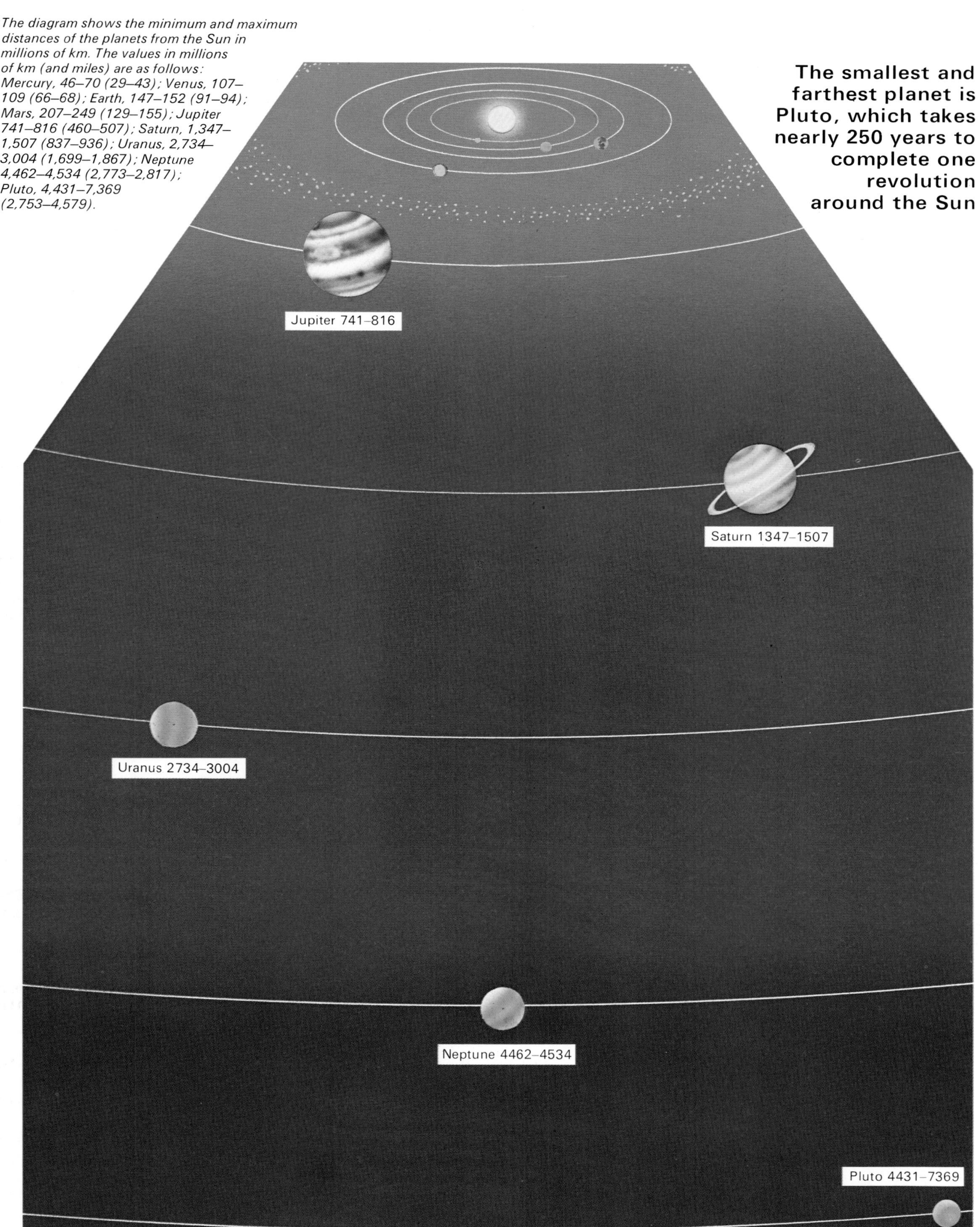

The diagram shows the minimum and maximum distances of the planets from the Sun in millions of km. The values in millions of km (and miles) are as follows: Mercury, 46–70 (29–43); Venus, 107–109 (66–68); Earth, 147–152 (91–94); Mars, 207–249 (129–155); Jupiter 741–816 (460–507); Saturn, 1,347–1,507 (837–936); Uranus, 2,734–3,004 (1,699–1,867); Neptune 4,462–4,534 (2,773–2,817); Pluto, 4,431–7,369 (2,753–4,579).

The smallest and farthest planet is Pluto, which takes nearly 250 years to complete one revolution around the Sun

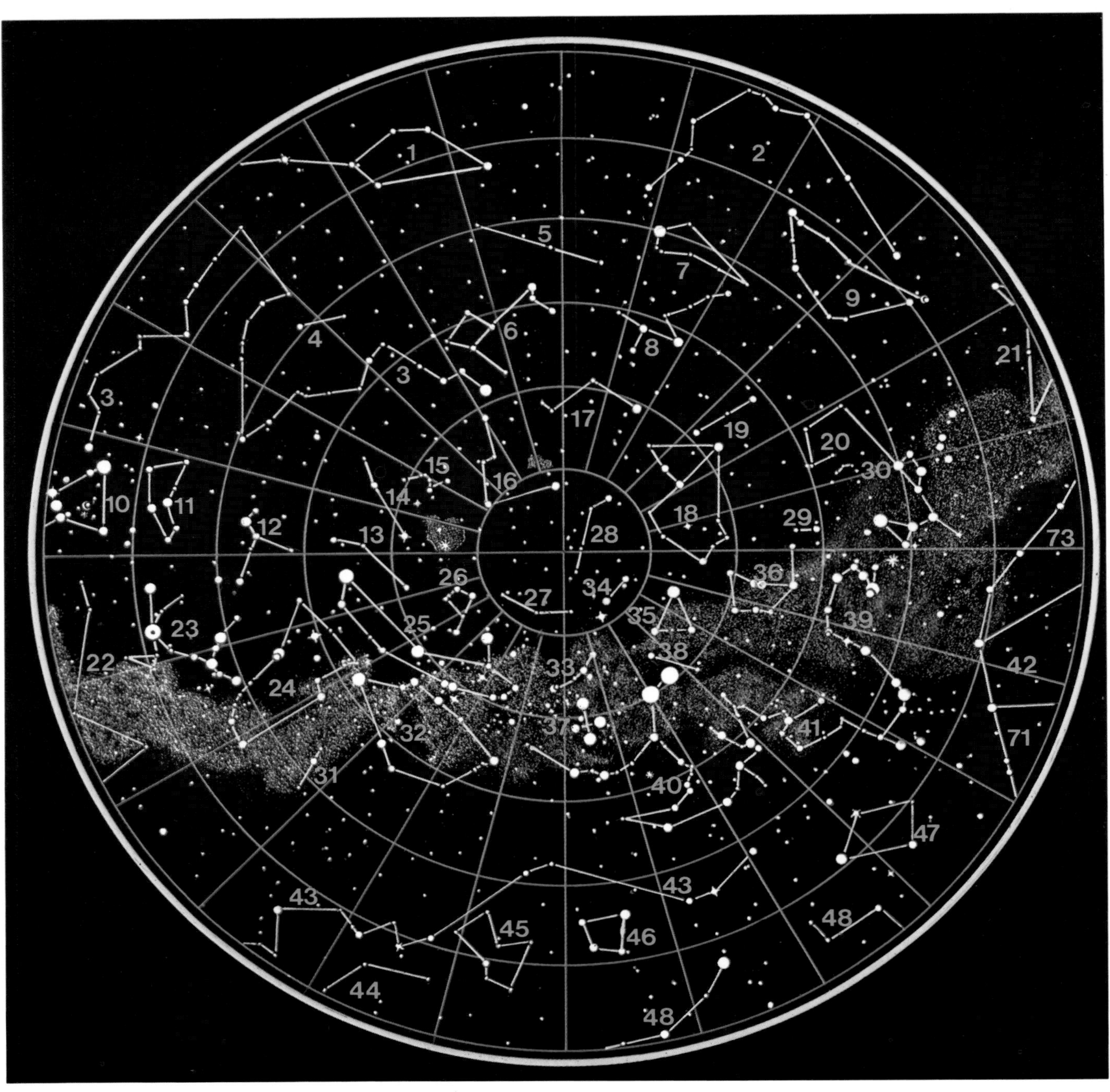

A map of the heavens

Constellations of the southern sky

1 Cetus
2 Aquarius
3 Eridanus
4 Fornax
5 Sculptor
6 Phoenix
7 Piscis Austrinus
8 Grus
9 Capricornus
10 Orion
11 Lepus
12 Columba
13 Pictor
14 Dorado
15 Reticulum
16 Hydrus
17 Tucana
18 Pavo
19 Indus
20 Sagittarius
21 Aquila
22 Monoceros
23 Canis Major
24 Puppis
25 Carina
26 Volans
27 Chamaeleon
28 Octans
29 Telescopium
30 Corona Australis
31 Pyxis
32 Vela
33 Musca
34 Apus
35 Triangulum Australe
36 Ara
37 Crux
38 Circinus
39 Scorpius
40 Centaurus
41 Lupus
42 Ophiuchus
43 Hydra
44 Sextans
45 Crater
46 Corvus
47 Libra
48 Virgo

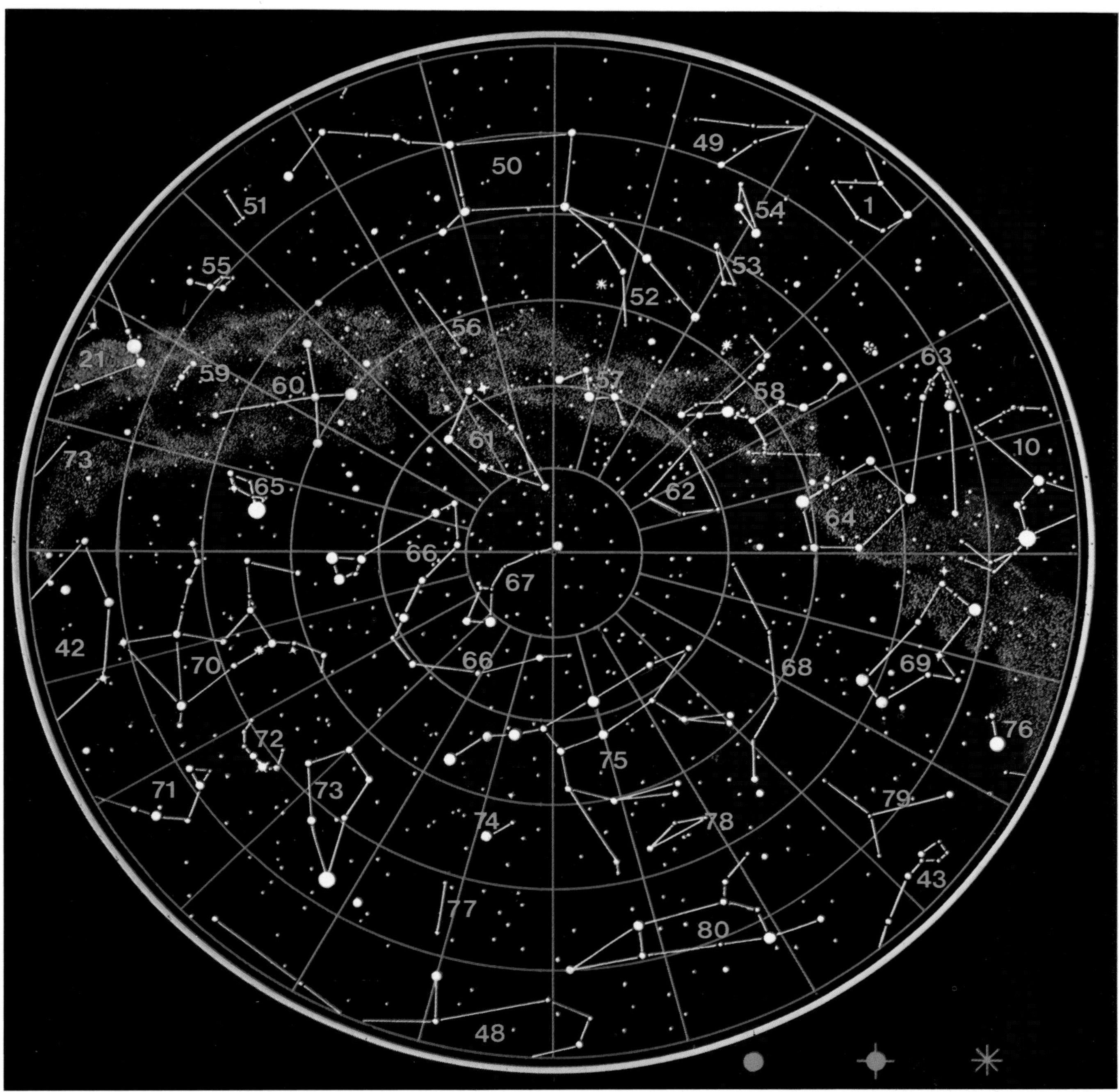

Constellations of the northern sky

49 Pisces
50 Pegasus
51 Equuleus
52 Andromeda
53 Triangulum
54 Aries
55 Delphinus
56 Lacerta
57 Cassiopeia
58 Perseus
59 Sagitta
60 Cygnus
61 Cepheus
62 Camelopardalis
63 Auriga
64 Taurus
65 Lyra
66 Draco
67 Ursa Minor
68 Lynx
69 Gemini
70 Hercules
71 Serpens
72 Corona Borealis
73 Bootes
74 Canes Venatici
75 Ursa Major
76 Canis Minor
77 Coma Berenices
78 Leo Minor
79 Cancer
80 Leo

Index

The alphabetical arrangement ignores accents. Page numbers in *italics* indicate the inclusion of illustrations.

Acknowledgments

Action Press – P. Curto 162 top left, F. Rho 163 centre, 163 bottom; Airviews Ltd 173, 197 top, 197 bottom right, 199 bottom, 201 bottom; G. Allegretti 90 right; Alpine Luftbild 176 top; Archivio IGDA 11 centre right, 164; Archivio IGDA – N. Cirani 8 top left, 8 bottom left, 9 top centre, 9 top right; Curzi 10-11; M. Fantin 8 top right; Archivio P2 11 top right, 42 top, 42-43, 95 top left, 166 centre, 167 top, 167 bottom, 175 top, 175 bottom, 181 top, 181 bottom, 205 bottom, 206-207 bottom, 219, 232 top; G. Arnaldi 111 right, 128 top; G. Barone 170-171 bottom; I. Barzilai 165 top right, 183 top left, 225 right; Beaujard-Titus 188-189, 190 top left, 190 bottom left; Berengo Gardin 193 bottom right, 199 top, 200 top left, 200 right, 201 top left, 201 top right, 202, 214 centre, 214 bottom, 224 bottom left; F. Bernini 59 bottom left; C. Bertinetti 113 bottom left, 114 bottom; M. Bertinetti 120; Blackstar – G. Neri 176 bottom; P. Boroli 58 bottom; S. Boroli 55 left; Camera Press – M. J. Gilson 174 bottom; G. Canuti 89; M. Carrieri 84, 121 top, 215; N. Celoria 222 top left, 228 top, 228 bottom; R. Cesati 227 top; N. Cirani 6-7, 54 top, 54 centre, 54 bottom, 58 top, 58 centre, 59 top, 60 top left, 60 top right, 60 bottom left, 62, 63 bottom right, 75 bottom left, 75 bottom right, 86-87 top, 86 bottom, 87 top, 87 bottom left, 87 bottom right, 113 top left, 113 bottom right, 114 top, 117 left, 117 right, 146-147 top, 146 bottom, 151 bottom left, 153 bottom; B. Coleman – Erre 59 bottom right; Colour Library International 209 top, 209 bottom, 210; G. Costa 160 bottom; A. Dagli Orti 178 top; G. Dagli Orti 20, 21 right, 80 bottom left, 80 top, 110 top, 118 bottom, 126 right, 138, 140 top right, 183 top right, 190 top left, 211 top, 217 top, 230 top, 235 top left, 235 top right; G. Dondio 212 top; A. Ducellier 174 top; Explorer 143 bottom; Explorer – Duboutin 97 bottom; A. Facchinetti 95 bottom right, 142; M. Falcioni 144 top; M. Fantin 126 top left, 152-153 top, 159 bottom, 237 top; Fototeca Storica Nazionale 169; E. Frisia 64 right, 239; M. Gandiano 85 bottom; O. Geddo 194 bottom, 233, 238 top; L. Gerosa 140 top left, 140 bottom; A. Gogna 11 bottom left; A. and O. Gogna 95 centre left, 112, 203; G. Hall 148-149 top, 150 top, 150 bottom; R. Harding 159 top; Alan Hutchison Library 16 right, 17, 23, 25 top, 25 bottom, 26, 27, 28, 29 top, 31 top, 31 bottom, 38 top left, 38 top right, 39 top, 39 bottom, 41 top, 41 bottom, 44, 45, 47, 48, 49 top, 50, 51, 64 left, 70 bottom, 72 bottom, 75 top, 81, 82, 83 left, 83 right, 100 bottom, 108 bottom right, 109, 116, 118 top, 119 top, 128 bottom, 129 top, 129 bottom, 131, 132 left, 133 left, 133 right, 134, 135 bottom, 152 bottom left, 155 top, 156, 157, 162 bottom, 163 top, 184, 230 bottom, 232 bottom, 249 bottom; Alan Hutchison Library – Timothy Beddow 91, S. Burman 148 bottom, S. Errington 35 left, 70 top, 72 top, 101 top and bottom, 139, D. Fleming 100 top, B. Gerard 128 bottom right, J. Goldblatt 15, P. Goycolea 33 top, 33 bottom, R. House 115, R. I. Lloyd 52, 137 top, 147 bottom, M. Macintyre 103 top, 103 bottom, 155 bottom, B. Moser 34 top, 34 bottom, 76, 78, 132 right, J. Pate 102, J. L. Peyromaure 135 top, P. Rankin Smith 70 bottom, J. Reditt 127 bottom, B. Régent 40, 73 top, 77 top, 127 top, 137 bottom left, M. Rock 137 bottom right, V. Southwell 119 bottom, 119 top, V. and A. Wilkinson 16 left, J. Wright 35 right; A. Hutchinson 94 left; Jacana 8-9 bottom, 9 top left; Jacana – Gens 67 top, Massari 162 top right, J. Prévost 158; R. König 94 bottom right; M. Leigheb 10 bottom, 60 bottom right, 65 bottom, 96-97 top, 122, 123 top, 123 centre, 123 bottom, 124 top, 124 centre, 124 bottom, 125 top, 125 bottom left, 125 bottom right, 126 bottom left, 136, 144 bottom, 145 bottom left; C. Lénars 95 top right; A. Luppi 108 top left, 141 bottom; C. Luppi 96 bottom left; Magnum – B. Barbey 108 top centre, 108 bottom centre, B. Glinn 92; G. Mairani 88 bottom left, 90 left, 165 bottom left, 195, 196 bottom, 218; Marka 66 top right, 66-67 bottom, 69 top left, 69 top right; G. Nimatallah 165 bottom right, 170-171 centre, 180 left, 180 right, 183 bottom right, 197 bottom left, 200 bottom left, 200 bottom centre, 205 top left, 224-225, 226-227; C. Novara 171 top right, 171 centre right, 206 top, 231; Orbis 10 top, 160 top; P. Pampolini 95 bottom left; G. Pavia 96 bottom right; M. Pedone 224 top; R. Portolese 68 left, 68 right; S. Prato 185 bottom; Publi-Aer Foto 165 top left, 166 bottom, 177, 178 bottom, 212 bottom, 214 top; E. Quéméré 46 bottom right, 188 top left; F. Rho 69 bottom, 161; G. Ricatto 32 bottom right; A. Risso 113 top right; C. Rives 145 top right, 186; G. A. Rossi 55 right, 121 bottom, 216 bottom; M. Saini 207 top; Salmer 227 bottom; C. Sappa 170 top, 189 top right, 216 top, 222 top right; Seemuller 183 bottom left, 220, 222 bottom; A. Sella 211 bottom; E. Shulthess 95 top centre; G. Sioen 18, 19 top, 19 bottom, 21 left, 22 top, 22 bottom, 79, 188 bottom left, 189 bottom right, 221; S. Spini 59 centre left; Studio IF 74 bottom; Tass 235 bottom, 236 top, 236 bottom, 237 bottom, 238 centre, 238 bottom; A. Tessore 104, 105 top, 105 bottom, 106-107, 108 bottom left, 196 top, 223, 229, 240 right; Titus 88 top left, 88 right, 240 left; J. Todd 208, 240 bottom; A. Tornielli 59 centre right; A. Vergani 11 bottom right, 14, 166 top, 167 centre, 171 bottom right, 172 left, 179 left and right, 185 top, 191, 193 top left, 193 bottom left, 194 top left, 194 top right, 205 top right; R. Villarosa 110-111 bottom; C. Zappelli 94 top right, 171 top left; Zefa 172 right; Zefa – Hugel 193 top right.

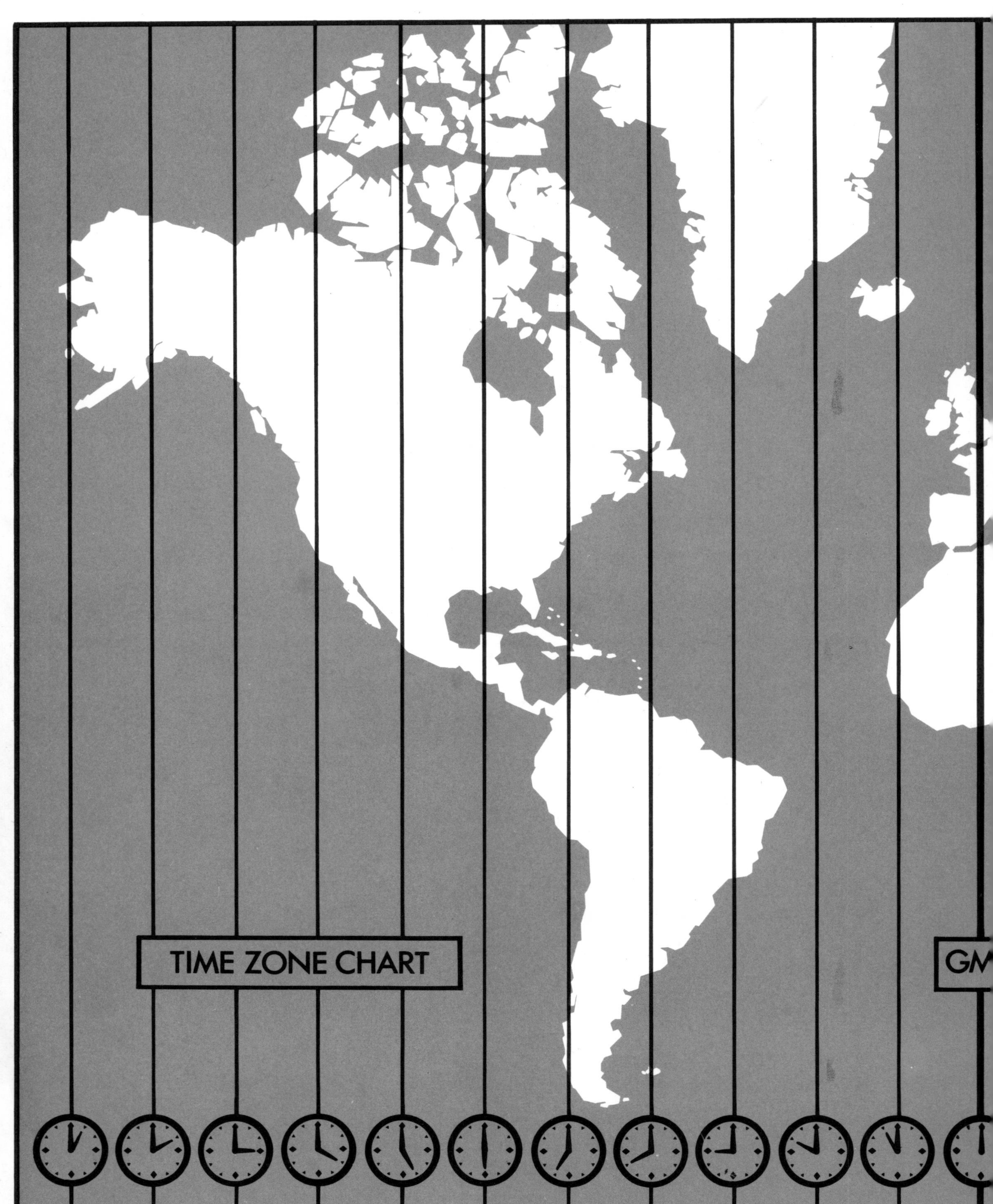
TIME ZONE CHART